THE CANADIAN YEARBOOK OF INTERNATIONAL LAW

1997

ANNUAIRE CANADIEN DE DROIT INTERNATIONAL

The Canadian Yearbook of International Law

VOLUME XXXV 1997 TOME XXXV

Annuaire canadien de Droit international

Published under the auspices of
THE CANADIAN BRANCH, INTERNATIONAL LAW ASSOCIATION
AND
THE CANADIAN COUNCIL ON INTERNATIONAL LAW

Publié sous les auspices de
LA SECTION CANADIENNE DE L'ASSOCIATION DE DROIT INTERNATIONAL
ET
LE CONSEIL CANADIEN DE DROIT INTERNATIONAL

UBC Press
VANCOUVER, B.C.

Printed in Canada on acid-free paper ∞

ISBN 0-7748-0679-6
ISSN 0069-0058

Canadian Cataloguing in Publication Data

The National Library of Canada has catalogued this publication as follows:

The Canadian yearbook of international law — Annuaire canadien de droit international

Annual.
Text in English and French.
"Published under the auspices of the Canadian Branch, International Law Association and the Canadian Council on International Law."
ISSN 0069-0058

1. International Law — Periodicals.
I. International Law Association. Canadian Branch.
II. Title: Annuaire canadien de droit international.
JC 21.C3 341'.05 C75-34558-6E

Données de catalogage avant publication (Canada)

Annuaire canadien de droit international — The Canadian yearbook of international law

Annuel.
Textes en anglais et en français.
"Publié sous les auspices de la Branche canadienne de l'Association de droit international et le Conseil canadien de droit international."
ISSN 0069-0058

1. Droit international — Périodiques.
I. Association de droit international. Section canadienne.
II. Conseil canadien de droit international.
III. Titre: The Canadian yearbook of international law.
JC 21.C3 341'.05 C75-34558-6E

UBC Press
University of British Columbia
6344 Memorial Road
Vancouver, BC V6T 1Z2
(604) 822-3259
Fax: 1-800-668-0821
E-mail: orders@ubcpress.ubc.ca
http: //www.ubcpress.ubc.ca

The Board of Editors, the Canadian Branch of the International Law Association, the Canadian Council on International Law, and the University of British Columbia are not in any way responsible for the views expressed by contributors, whether the contributions are signed or unsigned.

Les opinions émises dans le présent *Annuaire* par nos collaborateurs, qu'il s'agisse d'articles signés ou non signés, ne sauraient en aucune façon engager la responsabilité du Comité de rédaction, de la Section canadienne du Conseil canadien de droit international ou de l'Université de Colombie-Britannique.

Communications to the *Yearbook* should be addressed to:

Les communications destinées à l'*Annuaire* doivent être adressées à:

THE EDITOR, THE CANADIAN YEARBOOK OF INTERNATIONAL LAW
FACULTY OF LAW, COMMON LAW SECTION
UNIVERSITY OF OTTAWA
57 LOUIS PASTEUR
OTTAWA, ONTARIO K1N 6N5 CANADA

Contents / Matière

Articles

Notes and Comments / Notes et commentaires

Book Reviews / Recensions de Livres

THE CANADIAN YEARBOOK OF INTERNATIONAL LAW

1997

ANNUAIRE CANADIEN DE DROIT INTERNATIONAL

La zone économique exclusive dans la pratique des États

FRANCIS RIGALDIES

À LA FIN DE L'ANNÉE 1996, avec sa *Loi sur les océans,*[1] le Canada se dotait d'une authentique zone économique exclusive de 200 milles en lieu et place de la zone de pêche de même largeur qu'il avait établie en 1977. Il rejoignait ainsi près d'une centaine d'États, dont une soixantaine sont actuellement liés par la Convention des Nations Unies de 1982 sur le droit de la mer.[2] Il est de bon aloi de soutenir que s'il est un secteur où la "juridiction rampante" des États côtiers se manifeste volontiers, c'est bien celui de la zone économique exclusive. Les raisons de principe ne manquent pas puisque la plupart des États à s'être dotés d'une telle zone l'ont fait avant l'adoption de la Convention de 1982, plusieurs avant même qu'un consensus final ne soit établi sur l'ensemble du régime [j]uridique de la zone dans le cadre de la troisième Conférence sur le droit de la mer. Quant aux États qui ont créé une zone économique postérieurement à l'adoption de la Convention, ils ne se sentaient pas techniquement liés par celle-ci avant son entrée en vigueur le 16 novembre 1994, et ce même s'ils l'avaient ratifiée ou y avaient adhéré.

Pourtant, si l'on veut véritablement savoir si les États côtiers outrepassent les facultés que leur offre le droit international, il convient de faire un inventaire précis des types de zones de juridiction qu'ils ont établies au large de leurs côtes et de la juridiction qu'il y exercent

---

Francis Rigaldies est professeur titulaire, faculté de droit, Université de Montréal.

1 L.C. 1996, c. 31.

2 Doc. N.U. A/CONF 62/122 et Corr. 1 à 11 (1982), ci-après Convention de 1982. Au 23 mai 1997, cette Convention comptait 116 États parties.

effectivement.[3] À la suite de cette analyse, il sera possible d'établir si la pratique correspond ou non aux exigences de la Convention de 1982, s'il s'est ou non développé des normes coutumières conformes à la Convention ou permissives par rapport à celle-ci, ou bien encore si les États agissent dans la plus totale anarchie.

I Les divers types de zones de juridiction des États côtiers dans le domaine "économique"

Même si la présente étude porte principalement sur les zones économiques exclusives proprement dites, elle prendra en compte diverses zones de juridiction dans lesquelles les États revendiquent des compétences variables dans des domaines de compétence relevant normalement, selon la Convention de 1982, de la zone économique. Il s'agira essentiellement des mers territoriales supérieures à douze milles et des zones de pêche *stricto sensu*.[4]

A Mers territoriales supérieures à douze milles

Il convient de rappeler ici que la mer territoriale constitue une zone de pêche exclusive, ce qui permet à l'État côtier de réserver s'il l'entend ainsi la pêche à ses propres ressortissants. La Convention de 1982 confère en effet clairement à l'État côtier le droit d'édicter des lois et règlements relatifs à la pêche (voir Tableau 1).[5] Toute infraction à ces lois et règlements rendra non inoffensif le

[3] Pour une compilation de la pratique des États, voir R. W. Smith, *Exclusive Economic Zone claims, An Analysis and Primary Documents*, Martinus Nijhoff Publishers, Dordrecht, Boston, Lancaster, 1986, *Le droit de la mer, Législation nationale en matière de zone économique exclusive*, Division des Affaires maritimes et du droit de la mer, Bureau des Affaires juridiques, Nations Unies, New York, 1994. Pour une superbe étude de cette pratique des États, on consultera l'incontournable recherche de L. Juda, "The Exclusive Economic Zone: Compatibility of National Claims and the United Nations Convention on the Law of the Sea," (1986) O.D.I.L. à la p. 1. Les Nations Unies ont effectué une récente synthèse de la pratique des États dans le domaine maritime intitulée *Le droit de la mer, Pratique des États au moment de l'entrée en vigueur de la Convention des Nations Unies sur le droit de la mer*, Division des Affaires maritimes et du droit de la mer, Bureau des Affaires juridiques, Nations Unies, New York, 1994, ci-après *Le droit de la mer.*

[4] Nous excluons les zones contiguës (qui ne constituent en principe que les 12 premiers milles de la zone économique exclusive et n'ont pas d'intérêt d'ordre économique). Quant au plateau continental, qui constitue par définition selon la Convention de 1982 le sol et le sous-sol de la zone économique, il possède son propre régime juridique, lequel est acquis de longue date et ne fait pas problème.

[5] Convention de 1982, art. 21, § 1e.

TABLEAU 1

Mers Territoriales supérieures a douze milles

	Convention			*Acte Unilatéral*	
	Adoption	*Signature*	*Ratification (date)*	*Largeur*	*Date d'adoption*
A. Largeur de 20 à 50 milles					
Angola[a]	P	S	R (1990)	20	1975
Nigéria[b]	P	S	R (1986)	30	1971
Togo[b]	P	S	R (1985)	30	1977
République arabe syrienne	P	*na*	*na*	35	1991
Cameroun	P	S	R (1985)	50	1974
B. Largeur de 200 milles					
Bénin	P	S	*na*		1976
Congo	P	S	*na*		1977
El Salvador	P	S	*na*		1950
Équateur	NP	*na*	*na*		1966
Libéria	NP	S	*na*		1976
Nicaragua	P	S	*na*		1979
Panama	P	S	R (1996)		1967
Pérou	P	*na*	*na*		1947
Sierra Leone	P	S	R (1994)		1971
Somalie	P	S	R (1989)		1972
Uruguay	P	S	R (1992)		1969

Notes: P — pour; NP — non-participation au vote; S — signature; R — ratification. Tableau à jour au 23 mars 1997 pour les adhésions/ratifications et au 31 décembre 1996 pour les actes unilatéraux.

[a] Possède de plus une zone de pêche de 200 milles.

[b] Possède de plus une zone économique exclusive de 200 milles.

passage d'un navire étranger.[6] Soulignons de plus qu'une mer territoriale constitue davantage qu'une zone de pêche. L'État côtier y dispose de larges compétences en matière de recherche scientifique,[7] dans le domaine environnemental,[8] au chapitre de la navigation,[9] ainsi que dans la gestion des ressources du fond et du

6 *Id.*, art. 19, § 2i.

7 Il s'agit de compétences totalement exclusives (*id.*, art. 245).

8 L'État côtier peut légiférer librement, à la seule condition de ne pas réglementer la construction des navires étrangers, sauf à donner effet aux normes internationales généralement acceptées (*id.*, art. 2, § 1f et § 2).

9 L'État côtier a la faculté d'interdire tout passage qu'il estime non inoffensif d'un navire privé étranger (*id.*, art. 25, § 1).

sous-sol,[10] qui sont sans commune mesure avec celles dont il dispose en zone économique. Or, on sait que le droit international public, qu'il soit coutumier ou conventionnel,[11] s'il autorise l'État côtier à fixer la largeur de sa mer territoriale, précise désormais que celle-ci ne peut dépasser douze milles marins. Plusieurs États côtiers ont pourtant établi au large de leurs côtes une zone de mer territoriale supérieure à douze milles. C'est ainsi qu'un État (Angola) dispose de vingt milles, deux (Nigéria et Togo) de trente milles, un (République arabe syrienne) de trente-cinq et un (Cameroun) de cinquante. Ce choix n'empêche pas les trois premiers de ces États de disposer par ailleurs d'une zone économique exclusive (Nigéria, Togo) ou d'une zone de pêche (Angola) jusqu'à 200 milles de leurs lignes de base, créant ainsi un dégradé de juridiction au large de leurs côtes en matière halieutique. Ces "anomalies" se devraient d'être provisoires, d'autant plus que les trois États en cause sont parties à la Convention de 1982. La Syrie et le Cameroun, par contre, constituent des États géographiquement désavantagés qui n'ont pas la possibilité d'exercer leur juridiction loin de leurs côtes.

De plus, onze États disposent d'une mer territoriale de 200 milles. Quelques États africains font désormais partie de ce groupe aux côtés d'États latino-américains. Plusieurs détenteurs de mer territoriale de 200 milles semblent farouchement attachés à cette formule et n'ont d'ailleurs pas ratifié la Convention. D'autres (comme l'ont prouvé l'Argentine et — plus récemment — le Brésil) pourraient assez facilement se rallier dans l'avenir au concept de zone économique exclusive. La chose paraît d'autant plus probable que plusieurs titulaires de mers territoriales de 200 milles sont devenus parties à la Convention de 1982 (Panama, Sierra Leone, Somalie, Uruguay) et devraient ainsi mettre leur législation en accord avec leurs obligations internationales. En effet, même si ces États n'exploitent pas nécessairement toutes les possibilités que leur offre le droit international en mer territoriale (plusieurs acceptent la pêche étrangère[12]

10 L'État côtier exerce sur le sol et le sous-sol de sa mer territoriale une juridiction absolue, ce qui n'est pas le cas sur le sol et le sous-sol de la zone économique, qui constituent du plateau continental (lequel n'est pas la propriété de l'État côtier) (*id.*, art. 2, § 2).

11 *Id.*, art. 3.

12 J. Carroz, *infra* note 86 à la p. 728, constate que plusieurs des législations sur la mer territoriale de 200 milles contiennent des dispositions sur la gestion des ressources biologiques et l'accès des étrangers et que des permis de pêche sont délivrés en pratique à des pêcheurs étrangers.

ou affirment la liberté de navigation),[13] la possibilité qu'ils se donnent de le faire est en elle-même condamnable.

B ZONES DE PÊCHE DE 200 MILLES OU MOINS

Dix-sept États disposent d'une zone de pêche spécifique égale ou supérieure à douze milles (voir Tableau 2). Douze d'entre eux ont une zone de pêche s'étendant jusqu'à 200 milles de leurs côtes; quatre autres disposent de largeurs variables (douze pour la Finlande, vingt-cinq pour Malte, trente-deux et cinquante-deux pour l'Algérie, cinquante pour l'Iran). Un dernier (la Belgique) possède une zone de pêche s'étendant jusqu'à la ligne médiane avec l'État voisin. Même si ces cinq derniers cas correspondent à des situations d'États géographiquement désavantagés, les dix-sept États qui ont choisi la formule de la zone de pêche ont — *a priori* du moins[14] — renoncé aux compétences autres qu'halieutiques auxquelles ils pourraient prétendre dans une authentique zone économique exclusive. Dans plusieurs cas, on note le souci d'États qui ont décidé très tôt (en général en 1977: voir Tableau 3) de créer des zones de 200 milles au large de leurs côtes de faire montre de retenue, alors que le contenu exact de la juridiction de l'État côtier n'était pas définitivement arrêté à la troisième Conférence. Ceci explique que plusieurs d'entre eux (États-Unis, Union soviétique à l'époque, Dominique, Antigua et Barbuda, ainsi que, depuis peu, le Canada et les Bahamas), qui avaient initialement établi une simple zone de pêche de 200 milles, l'aient convertie ultérieurement en zone économique authentique. Il n'y a en revanche rien d'illégal pour un État à posséder une simple zone de pêche jusqu'à 200 milles de ses côtes. La juridiction que les États exercent dans le domaine de l'exploitation des ressources halieutiques se compare d'ailleurs généralement à celle qu'exercent les détenteurs d'authentiques zones économiques de 200 milles.

C ZONES ÉCONOMIQUES EXCLUSIVES DE 200 MILLES OU MOINS

Tout État doté d'un littoral a droit à une zone économique exclusive, sauf dans le cas de rochers ne se prêtant pas à l'habitation humaine ou à une vie économique propre.[15] L'État doit cependant

[13] Voir *infra* note 37.

[14] Le Canada, p. ex., aurait pu appliquer nombre de compétences d'ordre environnemental dans la zone de pêche de 200 milles qu'il possédait de 1977 à 1996.

[15] Convention de 1982, art. 121, § 3.

TABLEAU 2

Zones de pêche

	Convention			*Acte Unilatéral*
	Adoption	*Signature*	*Ratification (date)*	*Date d'adoption*
A. Largeur de 200 milles				
Afrique du Sud	*na*	S	*na*	1977
Allemagne	A		Ad (1996)	1977
Angola	P	S	R (1990)	1975
Danemark	P	S	*na*	1977
Gambie	Ab	S	R (1984)	1978
Guyana	P	S	R (1993)	1977
Irlande	P	S	R (1996)	1977
Japon	P	S	R (1996)	1977
Nauru	Ab	S	R (1996)	1978
Papouasie-Nouvelle Guinée	P	S	R (1997)	1975 (1977-78)
Pays Bas	A	S	R (1996)	1977
Royaume-Uni	A	*na*	*na*	1977
B. Largeur inférieure à 200 milles				
Algérie[a] (32 et 52)	P	S	R (1996)	1994
Finlande (12)	P	S	R (1996)	1975
[Iran][b] (50)	P	S	*na*	[1959]
Malte (25)	P	S	R (1993)	1978
C. Largeur variable				
Belgique	A	S	*na*	1978 (équidistance)

Notes: A — adoption; Ab — Absence; Ad — Adhésion; P — pour; S — signature; R — ratification. Tableau à jour au 23 mars 1997 pour les adhésions/ratifications et au 31 décembre 1996 pour les actes unilatéraux.

[a] Zone de pêche réservée (étrangers admis sur la base de permis pour la pêche aux grands migrateurs seulement).

[b] Les Nations Unies indiquent toujours cette zone de pêche, en plus de la ZÉE.

TABLEAU 3

Chronologie de la proclamation des zones économiques exclusives (ZÉE) et des zones de pêche de 200 milles

Année	*ZÉE*	*Zone de pêche*
1974 (2e session)	Bangladesh	
	Qatar	
1975 (TUNO)	Costa Rica[a]	Angola[a]
		Finlande[a]
		Papousie-Nouvelle Guinée
1976 (TUNOR)	Comores[a]	
	France[a]	
	Guatémala	
	Inde[a]	
	Luxembourg	
	Maldives	
	Mozambique	
	Norvège[a]	
	Pakistan	
	Sénégal[a]	
	Sri Lanka[a]	
1977 (TNCO)	Cap Vert[a]	Afrique du sud
	Côte d'Ivoire[a]	Allemagne[a]
	Cuba[a]	Bahamas[a]
	Îles Cook[a]	Danemark
	Maurice[a]	Guyana[a]
	Myanmar[a]	Irlande[a]
	Nioué	Japon[a]
	Nouvelle-Zélande[a]	Pays Bas[a]
	Portugal	Royaume-Uni
	République démocratique populaire de Corée	
	République dominicaine	
	Samoa occidental[a]	
	Seychelles[a]	
	Togo[a]	
	Tokelau	
	Vietnam[a]	
	Yémen[a]	
1978 (7e session)	Barbade[a]	Gambie[a]

(Suite à la page suivante)

TABLEAU 3 *(suite)*

Chronologie de la proclamation des zones économiques exclusives et des zones de pêche de 200 milles

Année	*ZÉE*	*Zone de pêche*
	Colombie	Malte[a]
	Djibouti[a]	Nauru[a]
	Espagne	
	Grenade[a]	
	Guinée Bissau[a]	
	Îles Salomon	
	Mauritanie[a]	
	Nigéria[a]	
	Philippines[a]	
	Sao Tomé et Principe[a]	
	Suriname	
	Tonga[a]	
	Vénézuela	
1979 (TNCO, Rev. 1)	Cambodge Islande[a]	
	Kenya[a]	
	République unie de Tanzanie[a]	
1980 (TNCO, Rev. 2; Projet de Convention, texte officieux)	Émirats arabes unis	
	Guinée[a]	
	Honduras[a]	
	Indonésie[a]	
	Maroc	
1981 (Projet de Convention)	Dominique[a]	
	Fidji[a]	
	Oman[a]	
	Thaïlande	
	Vanuatu	
1982 (Adoption et signature)	Antigua et Barbuda[a]	
1983	Égypte[a]	
	États-Unis	
	Fédération de Russie	
	Kiribati	

(Suite à la page suivante)

TABLEAU 3 *(suite)*

Chronologie de la proclamation des zones économiques exclusives et des zones de pêche de 200 milles

Année	*ZÉE*	*Zone de pêche*
	Saint-Vincent et Grenadines[a]	
	Trinité et Tobago[a]	
	Tuvalu	
1984	Gabon	
	Guinée équatoriale	
	Îles Marshall[a]	
	Malaisie[a]	
	Saint Kitts et Névis[a]	
	Sainte-Lucie[a]	
1985	Madagascar	
1986	Chili	
	Ghana[a]	
	Roumanie	
	Turquie	
1987	Bulgarie[a]	
1988	Micronésie[a]	
1989	Argentine[a]	
1990	Namibie[a]	
1991	Jamaïque[a]	
	Pologne	
1992	Suède[a]	
	Zaïre[a]	
1993	Brésil[a]	
	Brunei Darussalam[a]	
	Estonie	
	Iran	
1994 (Entrée en vigueur)	Australie[a]	
	Algérie	
1995	Ukraine	
1996	Bahamas[a]	
	Canada	

Notes: TUNO — texte unique de négociation officieux; TUNOR — texte unique de négociation officieux révisé; TNCO — texte de négociation composite officieux. En dessous des années figurent les principaux documents élaborés par la troisième Conférence sur le droit de la mer. Tableau à jour au 31 décembre 1996.

[a] Partie à la Convention de 1982.

proclamer formellement sa zone (à la différence de la mer territoriale ou du plateau continental).

La zone économique ne s'étend pas au-delà de 200 milles des lignes de base de la mer territoriale.[16] Puisqu'elle est adjacente à cette dernière,[17] elle n'aura donc jamais, en pratique, une largeur de 200 milles. Par ailleurs, si l'État s'est doté d'une zone contiguë, les compétences qu'il y exerce s'ajouteront à celles dont il jouit dans la zone économique, dans les limites de la zone contiguë naturellement.[18]

On compte aujourd'hui quatre-vingt-huit États disposant d'une zone économique s'étendant jusqu'à 200 milles de leurs côtes quand huit autres ont dû limiter leurs prétentions, compte tenu d'une situation géographiquement désavantagée (Tableau 4). En pratique, pour les quatre-vingt-huit États non enclavés, la largeur réelle de la zone économique varie (en fonction de la largeur de la mer territoriale) de 170 milles (Nigéria, Togo) à 194 milles (République Dominicaine.[19] La largeur la plus courante est naturellement de 188 milles, les États ayant généralement opté pour une mer territoriale de douze milles. Un État (Philippines) dispose même d'une zone économique (apparente) de 200 milles puisqu'il ne paraît pas avoir de mer territoriale déclarée.[20] Oman et le Togo, pour leur part, semblent inclure leur mer territoriale dans leur zone économique exclusive puisqu'ils n'affirment pas la "contiguïté" de cette dernière par rapport à leur mer territoriale.

Le nombre d'États revendiquant des zones de contrôle de pêche au large de leurs côtes est donc impressionnant. Rappelons que 124 États contrôlent d'une façon ou d'une autre la pêche au maximum

16 *Id.*, art. 57.

17 *Id.*, art. 55.

18 C'est ainsi que le Canada, en vertu de sa récente *Loi sur les océans* (réf. *supra* note 1), dispose désormais, au-delà de sa mer territoriale de 12 milles, d'une zone contiguë de 12 milles supplémentaires, qui recouvre les premiers 12 milles de sa zone économique.

19 On note le même phénomène pour les zones de pêche de "200" milles qui varient en pratique de 180 milles à 197 milles (Bahamas, Danemark).

20 En fait, ainsi que l'on vient de le souligner, la mer territoriale existe en dehors de toute proclamation expresse. La détermination de sa largeur constitue par contre, dans un cas de non proclamation, un problème. Le décret philippin précise d'ailleurs que la zone économique est contiguë à la mer territoriale.

TABLEAU 4

Zones économiques exclusives

	Convention			*Acte Unilatéral*
	Adoption	*Signature*	*Ratification (date)*	*Date d'adoption*
A. Largeur de 200 milles				
Antigua et Barbuda	Ab	S	R (1989)	1982
Argentine	P	S	R (1995)	1989 (1991)
Australie[1]	P	S	R (1994)	1994
Bahamas	P	S	R (1983)	1993 (1996)
Bangladesh	P	S	*na*	1974
Barbade	P	S	R (1993)	1978
Bélize	Ab	S	R (1983)	1992
Brésil	P	S	R (1988)	1993
Brunei Darussalam	*na*	S	R (1996)	1993
Bulgarie	A	S	R (1995)	1987
Cambodge	P	S	*na*	1979 (1982)
Canada	P	S	*na*	1996
Cap Vert	P	S	R (1987)	1977 [1978] (1992)
Chili	P	S	*na*	1965 (1986) (discutable)
Colombie	P	S	*na*	1978
Comores	Ab	S	R (1994)	1976 (1982)
Costa Rica	P	S	R (1992)	1975
Côte d'Ivoire	P	S	R (1984)	1977
Cuba	P	S	R (1984)	1977
Djibouti	P	S	R (1991)	1978 [1979]
Dominique	Ab	S	R (1991)	1981
Émirats Arabes unis	P	S	*na*	1980 (1993)
Espagne	A	S	R (1997)	1978
États-Unis	C	*na*	*na*	1983
Fédération de Russie	A	S	R (1997)	1983 [1984]
Fidji	P	S	R (1982)	1981
France	P	S	R (1996)	1976 [1977]
Gabon	P	S	*na*	1984
Ghana	P	S	R (1983)	1986
Grenade	P	S	R (1991)	1978
Guatemala	P	S	R (1997)	1976
Guinée	P	S	R (1995)	1980

(Suite à la page suivante)

TABLEAU 4 *(suite)*

Zones économiques exclusives

	Convention			*Acte Unilatéral*
	Adoption	*Signature*	*Ratification (date)*	*Date d'adoption*
Guinée Bissau	P	S	R (1986)	1978 (1985)
Guinée équatoriale	Ab	S	*na*	1984
Haïti	P	S	R (1996)	1977
Honduras	P	S	R (1993)	1980
Îles Cook	*na*	S	R (1995)	1977 [1978]
Îles Marshall	*na*	*na*	Ad (1991)	1984
Îles Salomon	Ab	S	*na*	1978 [1979]
Inde	P	S	R (1995)	1976 [1977]
Indonésie	P	S	R (1986)	1980 (1983)
Islande	P	S	R (1985)	1979
Jamaïque	P	S	R (1983)	1991
Kenya	P	S	R (1989)	1979
Kiribati	Ab	*na*	*na*	1983
Madagascar	P	S	*na*	1985
Malaisie	P	S	R (1996)	1984
Maroc	P	S	*na*	1980 [1981]
Maurice	P	S	R (1994)	1977
Mauritanie	P	S	R (1996)	1978 (1988)
Mexique	P	S	R (1983)	1976 (1986)
Micronésie	*na*	*na*	Ad (1991)	1988
Mozambique	P	S	R (1997)	1976 (1985)
Myanmar	P	S	R (1996)	1977
Namibie	P	S	R (1983)	1990 [1991]
Nigéria	P	S	R (1986)	1978
Nioué	*na*	S	*na*	1977 [1978]
Norvège	P	S	R (1996)	1976 [1977]
Nouvelle-Zélande	P	S	R (1996)	1977 [1978] (1980)
Oman	P	S	R (1989)	1981
Pakistan	P	S	R (1997)	1976
Philippines	P	S	R (1984)	1978 [1979]
Portugal	P	S	*na*	1977 [1978]
République démocratique populaire de Corée	P	S	*na*	1977

(Suite à la page suivante)

TABLEAU 4 *(suite)*

Zones économiques exclusives

	Convention			*Acte Unilatéral*
	Adoption	*Signature*	*Ratification (date)*	*Date d'adoption*
République Dominicaine	P	S	*na*	1977
République unie de Tanzanie	P	S	R (1985)	1979
Roumanie	P	S	R (1997)	1986
Saint-Kitts-et-Névis	*na*	S	R (1993)	1984
Sainte-Lucie	P	S	R (1985)	1984
Saint-Vincent-et-Grenadines	P	S	R (1993)	1983
Samoa occidental	P	S	R (1995)	1977 (1980)
Sao Tomé-et-Principe	P	S	R (1987)	1978
Sénégal	P	S	R (1984)	1976 (1987)
Seychelles	P	S	R (1991)	1977
Sri Lanka	P	S	R (1994)	1976 [1977]
Suriname	P	S	*na*	1978
Thaïlande	A	S	*na*	1981 [1982]
Togo	P	S	R (1985)	1977
Tokelau	*na*	*na*	*na*	1977 [1978]
Tonga	Ab	*na*	Ad (1995)	1978 [1979]
Trinité-et-Tobago	P	S	R (1986)	1983 (1986)
Turquie	C	*na*	*na*	1986
Tuvalu	Ab	S	*na*	1983 (proclamation) 1986 (loi)
Ukraine	A	S	*na*	1995
Vanuatu	Ab	S	*na*	1981 [1982]
Vénézuela	C	*na*	*na*	1978
Vietnam	P	S	R (1994)	1977
Yémen	P	S	R (1987)	1977 [1978]
B. Largeur variable				
Égypte	P	S	R (1983)	1983 (selon Convention)
Estonie	*na*	*na*	*na*	1993 (coordonnées)

(Suite à la page suivante)

TABLEAU 4 *(suite)*

Zones économiques exclusives

	Convention			*Acte Unilatéral*
	Adoption	*Signature*	*Ratification (date)*	*Date d'adoption*
Îles Maldives	Ab	S	*na*	1976 (coordonnées)
Iran	P	S	*na*	1993 (accord ou ligne médiane)
Pologne	A	S	*na*	1991 (accords)
Qatar[a]	P	S	*na*	1974 (accord ou équidistance)
Suède	P	S	R (1996)	1992 (accord ou ligne médiane)
Zaïre	P	S	R (1989)	1992 (accord)

Notes: A — abstention; Ab — absence; Ad — adhésion; C — contre; P — pour; S — signature; R — ratification. Les dates sont celles de l'établissement initial de la zone. La date entre parenthèses constitue la date d'entrée en vigueur (lorsqu'elle diffère). La date entre crochets correspond à l'acte unilatéral le plus récent. Tableau à jour au 23 mai 1997 pour les adhésions/ratifications et au 31 décembre 1997 pour les actes unilatéraux.

[a] Compétences sur ressources naturelles et halieutiques seulement.

des possibilités que leur offrent leurs conditions géographiques.[21] Si l'on estime à 192 le nombre d'États susceptibles de devenir partie à la Convention de 1982, soixante-huit États n'ont ainsi pas créé de zones de contrôle de pêche. Or, quarante-deux d'entre eux ne risquent pas d'en établir puisqu'ils sont enclavés.[22] Sur les vingt-six

21 Quatre-vingt-seize États disposent d'une zone économique exclusive, 17 d'une zone de pêche, 11 d'une mer territoriale de 200 milles. De plus, La Syrie a une mer territoriale de 35 milles et le Cameroun une mer territoriale de 50 milles. Nous retenons le chiffre de 124 (et non 125) afin de ne pas décompter deux fois l'Iran (qui dispose à la fois d'une zone de pêche de 50 milles et d'une ZÉE).

22 Il s'agit des États suivants: Afghanistan, Andore, Arménie, Autriche, Azerbaidjan, Bélarus, Bhoutan, Bolivie, Botswana, Burkina Faso, Burundi, Éthiopie, Hongrie, Kazakhstan, Kirghizistan, Lesotho, Liechstestein, Luxembourg, Macédoine, Malawi, Mali, Mongolie, Népal, Niger, Ouganda, Ouzbekistan, Paraguay, République centrafricaine, République démocratique du Lao, République de Moldova, République tchèque, Rwanda, Saint-Marin, Saint-Siège, Slovaquie, Suisse, Swaziland, Tadjikistan, Tchad, Turmekistan, Zambie, Zimbabwe.

qui restent, seize sont géographiquement désavantagés[23] et huit méditerranéens.[24] À l'exclusion de l'Égypte, ces derniers ont renoncé à établir des zones économiques exclusives et ont opté pour un contrôle concerté de la pêche (et de l'environnement). Il n'y a ainsi guère que la Chine et la République de Corée qui ne disposent pour contrôler la pêche que d'une mer territoriale de douze milles. La Chine a toutefois fait savoir qu'elle se doterait prochainement d'une zone économique de 200 milles.[25]

II La juridiction concrètement exercée par les États côtiers dans leur zone économique exclusive

Près de cinquante États (sur les quatre-vingt-seize qui en possèdent aujourd'hui) se sont dotés d'une zone économique exclusive entre 1976 et 1978 (Tableau 4). Si on y ajoute les États qui ont créé une zone de pêche de 200 milles à cette époque, ce chiffre dépasse les soixante. Si on y ajoute enfin les États qui ont opté pour une mer territoriale de 200 milles, plus de soixante-dix États exerçaient une juridiction sur la pêche jusqu'à 200 milles en 1978.[26] Il est bien évident que les États qui ont légiféré antérieurement à cette date ne se sentaient guère liés par ce qui n'était alors qu'un texte de négociation officieux.[27] Rappelons qu'en 1977, on discutait encore pied à pied à la troisième Conférence sur le statut de la zone, l'accès des États sans littoral et géographiquement désavantagés, ou la gestion des grands migrateurs pour ne citer que quelques problèmes non réglés.

La question du statut, en particulier, constituait un enjeu de taille, opposant le tiers-monde aux États développés. Les pays riches souhaitaient en effet que la zone constitue de la haute mer. De la

[23] Albanie, Arabie saoudite, Bahrein, Bosnie Herzégovine, Croatie, Erythrée, Georgie, Iraq, Jordanie, Koweït, Lettonie, Lithuanie, Singapour, Slovénie, Soudan, Yougoslavie.

[24] Chypre, Grèce, Israël, Italie, Libye, Liban, Monaco, Tunisie.

[25] L. Juda, "The Exclusive Economic Zone: Non-Claimant States," (1988) O.D.I.L. 431. En ratifiant la Convention de 1982, la Chine a fait une déclaration annonçant cette future création de ZÉE. Voir Bureau des affaires maritimes et du droit de la mer, *Bulletin du droit de la mer*, Nations Unies, New York, n° 31 à la p. 8 (ci-après *Bulletin du droit de la mer*).

[26] On pourra consulter à cet égard les statistiques et tableaux présentés dans R.W. Smith, *supra* note 3, en particulier p. 33.

[27] Le premier État à avoir légiféré, le Bangladesh, a créé sa zone en 1974, alors même qu'aucun texte de négociation n'avait été établi par la troisième Conférence (cf. R.W. Smith, *supra* note 3 à la p. 30).

sorte, les États côtiers ne pourraient y exercer de compétences que dans la mesure où la Convention le prévoirait expressément. Nulle compétence implicite ou résiduaire ne pourrait ainsi être revendiquée. De leur côté, les pays en développement souhaitaient pour la zone un statut plus territorial, impliquant que les compétences expressément reconnues aux États côtiers puissent être éventuellement complétées par le recours à la théorie des compétences implicites ou accessoires. La Convention de 1982 a finalement choisi une formule de compromis manifestement ambiguë. L'article 55 opte formule de compromis manifestement ambiguë. L'article 55 opte en effet pour un statut *sui generis* en indiquant que la zone est "soumise au régime juridique particulier établi par la présente partie en vertu duquel les droits et la juridiction de l'État côtier et les droits et libertés des autres États sont gouvernés par les dispositions de la présente convention." L'article 86, qui définit plus loin le champ d'application de la Partie VII sur la haute mer (ce qui ne constitue d'ailleurs pas une définition de celle-ci) retient une approche résiduelle selon laquelle "[l]a présente partie s'applique à toutes le[s] parties de la mer qui ne sont comprises ni dans la zone économique exclusive, la mer territoriale ou les eaux intérieures d'un État, ni dans les eaux archipélagiques d'un État archipel." Mais cet article, qui exclut formellement la zone économique de la haute mer, s'empresse d'ajouter qu'il ". . . ne restreint en aucune manière les libertés dont jouissent tous les États dans la zone économique exclusive en vertu de l'article 58." Or, cet article fait référence à l'ensemble des libertés de la haute mer (sauf la pêche, la recherche scientifique et le droit de construire des îles artificielles), en précisant toutefois que les États qui exercent ces libertés dans la zone d'un tiers doivent tenir compte des droits et obligations de l'État côtier dans sa zone. Et, comme pour compenser cette assertion, l'article 56, para. 2 vient, à l'inverse, souligner l'obligation pour l'État côtier qui exerce ces droits et obligations de tenir ". . . dûment compte des droits et des obligations des autres États . . ." Somme toute, un match nul entre les pays en développement et les grandes puissances maritimes . . .

En pratique, les législations nationales se prononcent rarement de façon expresse sur la question de la nature juridique de la zone économique. Le Bangladesh, pourtant, qui ouvrait le bal des créations de zone économique exclusive en 1974, qualifiait alors sa zone — de façon surprenante — de zone de haute mer. Il faut dire que sa loi précédait le premier texte de négociation établi par la troisième Conférence en 1975. Dans la déclaration qu'il émettait lors de la signature de la Convention de 1982, le Chili, par contre, affirmait en rapport avec la zone que:

> La Convention la caractérise comme une zone de juridiction côtière dépendant de la souveraineté territoriale et rattachée au territoire lui-même, dans des conditions semblables aux autres espaces marins, à savoir la mer territoriale et le plateau continental.[28]

Mais c'est plutôt de façon implicite que les États caractérisent leur zone et la tendance à la territorialisation est parfois évidente, en particulier au chapitre des compétences résiduaires. À cet égard, on se rappellera que, dans les cas où la Convention n'attribue de compétences dans la zone ni à l'État côtier ni à d'autres États et qu'un conflit se manifeste, ce conflit devrait être résolu sur la base de l'équité.[29] Compte tenu de l'absence de détermination précise du statut de la zone, cette problématique des compétences ancillaires, accessoires ou implicites de l'État côtier dans sa zone ne peut que générer des tensions.[30] C'est ainsi que, ignorant les subtiles balises de la Convention, plusieurs États n'hésitent pas à se doter de compétences résiduaires sans autre précision.[31] D'autres États se donnent des compétences résiduaires spécifiques de légalité contestable. Ainsi en est-il parfois dans le domaine de la sécurité. Le Brésil, par exemple, exige une autorisation avant tout exercice de manoeuvres militaires étrangères dans sa zone.[32] Les puissances

28 *Bulletin du droit de la mer*, n° 25, juin 1994 à la p. 29.

29 Convention de 1982, art. 59.

30 *Id.*, art. 56, § 2, qui laisse entendre p. ex. qu'il existe dans le domaine de l'exploration et de l'exploitation de la zone à des fins économiques d'autres activités que celles visant à la production d'énergie à partir de l'eau, des courants et des vents, citées à fins illustratives seulement.

31 Haïti, p. ex., affirme disposer de compétences résiduaires "selon la loi" et non selon le droit international.

32 Une survivance probable de l'époque où il disposait d'une mer territoriale de 200 milles. Dans le même sens, voir la Déclaration de Cap Vert lors de sa signature de la Convention de 1982 et celle, récente, de l'Inde, lors de la ratification de la Convention (*Bulletin du droit de la mer* n° 29 à la p. 8). L'Uruguay, à l'occasion de la Déclaration émise lors de la signature, retient la même formule relativement à la ZÉE. La chose ne manque pas de surprendre, puisque l'Uruguay précise dans la même déclaration que "[l]es dispositions de la Convention relatives à . . . la zone économique exclusive sont compatibles avec les objectifs et les principes fondamentaux dont s'inspire la législation de l'Uruguay en ce qui concerne sa souveraineté et sa juridiction sur l'espace maritime adjacent à ses côtes . . . jusqu'à 200 milles marins." L'Uruguay ayant

maritimes se sont montrées farouchement opposées à ce type d'attitude, tout particulièrement l'Allemagne, l'Italie et les États-Unis.[33] Haïti se confère lui aussi dans sa zone économique des compétences dans le domaine de la sécurité.[34] Cette approche va jusqu'à impliquer à ses yeux le contrôle du survol de la zone: "La République d'Haïti exerce sa souveraineté exclusive sur l'espace aérien de son territoire et de ses eaux juridictionnelles jusqu'aux limites [des 200 milles]."[35]

Plusieurs États enfin soumettent leur zone économique ou certaines parties de celle-ci éventuellement au régime du libre passage inoffensif, qui est celui de la mer territoriale,[36] chose d'autant plus paradoxale que certains États détenteurs d'"authentiques" mers territoriales de 200 milles y reconnaissent la libre navigation![37] De nombreuses puissances maritimes condamnent de tels agissements, au nombre desquelles l'Italie, qui rappelait en 1995 qu'

> [a]ucune des dispositions de la Convention, qui correspond à ce sujet à la coutume du droit international, ne peut être considérée comme donnant à l'État côtier le droit de subordonner le passage innocent de

---

ratifié la Convention de 1982, ceci revient à dire que la ZÉE constitue à ses yeux de la mer territoriale, puisque l'Uruguay dispose actuellement d'une mer territoriale de 200 milles.

33 L'Allemagne, dans la déclaration émise lors de son adhésion à la Convention de 1982 (*Bulletin du droit de la mer*, n° 27 aux pp. 7 et 8) estimait que les États côtiers ne peuvent y contrôler les manoeuvres militaires. L'Italie, lors de la ratification, spécifiait: "les droits de l'État côtier dans cette zone n'incluent pas le droit d'obtenir notification des exercices ou manoeuvres militaires ou de les autoriser" (*Bulletin du droit de la mer*, n° 27 à la p. 5). Les États-Unis ont récemment réaffirmé la liberté de navigation en ZÉE, même au profit des navires qui transportent des déchets dangereux selon la Convention de Bâle: *Bulletin du droit de la mer*, n° 31 à la p. 39.

34 Décret du 8 avril 1977.

35 Déclaration en date du 6 avril 1977, en vigueur dès publication et notifiée aux gouvernements concernés. Notons que le Décret du 8 avril 1977 (*supra* note 34) fait allusion à cette déclaration en préambule. Le Brésil et Haïti ont ratifié la Convention de 1982.

36 Par exemple, les Maldives (signataires de la Convention de 1982). L'Inde, le Pakistan, Maurice et les Seychelles prétendent pour leur part pouvoir imposer des corridors de navigation dans certains secteurs de leur zone économique (*infra* notes 40, 106 et 158-59).

37 Le Pérou, l'Uruguay et (autrefois) l'Argentine.

catégories particulières de navires étrangers à une autorisation ou à une notification préalable.[38]

Autre exemple: quelques États, dont Haïti, assimilent leur zone économique à une zone contiguë, reprenant ainsi la vieille revendication des "contiguïstes," principalement véhiculée par le Nigéria lors de la troisième Conférence sur le droit de la mer.[39] Certains de ces États limitent cependant leurs revendications (dans de possibles "zones désignées" au demeurant) à des compétences douanières et fiscales (à l'exclusion par conséquent des questions sanitaires et d'immigration.[40]

Ces prétentions territorialistes ont été fréquemment contestées par diverses puissances maritimes. On peut citer l'Italie qui, en ratifiant la Convention, réaffirmait que "l'État côtier n'a pas de droits résiduels dans la zone économique exclusive[41] ainsi que, lors de son adhésion, l'Allemagne, qui rappelait que "la notion d'une zone de 200 milles sur lesquels l'État côtier exercerait généralement des droits de souveraineté et de compétence ne peut pas être défendue ni en droit international général, ni en application des dispositions pertinentes de la Convention" et qui concluait, de la même façon que l'Italie, quant à l'absence de droits résiduels au profit de l'État côtier dans sa zone économique.[42] Une telle attitude est elle-même exagérée puisque la Convention prévoit l'éventualité de tels pouvoirs.

Quant aux compétences expressément attribuées à l'État côtier dans sa zone économique exclusive, elles sont globalement listées dans l'article 56 de la Convention de 1982, dont le paragraphe 1er dispose:

38 Déclaration émise lors de la ratification, *Bulletin du droit de la mer*, n° 27 à la p. 5. Les États européens se sont objectés de la même façon à toutes les interprétations de diverses conventions qui porteraient atteinte à la libre navigation en ZÉE. Voir sur ce point *Le droit de la mer*, *supra* note 3 à la p. 133.

39 Paradoxalement, le Nigéria ne semble pas revendiquer de compétences dans les domaines couverts par la zone contiguë. Il faut dire qu'il a opté pour une mer territoriale de 30 milles.

40 Inde, Maurice, Pakistan, Seychelles, p. ex. L'Inde et le Pakistan se donnent la possibilité d'appliquer toutes leurs lois en ZÉE, comme si celle-ci constituait une partie du territoire étatique. Voir *Le droit de la mer*, *supra*, note 3 à la p. 72. Nombre d'États africains réaffirment par contre dans leur législation le principe de la liberté de navigation et de survol dans leur ZÉE (*Le droit de la mer*, *id.* à la p. 36).

41 *Bulletin du droit de la mer*, n° 27 à la p. 5.

42 *Id.*, aux pp. 7-8.

Dans la zone économique exclusive, L'État côtier a:

(a) des droits souverains aux fins d'exploration et d'exploitation, de conservation et de gestion des ressources naturelles, biologiques ou non biologiques, des eaux surjacentes aux fonds marins, des fonds marins et de leur sous-sol, ainsi qu'en ce qui concerne d'autres activités tendant à l'exploration et à l'exploitation de la zone à des fins économiques, telles que la production d'énergie à partir de l'eau, des courants et des vents;

(b) juridiction, conformément aux dispositions pertinentes de la Convention, en ce qui concerne:

 (i) la mise en place et l'utilisation d'îles artificielles, d'installations et d'ouvrages;

 (ii) la recherche scientifique marine;

 (iii) la protection et la préservation du milieu marin;

(c) les autres droits et obligations prévus par la Convention.

Ces compétences attribuées concernent ainsi essentiellement les ressources naturelles, l'environnement et la recherche scientifique.[43] S'agissant des ressources naturelles, on ne retiendra ici que les compétences reliées aux ressources halieutiques de la colonne d'eau, les autres ressources naturelles aquatiques demeurant d'intérêt mineur pour l'instant. Quant aux ressources naturelles du fond et du sous-sol de la zone, elles relèvent de l'étude du plateau continental et présentent peu de difficultés juridiques.

L'intérêt premier de la zone économique concerne sans nul doute la gestion des ressources halieutiques (espèces vivantes) non sédentaires et, à cet égard, la zone ne mérite pas totalement son appellation d'"exclusive." La Convention est en l'espèce le fruit d'un compromis qui possède sa logique interne. Alors que les pays en développement souhaitaient initialement une zone de pêche à tous égards exclusive, les grandes puissances halieutiques défendaient plutôt en matière halieutique une approche non zonale et strictement préférentielle au profit des États côtiers et même parfois seulement de certains d'entre eux. La Conférence a fini par retenir dès 1974 une approche zonale qui est mi-exclusive et

43 Bien rares seront les États qui n'exploiteront pas les possibilités que leur offre la Convention, sauf ceux qui ont opté pour une simple zone de pêche de 200 milles. Pourtant, bien que disposant d'une authentique ZÉE, l'Argentine ne revendique de juridiction qu'à l'égard des ressources naturelles et Qatar (qui opte pour une "zone territoriale") limite sa juridiction aux ressources naturelles et halieutiques. On verra plus loin que quelques États ont renoncé à exercer des compétences dans certains secteurs comme la recherche scientifique (le tiers environ, dont les États-Unis). La quasi-totalité des lois accordent aux États côtiers — minimalement — des compétences sur les ressources naturelles et en matière environnementale.

mi-préférentielle. La Convention de 1982 opte en faveur de compétences exclusives au bénéfice de l'État côtier pour ce qui est de la conservation des ressources halieutiques de sa zone. Tel était le but premier recherché puisque la surexploitation antérieure découlait principalement de l'absence d'intérêt des États du pavillon à exercer une tutelle efficace sur leurs navires de pêche dans les espaces maritimes aujourd'hui englobés dans les zones économiques d'États tiers et qui constituaient alors de la haute mer. Toutefois, l'État côtier est tenu de respecter l'objectif de l'utilisation optimale des ressources. On voit ici toute la différence entre le plateau continental et la zone économique dans sa constituante aquatique. Alors que l'État côtier peut laisser en jachère son plateau, il se doit d'exploiter les ressources halieutiques de la colonne d'eau au maximum de leur potentiel. Ce concept d'utilisation optimale, joint à la constatation de l'incapacité pratique des États côtiers en développement à la réaliser, ouvrait la porte à la notion de droits strictement préférentiels (et non exclusifs) au bénéfice des États côtiers dans l'exploitation des ressources halieutiques non sédentaires de leur zone.[44]

Concrètement, l'exercice de ces droits par l'État côtier s'effectue selon la Convention de la façon suivante. Dans un premier temps, l'État fixe le total admissible des captures (TAC) dans sa zone économique,[45] par espèce et par saison de pêche (en tenant compte naturellement des mesures de conservation: utilisation optimale ne signifie pas ratissage). Dans un deuxième temps, L'État côtier détermine ses propres capacités de prises (par espèce et par saison toujours). Dans un troisième temps enfin, si cette capacité

44 La plupart des auteurs refusent ce qualificatif de "préférentiel." Cette terminologie, employée par la CIJ dans l'affaire des *Pêcheries* (Royaume-Uni/Islande; R.F.A./Islande), arrêt, Recueil C.I.J. 1974 à la p. 3, leur semble dépassée. Elle témoignait pourtant du souci de la Cour d'opposer une approche "exclusiviste" des droits de l'État côtier en matière halieutique au sens que donne à ce qualificatif le droit, tant conventionnel que coutumier, relatif au plateau continental et une approche strictement "préférentielle," c.-à-d. prioritaire, au bénéfice de l'État côtier. Même si la Cour retenait ce dernier concept au profit des seuls États en situation de "dépendance spéciale" à l'égard de la pêche (ce qui n'est pas le cas dans la Convention de 1982), il nous semble qu'il demeure tout-à-fait adapté au régime de l'exploitation des ressources halieutiques non sédentaires de la zone économique. Si l'on peut parler de compétences exclusives au bénéfice de l'État côtier, c'est seulement au chapitre de la conservation et de la gestion des ressources, et non de leur exploitation, sauf à prouver qu'il n'existe pas de surplus. Dans ce sens, J.E. Bailey, *infra* note 86 à la p. 1275 et sa note 49.

45 Convention de 1982, art. 61, § 1.

d'exploitation est inférieure à l'ensemble du volume admissible des captures, l'État côtier "autorise" d'autres États à exploiter le reliquat du volume admissible.[46] Il s'agit bien là d'une obligation, plus évidente au demeurant dans d'autres versions linguistiques de la Convention que la version française.[47] Elle est pourtant tempérée par le fait que l'État qui accorde l'accès aux tiers dans sa zone ". . . tient compte de tous les facteurs pertinents, entre autres: l'importance que les ressources biologiques de la zone présentent pour son économie et ses autres intérêts nationaux . . ."[48] Il doit tout de même prendre en considération ". . . la nécessité de réduire les perturbations économiques dans les États dont les ressortissants pratiquent habituellement la pêche dans la zone . . ."[49] Il doit aussi tenir compte des besoins des États en développement de la région, tout particulièrement ceux qui sont sans littoral ou géographiquement désavantagés.[50]

46 *Id.*, art. 62, § 2.

47 L'État côtier "shall . . . give access to the surplus of the allowable catch . . ." dans la version anglaise, et "dara acceso a ostros Estados al excedente de la capture permissible . . ." dans la version espagnole.

48 Convention de 1982, art. 62, § 3.

49 *Ibid.*

50 *Id.*, art. 69 à 71. Les "ESL-GD" sont en pratique les grands perdants de la Convention. Les ESL et les GD en développement réclamaient un droit d'accès égal aux ressources biologiques des États voisins afin d'obtenir une part équitable du TAC (les ESL développés ne pouvant bénéficier d'un tel droit que dans les ZÉE des États voisins développés). En pratique, les ESL n'ont obtenu que ". . . le droit de participer, selon une forme équitable, à l'exploitation d'une part appropriée du *reliquat* [nous italiques] des ressources biologiques . . ." des États voisins (art. 69, § 1), avec de nombreuses réserves (art. 69, § 2), les ESL développés ne disposant de ce droit que dans les ZÉE des États voisins développés. Les GD en développement et ceux qui ne peuvent prétendre à une ZÉE ont obtenu les mêmes droits, avec les mêmes restrictions (art. 70, § 1 et 2). Il existe quelques dispositions spécifiques concernant les ESL et les GD en développement (art. 69, § 3 et 70, § 4), mais qui ne génèrent aucune garantie supplémentaire à leur profit. Pire encore pour les ESL-GD, les faibles "droits" dont ils disposent ne contraignent pas les ". . . États côtiers dont l'économie est très lourdement tributaire de l'exploitation des ressources biologiques de leur zone économique exclusive" (art. 71). Il va sans dire que cette dernière disposition peut concerner des États par ailleurs développés. J. Carroz, *infra* note 86 à la p. 716, fait état du recul effectué à l'égard des ESL-GD entre 1977 (TNCO) et 1980 (TNCO Rév. 2). On note en effet une diminution des droits des ESL-GD (voir note 18) qui se double d'une augmentation des droits des États côtiers en raison de la baisse des cas de soumission à des modes obligatoires de règlement des différends (p. 717).

En pratique, l'État côtier jouit d'une très grande latitude[51] qui tempère sérieusement le "droit" d'accès au reliquat reconnu aux États tiers par la Convention. Ceci est d'autant plus vrai que la réglementation de l'État côtier est exécutoire.[52] L'article 73 confère en effet à l'État côtier la possibilité de "... prendre toutes mesures, y compris l'arraisonnement, l'inspection, la saisie et l'introduction d'une instance judiciaire, qui sont nécessaires pour assurer le respect des lois et règlements qu'il a adoptés ..."[53] Les sanctions ne devraient cependant pas comprendre l'emprisonnement (sauf accord contraire entre les États) ni aucun autre châtiment corporel.[54] La latitude de l'État côtier est aussi renforcée par le fait que les questions relatives à la gestion des ressources et à l'accès des pêcheurs étrangers en zone économique échappent dans la Convention de 1982 à toute forme de règlement obligatoire des différends.[55]

51 Selon la Convention de 1982, art. 62, § 4, l'État côtier peut légiférer, notamment, sur les questions suivantes: délivrance de licences assorties de paiement de droits ou autres contreparties; détermination des espèces dont la pêche est autorisée, des quotas de prises, par navire ou par État; fixation de l'âge et de la taille des poissons pouvant être pêchés; réglementation des zones de pêche, du type, du nombre, de la taille des navires et engins de pêche; fourniture de statistiques sur les captures et participation à des programmes de recherche; obligation d'accepter des observateurs à bord des navires; obligation de décharger tout ou partie des prises dans les ports de l'État côtier; participation à des entreprises conjointes; obligations de transfert de technologie, etc.

52 *Id.*, art. 62, § 4, al. K.

53 On voit le chemin parcouru avec l'établissement des zones économiques exclusives. Auparavant en effet, c'était l'État d'immatriculation qui veillait à ce que les navires immatriculés chez lui respectent les conventions internationales dans le domaine des pêches ou les quotas éventuellement établis par les organisations internationales compétentes, à supposer qu'il soit partie à ces accords ou membre de ces institutions. Il va sans dire, en tout état de cause, que l'État d'immatriculation manquait sérieusement de motivation pour assurer le respect de ces normes, ce qui n'est pas le cas pour l'État côtier dans sa propre zone.

54 T. Treves, *infra* note 86 à la p. 158, citant en sa note 169 une recherche de la FAO, estime qu'environ 35 États ont des législations prévoyant des peines d'emprisonnement. Antigua et Barbuda ainsi que le Bangladesh et le Portugal notamment prévoient des peines de prison en cas de violation de leurs lois sur la pêche, qui seraient en contradiction avec l'art. 73 de la Convention de 1982 si elles étaient appliquées à des étrangers.

55 Il est important à cet égard de noter que si les différends concernant l'interprétation ou l'application des dispositions de la Convention portant sur la pêche sont réglés par des procédures obligatoires aboutissant à des décisions

Si nous avons cru pouvoir qualifier de "préférentiels" les droits de l'État côtier dans le domaine de l'exploitation des ressources biologiques non sédentaires de sa zone, il est frappant de constater que nombre de législations nationales, une vingtaine au moins, n'hésitent pas à qualifier d'exclusifs les droits de l'État côtier en matière halieutique[56] ou, à tout le moins, n'effectuent pas la moindre référence à l'éventualité d'une pêche étrangère.[57] Ceci ne signifie pas nécessairement que les tiers seront exclus en pratique de tout accès, mais il faut convenir que le pouvoir réglementaire disposera d'une grande latitude, à moins d'avoir à respecter des accords bilatéraux éventuels.

D'autres États (une quarantaine) font allusion à une possibilité de pêche étrangère dans leur zone économique, mais simplement sur la base de licences ou d'accords internationaux, et sans effectuer la moindre allusion au volume admissible des captures ni donc à l'existence potentielle d'un reliquat au bénéfice des pêcheurs étrangers.[58] Là encore, l'accès des tiers, même s'il semble mieux

---

obligatoires, "... l'État côtier n'est pas tenu d'accepter que soit soumis à un tel règlement un différend relatif à ses droits souverains sur les ressources biologiques de sa zone économique exclusive ou à l'exercice de ces droits, y compris son pouvoir discrétionnaire de fixer le volume admissible des captures et sa capacité de pêche, de répartir le reliquat entre d'autres États et d'arrêter les modalités et conditions établies dans ses lois et règlements en matière de conservation et de gestion" (art. 297, § 3a)). Par contre, la Convention prévoit un recours à une formule de conciliation obligatoire si l'État côtier refuse arbitrairement de fixer un TAC ou d'attribuer une portion du reliquat à un autre État (art. 297 § 3b)i, ii, iii et section II de l'Annexe V). Voir J. Carroz, *infra* note 86 à la p. 717.

56 *Inter alia*, Antigua et Barbuda, qui parle d'"autorité exclusive" sur la pêche, terminologie aussi utilisée par la Dominique (alors que, pour le Bangladesh, c'est la propriété des ressources naturelles qui est exclusive), Costa Rica, Guinée (qui interdit même la pêche étrangère), Oman (qui se donne "all sovereignty" sur les ressources halieutiques).

57 *Inter alia*, Bélize, Cap Vert (sa loi de 1992 constitue un recul sur celle de 1977, *infra* note 59), Haïti, Kiribati, Iran, Jamaïque, Mauritanie, Micronésie, Namibie, République dominicaine, Saint-Vincent-et-Grenadines, Suède, Qatar.

58 *Inter alia*, Barbade, Birmanie, Bulgarie, Cambodge, Corée du Nord, Côte d'Ivoire (qui fait allusion à des accords de réciprocité), Djibouti, Émirats arabes unis (la loi de 1980 faisait référence à l'admission des tiers en cas de surplus, ce qui n'est plus le cas avec la loi de 1993), France (qui interdit la pêche étrangère en application d'une loi de 1888, sauf aux partenaires communautaires, ou sur la base d'accords ou de réglementation nationale), Gabon (qui affirme toutefois l'accès prioritaire des nationaux), Grenade, Guatémala, Guinée Bissau, Guinée équatoriale, Guyana (il s'agit d'une zone de pêche, mais une

garanti que dans la première formule législative décrite, devrait être largement tributaire d'éventuels accords internationaux.

Une dernière catégorie de législations nationales semble plus respectueuse des dispositions de la Convention de 1982. Une quinzaine d'États reprennent en effet dans leur législation le mécanisme prévu: ils fixent le TAC, déterminent leurs propres capacités et permettent l'accès des tiers au surplus éventuel.[59] Toutefois, alors que certains de ces États semblent se créer une obligation à cet égard, conformément à la Convention,[60] d'autres se contentent de faire référence à la simple potentialité de l'accès des tiers.[61] Les traités bilatéraux devraient, bien entendu, être ici encore déterminants pour fixer l'étendue concrète de cet accès.

L'analyse des législations nationales tend ainsi à prouver que les États n'excluent pas les tiers de leur zone. En revanche, ils exigent d'eux de nombreuses conditions et manifestent peu d'empressement à leur reconnaître un droit formel d'accès au surplus. Reste à savoir si les accords bilatéraux, en concrétisant ces lois, confirment ou infirment cette tendance. À cet égard, il est intéressant de constater que la jurisprudence accorde une place importante à ces accords puisque les compétences de l'État côtier relativement à la réglementation de la pêche étrangère dans sa zone doivent "céder

---

ZÉE pourrait être créée selon la loi), Inde, Kenya, Madagascar, Malaisie, Maldives, Maroc, Maurice, Nigéria (allusion aux accords internationaux), Pakistan, Philippines, Pologne, Saint-Kitts-et-Névis, Sainte-Lucie, Samoa occidental, Seychelles, Sénégal, Suriname, Tanzanie, Togo (qui s'engage à conclure des traités d'accès aux tiers dans le contexte de la "solidarité interafricaine"), Turquie, Vanuatu, Yémen. Soulignons que le Maroc manifeste de bonnes intentions à l'égard des États sans littoral de la région, sans pour autant leur reconnaître de priorité d'accès. C'est dans cette catégorie que l'on trouve le plus grand nombre de législations prévoyant des peines d'emprisonnement pour les pêcheurs étrangers: Barbade (jusqu'à 2 ans), Birmanie (jusqu'à 10 ans), Grenade (jusqu'à 5 ans), Inde (jusqu'à 3 ans), Maurice (jusqu'à 5 ans), Philippines (jusqu'à 10 ans), Seychelles (jusqu'à 5 ans), Suriname (jusqu'à 6 ans), Tanzanie (jusqu'à 5 ans), Vanuatu (jusqu'à 5 ans), Yémen (jusqu'à 3 ans).

59 Notons que la législation du Cap Vert en 1977 prévoyait l'accès des tiers au surplus dans le cadre d'accords bilatéraux, option abandonnée avec la loi de 1992, qui ne mentionne plus désormais la pêche étrangère. Ceci est d'autant plus surprenant que le Cap Vert, entre temps, a ratifié la Convention de 1982.

60 Comores, Cuba, Fiji, Mexique, Nouvelle-Zélande, Tonga, Vénézuela.

61 Fédération de Russie, Honduras, Indonésie, Nioué, Norvège, Portugal, Sao Tomé et Principe, Trinité-et-Tobago.

le pas" devant le texte d'un traité bilatéral qui porte sur ces questions.[62] D'ailleurs, la Convention de 1982 elle-même "... ne modifie en rien les droits et obligations des États parties qui découlent d'autres traités compatibles avec elle ..."[63] Des accords de pêche pourraient même contredire les dispositions de la Convention, "... à condition que ces accords ne portent pas sur une des dispositions de la Convention dont le non respect serait incompatible avec la réalisation de son objet et de son but, et à condition également que ces accords n'affectent pas l'application des principes fondamentaux énoncés dans la Convention ..."[64] Le droit d'accès des tiers au surplus éventuel de l'État côtier dans sa zone nous semble relever de ces "principes fondamentaux," compte tenu de l'importance du concept d'utilisation optimale. À l'instar des législations, ces accords bilatéraux retiennent diverses formules en rapport avec l'accès des tiers.[65] Leur analyse, toutefois, n'apporte pas un grand éclairage aux législations qui les fondent. Comme elles, ils multiplient les conditions d'accès des tiers et affirment, par contre, rarement l'existence d'un droit formel d'accès à leur bénéfice.

En matière environnementale, la Convention limite considérablement les initiatives des États côtiers dans leur zone économique, particulièrement au chapitre de la pollution par les navires, dans le but d'éviter certains abus qui pourraient porter atteinte à la liberté de la navigation. Leurs compétences ne sont en conséquence absolues que dans le domaine de l'immersion ou de la

[62] *Affaire de "La Bretagne"* (Canada-France), Tribunal arbitral, 17 juillet 1986, (1986), R.G.D.I.P. à la p. 713, § 53.

[63] Art. 311, § 2. Le Tribunal arbitral dans l'*Affaire de "La Bretagne," supra* note 62, écrit: "Même si la *Convention des Nations Unis sur le droit de la mer* faisait actuellement droit entre les deux Parties, le Tribunal note qu'elle ne porterait certainement pas atteinte au régime conventionnel établi par l'Accord de 1972, en raison de la clause contenue dans son article 311, paragraphe 2 ..."

[64] Art. 311, § 3.

[65] J. Carroz (*infra*, note 86 aux pp. 733 et s.), estime que les traités sont de trois sortes. Certains sont basés sur la réciprocité, d'autres prévoient un retrait graduel des étrangers, d'autres enfin, les plus nombreux, déterminent les conditions d'accès des tiers. Beaucoup de ces traités reprennent les mécanismes de l'art. 62 de ce qui était alors le TNCO (États-Unis, URSS en 1976, Canada, Mexique, Nouvelle-Zélande), sans toutefois reconnaître un droit d'accès aux tiers (constatation discutable pour le Canada, selon nous). Les traités font par ailleurs souvent allusion à la nécessité de réduire les perturbations économiques (Norvège-Pologne, Canada-Pologne, Japon-URSS, p. ex.).

pollution découlant de l'exploitation même de la zone.[66] En dépit de ce cadre conventionnel à certains égards étriqué, les États s'attribuent volontiers dans leur législation une juridiction sans limite, le

66 La Convention de 1982 accorde à l'État côtier des compétences variables au chapitre de la protection de l'environnement. Elles semblent importantes en matière d'immersion, puisqu'elles sont identiques à celles dont dispose l'État côtier dans sa mer territoriale (art. 210, § 5). C'est dire qu'il a le droit d'autoriser, réglementer et contrôler l'immersion en zone économique exclusive. Il peut donc la refuser. La réglementation nationale ne doit d'ailleurs pas être moins efficace que la réglementation de caractère mondial, c.-à-d. la Convention de Londres du 29 décembre 1975 sur la prévention de la pollution des mers résultant de l'immersion de déchets et autres matières, telle qu'amendée en 1978 et 1980, ST/LEG/SER.B/16, p. 464. L'État côtier doit aussi, selon l'art. 216, § 1a, assurer la mise en application dans sa ZÉE des normes en matière d'immersion établies par les organisations internationales compétentes ou découlant de conventions internationales. On ne peut malheureusement pas tenir le même raisonnement dans le domaine de la pollution par les navires. En l'occurrence, la victoire des grandes puissances maritimes est évidente. Il n'y a en effet que si les normes internationales s'avèrent inadéquates pour répondre à des problèmes environnementaux spécifiques dans certains secteurs de sa zone économique que l'État côtier peut recourir à l'adoption de règles nationales propres, lesquelles ne constituent que la mise en oeuvre de normes internationales établies par l'organisation internationale compétente pour répondre à de telles situations. Encore faut-il que ladite organisation ait décidé que les secteurs concernés de la zone économique répondent bien à une situation particulière. En tout état de cause, les règles nationales ne devront jamais imposer aux navires étrangers de normes de construction ou de conception autres que celles que détermine le droit international (art. 246, § 5 et 6). Dans le cas des zones économiques recouvertes de glace, toutefois, l'État côtier a le droit d'adopter et de faire appliquer toute réglementation nationale non discriminatoire visant à prévenir, réduire et maîtriser la pollution du milieu marin par les navires (art. 234). Il s'agit d'une victoire canadienne. Quant aux pouvoirs de l'État côtier à l'égard de navires étrangers dans sa zone économique en matière environnementale, ils sont pour le moins ténus. En effet, si un navire étranger enfreint les lois de l'État côtier ou la réglementation internationale applicable à la zone, il peut intervenir pour lui demander des informations (art. 220, § 3). Si cette infraction entraîne des rejets importants causant ou susceptibles de causer une pollution notable, l'État côtier peut procéder à l'inspection matérielle du navire (art. 220, § 5). Ce n'est que s'il y a preuve manifeste que l'infraction a entraîné des rejets causant ou susceptibles de causer des dommages importants que l'État côtier pourra intenter une action, notamment ordonner l'immobilisation du navire (art. 220, § 6). On n'insistera pas sur le caractère dérisoire de ces dispositions aux yeux des États côtiers soucieux de protéger leur littoral.

plus souvent qualifiée d'exclusive.[67] On y trouve parfois des dispositions à l'effet que l'État pourra "prendre toute mesure[68] ou fera "tout ce qui est nécessaire" ou "approprié" dans le domaine de l'environnement.[69] Certains États en font même expressément une zone de prévention de la pollution.[70]

Quant à la recherche scientifique, elle fait l'objet, selon la Convention de 1982, de compétences semi exclusives au bénéfice de l'État côtier.[71] À ce chapitre, on ne note pas d'abus criants dans les législations nationales. Bien plus, certains États ne revendiquent aucune juridiction dans ce domaine.[72] C'est le cas pour les États-Unis, qui n'en reconnaissent pas moins les droits des autres États côtiers en la matière:

67 *Inter alia*, Bangladesh, Barbade, Bélize, Birmanie, Brésil, Colombie, Côte d'Ivoire, Émirats arabes unis, Guinée équatoriale, Haïti, Îles Solomon, Inde, Iran, Jamaïque, Kiribati, Malaisie, Maroc, Maurice, Mauritanie, Nouvelle-Zélande, Pakistan (pour certaines régions définies), Philippines, Pologne, Saint-Vincent et Grenadines, Samoa occidental, Seychelles, Sri Lanka, Suriname, Suède, Tonga, Trinité et Tobago, Vanuatu, Yémen.

68 Côte d'Ivoire.

69 Haïti, Pakistan ("tout ce qui est nécessaire"); Bangladesh ("tout ce qui est approprié").

70 Sri Lanka, Pologne: "le droit polonais de l'environnement s'applique à la zone économique exclusive."

71 C'est en effet son droit que de réglementer, autoriser et mener la recherche scientifique. Aucune recherche ne peut être effectuée sans son consentement (art. 246, § 2). Si ce droit n'est pas qualifié d'exclusif par la Convention (à la différence de la mer territoriale selon l'art. 245), c'est que, dans le cas de recherches strictement scientifiques, qui ont pour but d'accroître les connaissances sur le milieu marin, l'État côtier consent normalement à la réalisation des projets (art. 246, § 3). C'est là une satisfaction pour les grandes puissances maritimes, attachées traditionnellement à la liberté de la recherche. Si par contre le projet a une incidence directe sur l'exploration et l'exploitation des ressources naturelles, l'État côtier disposera du pouvoir discrétionnaire de refuser son consentement à l'exécution du projet de recherche (art. 246, § 5). Le succès est ici celui des pays en développement, assurés de contrôler de façon absolue la recherche appliquée dans leur zone. On notera que l'ensemble des dispositions sur la recherche scientifique en zone économique s'applique aussi au plateau continental à ceci près que les États côtiers ne disposent généralement pas de leur pouvoir discrétionnaire de refuser leur consentement à l'exécution de projets de recherche appliquée pour la partie du plateau qui excède la zone. Il y a là compensation à la reconnaissance des droits des États à large plateau au-delà de 200 milles de leurs côtes.

72 Le tiers environ des États possédant une ZÉE n'ont aucune prétention en matière de recherche scientifique ou de contrôle des installations et ouvrages à fins économiques.

Les États-Unis reconnaissent néanmoins le droit des autres États côtiers d'exercer leur juridiction sur la recherche scientifique marine jusqu'à 200 milles marins au large de leurs côtes, pourvu que cette juridiction soit exercée de manière raisonnable et conforme au droit international.[73]

La recherche scientifique marine, ainsi que les autres activités reliées à l'exploration et l'exploitation des ressources naturelles de la zone et à son utilisation à des fins économiques, peuvent impliquer la mise en place d'îles artificielles, d'installations et d'ouvrages.[74] Or, à cet égard, la Convention de 1982 confère à l'État côtier le droit exclusif de procéder à la construction ou d'autoriser et réglementer la construction, l'exploitation et l'utilisation de tels engins marins.[75] Une exception toutefois à cette compétence exclusive: le cas des installations et ouvrages autres que ceux qui sont affectés à des fins d'exploration ou d'exploitation des ressources naturelles ou à d'autres fins économiques.[76] Certaines grandes puissances ont fortement insisté sur la nécessité de respecter la Convention à cet égard,[77] dans le but de prévenir certains glissements. Plusieurs États en développement souhaitent en effet se donner le droit exclusif de construire et de réglementer les installations et ouvrages quel que soit leur objet. Telle est la position du Brésil[78] du

73 *Exclusive Economic Zone of the United States of America*, Presidential Proclamation N° 5030, Statement by the President, The White House, Office of the Press Secretary, March 10, 1983, (1983) I.L.M. 465. Traduction de l'auteur.

74 Il convient de souligner ici les difficultés qu'il peut y avoir à distinguer les îles artificielles des installations et ouvrages. De façon générale, on peut dire que les îles artificielles sont des structures fixes qui se distinguent des îles en ce que leur création implique une intervention humaine (caractère artificiel). Les installations et ouvrages sont aussi des structures artificielles érigées en mer et caractérisées par leur fixité. Elles se distinguent des îles artificielles par une moindre permanence et une dimension généralement inférieure. Les plates-formes fixes de forage en font partie.

75 Convention de 1982, art. 60, § 1.

76 *Ibid.*

77 Voir p. ex. les déclarations de l'Allemagne et de l'Italie (*supra* note 33) à l'occasion respectivement de leur adhésion et ratification de la Convention de 1982.

78 Tant à l'occasion de la signature que de la ratification de la Convention de 1982, le Brésil affirme de tels droits exclusifs. Dans sa récente loi, il confirme ce principe avec plus de nuances toutefois puisque ce droit exclusif "de réglementer . . . la mise en place et l'utilisation d'îles artificielles, d'installations et ouvrages" semble ne devoir s'opérer que "dans l'exercice de sa juridiction." Il y a là un autre vestige hérité de l'ancienne mer territoriale de 200 milles.

Cap Vert[79] de l'Uruguay[80] et d'une dizaine d'autres États du tiers-monde.[81]

III Pratique des États et coutume

Nous avons pu constater jusqu'ici que tant à l'égard des divers types de zones à incidence économique qu'ils créent qu'à l'égard de la juridiction qu'ils y exercent, les États côtiers ne se conforment pas nécessairement en tout point aux dispositions de la Convention de 1982. Ce phénomène a été souvent dénoncé. Si l'on veut toutefois évaluer la légalité de ce comportement au regard du droit international public, il convient de déterminer si le droit conventionnel (la Partie V de la Convention de 1982) et le droit coutumier en matière de zone économique exclusive sont au même effet. Si tel est le cas, les États non respectueux de ces normes devraient revoir leur comportement (qu'ils soient ou non liés par la Convention). Si tel n'est pas le cas en revanche, il conviendra de se demander si des pratiques *a priori* aberrantes n'ont pas d'ores-et-déjà généré des coutumes permissives par rapport aux dispositions de la Convention de 1982.

Dans les Affaires du *Plateau continental de la mer du Nord*, la Cour internationale de Justice a décrit trois types de relations susceptibles de se présenter entre coutumes et traités.[82] Une convention peut en premier lieu être simplement déclaratoire de normes coutumières qu'elle se contente de consacrer.[83] Si par contre, au moment de l'ouverture de la conférence qui conduit au traité, la

79 Lors de la signature de la Convention, le Cap Vert déclarait que cette dernière "ne donne à aucun État le droit de construire, d'exploiter ou d'utiliser sans le consentement de l'État côtier des installations ou des structures dans la zone économique d'un autre État, qu'il s'agisse de celles prévues dans la Convention ou qu'elles soient de tout autre nature." Le Cap Vert a repris cette déclaration lors de la ratification de la Convention. Dans sa récente loi, il confirme (et spécifie) sa juridiction exclusive sur la mise en place et l'utilisation d'îles artificielles, d'installations et ouvrages.

80 En signant la Convention, l'Uruguay formulait la même déclaration que le Cap Vert (*supra* note 79). On sait que l'Uruguay possède encore une mer territoriale de 200 milles.

81 *Inter alia*, Birmanie, Honduras, Inde, Indonésie, Maldives, Maurice, Pakistan, Philippines, Seychelles, Sri Lanka, Vanuatu.

82 Ces trois types de relations sont rappelées par J. Charney, *infra* note 86 à la p. 238.

83 *Plateau continental de la mer du Nord* (Danemark/R.F.A.; Pays-Bas/R.F.A.) arrêt, Recueil C.I.J. 1969 à la p. 3, § 61.

pratique des États ne répond pas encore aux conditions d'existence de la coutume, il peut arriver que les travaux de la conférence définissent et consolident des normes coutumières en voie de formation. Dans ce cas, l'adoption de la convention permet la cristallisation de ces normes.[84] Enfin, dans un troisième scénario, il peut arriver qu'une norme purement conventionnelle au départ devienne coutumière du fait de l'influence de la convention et de la pratique ultérieure des États.[85]

Il serait difficile de soutenir que la troisième Conférence ait eu pour objectif de codifier des règles coutumières en matière de zone économique exclusive, faute de pratique générale antérieure à l'ouverture de la Conférence. L'activité unilatérale des États en la matière est concomitante aux travaux de la Conférence (voir Tableau 4). Les divers projets qu'elle a rédigés ne sont pas fondés sur la pratique des États. En revanche, cette pratique s'est manifestement inspirée des consensus minima établis dans le cadre de la Conférence à compter de 1975, sans pour autant que les États ne se sentent techniquement obligés par quelque norme que ce soit. Rappelons que la quasi totalité des zones économiques ont été créées avant l'entrée en vigueur de la Convention (1994), et que plus de la moitié précèdent l'adoption définitive de son texte (1982).

Toutefois, compte tenu du volume de cette pratique antérieure à 1982, on est en droit de se demander s'il n'existait pas dès avant l'adoption de la Convention des coutumes *in statu nascendi* relativement à certains éléments du régime de la zone, consolidées par la pratique des États et leur comportement dans le cadre de la Conférence, et cristallisées du fait de l'adoption de la Convention. Si l'on peut aller jusqu'à dire que certaines coutumes existaient dès 1982, la Convention aurait même réalisé à leur égard une certaine forme de codification non spécifiquement recherchée. Quant aux actes juridiques unilatéraux émis par les États postérieurement à l'adoption de la Convention en 1982, ils mériteront une attention toute particulière afin de déterminer s'ils confortent la pratique antérieure, s'ils se conforment à la Convention, ou s'ils manifestent des tendances nouvelles.

En tout état de cause, on ne peut échapper à une étude exhaustive de la pratique des États afin de déterminer si elle a généré des coutumes. Pour ce faire, nous devrons établir si cette pratique a été générale, constante et assortie de l'*opinio juris*. Pratique et coutumes

84 *Ibid.*

85 *Id.*, § 70.

éventuelles seront ensuite confrontées aux dispositions correspondantes de la Partie V de la Convention de 1982 sur la zone économique. Ce faisant, nous prendrons en compte le fait que la Convention est désormais en vigueur et lie un nombre croissant d'États développés, autant d'éléments qui ont rarement été pris en considération jusqu'ici par la doctrine.[86]

S'agissant tout d'abord de l'élément matériel de la coutume, soit la pratique des États, il découle surtout des proclamations et lois portant sur la zone, des règlements d'application de ces lois, des traités pertinents, des déclarations émises dans divers contextes diplomatiques ou des déclarations effectuées en vertu de la Convention de

86 La doctrine, en effet, pour l'essentiel, s'est manifestée entre 1987 et 1994. On consultera tout particulièrement D. Attard, *The Exclusive Economic Zone in International Law*, Clarendon Press, Oxford, 1987; J.E. Bailey, "The Exclusive Economic Zone: its Development and Future in International and Domestic Law," (1985) Louisiana L.Rev. 1270; W.T. Burke, "National Legislation on Ocean Authority Zones and the Contemporary Law of the Sea," (1981) O.D.I.L. 289; H. Caminos et M.R. Molitor, "Progressive Development of International Law and the Package Deal," (1985) A.J.I.L. 871; J. Carroz, "Les problèmes de la pêche à la Conférence sur le droit de la mer et dans la pratique des États" (1980) R.G.D.I.P. 705; J.I. Charney, "The Exclusive Economic Zone and Public International Law," (1985) O.D.I.L. 233; J. Grolin, "The Future of the Law of the Sea: Consequences of a Non-Treaty or Non-Universal Treaty Situation," (1983) O.D.I.L. 1; C. Hudson, "The EEZ as Customary International Law," (1980) S.D.L.R. 673; B. Kwiatkowska, *The 200 Mile Exclusive Economic Zone in the International Law of the Sea*, Dordrecht, Lancaster, Boston, 1989; L.T. Lee, "The Law of the Sea Convention and Third States," (1983) A.J.I.L. 541; J.P. Lévy, "Les Nations unies et la Convention de 1982 sur le droit de la mer," (1995) R.B.D.I. 11; L.M. Macrae, "Customary International Law and the United Nation's Law of the Sea Treaty," (1983) California Western Int'l L.J. 181; S.K.B. Mfodwo, B.M. Tsamenyi et S.K.N. Blay, "The Exclusive Economic Zone: State Practice in the African Atlantic Region," (1989) O.D.I.L. 445; F. Orrego Vicuña, "La zone économique exclusive: régime et nature juridique dans le droit international," Recueil des cours de l'Académie de droit international, Martinus Nijhoff Publishers, Dordrecht, Boston, Lancaster, 1986-IV 9, ci-après (1986); F. Orrego Vicuña, *The Exclusive Economic Zone, Regime and Legal Nature under International Law*, Cambridge University Press, Cambridge, New York, Port Chester, Melbourne, Sidney, 1989, ci-après (1989); F.H. Paolillo, "The Exclusive Economic Zone in Latin American Practice and Legislation," (1995) O.D.I.L. 105; L.B. Sohn, "The Law of the Sea: Customary International Law Developments," (1985) The American University L.Rev. 271; T. Treves, "Codification du droit international et pratique des États dans le droit de la mer," Recueil des cours de l'Académie de droit international, Martinus Nijhoff Publishers, Dordrecht, Boston, Lancaster, 1990-IV 9; R. Wolfrum, "The Emerging Customary Law of Marine Zones: State Practice and the Convention on the Law of the Sea," (1987) N.Y.I.L. 121.

1982.[87] Les lois demeurent l'élément privilégié de cette pratique, mais elles constituent trop souvent de simples cadres et n'ont pas toujours été complétées par des textes plus spécifiques ou des règlements d'application.[88] Elles sont alors difficiles à évaluer. L'impression générale fréquemment notée par les observateurs est à l'effet que dans leurs lois les États semblent se reconnaître plus facilement des droits qu'ils ne s'imposent d'obligations.[89] Le fait est que ces législations font par exemple rarement mention des droits des tiers (droit d'accès des étrangers à la pêche, respect à leur égard des libertés générales de la haute mer). S'il est difficile d'interpréter des silences, le comportement concret des États, parfois même les accords bilatéraux ou régionaux qu'ils concluent, permettent cependant de constater plus souvent qu'autrement leur adhésion aux principes de la Convention de 1982. Parfois en revanche, on notera que certaines dispositions législatives sont carrément contraires à la Convention (création de "zones désignées," atteintes diverses à plusieurs libertés de la haute mer, juridiction sur certains ouvrages). Dans de tels cas, les objections des États tiers se manifestent fréquemment. Le conflit est alors évident entre la volonté de certains États côtiers de "forcer" la création de normes dérogatoires au droit conventionnel et celles d'autres États, développés le plus souvent, de canaliser la pratique pour la maintenir conforme à la Convention.[90]

A CONCEPT ET LARGEUR

Le concept de zone de pêche de 200 milles ou — voisin — de mer épicontinentale[91] est reconnu de longue date,[92] mais il est

87 Rappelons que l'art. 310 autorise les États, lorsqu'ils signent la Convention, la ratifient ou y adhèrent, à émettre des déclarations qui ne sont pas des réserves, et qui visent notamment à harmoniser leurs lois et règlements avec la Convention.

88 Voir sur ce point, *inter alia*, J. Charney, *supra* note 86 aux pp. 240-41.

89 *Inter alia*, R. Wolfrum, *supra* note 86 à la p. 144: "National Legislation reflects the coastal State's rights, although not always to the same extent as corresponding obligations vis-à-vis other States."

90 Dans ce sens, voir T. Treves, *supra* note 86 aux pp. 179-80.

91 La zone de pêche de 200 milles, justifiée par le courant de Humboldt, couvrait à compter de 1945 le littoral pacifique de l'Amérique du sud, quand la mer épicontinentale s'étendait au large de la côte atlantique, recouvrant le large plateau continental.

92 Les législations établissant la juridiction sur la mer épicontinentale remontent à 1946 (Argentine, Panama). Celles sur les 200 milles à 1947 (Chili, Pérou).

longtemps resté régional. Toute création de semblable zone en dehors de l'Amérique latine eut alors été vouée à l'échec.[93] Il reste que ces zones pouvaient être considérées à l'époque comme constituant des coutumes régionales.

Aujourd'hui, on est en droit de soutenir, depuis le début des années 80, que le concept de zone économique exclusive est de nature coutumière. De ce fait, nul État ne saurait contester le fait même de l'établissement d'une zone économique exclusive par un autre.[94] Après une légitime période transitoire, la doctrine dominante s'est ralliée à cette approche.[95] De la même façon, à la suite de quelques hésitations compréhensibles,[96] les tribunaux internationaux l'admettent désormais. C'est ainsi que la Cour internationale de

93 Rappelons que la CIJ, dans l'Affaire des *Pêcheries, supra* note 44, avait refusé en 1974 l'extension de la zone de pêche islandaise de 12 à 50 milles. Il est vrai qu'il s'agissait d'une zone de pêche exclusive, qui remettait en cause les droits conventionnels de la Grande-Bretagne et de l'Allemagne.

94 Certains auteurs vont même jusqu'à soutenir — ce que nous contestons — l'existence automatique de la zone au bénéfice des États côtiers dès lors qu'ils sont parties à la Convention de 1982.

95 C'est le cas par exemple pour F. Orrego Vicuña (1989), *supra* note 86, qui cite cependant certains auteurs hésitants à cet égard (Akehurst, Flemming, Scovazzi, selon B. Kwiatkowska) et d'autres, soviétiques en particulier (Kolodkin, Zakharov) qui sont en désaccord. Il cite de nombreux auteurs à l'appui du caractère coutumier du concept de ZÉE (Elias, Evensen, Galindo Pohl, Goy, Quéneudec, Oxman, Treves, Dupuy, Vukas). On peut ajouter F.H. Paolillo (*supra* note 86) et S.K.B. Mfodwo *et al.* (*id.*) notamment. Voir enfin D. Attard, *supra* note 86, et les auteurs qu'il cite (aux pp. 303-7).

96 Dans l'*Affaire de la délimitation du plateau continental entre la France et le Royaume-Uni*, décision du 30 juin 1977, Documentation française, Paris, septembre 1977 (I.S.B.N.: 2-11-000064-3), la France soutenait qu'il existait un consensus sur la zone économique exclusive (§ 45). Le Royaume-Uni, pour sa part, estimait que ce relatif consensus n'impliquait pas que le concept soit devenu coutumier puisque plusieurs questions restaient à régler: contenu de la juridiction de l'État côtier, statut de la zone par rapport à la haute mer (§ 46). Le Tribunal arbitral ne se prononce pas directement sur la question. Il se contente d'admettre que "... un développement du droit coutumier [pourrait] permettre, dans certaines conditions, que les États concernés acceptent la modification ou même l'abrogation de droits et d'obligations conventionnels existant précédemment" (§ 47). Le Tribunal tiendra compte de ces développements récents pour affirmer que les règles coutumières en matière de délimitation du plateau continental sont comparables à celles établies par la Convention de 1958 (§ 65). Ces hésitations du Tribunal à se prononcer sur le caractère coutumier de la zone économique s'expliquent par le fait qu'il n'avait pas vraiment besoin de le faire. Par ailleurs, peu d'États avaient créé une zone économique exclusive avant la rédaction de l'arbitrage.

Justice a affirmé en 1982 que "... l'on peut considérer [la zone économique exclusive] comme faisant partie du droit international moderne."[97] Deux ans plus tard,[98] traitant de "... la nature et du but du nouveau régime des 200 milles," une Chambre de cette même Cour confirmait: "... les dispositions dont il s'agit, bien que portant parfois la marque du compromis qui a présidé à leur adoption, peuvent être considérées comme conformes actuellement au droit international public général en la matière."

Il est par contre important de souligner que si la Cour internationale de Justice se prononçait ainsi sur le caractère coutumier de la notion de zone économique, elle ne se prononçait nullement sur le caractère coutumier de son régime juridique. Elle n'avait pas besoin de le faire, puisqu'elle se contentait de rechercher un fondement au titre de l'État côtier sur la zone économique afin d'en tirer les conséquences en matière de délimitation.

Dans la même veine, il n'est guère risqué de soutenir que la largeur de la zone économique est coutumière.[99] Le "principe de distance" est d'ailleurs le fondement de la zone économique selon la Cour internationale de Justice.[100] Si, on l'a noté, quelques États possèdent des zones inférieures à 200 milles, c'est en général parce qu'ils sont géographiquement désavantagés et n'ont ainsi pas la faculté d'aller jusqu'à cette distance. En revanche, nul État ne dépasse formellement les 200 milles. On notera toutefois une regrettable tendance de la part de certains États à vouloir exercer

97 *Affaire Tunisie-Lybie*, Recueil C.I.J. 1982, § 100. À cette époque, une soixantaine d'États avaient créé une zone économique (et 16 une zone de pêche)

98 *Affaire du golfe du Maine*, Recueil C.I.J. 1984, § 94. À cette date, environ 70 États disposaient d'une zone économique. L'année suivante, dans l'*Affaire du plateau continental* (Jamahiriya arabe libyenne/Malte), arrêt, Recueil C.I.J. 1985, la Cour confirmait que "... les deux institutions du plateau continental et de la zone économique exclusive sont liées dans le droit moderne" (§ 33) et que "... l'institution de la zone économique exclusive ... s'est intégrée au droit coutumier" (§ 34). Le gouvernement britannique affirmait de même en 1984 que "the concept of the EEZ has developped into customary international law," *Hansard*, House of Lords, vol. 457, col. 1301: December 4, 1984, cité par D. Attard, *supra* note 86 à la p. 299, note 253.

99 Dans ce sens, D. Attard, *supra* note 86 aux pp. 288-89 et C. Hudson, *id.* à la p. 677.

100 Voir notamment *Affaire du plateau continental* (Jamahiriya arabe libyenne/Malte), *supra* note 98, § 34.

diverses formes de juridiction au delà de 200 milles en vue notamment de contrôler la gestion des stocks chevauchants.[101]

B CONCEPTION FONDAMENTALE

La répétition *ad nauseam* dans les législations étatiques de l'article 56 de la Convention de 1982, dont la législation canadienne constitue la dernière manifestation en date, accrédite l'idée que cet article, et donc la conception fondamentale de la zone, correspondent au droit coutumier. Les auteurs adhèrent de plus en plus à cette approche.[102] Dans l'*Affaire de "La Bretagne,"*[103] le Tribunal arbitral confirme partiellement cette thèse, sans autre démonstration doit-on préciser. Ce consensus sur la conception fondamentale de la zone nous incite à soutenir qu'il existe dans la pratique des États une reconnaissance générale du caractère *sui generis* de la zone, laquelle n'est ni tout à fait haute mer, ni tout à fait mer territoriale.[104] On remarque ainsi que les grandes puissances maritimes contrôlent les dérives de certains États en développement et que les rares tentatives de territorialisation semblent vouées à l'échec. Nous avons déjà noté les objections de certaines grandes puissances à l'égard des allocations unilatérales de compétences résiduaires au bénéfice d'États côtiers, ou de prétentions spécifiques limitant notamment la liberté d'exercice de manoeuvres

101 Voir notre article, "La nouvelle loi canadienne sur la protection des pêcheries côtières: légitimité n'est pas légalité" (1994) *Espaces et Ressources maritimes* à la p. 252.

102 Voir notamment Attard, Treves, Vicuña, Wolfrum. Ce dernier auteur (*supra* note 86 à la p. 144) estime: "... [t]he newly created regime on ... exclusive economic zone ... [has] already become part of international customary law ... However, the acceptance of the regime on ... the exclusive economic zones ... does not mean that all specific regulations of the Convention on the Law of the Sea have been accepted by State practice."

103 Le Tribunal arbitral est d'avis que "la troisième Conférence des Nations Unies sur le droit de la mer et la pratique suivie par les États en matière de pêches maritimes pendant le déroulement de cette conférence ont cristallisé et consacré une nouvelle règle internationale, selon laquelle dans la zone économique exclusive, l'État côtier dispose de droits souverains aux fins de l'exploration et de l'exploitation, de la conservation et de la gestion des ressources naturelles" (§ 49), terminologie qui reprend l'art. 56, § 1a) de la Convention. Réf. *supra* note 62.

104 Dans ce sens, F. Orrego Vicuña (1986), *supra* note 86 aux pp. 77-79.

militaires ou la libre navigation en général.[105] Nous pouvons y ajouter les objections américaines face à la plupart des législations émanant d'États riverains de l'océan indien, qui — on l'a mentionné — se donnent la possibilité de créer des "zones désignées" à l'intérieur de leur zone économique et dans lesquelles ils s'attribuent des pouvoirs potentiellement excessifs.[106]

Il résulte de ces constatations que la pratique nous semble assez clairement établie quant à la nature juridique de la zone et paraît correspondre à cet égard aux délicats équilibres de la Convention de 1982. Nous n'avons même aucune objection à endosser l'intéressante opinion de F. Orrego Vicuña à l'effet que la coutume comporte un ensemble de garde-fous qui constituent autant de garanties au profit des États tiers.[107]

C LES COMPÉTENCES NOMMÉES

Compte tenu des constatations qui précèdent, peut-on aller jusqu'à soutenir que l'ensemble du régime juridique établi par la Convention de 1982 correspond au droit coutumier? De rares auteurs ont franchi le pas.[108] L'opinion la plus tranchée à cet égard est celle de J.N. Moore, qui estime que:

> [t]he non sea-bed portions of [the 1982 Convention] are the best evidence of customary international law absent a pattern of State practice to the contrary.[109]

105 Voir à cet égard les développements de T. Treves, *supra* note 86 aux pp. 183-87. Dans l'affaire de la *Délimitation des espaces maritimes entre le Canada et la République française*, sentence du 10 juin 1992, reproduite dans J.-Y. Morin, F. Rigaldies, et D. Turp, *Droit international public, Notes et documents*, 2e éd., Les Éditions Thémis, Montréal, 1992 à la p. 645, le Tribunal arbitral, au § 88, parle du "principe de la liberté de la navigation dans la zone de 200 milles, garantie par l'article 58 de la Convention de 1982, disposition qui représente à n'en pas douter le droit international coutumier, au même titre que l'institution de la zone de 200 milles elle-même."

106 C'est le cas pour l'Inde, Maurice, le Pakistan et les Seychelles. Même si ces lois ne violent pas en elles-mêmes la Convention, le risque demeure (*supra* note 40).

107 *Supra* note 86 à la p. 262. Le juge Evensen, cité par D. Attard, *supra* note 86 à la p. 305, semble partager globalement ce point de vue.

108 On peut citer Galindo Pohl, tel que rapporté par D. Attard, *id.* à la p. 305. Voir aussi, de façon générale, L. Macrae, *supra* note 86 à la p. 222.

109 "Customary International Law After the Convention," dans R.B. Krueger et S.A. Riesenfeld (dir.), *The Developing Law of the Oceans* (Law of the Sea Institute Conference 1984), Honolulu, 1985 à la p. 45.

Cette approche a été fort critiquée. On lui a parfois reproché d'être plus politique que juridique.[110] Elle correspond pourtant à la position des États-Unis[111] depuis 1982, mais n'est guère partagée par les autres États.[112] Elle a permis aux États-Unis de s'objecter depuis cette date à une quarantaine de reprises à des législations étrangères jugées incompatibles avec la Convention et — partant — le droit coutumier.[113]

Il est pourtant impensable d'affirmer *a priori* le caractère coutumier de l'ensemble des dispositions de la Partie V de la Convention de 1982 sans en faire la démonstration préalable, opération à laquelle nous allons procéder.

1 Pêche

S'agissant de la pêche, il ne fait aucun doute qu'il existe un large consensus entourant les grands paramètres des droits souverains de l'État côtier sur l'ensemble des ressources naturelles de la zone (tels que définis en termes généraux dans l'article 56, § 1 de la Convention de 1982). Certains États transcrivent d'ailleurs

110 Voir en particulier F. Orrego Vicuña (1989), *supra* note 86 aux pp. 230-31.

111 Voir F. Orrego Vicuña (1989), *supra* note 86 à la p. 231 (et la référence à W. Burke en note 10). Dans son commentaire joint à sa Proclamation du 10 mars 1983 concernant la zone économique exclusive, le président Reagan affirmait que les dispositions de la Convention concernant les usages traditionnels de la mer "generally confirm existing maritime law and practice," tandis que l'exploitation des grands fonds marins "remains a lawful exercice of the freedom of the high seas open to all nations," The White House, Office of the Press Secretary, March 10, 1983, *supra* note 73. Lors de la succession en 1995, la Slovénie déclarait considérer la partie V de la Convention consacrée à la zone économique "comme faisant partie du droit commun international coutumier." *Bulletin du droit de la mer*, n° 28, juin 1995 à la p. 4.

112 T. Treves, *supra* note 86, cite le Royaume-Uni, qui s'inscrit en faux contre cette attitude (p. 49). Dans le même sens, l'Iran, en signant la Convention de 1982, émettait une déclaration à l'effet que la notion de zone économique exclusive et certaines autres dispositions "sont simplement issues d'un effort de compromis et ne visent pas nécessairement à codifier les coutumes ou les usages (la pratique) existant déjà et considérés comme ayant un caractère obligatoire." *Bulletin du droit de la mer*, n° 25, juin 1994 à la p. 32. Dans une note diplomatique récente, datée du 3 mai 1995, l'Iran reprend cette même thèse. *Bulletin du droit de la mer*, n° 31 à la p. 37.

113 Voir W. Burke, *supra* note 111 à la p. 231.

méticuleusement les termes de l'article 56, § 1 dans leur législation.[114] Reste à savoir si l'on peut aller plus loin et considérer que le dispositif de la Convention qui met en oeuvre le principe de l'article 56 a lui aussi acquis force coutumière. En ce qui concerne la gestion et la conservation des ressources, nous avons noté que l'État côtier possède d'après la Convention des compétences exclusives dans sa zone.[115] À cet égard, il nous semble que la pratique des États reconnaît clairement cette nouvelle responsabilité des États côtiers et la Convention correspond à cet égard à la coutume,[116] incluant, croyons-nous, l'obligation de respecter le principe du rendement constant maximum.[117]

Quant aux mécanismes précis d'exploitation des ressources halieutiques de la zone, on sait qu'ils reposent dans la Convention sur la notion de droits strictement prioritaires, que nous avons qualifiés de préférentiels, au bénéfice de l'État côtier. Or, nous avons pu constater que de nombreuses lois ne font pas allusion à une possibilité de pêche étrangère et que celles qui y font allusion ne mentionnent pas nécessairement l'existence d'un droit d'accès des pêcheurs étrangers au reliquat éventuel de l'État côtier, ce que confirment les accords bilatéraux. À vrai dire, concrètement, les États côtiers n'excluent pas souvent les étrangers de l'accès à leur zone.[118] Nombre d'observateurs craignaient pourtant que l'État

114 On peut fournir les exemples suivants: Australie, Bulgarie, Canada, Indonésie, Islande, Norvège, République dominicaine, Thaïlande, Tuvalu, Vénézuala, Vietnam. Remarquons que si la loi de Tuvalu se dit: "en accord avec le droit international," elle mentionne que cette conformité n'est pas un principe justiciable, compte tenu du caractère flou du droit international (en 1983).

115 Art. 61 et 62, § 1.

116 Telle est l'opinion du Tribunal arbitral dans l'*Affaire de la "Bretagne"* (*supra* note 62, § 51-53) qui semble admettre sans autre démonstration (ce que l'on peut déplorer) le caractère coutumier des articles 61 et 62 (sauf si l'État côtier a conclu avec des tiers des accords à l'effet inverse). Cette opinion est partagée par plusieurs auteurs, dont J. Charney, *supra* note 86, et T. Treves, *id.* aux pp. 152-53.

117 Opinion appuyée *inter alia* par D. Attard, *supra* note 86 à la p. 290.

118 La Guinée constitue une exception (*supra* note 56). De façon générale, les études de la FAO, notamment *Fisheries Regulations under Extended Jurisdiction and International Law (FAO Fisheries Technical Paper No. 223)* (1982) et *Report of the Expert Consultation on the Conditions of Access to the Fish Resources of the Exclusive Economic Zones (FAO Fisheries Report No. 293)* (1983) tendent à prouver que même si les législations qui reprennent les art. 61, 62 et 73 sont rares, la FAO est d'avis que ces articles constituent la base principale de la pratique des États,

côtier, doté de compétences fort larges en vertu de la Convention de 1982 ou de ses ébauches, n'établisse le volume admissible des captures dans sa zone au niveau de ses propres prises afin d'exclure toute pêche étrangère. Or, la pratique a plutôt établi que les États côtiers exploitaient au maximum les larges possibilités que leur offrait la Convention ou les consensus préalables à celle-ci pour rentabiliser l'accès des tiers (avantages pécuniers, commerciaux ou même "en nature": fourniture de bateaux, construction de quais.[119] Il en ressort que le principe même de l'accès des tiers au reliquat nous semble être consacré par la pratique dominante. L'expérience prouve d'ailleurs que les États côtiers ont évité bien des problèmes en ce qui concerne la détermination du TAC et des quotas en ayant souvent recours, lors de l'établissement de leur zone, aux normes établies préalablement par les organisations de pêche dans le secteur concerné (lorsqu'elles existaient naturellement). L'expérience prouve en outre que les États côtiers ont eu tendance, ainsi que les y incite la Convention, à tenir compte des intérêts spécifiques des États qui pêchaient traditionnellement dans la région. Elle prouve enfin que les États concernés ont encouragé, lorsque c'était pertinent, le principe de la réciprocité des droits d'accès.

Le professeur Carl Fleischer, qui a étudié les accords bilatéraux de pêche,[120] est d'avis qu'ils traduisent une tendance à l'exclusivité au profit des États côtiers.[121] Nul ne saurait s'en surprendre. En effet, la vocation d'une zone économique bien gérée dans le domaine halieutique était de devenir exclusive au fil des années. C'était la logique de la Convention. C'est ce qui se passe dans la réalité. L'État côtier qui gère habilement sa zone voit se développer son industrie de la pêche et de la transformation ainsi que ses

---

particulièrement en Amérique latine. Dans *Le droit de la mer, supra* note 3, les Nations Unies estiment que la pratique de ces États ne contrarie nullement les dispositions de la Convention, mais exploitent la latitude qu'elle leur offre (p. 181).

119 Pour des exemples de "rentabilisation," voir *Le droit de la mer, supra* note 3 à la p. 46.

120 C.A. Fleischer, "La pêche" dans R.-J. Dupuy et D. Vignes, (dir.), *Traité du nouveau droit de la mer*, Economica et Bruylant, Paris, Bruxelles, 1985 aux pp. 909-10.

121 *Id.* aux pp. 909-10.

débouchés commerciaux.[122] L'exemple canadien est typique à cet égard. Lorsque le Canada, en 1971, a créé les zones de pêche 1 (golfe du Saint-Laurent), 2 (baie de Fundy) et 3 (détroit d'Hécate, entrée Dixon, bassin de la Reine Charlotte), il s'agissait de zones de pêche véritablement exclusives.[123] Il en résulta la conclusion de traités bilatéraux qui prévoyaient le retrait graduel d'États qui, pour certains, évoquaient pourtant des droits de pêche historiques, en particulier dans le golfe du Saint-Laurent.[124] Avec la création, à l'extérieur de ces zones de pêche exclusives 1, 2 et 3, des zones de pêche 4 (côte atlantique), 5 (côte pacifique) et 6 (côte arctique) en 1977,[125] le Canada optait cette fois pour des zones de pêche strictement préférentielles au niveau de leur exploitation,[126] ainsi que le confirme la douzaine d'accords bilatéraux conclus à cette époque avec les États impliqués dans la pêche dans ces régions nouvellement contrôlées par le Canada.[127] En effet, les États étrangers se voient reconnaître dans ces traités un droit d'accès à une part du reliquat canadien éventuel. Ceci posé, il est vrai que les conditions d'accès qui suivent sont largement favorables au Canada, ce qui lui a permis de tirer profit de l'accès des tiers. Dans la logique

122 R.R. Churchill et A.V. Lowe, dans *The Law of the Sea*, Manchester University Press, 1988, constatent que beaucoup des États qui ont réduit l'accès des tiers à leur ZÉE ont accru leurs propres prises, qu'ils soient développés (Canada, États-Unis, Islande, Mexique, Nouvelle-Zélande) ou non (Guinée Bissau, Indonésie, Malaisie, Pakistan, Sri Lanka): pp. 148-49.

123 Le *Décret sur les zones de pêche du Canada (zones 1, 2 et 3)*, DORS/71.81, (1971) 105 Gaz. Can. II, 822, était basé sur la nouvelle *Loi sur la mer territoriale et les zones de pêche*, adoptée en 1970, L.R.C. 1985, c. T-8. On consultera à cet égard avec profit les excellents articles de A. Braën, "Le contrôle par le Canada des pêches étrangères dans sa zone de pêche exclusive," (1983) A.C.D.I. à la p. 3, et "La réglementation canadienne des pêches," (1996) *Annuaire de droit maritime et océanique* à la p. 97. Dans cet article, il rapporte (p. 102) que "le total des allocations réservées par le Canada en 1977 aux pêcheurs étrangers s'élevait à 59 800 tonnes. En 1992 ces allocations avaient chuté à 55 000 tonnes."

124 Voir F. Rigaldies, "Le statut du golfe du Saint-Laurent en droit international public," (1985) A.C.D.I. 80 aux pp. 126 et s.

125 *Décret sur les zones de pêche du Canada (zones 4 et 5)*, DORS/77-62, (1977) III Gaz. Can. II, 115 et *Décret sur les zones de pêche du Canada (Zone 6)*, DORS/77-173, (1977) III Gaz. Can. II, 652.

126 L'adoption de la nouvelle *Loi sur les océans*, *supra* note 1, ne change rien à l'état antérieur de la situation, en particulier la dualité des zones de pêche canadiennes (voir l'art. 16 de la *Loi*).

127 Voir G.A. Léger, "Les accords bilatéraux régissant la pêche étrangère dans les eaux canadiennes," (1978) A.C.D.I. 116.

des choses, ceux-ci sont chaque année de moins en moins présents et la zone, de préférentielle qu'elle est *de jure*, tend à devenir exclusive *de facto*.

Les États côtiers en développement, longtemps victimes des prédateurs extérieurs, souvent les anciennes puissances coloniales, peuvent ainsi mettre sur pied une industrie autochtone de la pêche (Fidji pour le thon, Inde pour la crevette, Thaïlande pour la pêche au chalut). Le Pérou, qui possède une zone de pêche depuis 1947, reste le quatrième État au monde pour le volume des prises (anchois principalement). Le problème technique majeur auquel sont confrontés les pays en développement demeure celui du contrôle effectif de la pêche étrangère, efficacement réglé cependant par certains (Îles Marshall, Fidji).[128] Quant aux victimes potentielles les plus évidentes de la création des zone économiques exclusives, soit les grandes puissances halieutiques[129] ou les communautés de certains États dépendantes de la pêche hauturière (Bretagne, nord-ouest de l'Espagne), elles bénéficient en pratique d'une manière de "retrait graduel" qui leur permet soit de se reconvertir, soit de se déplacer vers d'autres champs de pêche, voire même d'en créer (par l'aquaculture). En effet, ce n'est en général que de façon progressive que l'État côtier parviendra à pêcher à lui seul la totalité du volume admissible des captures dans sa zone.

L'accès des tiers aux surplus est donc une réalité, justifiée par les intérêts de l'État côtier. Certains auteurs en déduisent que l'existence d'un droit d'accès des tiers aux surplus est douteux, et qu'ils doivent plutôt leur admission à des considérations d'opportunité politique.[130] C'est faire fi de la reconnaissance généralisée du concept d'utilisation optimale des ressources de la zone. Avec d'autres auteurs, plus rares, nous sommes d'avis que les multiples conditions exigées par les États côtiers correspondent aux dispositions de la

128 La coopération régionale est parfois impressionnante à cet égard, tant dans le Pacifique sud qu'en Amérique latine.

129 R.R. Churchill et A.V. Lowe, *supra* note 122 à la p. 148, soutiennent que certaines puissances halieutiques ont tout de même accru leurs prises globales (Japon, URSS, Corée du Sud, Roumanie), quand d'autres ont été moins fortunées (Allemagne de l'Est, Portugal, Bulgarie).

130 C.A. Fleischer, *supra* note 120 aux pp. 909-10. D'autres auteurs (Orrego Vicuña, Burke) paraissent exclure l'existence d'un droit coutumier d'accès des tiers. Plus nuancés, R.R. Churchill et A.V. Lowe, *supra* note 122 à la p. 234, estiment que ". . . there may be a rule of customary international law that coastal States must give foreign vessels access where there is a surplus (academic opinion is divided on this question)."

Convention de 1982 (qui n'est d'ailleurs pas limitative) et traduisent indirectement l'existence d'un droit au bénéfice des tiers,[131] ce que ne nie pas la jurisprudence.[132] Ce droit reste mou cependant, à l'image d'une Convention qui le limite et le soustrait à toute forme de règlement obligatoire en cas de différend.[133] Il est évident, par contre, faute de dispositions législatives suffisantes ou de traités à cet effet,[134] qu'il n'existe pas de coutume prévoyant un droit d'accès des États sans littoral ou géographiquement désavantagés aux zones économiques de la région où ils se trouvent.[135] Cela dit, il serait bien difficile de soutenir qu'un tel "droit" existe dans la Convention de 1982 elle-même.[136]

Les dispositions de la Convention de 1982 relatives à la mise en application par l'État côtier des dispositions de la Convention en matière halieutique[137] se reflètent globalement dans la coutume.[138] Le seul problème concerne les États qui maintiennent des peines d'emprisonnement pour les étrangers commettant des infractions dans leur zone économique, mais il semblerait que ce type de législation soit en recul.[139]

131 J. Carroz et M.J. Savini, dans "The New International Law of Fisheries Emerging from Bilateral Agreements," 1979, *Marine Policy* 70.

132 Rappelons que le Tribunal arbitral dans l'*Affaire de "La Bretagne"* (*supra* note 62), soulignait le caractère coutumier de l'ensemble de l'art. 62 de la Convention.

133 T. Treves, *supra* note 86 à la p. 156, souligne "le caractère faible de l'obligation de l'État côtier." Il croit cependant pouvoir "penser que la pratique de reconnaître un accès au reliquat pourra s'étendre" (*id.*). D. Attard, *supra* note 86 aux pp. 161-63, partage globalement la même opinion.

134 T. Treves, *supra* note 86 à la p. 157, a cependant décelé l'ordonnance togolaise de 1977, ainsi que de rares lois (Maroc). Il n'y a pas, selon lui, d'accords bilatéraux concernant les ESL-GD. On peut toutefois citer des accords récents Bolivie-Pérou en date du 24 janvier 1992 (*Bulletin du droit de la mer*, n° 21 à la p. 87).

135 La doctrine confirme cette constatation. *Inter alia*, D. Attard, *supra* note 86 à la p. 308. Les Nations Unies (*Le droit de la mer*, *supra* note 3 à la p. 12) confirment cette opinion.

136 J. E. Bailey, *supra* note 86 aux pp. 1279-80), constatant qu'un tel droit n'existe que dans la ZÉE d'un État côtier voisin non dépendant de la pêche, constate que plus cet État côtier pêche, plus il est dépendant. Il s'ensuit que le prétendu droit d'accès des ESL-GD se réduit d'autant.

137 Art. 73.

138 Dans ce sens, D. Attard, *supra* note 86 aux pp. 291-92.

139 T. Treves, *supra* note 86 à la p. 159, mentionne que la Guinée Bissau, le Cap Vert et le Canada ont retiré leurs lois en ce sens.

2 *Environnement*

On a déjà noté que les dispositions de la Convention de 1982 sur l'environnement ne se reflètent pas toujours dans la pratique des États. De très nombreuses lois revendiquent au profit de l'État côtier une juridiction qualifiée d'"exclusive," ce qui est exagéré à certains égards. Plus souvent qu'autrement, ces lois demeurent cependant pour l'instant des coquilles vides et le comportement des États impliqués sera déterminant pour évaluer la création éventuelle de règles coutumières.[140] Les États qui ont légiféré de manière plus complète pèchent parfois par excès, parfois par défaut. Il devient difficile d'évaluer leur comportement à l'aune de la seule Convention de 1982, puisque celle-ci n'est jamais qu'un cadre qui détermine par ailleurs des obligations fondamentales, complétées par de nombreuses conventions spécifiques.[141] Chose certaine, l'histoire nous enseigne que les législations qui affecteraient clairement la liberté de navigation des tiers et qui ne seraient justifiées ni par la Convention de 1982, ni par des traités spécifiques, feraient l'objet de protestations et paraissent ainsi comme les autres tentatives de territorialisation, vouées à l'échec.

3 *Recherche scientifique*

Relativement à la recherche scientifique marine, nous avons noté une concordance générale entre la législation des États et une Convention qui a su se montrer généreuse à leur égard. Assez rares

140 La position du Canada est typique à cet égard. La *Loi sur les océans*, dans son art. 14b), donne au Canada compétence ". . . à la [*sic*] protection et la préservation du milieu marin," reprenant ainsi la formulation de l'art. 56, § 1b)(iii) de la Convention de 1982. Ce dernier article cependant subordonne la compétence de l'État côtier au respect des "dispositions pertinentes de la Convention," soit la partie XII consacrée à la "protection et préservation du milieu marin," ce que ne fait pas la loi canadienne. En pratique, la juridiction du Canada en matière environnementale dans sa zone économique s'exercera en vertu de lois établies, soit essentiellement la *Loi sur la marine marchande du Canada* (L.R.C. 1985, c. S-9), révisée pour la circonstance, la *Loi canadienne sur la protection de l'environnement* (L.R.C. 1985 (4e supp.), c. 16), révisée elle aussi, et la *Loi sur la prévention de la pollution des eaux arctiques* (L.R.C. 1985, c. A-12). Techniquement, s'agissant des deux premières lois, le Canada s'est contenté de substituer les termes "zone économique exclusive" à ceux de "zone de pêche," sans modifier aucunement le régime juridique préétabli.

141 Convention de 1982, art. 237. Il convient de remarquer qu'une vingtaine de conventions globales ou régionales ont été adoptées pendant la troisième Conférence ou depuis l'adoption de la Convention de 1982 (*Le droit de la mer, supra* note 3 à la p. 17).

sont les États côtiers qui outrepassent les compétences qui leur sont reconnues par la Convention.[142] En revanche, les législations reprennent rarement les limites prévues expressément par celle-ci.[143] En dépit de ces nuances, la pratique semble correspondre globalement à la Convention, avec semble-t-il une tendance à exiger un consentement formel et systématique de l'État côtier pour toute recherche effectuée dans sa zone par un tiers. T. Treves résume parfaitement la situation lorsqu'il soutient: ". . . au stade actuel de l'évolution du droit, il est très difficile de dire si l'on se trouve face à des violations du droit coutumier ou à des éléments qui contribuent à mieux en définir les contours."[144]

Reste la prétention de certains États en développement à vouloir exercer des compétences exclusives à l'égard de la totalité des installations et ouvrages situés dans leur zone, quelle qu'en soit la finalité, ce qui n'est acceptable, selon la Convention de 1982, que pour les îles artificielles. On pourrait certes y voir un regrettable épiphénomène d'une conception territorialiste de la zone.[145] Pourtant, on peut comprendre les États en développement lorsqu'on constate que, dans sa rédaction actuelle, la Convention de 1982 autorise l'implantation d'installations et ouvrages à caractère militaire en zone économique étrangère. L'intransigeance des grandes puissances à ce qu'il en soit ainsi, tant au cours de la troisième Conférence que par la suite, devrait toutefois empêcher toute autre prétention d'aspirer au statut de règle de droit international public positif.[146]

IV Conclusion

Le concept, la largeur, la conception fondamentale de la zone économique exclusive paraissent chaque jour mieux établis en coutume, et ce en conformité avec la lettre de la Convention de 1982. Le caractère *sui generis* de la zone s'est imposé dans la pratique des États au point où l'on est en droit de soutenir, avec le professeur F. Orrego Vicuña, que la coutume possède suffisamment de balises

142 J. Charney, *supra* note 86, dans sa note 96A, cite le cas du Mexique.

143 Dans ce sens, J. Charney, *supra* note 86, D. Attard, *id.* à la p. 92.

144 T. Treves, *supra* note 86 à la p. 169.

145 On ne se surprendra pas de voir cette position défendue par le Brésil et l'Uruguay, ainsi que par le Cap Vert.

146 B. Vukas, "L'utilisation pacifique de la mer, dénucléarisation et désarmement," dans R.-J. Dupuy et D. Vignes (dir.), *supra* note 120 aux pp. 1047, 1056-57.

pour équilibrer les intérêts en présence aussi bien que ne le fait le texte, à cet égard ambigu, de la Convention:

Even though custom has not incorporated all the detailed mecanisms of the Convention, being generally limited to the basic concepts, it is sufficiently balanced so as to guarantee an extent in which the coastal State's rights and obligations harmonize with those of other States. This means that it performs a complementary role with respect to other sources of the exclusive economic zone regime, confirming the approach of legal moderation that constitutes the central characteristic of this new regime in international law.[147]

On note, certes, une tendance de la part de certains États côtiers en développement à se doter unilatéralement de compétences résiduaires,[148] mais elle est l'objet de nombreuses protestations émanant des grandes puissances maritimes, soucieuses de contrôler de telles dérives. Si bien qu'après une période de craintes compréhensibles,[149] les auteurs reconnaissent aujourd'hui volontiers qu'il n'y a pas eu de territorialisation notable, ou en tout cas irréversible, de la zone.[150]

Que fur et à mesure que les textes de négociation se consolidaient et que la convention parvenait à son état de signature, la pratique nationale montrait un plus grand degré d'harmonie avec la convention . . . Rien ne permet de prévoir que la zone économique exclusive puisse être essentiellement dénaturée par la pratique nationale, situation où, de toute façon, il y aurait lieu d'utiliser les corrections diplomatiques ou les procédures correspondantes de règlement des différends.[151]

Pour autant, il ne paraît pas possible de soutenir que le régime juridique précis établi par la Convention pour chaque compétence fonctionnelle de l'État côtier trouve intégralement écho dans le droit coutumier. Pour les pêches, les compétences exclusives de l'État côtier en matière de conservation et de gestion se reflètent

147 F. Orrego Vicuña, *supra* note 86 (1989) à la p. 262.

148 Lorsque ces lois sont anciennes, elles peuvent être justifiées par l'absence de consensus dans le cadre de la troisième Conférence. Lorsqu'elles sont récentes, elles exploitent souvent les ambiguïtés de la Convention: voir l'article de F.H. Paolillo, *supra* note 86, pour la pratique latino-américaine à cet égard. La Convention constitue dans ce cas une caricature de ce que peut générer le consensus: une "rencontre d'arrière-pensées."

149 De telles craintes ont initialement été exprimées par B. Oxman et R.-J. Dupuy en particulier à de nombreuses occasions.

150 Cette opinion est partagée par plusieurs auteurs (Wolfrum, Paolillo). Voir tout particulièrement D. Attard, *supra* note 86 aux pp. 307-8.

151 F. Orrego Vicuña, *supra* note 86 (1986) à la p. 121.

dans la coutume. Il en va de même, croyons-nous, de ses droits préférentiels au chapitre de l'exploitation des ressources halieutiques non sédentaires. Le droit d'accès des tiers au reliquat des prises de l'État côtier dans les limites de l'utilisation optimale semble admis, en pratique tout au moins, car il est de l'intérêt de l'État côtier de le reconnaître.[152] Cette obligation d'admettre les tiers est d'ailleurs assez "molle" dans la Convention de 1982 elle-même, compte tenu à la fois des limites dont elle est flanquée et de l'absence de procédure de règlement obligatoire des différends à son sujet. Par ailleurs, la pratique des États ne confirme pas l'existence d'un droit privilégié d'accès des États sans littoral et désavantagés; si tant est qu'un tel "droit" existe dans la Convention, il semble voué à la désuétude,[153] en particulier en raison de l'absence de pressions véritables de la part des États sans littoral et géographiquement désavantagés, qui n'ont pas de tradition de pêche à évoquer en l'espèce.

Au chapitre de l'environnement, la Convention de 1982 constitue un traité-cadre, complété par de nombreux accords à vocation universelle ou régionale. Il s'avère de ce fait très délicat de déterminer si la législation des États est conforme à cet ensemble conventionnel complexe. La tendance est ici manifestement à la revendication de compétences, mais il faudrait vérifier si les États s'en prévalent concrètement. Puisque les États côtiers sont plus enclins à se reconnaître des droits qu'à se créer des obligations, on peut douter de la convergence absolue traité-coutume. En revanche, s'il existait des abus criants affectant la liberté de navigation, les grandes puissances ne tarderaient pas à se manifester. Même si les États non liés par la Convention de 1982 ne reprennent pas toujours dans leur législation les obligations que celle-ci impose en vue de la protection de la zone (contre les risques découlant, par exemple, de l'exploration et de l'exploitation du plateau continental), ce qui est regrettable, il n'en demeure pas moins que le droit

[152] Ce droit n'existe évidemment pas en cas d'absence de surplus. Voir T. Treves, *supra* note 86, note 363. Dans l'Union européenne, où il n'y a pas de surplus, l'accès des tiers est conditionné par la réciprocité. Notons qu'il n'existe pas de différence notable dans le comportement des États qui ont établi une simple zone de pêche (et non une ZÉE complète) au large de leurs côtes. Voir J.-P. Quéneudec, "Les rapports entre zones de pêche et zones économiques exclusives," (1990) *German Yearbook of International Law* 138.

[153] J. E. Bailey, *supra* note 86 à la p. 1280, conclut: "... it seems certain that coastal States will never permit such participation, and thus, articles 69 and 70 will never be more than words."

international coutumier leur impose en la matière certaines obligations de base.[154]

La recherche scientifique marine n'est pas toujours abordée dans les législations nationales sur la zone. Quand ils le font, les États semblent respecter globalement les dispositions de la Convention, sans pour autant s'encombrer des nuances qu'elle établit. On note ainsi une tendance des États côtiers à imposer leur consentement spécifique et systématique à toute forme de recherche envisagée par des tiers ou à combler, souvent à leur propre avantage, les vides de la Convention. Il en résulte ici encore une certaine tendance à la territorialisation:

> Tout en étant assez fidèle à la Convention dans l'ensemble de ses dispositions sur la recherche scientifique marine, la pratique ouvre ainsi certaines brèches dans l'équilibre entre les dispositions favorables aux droits de l'État côtier et celles visant à garantir les intérêts de la recherche.[155]

Quant à la volonté manifestée par certains États côtiers tiers-mondistes d'exercer une juridiction exclusive sur l'ensemble des installations et ouvrages situés dans leur zone, pour justifiable qu'elle soit en termes de sécurité, elle risque de ne pas résister longtemps aux attaques des grandes puissances.

Nous avons ainsi pu établir qu'à quelques exceptions près, la pratique des États est assez constante dans le sens des dispositions de la Partie V de la Convention de 1982. Pour reprendre les exigences de la jurisprudence, on peut aussi prouver sans difficultés qu'elle est générale puisqu'elle émane aujourd'hui de toutes sortes d'États, riches ou pauvres, provenant de tous horizons géographiques. Le facteur durée, compte tenu des faibles exigences de la jurisprudence récente à cet égard ainsi que du volume de la pratique, ne présente pas non plus de difficultés particulières. Reste donc à savoir si l'élément psychologique *(opinio juris)* poussait les États à se comporter ainsi qu'ils l'ont fait. À cet égard, le comportement des États dans le cadre de la troisième Conférence ne saurait être sous-estimé.[156] Nous

154 Voir en particulier le principe 21 de la *Déclaration de la Conférence de Rio sur l'environnement et le développement*, 13 juin 1992 (1992) R.G.D.I.P. 975.

155 T. Treves, *supra* note 86 à la p. 169.

156 Dans l'Affaire des *Activités militaires et paramilitaires au Nicaragua et contre celui-ci*, (Nicaragua/États-Unis), Fond, Recueil C.I.J., 1986 à la p. 14, la CIJ, au § 188, affirmait devoir "... s'assurer de l'existence, dans le droit international coutumier, d'une *opinio juris*... Cette *opinio juris* peut se déduire entre autres, quoique avec la prudence nécessaire, de l'attitude des parties et des États à l'égard de certaines

avons pu noter qu'une grande partie de leur activité unilatérale reposait sur des consensus acquis dès 1975 dans le cadre de la troisième Conférence. Ces mêmes États ont, en fin de Conférence, voté en faveur du texte de la Convention. Les dix-sept abstentions et les quatre votes négatifs ont été principalement justifiés par l'insatisfaction de certains États à l'égard de la Partie XI, consacrée à la zone internationale des fonds marins. Le désir de se conformer aux acquis de la Conférence a donc été déterminant pour les États, traduisant une *opinio juris* de leur part. On imagine mal quels ". . . autres facteurs [auraient] pu motiver leur action."[157]

Les pratiques aberrantes de certains États par rapport à quelques dispositions de la Convention (recherche scientifique, environnement en particulier), contestées par certaines objections formelles, incitent par contre à douter du caractère coutumier de ces dispositions, même si la Cour internationale de Justice, dans l'Affaire des *Activités militaires et paramilitaires au Nicaragua*, semble avoir quelque peu réduit ses exigences en matière d'uniformité.[158] Par ailleurs, ces comportements atypiques ne sont eux-mêmes pas suffisamment généraux et représentatifs pour constituer des coutumes dérogatoires par rapport à la Convention. Le seul groupe identifiable à se comporter collectivement en contradiction — souvent potentielle — avec certains articles de la Convention est constitué d'États riverains

---

résolutions de l'Assemblée générale . . ." Et la Cour de citer la Résolution 2625 (XXV) sur les relations amicales, précisément adoptée par consensus.

157 *Plateau continental de la mer du Nord, supra* note 83, § 78. On consultera avec profit les excellents développements consacrés à l'*opinio juris* par D. Attard, *supra* note 86 aux pp. 297 à 301. Dans l'*Affaire du golfe du Maine, supra* note 98, la CIJ fait un lien manifeste, au § 94 de son jugement, entre l'adoption de la majorité des dispositions de la Convention par consensus et l'existence de règles coutumières correspondantes: la non entrée en vigueur — à l'époque — de la Convention de 1982 "n'enlève rien au fait du consensus qui a été réuni sur des parties importantes de l'instrument et n'empêchent surtout pas de constater que certaines dispositions de la Convention relatives . . . à la zone économique exclusive . . . n'ont pas rencontré d'objections lors de leur adoption . . . Les dispositions dont il s'agit, bien que portant la marque du compromis qui a présidé à leur adoption, peuvent être considérées comme conformes actuellement au droit international général en la matière."

158 "La Cour ne pense pas que, pour qu'une règle soit coutumièrement établie, la pratique correspondante doive être rigoureusement conforme à cette règle. Il lui paraît suffisant, pour déduire l'existence de règles coutumières, que les États y conforment leur conduite d'une manière générale et qu'ils traitent eux-mêmes les comportements non conformes à la règle en question comme des violations de celle-ci et non pas comme la manifestation d'une règle nouvelle." Réf. *supra* note 156, § 186.

de l'océan indien.[159] On ne saurait toutefois déduire de ce constat l'existence d'une coutume régionale établie, compte tenu à la fois des objections nombreuses dont leur comportement a été l'objet et du fait que plusieurs des États concernés sont parties à la Convention de 1982 et désormais tenus de la respecter.[160] L'analyse du comportement à venir des États en ces domaines sera donc déterminante.[161]

159 On peut ainsi citer quelques cas de législations (Inde, Maurice, Pakistan, Seychelles) qui outrepassent les dispositions de la Convention de 1982 en matière de pêche (sauf Maurice), d'installations et d'ouvrages, d'environnement et qui accordent à l'État des compétences douanières et fiscales dans des secteurs désignés de la zone. Trois de ces États, en outre, prévoient des peines de prison pour non respect des règlements de pêche (Inde, Maurice, Seychelles). L'Inde prévoit aussi de fixer éventuellement des conditions d'entrée des navires dans des zones désignées ainsi que la détermination de voies de navigation. De façon générale, la poignée d'États qui se donnent la possibilité de créer des "zones désignées" à l'intérieur de leur ZÉE s'attribuent des pouvoirs potentiellement excessifs dans ces zones (ce qui est le cas pour l'Inde, Maurice, le Pakistan et les Seychelles). Voir en particulier T. Treves, *supra* note 86 à la p. 210.

160 L'Inde, Maurice, les Seychelles sont ainsi parties à la Convention, ce qui n'est pas le cas du Pakistan.

161 Ceci en vertu de la troisième hypothèse envisagée par la CIJ dans les Affaires *Plateau continental de la mer du Nord, supra* note 83, § 70, à l'effet qu'une disposition purement conventionnelle qui possède un caractère normatif et est insusceptible de réserves peut constituer la base d'une règle générale de droit. Cette règle, qui apparaît suite à la convention, résulte ". . . du fait pour une part de l'influence exercée par celle-ci et pour une autre de la pratique ultérieure des États." Cependant, plusieurs conditions s'imposent pour établir une telle règle. À cet égard, ". . . il se peut que, sans même qu'une longue période se soit écoulée, une participation très large et représentative à la convention suffise, à condition toutefois qu'elle comprenne les États particulièrement intéressés" (§ 73). On peut certes considérer qu'avec 116 États parties, cette condition est aujourd'hui remplie, mais de fraîche date seulement, compte tenu de la lenteur du processus de ratification par les grandes puissances maritimes tout particulièrement. À cet égard, la Cour constatait en 1969 que la signature de la Convention de 1958 sur le plateau continental remontait à plus de dix ans et son entrée en vigueur à moins de cinq ans. Elle ajoutait (§ 74):

> Bien que le fait qu'il ne se soit écoulé qu'un bref laps de temps ne constitue pas en soi un empêchement à la formation d'une règle nouvelle de droit international coutumier à partir d'une règle purement conventionnelle à l'origine, il demeure indispensable que dans ce laps de temps, aussi bref qu'il ait été, la pratique des États, y compris ceux qui sont particulièrement intéressés, ait été fréquente et pratiquement uniforme dans le sens de la disposition invoquée et se soit manifestée de manière à établir une reconnaissance générale du fait qu'une règle de droit ou une obligation juridique est en jeu.

Si nous nous croyons ainsi en droit de soutenir que l'essentiel de la Convention correspond à la coutume,[162] il est à prévoir que la récente entrée en vigueur de la Convention aura un impact bénéfique sur l'uniformisation de l'ensemble du droit positif, ce qu'anticipaient certains observateurs il y a quelques années:

> If the LOS Convention were to come into force for the vast majority of nations, both parties and nonparties would be under significant pressure to conform their national claims to the rules found in the Convention.[163]

Il est bien évident que les États liés par la Convention n'ont désormais d'autre choix que de se conformer à l'ensemble de la Partie V, insusceptible de réserves, sous peine de recours juridictionnels.[164] Plusieurs d'entre eux ont d'ores-et-déjà redressé la situation quand d'autres, à tort ou à raison, estiment que leur législation est conforme à leurs obligations conventionnelles.[165] Quant aux États non

---

Tel n'est précisément pas le cas à l'heure actuelle dans les secteurs de la recherche scientifique et de l'environnement. La CIJ semble de plus accorder peu de poids à l'activité unilatérale d'États qui sont ou sont bientôt devenus parties à une convention comme preuve de l'élément matériel de la coutume (§ 76).

162 D. Attard, *supra* note 86 à la p. 294, estime que le modèle de la ZÉE établi par la Convention de 1982 en tant que tel ("*as such*") passe le test de la constance et de l'uniformité (uniformité qui n'a pas à être absolue). F. Orrego Vicuña, *supra* (1986 et 1989) note 86, *passim*, estime lui aussi qu'une grande partie de la Convention reflète la coutume. De même, J.E. Bailey, *supra* note 86 à la p. 1284, dresse une liste généreuse des éléments de la Partie V qui se retrouvent dans la coutume. Voir aussi ses conclusions générales aux pp. 1294-97.

163 J. Charney, *supra* note 86 à la p. 237.

164 T. Treves, *supra* note 86 à la p. 286, estime que l'entrée en vigueur de la Convention de 1982 à l'égard des États parties aura pour effet de promouvoir la limitation des revendications excessives et d'autoriser la contestation des abus. J. E. Bailey, *supra* note 86, remarque que les États qui ont tendance à ne pas respecter la Convention sont souvent les pays en développement, qui sont ceux qui adhèrent le plus à la Convention. Ceci donne un intérêt tout particulier à son entrée en vigueur (p. 1295).

165 Tel est le cas pour le Brésil, Cap Vert, les Philippines (qui ont affirmé corriger leur constitution pour la rendre conforme aux dispositions de la Convention sur les eaux archipélagiques), Sao Tomé et Principe, l'Uruguay (respect douteux dans ce cas, puisque ce pays revendique une mer territoriale de 200 milles). En ratifiant récemment la Convention, la Grèce se disait prête à assumer l'ensemble des droits et obligations en découlant, tout en déterminant elle-même quand et comment elle exercera ces droits: *Bulletin du droit de la mer*, n° 29 à la p. 7. Compte tenu du caractère flou de certaines dispositions conventionnelles, il faut être conscient du fait que "si un État agit d'une manière apparemment inconciliable avec une règle reconnue, mais défend sa

parties, suite à une adhésion désormais "large" et "représentative" à la Convention, ils se retrouvent minorisés,[166] et vont en conséquence subir de très fortes pressions de la part des États parties afin qu'ils se conforment à la Convention, même s'ils n'y adhèrent pas formellement.[167] Il en résulte que la Convention exerce un rôle très bénéfique d'entraînement sur la coutume,[168] laquelle à son tour

---

conduite en invoquant des exceptions ou justifications contenues dans la règle elle-même, il en résulte une confirmation plutôt qu'un affaiblissement de la règle, et cela que l'attitude de cet État puisse ou non se justifier sur cette base" (Affaire des *Activités militaires au Nicaragua et contre celui-ci, supra* note 156, § 186. Dans *Le droit de la mer, supra* note 3, les Nations Unies estiment que ce sont souvent les lois les plus anciennes qui dérogent à la Convention. Ainsi en est-il des lois sur les "zones désignées" qui sont antérieures à 1982. En Asie, les dispositions législatives prévoyant des compétences exclusives sur l'ensemble des installations et ouvrages ainsi que les îles artificielles sont anciennes. Dans cette même région, les lois qui prévoient une "juridiction exclusive" de l'État côtier en matière environnementale datent des années 70, quand celles qui ont été adoptées dans les années 80 parlent de "juridiction," conformément à la Convention. En Afrique, 11 lois sur la ZÉE sont postérieures à 1982, 13 antérieures. Or, 6 de ces dernières ont été changées pour les mettre en accord avec la Convention (p. 35). En 1991 en particulier, la Namibie a exclu de sa loi les compétences qu'elle prétendait exercer en ZÉE dans les domaines fiscal, douanier, sanitaire et de l'immigration (p. 36). Dans sa récente loi en date du 16 mai 1995, l'Ukraine évoque explicitement en préambule le fait que sa législation est basée sur la Convention de 1982 et va, dans l'art. 32, jusqu'à préciser que la Convention (ou tout autre traité liant l'Ukraine) l'emporteront sur toute disposition incompatible de la loi: *Bulletin du droit de la mer*, n° 30 aux pp. 49 et 59.

166 Environ 40 États disposent d'une ZÉE ou d'une zone de pêche de 200 milles sans être parties à la Convention de 1982.

167 Les objections prennent plus de poids si la Convention est considérée comme représentative du droit coutumier.

168 J. Charney, *supra* note 86 aux pp. 257-58, donne l'exemple à cet égard des compétences résiduaires. Pour F. Orrego Vicuña (1989), *supra* note 86 à la p. 251, l'adhésion massive à la Convention aidera à régler les inadéquations Convention-coutume en incitant à la longue la pratique à se conformer à la Convention. Or, la coutume présente un intérêt tout particulier depuis que la CIJ a affirmé, dans les *Affaires du plateau continental de la mer du Nord, supra* note 83, son caractère objectif et — partant — son applicabilité universelle (p. 42, § 70). Pour la Cour, les règles coutumières doivent par nature ". . . s'appliquer dans des conditions égales à tous les membres de la communauté internationale et ne peuvent être subordonnées à un droit d'exclusion exercé unilatéralement et à volonté par l'un quelconque des membres de la communauté à son propre avantage" (*Id.*, pp. 39-40, § 63). Voir K. Marek, "Plateau continental et sources du droit international dans la décision de la C.I.J. du 20 février 1969," (1970) R.B.D.I. à la p. 53.

aidera à cerner les ambiguïtés du texte de la Convention.[169] Il est ainsi permis de présager que les deux instruments se mettront progressivement au diapason l'un de l'autre.

Summary

The Exclusive Economic Zone in State Practice

The use of the concept of an exclusive economic zone has increased since the adoption of the United Nations Convention on the Law of the Sea. However, the characterization of this zone varies greatly between States. This article presents an exhaustive survey of the concept of an exclusive economic zone. The author discusses the types of jurisdiction exercised by States in their uses of an exclusive economic zone. Disparity exists between the provisions of the Convention and State practice in some specific areas: for example, the provisions on the environment and on scientific research. Despite these exceptions, the author maintains that the basic tenets of the Convention are respected in State practice. State declarations as well as arbitral and judicial decisions show that the Convention and State practice are together evolving to reinforce the basic principles of the concept of an exclusive economic zone.

Sommaire

La zone économique exclusive dans la pratique des États

Depuis l'entrée en vigueur de la Convention des Nations Unies sur le droit de la mer, nous remarquons une augmentation de l'utilisation du concept de zone exclusive économique; cependant, la caractérisation de ces zones varie énormément entre États. Cet article offre un survol exhaustif de l'utilisation d'une zone exclusive économique. L'auteur discute des types de juridiction et de la juridiction actuelle exercée par les États dans leurs zones respectives. Il existe une divergence entre les dispositions de la Convention et la pratique des États dans certaines matières, telles l'environnement et la recherche scientifique. Malgré cela, l'auteur conclut que les déclarations d'État et les décisions juridiques et arbitrales nous indiquent que la Convention et la pratique des États évoluent de façon à renforcer les notions de base du concept d'une zone économique exclusive.

169 Dans ce sens, J. Charney, *id.* à la p. 258.

The Dispute Settlement Regime of the Straddling and Highly Migratory Fish Stocks Convention

TED L. MCDORMAN

INTRODUCTION

At the commencement of the United Nations Conference on Straddling Fish Stocks and Highly Migratory Fish Stocks in 1993, it was uncertain whether sufficient political will or common ground among participating states existed to achieve a consensus on a final product.[1] Whether this final product should be an international treaty or a non-legally binding statement of principles was a dividing issue throughout much of the conference.[2] In the end,

Ted L. McDorman, B.A. (Toronto), LL.B., LL.M. (Dalhousie), is an associate professor in the Faculty of Law at the University of Victoria in British Columbia and a member of the Oceans Institute of Canada in Halifax. This article is a revised and expanded version of a section of a forthcoming article on the 1995 Straddling Fish Stocks and Highly Migratory Fish Stocks Agreement being prepared with Peter Orebech and Ketill Sigurjonsson.

[1] An excellent presentation of the background that led to the Conference is Paul Fauteux, "L'initiative juridique canadienne sur la pêche en haute mer" (1993), 31 Canadian Yearbook of International Law 33-87, translated as "The Canadian Legal Initiative on High Seas Fishing" (1993), 4 Yearbook of International Environmental Law 51.

[2] See Ronald Barston, "United Nations Conference on Straddling and Highly Migratory Fish Stocks" (1995), 19 Marine Policy 159; David A. Balton, "Strengthening the Law of the Sea: The New Agreement on Straddling Fish Stocks and Highly Migratory Fish Stocks" (1996), 27 Ocean Development and Int'l L. J. 125 at 133-35; Moritaka Hayashi, "The Role of the United Nations in Managing the World's Fisheries" in G. H. Blake, et al., eds., *The Peace Management of Transboundary Resources*, 378-79 (Dordrecht: Graham & Trotman/ Martinus Nijhoff, 1995); and José A. de Yturriaga, "Fishing in the High Seas: From the 1982 UN Convention on the Law of the Sea to the 1995 Agreement on Straddling and Highly Migratory Fish Stocks" (1995), 3 African Yearbook of International Law 151 at 162-64.

the participants agreed (some reluctantly) that an international treaty had to be the final outcome of the deliberations. The inelegantly titled Agreement for the Implementation of the Provisions of the United Nations Convention on the Law of the Sea of 10 December 1982 Relating to the Conservation and Management of Straddling Fish Stocks and Highly Migratory Fish Stocks[3] was adopted in late 1995.

As the Conference edged towards accepting that a formal international treaty was the preferred result, it also accepted that a dispute settlement regime had to be a critical component of the 1995 Agreement. Conference Chair Satya Nandan referred to the provisions on the peaceful settlement of disputes as the third of three essential pillars upon which the 1995 Agreement was built.[4]

The events astride Canada's 200 nautical (200-n.) mile zone east of Newfoundland in the spring of 1995 heightened the attention given to the dispute settlement regime in the new Agreement. Canada seized a Spanish trawler on the high seas and charged it with fishing turbot (Greenland halibut) in a manner inconsistent with the governing regulations of the Northwest Atlantic Fisheries Organization (NAFO), which had been incorporated into Canadian law. Spain characterized the arrest as piracy, arguing that neither NAFO nor any other treaty or principle of international law justified Canada's seizure of a foreign fishing vessel on the high seas. An Easter 1995 accord cooled a tense standoff between

3 Reprinted at (1995), 34 International Legal Materials 1547 [hereinafter 1995 Agreement]. The choice of this title is described in Balton, *supra* note 2 at 135. For a detailed description of the 1995 Agreement, see André Tahindro, "Conservation and Management of Transboundary Fish Stocks: Comments in Light of the Adoption of the 1995 Agreement for the Conservation and Management of Straddling Fish Stocks and Highly Migratory Fish Stocks" (1997), 28 Ocean Development and Int'l L. J. 1. For a more succinct review of the 1995 Agreement, see Balton, *supra* note 2, and Ellen Hey, "Global Fisheries Regulations in the First Half of the 1990s" (1996), 11 Int'l J. of Marine and Coastal Law 459 at 472-82. As of Aug. 5, 1997, 15 states, including the U.S., had ratified the 1995 agreement. Canada is in the process of changing its domestic law to facilitate ratification. Pursuant to Art. 40, the Agreement is to come into force 30 days after the receipt of 30 ratifications.

4 Dr. Nandan's closing remarks at the conference are reprinted in "Deal Farreaching, Bold and Revolutionary" (Sept. 1995), Fishing News Int'l, at 2. The other two pillars of the 1995 Agreement were identified as the conservation and management principles for stocks, which include the precautionary approach and the enforcement and compliance provisions.

Canada and the European Union.[5] The perception is that the dispute settlement regime of the 1995 Agreement will be available to resolve or even prevent such a conflict in the future.[6]

However, little confidence can be placed in the dispute settlement regime of the 1995 Agreement as a method for resolving high seas fishing problems similar to those faced by Canada and Spain. First, the dispute settlement regime will be binding only upon states that become parties to the 1995 Agreement. While it can be expected that much of the Treaty will emerge as part of accepted state practice, the dispute settlement obligations will remain as contractual and therefore only binding upon states that formally accept them. Second, even in a situation where disputing states are both parties to the 1995 Agreement, if past practice is a guide, states will be reluctant to make use of formal, binding third-party dispute settlement or other modes of formal dispute settlement and will prefer to rely on direct negotiations to heal rifts.[7] Third, but

5 See generally T. L. McDorman, "Canada's Aggressive Fisheries Actions: Will They Improve the Climate for International Agreements?" (1995), Vol. 2, No. 3 Canadian Foreign Policy 5-28; G. L. Lugten, "Fisheries War for the Halibut" (1995), 25 Environmental Policy and Law 223; David Freestone, "Canada and the EU Reach Agreement to Settle the Estai Dispute" (1995), 10 Int'l J. of Marine and Coastal Law 397; Anthony Bergin, et al., "Marine Living Resources" in L. K. Kriwoken, et al., eds., *Oceans Law and Policy in the Post-UNCED Era: Australian and Canadian Perspectives* 193-98 (The Hague: Kluwer Law Int'l, 1996); Michael Keiver, "The Turbot War: Gunboat Diplomacy or Refinement of the Law of the Sea" (1996), 37 Les Cahiers de Droit 543; Christopher C. Joyner and Alejandro Alvarez von Gustedt, "The 1995 Turbot War: Lessons for the Law of the Sea" (1996), 11 Int'l J. of Marine and Coastal Law 425; and Allen L. Springer, "The Canadian Turbot War with Spain: Unilateral State Action in Defense of Environmental Issues" (1997), 6 J. of Environment and Development 26.

Numerous disputes have arisen regarding the activities of fishing vessels in high seas waters adjacent to 200-n. mile zones. An overview of these disputes is provided by Evelyne Meltzer, "Global Overview of Straddling and Highly Migratory Fish Stocks: The Nonsustainable Nature of High Seas Fisheries" (1994), 25 Ocean Development and Int'l L. J. 255 at 268-305. The Iceland-Norway dispute regarding the loophole in the Barents Sea is of particular interest, since Iceland, once an aggressive state regarding fisheries jurisdiction, is in the position of relying on high seas freedoms. See Thorir Gudmundsson, "Cold War on the High Seas: Norwegian-Icelandic dispute over 'Loophole' fishing in the Barents Sea" (1995), 64 Nordic J. of Int'l L. 557.

6 See Michael Rivlin, "A U.N. Treaty Takes on the World's Fisheries" (March 1996), National Fisherman 28 at 84.

7 An excellent statement of this reality is provided by Oscar Schachter, *International Law in Theory and Practice* 218 (Dordrecht: Martinus Nijhoff, 1991):

related to the second point, even when two disputant states have pre-agreed to make use of formal or binding third-party dispute settlement, it is unusual and frequently counter-productive for one state to "force" the other before a dispute settlement body in the absence of mutual consent regarding a specific dispute. Such "forcing" can lead to a state's refusal to participate in the dispute settlement process.[8] Actions of this type do little to resolve a dispute and can raise questions about the legitimacy and responsibility of the third-party body itself.

Both the Canada-Spain dispute and the Iceland cod war of the 1970s demonstrate the issues involved. Since neither Canada nor Spain were parties to the 1982 United Nations Convention on the Law of the Sea (the 1982 LOS Convention) at the time of the turbot dispute, the dispute settlement regime of the LOS Convention[9] was not available. While both countries had agreed to the compulsory jurisdiction of the International Court of Justice (ICJ), Canada had carefully crafted an exception to its acceptance that attempted to cover a situation like the high seas seizure of the Spanish trawler.[10] Canada and Spain are currently before the ICJ

> [Governments] recognize that there is a place, and even a necessity, for adjudication but as the record shows, the actual recourse to arbitration or courts is comparatively minimal in relation to the number of legal disputes that concern them. It is no great mystery why they are reluctant to have their disputes adjudicated. Litigation is uncertain, time consuming, troublesome. Political officials do not want to lose control of a case that they might resolve by negotiation or political pressures. Diplomats naturally prefer diplomacy; political leaders value persuasion, manoeuvre [*sic*] and flexibility. States do not want to risk losing a case when the stakes are high or to be troubled with litigation in minor matters.

8 Richard B. Bilder, "International Third Party Dispute Settlement" (1989), 17 Denver J. of Int'l Law and Policy 471 at 479 commented: "Recent experience . . . raises questions as to the usefulness or effectiveness of third-party intervention in the absence of real and continuing consent on the part of all the disputing parties." The recent experience referred to by Bilder was the non-participation of the U.S. in the *Nicaragua* litigation before the International Court of Justice: *Case Concerning Military and Paramilitary Activities in and against Nicaragua*, [1986] ICJ Rep. 14. Non-appearance as a litigation strategy is commented upon by Terry D. Gill, *Litigation Strategy at the International Court* 76-81 (Dordrecht: Martinus Nijhoff, 1989).

9 See *infra* note 17.

10 Foreign Affairs and International Trade, Press Release (May 10, 1994) "Canada Takes Action to End Foreign Overfishing."

arguing whether the Court has jurisdiction to resolve the dispute.[11] During the Iceland dispute in the 1970s, Iceland denied that the ICJ had competency over its fisheries dispute with the United Kingdom and Germany. Iceland declined to participate in the hearings respecting either the Court's jurisdiction or (once the Court decided it did have jurisdiction, based upon Iceland's pre-agreement to adjudicate) the merits of the action.[12] Accordingly, Iceland walked away from formal, adjudicative dispute settlement. In neither of these situations, however, was the jurisdiction of the ICJ as clear as might be the case in a dispute arising from a treaty that creates its own procedures for binding dispute settlement. However, the examples are cautionary. States do not like to be brought before international tribunals without agreement, and it is best for that agreement to occur after a dispute has arisen.

The only recent example of an adjudicative tribunal dealing directly with an international fisheries dispute occurred in the 1986 *La Bretagne Arbitration* between Canada and France.[13] The dispute arose over the interpretation of French fishing rights in Canadian waters set out in a 1972 Canada-France Agreement. Other third party dispute settlement processes dealing with ocean boundary disputes[14] and international trade disputes[15] have indirectly dealt with bilateral

[11] *Fisheries Jurisdiction (Spain v. Canada), Application Instituting Proceedings,* [1995] ICJ Rep 87.

[12] *Fisheries Jurisdiction Cases, Jurisdiction,* [1972] ICJ Rep. 3 and *Fisheries Jurisdiction Cases, Merits,* [1973] ICJ Rep. 3. See generally Hannes Jonsson, *Friends in Conflict: The Anglo-Icelandic Cod Wars and the Law of the Sea* (London: C. Hurst, 1982) and Jeffrey A. Hart, *The Anglo-Icelandic Cod War of 1972-1973* (Berkeley: Institute of Int'l Studies, Research Series No. 20, 1976).

[13] *Filleting within the Gulf of St. Lawrence between Canada and France* (1986), 19 U.N. Reports of Int'l Arbitral Awards 225. See generally concerning the Arbitration: William T. Burke, "A Comment on the 'La Bretagne' Award of July 17, 1986: The Arbitration between Canada and France" (1988), 25 San Diego L. Rev. 495 and T. L. McDorman, "French Fishing Rights in Canadian Waters: The 1986 La Bretagne Arbitration" (1989), 4 Int'l J. of Estuarine and Coastal L. 52.

[14] E.g., *Case concerning the Delimitation of the Maritime Areas between Canada and France,* June 10, 1992, reprinted in (1992), 31 Int'l Legal Materials 1148. For an excellent analysis of this decision, see G. P. Politakis, "The French-Canadian Arbitrarion around St. Pierre and Miquelon: Unmasked Opportunism and the Triumph of the Unexpected" (1993), 8 Int'l J. of Marine and Coastal Law 105.

[15] E.g., *Lobsters From Canada, Final Report of the Canada-U.S. Free Trade Agreement Panel,* May 25, 1990. At issue in this trade decision was a U.S. embargo on certain lobsters from Canada. The Panel held that the embargo was not inconsistent with the Canada-U.S. Free Trade Agreement.

fishing problems. The record of states using dispute settlement procedures to resolve international fisheries disputes is not encouraging.

While it cannot be expected that the dispute settlement regime in the 1995 Agreement will lead to a stampede in the use of binding dispute resolution, the existence of the regime in the Treaty is important. First, for disputing states that are parties to the Agreement, the regime creates an option that can be used and, through its use, may establish a framework for resolving and managing disputes. Second, the binding dispute settlement regime may be employed to hasten a negotiated solution or alter the negotiating dynamic of disputing states. This article focuses on the details of the dispute settlement regime that will be established when the 1995 Agreement enters into force.

The Link to the 1982 LOS Convention

Part VIII of the 1995 Agreement, "Peaceful Settlement of Disputes," inextricably links the dispute settlement regime of the 1995 Agreement with that of the 1982 LOS Convention.[16] The much-admired dispute settlement regime of the 1982 LOS Convention[17]

16 This direct link between the 1995 Agreement and the LOS Convention was the product of intense negotiations. See Tahindro, *supra* note 3 at 45-46.

17 A detailed history of the dispute settlement regime of the LOS Convention is provided by A. O. Adede, *The System for Settlement of Disputes Under the United Nations Convention on the Law of the Sea* (Dordrecht: Martinus Nijhoff, 1987) and Shabtai Rosenne and Louis B. Sohn, eds., *United Nations Convention on the Law of the Sea, 1982: A Commentary*, Vol. V, 3-146 (Dordrecht: Martinus Nijhoff, 1989). A convenient overview can be found in J. G. Merrills, *International Dispute Settlement*, 166-72 (2nd ed., Cambridge: Grotius, 1991). An excellent analysis of the workability of the LOS Convention dispute settlement regime is provided by John King Gamble, Jr. "The 1982 UN Convention on the Law of the Sea: Binding Dispute Settlement?" (1991), 9 Boston Univ. Int'l L.J. 39. A recent detailed study of the LOS Convention dispute settlement regime is provided by E. D. Brown, "Dispute Settlement and the Law of the Sea: the UN Convention Regime" (1997), 21 Marine Policy 17.

The LOS Convention dispute settlement regime has its detractors. See Shigeru Oda, "The International Court of Justice from the Bench" (1993), 244 Recueil des Cours 9 at 139-55. See also the response to Judge Oda in Jonathan I. Charney, "The Implications of Expanding International Dispute Settlement Systems: The 1982 Convention on the Law of the Sea" (1996), 90 Amer. J. of Int'l L. 69. This debate, as well as an insightful analysis of the LOS Convention dispute settlement regime, is canvassed in Alan E. Boyle, "Dispute Settlement and the Law of the Sea Convention: Problems of Fragmentation and Jurisdiction" (1997), 46 Int'l and Comparative L. Q. 37.

has only recently become fully operational as the Treaty entered into legal force in November 1994.[18]

The dispute settlement regime of the LOS Convention sets out an array of situations in which adjudication is compulsory but the choice of adjudicative body is flexible and of situations in which conciliation or a non-adjudicative process is required but the results are not binding. Article 280 of the LOS Convention provides an override to all processes and procedures by allowing states to use "any peaceful means of their choice" to resolve a dispute.

The presumption in the LOS Convention wording favours compulsory dispute resolution unless the issue in dispute is exempt under Article 297. Also, pursuant to Article 298, which lists such potential dispute subjects as conflicting maritime boundary claims, a state by declaration can elect to exempt a listed subject from the reach of compulsory settlement. Since no exemptions apply to disputes respecting the application of the provisions of the LOS Convention respecting high seas fishing, the clear presumption in the 1982 Treaty is that high seas fishing disputes between states party to the Treaty that engage the obligations of the LOS Convention would be subject to compulsory third-party dispute resolution.[19] The high seas fishing obligations in the 1982 LOS Convention favour fishers and harvesting rather than resource conservation and support the sanctity of flag state control over fishing vessels rather than interference with foreign fishers.[20]

The application of the LOS Convention dispute settlement regime to fisheries issue is discussed in M. Dahmani, *The Fisheries Regime of the Exclusive Economic Zone*, 117-23(Dordrecht: Martinus Nijhoff, 1987).

18 Canada has not yet become a party to the LOS Convention. See generally Aldo Chircop, "Canada and the Law of the Sea: Perspectives and Issues for Canadian Accession," in Kriwoken et al., *supra* note 5 at 75-96; Rob Huebert, "Canada and the Law of the Sea Convention" (1996-97), 52 Int'l J. 69-88 and T. L. McDorman, "Will Canada Ratify the Law of the Sea Convention?" (1988), 25 San Diego L. Rev. 535-579.

19 William T. Burke, *The New International Law of Fisheries*, 124 (Oxford: Clarendon Press, 1994); Dahmani, *supra* note 17 at 121 and Boyle, *supra* note 17 at 43.

20 See generally Burke, *ibid.*, 82-150; E. D. Brown, *The International Law of the Sea*, 286-314 and 317-25 (Aldershot: Dartmouth Publishing, 1994) and United Nations, *The Law of the Sea: The Regime for High-Seas Fisheries* (New York, United Nations, 1992).

The Dispute Settlement Regime of the 1995 Agreement

GENERAL OBLIGATIONS

State parties to the 1995 Agreement, pursuant to Article 27, have an obligation to resolve their disputes peacefully. A listing is given in the article outlining the traditional resolutive means available to states — that is, negotiation, inquiry, mediation, conciliation, arbitration, judicial settlement, and the use of regional agencies or arrangements.

Article 28 provides that states are to co-operate to avoid disputes. The Agreement suggests that one way of accomplishing this aim is to improve the decision-making procedures of the relevant regional fisheries management organizations.[21] For many straddling and highly migratory stocks, there exists an international fisheries organization with a management or scientific mandate.[22] The prime example for Canada is NAFO, which has management responsibility for straddling stocks on the high seas outside Canada's Atlantic Ocean 200-n. mile zone.[23] Much of the 1995 Agreement is directed to improving the state cooperation with, and the operation of, the appropriate regional fisheries management organizations.[24]

TYPES OF DISPUTES SUBJECT TO THE DISPUTE SETTLEMENT REGIME

Beyond the general obligations on dispute resolution are the specific provisions of the 1995 Agreement that create the mandate for the Treaty's dispute resolution processes.

21 See Tahindro, *supra* note 3 at 48.

22 The work of many of the international fisheries organizations that manage highly migratory and straddling stocks is discussed in Meltzer, *supra* note 5 at 268-322. See also Alberto Szekely and Barbara Kwiatkowska, "Marine Living Resources," in P. H. Sand, ed. *The Effectiveness of International Environmental Agreements: A Survey of Existing Legal Instruments*, 256-301 (Cambridge: Grotius Publications, 1992) and Ellen Hey, *The Regime for the Exploitation of Transboundary Marine Fisheries Resources*, 131-274 (Dordrecht: Martinus Nijhoff, 1989).

23 See L. S. Parsons, *Management of Marine Fisheries in Canada*, 263-83 (Ottawa: National Research Council of Canada, 1993). Respecting the role and operation of NAFO in the context of the 1995 Canada-EU dispute, see Douglas Day, "Tending the Achilles Heel of NAFO: Canada Acts to Protect the Nose and Tail of the Grand Banks" (1995), 19 Marine Policy 257.

24 See Arts. 8-13 and 17 of the 1995 Agreement and Tahindro, *supra* note 3 at 20-32.

Interpretation and Application of the 1995 Agreement

Article 30(1) provides that disputes concerning "the interpretation or application" of the 1995 Agreement are to be resolved using the dispute settlement regime (Part XV) of the 1982 LOS Convention. Unless disputant states agree to alternative procedures under Article 280 of the LOS Convention, disputes respecting the interpretation or application of the 1995 Agreement would be subject to the compulsory dispute settlement procedures of the 1982 LOS Convention. The disputing states need only be party to the 1995 Agreement and not to the 1982 LOS Convention, because the LOS Treaty procedures are directly incorporated into the 1995 Agreement dispute settlement regime.

Non-Application within 200-n. Mile Zones

Article 32 establishes a limit on the reach of the dispute settlement regime of the 1995 Agreement. The provision directs that Article 297(3) of the 1982 LOS Convention is applicable. Article 297(3) specifically exempts from the scope of compulsory adjudication any disputes arising from the exercise by a state of its sovereignty over living resources within its 200-n. mile zone.[25] This limitation exists even though the 1995 Agreement emphasizes the scientific and managerial need to treat straddling fish stocks and highly migratory fish stocks as indivisible units. A key component of the 1995 Agreement is that there should and must exist compatible management measures for marine living resources inside and outside the 200-n. mile zone.[26] One author has described the situation in the following manner:

25 Under Art. 297(3)(a) of the 1982 LOS Convention:

> Disputes concerning the interpretation or application of the provisions of this Convention with regard to fisheries shall be settled in accordance with section 2 [Compulsory Procedures Entailing Binding Decisions]; except that the coastal State shall not be obliged to accept the submission to such settlement of any dispute relating to its sovereign rights with respect to the living resources in the exclusive economic zone or their exercise, including its discretionary powers for determining the allowable catch, its harvesting capacity, the allocation of surpluses to other States and the terms and conditions established in its conservation and management laws and regulations.

See generally Dahmani, *supra* note 17 at 121-23.

26 See Art. 7 of the 1995 Agreement; Balton, *supra* note 2 at 136-37 and Tahindro, *supra* note 3 at 14-18.

> [T]he Agreement recognized in its strategy for conservation and management . . . the importance, inter alia, of the biological unity of the stocks and provided that compatible conservation and management measures be adopted for the stocks within and beyond areas under national jurisdiction. It may be inferred therefore that the recognition of the realities of biological unity . . . *should have led* to a uniting of the procedures for the settlement of disputes for the whole geographical distribution of these stocks. However, pursuant to Article 297(3)(a), conservation and management disputes . . . within the EEZ will be excluded from the compulsory settlement provisions . . . while disputes beyond the EEZ will be subjected to compulsory settlement procedures entailing binding decisions [emphasis added].[27]

Article 297(3)(a) directs that fishery disputes involving the exercise of state sovereignty within the 200-n. mile zone are to be resolved through the use of conciliation. However, Article 297(3)(c) states that: "In no case shall the conciliation commission substitute its discretion for that of the coastal state." Hence, no decision unacceptable to a coastal state can be imposed.

Article 32 emphasizes the relationship of the 1995 Agreement to the 1982 LOS Convention and the continuing explicit desire by states not to subject national decisions respecting marine living resource use within 200-n. mile zones to compulsory third-party adjudication.

Compatible Measures for Straddling Stocks

As noted above, the compatibility of conservation and management measures for marine living resources within and without the 200-n. mile zone is an important principle in the 1995 Agreement. While the dispute settlement regime of the 1995 Agreement has no application to activities within a national 200-n. mile zone, Article 7(4) states explicitly that the dispute settlement regime is available where, within a reasonable time, the relevant states cannot agree on compatible management measures for marine living resources beyond the 200-n. mile limit. This is the only explicit mention of the availability of dispute settlement outside Part VIII itself.[28] It gives a coastal state an important lever to achieve agreement with high seas fishing states on the adoption of conservation and management measures outside the 200-n. mile zone that are

27 Tahindro, *supra* note 3 at 49.

28 Art. 16(2) of the 1995 Agreement directs that Art. 7(4) applies where agreement is not reached on compatible conservation measures respecting a high seas area surrounded by a single state.

compatible with measures adopted for straddling stocks within the 200-n. mile zone.

Regional Fisheries Management Agreement Disputes

An innovative twist in the dispute settlement regime of the 1995 Agreement is in Article 30(2). Pursuant to this provision, any disputes concerning the interpretation or application of a regional fisheries management agreement relating to straddling or highly migratory fish stocks, "including any dispute concerning the conservation and management of such stocks," are to be resolved using Part XV of the 1982 LOS Convention. Hence, disputes that arise under regional fisheries management agreements can be subject to compulsory third-party resolution, since no exemption exists in the LOS Convention to redirect this type of dispute to a non-compulsory procedure.

It has long been a criticism of regional fisheries management organizations such as NAFO that they provide no dispute settlement processes.[29] Article 30(2) of the 1995 Agreement, which imposes the compulsory settlement regime of one treaty (the 1982 LOS Convention) on disputes arising from a different treaty (regional fisheries management agreements), attempts to remedy that deficiency.

Article 30(2) is clearly designed to deal with quota, gear, and over-harvesting disputes that arise under regional fisheries management agreements. However, many regional fisheries agreements have objection procedures that allow states to become exempt from quotas and other measures adopted by the regional organization.[30] While the use of the objection procedure may be troubling to some

29 See generally Burke, *supra* note 19 at 95-99 and M. J. Peterson, "International Fisheries Management" in P. M. Haas et al., *Institutions for the Earth: Sources of Effective International Environmental Protection*, 249-305 (Cambridge: MIT Press, 1995).

30 The use (or abuse) of the objection procedure within the Northwest Atlantic Fisheries Organization by Spain and the European Union was a key irritant in the 1995 Canada-Spain dispute. See Bergin, *supra* note 5 at 194 and Day, *supra* note 23 at 261-63. Before the 1995 dispute, Parsons, *supra* note 23 at 277 commented: "The evidence was overwhelming that the EC's extensive use of the objection procedure was eroding the authority and effectiveness of NAFO."

In 1996, NAFO created a working group to examine the use of a dispute settlement process to address misuse of the objection procedure: Fisheries and Oceans Canada, Press Release (Sept. 16, 1996) "NAFO Recognizes Canadian Decision-Making for Northern Cod."

organization members, proper use of the procedure and the establishment by an objecting state of an independent quota would not appear to be a dispute under the regional agreement that would be covered by Article 30(2) of the 1995 Agreement and thus would not be subject to compulsory settlement. Of course, each circumstance would have to be examined on its own merits.

However, establishing an independent quota or avoiding the management measures of a regional fishery management organization through the use of the objection procedure would undoubtedly result in the replacement measure (or quota) being incompatible with the adjacent coastal state's conservation and management measures. The coastal state, citing this failure to agree on compatible measures, could invoke Article 7(4) of the 1995 Agreement and obtain dispute settlement respecting the objecting country's action.

Article 30(2), which incorporates the LOS Convention dispute settlement regime into regional fisheries organization disputes, applies where the disputing states are *both* parties to the 1995 Agreement *and* to the relevant regional fisheries management agreement, although they need not be parties to the LOS Convention. In the past, states have been able to avoid regional fisheries organization regulations and quota restrictions by not becoming members of the organization.[31] The 1995 Agreement attempts to eliminate this evasion by prohibiting states that are not participating in regional fisheries organizations from fishing stocks that are subject to regional management regimes.[32] What this means with respect to dispute settlement is as follows. While Article 30(2) does not apply to a non-member of a regional fisheries agreement allegedly harvesting fish inconsistent with the regulations of the regional agreement, Article 30(1) would apply, because the alleged harvesting by a non-member of a regional fisheries agreement would engage "the interpretation and application" of the 1995 Agreement. Organization avoidance will not exempt states from the rules of an organization or from the dispute settlement regime.[33]

[31] The fishing actions of non-NAFO members has long vexed Canada. See Parsons, *supra* note 23 at 281 and Day, *supra* note 23 at 261-63.

[32] Arts. 17(1) and (2) of the 1995 Agreement. See also Art. 8(3) and (4) of the 1995 Agreement; Balton, *supra* note 2 at 138-39; Hey, *supra* note 3 at 476; and Tahindro, *supra* note 3 at 25-27.

[33] Clearly this situation only arises for states that are a party to the 1995 Agreement.

A "Short-Cut" for Technical Disputes

Article 29 creates a "short-cut" dispute settlement procedure for disputes that states consider to be of a technical nature. Where such disputes arise, states may employ an *ad hoc* expert panel to assist in resolution rather than employing the binding procedures of the 1995 Agreement. This provision merely signifies an option that would have been open to states in any event.

THE COMPULSORY DISPUTE SETTLEMENT PROCEDURE

A key characteristic of the compulsory dispute settlement process in the 1982 LOS Convention is the procedural choice given to states. Article 287(1) provides that, for disputes that may arise under the LOS Treaty, states can pre-select from the International Tribunal for the Law of the Sea, the International Court of Justice, an arbitral tribunal, or a special arbitral tribunal.[34] States can indicate their choice of procedure at the time of signing, ratifying, or acceding to the 1982 LOS Convention or at any time thereafter. Where a dispute arises and the disputing states have pre-selected the same dispute settlement procedure, that body is to have jurisdiction over the dispute. Where a dispute arises that is subject to compulsory settlement, and a disputing state has not pre-selected a procedure or the disputing states have pre-selected different procedures, Article 287(3) and (5) of the LOS Convention indicates that an arbitral tribunal is to be used, unless the parties otherwise agree.

Few of the 106 states that have ratified the LOS Convention have pre-selected an adjudicative procedure. Of the sixteen states that had pre-selected as of August 31, 1996, eight had opted for the LOS Tribunal.[35]

[34] Annex VII of the LOS Convention sets out the procedure for establishing an arbitral tribunal and Annex VII concerns special arbitral tribunals. The functional distinction is that the mandate of an arbitral tribunal is exclusively adjudicative, while a special arbitral tribunal can be either adjudicative or restricted to fact-finding. See Annex VII and VIII of the LOS Convention.

[35] United Nations, *Law of the Sea Bulletin*, No. 32, 101-2 (New York: United Nations, 1996). For an analysis of the selections made by states, see Louis B. Sohn, "Settlement of Law of the Sea Disputes" (1995), 10 Int'l J. of Marine and Coastal Law 205 at 207-10 and Brown, *supra* note 17 at 30-34.

In mid-1996, the LOS Tribunal, to sit in Hamburg, was elected and now operates to hear disputes.[36] The LOS Tribunal has twenty-one members elected by the parties to the LOS Convention. These judges were to have "recognized competence in the field of the law of the sea,"[37] such that the Tribunal would project the image of an adjudicative body with specialized knowledge, sensitivity, and capacity to resolve ocean disputes.[38]

An important distinction between the arbitral tribunals and the permanent court bodies is the composition of a panel to resolve a dispute. With both the arbitral tribunal and special arbitral tribunal, the disputants have maximum flexibility in the selection of panel members.[39] In both the ICJ and the LOS Tribunal, the membership is pre-determined, although disputants before either body can request chambers to hear a case,[40] and disputants are entitled to have a national judge as a member of the Court or Tribunal that is hearing a dispute.[41]

The 1995 Agreement has adopted the same adjudicative selection opportunities as the 1982 LOS Convention. Article 30(3) of the 1995 Agreement provides that if a state has opted for a specific procedure under the LOS Convention, that procedure shall be its selection for disputes arising under the 1995 Agreement, unless the state accepts another procedure for these disputes. A non-party to the LOS Convention can, pursuant to Article 30(4), opt for one of the procedures listed in Article 287(1) of the LOS Convention. Article 30(4) also directs that Article 287 is to apply where a state party to the 1995 Agreement has not selected a procedure; thus,

36 "Int'l Tribunal Starts Work" (1997), 27 Environmental Policy and Law 2-4 and see Brown, *supra* note 17 at 34-37.

37 Art. 2(1), Annex VI of the LOS Convention.

38 How successful the LOS Tribunal will be is a central part of the debate about the LOS Convention dispute settlement regime. *See* Oda, *supra* note 17; Charney, *supra* note 17; and Boyle, *supra* note 17.

39 See Art. 3, Annex VII and Art. 3, Annex VIII of the LOS Convention.

40 See Art. 15, Annex VI of the LOS Convention respecting the LOS Tribunal and Brown, *supra* note 17 at 37-38. Regarding chambers of the ICJ, see Art. 26 of the Statute of the International Court and, more generally, Eduardo Valencia-Ospina, "The Use of Chambers of the International Court of Justice" in V. Lowe and M. Fitzmaurice, eds., *Fifty Years of the International Court of Justice*, 503-27 (Cambridge: Grotius Publications, Cambridge Univ. Press, 1996).

41 See Art. 17, Annex VI of the LOS Convention respecting the LOS Tribunal and, for the ICJ, Art. 31 of the Statute of the International Court.

resort to an arbitral tribunal is the appropriate procedure where a state fails to select a procedure. In the event of conflicting pre-selected procedures, it is apparent that the 1995 Agreement relies on Article 287(5) of the LOS Convention so that resort to an arbitral tribunal is again the appropriate procedure.

Article 288(4) of the LOS Convention, which presumably applies to disputes arising under the 1995 Agreement, states that "in the event of dispute as to whether a court or tribunal has jurisdiction, the matter shall be settled by decision of that court or tribunal." However, it is always a delicate issue for an international tribunal to determine its own jurisdiction where the disputing states are in disagreement. Article 36(6) of the statute of the ICJ provides that, where there is a dispute as to whether the Court has jurisdiction, the matter shall be decided by the Court.[42] The ICJ's recent handling of questions regarding its jurisdiction has raised concerns that it may be overreaching both its role and its capacity.[43] At stake in jurisdictional decisions is the legitimacy of an international tribunal as a neutral third party capable of resolving a dispute and, particularly in regard to the ICJ, an international tribunal's fidelity to international legal principles.

The dispute settlement process in the 1995 Agreement retains the flexibility of the 1982 LOS Convention. As a result of the recent entry into force of the LOS Convention, however, there is no indication of whether the procedure-options approach encourages the employment and acceptance of compulsory third-party dispute settlement or whether the numerous options and potentially incompatible pre-selections in themselves become a significant source of disagreement between already disputing states. The minimal use made of the pre-selection options by states ratifying the LOS Convention and the minimal use of the options in Article 298 to exempt certain types of disputes from compulsory adjudication can be interpreted as meaning that states are not very concerned about the potential operation of the dispute settlement regime of the Treaty. Such a view is consistent with the practice of states to avoid formal third-party dispute settlement. Of course, the non-use of the various LOS Convention options also is indicative of state

42 Concerning Art. 36(6), see Renata Szafarz, *The Compulsory Jurisdiction of the International Court of Justice*, 14-16 (Dordrecht: Martinus Nijhoff, 1993).

43 A summary of the recent controversy is provided in E. Lauterpacht, "Partial Judgments and the Inherent Jurisdiction of the International Court of Justice" in Lowe and Fitzmaurice, *supra* note 40 at 465-86.

contentment with the dispute settlement regime. It is strongly suggested that the first view more closely mirrors past state practice.

THE LAW TO BE APPLIED

Another novel aspect of the dispute settlement regime of the 1995 Agreement is found in Article 30(5), which directs courts and tribunals faced with resolving a dispute as to what law and considerations it must follow in reaching a decision. The equivalent provision in the 1982 LOS Convention, Article 293(1), merely states that a court or tribunal is to apply the LOS Convention and other non-incompatible rules of international law.

Article 30(5) indicates that the sources of law, rules, or norms that a court or tribunal are to consider are the applicable provisions of the 1982 LOS Convention, the 1995 Agreement, and relevant regional fisheries management agreements. In addition, a court or tribunal is to apply "generally accepted standards" for the conservation and management of marine living resources and other rules of international law not incompatible with the LOS Convention. It is unclear whether "generally accepted standards" implies customary law or whether, and more likely, it allows a court or tribunal to examine appropriate resource management practices that are not of a law-creative quality.[44]

The most interesting part of Article 30(5) is the final phrase, which directs that a court or tribunal is to apply the above noted sources, rules, and standards "with a view to ensuring the conservation of the straddling fish stocks and highly migratory fish stocks concerned." The thrust of Article 30(5) is to condition a court or tribunal to place marine living resource conservation above legal or quasi-legal considerations.

From an environmental or resource protectionist perspective, this outcome is as it should be. However, it is uncertain whether a court or tribunal, by its very nature a legal rather than a scientific or environmental body, would relegate law to a sub-factor in reaching a decision, particularly, if it is faced with well-settled international law. Moreover, allowing conservation/environmental considerations to trump well-established legal rules may encourage unilateral state action under the guise of conservation and thus encourage chaotic high seas practices. The Canada-Spain situation is relevant. The international law of the sea, while somewhat ambiguous,

44 Brown, *supra* note 17 at 29 commented: "What precisely is included among these additional standards and rules of international law is not clear."

favours the view that the Canadian seizure of a Spanish vessel on the high seas was inconsistent with international law. On the other hand, the Canadian action was morally justified as being necessary to protect endangered marine living resources. Moreover, Spain had a well-known track record for abusive fishing practices. However, Canada's moral position was clearly not shared by Spain or by the European Union, which strongly resisted Canada's actions. A court or tribunal that sided with Canada, absent a legal rationale,[45] would be setting the moral or ethical principles of one country on a higher level than those of another country. Such a triumph of moral superiority (and consequent moral inferiority) neither enhances constructive international relations nor resolves international disputes.[46]

The real hope of Article 30(5) must be, not that resource morality will trump law, but that legal rules will be interpreted and developed to take into account more fully the needs of marine living resource conservation.

PROVISIONAL MEASURES

Article 290 of the 1982 LOS Convention provides that, where a dispute has been submitted to a court or tribunal, at the request of one of the parties and following the parties' right to be heard, provisional measures "appropriate under the circumstances to preserve the respective rights of the parties" or "to prevent serious harm to the environment" may be prescribed. Article 31(2) of the 1995 Agreement tracks this wording, recognizing that a properly seized court or tribunal may prescribe provisional measures both to preserve the rights of disputants and also "to prevent damage to the stocks in question."

Article 31(2) refers to two additional circumstances when provisional measures may be prescribed. First, Article 7(2) of the 1995 Agreement obliges states harvesting straddling stocks both within

45 Concerning the international legal rationales employable by Canada, see Bergin, *supra* note 5 at 194-95. More generally, see Springer, *supra* note 5.

46 It may also not be a good way to deal with international environmental concerns. Increasingly international environmental "issues" are ones of conflicting moral values rather than scientific or legal disputes. Particularly respecting marine living resource "issues," the rhetoric of preservation is replacing conservation and different communities may not feel as strongly about preservation. The debates surrounding dolphins, turtles, whales, and driftnet fishing reflect this increasing divide. See Burke, *supra* note 19 at 145-6.

and without a national fishing zone to adopt "compatible" conservation and management measures. Article 7(5) directs that, pending agreement on such compatible measures, states are to attempt to establish "provisional arrangements of a practical nature." Where no such arrangements are made, an aggrieved state can submit the dispute to the appropriate court or tribunal "for the purpose of obtaining provisional measures." Second, in the circumstance of a high seas enclave surrounded by the national jurisdiction of a single state, where the coastal state and the fishing states cannot agree on appropriate conservation and management measures, an aggrieved state, using Article 7(5), can seek provisional measures from the appropriate court or tribunal.[47] The intent of the additional circumstances for the possibility of provisional measures is to pressure reluctant states to agree to interim arrangements for high seas fishing.

Article 290(5) of the 1982 LOS Convention attempts to deal with the situation where the request for provisional measures is made before it is ascertained or agreed which court or tribunal has jurisdiction over the dispute or where the adjudicative body has not yet been constituted. Article 290(5) directs that, where urgency is an issue, the LOS Tribunal may prescribe provisional measures irrespective of whether the LOS Tribunal has been selected or agreed upon by the disputing states. The 1995 Agreement modifies this "fail-safe" mechanism to avoid the situation of states that are not parties to the 1982 LOS Convention from being forced to accept the LOS Tribunal. Article 31(3) of the 1995 Agreement provides that non-parties to the LOS Convention can declare their non-acceptance of the role of the LOS Tribunal in prescribing provisional measures. Presumably, where such a declaration is made, no "fail-safe" body has jurisdiction respecting provisional measures.[48]

Article 290(6) of the LOS Convention, which is also part of the dispute settlement regime of the 1995 Agreement, states that "the parties to the dispute shall comply promptly with any provisional measures prescribed under this article." While innocent and apparently self-evident, the paragraph is a major step forward in the judicial settlement of disputes. While the ICJ has asserted jurisdiction to order interim measures, there has long been debate about

47 Art. 16(2) of the 1995 Agreement.

48 See Brown, *supra* note 17 at 30.

whether such orders were binding on disputants and, as a consequence, the record of compliance with ICJ interim measures orders has been poor.[49]

PROMPT RELEASE OF DETAINED VESSELS

Article 73(1) of the 1982 LOS Convention explicitly permits a coastal state to arrest foreign fishers that have, while in the arresting state's waters, allegedly violated its fisheries laws. The physical execution of a fishing vessel seizure under Article 73(1) may take place either within the waters of the coastal state or, if the conditions of hot pursuit are met,[50] on the high seas. Article 73(2) provides that arrested vessels and crews, upon posting of reasonable bond or security, are to be promptly released. No such prompt release provision exists regarding fishing vessels seized on the high seas, other than one seized as a result of hot pursuit, since it is inconsistent with the LOS Convention for such an arrest to take place.[51] But, as one authority has written: "It would seem absurd . . . that the prompt release procedure should be available in cases in which detention is permitted by the Convention . . . and not available in cases in which it is not permitted by it."[52] Thus, for fishing vessels arrested on the high seas, where the states involved

49 See Jerome B. Elkind, *Interim Protection*, 153-66 (The Hague: Martinus Nijhoff, 1981); Jerzy Sztucki, *Interim Measures in the Hague Court*, 260-302 (Deventer: Kluwer, 1983); and H. W. A. Thirlway, "The Indication of Provisional Measures by the International Court of Justice" in R. Bernhardt, eds., *Interim Measures Indicated by International Courts*, 28-33 (Berlin: Springer-Verlag, 1994).

50 Art. 111 of the 1982 LOS Convention codifies the criteria that must be met for hot pursuit. See Brown, *supra* note 20 at 295-99 and Robert C. Reuland, "The Customary Right of Hot Pursuit onto the High Seas: Annotations to Art. 111 of the Law of the Sea Convention" (1993), 33 Virginia J. of Int'l L. 557. Brown discusses the 1986 Canadian hot pursuit case of *Regina* v. *Sunila and Solayman* (1986), 28 D.L.R. (4th) 450 (N.S.S.C. A.D.).

51 High seas arrests for activities that take place on the high seas are sanctioned by the LOS Convention only for piracy, Art. 105, and unauthorized broadcasting, Art. 109(3). However, the right to visit a vessel on the high seas, Art. 110, may also lead to seizures respecting vessels engaged in the slave trade and vessels without nationality. See generally Brown, *supra* note 20 at 299-314 and Moritaka Hayashi, "Enforcement by Non-Flag States on the High Seas under the 1995 Agreement on Straddling and Highly Migratory Fish Stocks" (1996), 9 Georgetown Int'l Environmental L. Rev. 1 at 4-10.

52 Tullio Treves, "The Proceedings Concerning Prompt Release of Vessels and Crews before the International Tribunal for the Law of the Sea" (1996), 11 Int'l J. of Marine and Coastal Law 179 at 186.

are parties to the LOS Convention, the process for prompt release in the LOS Convention must apply. The process for dealing with prompt release of vessels is set out in Article 292, part of the dispute settlement section of the LOS Convention.[53]

The issue of non-flag state enforcement on the high seas was highly contentious during the negotiation of the 1995 Agreement.[54] The final result is that, without the consent of the flag state, a fishing vessel allegedly in breach of the 1995 Agreement or an appropriate regional fisheries arrangement cannot be arrested or seized on the high seas. However, Article 21 of the 1995 Agreement creates the possibility of a foreign fishing vessel on the high seas being boarded, inspected, and, where "clear grounds" exist of "a serious violation," the offending vessel may be brought into port for further investigation.[55] The keys to the exercise of these powers are: (1) that the boarding/inspection state must be a member of a regional fisheries management arrangement; (2) that there are clear grounds for believing that the offending vessel is violating the regional fisheries management regulations; and (3) that the flag state does not intervene.[56] It is important to reiterate that even under Article 21, without flag state consent, an inspected vessel cannot be prosecuted.

Disputes about the application of the enforcement provisions of the 1995 Agreement fall under either Article 30(1) or, where there are relevant regulations regarding these issues in a regional fisheries agreement, under Article 30(2). The exercise of the above noted inspection powers or the direct seizure of foreign fishing vessels, however, could lead to demands for prompt release of the vessels. Article 21(12) of the 1995 Agreement explicitly provides

53 Art. 292 is discussed in detail in Treves, *ibid.* at 179-200; David H. Anderson, "Investigation, Detention and Release of Foreign Vessels under the UN Convention on the Law of the Sea of 1982 and Other International Agreements" (1996), 11 Int'l J. of Marine and Coastal Law 165; and Rainer Lagoni, "The Prompt Release of Vessels and Crews before the International Tribunal for the Law of the Sea: A Preparatory Report" (1996), 11 Int'l J. of Marine and Coastal Law 147.

54 Hayashi, *supra* note 51 at 10-27 describes the negotiations about this issue in detail.

55 While "clear grounds" is not defined in the 1995 Agreement, "a serious violation" is defined in detail in Art. 21(11).

56 For a detailed description of the enforcement provisions of the 1995 Agreement, see Hayashi, *supra* note 51 at 10-27 and Tahindro, *supra* note 3 at 37-40.

for prompt release of a fishing vessel being detained by an inspecting state "at the request of the flag state."

There is some debate whether fishing vessels seized or detained in contravention of the 1995 Agreement would trigger Article 292 of the LOS Convention.[57] An explicit reference in the 1995 Agreement to Article 292 of the LOS Convention was deleted at the last moment because the negotiators decided that such a reference might be interpreted as sanctioning high seas vessel arrests.[58] Article 30(1) integrates all of the LOS Convention dispute settlement regime into disputes regarding the interpretation and application of the 1995 Agreement, and this would apparently include Article 292.[59] Article 292 is not a perfect fit, however, in part because it presumes that prompt release can occur where a reasonable bond is posted, yet Article 21(12) of the 1995 Agreement requires release upon flag state request without reference to the posting of a bond.[60] While there may be problems in directly applying Article 292 to vessel detentions under the 1995 Agreement, the better view is that the procedures under Article 292 are available to disputing states under the 1995 Agreement.

Pursuant to Article 292 of the LOS Convention, where a vessel has been detained and it is alleged that the detaining state has not complied with the prompt release requirement, "the question of release from detention" may be submitted to an agreed-upon court or tribunal. If no agreement is reached within ten days of the detention, the issue may be submitted by the flag state of the arrested vessel to the court or tribunal pre-selected by the detaining state pursuant to Article 287 or, if no pre-selection has been made, to the LOS Tribunal. In either situation, Article 292(3) indicates that the jurisdiction of the relevant body is restricted to questions respecting the release of the vessel. Another restriction is that, irrespective of the nationality of the master or crew, the application for prompt release can be made only by the flag state of the arrested vessel.[61]

One obvious process problem with incorporating Article 292 of the LOS Convention into the 1995 Agreement is the "fail-safe" role of the LOS Tribunal. The situation could arise where the LOS

57 See Treves, *supra* note 52 at 186-87 and Anderson, *supra* note 53 at 171-74.

58 Treves, *ibid.*, 187.

59 Art. 30(2) also integrates all the LOS Convention dispute settlement regime into disputes regarding regional fisheries management arrangements.

60 As noted by Anderson, *supra* note 53 at 172-73.

61 Art. 292(2) of the 1982 LOS Convention.

Tribunal could have jurisdiction, however temporary, respecting prompt release of an arrested fishing vessel and the relevant states not be a party to the LOS Convention and thus not technically bound by the activities of the LOS Tribunal.

CONCILIATION

While conciliation is not explicitly noted in the 1995 Agreement, it is given a prominent place in the dispute settlement regime of the LOS Convention as an alternative method to resolutive dispute settlement.[62] While disputing states can create their own conciliation process, Annex V of the LOS Convention establishes both a process and a mandate for a conciliation commission. Conciliation has the benefit of involving independent third parties in disputes while not removing from the disputants ultimate control over resolution. However, conciliation is non-binding and has not been frequently used by states.[63]

The LOS Convention provides that, in disputes respecting the exercise of jurisdiction over marine living resources within a national zone, an aggrieved party may request that the dispute be submitted to conciliation.[64] Hence, conciliation may play an important role in fishery disputes where what is in question is actions both within and without a national fishery zone.

CONCLUSION

The dispute settlement regime of the 1995 Agreement, which carefully integrates the regime of the 1982 LOS Convention, attempts to provide a resolutive path to states faced with a dispute under the Agreement. While the regime favours compulsory dispute resolution, which allows one state to force another before an independent third-party body with a binding result, states have been reluctant to use "forcing" procedures on unwilling states. Thus, while the path appears to encourage compulsory adjudication, one should not expect the resolutive path to be greatly used.

It must be emphasized that the dispute settlement regime of the 1995 Agreement is available only for states and between states that are party to the Agreement. Recalcitrant high seas fishing states and

62 Art. 284 of the 1982 LOS Convention.

63 There is a growing international literature respecting conciliation. For a useful overview, see Merrills, *supra* note 17 at 59-79.

64 Art. 297(3)(b) of the 1982 LOS Convention and *supra* notes 25-27.

adventurist coastal states can avoid the dispute settlement regime, although not the principles of the 1995 Agreement, by not ratifying the Agreement.

One should not judge a dispute settlement regime solely by the use made of it by disputing states. This is only one criterion. The existence of a viable dispute settlement regime may assist (or force) disputing states to negotiate arrangements to avoid the regime. This criterion is difficult to document but clearly an important one in evaluating an international dispute settlement regime. Until there is a practice of use or avoidance of either the 1982 LOS Convention or the 1995 Agreement dispute settlement procedures and processes, one cannot truly evaluate them except to conclude that every effort was made by the negotiators to accommodate state choice of resolutive procedures while retaining the integrity of the regime to provide a binding, acceptable resolution of a dispute.

Sommaire

Le régime de règlement des différends de la Convention sur les stocks de poissons chevauchants et grands migrateurs

L'entente de 1995 sur l'Application des dispositions de la Convention sur les stocks de poissons chevauchants et grands migrateurs complète un aspect du travail innovateur de la Convention des Nations Unies sur le droit de la mer. Cet article présente un inventaire des dispositions de l'entente de 1995 et de leur lien avec la Convention de 1982. L'auteur évalue l'efficacité de certaines dispositions et conclut que l'Accord de 1995 offre aux états un régime stable pour le règlement des différends dans le domaine des pêches et des affaires maritimes. Il reste à voir si les États profiteront du régime.

Summary

The Dispute Settlement Regime of the Straddling and Highly Migratory Fish Stocks Convention

The 1995 Agreement on the Regime for Straddling and Highly Migratory Fish Stocks completes one aspect of the work of the 1982 Convention on the Law of the Sea. This article presents a summary of the provisions of the 1995 Agreement and their relationship to the 1982 Convention. The author offers insights into the possible effectiveness of several articles and concludes that the 1995 Agreement offers states the possibility of a stable and predictable dispute resolution mechanism. Whether states will take advantage of this regime is another question.

The NAFTA Panel Decision on Supply Management: Gamble or Bargain?

ALLAN WILLIS AND MICHAEL G. WOODS

The United States has argued that Canada "gambled" that it could convince participants in the Uruguay Round to preserve the right to maintain agricultural quotas. But, if FTA Article 710 had frozen GATT rights and obligations as of 1989 or 1994, then there can have been no "gamble" by Canada, at least in relation to the United States . . .[1]

You never know how panels are going to come out . . . It's a crap shoot . . .[2]

Introduction

On July 14, 1995, the United States requested the establishment of the first Panel under the Chapter 20 procedures set out for the resolution of disputes between the parties of the North American Free Trade Agreement (NAFTA).[3] At issue were Canada's duties on dairy, poultry, egg, barley, and margarine products of industries that had grown and prospered under Canada's "supply

---

Allan Willis is formerly of the International Law and Activities Section in the Department of Justice, and Michael G. Woods is formerly Counsel of the Trade Law Section in the Department of Foreign Affairs and International Trade/ Department of Justice. Willis was one of the counsel appearing for Canada in this case. The authors wish to thank Rambod Behboodi, Counsel, Trade Law Division in the Department of Foreign Affairs and International Trade/Department of Justice for his comments and critique and Patricia L. Shaefer, Account Manager, Information Management and Technology in the Department of Foreign Affairs and International Trade for her assistance. The views expressed are solely those of

[1] *In The Matter of Tariffs Applied by Canada to Certain U.S.-Origin Agricultural Products,* NAFTA Secretariat File No. CDA-95-2008-01, December 2, 1996, para. 160 [hereinafter Panel Report].

[2] Peter Clark, quoted in "Canada Bracing To Fight for Tarrifs," *Globe and Mail,* July 9, 1995, A1.

[3] Panel Report, *supra* note 1. Full text and other information about NAFTA available at the Secretariat website <http//www.nafta-sec-alena.org>.

management" system — a system that was intended to establish stability in a domestic market afflicted by unpredictable production cycles.

Supply management depended upon import controls designed in conformity with international trade rules set out in the General Agreement of Tariffs and Trade (GATT).[4] The rules changed significantly in 1995 as a result of the World Trade Organization (WTO)[5] Agreement on Agriculture,[6] under which Canada and WTO members replaced quantitative import restrictions with tariffs and tariff-rate quotas. At the heart of the United States challenge was the question of the relationship between obligations set out in NAFTA and the subsequently negotiated WTO Agreement on Agriculture.

The United States claim was that the new tariffs contravened a basic NAFTA obligation not to raise tariffs. Canada countered that the new tariff rates were justified under the new WTO Agreement on Agriculture, which had been negotiated in Geneva after NAFTA. A key element in the dispute was the relationship between obligations set out in these two separate agreements. The decision in favour of Canada was released on December 2, 1996. It was both praised for its consideration of the case in the context of the complex interplay of relevant trade obligations and criticized for finding "an implied bargain . . .that was never struck."[7]

The United States submitted that Canada was entitled to apply *neither* the Article XI quotas previously permitted under the GATT nor the tariff equivalents that replaced them. The Canadian market was to be opened to unlimited quantities of U.S. dairy and poultry exports, even if the supply management system were destroyed as a result. According to the United States, the "price of admission" to the WTO was the abandonment of quotas, and the "price of admission" to the NAFTA was a prohibition on new or increased tariffs. If Canada wanted to adhere to both agreements it had to comply with both of these prohibitions.

4 General Agreement on Tariffs and Trade, done at Geneva, Oct. 30, 1947, in force Jan. 1, 1948, 55-61 UNTS 194, 4 *Basic Instruments and Selected Documents (BISD)* (Geneva, 1969) [hereinafter GATT 1947].

5 Agreement Establishing the World Trade Organization (1994) 33 ILM 1144 [hereinafter WTO Agreement].

6 [Hereinafter WTO Agreement on Agriculture].

7 Dale E. McNeil, "The NAFTA Panel Decision on Canadian Tariff Rate Quotas: Imagining a Tariffying Bargain" (1997) 22 Yale Journal of International Law 346.

Fundamental to the U.S. position was the contention that Canada had gambled and lost. It gambled — so the United States argued — by failing to negotiate tariffication in NAFTA with the hope that the WTO negotiations would not result in the elimination of quantitative restrictions (QRs) on agricultural products. But that was not the outcome. The WTO agreement did provide for the elimination of QRs and for their replacement with tariffs for which NAFTA had made no provision. Canada was therefore faced with both a prohibition on QRs in the WTO and a prohibition on tariffication in NAFTA, and it was thus compelled — according to the United States — to open its agricultural markets to the U.S. without limitation and without delay. The Canadian response was that NAFTA, properly construed, allowed for tariffication. Nothing had been gambled and nothing had been lost because the protection of the agricultural sector had been fully provided for in the provisions of the 1988 Free Trade Agreement (FTA),[8] which were carried forward into NAFTA. Canada was under no obligation to "pay twice" for concessions that had been agreed upon and maintained from the outset of the free trade relationship between the parties.

The Background

If Canada had indeed gambled, the stakes had been very high. In Canada, the matter was seen in terms of the survival of the country's $10 billion-a-year dairy and poultry industries.[9] The United States challenge was described as going "to the very heart of Canada's vast complex supply management system, which has provided stable incomes for about 35,000 farmers . . ."[10] One Canadian trade policy veteran observed that "in political terms, this is the most serious threat Canada has experienced since free trade with the United States began in 1989 . . ."[11] There were predictions that if Canada's supply-management industries lost the challenge as well as the protection from unlimited United States imports, "rural Canada could be devastated . . ." and there would be a loss of 138,000 jobs and $16 billion in government revenues by the year 2000.[12]

8 Canada-United States Free Trade Agreement, 2 January 1988; in force 1 January 1989 (1988) 27 ILM 281 [hereinafter FTA].

9 *Globe and Mail*, July 9, 1995, A1.

10 *Ibid.*

11 Mel Clark, quoted in Francis Russell, "Canada's Lame Defence," *Winnipeg Free Press*, February 5, 1995, A6.

12 Russell, *ibid.*, A6.

In the United States, the challenge was driven by long-standing concerns over Canada's "protected" supply-management industries. The U.S. administration was pressed by domestic interests to use NAFTA to open access to a market that "would have provided them with export sales of over $1 billion":[13]

> The U.S. dairy organizations are now prepared to see their own tariff protection eliminated for trade with Canada because they are convinced they would be the big winners in the new open border arrangement. That's why they pushed the Clinton administration to launch the challenge to Canada's tariffs last month under the terms of the North American Free Trade Agreement.[14]

SUPPLY MANAGEMENT SYSTEM

Supply management in Canada has evolved over the last fifty years. It began when farmers tried to organize themselves to establish some degree of stability in a domestic market afflicted by unpredictable production cycles.[15] As farmers joined together to cooperate, marketing boards were introduced to help set and monitor overall production targets and common floor prices. Provincial governments stepped in to give marketing boards legally binding, province-wide authority to establish pricing and supply restrictions. Since the authority of these boards was limited to provincial territory, surplus production from other provinces and imports from beyond national borders could undermine attempts to regulate the local market. For this reason, the federal government stepped in to ensure coordinated marketing plans. National marketing boards were created and import restrictions were introduced.[16]

Canada's supply management system is used to manage the national supply of dairy products, chicken, turkey, and eggs by matching total supply with domestic demand.[17] It is designed to ensure a stable income to producers and a stable supply of high

13 *Globe and Mail*, July 9, 1995, A1.

14 Drew Fagan, "U.S. Mega-Farms Do Mean Business," *Globe and Mail*, August 12, 1995.

15 *Ibid.*

16 Department of Foreign Affairs / Agriculture and Agri-Food Canada, "The Supply Management System," see website at <http//accis.agc.cc/cb/news/n60227.ec.html>; John Kenny, "Structure and Issues of the Dairy Industry," see website at <http.//www.ofns.ualberta.ca/dairt/dp472.1htm>; Michael Hart, *Damned If You Do and Damned If You Don't: The Trials and Tribulations of Canada-U.S. Agricultural Trade* (Ottawa: Centre for Trade Policy and Law, 1996), 7-12.

17 "The Supply Management System," *supra* note 16.

quality products at reasonable prices to processors and consumers. Supply-managed commodities represent major sectors of Canada's farm economy, accounting for about 25 per cent of total farm cash receipts.

SPECIAL STATUS FOR AGRICULTURE: GATT 1947

The import quotas associated with Canada's supply management regimes were justified under the original GATT of 1947.[18] While Article XI of the agreement sets out a basic rule against import prohibitions and restrictions, an exception for agricultural products is provided for by Article XI:2(c)(i) in the following terms:

> The provisions of paragraph 1 of this Article shall not extend to the following: . . .
>
> (c) Import restrictions on any agricultural or fisheries product, imported in any form necessary to the enforcement of governmental measures which operate:
>
> (i) to restrict the quantities of the like domestic product permitted to be marketed or produced, or, if there is no substantial domestic production of the like product, of a domestic product for which the imported product can be directly substituted . . .

Agricultural protectionism was not limited to the exceptions in Article XI. In 1955, the United States sought and obtained a GATT waiver for products covered under section 22 of its Agricultural Adjustment Act. The contracting parties found it politically expedient to push for the means to protect a sector that was considered both critically important, not just in terms of food security, and highly vulnerable to both the effects of nature and cheap imports. In any case, given the problems of transportation and the related difficulty of ensuring that products arrive at market in fresh and consumable condition, closed markets were not difficult to accept. As the GATT Panel review of a complaint about Canada's supply management system for dairy products noted in 1989: "there was virtually no international trade in raw milk."[19]

"TARIFFICATION"

The rules changed significantly in 1995 as a result of the WTO Agreement on Agriculture. Under the agreement, WTO members

18 GATT, *supra* note 4.

19 *Ice Cream and Yogurt*, 5 December 1989 L/6568, BISD 36S/68, p. 87. See also EPCT/A/PV/19, p. 42.

replaced quantitative import restrictions with tariffs and tariff-rate quotas. The WTO members agreed to convert their non-tariff quantitative import restrictions on agricultural products, such as licensing regimes or quotas, to tariff equivalents. The process is known as "tariffication." The tariff equivalents were initially set at levels intended to provide protection that would be equivalent in effect to the restrictions that were replaced. This approach, which was based on a 1989 U.S. proposal, was considered by many to be a significant step forward, providing improved transparency, a staged process of tariff reductions, and the prospect of further reduction in future negotiations.[20] It was seen as a significant step towards the longer term goal of normalizing agriculture within the WTO.

The tariffication process included a quota element. For each "tariffied" product, WTO members were required to provide access at lower tariff rates for imports up to specified levels, with imports in excess of the specified limits made subject to higher tariff equivalents. The quantity that is eligible for importation at the lower tariff rate is known as a tariff-rate quota (TRQ). Market access up to the specified limit is known as in-quota access and access over the limit as over-quota access. Under these terms, members are committed to reducing tariffs on agricultural goods by 36 per cent over six years, with a minimum reduction of 15 per cent for each tariff line. Canada introduced tariff equivalents to replace import restrictions on supply-managed dairy, poultry, and egg products. Canada also "tariffied" its import licences on barley and barley products and its import prohibition on margarine. The United States "tariffied" import restrictions on a number of products.[21]

Tariffication was essentially a compromise. Instead of simply abolishing the existing non-tariff barriers with no replacements — a political impossibility — these barriers would be converted into tariffs of equivalent effect, referred to as tariff equivalents. From the perspective of the protected industries, tariffication offered the comfort of continued protection from international competition. But it also offered, in the long term, the ultimate promise of trade liberalization.

20 Nathalie J. Chalifour and Donald Buckingham, "Counting Chickens Before They Hatch: New Hope or No Hope for Discipline to International Agricultural Trade" (1994) 22 Canadian Yearbook of International Law 122.

21 Department of Foreign Affairs and International Trade / Agriculture and Agri-Food Canada, "World Trade Orgânization Tariffication," see website at <http//aceis.agr.ca/cb/news/n60227ce.html>.

FTA AND NAFTA PROVISIONS ON AGRICULTURE

Chapter 7 of NAFTA addresses agricultural trade. During the negotiation of this chapter, the three parties decided that a special approach was required with respect to agriculture. Separate bilateral arrangements were reached between Canada and Mexico and the United States and Mexico, respectively. Canada and the United States agreed through Annex 702[22] to maintain, and incorporate into NAFTA, the key agricultural provisions of Chapter 7 of the 1988 FTA.

Thus, under NAFTA, the rules of the FTA regarding agricultural trade continued to apply between Canada and the United States. It was common ground that the incorporation of GATT rights and obligations under FTA Article 710 and NAFTA Annex 702.1 permitted Canada to maintain quantitative restrictions in support of its supply management system, pursuant to Article XI of GATT 1947. The United States, as noted in its "Statement of Administrative Action,"[23] was permitted to retain most of the restrictions covered by the 1955 GATT Section 22 Waiver. The United States case was that Canada had violated NAFTA Article 302, paragraphs (1) and (2), which prohibited new or increased tariffs. Canada's response was that NAFTA Annex 702.1(1) incorporates Article 710 of the FTA, which provides:

> Unless otherwise specifically provided in this Chapter, the Parties retain their rights and obligations with respect to agricultural, food, beverage and certain related goods under the General Agreement on Tariffs and Trade (GATT) and agreements negotiated under the GATT, including their rights and obligations under GATT Article XI.

Canada took the view that Article 710 authorizes the tariff equivalents on agricultural products that were adopted pursuant to the WTO agreement. In the end, the Panel adopted the Canadian position in a decision that was notable for its detailed analysis of the interrelationship of several international agreements and obligations, including the FTA. The decision was both praised for its

22 Jon Johnson, *The North American Free Trade Agreement: A Comprehensive Guide* (Aurora, ON: Canada Law Book, 1994), 181.

23 See United States-Canada Free Trade Agreement: Communication from the President of the United States Transmitting the Final Legal Text of the Canada-U.S. Free-Trade Agreement, the Proposed U.S.-Canada Free Trade Implementation Act of 1988, and a Statement of Administrative Action, H.R. Doc. No. 216, 100th Congress, 2d Sess. 196-97 (1988) [July 26, 1988] [hereinafter Statement of Administrative Action].

consideration of the complex interplay of relevant trade obligations and criticized for finding "an implied bargain among negotiators . . . that was never struck."[24]

The Positions of the Parties

the united states position

The reduction or elimination of tariffs below general most-favoured nation (MFN) levels is an essential feature of a free trade agreement and is incorporated in Chapter III of NAFTA ("National Treatment and Market Access in Goods") by paragraphs 1 and 2 of Article 302 ("Tariff Elimination"). These provisions, as noted earlier, prohibit any new customs duty or increased customs duty on trade between the parties and require the progressive elimination of duties in accordance with an agreed schedule. The United States position in this dispute was that the Canadian tariffication of the quotas or "quantitative restrictions" (QRs) applied under Article XI of the GATT to agricultural products subject to supply management in Canada — poultry and dairy products as well as margarine and barley — was plainly inconsistent with this undertaking.[25]

Tariffication by definition involves the creation of new or increased tariffs. The United States position — stated with stark simplicity in its initial submission — was that whatever might have been agreed to in the Uruguay Round and whatever measures Canada might be entitled to apply to its other trading partners, tariffication could not be applied within the NAFTA trading area. It was incompatible with NAFTA, which takes precedence over GATT 1994 by virtue of Article XXIV of the latter agreement.[26]

The United States recognized that Chapter III of NAFTA contemplates exceptions. Article 300 — the introductory provision on "Scope and Coverage" — states that the chapter applies "except as provided" in any other chapter of the agreement. Paragraphs 1 and 2 of Article 302 on the reduction and elimination of tariffs, on which the United States relied, were each introduced by the same phrase: "Except as otherwise provided in this Agreement." However, the NAFTA "Model Rules" governing Arbitral Panels provide in Article 34 that when exceptions are at issue, the burden

24 McNeil, *supra* note 7, 346.

25 Panel Report, *supra* note 1, paras. 55-80.

26 GATT 1994 consists of GATT 1947 and all protocols, decisions, and understandings in effect on the entry into force of the WTO.

of proof or justification is on the party invoking the exception. In the United States view, therefore, it was up to Canada to demonstrate the existence of an exception to the prohibition on new or increased tariffs.[27]

THE CANADIAN POSITION

In a nutshell, the Canadian position was that the WTO tariff equivalents for agricultural products established as a result of tariffication had been incorporated by reference into the NAFTA by the provisions of Chapter 7 of that agreement. The Canadian argument relied on an intricate network of provisions — some of them obscure in their wording — from three separate agreements: Chapter 7 of NAFTA ("Agriculture and Sanitary and Phytosanitary Measures") and the annexes to that chapter; the FTA, predecessor to NAFTA; and the WTO Agreement on Agriculture, which entered into force as part of the WTO Agreement one year after NAFTA in January 1995.

For the most part, Chapter 7 of NAFTA consists of three separate bilateral agreements: Canada-U.S., U.S.-Mexico, and Canada-Mexico. The bilateral agreement between Canada and the United States consists largely of a renewal of much of Chapter 7 of the 1988 FTA. Article 710 of the FTA,[28] incorporated without alteration into NAFTA, provides that rights under the GATT, and also under agreements negotiated under the GATT, are "retained" with respect to agricultural goods. Paragraph 4 of Annex 702.1 of NAFTA adds that the parties' intention was to incorporate the GATT rights and obligations of Canada and the United States with respect to agricultural and related goods, including exemptions

[27] *Ibid.*, paras. 49-50. Rule 34 reads as follows: "A Party asserting that a measure is subject to an exception under the Agreement shall have the burden of establishing that the exception exists." Despite the language of Chapter 3 with respect to exceptions, Canada did not accept the proposition that it bore the burden of justification as the party invoking an exception. Chapter 3 and 7 did not, in its view, stand in the relation of rule and exception. The introductory article of Chapter 7 — Article 701 — provided that Chapter 7 would be given overriding effect in the event of inconsistency — a relationship that was inconsistent with the treatment of the provisions on agriculture as mere "exceptions" to the general provisions on tariffs.

[28] In this article, a reference to Article 710 refers to Article 710 of the 1988 FTA as incorporated into NAFTA by Annex 702.1 of the latter agreement. See *supra* note 8.

under the Protocol of Provisional Application and waivers under Article XXV of the GATT.[29]

It was the Canadian position that the WTO Agreement on Agriculture was an "agreement under the GATT," within the meaning of Article 710, and that the rights and obligations of Canada and the United States under that agreement were therefore retained. This position led to a consideration of Article 4.2 of the WTO Agreement on Agriculture, which was the treaty provision under which the tariffication program was carried out — though it, too, was written in cryptic language that could not easily have been understood by the uninitiated: "Members shall not maintain, resort to, or revert to any measures of the kind which have been required to be converted into ordinary customs duties . . ." A footnote to this article explained that the measures that had been "required" to be converted into customs duties (that is, "tariffied") included quantitative import restrictions as well as a wide range of other non-tariff barriers.[30]

Some of the interpretative issues are readily apparent. Did Article 710 of the FTA apply to tariffs or only to non-tariff barriers? Did the word "retain" in that provision have a purely retrospective application barring its application to *future* agreements under the GATT, including those under the Uruguay Round? And finally, what

29 Paragraphs 1 and 4 of NAFTA, Annex 702.1, read as follows:

1. Articles 701, 702, 704, 705, 706, 707, 710 and 711 of the *Canada — United States Free Trade Agreement*, which Articles are hereby incorporated into and made a part of this Agreement, apply as between Canada and the United States.

4. The Parties understand that Article 710 of the *Canada — United States Free Trade Agreement* incorporates the GATT rights and obligations of Canada and the United States with respect to agricultural, food, beverage and certain related goods, including exemptions by virtue of paragraph (1)(b) of the Protocol of Provisional Application of the GATT and waivers granted under Article XXV of the GATT.

30 The footnote to Article 4.2 of the WTO Agreement on Agriculture reads as follows: "These measures include quantitative import restrictions, variable import levies, minimum import prices, discretionary import licensing, non-tariff measures maintained through state-trading enterprises, voluntary export restraints, and similar border measures other than ordinary customs duties, whether or not the measures are maintained under country-specific derogations from the provisions of GATT 1947, but not measures under balance-of-payments provisions or under other general, non-agriculture-specific provisions of GATT 1994 or of the other Multilateral Trade Agreements in Annex 1A to the WTO Agreement."

should the Arbitral Panel make of Article 4.2 of the WTO Agreement on Agriculture, which did not *state* an obligation to tariffy, but nevertheless appeared to assume that such a requirement had in fact been imposed?

In Canada's view, these difficulties could be resolved only by considering the substance of the bargain between the parties — "the deal" — in the light of the negotiating history of the FTA, NAFTA, and the Uruguay Round. The deal, Canada argued, was that in negotiations for the 1988 FTA, the parties had agreed to liberalize agriculture trade *within* the limits established under GATT Article XI, but to leave any liberalization *above* those limits to the multilateral negotiations. In other words, in-quota trade would benefit from reduced NAFTA tariff treatment. Over-quota trade, however, would be subject to whatever outcome emerged from the Uruguay Round — be it the status quo, a re-negotiated system of quantitative restrictions under Article XI, or — as it actually turned out — tariffication.

That was the bargain in 1988 when the FTA was concluded. When NAFTA entered into force in 1994 there was no new deal; on the contrary, the original understanding was specifically reconfirmed by the incorporation of the FTA provisions into NAFTA.

THE UNITED STATES REJOINDER

As the proceedings developed, the United States joined issue with each of these contentions. Article 710 of the FTA, it contended, was inapplicable on three separate counts.[31] First, the word "retain" is retrospective. It could not have the effect of bringing future rights into the FTA or into NAFTA. Article 710, as a result, was simply a grandfathering clause. Second, the United States urged that the distinction between tariffs and non-tariff barriers was fundamental to trade law and should control the interpretation of Article 710. This provision had never been intended to apply in relation to tariffs. It was an incorporation of rights pertaining to non-tariff barriers alone, in particular, to Canada's Article XI quotas and the Section 22 restrictions applied by the United States. Third, Article 710 referred to GATT rights and obligations, but tariffication was neither: it was simply a part of the Uruguay Round negotiating process.

On the first point, the United States submitted that Article 710 of the FTA was irrelevant because, in using the word "retain," it

[31] Panel Report, *supra* note 1, paras. 81-104.

referred back to existing agreements. It could not be interpreted as being applicable to *future* GATT obligations or rights, including those under the Uruguay Round.[32]

On the second point — whether Article 710 applies to the tariff measures under challenge — the United States position was that "a tariff is a tariff." In law, it contended, the "tariff equivalents" resulting from the tariffication process were indistinguishable from the general body of MFN tariff bindings in the WTO schedules. If one applied any of the MFN tariff bindings through FTA Article 710, then logically one had to apply all of them. And this act, quite obviously, would be an absurdity because the very purpose of a free trade agreement is the substitution of preferential treatment for that accorded to the world at large. The entire schedule of preferential tariffs, the United States argued, would fall apart under the Canadian approach.

On the third point — whether tariffication is a GATT right or obligation within the meaning of Article 710 — the United States took a radically different position on the nature of tariffication and on the effect of Article 4.2 of the WTO Agreement on Agriculture. It was no accident, the United States argued, that Article 4.2 failed to state an explicit obligation to tariffy. There was no such obligation as a matter of law. Tariffication was a "facility" — a negotiating process — and not a treaty requirement. The wording of Article 4.2 ("required" to be converted) pointed not to a legal obligation but merely to the agreed negotiating procedures of the Uruguay Round.

A key document in the negotiating history was the Agreement on Modalities for the Establishment of Specific Binding Commitments

32 The United States found support in the wording of para. 4 of NAFTA Annex 702.1, which referred to the retention of GATT rights and obligations, but which, in contrast to FTA Article 710, made no reference to "Agreements under the GATT," such as the WTO Agreement on Agriculture. Canada noted, however, that the paragraph had been included to clarify one particular aspect of Article 710 — its application to alcoholic beverages — but not to amend it or reduce its scope. The United States also disputed the proposition that the non-tariff barriers that Canada had tariffied were consistent with the GATT. The *Ice Cream and Yoghurt* decision of a 1989 GATT Panel (*supra* note 19) showed that some, at least, of the measures were not GATT-consistent. Canada replied that the tariffication provision of the WTO Agreement on Agriculture was intended to be comprehensive and to provide an "amnesty" with respect to tariffied non-tariff measures that might have been inconsistent with the GATT prior to their conversion into tariffs.

under the Reform Program,[33] which was referred to by the Panel as the Modalities Document. It was in this document, and only here, that one could find a clear description of the "tariffication" concept and of a requirement to tariffy. Annex 3, paragraph 3, of the Modalities Document provided that "[t]ariff equivalents *shall* be established for all agricultural products subject to border measures other than ordinary customs duties . . ." (emphasis added). There was, therefore, a clear "requirement" to tariffy — but, as both parties agreed, the Modalities Document was not a treaty instrument. It did not form part of the final WTO Agreement and, therefore, it did not set out obligations that would have binding legal force in their own right. It was a step in the negotiating process but not the final product. Thus, in the view of the United States, the Modalities Document could not be the source of a GATT right or obligation for the purposes of Article 710.

The United States summed up its theory of the case in two striking phrases: that Canada had made a "high-stakes gamble" and lost and that Canada had to pay the "price of admission" to both the WTO and NAFTA if it wanted to adhere to both agreements. The "gamble," according to the United States, was taken when Canada failed to negotiate a tariffication deal in NAFTA, in the hope that it would not be forced to tarrify as a result of the multilateral trade negotiations. Mexico, in contrast, had anticipated tariffication in the NAFTA negotiations and had therefore negotiated detailed annexes to NAFTA Chapter 7, providing for both tariffication on a bilateral basis and for the eventual application of GATT tariff equivalents.[34] This fact, according to the United States, showed that when the parties to NAFTA intended to allow tariffication, they negotiated the necessary language and incorporated it into the agreement. Canada had failed to negotiate similar language for its own supply-management system. This failure, according to the United States, was based on a mistaken expectation that Canada would ultimately succeed in its multilateral negotiating objective of maintaining an improved form of quantitative restrictions under GATT Article XI or, as an alternative, that it could reach a separate agreement with the United States if the Uruguay Round opted for tariffication. This expectation, in the United States view, was the "gamble" that Canada had made when it signed NAFTA without language expressly providing for tariffication. The gamble

[33] GATT Document, MTN. GNG/MA/W/24.

[34] See NAFTA Annex 703.2, sections A and B.

was lost when the WTO Agreement, as it emerged a year after the conclusion of NAFTA, abolished the Article XI quota system in favour of a comprehensive tariffication of non-tariff barriers and when no subsequent separate agreement with the United States was concluded in order to allow for tariffication.

The United States also submitted that the "price of admission" to the WTO was the abolition of non-tariff barriers and that the "price of admission" to NAFTA was the prohibition of new or increased tariffs. Canada would have to pay the price of admission to *both* agreements if it wanted the benefits of membership in both organizations. This would also mean that Canada was obliged to abandon quantitative restrictions and would be prohibited from substituting tariff equivalents. Border protections in either form, however necessary to supply management, would be ruled out.

THE CANADIAN RESPONSE

Canada based its response on the principles of interpretation applicable to treaties, in particular, those principles codified in the Vienna Convention on the Law of Treaties (Vienna Convention).[35] The United States interpretation, in Canada's view, did not reflect the language of the relevant treaties nor did it reflect the intention or the object and purpose, and it left Article 710 with no effect — a spent force — contrary to the principle of effectiveness or *effet utile* in the interpretation of treaties, which requires that some effect should be given to every provision of a treaty.

With respect to the language of the relevant treaty provisions, Canada pointed out that Article 710 was not, in its terms, limited to non-tariff barriers. There might indeed be an implied limitation because the United States was right in saying that a wholesale application of *all* MFN tariffs would be inconsistent with the nature of the agreement. However, an implied limitation should be no broader than that which is required to avoid an obvious anomaly. Just as it made no sense to place all tariffs under the umbrella of Article 710, it made no sense to exclude all tariffs from the application of this provision. There was a clear and relevant distinction, Canada argued, between the general body of MFN tariffs and the special-purpose tariff equivalents established pursuant to the tariffication process. The latter were direct replacements for the non-tariff barriers that originally were the principal, and undisputed,

[35] Vienna Convention on the Law of Treaties, May 23, 1969, Can.T.S. 1980 No.37, 1155 U.N.T.S. 331, (1989) 8 ILM 679 [hereinafter Vienna Convention].

target of Article 710. They were the "functional equivalents" of the old quantitative restrictions. As such, given the essential purpose of Article 710, it was inappropriate to exclude them from the scope of Article 710 by virtue only of an implied limitation.[36]

The United States approach, in short, was that either all tariffs or no tariffs were covered — "everything or nothing at all." However, when the underlying function and purpose of the different kinds of tariffs were considered, a valid distinction could be made with less damage to a purely textual reading of the provision than that required by the United States interpretation.

The United States also failed, in Canada's view, to respect the language of Article 4.2 of the WTO Agreement on Agriculture. If there was no genuine requirement to tariffy, then the language used was inexplicable: in fact, the United States admitted as much when it said that the provision — in particular, the words "required to be converted" — was "poorly drafted." The contention that only existing rights could be "retained" overlooked the nature of the GATT. The GATT is not a static instrument; it is an evolving system of law. This fact is evident in the sequence of negotiating rounds and the proliferation of subsidiary agreements and "codes" that now make up the WTO Agreement. Thus, what was retained under Article 710 could hardly be frozen in time. As a practical matter, moreover, it would have made no sense for the FTA and NAFTA negotiators to lock into place a system of rights and obligations that they knew would become obsolete as soon as the Uruguay Round reached its goal.

More fundamentally, Canada said, the United States approach failed to respect the intentions of either NAFTA or the WTO

36 As confirmation of its reading of the intentions of the parties, Canada saw further support for its position in two other NAFTA provisions, although neither was central to its argument. Article 309, under the heading "Non-Tariff Measures," provided that not only Article XI of the GATT, but any "equivalent provision of a successor agreement . . ." would be incorporated into and made part of NAFTA. The provision might be seen as an indication of a general intention to give effect to any replacement regime negotiated at the Uruguay Round to replace the Article XI quotas. On the other hand, as the United States pointed out, the "equivalent provision of a successor agreement" could simply be Article XI of GATT 1994, which was identical in every respect to Article XI of the GATT 1947. Canada also referred to Note 5 of the agreement, which states that Article 301(1) and (2) were not intended to prevent a party from increasing a customs duty as authorized by "any dispute settlement provision of the GATT or any agreement negotiated under the GATT." The United States replied that Note 5 was addressed solely to the issue of GATT-approved trade retaliation.

Agreement. As far as the FTA and NAFTA were concerned, the intention, which was manifest throughout the negotiations, was to adopt the multilateral Uruguay Round solution for over-quota trade. Whatever was agreed to multilaterally was to be adopted for the purposes of the FTA and NAFTA. By refusing to accept tariffication, which was the multilateral outcome, the United States interpretation failed to reflect the intentions of the FTA and NAFTA. It also failed to reflect these intentions by substituting *unlimited* preferential access for *limited* preferential access: a fundamental change in the "deal" to which the parties had originally agreed.

With regard to the WTO, the intention behind the "tariffication" compromise, in Canada's view, was never to impose an absolute, immediate, and total abolition of the protection provided by the non-tariff barriers that had to be converted. The intention was, in fact, to preserve a similar level of protection, albeit in a different form. This intention was inherent in the notion of tariffication as a *conversion* of non-tariff barriers to tariffs of equivalent effect, which was reflected in the relevant documentation and in the expression "tariff equivalents." The basis of the WTO compromise was thus the understanding that through the substitution of tariff equivalents there would be a gradual, and not an abrupt, liberalization — a "soft landing." The United States approach failed to give effect to these intentions.

In fact, by saying to Canada that the "price of admission" to NAFTA was no new tariffs and that the "price of admission" to the WTO was the dismantling of quantitative restrictions, the United States was saying that the protection "necessary to the enforcement" of Canada's supply-management system could no longer be maintained — even though abolishing the system had never been agreed to in either forum. In oral argument, Canada described it as a "Catch 22" result and submitted that the United States interpretation brought about the unreasonable outcome that, through the combined operation of two separate treaties, a result that was not intended by the authors of either treaty would be obtained.

Canada argued, finally, that the United States interpretation offended the principle of effectiveness or *effet utile* in the interpretation of treaties. The United States interpretation indisputably made Article 710 a spent force — a dead letter — yet the agreement to retain GATT rights with respect to supply management was an essential component of the FTA/NAFTA bargain on agriculture. If the United States view were to prevail, Canada submitted, a provision that was originally the keystone of the whole scheme would simply fall by the wayside — a result that could not be reconciled with the principle of effectiveness.

Canada also relied, in a subsidiary way, on other provisions of the Vienna Convention. It submitted that if the United States were right in its interpretation, there would be a conflict between NAFTA and the WTO Agreement. The WTO Agreement *required* tariffication, while NAFTA, in the United States's view, precluded it. Such a conflict, Canada argued, could properly be resolved by applying the "later-in-time" rule of Article 30, paragraph 3, of the Vienna Convention: which states that an earlier treaty applies only to the extent that it is compatible with a later treaty on the same subject matter and binding upon the same parties. Thus, the tariffication provisions of the later (1995) WTO Agreement would prevail over any inconsistent provisions of the earlier (1994) NAFTA.

Moreover, the United States position was self-defeating. Article XI of the GATT had never been abrogated. If Article XI quotas could not be tariffied because of NAFTA, then they remained intact: they could not, in the words of Article 4.2 of the WTO Agreement on Agriculture, have been "required to be converted" because the conversion would have been precluded by a free trade agreement with overriding effect. Thus, the U.S. position led, at best, to a paradox: although both parties had been committed to agricultural reform at the multilateral level, an obsolete system, abandoned by the rest of the world, would have been locked into place for the North American continent.

Finally, Canada relied upon various statements of administration officials, which were made when NAFTA was being brought into force, and on the subsequent practice of the parties. Both are recognized as valid aids to interpretation under Articles 31 and 32 of the Vienna Convention. Canada attached particular importance to the fact that the United States had itself tariffied its Section 22 restrictions and had applied the resulting tariff equivalents to Canada. But the United States dismissed this fact as a purely defensive move, taken to protect its position pending the settlement of the dispute.

The Decision

The Panel found in favour of Canada. The "tariffied" customs duties applied in connection with the Canadian supply-management programs were found to be consistent with NAFTA.

THE INTERPRETATIVE FRAMEWORK

The principles of interpretation in Articles 31 and 32 of the Vienna Convention were found to be applicable not only because NAFTA is a treaty but also because NAFTA itself provides in Article 102(2) that the agreement is to be interpreted and applied "in accordance with the applicable rules of international law." The Vienna Convention was applied not as a treaty binding on the parties, since it has not been ratified by the United States, but rather as a codification of principles of customary international law.[37]

The basic rule in Article 31 of the Vienna Convention provides that "[a] treaty shall be interpreted in good faith in accordance with the ordinary meaning to be given to the terms of the treaty in their context and in the light of its object and purpose." While succinct, the formula encapsulates a number of potentially competing principles. It reflects both the textual approach ("ordinary meaning") and the purposive or teleological approach ("object and purpose" and the related concept of "good faith"). The terms of the treaty are to be read, moreover "in their context," requiring that specific provisions should not be read in isolation but in the light of the entire treaty — a factor that played an important role in the Panel's decision. Article 31 also requires subsequent agreement, or subsequent practice establishing an agreement, to be taken into account, along with "relevant rules of international law." While the terms of Article 31, on the surface, leave no discretion to a tribunal, in reality they leave decisionmakers with a range of complementary or alternative approaches to interpretation.

Article 32 of the Vienna Convention allows — on a discretionary basis — recourse to "supplementary means of interpretation," including the negotiating history (*travaux préparatoires*), either to *confirm* an interpretation based on Article 31 or to *determine the meaning* when an interpretation based on Article 31 leaves the meaning "ambiguous or obscure" or leads to a result that is "manifestly absurd or unreasonable." The fairly liberal use of extrinsic evidence thus permitted is perhaps the main distinction between treaty interpretation and statute interpretation in the Canadian courts.

37 The application of the principles codified in the Vienna Convention, Panel Report, *supra* note 1, para. 119. The Vienna Convention reflects the practice of arbitral panels under the FTA and of panel and appellate body decisions of the WTO Dispute Settlement Body.

Taking account of the "object and purpose" of NAFTA, the Panel stated that it attached importance to the objective of trade liberalization and that exceptions to obligations of trade liberalization would be "viewed with caution."[38] The Panel did not, however, find it necessary to base its decision on the burden of justification as set out in Articles 33 and 34 of the Model Rules.[39] It found that the United States had established a *prima facie* case of inconsistency as required by Article 33 of the NAFTA Model Rules[40] and that the principal concern of the Panel was to determine whether Canada had shown either that its actions were not inconsistent with NAFTA Article 302 or that they fell within an exception to that provision. While the Panel did not expressly determine whether the provisions of Chapter 7, on which Canada relied, constituted an "exception," thus, formally shifting the burden to Canada under Rule 34, the practical effect of the approach was that Canada did bear the burden of justification.

The Panel organized its analysis around two of the main points of debate. First, it considered the "temporal application" of Article 710 — whether it applied prospectively to Uruguay Round agreements. Second, it considered the substantive meaning of Article 710. On the first point, it concluded that Article 710 did in fact apply to future agreements. On the second point, it concluded that the effect of Article 710 was to justify the Canadian tariff equivalents, largely because tariffication had to be seen as the *quid pro quo* of the obligation to abandon agricultural non-tariff barriers, and the parties could not have intended either to remain outside the new WTO regime or to adopt only isolated elements of an integrated "package deal." Finally, the Panel concluded that while Article 710 created an "inconsistency" with Chapter 3 of NAFTA, it had to be given overriding effect because of the introductory clauses to Chapter 7.

THE TEMPORAL ISSUE

The Panel first addressed the competing interpretations on the "temporal" aspect of Article 710: should it be given a dynamic interpretation, encompassing future GATT agreements, as Canada

38 Panel Report, *supra* note 1, para. 122.

39 Model Rules of Procedure for Chapter Twenty of the North American Free Trade Agreement, 13 July 1995.

40 Panel Report, *supra* note 1, para. 127.

argued; or should the "frozen-in-time" theory of the United States be endorsed?

The Panel recognized that the use of the word "retain" in Article 710 created an ambiguity.[41] The word is capable of bearing two meanings: it could refer only to existing rights, as the United States contended, or it could refer to "rights under a regime that evolves and extends into the future." The Panel resolved the ambiguity by reference to a range of considerations: the wording of other clauses in the agreement; the circumstances under which the provision was negotiated; the anomalous consequences of a static approach; and the nature of the GATT as an evolving body of law.

Article 710, of course, was originally part of the 1988 FTA. The Panel therefore found it appropriate to compare the wording to a fair number of other clauses in the FTA, in which references to provisions in other instruments were explicitly qualified by the word "existing." In FTA Article 104, for example, the parties reaffirmed their *existing* rights and obligations with respect to each other. The absence of any similar limiting adjective in Article 710 was clearly significant and carried an implication that future rights and obligations were not excluded.[42] The Panel noted that:

> The GATT is more than a static set of rights and obligations. Based on a set of principles embodied in the *General Agreement*, the GATT has been developed, clarified and supplemented by subsequent legal instruments through successive negotiating rounds into a complex of substantive and procedural rules.[43]

41 *Ibid.*, para. 135.

42 *Ibid.*, para. 137. As a countervailing consideration, the United States had pointed to a number of clauses in NAFTA, in which "successor agreements" are referred to, and submitted that the absence of such language in Article 710 and other relevant provisions was significant. However, the Panel answered this point by noting that Article 710 was open to a "forward-looking" interpretation. Furthermore, the effect of the U.S. interpretation was that some provisions relevant to agricultural trade would be prospective (such as Article 309, which refers to "successor agreements"), while others would be static. The Panel thought this was not likely to have been the intention. The United States had also noted that while Article 710 refers to "agreements under the GATT," the latter phrase was not to be found in paragraph 4 of Annex 702.1, where the parties set out their understanding of the intent of Article 710. The Panel agreed, however, with the Canadian position that this paragraph was intended to clarify Article 710 — notably by providing that waivers and Protocol of Provisional Application (PPA) exemptions were covered — but not to change the meaning or to narrow its scope.

43 Panel Report, *supra* note 1, para. 139.

The Panel thus accepted Canada's submission that the GATT, as referred to in Article 710, is an evolving system — a moving target.

The anomalous practical consequences of a "frozen-in-time" interpretation of Article 710 weighed heavily with the Panel. The Uruguay Round negotiations began just after negotiations on the FTA were launched. The multilateral negotiations were expressly referred to in the FTA. The parties knew, or at least expected, that new agreements were likely to result from the multilateral initiative. This fact by itself made it implausible that "agreements negotiated under the GATT" were intended to refer only to prior agreements.[44]

This pointed towards a more fundamental consideration. The whole premise of the United States case was that Canada was entitled to apply *neither* the Article XI quotas nor the tariff equivalents that replaced them. In other words, the Canadian market was henceforth to be opened to unlimited quantities of United States dairy and poultry exports, even if the supply-management system were destroyed as a result. The Panel did not see the alternatives in this way. It assumed that if tariff equivalents could not be applied — which in effect would render Article 4.2 of the WTO Agreement on Agriculture inoperative — the result would be that the parties would be entitled to apply Article XI restrictions as if the Uruguay Round had never happened.[45]

The logic of this reasoning is impeccable. Article XI of the GATT remains in legal force as does Article 710, which incorporated Article XI into NAFTA. If the Article XI restrictions could not be converted, then Article 4.2 of the WTO Agreement on Agriculture, which contemplated tariffication and a *consequential* undertaking not to revert to the old non-tariff barriers, could not be applied. And if Article 4.2 could not be applied, the Article XI regime would remain fully intact. The result of the United States interpretation, the Panel said, was not at all what the United States assumed: it was rather "to preserve the rights of both Parties to maintain agricultural quotas as between themselves." The "frozen-in-time" theory, in other words, would have preserved GATT Article XI in its pre-Uruguay Round version between Canada and the United States.[46]

Such a result could not be accepted. The Panel was not convinced that the parties had a common intention "to turn the clock

44 *Ibid.*, para. 139.

45 *Ibid.*, para. 158.

46 *Ibid.*, para. 159.

back to agricultural quotas."[47] The United States itself was the author of the tariffication proposal in the Uruguay Round. Tariffs were to be substituted for non-tariff barriers precisely because they were ultimately more trade liberalizing, more transparent, and "the least trade-distortive" type of import barrier. Since the object and purpose of NAFTA is trade liberalization, such a retrograde result was unacceptable.

Not only was it unacceptable: it was inconsistent with the evidence. The evidence was that the United States *wanted* Canada to tariffy at the time of the NAFTA negotiations. Further, the Panel noted:

> The difficulty with the frozen-in-time theory is that nothing in the record indicates any intention by either party to preserve agricultural quotas under the NAFTA regardless of the outcome of the Uruguay Round. To the contrary, various statements by United States officials in 1988 following the conclusion of the FTA contemplated that these issues would be dealt with in the *Uruguay Round*.[48]

Other aspects of the "frozen-in-time" theory were more briefly considered. In the GATT Article XXIV Working Party, Canada had made statements that the United States considered inconsistent with the notion that future GATT rights might be incorporated. The Panel was not persuaded. In its view, these statements were inconclusive or they had been made in different contexts. The Canadian argument, which was based on U.S. practice in tariffying certain measures, was also set aside largely because the conduct occurred after the dispute had crystallized. However, the conclusion on the temporal issue was clear. With Article 710, the parties had retained *future* GATT rights and obligations in "agreements negotiated under the GATT," of which the WTO Agreement on Agriculture was an instance.

TARIFF EQUIVALENTS AS A *QUID PRO QUO*

The substantive question was as difficult as the temporal question. Article 710 refers to rights and obligations. As explained earlier, the United States submitted that tariffication was neither a right nor an obligation. Instead, it was a step in the negotiating process, not a treaty obligation or a requirement. As such, it could not have been incorporated by Article 710.

47 *Ibid.*, para. 167.

48 *Ibid.*, para. 162.

The Panel agreed with the United States that Article 4.2 of the WTO Agreement on Agriculture did not, by itself, state an obligation to tariffy. It did, however, imply the existence of "an antecedent obligation to tariffy," through its use of the words "required to be converted into ordinary customs duties."[49] This antecedent obligation was clearly set out in Annex 3 of the Modalities Document. The Modalities Document, however, was not a part of the treaty. At one point of the Uruguay Round, it had been included as Part B of a draft Text on Agriculture and had formed part of the Dunkel Draft (named for the chairman of the Uruguay Round Trade Negotiating Committee).[50] But in the end, it was left out of the WTO treaty package. So the Panel had to decide what legal status it had, if any.

The Panel treated the Dunkel Draft and the Modalities Document as part of the *travaux préparatoires* of the WTO Agreement on Agriculture.[51] With respect to the patent ambiguity of Article 4.2 of this agreement, it was proper to take account of such *travaux préparatoires* (that is, negotiating history relevant as a "supplementary means of interpretation") under Article 32 of the Vienna Convention. What the negotiating history, including the Modalities Document, demonstrated was that the right to establish tariff equivalents — in other words, to tariffy — was the *quid pro quo* for the removal of the non-tariff barriers. The two were inseparable, "inextricably linked."[52] It was a package deal. Article 4.2 was "nothing more than an imprecise method of referring to a complex of rights and obligations by which non-tariff barriers were replaced with tariffs."[53] As such, whether or not there was an obligation to tariffy, there was a *right* to tariffy:

> States, nevertheless, had the *right* to establish "tariff equivalents" in place of these non-tariff barriers. In other words, they were entitled to equivalent protection through the establishment of over-quota tariffs. To bring into the NAFTA only the obligation to eliminate non-tariff barriers without the *quid pro quo* for their elimination would ignore the agreement that made the elimination of non-tariff barriers acceptable.[54]

49 *Ibid.*, para. 171.

50 *Ibid.*, paras. 176-79. Draft Final Act Embodying the Results of the Uruguay Round of Multilateral Trade Negotiations [hereinafter Dunkel Draft] was circulated on 20 December 1991 as GATT Doc. MTN. TNC/W/FA.

51 *Ibid.*, para. 179.

52 *Ibid.*, para. 181.

53 *Ibid.*

54 *Ibid.*, para. 183. See also *ibid.*, para. 198.

The next question was whether this right was incorporated by Article 710, given the United States position that Article 710 applies only to non-tariff barriers. The Panel agreed that Article 710 could not have been intended to provide for the "wholesale incorporation" of all GATT rights and obligations or for "the simple substitution of the WTO tariff schedule for the NAFTA tariff schedule."[55] However, this fact was not the issue: the only issue was whether the tariff equivalents resulting from tariffication could be applied under this provision. The Panel noted that nothing in the language of Article 710 suggested that the provision could never apply to tariff measures and that other provisions of Chapter 7 touched on tariff matters, as evidenced by Article 702, which allowed for the "snapback" of MFN duties on fruits and vegetables.

What was critical for the Panel was the substance of the original bargain of the parties, not the instruments used to give effect to that bargain. It was therefore immaterial whether tariffs or quotas were used. The object and purpose of Article 710 "was to preserve for both Parties the agricultural protection permitted by the GATT . . ."[56] Whether tariffs or quotas were used as the instrument to achieve that end was not important: "The fact that they [the quotas] were turned into tariffs is, in a sense, incidental."[57] The essential point was that the tariff equivalents were "all part of a 'package' on agricultural trade"[58] — a package that Article 710 was designed to incorporate in its integrity, without divorcing the obligation from the *quid pro quo.* In these circumstances, therefore, there was no reason why Article 710 could not be interpreted as applying to the tariff equivalents substituted for agricultural non-tariff barriers pursuant to the WTO Agreement on Agriculture.

THE RESULT

The final question was the relationship between Article 302, which prohibited new or increased tariffs, and Article 710, which incorporated a right to tariffy. The Panel noted that Chapter 3 and Article 302, in particular, expressly provided for exceptions. Moreover, Article 701(2) of Chapter 7 provided that in the event of an inconsistency between Section A (Agriculture) of that chapter and

55 *Ibid.*, para. 196.

56 *Ibid.*, para. 197.

57 *Ibid.*, para. 198.

58 *Ibid.*

another provision of the agreement, the provisions of Section A would prevail. In the event, the Panel decided that there was an inconsistency, and that Article 710 should prevail.[59] It is not clear why the Panel treated the case as one of inconsistency and not as an exception recognized by the terms of Article 302 itself. The characterization did, perhaps, eliminate any question of a burden of justification under Model Rule 34, but it is clear from the terms of the decision, itself, that if a burden of justification had been applied, it would have been discharged. But, while there is a conceptual difference between the two approaches, the practical result is the same.

Conclusion

FURTHER LIBERALIZATION OR FUTURE LITIGATION — OR BOTH?

There have been Canada-United States disputes over agricultural trade since the nineteenth century, when United States legislators were already complaining about Canadian grain preferences in the United Kingdom market. Canada has often been the complainant as well and has consistently sought rules to reduce the capacity of the United States to use its size, power, and proximity to overwhelm Canadian interests. A seasoned observer of Canada-United States trade relations has described the relationship with some irony:

> [T]his case is but the latest example of a continuing theme in the history of Canada-United States trade in agriculture: US officials prefer that Canadians do as they say, not as they do. To their regret, Canadian governments have never learned this lesson. Rather, they learned to emulate what the US Congress did rather than what US officials counselled.[60]

The FTA, NAFTA, and now the WTO Agreement make clear the obligation on states to facilitate freer trade in agriculture goods. The tariffication of Canada's supply-management system, the European Union's variable import levies under the Common Agricultural Policy, and GATT waivers permitting the United States use of its Agricultural Adjustment Act, all create tariffs that are amenable to reduction in future multilateral trade negotiations. The concept and conclusion of the WTO Agreement on Agriculture was therefore a major accomplishment. The legal framework created by the agreement, however, set up new disciplines that may have been

59 Annex 702.1, incorporating Article 710, forms part of Section A of Chapter 7.

60 Hart, *supra* note 16.

insufficiently defined, particularly in their relationship to plurilateral and bilateral agreements such as NAFTA. The resulting ambiguities were at the heart of the case under review. In an earlier era, such ambiguities might have led to a continuing impasse. The existence of effective third-party settlement provisions in both NAFTA and the WTO Agreement ensure that ambiguities will no longer frustrate the operation of the agreements. These provisions also ensure that outcomes will depend, increasingly, upon principles of law rather than upon pure economic or political power; that the underlying intention will be sought out through all possible means; and that when ascertained, this intention will govern the resolution of the dispute.

A BARGAIN OR A GAMBLE?

The interplay of "tariffication" and the application of Article 302 was anticipated even before NAFTA came into force.[61] Some observers focused on matters that Canadian and U.S. trade negotiators had left open. In an article in the 1994 *Canadian Yearbook of International Law*, the authors point out:

> Since the NAFTA and GATT negotiators from Canada, the United States, and Mexico were well aware that any GATT agreement would benefit from the interpretative rule found in Article 30 of the Vienna Convention, it is odd that this issue of precedence was not clarified either through provisions in the GATT itself, or in a side agreement between the NAFTA parties.[62]

The ambiguity was widely perceived. It was the position of the United States that the ambiguity should be resolved in its favour because Canada had gambled on the retention of QRs in the Uruguay Round and had failed to negotiate provisions for tariffication in NAFTA. However, it takes two to gamble, and the reality is that both sides took a risk in allowing a degree of ambiguity to subsist in the NAFTA text. Contrary to the United States's contention, moreover, Canada did not place all its bets on maintaining QRs in the Uruguay Round. Canada had a safety net, which was that the original FTA "deal" providing the multilateral outcome would

61 See "At the Department of External Affairs in 1991-2 / Au Ministère des Affaires extérieures en 1991-2" (1992) 20 Canadian Yearbook of International Law 352-55.

62 Chalifour and Buckingham, *supra* note 20 at 131. Article 30 of the Vienna Convention, which is referred to here, includes the rule that of two inconsistent treaties, the later-in-time will prevail.

be accepted, that GATT rights would be retained, and that the FTA/NAFTA commitments to preferential market access would be limited to in-quota imports.

NAVIGATING THROUGH THE "COMPLEX INTERRELATIONSHIP" OF THE FTA, THE NAFTA, AND THE GATT

One of the most intractable elements of the dispute was the problem of dealing with "the complex interrelationship of the FTA, the NAFTA, the GATT, and the agreements of the WTO, in particular the *WTO Agreement on Agriculture.*" As the Panel noted:

> The NAFTA incorporates obligations from other agreements including both the FTA and the GATT. The terminology used in the drafting of various provisions, both within and across these agreements, is not marked by uniformity or consistency. As discussed more fully below, words like "existing," "retain" or "successor agreements," appear in some contexts yet do not appear in others where their presence might have been thought apposite. As a result, *the Panel has been faced not only with the task of determining meaning from the presence of certain words, but also with the more difficult task of divining meaning from the absence of particular words* [emphasis added].[63]

The Panel's reference point in beginning its task was NAFTA Article 102(2):

> The Parties shall interpret and apply the provisions of this Agreement in the light of its objectives set out in paragraph 1 and in accordance with applicable rules of international law.

The Panel turned to the "applicable rules of international law," as set out in Articles 31 and 32 of the 1969 Vienna Convention, as these provisions were "generally accepted as reflecting customary international law."[64] Taking into account the "object and purpose" of the parties, as required by Article 31, the Panel observed:

> The Panel also attaches importance to the trade liberalization background against which the agreements under consideration here must be interpreted. Moreover, as a free trade agreement the NAFTA has the specific objective of eliminating barriers to trade among the three contracting Parties . . . Any interpretation adopted by the Panel must, therefore, promote rather than inhibit the NAFTA's objectives . . .[65]

63 Panel Report, *supra* note 1, para. 123.

64 *Ibid.*, para. 119.

65 *Ibid.*, para. 122.

The Panel also relied on Article 32 of the Vienna Convention in treating the Dunkel Draft, the Modalities Document, and the documents on which they were based as *travaux préparatoires* to be considered in clarifying the obscurity of the WTO Agreement on Agriculture.[66]

The Panel's reliance on the Vienna Convention was significant and reflected the application of general principles of international law to the settlement of international trade law disputes. It is of interest that in its early decisions, the new Appellate Body of the WTO Dispute Settlement Body has followed a similar path. In the *Japan — Taxes on Alcoholic Beverages* case, the Appellate Body cited Article 3.2 of the WTO Dispute Settlement Understanding, which directs the Appellate Body to clarify the provisions of the 1994 GATT and the other "covered agreements" of the WTO Agreement "in accordance with customary rules of interpretation of public international law." It stressed the need to:

> [A]chieve such clarification by reference to the fundamental rule of treaty interpretation set out in Article 31(1) of the *Vienna Convention* . . . this general rule of interpretation "has attained the status of a rule of customary or general international law" . . . There can be no doubt that Article 32 of the *Vienna Convention*, dealing with supplementary means of interpretation, has also attained the same status.[67]

AN IMAGINARY BARGAIN?

While the decision was obviously welcomed in Canada, it has encountered sharp criticism in the United States trade law community. A recent comment in the *Yale Journal of International Law* concludes that the decision "sided with the interests of protectionism rather than the interests of trade liberalization, casting an ominous shadow over the future of the NAFTA."[68] The case comment provides a useful and in-depth analysis of the history of the dispute and the negotiating record, particularly, the record of the agricultural negotiations in the Uruguay Round. It is submitted, however, that its central proposition is wrong. The author of the comment contends that the implementation of the impugned tariff-rate quotas cannot be justified under Article 710 as a "right" retained under the GATT because there is no such right under the

66 *Ibid.*, para. 179.

67 *Japan — Taxes and Alcoholic Beverages*, AB-1996-2 WT/DS8/AB/R, Report of the Appellate Body, pp. 10-11.

68 Dale E. McNeil, *supra* note 7 at 346.

GATT. Under Article II:1(b) of the GATT, tariff bindings — including tariff bindings from prior negotiating rounds — remain in effect until superseded by an agreement negotiated pursuant to the terms of Article XXVIII of the GATT, which deals with the "modification of schedules." The author takes the view that the mere filing of a schedule of concessions at the Uruguay Round does not satisfy the requirements of Article XXVIII. This fact, he argues, is demonstrated by a provision of the Marrakech Protocol, which creates a strictly limited exemption from Article XXVIII in favour of four specified non-NAFTA countries (presumably for reasons that are distinct from the general tariffication program), and by the rejection of a proposal providing for "deemed compliance" with Article XXVIII in the case of agricultural products subject to tariffication. In the result he argues, "the negotiating parties explicitly refused to bless automatically tariffication that produced tariff equivalents that exceeded prior tariff bindings."[69]

This novel argument was never made by the United States in this case, and the Panel cannot, therefore, be criticized for failing to consider it. The argument, if accepted, would threaten the legal basis of the entire WTO tariffication initiative not only for states under a free trade agreement, such as NAFTA, but for all WTO members. As a consequence, it strikes at one of the foundations of the Uruguay Round settlement. Although it seems unthinkable that tariffication without an agreement, which is expressly based on Article XXVIII, is a legal nullity under the GATT itself, this seems to be the implication of this comment. If this manifestly unreasonable outcome is to be avoided, then Article 4.2 of the WTO Agreement on Agriculture must be treated as importing a genuine requirement to tariffy that either satisfies Article XXVIII or else overrides Article XXVIII by reason of Article 21 of the WTO Agreement on Agriculture. Article 21 provides that the 1994 GATT and other multilateral agreements apply "subject to the provisions of this Agreement," implying that in the event of any inconsistency, the WTO Agreement on Agriculture — with tariffication as its central feature — has overriding effect.

LESSONS LEARNED

Dura lex sed lex was, in effect, the United States position, although the words were never spoken. It would have been a hard bargain

69 *Ibid.*, 369.

indeed if Canada were found to have paid twice — once in NAFTA and once in the WTO — and received nothing in return for its agricultural community. Only in the face of clear and compelling language could such an outcome be accepted, and, in fact, the language was far from clear. The Panel, therefore, looked to the underlying objective of the negotiators, which was to adopt the eventual Uruguay Round solution — a gradual and incremental liberalization of agricultural treaties through the device of tariffication and a rejection of the immediate and absolute dismantling of all barriers to trade that was called for by the United States position. The decision also displayed a desire to maintain the intended balance of concessions and benefits, reflecting a principle that is central to the interpretation and application of trade agreements.

Faced with several difficult issues of interpretation, the Panel chose substance over form. It also looked beyond the language to the nature of the bargain between the parties. What counted most was not the form of the instrument — tariffs versus quotas — but the function of the tariff equivalents in replacing the quantitative restrictions necessary to the enforcement of supply-management programs, as contemplated by GATT Article XI and FTA Article 710. The text was by no means disregarded, but the ambiguities were very real. In looking to the nature of the bargain and the intentions of the parties, the Panel adhered to the principle that a treaty is to be interpreted in good faith, in accordance with its object and purpose, as required by the basic rule in Article 31 of the Vienna Convention.

As noted earlier, the reliance on the general principles of the Vienna Convention is typical of the approach taken by recent panels in the WTO and by the FTA and NAFTA. The implication is that although trade agreements are in some respects *sui generis*, they are nevertheless genuine international treaties and that trade law is an integral part of the corpus of public international law. This fact has further implications not only with respect to the relationship between trade agreements but also with respect to the "interface" of trade law with other important concerns of the international community, including culture, the environment, and human rights.

The response of the Panel to the patent ambiguity — indeed the *intended* ambiguity — of the texts is also significant. Deliberate ambiguity, or "constructive" ambiguity, is a typical feature of international agreements. It plays an essential and positive role, allowing agreements to be concluded on subjects too politically sensitive to allow for clear and explicit language. One lesson of this decision, however, was that negotiators cannot expect such ambiguities to secure their objectives when there is convincing evidence of a contrary intention in the negotiating history, the surrounding circumstances, or even in subsequent statements "against interest," such as the U.S. "Statement of Administrative Action."[70] The principles of general international law ensure that the real bargain, ascertained through such materials, will not be defeated by textual imprecision.

Sommaire

La décision du premier groupe spécial de l'ALÉNA

En juillet 1995, les États-Unis ont demandé la formation du premier groupe spécial en vertu des procédures du chapitre 20 de l'Accord de libre-échange nord-améericain (ALÉNA) en contestant les droits de douane appliqués par le Canada aux produits laitiers, à la volaille, aux oeufs, à l'orge et à la margarine "soumis à la gestion de l'offre." Ces industries se sont développées et ont prospéré grâce à la gestion de l'offre, système qui vise à stabiliser un marché national soumis à des cycles de production imprévisibles. Les restrictions à l'importation étaient conformes aux régles du commerce international énoncées dans l'Accord géneral sur les tarifs douaniers et du commerce (GATT). Elles ont été modifiées en 1995, à la suite de l'Accord sur l'agriculture de l'OMC, aux termes duquel le Canada et les membres de cette organisation ont remplacé les restrictions à l'importation quantitative par des droits de douane et des contingents tarifaires. Les États-Unis alléguaient que les droits de douane contrevenaient à l'obligation fondamentale contractée aux termes de l'ALÉNA de ne pas augmenter les tarifs douaniers. Le Canadia a riposté que les nouveaux taux étaient justifiés en raison de l'Accord sur l'agriculture de l'OMC, qui a été négocié à Genève après l'ALÉNA. La décision en faveur du Canada qui en a résulté a été à la fois louée pour son analyse de l'affaire dans le contexte de l'interaction complexe des obligations commerciales pertinentes, et critiquée pour avoir invoqué "un marché implicite entre les négociateurs . . . qui n'a jamais été conclu." Le groupe spécial a présumeé que si des équivalents tarifaires ne pouvaient pas être appliqués, ce qui en fait rendrait l'Accord sur l'agriculture de l'OMC inopérant, il en résultaerait que les parties auraient le droit d'appliquer les restrictions prévues à l'article XI, comme si l'Uruguay Round n'avait jamais eu lieu. Le raisonnement était sans faille — l'ALÉNA, ne devait "pas être isolé cliniquement de droit international public."

[70] Statement of Administrative Action, supra note 23.

Summary

The NAFTA Panel Decision on Supply Management: Gamble or Bargain?

In July 1995, the United States requested the establishment of the first Panel under Chapter 20 procedures of the North American Free Trade Agreement (NAFTA) and challenged Canada's duties on its "supply-managed" dairy, poultry, egg, barley, and margarine products. These industries had grown and prospered under supply management — a system intended to establish stability in a domestic market afflicted by unpredictable production cycles. The import restrictions were designed in conformity with the international trade rules as set out in the General Agreement of Tariffs and Trade (GATT). These rules changed in 1995 as a result of the WTO Agreement on Agriculture under which Canada and WTO members replaced quantitative import restrictions with tariffs and tariff-rate quotas. The United States claimed that the duties contravened the basic NAFTA obligation to not raise tariffs. Canada countered that the new tariff rates were justified under the new WTO Agreement on Agriculture that had been negotiated in Geneva after NAFTA. The resulting decision in favour of Canada was both praised for its consideration of the case in the context of the complex interplay of relevant trade obligations and criticized for finding "an implied bargain among negotiators . . . that was never struck." The Panel assumed that if tariff eqivalents could not be applied — which in effect would render the WTO Agreement on Agriculture inoperative — the result would be that the parties would be entitled to apply Article XI restrictions as if the Uruguay Round had never happened. The logic was impeccable — the NAFTA was "not to be read in clinical isolation from public international law."

Notre Mer? An Independent Québec's Maritime Claims in the Gulf of St. Lawrence and Beyond

JEFFREY J. SMITH

INTRODUCTION

THE PROSPECT OF Québec's secession from Canada creates potentially complex issues of maritime law. The ability of a nation to exercise sovereignty over its adjacent seas is a significant element and right of modern statehood. Consideration of such a right should feature prominently and early in the new state's accession to full international recognition and national status. However, during the lengthy and often contentious debate over Québec's possible departure from the Canadian Confederation, little seems to have been said regarding maritime issues.[1] Even the most emphatic of *indépendantiste* scholars have stopped short of considering the extent of maritime rights that Québec might possess upon leaving Confederation.[2] If Québec's separation is an issue for Canadians that is fraught with uncertainty, the lack of discussion over its resulting maritime implications is, or should be, cause for concern.

While an independent Québec could claim expansive maritime areas about its northern, western, and southern shores, the Gulf of

---

Jeffrey J. Smith, B.Sc. (RRMC), LL.B. (U. Vic), is a barrister at Thompson & McConnell, White Rock, British Columbia, Canada.

1 See, e.g., R. Howard, "Quebec Divisible, Chrétien Says," *Globe and Mail* (Jan. 30, 1996) A1.

2 See, e.g., J. Brossard, *L'accession à la souveraineté et le cas du Québec* (Montréal: Les Presses de l'Université de Montréal, 1976). The most comprehensive English language discussion concerning the maritime claims of an independent Québec is found in Jonathan I. Charney, "Maritime Jurisdiction and the Secession of States: The Case of Quebec" (1992) 25 Vand. J. Transnat'l L. 343.

St. Lawrence would initially be the focal point of its assertion of maritime sovereignty, given the importance of the Gulf's waters as the primary shipping route into North America, the population about its shores, and Canada's historic claims over it. For reasons of national status and access to maritime resources, the second ocean "front" that an independent Québec might claim about its northern shores could be equally important and should not be discounted.[3] However, the considerations of the international community and the bilateral agreements or disputes between Canada and Québec will first centre on the maritime area of greatest importance to the new state, the Gulf of St. Lawrence and its Atlantic Ocean environs.

A consideration of the prototypical maritime claim suggests a structure for the present analysis. First addressed is the scope of Québec's present maritime jurisdiction in the Gulf of St. Lawrence as a province within Confederation. This might be the foundation for its maritime claims at the instant of secession or, at least, upon effective independence. Second, a review of customary and conventional international law can be applied predictively to develop those maritime zones within the Gulf that Québec might legitimately claim after independence. With international jurisprudence now offering an extensive, if still uncertain, catalogue of principles and demarcation methods, those circumstances relevant or unique to bilateral boundary-making in the Gulf can be assessed to arrive at possible outcomes of negotiated or judicially resolved maritime delimitation.[4] Finally, this article addresses the potential for joint use of the Gulf of St. Lawrence and claims by Québec to the Canadian continental shelf and its exclusive economic zone in the Atlantic Ocean. On these latter issues, the principles of international law and equitable considerations remain uncertain, and may yet be sufficiently flexible to allow for an unprecedented regime of joint sovereignty and shared ocean use.

3 "Independence" is applied here neutrally. Quebec might become independent through secession, grant of independence (devolution), or the dissolution of the Canadian federation. For a review of these doctrines, see R. Y. Jennings, *The Acquisition of Territory in International Law*, 6 ff (Manchester: Manchester Univ. Press, 1963) and J. Crawford, *The Creation of States in International Law* 9 (Oxford: Clarendon Press, 1979). Consider also Professor Monahan's use of the phrase "Unilateral Declaration of Independence," in Patrick Monahan, "The Law and Politics of Quebec Succession" (1995) 33 Osgoode Hall L. J. 1.

4 Preliminary predictions about maritime claims in and around the Gulf are depicted in Figures 2 and 3.

Québec's Present Maritime Boundaries

COASTAL FRONT AND MARITIME SOVEREIGNTY

It is both a logical tenet and fundamental rule of international law that a state must possess a land territory adjacent to the maritime area claimed. If maritime rights are a fundamental part of statehood, the extent to which an independent Québec might assert its sovereignty in the Gulf of St. Lawrence will be founded on the coastline it ultimately possesses within it.[5] This basic principle of customary international law was emphasized recently by the International Court of Justice in the *Greenland-Jan Mayen* case:

> The Court would observe that the attribution of maritime areas to the territory of a State, which, by its nature, is destined to be permanent, is a legal process based solely on the possession by the territory concerned of a coastline.[6]

International custom,[7] which provides that a state's territorial sea and other, more expansive maritime zones[8] are predicated upon its

5 P. Weil, *The Law of Maritime Delimitation — Reflections* (Cambridge: Grotius Press, 1989). Professor Weil writes, at 51-52, that "[m]aritime rights derive from statehood. They are its 'prolongation,' 'extension,' 'emanation,' 'automatic adjunct.' They adhere to statehood as his shadow does to man . . . Whether it is large or small, whether it is endowed with a long coast and a short hinterland or an extensive territory with a short coastline, whether it is a large continental State or a small island State, in every case its statehood gives it the same potential for generating maritime projections under the conditions laid down by international law."

6 *Maritime Delimitation in the Area between Greenland and Jan Mayen*, [1993] ICJ Rep. 38 at 74 (para. 80) [hereinafter *Greenland-Jan Mayen* case]. See also the *Continental Shelf (Tunisia* v. *Libyan Arab Jamahiriya) Judgment*, [1982] ICJ Rep. 18 at 61 (para. 73) [hereinafter *Tunisia-Libya* case]: "[T]he coast of the territory of the State is the decisive factor for title to the submarine areas adjacent to it." And see the Court's judgment in the *Continental Shelf (Libyan Arab Jamahiriya* v. *Malta)*, [1985] ICJ Rep. 13 at 30 (para. 27) [hereinafter *Libya-Malta* case]: "The juridical link between the State's territorial sovereignty and its rights to certain adjacent maritime expanses is established by means of its coast."

7 R. R. Churchill and A. V. Lowe, *The Law of the Sea* 5-6 (2d ed., Manchester: Manchester University Press, 1988) write that "international custom, as evidenced by a practice generally accepted as law" is composed of two necessary elements: "a general and consistent practice adopted by States" and "the so-called *opinio juris* — the conviction that the practice is one which is either required or allowed by customary international law."

8 See *ibid.* for definitions of these progressive zones of maritime territory and sovereignty.

coastal presence,[9] is now codified in the UN Convention on the Law of the Sea (UNCLOS).[10] Article 2 of UNCLOS states that the maritime sovereignty of a coastal state extends "beyond its land territory and internal waters . . . to an adjacent belt of sea, described as the territorial sea." There should be few doubts that a truly independent Québec would generate, by claim or by right, an area of exclusive maritime jurisdiction, subject to international recognition and the competing or constraining claims of Canada.

A first step, however, is to determine what ocean areas are to be found at present within the provincial boundaries of Québec. This is integral to the more significant and often contentious debate over the boundaries of Québec that might exist at the instant of its independence. To consider a state's nascent maritime jurisdiction, it is a generally accepted doctrine that a grant of independence or the dissolution of a state carries with it the right of the new state to claim the former maritime areas of the predecessor. Examples can be seen in the dissolution of the Soviet Union and, to a less certain extent, in the fragmentation of the Yugoslav Federation, with several successor states able to claim areas of the Baltic, Black, and Adriatic Seas. International law underwrites the legality of such successor states filling *lacunae* in maritime zones. Similarly, the devolution of independence to a new state may also be rooted in the doctrine of *uti posseditis, ita possideatis*, which can allow for the certainty of territorial integrity between newly neighbouring states after the departure of a colonial state. The International Court of Justice defined the doctrine of *uti posseditis* in its 1992 *Gulf of Fonseca* decision:

> The two Parties . . . are states that came into existence with the break-up of the Spanish Empire in Central America, and their territories correspond to administrative sub-divisions of that empire. While it was from the outset accepted that the new international boundaries should be determined by the application of the principle generally accepted in

[9] Baselines can be drawn along the mean low water mark of a state's coast or by straight lines between geographical co-ordinates. For a discussion of baselines see *ibid.* and see The Law of the Sea, *Baselines: National Legislation With Illustrative Maps* (New York: UN Office for Ocean Affairs and the Law of the Sea, 1989). Professor Donat Pharand provides a useful summary of Canadian baseline practice in *Canada's Arctic Waters in International Law* at 147ff (Cambridge: Cambridge University Press, 1988). See also the Oceans Act, S.C. 1996, c. 31, s. 5.

[10] United Nations Convention on the Law of the Sea, opened for signature Dec. 10, 1982 at Montego Bay, in force Nov. 16, 1994, UN Doc. A/CONF. 62/122 (1982) reprinted in (1982) 21 ILM 1245 [hereinafter UNCLOS].

Spanish America of the *uti possiditis juris*, whereby the boundaries were to follow the colonial administrative boundaries, the problem, as in the case of many other boundaries in the region, was to determine where those boundaries actually lay.[11]

While either doctrine might provide some certainty of territorial sovereignty for Québec, it is generally considered that Québec's departure from Canada will not be through a grant of independence or through outright dissolution of the Canadian Federation.[12] Comparison to the recent *de facto* independence of the Baltic states Latvia, Lithuania, and Estonia also provides scant assistance in defining an independent Québec's preliminary ocean boundaries. The Baltic states were guaranteed the formal right of secession by the Soviet Union's constitution and, in any event, are generally considered in international law to have been occupied by the USSR with their pre-existing maritime boundaries intact after 1940.[13] Québec does not enjoy a similar position. Thus, defining

11 *Land, Island and Maritime Frontier Dispute (El Salvador* v. *Honduras: Nicaragua Intervening)*, Judgment of Sept. 11, 1992, [1992] ICJ Rep. 351 at 380 (para. 28) [hereinafter *Gulf of Fonseca* case]. Yehuda Z. Blum, *Historic Titles in International Law* 341-42 (The Hague: Martinus Nijhoff, 1965) stated:

> The term *uti possiditis* ["as you possess, so you may possess"] should be used with caution in international law. The term is derived from Roman law, in which it was used to denote an edict of the *praetor*, the purpose of which was to preserve, pending litigation, an existing state of possession of an immovable *nec vi, nec clam, nec precario*, as between individual claimants. The meaning of this term, when used with regard to international boundaries in Latin America, is somewhat different from that ascribed to it in civil law and is intended to denote *permanent* rather than temporary possession . . . In any event, the doctrine of *uti possiditis* can be considered merely as 'a principle by which the American Republics have decided to adjust their boundary differences. But in no case has the International Community recognized, as an institution of international law, the principle of *uti possiditis* . . . It remains . . . derogatory to general international law . . . binding only on those . . . [who] have, by a convention, expressly agreed to it.'

12 Professor Monahan notes "that the principle *uti possiditis* has no application to a border or any other territorial dispute between Canada and Quebec. In my view, Quebec's territorial integrity is not guaranteed under any principle of public international law in the event that it attempts to secede unilaterally from Canada": Monahan, *supra* note 3 at 28.

13 See especially A. G. O. Elferink, *The Law of Maritime Delimitation: A Case Study of the Russian Federation* (London: Martinus Nijhoff, 1995) and Jeffrey Lee Canfield, "The Independent Baltic States: Maritime Law and Resource Management Issues" (1993) 24 Ocean Dev. & Int'l L. 1.

the present status quo of its provincial maritime sovereignty is of practical significance in determining its possible claims at the instant of its secession or nascent independence.[14]

QUEBEC'S EARLY BOUNDARIES: 1686-1867

The earliest formal European incidents of sovereignty in the Gulf of St. Lawrence resulted from fishery agreements between France and the United Kingdom. In part, the agreements defined control of resources and the maintenance of sovereignty over lands in the New World. France accepted in 1686 and in the 1713 Treaty of Utrecht that it was to limit fishing by its subjects off the coasts of Newfoundland and Nova Scotia.[15] By 1763, only limited guarantees of fishing rights and the possession of St. Pierre and Miquelon remained.[16] The 1763 Treaty of Paris defined the extent of Québec, with the Royal Proclamation of October 7 of that year further refining its territorial position in the New World:

> Quebec [is] bounded on the Labrador Coast by the River St. John flowing into the north shore of the St. Lawrence opposite Anticosti Island, and from thence by a line drawn from the Head of that River through the Lake St. John, to the South end of the Lake Nippissim [just to the east of Georgian Bay]; from whence the said Line, crossing the River St. Lawrence, and the Lake Champlain, in 45 Degrees of North Latitude, passes along the High Lands which divide the Rivers that Empty themselves into the said River St. Lawrence from those which fall into the Sea; and also along the North Coast of the Bayes des Chaleurs, and the Coast of the Gulph of St. Lawrence to Cape Rosiere, and from thence

[14] Professor Peter Hogg notes that "[t]he boundaries of a province will be ascertained by reference to the instruments by which the province was initially created or defined, to the terms of union with Canada (where applicable), to any modifications after confederation . . . and to any judicial decisions on boundaries": P. W. Hogg, *Constitutional Law of Canada*, s. 13.3(b)(3d ed, Scarborough: Carswell, 1992).

[15] See Gérard V. La Forest, "Canadian Inland Waters of the Atlantic Provinces and the Bay of Fundy Incident," (1963) Canadian Yearbook of International Law 149 at 150.

[16] Louise de La Fayette, "The Award in the Canada-France Maritime Boundary Arbitration" (1993) 8 The Int'l J. of Marine and Coastal Law 77, note 1. See also F. Morrissette, "Le statut du golfe du Saint-Laurent en droit international et en droit interne" (1985) 16 RGD 273 at 295: "[L]e *Traité de Paris* de 1763 empêchait les français de pendre poisson à l'interieur de trois lieues du littoral du golfe du Saint-Laurent."

crossing the Mouth of the River St. Lawrence by the West End of the Island of Anticosti; terminates at the aforesaid River of St. John.[17]

The Royal Proclamation also defined British Imperial colonies in the Gulf, with Prince Edward Island and Cape Breton being annexed to Nova Scotia. New Brunswick, originally a part of Nova Scotia under the 1763 Treaty, was separated from it by a 1784 Order-In-Council.[18] The coast of Labrador east of St. John River (Rivière St. Jean) had also been ceded by France to Newfoundland in 1763, but was re-attached to it by effect of the Québec Act,[19] then re-annexed to Newfoundland in 1809 and finally ceded to Lower Canada in 1825.[20] Importantly, however, this last transfer of the northern Gulf coast to Lower Canada included an expanded area east of St. John River to Sablon Cove (Anse Sablon) on the northern shores of the Strait of Belle Isle. The certainty of Québec's eastern land boundary at this point would be questioned a century later. From 1825, however, Québec's Gulf coast consisted of a crescent-shaped coastal front centred on the St. Lawrence River estuary, extending from the Restigouche River in the Gaspé to Sablon Cove in the northeast.

The sole maritime boundary in the Gulf of St. Lawrence at the time of Confederation had been enacted following an 1851 arbitral decision. Uncertainty over the land boundary between Lower Canada, the United States, and New Brunswick, stemming from imprecise wording in the Royal Proclamation of 1763, had been partly resolved by an 1842 treaty with the United States. The 1851 Imperial statute affirmed the result of an arbitral decision between Lower Canada and New Brunswick, which almost incidentally established a maritime boundary between New Brunswick and Québec as follows:

New Brunswick shall be bounded . . . by a line . . . down the centre of the Stream of the Restigouche to its Mouth in the Bay of Chaleurs; and thence through the Middle of that Bay to the Gulf of the Saint Lawrence,

17 A. F. N. Poole, "The Boundaries of Canada" (1964) 42 Can. Bar. Rev. 101 at 125 (see Figures 1 and 2). For geographic details, see Canadian Hydrographic Services Chart LC 4002.

18 Poole, *ibid.*, 124.

19 (U.K.), 14 Geo. 3, c. 83.

20 Poole, *supra* note 17 at 121.

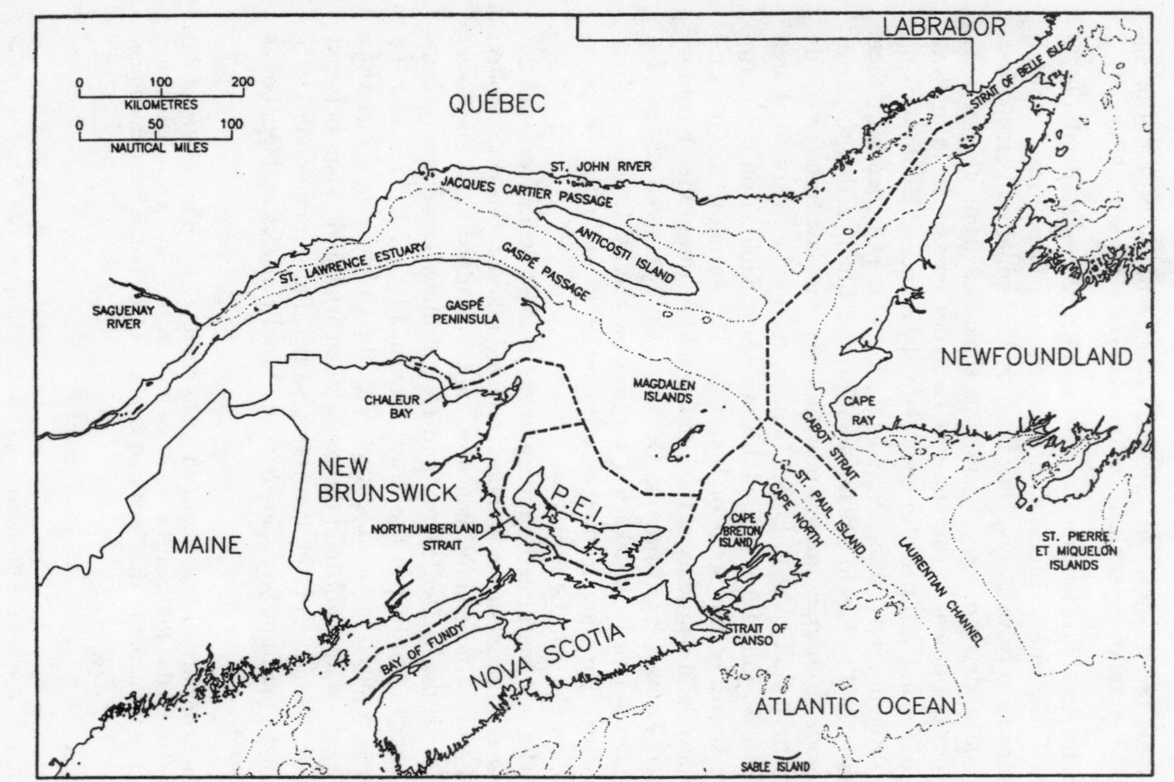

Figure 1 Delimitation line between Québec and the Maritime provinces resulting from the 1964 Interprovincial Boundary Agreement.

the Islands in the said Rivers Mistouche and Restigouche to the Mouth of the latter River at Dalhousie being given to New Brunswick.[21]

France's island possessions in the Gulf, Anticosti, and the Magdalens were transferred to Newfoundland in 1763 and then attached to Lower Canada in 1774. In 1809, however, Anticosti Island was ceded to Newfoundland under the Newfoundland Act, 1809,[22] on the probable basis that it lay to the east of the St. John River and was therefore considered a feature of the Labrador coast. The island was finally annexed administratively to Lower Canada under the British North America (Seignorial Rights) Act 1825.[23] The Magdalen Islands have formed part of Québec since 1774,[24] although the British North America Act 1840 made provision for their annexation to Prince Edward Island at the discretion of the Crown.[25]

21 An Act for the Settlement of Boundaries between the Provinces of Canada and New Brunswick, 1851 (U.K.), 9 & 10 Vic., c. 63. This maritime boundary continues by force of ss. 6, 7 of the British North America Act, 1867 (U.K.), 30 & 31 Vic., c. 3. This is one of the earliest maritime boundaries between British colonies and may have been enacted, in part, to regulate fishing in the Bay. See Figure 2.

The application of the Act and the nature of the Bay of Chaleur as internal waters were affirmed in *Mowat* v. *McFee* (1880), 5 S.C.R. 66. "Under the [1851 Act], regulating the boundary line between old Canada and New Brunswick, the whole of the Bay of Chaleurs is within the present boundaries of the Provinces of Quebec and New Brunswick, and within the Dominion of Canada and the operation of the *Fisheries Act* . . . Therefore the act of drifting for salmon in the Bay of Chaleurs, although that drifting may have been more than three miles from either shore of New Brunswick or of Quebec abutting on the Bay, is a drifting in Canadian waters."

See also *United States-Great Britain, In the Matter of the North Atlantic Coast Fisheries* (1910), 4 A.J.I.L. 948 at 984. Jonathan Charney notes this decision "probably fixes the provincial boundary at the closing line described as 'the line under international law the Light at Birch Point on Mescon Island to Macquereau Point Light'": "The Offshore Jurisdiction of the States of the United States and the Provinces of Canada — A Comparison" (1983) 12 Ocean Dev. & Int'l L. J. 301 at 330.

22 (U.K.), 49 Geo. 3, c. 27. The Act was intended primarily to establish Newfoundland's courts.

23 (U.K.), 6 Geo. 4, c. 59.

24 This was affirmed in the Newfoundland Act, 1809.

25 1840 (U.K.), 3 & 4 Vic., c. 35, s. 60. Poole, *supra* note 17 at 124 notes, erroneously, that the Magdalen Islands were added to P.E.I. in 1840. This Act, apparently never repealed by the Imperial Parliament, is likely spent. In any event, the British North America Act, 1871 (U.K.), 34 & 35 Vic., c. 28, s. 3 permits the federal government to alter provincial boundaries only with the consent of an affected province.

Thus, at the time of Confederation, Québec possessed its present coastline in the Gulf of St. Lawrence, from along the northern shore of the Restigouche River and the Bay of Chaleur (including the northern half of the bay's seabed and superjacent waters), to the Gaspé peninsula across the mouth of the St. Lawrence River and along the shore of the northern Gulf coast to Anse Sablon, in the Strait of Belle Isle opposite Newfoundland. By 1867, Anticosti Island and the Magdalens were established firmly as part of the province. With the exception of the pre-existing boundary in the Bay of Chaleur, no grant by Confederation nor historical right created for the province a coastal zone even remotely resembling a territorial sea. By all accounts, Québec entered Confederation seized solely of land territory.[26]

QUÉBEC'S BOUNDARIES: 1867-1949

A further impetus to refine boundaries along Québec's Gulf coast resulted from settlement into the eastern hinterlands after Confederation.[27] Colonization prompted the federal government in 1898, with the acceptance of Québec, to legislate the expansion of the province northwards.[28] The province's boundaries were enlarged again to the shores of Hudson Strait and the Bay of

26 See H. Brun, *Le Territoire du Québec* 233 (Ville de Québec: Les Presses de l'Université Laval, 1974): "Canadian law obliges us to conclude that the territory of Quebec in 1867 terminated at the coast. Quebec did not enter Confederation seized with a territorial sea . . . its territory terminated at the low water mark. Nothing, definitively, allows us to think differently" [translation with notes omitted]. It should be noted that Quebec did possess certain waters now defined as "internal" and "inland," such as those within harbours and estuaries.

In 1867 the legal concept of exclusive territorial waters was in its infancy, although international law generally recognized zones of sovereignty adjacent to a coast. The Territorial Waters Jurisdiction Act, 1878 (U.K.), 41 & 42 Vic., c. 73 enacted the "cannonshot principle" of a territorial sea. See Churchill and Lowe, *supra* note 7 at 59 ff.

27 P. Linteau, R. Durocher, and J. Robert, *Quebec: A History (1867-1929)* (Toronto: James Lorimer & Co., 1983) 387, note "[t]he colonization movement continued to open up new areas of Quebec after 1896."

28 See An Act Respecting the North-western, Northern and North-eastern boundaries of the Province of Quebec, SC 1898, c. 3. The requirements of the British North America Act, 1871, *supra* note 25, for provincial consent to boundary modifications are noted in the 1898 Act.

Ungava in a 1912 federal statute.[29] Boundary conflict between Québec and Labrador followed the 1912 expansion. The 1763 Treaty of Paris had ceded the Labrador coast of Québec to the United Kingdom in somewhat uncertain terms.

At the turn of the nineteenth century, the government of Newfoundland and Labrador proclaimed a right to issue timber licences in the inland area north of 52 degrees latitude. Québec disputed this act. Reference of the matter to the Judicial Committee of the Privy Council resulted in the upholding of Newfoundland's claim to an expansive inland territory inland from the east coast of Labrador. The Judicial Committee found that the coastal starting point of this interprovincial boundary was at the head of Sablon Cove. The boundary determined by the Privy Council proceeded north from the Cove to the 52nd parallel of latitude before turning westward, and affirmed the 1825 eastern terminus of Québec's Gulf coastline.[30] It would be another half century before the extent, if any, of Québec's seaward expanse would receive consideration.[31]

Next, two events further eroded any maritime claim that Québec might pursue in the Gulf of St. Lawrence. First, the 1931 Statute of Westminster ousted the jurisdiction of the Imperial Parliament to impose laws of external application upon Canada.[32] Boundary claims by Canada would henceforth be advanced by the Dominion on a nation-to-nation basis. Second, the entry of Newfoundland

29 An Act to Extend the Boundaries of the Province of Quebec, S.C. 1912, c. 45.

30 See *In re Labrador Boundary*, [1927] 2 D.L.R. 401, 137 L.T.R. 187. P. Linteau et al, *supra* note 27 at 8 remark that "[t]he Privy Council decision is still a subject of debate, and Quebec wants to reopen the case."

31 P. Linteau et al, *ibid.*, 8, write in respect of Quebec's changing territory that "[i]t should be stressed that all these additions to or subtractions from the territory of Quebec were imposed by outside governments, in London and in Ottawa; in other words, Quebec has never really had control over the formation of its territory. In addition, it is clear that in some cases the central government hesitated seriously before allowing Quebec's borders to be extended . . . The question of Labrador also shows the federal government's reticence about extending Quebec's borders; in 1927 it was Ottawa's responsibility to protect the interests of Quebec and Canada against the claims of Newfoundland, at that time still a separate dominion."

32 1931 (U.K.), 22 Geo. 4, c. 4, s. 3: "It is hereby declared and enacted that the Parliament of a Dominion has full power to make laws having extra-territorial application."

into Confederation in 1949[33] resulted in the Gulf of St. Lawrence being bounded by a single state.[34]

QUÉBEC'S MARITIME CLAIMS AFTER 1964

Technical and economic developments, as well as the growth in international maritime claims during the years following the Second World War, generated renewed contemplation of provincial jurisdiction over adjacent seas and the continental shelf. By this time, it had been commonly accepted that "inland waters" came within provincial jurisdiction through the common law doctrine of *inter fauces terrae*,[35] with such maritime areas consisting of "harbours, bays, estuaries, and other waters 'lying between the jaws of the land.'"[36] In 1964, Professor Gérard La Forest assessed the status of Québec's maritime jurisdiction:

33 Newfoundland Act, 1949 (U.K.), 12-13 Geo. 6, c. 22.

34 Prime Minister Louis St. Laurent announced shortly before Newfoundland's union with Canada that "[w]e intend to contend, and hope to be able to get acquiescence in the contention that the waters west of Newfoundland constituting the Gulf of St. Lawrence shall become an inland sea. We hope that, with Newfoundland as part of Canadian territory, the Gulf of St. Lawrence west of Newfoundland will all become territorial waters of Canada": House of Commons Debates (Feb. 8, 1949) at 368.

This was affirmed by the Diefenbaker government (House of Commons Debates (Nov. 14, 1957) at 1168-9) and by the Trudeau government (House of Commons Debates (Mar. 7, 1975) at 3884). The nature of the Gulf as an historic bay is discussed below.

35 The Canadian regimes of internal and inland waters must be distinguished. "Internal waters," landward of maritime baselines, are defined in the Oceans Act, S.C. 1996, c. 31, s. 6.

The Canada Shipping Act, R.S.C. 1985, c. S-9, defines "inland" waters as including the St. Lawrence River estuary west of a "straight line drawn (a) from Cap des Rosiers to West Point Anticosti Island, and (b) from Anticosti Island to the north shore of the St. Lawrence River along the meridian of longitude sixty-three degrees west." These two closing lines are shown in Figure 2.

36 Hogg, *Constitutional Law of Canada*, *supra* note 14 at s. 13.3 (b). See also *In Re Provincial Fisheries*, [1897] 26 S.C.R 444 at 444: "The beds of public harbours not granted before confederation are the property of the Dominion of Canada . . . The beds of all other waters not so granted belong to the respective provinces in which they are situate, without any distinction between the various classes of waters." Sir Henry Strong C.J. states, at 514: "At the time of confederation the beds of all lakes, rivers, public harbours and other waters within the territorial limits of the several provinces which had not been granted by the Crown were vested in the Crown as representing the provinces respectively."

Quebec clearly possesses all the waters of its rivers, lakes, and watercourses, as well as the resources of their subjacent beds. Quebec is also vested with title to internal waters situated within the province as of 1867; these comprise bays and coves with openings of less than six miles in width (and perhaps somewhat greater distances), the north half of the Bay of Chaleurs and all the estuary of the [same] river, and also the waters of the St. Lawrence River which terminate in a line drawn across its mouth from Cap des Rosiers to the extreme western point of Anticosti Island and thence [north] to St. Jean [John] River. *The weight of legal tradition also equally affords Québec a marginal zone of three [nautical] miles extending outward from its coasts or from internal water closing lines located in the Gulf of St. Lawrence. Although without direct precedent, legal tradition also favours the division of continental shelf resources in the Gulf of St. Lawrence between Québec, the Maritimes and Newfoundland* [translation, with emphasis added].[37]

Canada asserted a three nautical mile territorial sea through its enactment in 1964 of the Territorial Sea and Fishing Zones Act.[38] This did little to resolve the uncertain reach of provincial maritime sovereignty, perhaps best exemplified in Professor La Forest's remarks about a three-mile "provincial littoral zone." This question, along with that of the competing jurisdictions over continental shelf resources, would be clarified over the next two decades by the Supreme Court of Canada.[39]

However, before a judicial assessment of provincial maritime rights could commence, certain provinces, through mutual agreement, began to assert claims over the continental shelf. In the Gulf of St. Lawrence, this process began with the 1964 Interprovincial Boundary Agreement. A meeting of three Maritime premiers in September 1964 resulted in the adoption of a "Submission on

37 G. V. La Forest, "Les droits de propriété du Québec sur ses eaux," in J. Brossard et al, *Le Territoire Québécois* 105 at 150 (Montréal: Les Presses de l'Université de Montréal, 1970).

38 S.C. 1964, c. 22. Section 3 provides that the territorial sea of Canada extended 3 nautical miles seaward of baselines defined in s. 5. The Act was a consolidation of amendments to the Customs Act, S.C. 1936, c. 30, which defined Canadian waters for customs purposes.

39 Jonathan Charney wrote in 1983 that "[t]he question of provincial jurisdiction in the adjacent seas of Canada appears to be an open political question and perhaps even an open legal question for all the provinces except, perhaps, British Columbia": "The Offshore Jurisdiction of the States of the United States and the Provinces of Canada — A Comparison," *supra* note 21 at 306. Professor Charney compares Canadian provincial maritime claims with American seaward boundary delimitation practice under the Submerged Lands Act, 43 USC, ss. 1301-14 (1953).

Submarine Rights."[40] Québec joined this request, essentially an apportionment proposal for the Gulf of St. Lawrence, immediately before its transmission to the federal government. The proposed scheme of division was more comprehensive than was suggested by its title since the four provinces' signatory requested a vesting of both the continental shelf and its superjacent waters. However, the effect of the agreement was minimal, calling as it did "for federal legislation implementing this agreement, [with] none . . . forthcoming."[41] Although the Interprovincial Boundary Agreement was disregarded by the federal government, the maritime areas created by it and the consensus between Gulf provinces in the Agreement's development provide some basis for a sovereign Québec to claim a limited degree of sovereignty in the Gulf of St. Lawrence.[42]

Four methods of delimitation, now notable for their simplicity, were applied by the provincial premiers in formulating the 1964 Agreement:

(1) Mineral deposits under shelf waters [*sic*] between Provinces pertain to one or another Province.
(2) Islands lying between Provinces and belonging to one or another Province are considered as if they were peninsulas [i.e., islands were not regarded as discrete boundary generating entities in their own right, but as extensions of the continental landmass of a province.]
(3) Mineral rights boundaries are drawn to join median points between prominent landmarks selected so far as possible along parallel shores.

40 See especially Charney, *supra* note 2 at 397.

Paul Evans notes that "[t]he final decision of this Conference was to reaffirm the Premiers' position of provincial responsibility for the mineral rights and possible oil and gas deposits on the Continental Shelf. In order to strengthen their case, the Premiers drew up a map, outlining the extent of each province's ownership. In order to secure their position on ownership with the federal government, they decided to involve the other provinces, (except Alberta and Saskatchewan). Each of these provinces would recognize each other's offshore claim. (The Atlantic Provinces secured the agreement of Manitoba and Ontario in this way by supporting the [interprovincial] division of Hudson Bay)": *Report on Atlantic/Maritime Interprovincial Cooperation Between 1950 and 1971* 100 (Halifax: Dalhousie Univ., Apr. 1985). See also Charney, *supra* note 21 at 330.

41 Charney, *supra* note 2 at 397.

42 Professor Charney, *ibid.*, 398 concludes that "the maritime provinces and Québec appear to agree generally on the location of the boundaries between their maritime claims in the Gulf of St. Lawrence area. [However,] this agreement has questionable legal status because Canada has never legislatively implemented the agreement. Furthermore, the Canadian government denies the provinces jurisdiction over most, if not all, of the area of interest."

(4) In cases where three Provinces meet but boundaries for one pair would overlap on the third, an N-S line or other prime directional line is used to connect the closest point definable from the considerations in paragraph 3 above to the conflicting boundary.[43]

The simplicity of this agreement, relying strongly on the application of equidistance,[44] is remarkable in the light of subsequent international maritime boundary jurisprudence. Negotiations over continental shelf rights continued through the ensuing years, and by 1977 three of the Maritime premiers and Prime Minister Pierre Trudeau had agreed to divide revenues and administrative responsibilities in the offshore areas of the signatory provinces, including within the Gulf of St. Lawrence, on the basis of the 1964 Interprovincial Boundary Agreement.[45] The three Maritime provinces, which did not include Newfoundland, anticipated that the newer agreement would be ratified by federal statute, but no legislation was introduced.[46]

Further restricting Québec's maritime aspirations during this period were two federal-provincial agreements. An agreement in August 1975 defined the shore as the low water line and a second agreement concluded in March 1976 provided that rivers would "be closed at their mouths."[47] The three nautical mile "provincial

43 *Ibid.*, 398, note 213. See Figure 1.

44 The equidistant lines in the Gulf of St. Lawrence between Québec and the three Maritime provinces were drawn from prominent geographic features.

45 The 1977 agreement was styled "Memorandum of Understanding in Respect of the Administration and Management of Mineral Resources Offshore of the Maritime Provinces."

46 Charney, *supra* note 2 at 397. The 1977 agreement was concluded only between Nova Scotia, New Brunswick, Prince Edward Island, and the federal government.

See also Rowland Harrison, "The Offshore Mineral Resources Agreement in the Maritime Provinces" (1978) 4 Dalhousie L.J. 245: "In summary, the [1977] Understanding sets aside the competing claims to jurisdiction by Canada on the one hand and the Provinces on the other; provides that the Federal Parliament and the provincial legislatures will be asked to implement an administrative and management regime by joint legislative action; provides for the joint constitution of a Maritime Offshore Resources Board to issue rights in respect of off-shore mineral resources . . . and evidences the agreement of the parties that direct revenues . . . will be shared on the basis of 25 per cent to Canada and 75 per cent to the adjacent province, subject to a regional revenue sharing pool."

47 Charney, *supra* note 21 at 329. Conclusion of the agreements was contrary to the "expansionistic" aims of Quebec during the preceding decade. It is likely

sea" postulated by Professor La Forest in 1964 had been effectively nullified.

Provincial attempts to delimit and control the resources of the Gulf of St. Lawrence were dealt a definitive blow by the Supreme Court of Canada in its trilogy of provincial maritime claims decisions.[48] First, the 1967 decision of the Court in *Re Offshore Mineral Rights of B.C.* found that, absent a constitutional provision or the possession of a territorial sea by a province prior to its entry into Confederation, the maritime extent of a Canadian province ended at the low water mark.[49]

> [W]e are of the opinion that the territorial sea lay outside the limits of the Colony of British Columbia in 1871 and did not become part of British Columbia following union with Canada. We are also of the opinion that British Columbia did not acquire jurisdiction over the territorial sea following union with Canada.[50]

The Court added:

> Canada now has full constitutional capacity to acquire new areas of territory and new jurisdictional rights which may be available under international law. The territorial sea now claimed by Canada was defined in the *Territorial Sea and Fishing Zones Act* jurisdiction of 1964 . . . The effect of that Act, coupled with the Geneva Convention [on the Continental Shelf] of 1958, is that Canada is recognized in international law as

---

that they were part of a larger effort to clarify and even limit the seaward boundaries of the provinces. Charney adds at 329: "I understand that Quebec along with Manitoba and Ontario have submitted several proposals to the federal government seeking a political decision to extend their northern boundaries to the middle of James and Hudson Bays."

48 *Reference Re Off-Shore Mineral Rights of B.C.*, [1967] S.C.R 792, *(sub nom. Reference Re Ownership of Off-Shore Mineral Rights)* (1968), 65 D.L.R. (2d) 353 [hereinafter *Re Offshore Mineral Rights of B.C.* cited to S.C.R.]; *Reference Re the Seabed and Subsoil of the Continental Shelf Offshore Newfoundland*, [1984] 1 S.C.R. 86, 5 D.L.R. (4th) 385 [hereinafter *Newfoundland Reference* cited to D.L.R.]; *Reference Re Ownership of the Bed of the Strait of Georgia and Related Areas*, [1984] 1 S.C.R. 388 (*sub nom. A.G. Can.* v. *A.G. B.C. et al.*), [1984] 4 W.W.R. 289 [hereinafter *Georgia Strait Reference* cited to S.C.R.].

49 This is referred to as the doctrine in *R.* v. *Keyn* (1876), 2 Ex. D. 63 (hereinafter *Franconia* case). The court held that the territory of the realm, absent express extension, terminated at the low water mark about the United Kingdom's shores. The refusal of the court to find British sovereignty over a three mile coastal sea resulted in the enactment of the Territorial Waters Jurisdiction Act, 1878, *supra* note 26.

50 *Re Offshore Mineral Rights of BC*, *supra* note 48 at 814.

having sovereignty over a territorial sea three nautical miles wide. It is part of the territory of Canada.[51]

The Court continued:

The sovereign state which has property in the bed of the territorial sea adjacent to British Columbia is Canada. At no time has British Columbia, either as a colony or a province, had property in these lands . . . British Columbia has no legislative jurisdiction since the lands in question are outside its boundaries.[52]

It should be noted that this reasoning concerned the asserted claim of British Columbia to the seabed in the Pacific Ocean off its west coast. Fifteen years later, the Court would consider the question of maritime jurisdiction between Vancouver Island and the province's mainland.

The limits upon provincial maritime jurisdiction were confirmed by the Court in its 1984 *Newfoundland Reference* decision. The Supreme Court was asked to determine whether Canada or Newfoundland had the right to explore the resources of the Hibernia oilfield, about 170 nautical miles east of St. John's, and which government had legislative jurisdiction over the continental shelf off Newfoundland.[53] Despite the persuasive arguments of Newfoundland that it had possessed these rights over the continental shelf upon entering Confederation in 1949, the Court found that such sovereignty, being extra-territorial, was vested in Canada.[54] This was based on claims to the continental shelf having been made solely in the international sphere consistent with the 1958 Continental Shelf Convention.[55] The Court further applied the peace,

51 In 1970, Canada extended its territorial sea to 12 nautical miles. See An Act to Amend the Territorial Sea and Fishing Zones Act, R.S.C. 1970, c. 45, s. 3 and Territorial Sea and Fishing Zones Act, R.S.C. 1985, c. T-8. See now the Oceans Act, S.C. 1996, c. 31.

52 *Re Offshore Mineral Rights of B.C., supra* note 48 at 816-17.

53 *Newfoundland Reference, supra* note 48 at 390.

54 Ross Hornby notes that Newfoundland was "the province with perhaps the strongest claim to jurisdiction over the offshore": R. Hornby, "The Canadian Laws Offshore Application Act: The Legislative Incorporation of Rights over the Continental Shelf" (1991) Canadian Yearbook of International Law 55 at 356.

The Newfoundland Court of Appeal determined earlier that Newfoundland had continuing jurisdiction over a territorial sea and continental shelf: *Reference Re Mineral and Other Natural Resources of the Continental Shelf* (1983), 145 D.L.R. (3d) 9 (Nfld. C.A.). The claim to a territorial sea was not raised on subsequent appeal to the Supreme Court of Canada.

55 Geneva Convention on the Continental Shelf, Apr. 29, 1958, 499 UNTS 311, ND 1 at 101 (CIF, June 10, 1964).

order, and good government provision of section 91 of the British North America Act, 1867, in confirming the federal government's legislative jurisdiction over the continental shelf.[56]

The third judgment of Canada's Supreme Court, the *Georgia Strait Reference*, added further detail with certain principles relevant to Québec's possible maritime claims. On appeal from the British Columbia Court of Appeal, which had found in favour of British Columbia, the following question was asked of the Supreme Court:

> Whether the lands, including mineral and other natural resources of the seabed and subsoil covered by the waters between mainland British Columbia and Vancouver Island are the property of Canada or of British Columbia?[57]

The Court held that, although the presumption that a Crown colony's territory terminates at the low water mark would normally prevail, British Columbia had entered Confederation possessed with the seabed of internal straits contiguous with its mainland. This seemingly inconsistent result stemmed from the 1846 boundary division between the colonies of British Columbia and Vancouver Island and the United States in the Straits of Juan de Fuca, Georgia, and Haro, in which "Britain asserted ownership over 'all the territories' up to the mid-channel mark of the straits."[58]

The Court's reasoning in the *Georgia Strait Reference* has been reconciled with the *Newfoundland Reference* by one scholar as follows:

56 Constitution Act, 1982 being Schedule B to the Canada Act (U.K.), 1982, c. 11. Scholarly comment on the decision in *Newfoundland Reference, supra* note 48, supports the reasoning of the Court. "This characterization is surely correct. The right to explore and exploit the natural resources of the continental shelf is in substance a right to exercise a limited sovereignty over a new territory. As such it is a form of annexation, one of the classic incidents of external sovereignty": R. E. Sullivan, "Interpreting the Territorial Limitations on the Provinces" (1985) 7 Supreme Court L. Rev. 511 at 523. See also W. D. Moull, "Newfoundland Resources: The Supreme Court Strikes Again" (1985) 7 Supreme Court L. Rev. 419.

57 *Georgia Strait Reference, supra* note 48 at 391. This area includes the Strait of Juan de Fuca, Haro Strait, Georgia Strait, and Johnstone Strait. See Canadian Hydrographic Service Charts 3000 and 3001. In a similar Australian context, see *New South Wales* v. *The Commonwealth (Australian Seas and Submerged Lands Case)* (1975), 50 A.L.J.R. 218, 135 C.L.R. 337 (Aust. H.C.).

58 In *Georgia Strait Reference, ibid.* at 451, Wilson J. argued in dissent that the 1846 Oregon boundary treaty did not define seabed sovereignty to justify a departure from the common law presumption that a colony's territory is limited to the low water mark at its coast, as the Court held earlier in *Re Offshore Mineral Rights of B.C., supra* note 48.

So it seems that British Columbia *had* pre-existing rights in these areas to bring into Confederation — unlike Newfoundland with respect to the continental shelf, and in contrast to British Columbia's own position regarding the area underlying the Pacific Ocean to the west of Vancouver Island — because the requisite step of an express claim had been taken on its behalf. To some it may seem rather odd that important federal-provincial issues are settled by the Court today on the basis of the words used by an eighteenth-century explorer to describe what he was claiming for his King. Still, the principles applied by the Court in the *Strait of Georgia Reference* seem consistent with those expressed in the *Newfoundland Offshore Reference* and thus cast no shadow on its persuasiveness.[59]

For Québec, these decisions confirm the present limit of its territorial extent to the low water mark about the shores of the Gulf of St. Lawrence and the maritime boundary of Québec at Confederation, except in the St. Lawrence River estuary proper and in the Bay of Chaleur. Even the seabed under the shallow waters about the Magdalen Islands is thus vested in the federal Crown.[60] No historical claim has been, or seemingly can be, advanced to the contrary.[61] In any event, the maritime aspirations of all provinces have been effectively eliminated by the comprehensive federal jurisdictional regime in the Oceans Act, which provides by its preamble that "Parliament wishes to affirm in Canadian domestic law Canada's sovereign rights, jurisdiction, and responsibilities in the exclusive economic zone of Canada."[62]

59 See Moull, *supra* note 56 at 428. See also P. Finkle and A. Lucas, "The Concept of the British Columbia Inland Marine Zone" (1990) 24 U.B.C. L. Rev. 37 at 52: "The fact that the Supreme Court of Canada did not go further to clearly establish the right to an inland marine zone for all coastal provinces regardless of their historic circumstances raises the prospect of further litigation to defend such claims. This is unfortunate because the concept [of a provincial maritime area], if it had been fully vindicated, would have been a convenient means to place the provinces on an equal footing with regard to their maritime claims without legislation."

60 See Charney, *supra* note 2 at 401-25 for a description of Québec's present boundaries in James Bay, Hudson Bay, and the Hudson Strait.

61 An independent Québec might argue that, before the 1713 Treaty of Utrecht and the 1763 Royal Proclamation, New France had been seized solely of the waters in the Gulf of St. Lawrence and that a measure of historic title thus remains. Such reasoning would be tenuous, since the right, if it ever existed (and it did not in respect of submarine resources), would have been extinguished by passage of time.

62 S.C. 1996, c. 31 (CIF, Jan. 31, 1997). The Act repeals the Canadian Laws Offshore Application Act and the Territorial Sea and Fishing Zones Act. The Territorial Sea and Fishing Zones Regulations continue to apply.

THE EFFECT OF RESOURCE REVENUE SHARING AGREEMENTS

The legislation and judicial authorities curtailing provincial maritime jurisdiction have yielded partly to the *realpolitik* of resource exploitation and federal-provincial relations. A regime for development of the continental shelf off Nova Scotia and Newfoundland is now in place, founded upon the 1977 offshore administration agreement between Ottawa and three Maritime provinces.[63] Resource exploration of Nova Scotia's continental shelf is provided for in the Canada-Nova Scotia Offshore Petroleum Resources Accord Implementation Act[64] and the Canada-Nova Scotia Offshore Petroleum Resources Accord Implementation Act.[65] The federal government and Newfoundland will share resources from the Hibernia and other oil fields, and otherwise from the continental shelf as defined in the Canada-Newfoundland Atlantic Accord Implementation Act[66] and the Canada-Newfoundland Accord Implementation Act.[67] The effect of these two legislated resource and revenue allocation schemes upon Québec's possible maritime interests suggests a basic requirement for equitable intergovernmental management and the sharing of resource revenues.

Whether the resolution of the continental shelf claims of two maritime provinces further confirms the 1964 division of the Gulf of St. Lawrence is open to question. Even without legislation enabling provincial sovereignty over offshore areas, the 1964 Interprovincial Boundary Agreement seems to have been largely adopted in the above legislation for the provinces concerned. Although no similar legislation has put it on a similar footing, Québec has not been reticent concerning its maritime claims and has "consistently pursued [them] by citing the 1964 Agreement and depicting [its]

63 See *supra* note 45 and accompanying text. See especially T. L. McDorman, "Canadian Offshore Oil and Gas: Jurisdiction and Management Issues in the 1980s and Beyond," in D. McRae and G. Munro, eds., *Canadian Oceans Policy: National Strategies and The New Law of The Sea* 39 (Vancouver: UBC Press, 1989).

64 S.N.S. 1986, c. 37.

65 S.C. 1988, c. 28. Preceding these legislative arrangements was an agreement in 1982 between the federal government and the government of Nova Scotia for oil and gas resource management and revenue sharing. Jonathan Charney notes that the agreement used, in part, a map delimiting the Gulf of St. Lawrence that is markedly similar to the one agreed upon in 1964. See Charney, *supra* note 2 at 398. The Act provides specifically for continental shelf delimitation between Nova Scotia and other provinces.

66 S.N. 1986, c. 37.

67 S.C. 1987, c. 3. See also the Hibernia Development Act, S.C. 1990, c. 41.

boundary line on official maps of Québec."[68] The lack of progress over administrative boundaries within the Gulf of St. Lawrence might be attributable to the limited extent of hydrocarbon exploration in that area. The practical, if effectively limited, application of the 1964 division between Canada and two other provinces might be relied upon to provide an independent Québec with further arguments for equidistant delimitation of the Gulf of St. Lawrence.

If intergovernmental harmony over resource exploitation has advanced Québec's potential claim to division of the Gulf of St. Lawrence, then the clarifying of Canadian federal jurisdiction over the offshore has likely restricted it. The 1990 Canadian Laws Offshore Application Act[69] resulted in:

> [A] general framework for the application of all laws to the [continental] shelf . . . particularly in relation to the extraterritorial application of the Criminal Code. With its entry into force, the whole body of federal legislation applie[d] to the internal waters, territorial sea and to "marine installations or structures" that are "attached" to the continental shelf. In addition, the Governor in Council [was] authorized to apply federal laws in or above the shelf, or to any part of it, by regulations . . . The impetus for the new legislation, apart from the increased jurisdiction accorded to coastal states by international law, was the positive result from the federal perspective of the 1984 [Newfoundland Reference Case].[70]

The Canadian Laws Offshore Application Act has been superseded by the Oceans Act[71] with certain substantive provisions unaltered. The former Act had three ostensible objectives.[72] First, an application of federal laws to "marine installations" was intended to regulate oil platforms and drilling operations over the continental shelf.[73] This was consistent with similar offshore legislation in the United States and the United Kingdom.[74] Second, the inconsistent reach of Canadian law into historic waters, exemplified by the prosecution of criminal cases originating in the Gulf of St.

68 Charney, *supra* note 2 at 398. See also Figure 2.

69 S.C. 1990, c. 44 (CIF, Feb. 4, 1991. Section 7 was to CIF by order of Governor-in-Council).

70 R. Hornby, *supra* note 54 at 355-56.

71 *Supra* note 62.

72 Section 3 of the Act, *supra* note 69, also codified the judgment of the Supreme Court of Canada in *Re Offshore Mineral Rights of B.C.* and *Newfoundland Reference, supra* note 48.

73 See now s. 20 of the Oceans Act, *supra* note 62.

74 See 43 U.S.C., ss. 1331-34 (1953) and Continental Shelf Act, 1964 (U.K.), c. 29.

Lawrence, was now rendered certain through a mechanism for ministerial declaration of such waters being unreservedly Canadian.[75] Finally, the Act provided for the application of provincial law in offshore areas, enabling fuller legislation in respect of "property and civil rights" during continental shelf exploration and exploitation.[76]

Importantly for Québec, because the Oceans Act[77] provides for dual jurisdiction of the law in offshore areas, the provision in the Act for delimitation of the areas in which the legal regimes of the provinces will apply supports the claim that Québec might make in the Gulf of St. Lawrence. It should be noted that no regulations defining the areas of application of provincial law have yet been formulated, consistent with section 7 of the Canadian Laws Offshore Application Act, which was itself never brought into force. Presumably the recent commencement of operations at the Hibernia drilling site will lead to such regulations, which are expected to be based on the delimitation principles expressed in the earlier legislation:

> The means to establish the extent of the offshore area adjacent to any particular province is set out in section 2 of the [Canadian Laws Offshore Application] Act. Basically, the offshore area is a zone determined in accordance with the equidistance method, that is, in the terms of the legislation, "any area of the sea that *is not within any province* that is . . . nearer to the coast of the province than to the coast of any other province" [emphasis in original].[78]

75 See s. 5 of the Oceans Act, *supra* note 62, which provides for baselines encompassing historic waters including, impliedly, those of the Gulf of St. Lawrence. The Act also permits the Minister of Foreign Affairs to issue a certificate as conclusive evidence that historic waters are internal to Canada. The first such certificate, issued in 1991 under the former Canadian Laws Offshore Application Act, stated that the waters of the Gulf of St. Lawrence were internal waters. See especially Hornby, *supra* note 54 at 360. Professor Morrissette reviews the previous uncertain application of Canadian law within the Gulf of St. Lawrence in "La statut du golfe du Saint-Laurent en droit international et en droit interne" (1985) 16 R.G.D. 273. See also *R.* c. *Paul Frank Watson*, Cour de la sessions de la paix, Province de Québec, District de Gaspé, n° 110-01-000306-83.

76 See Oceans Act, *supra* note 62, s. 9. This section is in effect with the arrival of the Hibernia platform at its ocean drilling site in June 1997. In addition to the Hibernia Project, two other oilfields are under study off Newfoundland: B. Jang, "Oil Projects Put Spotlight on Newfoundland," *Globe and Mail* (Dec. 27, 1996) B1.

77 *Supra* note 62.

78 Hornby, *supra* note 54 at 368.

However, the application of equidistance was to be varied by the governor-in-council[79] "to permit recourse to some other method of delimitation, such as an enclave, parallels and meridians and so on, where the coastal geography is such that an application of the equidistance method would produce an unusually shaped or unworkable offshore area."[80] For greater certainty, section 9(5) of the Oceans Act now limits potential claims by provinces to offshore areas, notwithstanding the application of their laws within such defined areas.[81]

The legal and political effect of the 1964 Interprovincial Boundary Agreement has been muted by the Supreme Court's reference decisions and by increasingly exclusory federal legislation. However, the principles underlying the agreement — an equidistant division of the Gulf and the practical management and sharing of resources — survive and are respected between provinces with active offshore development and a jurisdiction-sensitive federal government. The result is one further presumption in favour of the independent Québec in its case for maritime sovereignty and points to an initial application of equidistance in the delimitation of its jurisdiction within the Gulf.

CONCLUSION

As a province of Canada, Québec's maritime extent in the Gulf of St. Lawrence is limited to the low water mark about its shores and those of the Magdalen Islands in the Gulf, save for the historical anomaly of vaguely defined "provincial waters" in the northern half of the Bay of Chaleur and the inland waters of the St. Lawrence River estuary proper. Neither federal-provincial agreement nor judicial authority allows for any seaward expansion of the maritime areas that Québec has always possessed. Indeed, the tide of domestic Canadian

79 Pursuant to s. 2(2)(c) of the Act, *supra* note 69.

80 Hornby, *supra* note 54 at 368. Further, at 369: "The Act provides no guidance to the Governor in Council on when to exercise this power to abandon equidistance. One plausible situation would be where the equidistance method would produce inequitable results in a delimitation between sovereign states effected in accordance with principles of international law."

By way of comparison, international legal principles in the setting of a domestic boundary were applied by the United States Supreme Court in *Texas* v. *Louisiana*, 426 U.S. 465 (1976).

81 *Supra* note 62. "[T]his section shall not be interpreted as providing a basis for any claim, by or on behalf of a province, in respect of any interest in or legislative jurisdiction over any area of the sea": see also s. 9(2).

maritime law has run contrary to Québec's aspirations, with increasing curtailment of any possible provincial expansion since the Second World War. Notwithstanding Québec's continued pressure since 1964 for a divided share of resources within the Gulf (and other maritime areas), its claims have been remarkably muted during successive sovereignty debates. How, then, might principles of international law and recognized methods of maritime boundary delimitation come to its aid in the event of independence?

Québec's Claims in the Gulf of St. Lawrence at the Time of Independence

At the moment of its purported independence, whether by dissolution of the Canadian federal state or through unilateral declaration, Québec can be expected to define its territory and to attempt to exercise some measure of sovereignty over it. The extent to which maritime claims might be pursued will depend upon several factors, including a threshold international recognition of the new state, its possession of a relevant coastal area, and, principally, a realization of the classic incidents of statehood.[82]

To begin with Québec's capacity to claim maritime sovereignty, the judgment of the International Court of Justice in the *North Sea Continental Shelf* cases favoured the automatic attachment of rights to an independent state: "The land is the legal source of the power which a State may exercise over territorial extension to seaward."[83] In response to this, and within the context of a unilateral declaration of independence (UDI), however, an expected argument by the federal government could be that the province did not have legal competency to determine its boundaries and that the *status quo ante* must prevail. This would, in effect, freeze the present

[82] The condition precedent to the exercise of maritime sovereignty is statehood, the classic incidents of which are a permanent population, defined territorial expanse, an existing government, and a capacity to enter into relations with other states. These principles are embodied in the Montevideo Convention of 1933, Art. 1, 165 LNTS 19. See also J. Crawford, *The Creation of States in International Law* 36 ff (Oxford: Clarendon Press, 1979) and J. Dugard, *Recognition and the United Nations* 127 (Cambridge: Grotius Publications, 1987).

The criterion of "effective independence" from a central government should also be added, otherwise all Canadian provinces might be recognizable as sovereign states under customary international law: Crawford, *ibid.*, 232.

[83] *North Sea Continental Shelf (Federal Republic of Germany/Denmark and Federal Republic of Germany/Netherlands)* [1969] ICJ Rep. 3; 41 ILR 29 [hereinafter *North Sea Continental Shelf* cases cited to ICJ Rep.].

boundaries until legal resolution of the UDI is accomplished. As to the contrary argument, it must be recognized that even Canadian domestic law recognizes an inherent right of the littoral or riparian property owner to access to the sea.

For Québec to acquiesce to its present territorial *status quo* would be contrary to the general expectations of any new state seeking legitimacy through sovereign aspirations and recognition of territorial claims. In reviewing an independent Québec's prospective territorial status, one *indépendantiste* legal scholar has asserted:

> [It is essential that the question of Quebec's frontiers be resolved prior to independence . . .] It would be otherwise absurd and unacceptable that the territory of a sovereign Quebec would be restricted by Canadian territorial waters, *a fortiori* as international law would recognize sovereign rights over *her* territorial sea but also the exploitation of natural resources of *her* portion of the continental shelf . . . The delimitation lines between coastal provinces in Hudson Bay and the Gulf of St. Lawrence, established for 12 years, will certainly serve as the bases of discussion [translation, emphasis in original].[84]

Québec will not immediately be able to assert maritime sovereignty, at least within the Gulf of St. Lawrence, at the instant of any unilateral declaration of independence.[85] The principles of international law are sufficiently clear to deny Québec an initial maritime claim should a UDI occur. One current argument by Québec, that the doctrine of *uti posseditis* renders its territory indivisible or "frozen" as of the moment of independence, also preserves the present restrictive maritime *status quo.* Jonathon Charney writes:

84 Brossard, *supra* note 2. Interestingly, Brossard notes, at 503, that Québec might also seek an adjustment of the Gulf's 1964 interprovincial marine boundary ("ligne de partage"), stating that certain commentators "have judged that it favours . . . New Brunswick and Prince Edward Island to the detriment of Quebec" [translation].

85 The debate over the territory with which Québec would remain seized upon independence focused first upon Aboriginal lands in the northern reaches of the province. The debate has shifted recently to partition of areas within the province that might choose to remain with Canada. Should there be any consideration of partition of the littoral areas around the Gulf, possibly allowing more of its maritime area proper to remain within Canada, it should be noted that the electoral areas of Québec around the Gulf of St. Lawrence indicated a strong desire for secession in the October 1995 sovereignty referendum. See H. Winsor, "Poll Results Challenge Old Notions," *Globe and Mail* (Nov. 1, 1995) A5. If only from a spatial perspective, it would benefit the federal government if the Magdalen Islands could be partitioned from an independent Québec.

[U]nlike the case of the Soviet Union, secession of Quebec may not be tied to the disintegration of the entire Canadian Confederation. Canada would probably continue to exist as a state and retain much of its land and maritime jurisdiction. *A seceding province may have no right to areas held by the Canadian government because the nation will endure and benefit from those areas. The Canadian government could also argue that the acquisition of maritime zones has been the result of Canadian federal efforts and that equity requires the fruits of those efforts to remain with Canada.* The conclusion that the waters in question are internal waters under international law and not territorial sea, exclusive economic zone, or the like further supports this view. Internal waters are the subject of complete state sovereignty . . . *Absent an agreement, Quebec would have no legal right under Canadian or international law to a transfer of Canadian waters or land territory outside the defined boundaries of Quebec. At present, those boundaries do not expressly include the areas in question in Quebec* [emphasis added].[86]

Integral to any consideration of secession or UDI is whether Québec could later achieve "effective independence."[87] Such an outcome would rest upon international recognition, "formal independence," internal sovereignty, and, importantly in the Canadian context, the absence of central government authority and control. At present, none of these criteria are certain for Québec, particularly if it chooses to seek independence by a unilateral declaration of independence.[88]

Assuming that Québec can attain such effective independence, as the term is recognized in international law, a normal set of maritime zones can then be expected to attach to it:

86 Charney, *supra* note 2 at 355-66. This reasoning heightens the requirement for a pre-independence negotiation of boundaries, as noted by Brossard, *supra* note 2. Professor Charney concludes that "the doctrine [of *uti possedit*is] might deny the new state the full complement of maritime zones." Enhancing Canada's claim to all waters of the Gulf of St. Lawrence is the *de facto* shift of its internal waters boundary line from the mouth of the St. Lawrence River to the Gulf closing line across the Cabot Strait. See Figure 2 and Canadian Hydrographic Services Charts LC 4001 and 4002.

While a different legal and geographical context, it should be noted that the People's Republic of China continues to claim sovereignty over maritime areas adjacent to the Island of Taiwan. See "Declaration of the Government of the People's Republic of China on China's Territorial Sea 4 September 1958" in The Law of the Sea, *supra* note 9 at 104.

87 Crawford, *supra* note 82 at 48. Further, "A new State formed by secession from a metropolitan State will have to demonstrate substantial independence, both formal and real, before it will be regarded as definitively created": *ibid.*, 52-53.

88 See generally *ibid.*, 48-76 for a discussion of the requisites of independent statehood.

International law provides that, where an entity qualifies as a State, certain rules *prima facie* enure to its benefit: it is entitled to the control and governing of its territory (subject to boundary disputes and the like).[89]

The creation of a truly independent state normally brings recognition by the international community of its minimum entitlement to a territorial sea, thus allowing consideration of competing claims. In this respect, the recent declarations and international acceptance of territorial seas for Lithuania, Latvia, and Estonia confirmed customary international law.[90] Further, the judgment of the International Court of Justice in the *Greenland-Jan Mayen* case implies that the newest of maritime rights — the 200 nautical mile exclusive economic zone — automatically inheres in the coastal state.[91] The acceptance of an independent Québec's maritime claims will

89 *Ibid.*, 397. This view is supported by Jonathan Charney in the situation of Québec, *supra* note 2 at 426: "The law of the sea reflects a strong policy in favour of the right of coastal states to the normal complement of maritime zones, subject to appropriate boundaries."

90 See, e.g., J. L. Canfield, "The Independent Baltic States: Maritime Law and Resource Management Issues" (1993) 24 Ocean Dev. & Int'l L. 291. Churchill and Lowe, *supra* note 7 at 68, note the operation of customary international law in providing at least a territorial sea to a coastal state: "The notion of a territorial sea automatically appurtenant to coastal States, which has been expressed by the Permanent Court of Arbitration in the *Grisbadarna* case as early as 1909, is also implicit in both the 1958 Territorial Sea Convention . . . and the Law of the Sea Convention . . . It follows, therefore, that international law should lay down a *minimum* breadth for the territorial sea . . . The time may come, however, when customary international law moves beyond the Law of the Sea Convention and regards twelve miles not merely as the maximum, but as the minimum, mandatory limit for the territorial sea" [emphasis in original].

91 *Supra* note 6 at 57 (para. 43). "[T]he two lines [delimiting the EEZ and the continental shelf, respectively], even if coincident in location, stem from different strands of the applicable law, the location of the one being derived from the 1958 Convention, and the location of the other being derived from customary law."

The customary nature of continental shelf and EEZ rights was affirmed by the Court of Arbitration in the *St. Pierre and Miquelon* case, infra note 129. See Figure 2. See also S. C. Vasciannie, *Land-Locked and Geographically Disadvantaged States in the International Law of the Sea* 68 (Oxford: Clarendon Press, 1990): "Even on the basis of a very cursory review, it can be established that the EEZ concept is now firmly enshrined in customary international law . . . coastal State proclamations in favour of the EEZ and similar zones have grown to the point where States without exclusive jurisdiction and sovereign rights over maritime fisheries beyond the twelve-mile territorial sea find themselves in a highly exceptional situation" [citation omitted].

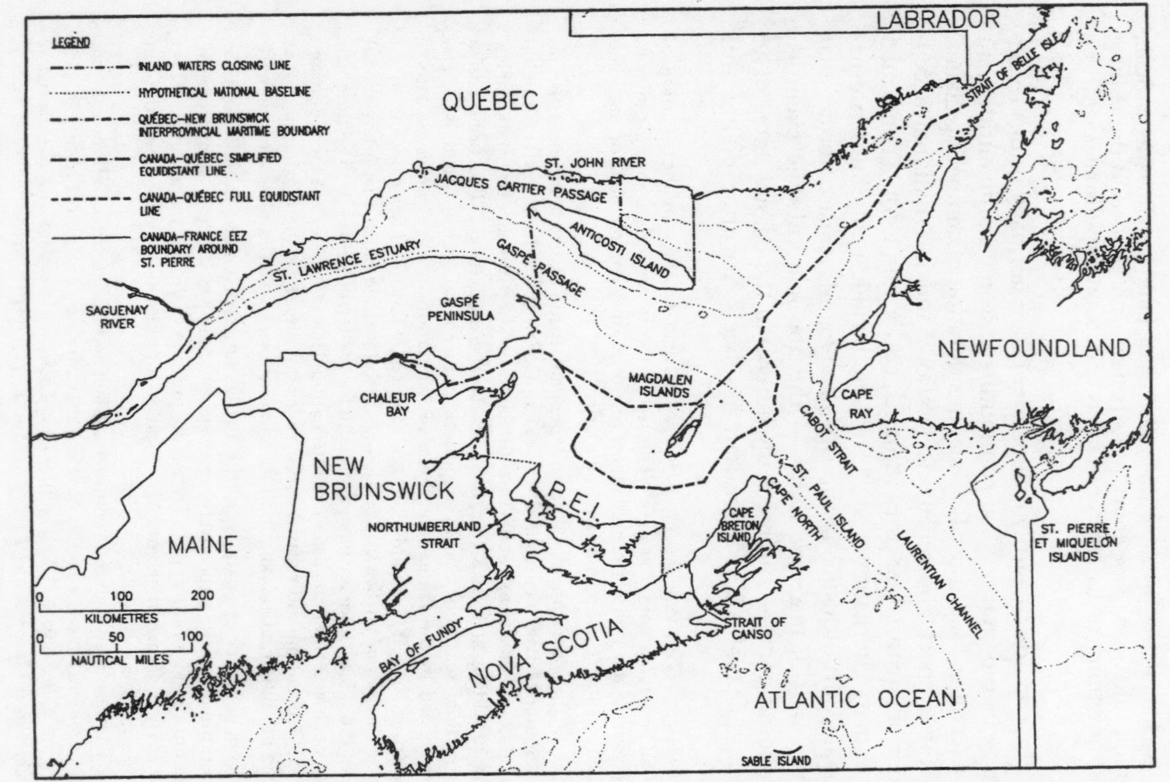

Figure 2 Equidistant boundaries, closing lines, and hypothetical baselines in the Gulf of St. Lawrence.

depend on its viability and, to a limited extent, on its international recognition as a nation-state. If and when Québec achieves such independence, it might look to the United Nations Convention on the Law of the Sea (UNCLOS) to define its maritime sovereignty.[92]

UNCLOS is not yet binding upon Canada nor a putatively independent Québec.[93] However, custom dictates that states signatory to multilateral treaties should not act contrary to their expressed intent. This is reinforced by the Vienna Convention on the Law of Treaties to which Canada is a party.[94] Article 18 of the Convention obliges Canada "not to defeat the object and purpose of a treaty not yet in force."[95] Whether an independent Québec would assume Canada's inchoate obligations to respect UNCLOS is open to conjecture. A newly independent country, in contrast to a successor state, would not likely acquire the treaty obligations of its parent state. However, when a state "has in fact had a part in the formation of its predecessor's commitments there is a substantial continuity and commitments are transmitted to the successor State as far as compatible with their character."[96] The Vienna Convention on the

92 *Supra* note 10.

93 Canada was an initial proponent of UNCLOS and is a state signatory. Alan MacEachern, Canada's minister for external affairs at the time, stated to the 11th session of the Third United Nations Conference of the Law of the Sea on Dec. 6, 1982: "The Convention sets out a broad range of new rights and responsibilities. If States arbitrarily select those they will recognize or deny, we will not only see the end of our dreams of a universal comprehensive convention on the law of the sea but perhaps the end of any prospect for global co-operation on issues that touch the lives of all mankind . . . The United Nations Convention on the Law of the Sea, and that alone, provides a firm basis for the peaceful conduct of ocean affairs for the years to come": Third United Nations Conference on the Law of the Sea Official Records: Vol. XVII (New York: UN, 1984) at 16 (para. 74).

94 Vienna Convention on the Law of Treaties, May 23, 1969, (1980) UKTS 58, reprinted in P. Reuter, *Introduction to the Law of Treaties* (London: Pinter Publishers, 1989).

95 Art. 18, *ibid.* at 169 further requires that "a state is obliged to refrain from acts which would defeat the object and purpose of a treaty when:

(a) it has signed the treaty . . . subject to ratification, acceptance or approval, until it shall have made its intention clear not to become a party to the treaty; or

(b) it has expressed its consent to be bound by the treaty, pending the entry into force of the treatyand provided that such entry into force is not unduly delayed."

96 Reuter, *supra* note 94 at 87 (para. 173).

Succession of States in Respect of Treaties[97] attempts to clarify successor state obligations:

> [T]he 1978 Convention provides for either the non-transmission of treaty obligations (clean slate) or for their transmission (continuity of undertakings) to the successor State. The clean slate solution applies to newly independent States, whereas continuity applies to the unification or separation of States (irrespective of whether or not the State which has undergone the separation remains in existence).[98]

The uncertainty of an independent Québec's *obligation* to adhere to UNCLOS must be contrasted with the obvious advantage of its insistence on the recognition of the maritime rights and areas defined in the Convention. Indeed, it would be to Québec's advantage to have Canada ratify the Convention. For example, Article 3 of UNCLOS explicitly permits an independent Québec to possess at least a littoral band of territorial sea: "Every State has the right to establish the breadth of its territorial sea up to a limit not exceeding 12 nautical miles."[99] This is reinforced by Article 15, which obliges states with opposite or adjacent coasts, failing agreement to the contrary, to extend territorial waters to the median line between them.[100]

The truly independent Québec can be expected to seek and exercise its sovereignty over more expansive maritime zones than simply a territorial sea. This would be the basis for expansive claims, and possibly conflict with Canada, in the Gulf of St. Lawrence. For example, Article 33 of UNCLOS allows a state to exercise its surveillance jurisdiction in a contiguous zone extending from twelve to twenty-four nautical miles offshore.

Of greater importance from the perspectives of economic expectation, spatial control, and national prestige, Article 74(1) of UNCLOS provides for recognition of the maritime state's exclusive economic zone (EEZ):

> The delimitation of the exclusive economic zone between States with opposite or adjacent coasts shall be effected by agreement on the basis of international law, as referred to in Article 38 of the Statute of the

97 Aug. 23, 1978.

98 Reuter, *supra* note 94 at 87 (para. 172).

99 UNCLOS, *supra* note 10. See also Art. 5 "Normal baseline" and Art. 7 "Straight baselines."

100 Art. 15 further reads: "[This] provision does not apply, however, where it is necessary by reason of historic title or other special circumstances to delimit the territorial seas of the two States in a way which is at variance therewith."

International Court of Justice, in order to achieve an equitable solution.[101]

The equivalent right of a claim to sovereignty over the continental shelf would be available to an independent Québec under UNCLOS and through the operation of customary international law, although the incidents of such national jurisdiction would be likely indistinguishable from those exercised over an EEZ as a result of the trend towards single maritime boundaries.[102] National claims to continental shelves are historically more pronounced than those advanced for EEZ regimes, although this pattern of state practice is evolving. The provisions of UNCLOS, especially Article 77(1), effectively codify the entitlement provided by customary international law.[103] In this context, it should be noted that Canada is a party to the 1958 Geneva Convention on the Continental Shelf, and thus recognizes the rights of coastal states to sovereignty over their adjacent continental shelves.[104]

It can be concluded that an independent Québec would possess a valid claim to the normal complement of maritime zones as is

101 See also UNCLOS Arts. 55 and 56. Canada now claims an EEZ in place of an "Exclusive Fishery Zone." See Oceans Act, *supra* note 62, s. 13.

102 See especially *Greenland-Jan Mayen* case, supra note 6 at 79 (para. 90): "In the view of the Court, the delimitation now to be described, whereby the position of the delimitation lines for the two categories of marine spaces is identical, constitutes, in the circumstances of this case, a proper application both of the law applicable to the continental shelf and of that applicable to the fishery zones." In a separate concurring opinion, Judge Oda, vice president of the Court, expressed concern over delimiting two separate maritime areas into a single boundary: "One cannot presuppose a single delimitation line for two separate and independent régimes, the exclusive economic zone and the continental shelf, although the possibility of an eventual coincidence of the two lines may not be excluded": *ibid.*, 109 (para. 70).

103 *Supra* note 10. Further, Article 77(2) and (3) provides that such rights are "exclusive" and that they "do not depend on occupation, effective or notional, or on any express proclamation." As well, Art. 83(1) requires delimitation of the continental shelf in accordance with equitable principles.

The Court in the *North Sea Continental Shelf* cases (1969), ICJ Rep. 3 at 23 held that "[t]he rights of the coastal state in respect of the area of continental shelf that constitutes a natural prolongation of its land territory into and under the sea exist *ipso facto* and *ab initio*, by virtue of its sovereignty over the land, and as an extension of it in an exercise of sovereign rights for the purpose of exploring the seabed and exploiting its natural resources. In short there is here an inherent right."

104 Geneva Convention on the Continental Shelf, *supra* note 55. Canada ratified the Convention on Feb. 6, 1970.

currently sanctioned and recognized by international law. The foundations for such full maritime sovereignty include state practice, the principles of international equity and the UNCLOS regime.[105] However, it is a task less certain to properly define the extent of such maritime areas and to resolve possible conflicts with the competing claims of the Canadian federal state in and around the Gulf of St. Lawrence.

Defining Canada's and Québec's Maritime Claims in the Gulf of St. Lawrence

Introduction

Canada and an independent Québec would face complex issues in their exercise of national sovereignty and the definition of respective maritime claims in and around the Gulf of St. Lawrence.[106] An initial boundary delimitation of the Gulf might *prima facie* be a simple task for an area that is a semi-enclosed body of water with defined coastlines.[107] However, even with such preliminary analysis, further complexities arise. What if an independent Québec, by result of being shelf-locked in the Gulf of St. Lawrence (and in Hudson and Ungava Bays), and thus at a geographic disadvantage, was to demand its "equitable share" of the resources of the *outer* continental shelf?

105 Canada has affirmed UNCLOS's role in international maritime law by declaring in 1994 that it would ratify the Convention. See House of Commons Debates (Mar. 15, 1994) at 2255.

106 L. A. Willis has written that "[t]here are no legally preferred methods" of maritime boundary making: "From Precedent to Precedent: The Triumph of Pragmatism in the Law of Maritime Boundaries" (1986) 24 *Canadian Yearbook of International Law* 1 at 48. It is submitted that more certain principles have emerged in three judgments rendered in 1992-93. Jonathan Charney writes that, as a result of these judgments, "[t]he Court is now in a position to make further contributions that will promote greater consistency and certainty in these matters": "Progress in International Maritime Boundary Delimitation Law" (1994) 88 A.J.I.L. 227 at 256.

The lengthy Canadian Memorials and Counter-Memorials filed before the Arbitration Court in the *Case Concerning the Delimitation of the Maritime Boundary in the Gulf of Maine Area (Canada* v. *United States)*, [1984] ICJ Rep. 246 are typical of the arguments submitted by parties in a maritime boundary adjudication.

107 The Adriatic, Baltic, and Black Seas are examples of semi-enclosed seas that have been delimited by negotiation. Their delimitation is discussed *infra* notes 117-24 and accompanying text.

State and judicial practice regarding ocean boundary-making has defined the elementary criteria that could be applied to boundary delimitation in the Gulf of St. Lawrence.[108] This is a suitable starting point in the analysis of Québec's most basic, proximal, and likely initial claims. International law defines the foundational elements for the process of defining maritime claims and delimiting areas of the sea, and the most persuasive law, of course, is that of the International Court of Justice:

> *De facto*, the International Court, with some assistance from *ad hoc* arbitrations, exercises substantial authority over international maritime boundary law. These tribunals take account of the jurisprudence on the subject and the state practice in agreements settling maritime boundaries. The judgments and awards articulate and shape states' obligations in this regard. Even though there is no doctrine of *stare decisis* in international adjudication, it is not inaccurate to consider the impressive line of maritime boundary decisions as forming a common law in the classic sense [citations omitted].[109]

Nine ocean boundary adjudications are further refined with the addition of numerous bilateral boundary agreements over territorial seas, economic zones, and continental shelves.[110]

Application of the recognized criteria of ocean boundary-making could result in a paradox. The underlying rationale for multilateral agreement over maritime claims — the apportionment of seas in order to establish definitive rights and obligations over them — will be defeated if the states turn to third party resolution. This is because the equitable principles that will be applied through curial or arbitral

108 Paul Bravender-Coyle notes that "there is an emerging general rule for the delimitation of maritime boundaries between littoral states, and that customary international law is slowly evolving towards this formula": "The Emerging Legal Principles and Equitable Criteria Governing the Delimitation of Maritime Boundaries between States" (1988) 19 Ocean Dev. & Int'l L. 171.

The ICJ appears to have considered the unsettled state of *opinio juris* in the *Greenland-Jan Mayen* case, *supra* note 6 at 63 (para. 58): "A court called upon to give a judgment declaratory of the delimitation of a maritime boundary, and *a fortiori* a court called upon to effect a delimitation, will therefore have to determine the relative weight to be accorded to different considerations in each case; to this end, it will consult not only 'the circumstances of the case' but also previous decided cases and the practice of States. In this respect, the Court recalls the need, referred to in the *Libya/Malta Case*, for 'consistency and a degree of predictability'" [parenthetical note omitted].

109 J. I. Charney, "Progress in International Maritime Boundary Delimitation Law." *supra* note 106 at 228.

110 S. P. Jagota summarizes ocean boundary agreements in *Maritime Boundary* 121ff (Dordrecht: Martinus Nijhoff, 1985).

reasoning are anchored largely in considerations of geographic circumstances and often fail to take into account the parties' true interests, such as resource exploitation or national prestige, that most often are the source of maritime boundary disputes.[111]

The nature of the Gulf of St. Lawrence, the vital interests of its littoral provinces, and its important status as the outer basin of the St. Lawrence Seaway suggest the pragmatic result of a negotiated settlement between Canada and an independent Québec. The importance of such co-operation between states bordering upon semi-enclosed seas is emphasized by Article 123 of UNCLOS.[112] One ideal outcome is that a delimitation of the continental shelf and an economic zone within the Gulf would not be sought. Instead, a comprehensive management scheme might be created for the shared use of a joint development zone, with possible provision for the parties to retain marginal territorial seas. Unfortunately, the likelihood of strained post-independence relations between the two states, and Canada's historic inability to settle ocean boundary disputes except by third party adjudication, militate against this result.[113] Nonetheless, joint use and sovereignty

111 Professor Phillip Saunders sums up the problem of a geographically oriented approach to boundary delimitation in writing that "[t]he result . . . is a body of law which is oriented to *spatial* rather than *functional* aspects of delimitation . . . If there is a fundamental lesson for other states in the *Gulf of Maine Case*, it may simply be the unsuitability of litigation for the full resolution of similar disputes": "The Gulf of Maine Boundary Decision: International Adjudication and Regional Marine Management" (1985) 1 Int'l. Insights 1 at 5-6.

112 *Supra* note 10. Art. 122 defines an "enclosed or semi-enclosed sea" to include a gulf "surrounded by two or more States and connected to another sea or the ocean by a narrow outlet or consisting entirely or primarily of the territorial seas and exclusive economic zones of two or more coastal States." Art. 123 provides that "States bordering an enclosed or semi-enclosed sea should co-operate with each other in the exercise of their rights" with particular attention to living resources, marine environmental protection, scientific research, and multilateral relations.

113 "The predominant feature of Canada's bilateral maritime boundary practice has been the failure of negotiations to resolve outstanding disputes and the willingness of Canada to utilize adjudication to draw bilateral maritime boundaries": T. L. McDorman, *Canada's Ocean Limits and Boundaries: An Overview* 24 (Victoria: Univ. of Victoria Faculty of Law, 1995) [unpublished]. See also Alan C. Cairns, *Looking into the Abyss: The Need for a Plan C*, C.D. Howe Institute Commentary 96 at 3 (Toronto: C.D. Howe Institute, 1997): "Federalists may not be able to keep Quebec in Canada; if Quebec goes, Canadians and their governments in the rest of Canada (ROC) may mismanage the terms of secession, making more difficult a subsequent harmonious coexistence with an independent Quebec."

over the Gulf of St. Lawrence is possible and is supported to a limited extent by state practice and international law.[114]

OCEAN BOUNDARIES: STATE PRACTICE AND AGREEMENTS

The precedent derived from bilateral agreements suggests that a single maritime boundary in the Gulf of St. Lawrence would be based initially upon an equidistance line.[115] This method of delimitation formed the basis for the continental shelf agreement between Canada and Denmark (Greenland) in the Davis Strait.[116] Agreements delimiting the economic zones and continental shelves of semi-enclosed seas have also employed equidistance: for example, in the Black Sea between the former USSR and Turkey,[117] and in the Adriatic between Italy and the former Yugoslavia.[118]

114 Specifically by the 1992 judgment of the ICJ in the *Gulf of Fonseca* case, supra note 11.

115 An equidistant boundary is defined as "[a] line composed of relatively short segments connecting points that are equidistant from the normal baselines, or from claimed (or assumed) baselines from which the breadth of the territorial sea is measured. This is sometimes called a median line": J. I. Charney and L. M. Alexander, eds., *International Maritime Boundaries* xix (Dordrecht: Martinus Nijhoff, 1993). Two equidistance lines between Québec and Canada in the Gulf of St. Lawrence are shown in Figure 2. The northern line indicates a simplified equidistance line that discounts fully any effect of the Magdalen Islands. The southern line conforms to the division agreed upon by the Atlantic premiers in 1964, giving full effect to the Magdalen Islands.

116 Agreement between the Government of Canada and the Government of the Kingdom of Denmark Relating to the Delimitation of the Continental Shelf between Greenland and Canada, Dec. 17, 1973, Can. T.S. 1974 No. 9 (CIF, Mar. 13, 1974). Art. I reads: "The dividing line in the area between Greenland and the Canadian Arctic Islands, established for the purpose of each Party's exploration and exploitation of the natural resources of that part of the continental shelf . . . is a median line which has been determined and adjusted by mutual agreement." The delimitation is in accordance with Art. 6 of the Geneva Convention on the Continental Shelf, *supra* note 55.

117 See Protocol between the Government of the Union of Soviet Socialist Republics and the Government of the Republic of Turkey Concerning the Establishment of the Maritime Boundary between Soviet and Turkish Territorial Waters in the Black Sea, Apr. 17, 1973 in The Law of the Sea: *Maritime Boundary Agreements (1970-1984)* 191 (New York: UN Office for Ocean Affairs and the Law of the Sea, 1987).

118 Agreement between Italy and Yugoslavia Concerning the Delimitation of the Continental Shelf between the Two Countries in the Adriatic Sea, Jan. 8, 1968 in *Maritime Boundary Agreements (1970-84)*, *ibid.*, 186. The equidistance line was modified to account for certain islands near the middle of the Adriatic Sea.

However, the lessons of state practice in defining an independent Québec's maritime boundaries must be used with caution. Negotiated maritime boundaries do not always apply referable principles of maritime delimitation. The parties are free to choose among fluid principles and may not necessarily express their bilateral consensus in the boundary instrument:

> [T]he circumstances related to the negotiations of bilateral delimitation agreements rather must be considered as evidence that there is no agreement within the community of states over the principles of maritime delimitation law, which prescribes that the delimitation has to be effected by agreement in accordance with equitable principles taking into account all the relevant circumstances, in order to achieve an equitable result.[119]

As well, the use of an equidistant line has been accepted in instances where bilateral agreement can be readily achieved.[120] Generally only the problematic, complex cases upon which states cannot agree result in adjudication from which the legal principles of maritime delimitation arise.[121] Finally, the distinction in negotiated boundaries between adjacent and opposite coastal profiles of states must be considered:

> The relationship of the coasts of the abutting states may be one of pure lateral adjacency, mixed oppositeness or adjacency, or pure oppositeness in relation to any particular part of the area to be delimited. Thus, the relationship of these coasts to each other *relative to an imaginary or real line drawn through the maritime area* can progress by stages from one of essential oppositeness, through one that combines elements of oppositeness and

---

Islands close to the Dalmatian Coast of Yugoslavia were given full effect in the generation of baselines. With the dissolution of the former Yugoslav Republic, the present status of this agreement is unknown.

119 Elferink, *supra* note 13 at 373.

120 The application of equidistance is synonymous with the drawing of a median line.

121 Jonathan Charney notes that "[j]udgments of the International Court of Justice (ICJ) and awards of ad hoc arbitration panels carry special weight in international maritime boundary law . . . Negotiated settlements, however, should be more influential since, in theory, a principal source of maritime boundary law ought to be customary international law grounded upon state practice as represented by the many various elements. But this practice does not seem to be very instructive and, thus, is less influential than the adjudications": Charney, *supra* note 106 at 227-28.

adjacency in varying degrees, to one of predominant adjacency [footnote omitted, emphasis in original].[122]

Equidistance is a method most appropriately used in the delimitation of maritime claims between states with sea coasts directly facing each other. Its application is illustrated by the *Greenland-Jan Mayen* and *Libya-Malta* cases.[123] Similarly, in the formulation of bilateral agreements, equidistance has been used overwhelmingly to define maritime areas between opposing coastal fronts.[124] As well, this method of boundary-making seems to be best applied in delimitations where the coastal maritime projections are classified as "situations of mixed oppositeness and adjacency."[125] It is where the coastlines of states are adjacent that the method ceases to be reliable and relevant. The reason is simple. Distortions or anomalies in the relevant coastline, generated by the presence of islands that are inevitable in every geographical situation, are frequently magnified by the projection of a line bisecting adjacent sea front projections. A judicial recognition of the need for caution in cases of adjacency is found in the *Tunisia-Libya* case in which the International Court of Justice wrote that the use of equidistance is not "a mandatory legal principle, nor a method having some privileged status in relation to other legal methods."[126] In addition, the line drawn by

122 L. Legault and B. Hankey, "Method, Oppositeness and Adjacency, and Proportionality in Maritime Boundary Delimitation," in J. I. Charney and L. M. Alexander, eds., *International Maritime Boundaries*, *supra* note 115, 203 at 215.

123 *Supra* note 6. The ICJ wrote in the *Greenland-Jan Mayen* case, at 66 (para. 64), that "[*p*]*rima facie*, a median line delimitation between opposite coasts results in general in an equitable solution, particularly if the coasts in question are nearly parallel." This statement follows the reasoning of the Court in the *North Sea Continental Shelf* cases that an equitable solution between opposite coasts can often be achieved by use of an equidistant line: *supra* note 83 at 36 (para. 37).

124 Legault and Hankey, *supra* note 122 at 215 note that equidistance was used in 89 per cent of 62 instances of opposing state boundary delimitation. One-half followed a strict equidistance line (as in the Black Sea between Turkey and Russia) and one-half used a modified equidistance line (as in the Adriatic Sea between Italy and the former Yugoslav Republic).

125 *Supra* note 122 at 215. In this category, 86 per cent of bilateral agreements use equidistance "for a substantial portion of the boundary": *ibid.*, 216.

126 *Tunisia-Libya* case, supra note 6 at 79 (para. 110). See also *Guinea/Guinea Bissau Maritime Boundary Arbitration (1985)*, [1986] 25 ILM 251, where the adjacent coastlines of the parties projected into the Atlantic Ocean in a convex manner. The delimitation line chosen was a perpendicular drawn outward from the general direction of the coasts of six African states.

the Court in the *Gulf of Maine* case reflects the difficulties of boundary-making in areas of varying coastal projections.[127] Thus equidistance, although a method common in state practice, is clearly not suitable to every delimitation.[128]

Finally, bilateral ocean boundary agreements, while persuasive, do not carry the weight of *opinio juris.* Seven judgments following the *North Sea Continental Shelf* case of 1969, as well as the decision in the *Gulf of Fonseca* case provide the most determinative criteria and principles of maritime boundary delimitation. While state practice will have an important role to play, especially for the delimitation of a semi-enclosed ocean area for which there is not a juridical precedent, the credible definition of Québec's ocean claims will rest upon an application of the common law principles of international maritime boundary-making.

JURIDICAL PRINCIPLES OF DELIMITATION

No exhaustive catalogue of delimitation principles can be derived from maritime boundary judgments. All circumstances in each boundary adjudication, whether termed relevant or special, have been weighed to various degrees in the attempt to achieve equitable results. However, nine judgments and awards provide the analytical framework to assist in predicting the maritime claims of an independent Québec. The recent judgments of the International Court of Justice in the *St. Pierre and Miquelon-Canada* case and the *Greenland-Jan Mayen* case are the most persuasive, in part because of the cumulative jurisprudence relied upon in them.[129] In the Québec context, the approach of the Court in delimiting the Gulf of Maine must also be considered because the geography of its

[127] *Delimitation of the Maritime Boundary in the Gulf of Maine Area Judgment* (Canada v. United States), [1984] ICJ Rep. 246 [hereinafter *Gulf of Maine* case]. The boundary consists of three segments: a modified equidistant line between Maine and Nova Scotia at the entrance to the Bay of Fundy, a short median line between the opposing coastal fronts of Cape Cod and Cape Sable, and a perpendicular drawn outward from the closing line of the Gulf of Maine.

[128] "It is now commonplace that every maritime delimitation is a *unicum* and can be determined only in the light of the factors particular to each case": M. D. Evans, "Less Than an Ocean Apart: The St Pierre and Miquelon and Jan Mayen Islands and The Delimitation of Maritime Zones," (1993), 43 ICLQ 678 at 690.

[129] *Supra* note 6. See also *Case Concerning the Delimitation of the Maritime Areas Between Canada and France* (1992), 31 ILM 1149 [hereinafter *St. Pierre and Miquelon* case]. See also Figure 2.

indented coastal fronts bears some resemblance to the concave nature of the Gulf of St. Lawrence.[130]

The primary principle of ocean boundary delimitation, since the 1969 *North Sea Continental Shelf* cases, is that an equitable result must result from adjudication.[131] Equity in international maritime law has been defined as:

> [A] matter of abstract justice, while "equitable principles" are "actual rules of law based on general precepts of justice and good faith." "Equity," in other words, is understood in the sense of natural justice, whereas "equitable principles," in the sense of the judgment of the Court in the *North Sea Continental Shelf* cases in which the applicable law was found not in the conventional law but in customary law, are part of customary international law. Thus the distinction, however qualified it may be, would seem in itself to be fundamental, for "equity" is understood in the sense of natural or abstract justice while "equitable principles" are understood to form part of the positive law.[132]

The International Court of Justice added, in the *North Sea Continental Shelf* cases, that:

> [D]elimitation is to be effected by agreement in accordance with equitable principles, and taking account of all the relevant circumstances in such a way as to leave as much as possible to each Party all those parts of the continental shelf that constitute a natural prolongation of its land territory into and under the sea, without encroachment on the natural prolongation of the land territory of the other.[133]

An important initial consideration between Canada and the independent Québec will be the type of boundary to be demarcated.

130 *Gulf of Maine* case, supra note 127. See especially paragraphs 208 to 221 of the judgment, justifying the drawing of the northern two segments of the delimitation line.

131 *Supra* note 83.

132 Masahiro Miyoshi, *Considerations of Equity in the Settlement of Territorial and Boundary Disputes* 13 (Dordrecht: Martinus Nijhoff, 1993) [endnote omitted].

133 *Supra* note 83 at 53 (para. 101). Two schools of thought have considered the application of the Continental Shelf Convention. The first, exemplified by Professor Prosper Weil of France, contends that delimitation is to commence with the drawing of an equidistant or median line and is only then to account for equitable considerations in its adjustment. The opposing school argues that all principles have equal weight in a delimitation, with equidistance having no special status. The latter won the day in the drafting of UNCLOS EEZ and continental shelf provisions, with Arts. 74 and 83 reading "[t]he delimitation of the [EEZ and continental shelf] between states with opposite or adjacent coasts shall be effected on the basis of international law, as reflected in Article 38 of the Statute of the International Court of Justice, in order to achieve an equitable solution."

The present maritime agreements between the federal government and the Atlantic provinces are based upon a simple division of continental shelf resources and revenues. It can be expected that an eventual resolution of Québec's maritime claims would include the full complement of maritime zones as they are presently recognized and provided for under international law. In other words, the creation of a single maritime boundary to encompass both the continental shelf and its superjacent waters would be logical. Indeed, the relevant distinctions between the two types of maritime zones have all but merged with the judgment of the International Court of Justice in the *Greenland-Jan Mayen* case.[134] Given this, the consideration must address how and where Québec's maritime boundary would be defined in the Gulf of St. Lawrence.

The overriding element of geography in maritime boundary adjudication has resulted in the following approach. First, the maritime area in dispute and the nature of the claim must be defined.[135] Within the Gulf of St. Lawrence proper, bounded by land around 90 per cent of its periphery, this would not pose a problem.[136] Next, a simplification of coastal profiles logically follows, through a drawing of straight baselines across the mouths of rivers and bays and, perhaps, to enclose channels between and

134 *Supra* note 6 at 57-79 (paras. 44-90). Note also the separate opinion of Judge Oda, *ibid.*, 108 (para. 70): "In the absence of an agreement between the States concerned, one cannot presuppose a single delimitation for two separate and independent régimes, the exclusive economic zone and the continental shelf, although the possibility of an eventual coincidence of the two lines may not be included."

On the trend towards a single maritime boundary for EEZs and continental shelves, see B. H. Oxman, "Political, Strategic, and Historic Considerations" in J. I. Charney and L. M. Alexander, eds., *supra* note 115 at 35 and Charney, *supra* note 106 at 246.

135 "The *sine qua non* of a delimitation is the basic and often unarticulated premise that there must be an area over which each party in dispute claims sole jurisdiction": M. D. Evans, *Relevant Circumstances and Maritime Delimitation* 64 (Oxford: Clarendon Press, 1989). Evans identifies three components of a maritime area for consideration: (1) "Area for the delimitation" — the area through which the delimitation will be made; (2) "The relevant coasts" — generally, the coastline fronting upon the relevant area; and (3) "The relevant framework" — "just as coasts outside the delimitation area influence the delimitation, features and factors derived from a wider area also influence it": *ibid.*, 68.

136 See Figures 1 and 2, and Canadian Charts LC 4001 and 4002.

around islands.[137] Contemporaneous with these first steps, the general direction of coastal projections is also assessed. With the exception of the Bay of Chaleur, an independent Québec and Canada would face each other oppositely across the expanse of the Gulf of St. Lawrence. Even if it were argued that the two states share an adjacent coastline in the Bay of Chaleur, an equidistant boundary has existed there for almost 150 years. Thus, the "dual concavities" of coastal profiles within the Gulf create a situation of near oppositeness.[138] Given that maritime delimitation in the Gulf would likely result in Québec being shelf-locked, such a geographic disadvantage might be relevant to a later equitable adjustment of a provisional boundary line.[139]

137 Hypothetical closing baselines within the Gulf are shown in Figure 2. The maritime "boundary" in the Bay of Chaleur and the St. Lawrence River inland waters closing lines would also be considered. See Figure 2.

Baselines may be used as a matter of customary international law to close "juridical bays" (and rivers) with mouths less than 24 nautical miles in width. See G. S. Westerman, *The Juridical Bay* (New York: Oxford Univ. Press, 1987) and Art. 7, "Straight Baselines," UNCLOS, *supra* note 10.

Baselines to smooth the coasts of an independent Québec and the Canadian maritime provinces abutting the Gulf would be drawn at this stage. Two such baselines, the Gulf closing lines for the (former) Canadian EFZ, already exist and are depicted on Canadian Charts LC 4001 and 4002. Baselines enclosing internal waters must follow the general direction of the coast to be consistent with international practice. It is possible that Canada might choose to close Northumberland Strait between P.E.I. and Nova Scotia with the use of baselines. Such a suggestion was advanced by the arbitral tribunal in the *North Atlantic Coast Fisheries Arbitration Case of 1910* (Proceedings: Washington, 1912). Professor La Forest once remarked that "under [the rule of straight baselines] Canada could easily claim the Northumberland Strait as inland waters": *supra* note 15 at 169. Application of this Canadian practice might allow Québec to draw straight baselines enclosing the Magdalen Islands and the Cartier Strait north of Anticosti Island.

138 This would tend to bring a juridical analysis closer to the initial use of an equidistance line proposed by the ICJ in the *Greenland-Jan Mayen* case, supra note 6 at 66 (para. 64ff). R. R. Churchill remarks that "[t]he court decided that what it should do, in the case of both a continental shelf and a fishery zone boundary, was to start with the median line as the provisional boundary and then see whether such a line required any adjustment in the light of special circumstances (as regards the continental shelf boundary) or relevant circumstances (as regards the fishery zone boundary), with the aim in each of these being to reach an equitable result": "The *Greenland-Jan Mayen* Case and its Significance for the International Law of Maritime Boundary Delimitation" (1994) 9 Int'l J. of Coastal and Marine Law 1 at 8.

139 UNCLOS, *supra* note 10 at Art. 70 provides for the "Right of Geographically

Next, the process of maritime boundary delimitation requires an examination of the relevant/special circumstances. Here, in determining a provisional boundary, the inquiry may broaden beyond geography. The past conduct of the parties and any subsisting agreements, by direct expression or through *modus vivendi*, are analyzed.[140] At this stage, the following argument can be expected to emerge. Canada is likely to maintain that it denied provincial maritime claims in the Gulf by ignoring the 1964 premiers' agreement. An independent Québec would adopt the contrary position.[141] Of some persuasive effect will be the existing boundary in the Bay of Chaleur and the federally imposed inland waters closing

---

Disadvantaged States." A geographically disadvantaged state is defined, in Art. 70(2), to include "coastal States, including States bordering upon enclosed or semi-enclosed seas, whose geographical situation makes them dependent upon the exploitation of the living resources of the exclusive economic zones of other States in the subregion or region for adequate supplies of fish for the nutritional purposes of their populations or parts thereof, and coastal States which can claim no exclusive economic zones of their own." No similar provision exists for a confined continental shelf. So defined, an independent Quebec would have to demonstrate limited access to the fishery in the Gulf of St. Lawrence to justify greater access to other resources within and without the Gulf.

S. C. Vasciannie remarks that "[t]he case for special privileges for GDS [Geographically Disadvantaged States] seems even less cogent than that of their land-locked allies. More particularly, the GDS do not have the problem of access to the sea and its resources which may be used to suggest that non-coastal States should be preferentially treated. Instead . . . these States claim to be disadvantaged primarily because they have limited coastlines or do not stand to benefit significantly from extended zones of national jurisdiction. In this situation, it seems quite difficult for them to maintain that they face problems of nature which entitle them to special treatment. They may be less fortunately endowed with coastal resources than most States, but at the same time some of them have natural resources, climatic conditions, or advantages of location which could be said to compensate them for their maritime problems. Conversely, some coastal states may well experience greater overall difficulties with nature than the GDS. In other words, *it is reasonable to assume that the GDS cannot discharge the onus of proof required to justify preferential treatment in the furtherance of equality*" [citations omitted, emphasis added]: *Land-Locked and Geographically Disadvantaged States in the International Law of the Sea* 32-33 (Oxford: Clarendon Press, 1990).

140 The tacit agreement of the parties preceding the *Tunisia-Libya* case, *supra* note 6 was considered by the ICJ in setting the continental shelf boundary in the Mediterranean Sea. Each state had accepted the issuance by the other of petroleum concessions and control over sponge banks off the coast.

141 See text at note 148-53.

line across the mouth of the St. Lawrence River.[142] The position of these two "boundaries," although strictly creations of Canadian domestic law, are reconcilable with the common law principle of the seabed and superjacent waters in nearly enclosed waterways *inter fauces terrae* being vested in the littoral jurisdiction concerned. Perhaps, then, within the specific and limited area enclosed by such domestic "boundaries," Québec will have an immediate maritime claim.[143] *Modus vivendi,* however, must be distinguished from historic title within the Gulf of St. Lawrence. The latter clearly enures to Canada given the now successful efforts of the federal government to assert complete sovereignty over the Gulf's waters.[144]

Some attention should also be accorded to the *thalweg* as a delimitation method. The *thalweg* permits a boundary to be drawn through the middle of a navigable deep water channel.[145] This delimitation method might afford the independent Québec a starting point for its boundary in the northern reaches of the Strait of Belle Isle, although the opposing coastlines in both locations readily suggest use of the equidistance method. From a Canadian federal perspective, defining the *thalweg* would result in minimal impact on Québec's claim in the sea lanes to the north of the Magdalen Islands, because the navigable channel south of Anticosti Island will no longer be shared in the customary sense of the doctrine.

These considerations permit the third step of delimitation — the drawing of a tentative or provisional boundary line — to be later adjusted with regard to all equitable factors. The timing of this step in the delimitation process has been the subject of much contention. Essentially, there is a debate over the extent to which equitable principles should be assessed before more definitive criteria —

142 See text at note 15-62.

143 See Figure 2.

144 The historic waters status of the Gulf of St. Lawrence is considered later. See text at note 174.

145 "The main application of the equitable doctrine of the thalweg is in situations where the preservation of equal access and navigational rights are of prime importance, in the sense that equal division of the surface of the water is far less significant than the mutual ability to navigate along the navigable channel, where large vessels can travel. The equitable doctrine of the thalweg is prima facie applicable to, and has, in fact, been applied by states and tribunals to, the delimitation of maritime boundaries in bays, in the territorial sea, including straits, and even in the continental shelf": P. Bravender-Coyle, *supra* note 108 at 180.

notably the use of the equidistance method — are employed. Since much of the Gulf of St. Lawrence consists of opposing coastal fronts, the drawing of a provisional boundary would be needed at an early stage. Given the geography of the Gulf, the use of equidistance is likely to feature prominently.[146] The tentative boundary would then need to be adjusted to account for relevant considerations and special circumstances, notably the distorting effect of islands and proportionality might then be used to check the result of final demarcation.[147]

EQUIDISTANCE AND THE PROVISIONAL SINGLE MARITIME BOUNDARY

The drawing of a provisional EEZ and continental shelf boundary line between Canada and an independent Québec that is based primarily upon an application of equidistance is supported curially by the *Greenland-Jan Mayen* case:

> [I]n two of the cases mentioned (*Gulf of Maine* and the *Libya/Malta* cases), where the delimitation was between opposite coasts, it was found entirely appropriate to begin with such a provisional line . . . it is in accord with precedents to begin with the median line as a provisional line

146 Consider Professor Charney's view: "Due to the configuration, the small area, and the nature of the coastline, the equidistant line would be appropriate. It could be argued that the equidistant line or an adjustment thereof should not be used because of the presence of three islands in the Gulf [the Magdalens, P.E.I. and Anticosti]. However, Anticosti and Prince Edward Island do not present a strong case for the use of a line other than equidistance. They are relatively large islands, close to the shore and well integrated therein. The projection to the east from Newfoundland containing Cape St. George might also suggest an inequitable situation, but it is countervailed by Anticosti Island near the Quebec shore": *supra* note 2 at 399-400.

147 Whatever the view held on the structure of the delimitation process, geographic considerations as defined above play a decisive role in judicially decided, i.e., legally mandated delimitations. According to one view, the delimitation decision is a unique and global operation whereby all the equities of the case are balanced up . . . According to another view, the delimitation process begins with a starting point in which the equidistant line serves as a first stage. This is followed in a second stage by a possible adjustment of the provisional equidistant line in order to achieve an equitable result. According to this view, geography fulfils its positive function in the first stage, and its negative (corrective function) in the second stage, when it gives rise to the definitive delimitation." P. Weil, "Geographic considerations in Maritime Delimitations," in J. I. Charney and L. M. Alexander, eds., *International Maritime Boundaries*, *supra* note 115 at 120.

and then to ask whether "special circumstances" require any adjustment or shifting of that line.[148]

Moreover, there is Canadian state practice, both domestic and international, and state practice in general, particularly in semi-enclosed seas.[149] The Canada Nova Scotia Offshore Petroleum Resources Accord Implementation Act underscores the application of the equidistance method in the Gulf of St. Lawrence proper.[150] The Act provides for continental shelf delimitation between Nova Scotia and other maritime provinces to the outer edge of the continental shelf, within which Nova Scotia and the federal government have agreed to undertake joint management of hydrocarbon exploration and revenue sharing.[151] The line established by the Act, which commences at the land boundary between Nova Scotia and New Brunswick in Baie Verte and then proceeds east through the Northumberland Strait and northeast between Nova Scotia and the Magdalen Islands before turning southeast between Nova Scotia and Newfoundland, explicitly follows a simplified equidistant course. Notably, even small, isolated islands within the Gulf were given full effect in the drawing of this continental shelf line.[152]

Two principles of maritime boundary delimitation will play a significant role in possible adjustments to Québec's provisional maritime boundary line so that equitable result might be achieved. These are (1) modifications to account for the distorting effects of islands, and (2) a "check" to compare coastal proportionalities.[153]

THE EFFECT OF THE MAGDALEN ISLANDS

The position of the Magdalen Islands poses particular problems in drawing any maritime boundary in the Gulf of St. Lawrence. Geographically, the islands are the northernmost extension of the Prince Edward Island group. Their attachment to the province of Québec under the 1964 Maritime Premiers' Agreement as a

148 *Supra* note 6 at 61 (para. 51).

149 See text at note 114-28.

150 *Supra* note 65.

151 See Schedule I to the Act, *ibid.*

152 Consider, e.g., Pictou Island in Northumberland Strait and St. Paul Island in Cabot Strait.

153 Two equidistant lines are shown in Figure 2. The northern line is a simplified line that disregards the distorting effect of the Magdalen Islands entirely. The southern portion of the second line gives full effect to the Islands.

"peninsula" could not have been a more inaccurate geophysical characterization.[154] However, as permanently inhabited islands and politically part of an independent Québec, the Magdalens would be entitled at international law to generate a full maritime zone. This is affirmed in the *Greenland-Jan Mayen* case and by the arbitral award in the *St. Pierre and Miquelon* case.[155] Customary international law in this regard is further supported by Article 121(2) of UNCLOS:

> [T]he territorial sea, the contiguous zone, the exclusive economic zone and the continental shelf of an *island* are determined in accordance with the provisions of this Convention applicable to other land territory [emphasis added].[156]

The giving of full effect to the Magdalens in boundary-making would generate an EEZ/continental shelf claim allowing Québec to claim, and possibly acquire, an additional one-seventh area of the Gulf.[157]

However, where islands are not themselves the principal feature in a coastal projection, a provisional boundary line based upon their distorting effect may be modified to achieve the desired equitable result. Four techniques are available in a continuum of assessing the effects of islands — a combination of which might be applied to adjust a provisional equidistant line. They are "full effect," "partial or semi-effect," "no effect," and "enclavement."[158] An independent Québec would be expected to argue for full effect to be given to the Magdalen Islands, possibly as one *quid pro quo* for its shelf-locked status. Equity, the argument might go, must take account of the fact that, while delimitation within the Gulf of St. Lawrence is sought, Canada additionally possesses sea coasts outside the relevant area. It might be maintained that a seemingly expansive claim within the Gulf must be distinguished with the relative apportionment of maritime areas on all of Canada's Atlantic coast.

154 See *supra* note 40 and accompanying text.

155 *Supra* notes 6 and 129, respectively.

156 *Supra* note 10.

157 This area is based on the proposed baselines discussed above.

158 Paul Bravender-Coyle identifies six equitable concepts to correct the effect of geographic distortions in maritime boundary making: (1) tout l'effet; (2) quid pro quo; (3) n'en tenant aucun compte simpliciter; (4) demi-effect; (5) n'en tenant aucun compte pour une partie; and (6) enclavement: *supra* note 108 at 188.

Assessing the impact of the Magdalens in the light of the adjudicative treatment of the effects of islands suggests the following approach. First, islands that are distant from the parent state generate complete maritime zones in their own right. This principle featured prominently in the *St. Pierre and Miquelon* and *Greenland-Jan Mayen* cases.[159] The Magdalen Islands are not in such a position.[160] Second, islands must always be given consideration in achieving an equitable result, even if they are ultimately accorded no effect at all.[161] Third, and a corollary of the first proposition, is that islands lying close to a mainland coast might not be given full effect.[162] Finally, islands that fall on the "wrong side" of a provisional equidistance line between opposite mainland coasts may be enclaved.[163]

The enclaving method can produce either a full enclave, where the maritime belt accorded to the island is wholly separated from the offshore zone of the mainland coast of the state to which the island belongs, or, alternatively, a semi-enclave, where the maritime zone appertaining to the island merges with the maritime zone of the mainland coast. The semi-enclave effect occurs when the island is situated on or close to the equidistant line.[164]

159 *Supra* note 129 and note 6, respectively.

160 The Magdalen Islands are about 120 nautical miles from the closest point on the Québec mainland at the Gaspé Peninsula.

161 The reasoning of the Chamber of the ICJ in the *Gulf of Maine* case, *supra* note 127 at 327 (para. 196) is notable. "[The Chamber] also has in mind the . . . criterion — it too being of an auxiliary nature — involving the necessity of granting some effect, however limited, to the presence of a geographical feature such as an island or group of small islands lying off a coast, when strict application of the basic criterion might entail giving them full effect, or, alternatively, no effect."

162 See especially the discussion by the Court in the *Tunisia-Libya* case, *supra* note 6 at 74-75 (para. 128). The Kerkennah Islands near the Tunisian coast were given "some effect" while the Island of Jerba was disregarded. Consider also the "half effect" accorded to Canada's Seal Island in the *Gulf of Maine* case, *supra* note 127 at 94-95 (para. 222).

163 The *Anglo-French Continental Shelf* case, in which the Channel Islands of the United Kingdom were isolated within a circle of territorial sea to the south of the Anglo-French continental shelf boundary in the English Channel, is a classic application of enclaving: *Delimitation of the Continental Shelf,* Decision of June 30, 1977 *(U.K.* v. *France),* [1979] 54 ILR, 18 ILM 398.

164 Legault and Hankey, *supra* note 122 at 212. The authors cite agreements that create enclaves and semi-enclaves.

This fourth approach is perhaps the most logical and curially supported modification to a provisional line delimiting the Gulf of St. Lawrence. The Magdalen Islands are the single most distorting boundary feature in the Gulf. Correcting their geographic effect, which could possibly create inequity for Canada, could take many forms. One outcome between the extremes of full effect and insular enclaving could be the creation of a twenty-four nautical mile radius of maritime area surrounding the islands encompassing territorial and contiguous zones as defined in the *St. Pierre and Miquelon* case, resulting in a situation of partial enclavement, or attachment of such a maritime zone to the rest of Québec's waters. The result could receive favourable attention in view of the Gulf's relatively confined waters.[165]

THE CORRECTIVE EFFECT OF PROPORTIONALITY

Proportionality has been occasionally applied as a further check of the equitable outcome of a maritime boundary allocation. However, this equitable check, which was never well developed nor applied extensively, has fallen into disrepute. Proportionality is a comparison of the ratios of the parties' coastal fronts to the areas of their delimited maritime zones and is applied either as a positive tool of boundary-making early in the process or as an after-the-fact check of equity. It was used in the *Gulf of Maine* case to correct the median line drawn between opposing coastal fronts to prevent "untoward consequences."[166] However, its unorthodox application in the *St. Pierre and Miquelon* case and the limited consideration it received by the International Court of Justice in the *Greenland-Jan Mayen* case have cast doubt on its utility.[167] It is submitted that both

165 *Supra* note 129 at para. 69. The Court was clearly concerned with encroachment of the St. Pierre and Miquelon Islands into a Canadian coastal projection: "A reasonable and equitable solution for the western sector would be to grant to St. Pierre and Miquelon an additional twelve nautical miles from the limit of its territorial sea, for its exclusive economic zone." Delimitation of a hypothetical territorial sea/contiguous zone, with partial enclavement, creating a 24 nautical mile radius EEZ about the Magdalen Islands is shown in Figure 3.

166 *Supra* note 127 at 334-37 (paras. 217-22). Canada had reservations about the use of proportionality as an "auxiliary criterion" in the *Gulf of Maine* case.

167 *Supra* note 129 and *supra* note 6, respectively. The Court wrote in the *Greenland-Jan Mayen* case, at 69 (para. 69) that "it follows that, in light of the disparity of the coastal lengths, the median line should be adjusted or shifted in such a way as to effect a delimitation closer to the coast of Jan Mayen. It

these decisions departed from the optimum use of proportionality as a final corrective factor, where the method "is best used in clearly defined closed areas such as the Gulf of Maine where third states are not relevant."[168] The Gulf of St. Lawrence constitutes such a discrete and ascertainable maritime area in which to apply proportionality.[169] Far from falling into disfavour, an adjudication of the Gulf would likely afford it new utility.[170]

If straight baselines are drawn in the Gulf to smooth coastal profiles, and the effect of the Magdalens is disregarded, proportionality affirms the larger maritime area that Québec might claim and be awarded. The parties would certainly not be as far apart as the claimed ratios in the *St. Pierre and Miquelon* case, with Québec enjoying a proportionality of its coastal front to Canada's with a ratio of about 1.3:1. Canada might argue that the use of proportionality would thus limit the increased maritime area generated by

should, however, be made clear that taking account of the disparity of coastal lengths does not mean a direct and mathematical application of the relationship between the length of the coastal front of eastern Greenland and that of Jan Mayen." In the *St. Pierre and Miquelon* case, France claimed a proportionality of Canadian to French coastal fronts of 6.5:1. Canada claimed a ratio of 21.4:1. The Court decided upon a ratio of 16.4:1: *id.* at para. 93. Malcolm Evans remarked "[t]he demonstration of a proportionality verified by reference to so malleable a set of figures shows nothing but the capacity of the Court to produce whatever result it wished": "Less Than An Ocean Apart: The St Pierre and Miquelon and Jan Mayen Islands and the Delimitation of Maritime Zones" (1993) 43 I.C.L.Q. 678 at 688.

168 J. I. Charney, "The Delimitation of Ocean Boundaries" (1987) 18 Ocean Dev. and Int'l L. 497 at 515.

169 See generally the hypothetical baselines in Figure 2. A further smoothing of coastal profiles in the Gulf of St. Lawrence before proportion distances were measured would likely be undertaken to account for deeply indented areas, akin to the process in the *St. Pierre and Miquelon* case, supra note 129 at 175 (paras. 92-93).

170 Professor Weil is outspoken against the use of proportionality: "Theoretically unjustifiable, impossible to put into practice, the test of proportionality is, moreover, useless. Conceived basically as a warning signal for detecting an inequitable deviation in the line of equidistance caused by a minor geographical feature, unreasonable disproportion between areas and coastal lengths can, as we shall see, today be replaced by a simpler indicator, the proximity of the equidistance line to the coast of the parties": *supra* note 5 at 244. Cf. Paul Bravender-Coyle: "[I]n every case in which an equitable solution is sought, the juridical concept of proportionality, as the handmaiden of equity, must be employed in order to determine whether the proposed delimitation is in fact equitable. Proportionality is, therefore, the golden metewand of equity": *supra* note 108 at 185.

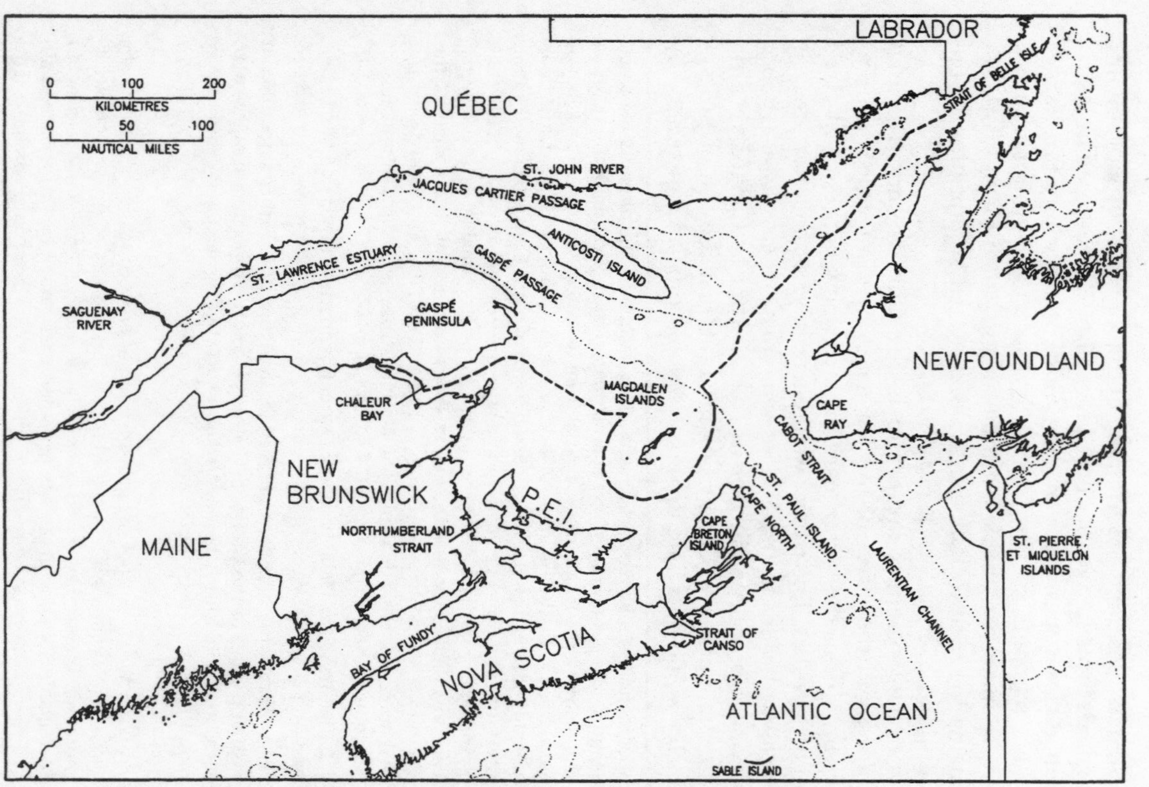

Figure 3 Delimitation by partial enclavement of the Magdalen Islands.

a full effect accorded to the Magdalens. One certainty is that the baselines adopted by the parties to support each of their claims to a favourable ratio would be scrutinized carefully.

THE ELEMENTS OF OCEAN BOUNDARY-MAKING AS APPLIED IN THE GULF OF ST. LAWRENCE

Sufficient principles can be found in the law of maritime delimitation, as a matter of state practice and by application of judicial precedent, that the Gulf of St. Lawrence could be divided without great complexity between Canada and an independent Québec. Given the Canadian experience and the tendency of maritime boundaries to be founded almost exclusively on geographic considerations, such an apportionment could be successful in the formalistic sense of determining the equitable share of each party over areas of the Gulf. On a cursory analysis, it is probable that an equidistance or median line that is adjusted to account for coastal projections, the effect of the Magdalen Islands, and possibly Québec's shelf-locked status within the Gulf would be arrived at. What is conspicuously absent from the result of such boundary-making is the practical effect upon the actual exercise of state sovereignty and uses of the Gulf of St. Lawrence. The geographic artificiality of a single maritime boundary, for example, excludes those anticipated shared uses of the Gulf, such as shipping lanes reaching into the industrial centre of North America, possible shared regimes of environmental monitoring and protection, and a host of other activities, none of which will be dependent upon the drawing of a line referable to state coastal projection. In an opportunistic sense, it could be advantageous to Canada and Québec for a public contest over exclusive national sovereignty to emerge, possibly attracting international approval of the claims of each. Paradoxically, however, the contest over a division of what are now recognized territorial waters of Canada would result in the Gulf, once again, being considered as international waters. Rather than an expansion of national claims by either party, their actions might foster a diminished mutual international presence in the Atlantic Ocean.

CANADA-QUÉBEC JOINT SOVEREIGNTY IN THE GULF OF ST. LAWRENCE

The Nature of Joint Sovereignty

Delimitation of the Gulf of St. Lawrence using the principles developed in judicial decisions, customary international law, and

UNCLOS could prove impractical or undesirable. If a traditional maritime boundary must inevitably be drawn between Canada and an independent Québec, mutual compromise over the allocation and sharing of maritime resources may provide at least a short-term solution. As the political solutions to Québec's departure from Confederation are unlimited, so too are the possible agreements on maritime issues.[171] At one extreme of a *continuum* of possible outcomes is a formal assertion and delimitation of maritime sovereignty claims. At the other is the maintenance of the *status quo*, where an independent Québec would not assert any claim to maritime sovereignty, but simply claim the equitable use of, and access to, resources.[172]

171 Douglas M. Johnston and Mark J. Valencia, in *Pacific Ocean Boundary Problems: Status and Solutions* 24 (Dordrecht: Martinus Nijhoff, 1991) suggest that a "spectrum of diplomatic options" is possible in resolving maritime boundary disputes, as follows: (i) disagreement; (ii) designation of an area in dispute; (iii) limited cooperation in designated area; (iv) access for specified purpose(s); (v) preliminary joint undertaking; (vi) development contemplating production; (vii) sharing of specified state services; (viii) uni-sectorial joint ocean management; and (ix) integrated joint ocean management.

Professor Donald McRae outlines two departures from maritime boundary making: "These are the agreement to separate the continental shelf and water boundaries, and the negotiation of joint management regimes in lieu of establishing a boundary . . . Both the approach of separate boundaries and joint management of development regimes offer more flexibility to states in the settlement of boundary area problems. Yet they are not without difficulty; they require the resolution of competing claims to apply civil and criminal jurisdiction and to apply environmental and fiscal regulations. They may require collaboration by non-state operating entities which have never had to cooperate before. Although these difficulties are great, they are not insurmountable. They require, however, a reorientation in thinking about the resolution of boundary problems, and an acceptance of the idea that neither state will be sovereign over the area in question" [footnote omitted]: "Canada and the Delimitation of Boundaries," in D. McRae and G. Munro, eds., *Canadian Oceans Policy: National Strategies and the New Law of the Sea* 145 at 158 (Vancouver: UBC Press, 1989).

172 See, e.g., "Treaty Proposal: Sovereigntist Plan for Partnership with Canada," *Globe and Mail* (Oct. 31, 1995) A2. The proposed partnership agreement was agreed to, and publicly released, by leading figures of the Québecois sovereigntist movement on June 12, 1995. The treaty plan was silent on maritime issues, although it implied a limited cooperation. "[T]he two member States will be free to make agreements in any other area of common interest, such as: . . . transportation (to facilitate, for example . . . inland navigation policies) [and] environmental protection (in order to set objectives in such areas as cross border-pollution . . .)."

The latter approach implies that the Gulf of St. Lawrence be considered as a joint development zone, with an understanding as to how shipping, resource use, and environmental protection would be regulated. The desirability of such a co-operative approach is emphasized in Article 123 of UNCLOS, which calls for states bordering semi-enclosed seas to co-operate "in the exercise of their rights and the performance of their duties" under the Convention. However, the concept of a joint development zone would demand that the relevant shared area be first identified, possibly leading to a reassertion of maritime sovereignty. The range of potential joint uses of the Gulf is extensive and would depend largely on the mutual commitments of Canada and an independent Québec to their bilateral agreements.[173]

Joint development of the Gulf of St. Lawrence prompts a consideration of the likelihood of mutual sovereignty. Would it be possible for Canada and an independent Québec to agree upon and then secure international recognition of the Gulf as a single legal entity consisting of undivided internal waters, although bounded by the two sovereign states? To phrase the question another way, following Québec's separation, might sovereignty over the sea and continental shelf in the Gulf of St. Lawrence arrogate with undiminished unity and equality of interest to the two states encompassing it? Such an arrangement has an uncertain foundation in customary international law since it would be based on the application of the principles of historic waters. The possibility that Canada and Québec might agree to avoid delimiting the Gulf of St. Lawrence, or that Québec could claim, on the basis that its waters are internal to both nations, additional rights to the Canadian maritime zone *outside* the Gulf of St. Lawrence adds further intrigue. A starting point for this discussion is the present status of the Gulf of St. Lawrence in international law.

The Historic Status of the Gulf of St. Lawrence

The Canadian claim to the Gulf of St. Lawrence as internal waters is not without controversy. It dates from at least the time of Newfoundland's entry into Confederation and has been asserted with varying degrees of success since the *de jure* loss of French sovereignty

173 Consider possible joint activities such as fishing, environmental monitoring and protection, shipping traffic control, navigational aids, marine pilotage, icebreaking, meteorological services, search and rescue, naval exercises, and hydrocarbon exploration.

in the Gulf in 1763.[174] The prevailing academic opinion holds that Canada has sufficiently subjected the Gulf of St. Lawrence to such sovereignty that the contrary claims of other states have been all but nullified.[175]

Canada's present and continuing sovereignty over the Gulf of St. Lawrence appears to satisfy the basic requirements at customary international law for a historic claim.[176] Such a claim rests on the continuing assertion of sovereignty over an extensive period of time with the acquiescence of other nations.[177] Recent acts of the federal

174 See the remarks of Prime Minister St. Laurent, *supra* note 34. See also La Forest, *supra* note 15 at 160 ff. The nature of historic waters was defined by the ICJ in the *Anglo-Norwegian Fisheries* case, [1951] ICJ Rep. 116 at 130. "By 'historic waters' are usually meant waters that are treated as internal waters but which would not have that character if it were not for the existence of an historic title. The United Kingdom Government refers to the notion of historic titles both in respect of territorial waters and internal waters, considering such titles, in both cases, as derogations from general international law. In its opinion, Norway can justify the claim that these waters are territorial or internal on the ground that she has exercised the necessary jurisdiction over them for a long period without opposition from other States, a kind of *possessio longi temporis*, with the result that her jurisdiction over these waters must now be recognized although it constitutes a derogation from the rules in force. Norwegian sovereignty over these waters would constitute an exception, historic titles justifying situations which would otherwise be in conflict with international law."

175 See Lawrence L. Herman, "Proof of Offshore Territorial Claims in Canada" (1982) 7 Dalhousie L. J. 3 at 7. Cf. Morrisette, *supra* note 16 at 313 (para. 84): "In sum, by virtue of international law, the Gulf of St. Lawrence will be considered, in my opinion, as high seas or an EEZ outside of a 12 nautical mile territorial sea upon baselines which existed prior to the *Territorial Sea and Fishing Zones Act* of 1964 [translation, footnote omitted].

176 UNCLOS, *supra* note 10 makes no provision for historic waters. See Art. 10, "Bays." The requirements for such claims have diminished with the increase in the extent of the territorial sea, such that a "juridical bay" results where the total length of a closing line drawn across its mouth is less than 24 nautical miles or where the "semi-circle" test is satisfied. See especially G. S. Westerman, *The Juridical Bay* (New York: Oxford Univ. Press, 1987). See also Churchill and Lowe, *supra* note 7 at 33 ff. Judge Shigeru Oda, vice-president of the ICJ has called the doctrine of historic waters "practically a redundancy": *Gulf of Fonseca* case, supra note 11 at 756 (para. 44 of his dissenting opinion). "[B]ut by now, most bays known as 'historic bays,' such as Delaware Bay, Chesapeake Bay, the Bristol Channel, have become, as I already stated above, ordinary bays because of the new rule of the 24-mile closing line": *ibid.*, 755 (para. 43).

177 See especially Yehuda Z. Blum, *supra* note 11 at 259: "It would therefore appear that the geographical factor, as well as the economic considerations

government emphasize its continued claim over the Gulf. First, the imposition of fishery zone lines across the northern entrance to the Strait of Belle Isle and Cabot Strait to close the Gulf to foreign fishing received little international comment, except perhaps as to their uniqueness.[178] Second, the Canadian Laws Offshore Application Act and its successor, the Oceans Act, have extended the reach of Canadian jurisdiction into the Gulf of St. Lawrence, setting aside a source of ambiguity that had previously resulted in contradictions over Canada's historic claim.[179] The Oceans Act allows the minister of foreign affairs to issue certificates declaring certain waters as historic or territorial seas or an "area created by Canada as an

---

and the elements of national defence and other vital interests of the coastal State, are relevant in the establishment of an historic title to the extent that they indicate the degree of consent accorded to historic claims by the nations affected by such national pretensions; in the case of a maritime historic claim, 'the nations affected' are the entire international community. See also Churchill and Lowe, *supra* note 7 at 36.

D. P. O'Connell, in *The International Law of the Sea*, Vol. 1 417 (Oxford: Clarendon Press, 1982) describes the historic waters doctrine as "essentially a doctrine of exception to the standard rules for delimitation of maritime territory . . . [which] can be thoroughly examined only in the light of the specific circumstances of each case."

178 "In 1971 Canada drew fishery closing lines across the mouths of the Bay of Fundy, Gulf of St. Lawrence and Queen Charlotte Sound. The fishery closing line was a Canadian invention which has not been emulated by other states. The purpose of the fishery closing lines was to delineate Canadian near-shore waters from which foreign fishing vessels were to be excluded. Waters landward of the fishery closing lines were described as fishing zones . . . On the east coast, the effect of the fishery closing lines was to delineate the historic waters of the Bay of Fundy and the Gulf of St. Lawrence, hence the fishery closing lines are the functional equivalent of straight baselines" [citations omitted, emphasis added]: McDorman, *supra* note 113 at 7.

The locations of fishery closing lines in the Strait of Belle Isle and Cabot Strait are still depicted on Canadian Charts LC 4001 and 4002. The ambiguous position of territorial sea limits near these straits should be noted.

179 *Supra* notes 62 and 69. The status of the Gulf was raised in the House of Commons in 1979 through questions about protests over the seal hunt put to the Minister of Fisheries, the Honourable Roméo LeBlanc (as he was then). "I have searched the *Fisheries Act* very carefully and found that there is no way the act would give me the power to stop a vessel from sailing on the Gulf of St. Lawrence": House of Commons Debates (Mar. 8, 1979) at 3943. Cf. application of the Coastal Fisheries Protection Act, R.S.C. 1985, c. C-33 and its regulations.

Exclusive Economic Zone."[180] The first such certificate declared the Gulf of St. Lawrence to be waters internal to Canada.[181] The Act also permits Canada to establish its maritime baselines "at the outer limits of any area . . . over which Canada has a historic or other title of sovereignty."[182]

The basis of Canada's sovereignty over the Gulf is further strengthened by the development of the baseline regime in international maritime law. The general state practice and operation of Article 7 of UNCLOS allow for an application of baselines to delimit irregular coastal fronts:

> In localities where the coastline is deeply indented and cut into, or if there is a fringe of islands along the coast in its immediate vicinity, the method of straight baselines joining appropriate points may be employed in drawing the baseline from which the breadth of the territorial sea is measured.[183]

> The drawing of straight baselines must not depart to any appreciable extent from the general direction of the coast, and the sea areas lying within the lines must be sufficiently closely linked to the land domain to be subject to the régime of internal waters.[184]

Canada's baselines on its east and west coasts have not attracted much international concern. The baselines drawn in Canada's Arctic, however, have received justifiable attention on the basis of their length and extensive closing of the Northwest Passage.[185] State practice and UNCLOS, thus, seem to allow the closing of the Gulf

180 *Ibid.* Ross Hornby notes that "[s]uch certificates will be particularly useful with respect to areas where the extent of Canada's internal waters claims have not been clarified by the creation of straight baselines, such as, in the Gulf of St. Lawrence or Dixon Entrance": *supra* note 54 at 360. Aside from its declaratory function, the Act has an equal effect to apply Canadian federal and provincial laws into an economic zone and especially to marine installations and structures.

181 Hornby, *supra* note 54 at 361.

182 *Supra* note 62 at s. 5(3).

183 UNCLOS, *supra* note 10 at Art. 7(1).

184 *Ibid.*, Art. 7(3). Vietnam and Myanmar have departed markedly from this requirement. See The Law of the Sea, *supra* note 9.

185 For a summary of Canadian baselines see The Law of the Sea, *supra* note 9 at 69. Professor Donat Pharand concludes that "[t]he practice of States in general and that of four of the five Arctic States in particular reflect a liberal interpretation of the geographic requirements for the applicability of straight baselines and lend strong support to the baselines drawn around the Canadian Arctic Archipelago": Pharand, *supra* note 9 at 178.

of St. Lawrence by the establishment of formal baselines, irrespective of historic title over the waters within, given the short distances spanned by the Strait of Belle Isle and Cabot Strait[186] and the undisputed importance of Canadian interests in the region.[187]

The possibility of Canada and an independent Québec exercising joint sovereignty over the Gulf of St. Lawrence on the basis of a single state's historic title is highly uncertain. The notion of a multistate bay held in common is contrary to the basis of historic title — namely, unity of possession by a single state through a prolonged period of time sufficient to justify an extraordinary territorial claim.[188] A degree of scholarly support for joint maritime sovereignty is evident, but with the *caveat* that states may agree to such an arrangement only if general international rights to the high seas are not obstructed:

> I agree that a condominium may be created with the consent of the States concerned with respect to the area to which those States could have originally been entitled. I am not suggesting any general rule that the concept of a condominium should not be applicable in maritime areas. The present Judgment refers to the case of the Baie du Figuier, where there has existed a zone of condominium possessed jointly by France and Spain since 1879. This precedent does not, however, give any ground for justifying the status of a condominium for the Gulf of Fonseca, in connection with which no agreement between the States concerned has ever existed. The rationale underlying the Baie du Figuier solution was that France and Spain agreed to keep the small area in that bay . . . under their joint administration for the common use of the anchorages in the

186 Approximately 40 and 58 nautical miles, respectively.

187 Professor La Forest wrote in 1963 that "lines closing off the Gulf of St. Lawrence could be drawn to follow the general direction of the coast . . . Equally, the intimate relationship between the gulf and the land areas surrounding it are immediately evident. And there are important economic interests involved; the gulf is the chief means of communication between the Province of Newfoundland and the rest of Canada, and the fisheries therein have long been the main source of livelihood for many of the inhabitants of the four Atlantic provinces": La Forest, *supra* note 15 at 171.

188 Churchill and Lowe discuss the unique nature of historic bays bounded by more than one state. "The normal rule of customary international law in relation to such bays would appear to be that, unlike bays governed by article 7 of the Territorial Sea Convention and article 10 of the Law of the Sea Convention, or historic bays, they cannot be closed by a line drawn across their mouth. Instead the baseline is constituted by the low water mark around the shores of the bay. The matter, however, is not free from controversy. Exceptionally, it may be possible for the riparian States to show that the position is different by reason of historic title. Such is the case with the Gulf of Fonseca": *supra* note 7 at 38.

roadsteads therein located; the question of separate title thus yielded to practicality.[189]

The modern legal situation of the multi-state bay was considered during the Gulf of Aqaba dispute. Following the creation of Israel after the Second World War, the waters of this narrow gulf were disputed by the four parties bordering upon it.[190] Analogous to the geographic location of Québec was Israel's location at the confined headwaters of the Gulf. The Gulf had been blockaded against shipping bound for the Israeli port of Eilat on the premise that its waters were historic in nature and fell within the sovereignty of adjacent Islamic states by right of prior unitary possession under the Ottoman Empire.[191] The denial of Israeli rights in the Gulf was challenged at the Eleventh General Assembly of the United Nations in 1957 and was remedied through the deployment of the United Nations Emergency Force into the Sinai Peninsula.[192] The prevailing opinion held that an historic embayment could not be closed to one of its littoral states, a proposition put into greater relief by the willingness of Egypt to allow Jordan right of access to, and transit

189 *Gulf of Fonseca* case, *supra* note 11 at 754-55 (para. 41 of the dissenting opinion of Judge Oda). Y. Z. Blum adds, *supra* note 11 at 310, that "even [an agreement between states] to 'close' a multinational bay is not sufficient to achieve this legal effect unless such measure receives the recognition, or at least the acquiescence, of other States" [footnote omitted]. A "maritime condominium" was defined by the ICJ in the *Gulf of Fonseca* case, *ibid.*, paras. 399-401 as "'co-ownership,' to describe . . . the legal result where . . . States jointly inherited by succession waters which for nearly three centuries had been under the single sway of the State from which they were the heirs; and in which waters there were no maritime administrative boundaries at the time of inheritance." The court added, at para. 410, that such a historic bay requires a defined closing line.

190 The Gulf of Aqaba measures about 96 miles in length and varies in width from 5.75 miles at its entrance in the Strait of Tiran to as much as 14.5 miles. Israel and Jordan are located at its head, with 6 mile and 3.5 mile long bordering coastlines, respectively. Egypt and Saudi Arabia form the western and eastern shores of the Gulf.

191 See M. El Baradei, "The Egyptian-Israeli Peace Treaty and Access to the Gulf of Aqaba: A New Legal Regime" (1982) 76 A.J.I.L. 532.

192 Canada supported the general international view, expressed by France, that "the Gulf of Aqaba, by reason partly of its breadth and partly of the fact that its shores belong to four different states, constitutes international waters" [citation omitted]. Blum, *supra* note 11 at 276-77.

within, the Gulf of Aqaba.[193] An interesting footnote to the matter was the statement of American Secretary of State John Foster Dulles that "[i]f the four littoral States which have boundaries upon the Gulf should all agree that it should be closed, then it should be closed."[194]

The ramifications for Canada and Québec from the Gulf of Aqaba situation are apparent. A loss of the Gulf of St. Lawrence's status as historic waters in the eyes of the international community could result from Canada attempting to limit Québec's coastline to the low water mark or otherwise at the mouth of the St. Lawrence River. In contrast, the preservation of the Gulf as a shared *mare clausum* will require at minimum a joint agreement and the acquiescence of other states.[195] If such joint sovereignty between Canada and an independent Québec is possible, then a claim by Québec to a defined portion of continental shelf and exclusive economic rights *outside* the Gulf might also be within the realm of possibility. The basis for such a unique proposition would be founded on the *Gulf of Fonseca* case.[196]

The Gulf of Fonseca *Case: A Canada-Québec Condominium?*

The Gulf of Fonseca is a small embayment at the confluence of the Pacific Ocean coasts of El Salvador, Honduras, and Nicaragua.[197] The International Court of Justice described the political history of the Gulf in its 1992 boundary decision:

> The Gulf was discovered by the Spanish navigator Andrés Nino in 1522, who named the Gulf after Juan Rodriguez de Fonseca, Bishop of Burgos, patron of his expedition, which had been organized by Captain Gil Gonzalez Davila. It appears that the Spanish Crown thereafter claimed and exercised continuous and peaceful sovereignty over the waters of the Gulf, without serious or more than temporary contestation until the

193 See generally L. Gross, "The Geneva Conference on the Law of the Sea and the Right of Innocent Passage through the Gulf of Aqaba" (1959) 53 A.J.I.L. 564.

194 News Conference Statement (Feb. 19, 1957) 36 *Department of State Bulletin* 404 (Jan.-June, 1957). See Gross, *ibid.* at 570, and Blum, *supra* note 11 at 309.

195 The role of the United States will feature prominently, not least because of its interests in the St. Lawrence Seaway.

196 *Supra* note 11.

197 The Gulf is approximately 20 nautical miles wide at its mouth and about 30 miles in diameter. On the geographic nature of the Gulf see the *Gulf of Fonseca* case, supra note 11 at 588 (para. 383).

three riparian states gained their independence in 1821. For the greater part of its long, known history, therefore, the Gulf was a single-State bay, the waters of which were under the single sway of the Spanish Crown . . . The rights in the Gulf of Fonseca of the present coastal States were thus acquired, like their land territories, by succession from Spain.[198]

The Central American Court of Justice held in a 1917 decision that the Gulf of Fonseca was an embayment possessed jointly or in "condominium" among its three littoral states.[199] The judicial search in this judgment for certainty and stability among the former colonies of Spain was to be followed by the International Court of Justice in 1992.

The origins of the 1992 *Gulf of Fonseca* case were rooted in a continuing dispute over uncertain boundaries that were ill-defined from the time of independence from Spain and had been contested periodically in armed conflict between El Salvador and Honduras.[200] A land boundary was partly drawn by agreement between the two states in 1980, but several issues remained unresolved, including the status of the Gulf of Fonseca, sovereignty over two small islands, and the entitlement of Honduras to a maritime zone outside the Gulf. El Salvador and Honduras sought adjudication by Special Agreement in 1987 at the International Court of Justice, and Nicaragua thereafter joined as an intervener.[201] In the result, the Court decided that the Gulf of Fonseca was held undivided and jointly by the three. To make the result even more unique, a vaguely defined three-nautical-mile-wide "coastal band" was awarded to each party. The Court held finally that all three states were possessed of the right to claim a full complement of maritime zones seaward of the Gulf.[202]

198 *Ibid.*, 589 (para. 385).

199 An English language translation of the Spanish judgment appears in (1917) 11 A.J.I.L. 674. The Court of Justice held that "[t]he legal status of the Gulf of Fonseca having been recognised by this Court to be that of a historic bay possessed of the characteristics of a closed sea, the three riparian states of el Salvador, Honduras and Nicaragua are, therefore, recognized as co-owners of its waters." *Ibid.*, para. 716.

200 See the adjudication of the land boundary dispute between El Salvador and Honduras in [1992] ICJ Rep. 351 at 380-553 (paras. 27-322).

201 See *Nicaraguan Intervention Judgment*, [1990] ICJ Rep. at 137 (para. 105). For comment on this case, see Iain Scobbie "The ICJ and the Gulf of Fonseca" (1994) 18 Marine Policy 249 at 261.

202 *Gulf of Fonseca* case, *supra* note 11 at paras. 404-420.

The reasoning of the Courts in the 1917 and 1992 *Gulf of Fonseca* decisions has been subject to much criticism. One academic has written: "Given some of the views expressed, [the 1992] decision might prove to be a thoroughly misleading statement of doctrine and accordingly it should be handled with a great deal of caution."[203] To the Court's credit, it was careful to limit the application of the condominium doctrine:

> It might, therefore, be sensible to regard the waters of the Gulf, insofar as they are the subject of the condominium or co-ownership, as *sui generis* . . . Nevertheless, the essential juridical status of these waters is the same as that of internal waters, since they are claimed à *titre de souverain* and, though subject to certain rights of passage, they are not territorial sea.[204]

It would be easy to discount the reasoning in the *Gulf of Fonseca* case as applicable solely to unique circumstance. The length of time that the Gulf had been held in condominium, coupled with the weight of 1917 judicial precedent and the nature in which colonial control was ceded militate against a wide application of the International Court of Justice's decision. However, the principles of historic and vital interests in waters that have become internal to a state cannot be dispensed with so readily.[205]

203 Scobbie, *supra* note 201 at 262. See also Blum, *supra* note 11 at 279. See especially the dissenting opinion of Vice-President Judge Oda, *supra* note 11 at 732 ff. In his review of historical bays, he found that a "pluri-State bay" could not be other than international waters. He continued (at 745-46 (para. 24)) "It may be concluded that the simple outcome of this study of the development of the law of the sea is that there did not and still does not (or, even, cannot) exist any such concept as a 'pluri-State bay' the waters of which are internal waters. It is not surprising that no rule covering such a pluri-State bay has ever been presented in international law. The very concept of 'internal waters,' which only appeared — under the term of 'inland waters' — in parallel with the fixing of the limit of the territorial waters (sea), implies, as a norm, the enclosure or semi-enclosure of the waters concerned within the embrace of a given jurisdiction. This element of embracement is absent or disappears when the shores of a geographical bay are so divided up between States as to render the criteria and rationale of a legal bay incapable of fulfillment. This is implicitly confirmed by the absence of any provision concerning the delimitation or division of internal waters either in the 1958 or the 1982 Conventions; the internal waters of one State cannot abut the internal waters of another State."

204 *Supra* note 11 at 605 (para. 412).

205 The Gulf of Fonseca has been characterized by some as more a "vital bay" than one which is historic. This is consistent with the reasoning of the Central American Court of Justice in its 1917 decision: "It is necessary to specify the

It would be obviously in the interest of an independent Québec that it maximize the extent of ocean sovereignty. However, the mutual assertion to the international community of the claim over the Gulf of St. Lawrence as waters shared in condominium would be tenuous, in that the generally accepted means of accomplishing such joint sovereignty, agreement between littoral states, is not likely to emerge from maximalist claims by Québec or a Canada anxious to preserve the jurisdictional *status quo*. However, the possibility of shared sovereignty over the Gulf could be too attractive for the two to forego.[206] With even further possible consequences, the *Gulf of Fonseca* case explicitly permitted a seaward division of exclusive economic waters.

In order to establish the waters (and the continental shelf) of the Gulf of St. Lawrence as an historic condominium, Québec would find itself in a contradictory tide of international law. At minimum, to limit the expansion of Québec, the federal government would be expected to assert its continuing jurisdiction over Canada's offshore. Canada's established maritime claims, supported by the weight of judicial decisions regarding the maritime limits of the provinces, would provide much evidence that historical title to the Gulf of St. Lawrence is vested in the Canadian central government. Two possibilities, both tenuous, can be suggested as a means for creation of joint maritime sovereignty in the Gulf of St. Lawrence.

A first scenario following the secession of Québec might be the dissolution of the entire Canadian federation. Into such a vacuum the two nations would be free to express a claim to the Gulf of St. Lawrence as shared internal waters. However, not only does such an outcome appear remote, but the loss of Canadian sovereignty *per se* in the Gulf suggests that its historic title by continuous possession

---

characteristics proper thereto from the threefold point of view of history, geography and the vital interests of the surrounding states": (1917) 11 A.J.I.L. 674 at 700.

206 The majority decision of the ICJ in the *Gulf of Fonseca* case is notable. "Given that there is a condominium of the waters of the Gulf, it follows that there is a tri-partite presence at the closing line of the Gulf and that Honduras is not locked out from rights in respect of the ocean waters outside the bay. This also seems equitable . . . Since the legal situation on the landward side of the closing line is one of joint sovereignty, it follows that all three of the joint sovereigns must have entitlement outside the closing line to territorial sea, continental shelf and exclusive economic zone," *supra* note 11 at 607-8 (paras. 418-20). The court left the issue of the delimitation of external maritime zones for future consideration by the parties.

would also dissipate, leaving the parties to agree upon claims over an area that had essentially reverted to a high seas regime.

A second possibility suggests itself through maintenance of the *status quo* in the Gulf of St. Lawrence for a lengthy period after Québec's secession. Should Canada and Québec make no effort to assert individual jurisdictions in the Gulf, then mutual sovereignty could emerge, analogous to the continuous possession of the Gulf of Fonseca by its three littoral states after the dissolution of the Federal Republic of Central America in 1839. The reasoning of the Court in adopting the 1917 decision in the 1992 *Gulf of Fonseca* case illustrates this possibility:

> [T]here was, at the time of independence, no delimitation between the three countries; and while the absence of delimitation does not always result in community, the undelimited waters of the Gulf have remained undivided and in a state of community, which entails a condominium or co-ownership of these waters. Further, the existence of a community was evidenced by continued and peaceful use of the waters by all the riparian States after independence . . . What matters, however, is . . . what was the position in this particular case, in which the maritime area in question had long been historic waters under a single State's sovereignty, apparently without any demarcated administrative limits, and was in 1821 jointly acquired by the three successor States by reason of the succession.[207]

From the present perspective of international law, the possibility of a joint sovereignty over the Gulf of St. Lawrence seems remote. An agreement between Canada and Québec to a condominium over the Gulf and the waters in the present Canadian EEZ has some precedent but does not have incontrovertible certainty. Thus, a replication of the result in the *Gulf of Fonseca* case, a shared regime of internal waters and full entitlements to sovereignty seaward of a Gulf closing line, seems unlikely. Sovereignty over the Canadian offshore is vested firmly in Canada's central government, and the spectre of Confederation dissolving and such sovereignty thereby dissipating remains speculative.

Conclusion

The establishment and recognition of an independent Québec's maritime sovereignty is laden with uncertainty. The international community has in recent years come to accept the progressive

207 *Supra* note 11 at 599-600 (para. 401). Judge Oda took emphatic exception to the ICJ's adoption of the 1917 decision of the Central American Court of Justice. See his dissenting opinion, *ibid.*, 751 (para. 35) ff.

seaward expansion of maritime areas and claims. Maritime delimitation methods and their underlying principles are now almost wholly codified in UNCLOS, which provides an oceans regime for all independent states. Québec would logically turn to the Convention in support of its claims, seeking to establish a territorial sea and sovereign rights to the continental shelf and an EEZ.

However, the validity of such claims to ocean areas will be anchored in the effectiveness of Québec's independence, recognition of its territorial rights by the international community, and the position adopted by Canada. Québec could be content to adhere to the territorial *status quo* in the Gulf of St. Lawrence, secure that its ocean interests would be best provided for through agreement and international confidence in its relationship with Canada. At least one scenario to the contrary, outright assertion over, and even attempted control of, a maritime area, is also possible.

The preferred course to resolve jurisdictional claims in the Gulf of St. Lawrence is through agreement. The critical interests of Canada and Québec in this region are part of the high stakes issues of separation, in which conflict can only result in lasting damage to the ocean interests of both. Fortunately, if legal conflict must be the result, there is a sufficient body of juridical principles and accepted state practice to permit Canada and an independent Québec to arrive at an equitable agreement in the Gulf of St. Lawrence. Canada's acceptance of Québec as a coastal state, generating in its own right a projecting complement of maritime zones, will be a vital first step. With the effects of geography considered upon a proposed delimitation of the Gulf, a negotiated agreement over sovereignty can encompass the substantive claims of the two states. The practical difficulties of classic ocean boundary-making, notably in the Gulf because of the distorting effects of islands and Québec's position as a shelf-locked state, could then be avoided.

Whatever the merits and disadvantages to Québec's departure from the Canadian federation, the resulting definition and assertion of the two nations' maritime rights will have lasting effects upon the international law of the sea.

Sommaire

Notre mer? les revendications maritimes du Québec indépendant dans le Golfe du St. Laurent

La géographie maritime du Québec ouvre des possibilités intéressantes dans le cas de son indépendance du Canada. Un survol historique de ses frontières maritimes révèle clairement l'importance des frontières maritimes pour l'avenir du Québec. L'auteur examine les aspirations du Québec à la lumière de la jurisprudence et des conventions internationales récentes. Ensuite, il évalue l'impact des différentes méthodes de délimitation maritimes pour le Canada et le Québec. Finalement, l'auteur explore la possibilité d'une souveraineté conjointe dans le Golfe du St. Laurent ainsi que l'application du concept de condominium à la situation Canada-Quebec.

Summary

Notre Mer? An Independent Québec's Maritime Claims in the Gulf of St. Lawrence and Beyond

The basic fact of Québec as a coastal entity creates interesting questions when considering the implications of its independence. A historical survey of its maritime boundaries further confirms the importance of maritime boundaries for an independent Québec. The author examines Québec's possible claims in the light of recent international law cases and conventions. He also explores the application of various methods of maritime boundary delimitation on Québec and Canada. Finally, the author explores the possibility of joint sovereignty in the Gulf of St. Lawrence and the application of the condominium concept to Canada and Québec.

Trials, Tribulations, and Triumphs: Major Developments in 1997 at the International Criminal Tribunal for the Former Yugoslavia

DARRYL ROBINSON

Introduction

Nineteen ninety-seven was a watershed year for the International Tribunal for the Prosecution of Persons Responsible for Serious Violations of International Humanitarian Law Committed in the Territory of the Former Yugoslavia since 1991. Since its creation by the Security Council in 1993,[1] the Tribunal has experienced difficulty in fulfilling its mandate due to a shortage of personnel and equipment, a lack of co-operation from key states and entities in the region, and an apparent reluctance on the part of the international community to apprehend indicted persons. As of January 1997, a great deal of money and effort had been invested with little in the way of visible results. The Tribunal had publicly indicted seventy-four persons but only seven were in custody, and many discouraged voices expressed doubt about the future prospects of the endeavour.[2]

A former law clerk to Mr. Justice John Major of the Supreme Court of Canada, Darryl Robinson now works in the United Nations, Criminal and Treaty Law Division of the Legal Affairs Bureau of the Department of Foreign Affairs and International Trade.

1 The Security Council created the Tribunal and adopted its Statute in Resolution 827 (S/RES/827(1993)), thus completing a process initiated in Resolution 808 (S/RES/808(1993)).

2 See, e.g., Tracy Wilkinson, "Problems Outweigh Progress of UN Tribunal," *Los Angeles Times*, (May 6, 1997); Rasim Cerimag, "Tried and Found Wanting," *The Tribunal*, No. 8, (April/May 1997); Morris Abram, "Will War Criminals Escape Justice?," *Wall Street Journal* (Apr. 11, 1997).

Over the course of 1997, several impasses were broken. Chief prosecutor, Louise Arbour,[3] appears to have been instrumental in turning around the fortunes of the Tribunal. She has been credited with successfully prompting the international community to take necessary action where local states and entities had failed to co-operate in arresting indictees.[4] In June 1997, a joint operation between the United Nations Transitional Administration for Eastern Slavonia (UNTAES) and the Office of the Prosecutor resulted in the arrest of suspected war criminal Slavko Dokmanovic.[5] In July 1997, the NATO-led Stabilization Force (SFOR)[6] detained suspected war criminal Milan Kovacevic at a hospital in Prijedor. In a separate action, SFOR forces approached and challenged suspected war criminal Simo Drljaca. Drljaca fired at them, and SFOR troops returned fire in self-defence, as a result of which Drljaca later died.[7] All three men had been indicted in "sealed" or non-public indictments, pursuant to the Rules of Procedure of the Tribunal.[8]

[3] Madam Justice Louise Arbour, formerly of the Ontario Court of Appeal, assumed the position of Chief Prosecutor in October 1996.

[4] Observers have noted that Arbour has been "stepping on toes . . . but . . . those toes needed stepping on" and "has been pulling every lever . . . to raise pressure on the villains in her sights": Timothy Appleby, "Tribunal Adopts Get-Tough Strategy," *Globe and Mail* (Aug. 4, 1997) 1. See also Timothy Appelby, "Ontario Judge Speeds War Crimes Arrests," *Globe and Mail* (July 11, 1997) A1; Charles Trueheart, "UN Prosecutor Sees Breakthrough in Arrest of Serb War Crime Suspects," *Washington Post* (July 1, 1997) A12.

[5] Tribunal, Press Release CC/PIO/221(27 June 1997). Tribunal press releases may be found at <www.un.org/icty>.

[6] This is the successor to the NATO Implementation Force (IFOR).

[7] NATO, Press Release, "Statement by Secretary-General of NATO, Mr. Javier Solano on action by SFOR to detain indicted war criminals at Prijedor" (July 10, 1997); Robert Fox, "Bosnian Swoop Indicates Change in NATO tactics," *Electronic Telegraph* (July 11, 1997); Tribunal, Press Release CC/PIO/225 (July 10, 1997).

[8] Rule 53 of the Rules of Procedure and Evidence (revised Oct. 20 and Nov. 12, 1997), "Non-disclosure" allows the judge confirming the indictment to issue a non-public indictment. A challenge to the legality of the arrest was rejected by the Trial Chamber (Tribunal, Press Release CC/PIO/251 (Oct. 27, 1997)) and by the Appeal Chamber (Tribunal, Press Release CC/PIO/260 (Nov. 12, 1997)). As noted by Chief Prosecutor Arbour, "there is nothing tricky about arresting people without giving them advance warning. That's the way police forces operate all over the world." Trueheart, *supra* note 4.

The arrests were followed by a wave of threats and attacks against international personnel in the region, fueled by local media.[9] Nevertheless, the international community has continued to demonstrate its resolve to bring war criminals to justice. SFOR has been playing a more active role, which has included crackdowns on special police units controlled by hardliners and the seizure of transmitters used for inflammatory broadcasts.[10] Further arrests have continued to take place, such as on December 18, 1997, when Dutch SFOR troops detained two more indictees. The first, Anto Furundzija, was indicted in a "sealed" indictment and was detained without incident; the second, Vlatko Kupreskic, who was publicly indicted, fired on SFOR troops and was wounded by return fire.[11]

The Tribunal has also enjoyed improved co-operation from the states and entities in the region. Following a visit to The Hague in July 1997 by Montenegro's state prosecutor, Vladmir Susovic, Montenegro has pledged active co-operation with the Tribunal.[12] In April 1997, Croatia transferred indicted war crimes suspect Zlatko Aleksovski to the Tribunal.[13] More dramatically, on October 6, 1997, Croatia assisted in the voluntary surrender of ten Bosnian Croats to the Tribunal, including Dario Kordic, the vice-president of the Croatian Community of Herceg-Bosna.[14] This followed a pledge by the United States to make every effort to strengthen the Tribunal's resources to facilitate speedy trials for the indictees. Chief prosecutor Louise Arbour welcomed the co-operation by Croatia and the surrender of the ten indictees, but clarified that the

9 Edward Cody, "U.S. Soldier in Bosnia Wounded in Sickle Attack," *Washington Post* (July 17, 1997); Mike O'Connor, "Serbs Threaten NATO Soldiers," *Globe and Mail* (July 17, 1997).

10 Tom Walker, "NATO Targets Karadzic TV Link," *London Times* (Aug. 22, 1997); Tracy Wilkinson, "Standoff in Bosnia: Karadzic Loyalists Trapped for Hours in Hotel," *Montreal Gazette* (Sept. 10, 1997) B4; "Hardline Serbs Clash with NATO-led Troops," *Reuters* (Sept. 24, 1997); Chris Hedges, "NATO Troops in Bosnia Silence Karadzic's Television Station," *New York Times* (Oct. 1, 1997); Angus Mackinnion, "NATO 'Tightening the Screw' on Bosnian Serb Hardliners," *Agence France Presse* (Oct. 1, 1997).

11 Chris Hedges, "Dutch Troops Seize Two War Crimes Suspects, Wounding One," *New York Times* (Dec. 19, 1997) A20; Tribunal, Press Release CC/PIO/277 (December 18, 1997).

12 Tribunal, Press Release CC/PIO/203 (May 29, 1997); Drasko Duranovic, "The Tribunal Goes to the Coast," *The Tribunal*, No. 10, Aug./Sept. 1997.

13 Tribunal, Press Release CC/PIO/185 (Apr. 28, 1997).

14 Mike Corder, "Bosnian War Crimes Suspects Surrender," *Globe and Mail* (Oct. 7, 1997).

Tribunal itself had not and could not give any guarantees of trials within three to five months.[15]

These developments signal a turnaround in the fortunes of the Tribunal. By mid-December 1997, the Tribunal had obtained custody over twenty-two indictees.[16] The resulting increase in the Tribunal's workload has prompted the United Nations to provide a substantial increase in the Tribunal's budget.[17] In addition, the international community has stepped up its support for the Tribunal, contributing personnel, equipment, facilities, financial assistance, and other programs such as the enforcement of sentences and witness relocation.[18] Finally, new judges were elected in 1997 and assumed office in November, with U.S. judge Gabrielle Kirk McDonald (who played an active role in all three of the cases discussed below) selected as the new president of the Tribunal.[19]

As the Tribunal swung into action in 1997, it encountered many hitherto unsettled legal issues and has therefore provided seminal analyses of these issues. This article focuses on the major legal developments in the jurisprudence of the Tribunal during 1997. It will examine the Trial Chamber's Opinion and Judgment in the *Tadic* case, particularly its treatment of war crimes and crimes against humanity, the Appeal Chamber's *Erdemovic* judgment, which

[15] With respect to six of the ten accused, the office of the prosecutor would be ready for trial within three to five months, but no such guarantee could be offered with respect to the others. In all cases, it is for the judges to set dates for trial and not the prosecutor: Tribunal, Press Release CC/PIO/246 (Oct. 6, 1997).

[16] This figure dropped to nineteen when judges ordered the release of three individuals following a request by the prosecutor to withdraw the indictments due to lack of evidence: Tribunal, Press Release CC/PIO/279 (Dec. 19, 1997).

[17] UNGA resolution 52/217, adopted by consensus Dec. 15, 1997, increased the Tribunal's budget to $64 million U.S., an increase of approximately 33 per cent.

[18] Discussed *infra* in the conclusion of this article.

[19] Election of judges for the next four-year term took place in the General Assembly on May 20, 1997 (Tribunal, Press Release CC/PIO/197 (May 21, 1997)), with the new judges taking office on Nov. 17, 1997 (Tribunal, Press Release CC/PIO/261 (Nov. 12, 1997)). Judge Gabrielle Kirk McDonald was elected president of the Tribunal by her peers on Nov. 19 (Tribunal, Press Release CC/PIO/264 (Nov. 19, 1997)). Judges Sidwa and Li passed away during 1997 (Tribunal, Press Release CC/PIO/173 (Apr. 1, 1997) and CC/PIO/257 (Nov. 6, 1997) respectively), and Judge Jules Deschênes, a Canadian, retired on Apr. 18, 1997, for health reasons (Tribunal, Press Release CC/PIO/187 (Apr. 29, 1997)).

dealt with guilty pleas and the defence of duress, and the Appeal Chamber's decision on subpoena orders.

TADIC JUDGMENT

PROCEDURAL HISTORY

On May 7, 1997, Trial Chamber II[20] handed down its Opinion and Judgment in *Prosecutor* v. *Dusko Tadic a.k.a "Dule"*[21] after the first war crimes trial by an international tribunal since the Nuremberg and Tokyo tribunals at the close of the Second World War.

Dusko Tadic was arrested in February 1994 in Germany, where he was then living, on suspicion of having committed offences at the Omarska camp in the former Yugoslavia, including torture and aiding and abetting the commission of genocide. In November 1994, the Tribunal issued a formal request asking the Federal Republic of Germany to defer the *Tadic* case to the competence of Tribunal.[22] Germany accordingly enacted the necessary legislation to permit the transfer of suspects to the Tribunal and transferred Tadic to the Tribunal in April 1995.

The indictment charged Tadic with 132 counts involving grave breaches of the Geneva Conventions and violations of the laws and customs of armed conflict and crimes against humanity for acts including murder, torture, rape, inhumane treatment, and persecution. Tadic pleaded not guilty to all charges in the indictment. The defence raised several jurisdictional arguments, *inter alia* challenging the legality of the establishment of the Tribunal. These arguments were heard by the Trial Chamber and then by the Appeal Chamber, which ruled in October 1995 that the establishment of the Tribunal was lawful under the United Nations Charter and under international law.[23] The trial, which has been described as

20 The eleven judges of the Tribunal are divided into two Trial Chambers with three judges each, and an Appeals Chamber with five judges.

21 Case No. IT-94-1-T, May 7, 1997 [hereinafter Judgment]. Complete copies of all Tribunal decisions can be found at <http://www.un.org/icty/index.html>.

22 Pursuant to para. 2 of Art. 9 of the Statute, the Tribunal has primacy over national courts and may request national courts to defer to the competence of the Tribunal.

23 Appeals Chamber, Decision on Defence Motion for Interlocutory Appeal on Jurisdiction, *Prosecutor* v. *Dusko Tadic a/k/a "Dule,"* Case No. IT-94-1-AR72, Oct. 2, 1995 [hereinafter *Tadic* decision].

"the *real* trial of the century,"[24] commenced on May 7, 1996 and continued for seven months, during which 125 witnesses testified and 473 exhibits were entered as evidence.

FACTUAL FINDINGS

General Observations

In a 301-page judgment, 173 pages are devoted to a review of the massive body of evidence and a determination of the facts. The factual findings by the Trial Chamber are possibly even more important that the legal findings. First, these findings were made by an independent, international body of judges in accordance with the criminal law standard of proof and will therefore serve as an objective and reliable historic record. As stated by President Antonio Cassese, the "records and reams of evidence collated by the Prosecutor and scrutinized by the judges will impede revisionists from denying what happened in Opstina Prijedor and elsewhere in the former Yugoslavia."[25]

Second, the findings should help inform public opinion outside the territory of the former Yugoslavia. By giving concrete form to the atrocities committed, the *Tadic* judgment may help galvanize international will and serve as a reminder of the need for action.

Finally, the judgment's review of the context of the conflict offers a chilling reminder of how easily a climate of political uncertainty combined with an intense campaign of hate propaganda can strip away the fragile veneer of civilization. The judgment recounts the success of nationalists in converting an apparently friendly atmosphere into one of fear and hostility,[26] which was accompanied by the suppression of moderate voices, the formation of "Serb Autonomous Regions," the assumption of power by "Crisis Staffs,"

24 William Horne, "The Real Trial of the Century," *American Lawyer* available at <http://courttv.com/casefiles/warcrimes/reports/realtoc.html>.

25 Statement delivered by Antonio Cassese, President of the Tribunal, to the UN General Assembly, Nov. 4, 1997 (available at <http://www.un.org/icty/spch97e.htm>).

26 The Judgment notes that, despite a history of atrocities and repression, the population of Bosnia and Herzegovina had been multi-ethnic for centuries and had enjoyed good intercommunal relations, friendships, and intermarriages in the post-Second World War era: *supra* note 21, paras. 56-64.

and the implementation of a policy of ethnic cleansing.[27] As part of this policy, thousands of Muslim and Croat civilians were confined in the Omarska, Keraterm, and Trnopolje camps, where "the situation was horrendous, with . . . brutal beatings, rapes and torture commonplace and the conditions of life appalling."[28] The events recounted in the judgment present an objective lesson on the need to guard against the culture of impunity that permits these crimes to occur.

Specific Crimes Alleged in the Tadic *Case*

Before the outbreak of hostilities, Dusko Tadic was the owner of a café and an accomplished karate expert. Tadic became increasingly involved in nationalist politics and helped to implement a policy of ethnic cleansing. The numerous counts in the indictment related primarily to the killing, torture, and abuse of Muslims and Croats within the camps, participation in beatings, killings, plunder, and

27 Pursuant to this policy, non-Serbs were subjected to persecution, beatings, destruction of property, and terror tactics, which eventually escalated into deportation, disappearances, confinement in concentration camps, and finally, liquidation. It must be kept in mind that although the Judgment focuses on atrocities committed by Bosnian Serbs, because these were the events relevant to the *Tadic* case, further atrocities committed by other groups will come to light in cases involving other defendants.

28 Judgment, *supra* note 21 at para. 151. Many of the allegations against Tadic related to the Omarska camp, which was perhaps the most notorious of the camps. The Trial Chamber heard from 30 witnesses who survived the brutality of the conditions to which they were systematically subjected at Omarska (para. 157). When prisoners arrived by bus at Omarska, they were usually searched, robbed, and beaten (para. 158). Hundreds of prisoners were confined in small rooms, with prisoners "packed one on top of the other and often they had to lie in the midst of excrement"(para. 159). One meal a day was provided, consisting of a plate of watery potato soup and a small slice of bread, and prisoners were often beaten by guards as they came for the daily meal (para. 160). Prisoners were called out for interrogation, during which they would be severely beaten (para. 163). In the evening, members of paramilitary organizations and local Serbs were routinely allowed to enter the camps to abuse, beat, and kill prisoners. These groups would call out particular prisoners from their rooms and attack them with sticks, iron bars, or lengths of heavy electric cable. Nails and knives were also among the weapons used (para. 164). Women were routinely called out of their rooms at night and raped (para. 165). The "white house" was a place of particular horror, reserved for especially brutal treatment of selected prisoners. Prisoners who were forced to clean the area after beatings reported finding the blood, teeth, and skin of victims on the floor. Dead bodies of prisoners, lying in heaps, were often seen (para. 166).

destruction outside the camps, and participation in the seizure, selection, and transportation of persons to the camps.[29]

The factual findings are remarkable in a number of respects; first, the sheer amount of evidence reviewed; second, the stringent standard of proof applied by the Trial Chamber; third, the shocking severity of the crimes; and fourth, the fact that so many of the victims were acquaintances, neighbours, and schoolmates of the accused.

On the first point, the body of evidence considered by the Trial Chamber was massive, including 125 witnesses and 473 exhibits. Credible testimony was received from scores of witnesses who had personally seen the accused beating and torturing prisoners in a variety of settings and with a variety of weapons. The defence asserted that the accused had never been to the Omarska camp and that he was working as a reserve traffic policeman at all relevant times. However, the accused's shift records generally did not cover the times of the offences alleged and therefore afforded no alibi. Moreover, the accused had been positively identified by numerous credible witnesses and the Trial Chamber concluded that "the accused's general denial of ever having been at the Omarska camp is rejected in view of the overwhelming credible evidence to the contrary."[30]

The second striking aspect of the factual findings was the stringent standard applied by the Trial Chamber in determining whether a fact had been proven by the prosecution beyond a reasonable doubt. One example of this cautious approach was the refusal by the Trial Chamber to infer that a particular victim had been killed, even though it was established beyond a reasonable doubt that Tadic and others had severely beaten the victim with iron bars, after which another prisoner was forced to bite off one of the victim's testicles.[31] The victim was dragged to a nearby table, the other prisoners were ordered to leave and the victim was never seen or heard from since. Despite the fact that heaps of bodies were often seen and dead bodies were buried in makeshift graves,[32] and despite the severity of the injuries and the extreme unlikelihood

29 *Ibid.*, paras. 38-51.

30 *Ibid.*, para. 434 The value of the shift records as alibi evidence was further undermined by the fact that the records were completed in advance (para. 509) and there was no record of actual attendance (para. 277).

31 *Ibid.*, para. 235-41.

32 *Ibid.*, para. 240.

that medical attention was administered, the Trial Chamber refused to infer that the victim had died.[33] This refusal may be disappointing, but it does have the advantage of making the findings of the Trial Chamber all the more credible and unimpeachable.[34]

A third notable feature of the factual findings is the shocking severity of the crimes committed by Tadic. In sum, it was proven beyond a reasonable doubt that the accused brutally assaulted several prisoners on several occasions using a number of different instruments, participated in mass beatings, and participated in an exceptionally sadistic episode of torture and beatings.[35] Outside the camps, he participated in the rounding up of non-Serbs and in several brutal and violent beatings and killings.[36] The clinical descriptions in the judgment help make these atrocities less abstract and demonstrate the moral imperative of bringing the transgressors to justice and deterring future transgressors.

The final striking aspect of the factual findings is that many of the victims and witnesses had known the accused since childhood, through school, through karate classes, through family friendships, or through the community.[37] Tadic himself testified that before the

33 *Ibid.*, para 241. There was in fact more than one victim who was never seen again after that particular episode. Another victim had been beaten with an iron bar, had black liquid poured on him, and was cut by the accused with a knife "as one slices chops." He was later seen lying on the hangar floor, with no signs of life. To confirm that he was dead, a guard put his foot on the victim's neck, turned his head backwards and forwards, and then ordered prisoners to drag his body to and fro across the hangar floor. He was never seen or heard from again: *ibid.*, para 238. Nevertheless, the Trial Chamber declined to infer that he was dead.

34 Moreover, given the political climate in wich the Tribunal operates, it would be most inopportune to convict an accused for murder and have the murder victim turn up alive. This very situation has allegedly occurred in domestic proceedings, as two Serbs, Sretko Damjanovic and Borislav Herak, were reportedly convicted by the Bosnian government for the murder of two Muslims who were later found to be alive.

35 See, e.g., Judgment, *supra* note 21 at paras. 235-37, 257-61, 279, 302, 316, 435, and 448.

36 See, e.g., *ibid.* at paras. 341, 366-75, 397, 455, and 461.

37 E.g., one prisoner had been Tadic's teacher in school, had helped Tadic gain access to the school gym for karate lessons, and his son had helped Tadic build his house and café: *ibid.*, para. 414. Another victim had been a friend of the accused for five years before the conflict and had seen the accused regularly for business and social purposes: *ibid.*, para. 440. One witness, Hase Icic, had known Tadic since school days and also went to school with, and played soccer

conflict most of his friends were Muslims.[38] The familiarity between victims and oppressors makes the severity of the violence unleashed in the conflict all the more disturbing and bewildering.[39]

In sum, the facts of the *Tadic* case provide a deeply disturbing account of brutal and sadistic treatment in a lawless environment. Although troubling, the factual findings demonstrate the importance of the work of the Tribunal and the need to bring to justice those responsible for these atrocities. The establishment of a factual record with such objective dispassion and clarity may prove to be one of the most important legacies of the *Tadic* case.

LEGAL CONCLUSIONS

The *Tadic* judgment significantly develops the jurisprudence of the Tribunal, and is certain to have an impact on international humanitarian law and the development of international criminal law and procedures generally. Since this was the first international criminal trial in decades, it was necessary for the Trial Chamber to interpret and clarify some pivotal concepts, particularly with respect to the definition of crimes against humanity and the preconditions for finding a grave breach of the Geneva Conventions.[40]

---

with, Tadic's brother. Icic was taken to a small room in the Omarska camp, where a noose was put around his neck. He stood face to face with Tadic before he was beaten unconscious by Tadic and others with cable, iron balls, an iron bar, a wooden bat, and rubber truncheons: *ibid.*, para. 251-52.

38 *Ibid.*, para. 181.

39 Leonard Stern captures this bewilderment in "Judgment at The Hague," *Ottawa Citizen* (Nov. 2, 1997), where he reports the testimony of witnesses that one of Tadic's victims was heard to plea, "Dule, brother, how have I wronged you?"

40 The Trial Chamber also made several evidentiary and procedural rulings con cerning the specificity of charges, corroboration, hearsay evidence, identification evidence, the reliability of witnesses who were victims in the conflict, and the effect of pre-trial media coverage: Judgment, *supra* note 21 at Section 5, paras. 532-56. The approach of the Trial Chamber was to consider the practice of the major legal systems of the world and to develop a common-sense approach free from technicalities and consistent with the twin goals of fairness and truth-seeking. E.g., the Trial Chamber rejected the suggestion that the testimony of all victims in the conflict should be discarded as inherently unreliable, and instead ruled that the reliability of each witness should be assessed on a case-by-case basis: Judgment, *ibid.*, para. 541. The rulings will be of interest in future Tribunal proceedings and may also establish a helpful precedent for the Rwanda Tribunal and the proposed International Criminal Court.

Crimes against Humanity

After reviewing the Tribunal's Statute and other relevant authorities, the Trial Chamber concluded that a "crime against humanity" entails (1) the commission of an offence enumerated in Article 5 of the Statute[41] (for example, murder, torture, etc.); (2) during an armed conflict; (3) as part of a widespread or systematic attack directed against a civilian population; (4) on discriminatory grounds; and (5) with the requisite intent and knowledge of these elements.[42] Given the relative dearth of jurisprudence on international humanitarian law, the Trial Chamber was faced with the task of further elaborating upon these elements in order to apply them.

Connection to Armed Conflict

The need for a connection to armed conflict had been considered by the Appeals Chamber in the *Tadic (Jurisdiction)* decision.[43] Although the Appeals Chamber concluded that a connection to armed conflict was *not* required under customary international law,[44] the Chamber was constrained by the express wording of the Statute, which explicitly requires the commission of the crime during an international or internal armed conflict.[45] In determining the degree of connection required, the Trial Chamber adopted a simple temporal and geographic test, holding that the act need only be committed during the armed conflict (the temporal requirement) and in territory under control of a party to the

41 Art. 5 of the Statute defines crimes against humanity as "the following crimes when committed in an armed conflict, whether international or internal in character, and directed against any civilian population: murder; extermination; enslavement; deportation; imprisonment; torture; rape; persecution on political, racial and religious grounds; and other inhumane acts."

42 Judgment, *supra* note 21 at para. 626.

43 *Supra* note 23

44 *Ibid.*, paras. 140-42. Although a nexus requirement appeared in the Nuremberg Charter, it was not included in subsequent instruments such as Control Council Law No. 10, the Genocide Convention, or the Statute of the International Criminal Tribunal for Rwanda. The nexus requirement in the Nuremberg Charter arguably related to the jurisdiction of the Nuremberg Tribunal rather than the definition of crimes against humanity. On this topic, see Joseph Rikhof, "Crimes against Humanity, Customary International Law and the International Tribunals for Bosnia and Rwanda" (1996) 6 N.J.C.L. 233, and James C. O'Brien, "The International Tribunal for Violations of International Humanitarian Law in the former Yugoslavia" (1993) 87 A.J.I.L. 639.

45 *Tadic (Jurisdiction)* decision, supra note 23 at paras. 138-42.

conflict (the geographic requirement). This simple test is subject to an important caveat, that the crime *must not be unrelated* to the conflict. A crime committed for purely personal motives would therefore not have sufficient connection to the armed conflict.[46]

Widespread or Systematic

The Trial Chamber confirmed that the requirement that the crime be "directed against any civilian population" is intended to exclude isolated or random acts and restrict jurisdiction to acts committed on a widespread or systematic basis. The term "widespread" refers to the number of victims and the term "systematic" refers to a pattern or methodical plan or policy.[47]

Intent

The Trial Chamber held that the perpetrator must be aware of the broader context (that is, the widespread or systematic attack on a civilian population) in which his acts occurred.[48] In this respect, the decision is consistent with *R.* v. *Finta*,[49] a Supreme Court of Canada decision that has been widely criticized.[50] It is respectfully submitted that the conclusion of the Trial Chamber (and the Supreme Court of Canada on this issue) is entirely supported by

46 The framing of the proposition (the crime "must *not* be *un*related") is significant because in most cases there will be many possible motives and it would be difficult to establish one predominant motive. Thus, the prosecution is relieved of the onerous burden of establishing a single predominant motive that was related to the armed conflict, and yet a "safety valve" is provided for those rare cases where there truly is no connection and the act is committed for purely personal motives. Such a flexible approach is all the more warranted when one recalls that customary international law would not have required any nexus at all.

47 Judgment, *supra* note 21 at para. 648. The Trial Chamber clarified the term "civilian population," noting that it means "predominantly civilian," so that the presence of a few non-civilians (combatants or prisoners of war) does not change the character of the population: para. 638. The Trial Chamber also confirmed that non-state actors can perpetrate crimes against humanity: paras. 654-55. Finally, the Tribunal indicated, albeit in *obiter*, that a single act can constitute a crime against humanity, provided it is part of a widespread or systematic attack: para. 649.

48 *Ibid.*, paras. 656-57.

49 [1994] 1 S.C.R. 701.

50 Irwin Cotler, "War Crimes Law and the *Finta* Case" (1995) 6 Supreme Court L. Rev. 577; David Matas, "The Case of Imre Finta" (1994) 43 Univ. of New Brunswick L.J. 281.

generally recognized principles of criminal liability. The very fact that the acts of the accused take place in the context of a widespread or systematic attack against a civilian population transforms the acts from a simple domestic crime to a crime against humanity. The widespread or systematic attack is an indispensable element of a crime against humanity. Therefore, in order to have the *mens rea* for a crime against humanity, the accused must be aware of the widespread or systematic attack.[51] This obligation on the prosecution to establish all mental elements of the offence is not unusually onerous. Knowledge may be implied from an objective examination of the circumstances.[52] Moreover, the mental element can be established by showing that the accused was either aware of, *or wilfully blind to,* the widespread or systematic attack.[53] Given the inescapable notoriety involved in any widespread or systematic attack on a civilian population, it would be a truly extraordinary case where an accused could credibly claim to have been completely unaware of the circumstances.

Discriminatory Motive

The final aspect of the Trial Chamber's discussion of crimes against humanity was the identification of an additional requirement that the offence must be committed on certain discriminatory grounds.[54] A requirement of discriminatory intent does not appear in the Statute, nor does it appear in other instruments indicative of customary international law, such as the Nuremberg Charter, the Tokyo Charter, Control Council Law No. 10, or the International Law Commission ("ILC") Draft Code of Crimes. Nor was the issue raised by either the prosecution or defence.[55] Nevertheless, the Trial Chamber imputed such a requirement because it was mentioned in the Report of the Secretary General and the statements of

51 If an accused committed a spontaneous assault but was somehow unaware of the ongoing widespread or systematic attack, the accused would have the *mens rea* for the crime of assault but not for the much more serious offence of a crime against humanity. Fundamental justice requires a mental blameworthiness (*mens rea*) reflecting the particular nature of the crime.

52 Judgment, *supra* note 21 at para. 657; *Finta, supra* note 49 at 819. In the absence of an admission by the accused, this is generally how knowledge must be proven.

53 Judgment, *ibid.*, para. 657; *Finta, ibid.*, 820.

54 Judgment, *ibid.*, para. 652.

55 *Ibid.*

some Security Council members.[56] Although reference to these sources is a useful practice established in Tribunal jurisprudence,[57] to do so in the absence of any statutory ambiguity was regrettable. Unlike the question of nexus to armed conflict, where the Tribunal was compelled to depart from customary international law due to the clear wording of the Statute, on the discrimination issue there was no such statutory constraint. Unlike the other inferred mental elements, on this issue there was no principle of customary international law requiring the insertion of the discrimination requirement. The addition of the discrimination requirement imposes an onerous and unnecessary burden on the prosecution. Moreover, the closed list of prohibited grounds could inadvertently exclude other equally invidious forms of discrimination.

In summary, the understandable but perhaps unwarranted reliance on statements supporting a discrimination requirement may complicate prosecutions in the future, but the judgment otherwise provides a useful and balanced elaboration of the definition of "crimes against humanity."

Grave Breaches: International Armed Conflict

The most controversial aspect of the judgment was the dismissal of eleven counts under Article 2 of the Statute (grave breaches of the Geneva Conventions) because of the conclusion that, at the relevant time and place, the armed conflict was not international.[58] On this point, there was a strong dissent from Judge Gabrielle Kirk McDonald.[59] All of the judges agreed that, before May 19, 1992, the conflict was international, but they split over the question of

56 Report of the Secretary-General Pursuant to Paragraph 2 of Security Council Resolution 808 (1993), (S/25704), presented May 3, 1993, at para. 48.

57 See, e.g., *Tadic (Jurisdiction)* decision, *supra* note 23 at paras. 75, 88, and 143.

58 The characterization of the conflict as international or non-international determines the applicability of Art. 2 of the Statute, "grave breaches of the Geneva Conventions of 1949." An offence under Art. 2 of the Statute can only be established where the victim is a "protected person" under the 1949 Geneva Conventions, which is a person "in the hands of a party to the conflict . . . of which they are not nationals." Thus, for the Bosnian Croats and Muslims to enjoy the status of "protected persons," triggering the grave breaches regime and Art. 2 of the Statute, it must be shown that they were effectively in the hands of agents of another State—in this case, the Federal Republic of Yugoslavia (Serbia and Montenegro).

59 Separate and Dissenting Opinion of Judge McDonald Regarding the Applicability of Art. 2 of the Statute: *Prosecutor* v. *Dusko Tadic a/k/a "Dule"* case IT-94-1-7 [hereinafter McDonald Opinion].

whether the conflict was international following the purported withdrawal of the JNA (the army controlled by the Federal Republic of Yugoslavia) on May 19, 1992.

The facts were as follows. Before May 19, 1992, military activities were carried out in the territory of Bosnia and Herzegovina ("Bosnia") by the JNA[60] — an army headquartered in Belgrade and controlled by the Federal Republic of Yugoslavia (Serbia and Montenegro) ("the FRY"). The Trial Chamber had no difficulty identifying the conflict during this period as international.[61]

On May 15, 1992, the Security Council, by Resolution 752, demanded the immediate cessation of all interference from outside Bosnia by units of the JNA, and that those units be withdrawn, disbanded, or subjected to the authority of the Bosnia government. The FRY responded by transferring JNA soldiers of Bosnian origin into a newly-created army, the army of the Republica Srpska (VRS), which remained in Bosnia. In this manner, the JNA formally withdrew from Bosnia while leaving behind a substantial force. There were many reasons to question the legitimacy of this withdrawal. Although the non-Bosnian *soldiers* were transferred, the *officers* of the JNA remained in Bosnia as part of the VRS, regardless of the fact that many officers were Serbs from the FRY rather than from Bosnia. Salaries and pensions for the soldiers and officers of the VRS continued to be paid by the FRY. Moreover, the VRS was financed by the FRY, received its supplies from the FRY, and used the arms and equipment provided by the FRY. The VRS used the same command structures, the same units, and the same methods of operation as it had as the JNA, and continued to work in coordination with FRY forces.[62]

Since Article 2 (grave breaches) applies only to international armed conflicts,[63] the applicability of the counts alleged under Article 2 hinged on whether the acts of the VRS were attributable to the FRY. The fundamental question was whether the FRY had sufficiently distanced itself from the VRS so that those forces could

60 The JNA had formerly been the multi-ethnic national army for the former Yugoslavia, but in the early 1990s it was transformed from 35 per cent to 90 per cent ethnic Serbs through disbanding non-Serb units, recruiting ethnic Serbs, and encouraging non-Serbs to leave: Judgment, *supra* note 21 at paras. 106-109.

61 *Ibid.*, paras. 581-82.

62 *Ibid.*, paras. 114-21.

63 See *supra* note 58.

not be regarded as *de facto* organs or agents of the FRY.[64] The majority[65] referred to the International Court of Justice (ICJ) *Nicaragua (Merits)* decision, which adopted a high threshold test of "effective control" in determining whether an armed band could be regarded as a *de facto* organ of a state.[66] The majority of the Trial Chamber concluded that it is not enough to prove the existence of a relationship of dependency; rather it is necessary to show that the state "exercised the potential for control inherent in that relationship of dependency."[67] The majority acknowledged that, in the light of the dependence of the VRS on the FRY, the FRY had the *capacity* to exert great influence, but there was no evidence that the FRY had *actually directed* operations.[68] The majority concluded that, in the absence of direct evidence of orders from the FRY overriding the authority of the VRS Corps Commander, it could not be said that those acts were carried out on behalf of the FRY.[69]

The majority acknowledged that:

> It is of course possible . . . to view the acts of the JNA and the [FRY] . . . as nothing more than a cynical and intentional creation of the objective factors necessary to distance themselves from direct legal responsibility for the acts of the [VRS], while doing everything to ensure that the material factors necessary to ensure the successful continuation of the armed conflict to achieve the same military and political goals were kept in place.[70]

However, the majority concluded that "that is not the only nor the most reasonable conclusion open on the evidence presented." The majority held that the FRY had given up effective control over the relevant parts of Bosnia after May 19, 1992, that the victims of the acts of the accused were therefore not "in the hands of" a foreign power, and that the victims were therefore not "protected persons."

64 Judgment, *supra* note 21 at para. 587.

65 Judges Stephen and Vohrah comprised the majority.

66 *Case Concerning Military and Paramilitary Activities in and Against Nicaragua (Nicaragua v. USA) (Merits)*, [1986] ICJ Rep 14. The ICJ concluded that proof of U.S. participation in the financing, organizing, training, supplying, and equipping of the contras was insufficient, since it was not proven that the U.S. had effective control of the operations. Likewise, the ICJ held that Nicaraguan assistance to rebels in Ecuador did not amount to armed attack.

67 Judgment, *supra* note 21 at para. 588.

68 *Ibid.*, para. 605.

69 *Ibid.*, paras. 596-601.

70 *Ibid.*, para. 606.

Accordingly, Article 2 (grave breaches) could not apply, so the accused was found not guilty of the eleven counts under Article 2.

Judge McDonald, in dissent, argued that the standard applied by the majority was even more demanding than the high threshold set by the ICJ in the *Nicaragua (Merits)* case. In her opinion, the evidence showed that the creation of the VRS was a legal fiction. The FRY continued to pay all salaries and pensions of the VRS, and several FRY Serb officers remained in the VRS. Although the name of the organization and the insignia had been changed,

> [t]here remained the same weapons, the same equipment, the same officers, the same commanders, largely the same troops, the same logistics centres, the same suppliers, the same infrastructure, the same source of payments, the same goals and mission, the same tactics, and the same operations. Importantly, the objective remained the same: to create an ethnically pure Serb state.[71]

Judge McDonald noted that, although there was little evidence of formal command by the FRY over the VRS, the VRS clearly continued to operate as an integrated and instrumental part of the FRY war effort. After reviewing the evidence of co-ordination and daily communication between the VRS and the FRY forces, she concluded that the re-designation was a ruse calculated to feign compliance with the Security Council resolution, while assuring that military operations continued successfully.[72] She concluded that the change was a change in name only, and that the FRY had not sufficiently distanced itself from the VRS so that those forces could not be regarded as *de facto* organs or agents of the FRY.

There is considerable reason to favour the dissenting position of Judge McDonald. The caution exhibited by the majority is understandable, given the uncertain ramifications in the field of state responsibility with respect to the funding and equipping of armed bands. Nevertheless, the decision of the majority as it now stands will essentially serve as an instruction manual for states on how to evade their international humanitarian law obligations through the

71 McDonald Opinion, *supra* note 59 at para. 7.

72 *Ibid.*, paras. 8-10. Other factors supporting McDonald's position are that (1) the FRY essentially depleted its own army to establish the VRS (*ibid.*, para. 14); (2) some officers had direct telephone lines between Belgrade and Pale, which were used in everyday communication (para. 8); (3) after its creation the VRS immediately carried out complex operations that had been planned by the JNA (para. 31); and (4), usually it would be illegal for JNA soldiers to serve any other force, yet service in the VRS was permitted: Judgment, *supra* note 21 at para. 594.

use of proxy forces. The approach of the majority appears to be even more stringent than the approach of the ICJ in the *Nicaragua (Merits)* decision — an approach that has been harshly criticized for imposing an inappropriately high threshold.[73]

Moreover, this was not a case of an outside state supporting an already-existing local insurgent movement; in this case, the FRY *created* the VRS. As the majority observed, the real question was whether the FRY "notwithstanding its continuing support for the VRS, had sufficiently distanced itself from the VRS so that those forces could not be regarded as *de facto* organs" of the FRY. Given the evidence that the change was essentially only a change of shoulder patches, most observers, including academic commentators,[74] the Security Council,[75] domestic courts,[76] and other expert

[73] The ICJ pronouncement that proof of funding, supplying arms, and providing logistic support to an armed band does not establish an armed attack has been rejected by many commentators and described as "flatly wrong as a principle of international law." This "purported rule would have disastrous consequences" because it would "encourage secret aggressive attack through support for terrorists and guerillas and discourage effective defence in response": John Norton Moore, "The *Nicaragua* Case and the Deterioration of World Order" (1987) 81 A.J.I.L. 151 at 154-55. See also John Lawrence Hargrove, "The *Nicaragua* Case and the Future of the Law of Force and Self Defence" (1987) 81 A.J.I.L. 135; Francis A. Boyle, "Determining U.S. Responsibility for Contra Operations under International Law" (1987) 81 A.J.I.L. 86; Dinstein, *War, Aggression and Self-Defence* 190 (Cambridge: Grotius, 1988); Dissenting Opinion of Judge Schwebel, Dissenting Opinion of Judge Sir Robert Jennings. A question can legitimately be raised whether the decision of the ICJ is inconsistent with the definition of aggression articulated by the General Assembly after decades of negotiation, which includes "the sending by, on, or behalf of a State of armed bands . . . which carry out acts of armed force against another State of such gravity as to amount to the acts listed above, *or substantial involvement therein*": UN General Assembly Resolution 3314 (1974).

[74] Extensive reference to documents indicating that the FRY exercised operational command-and-control over Serbian forces in Bosnia are made by Jordan J. Paust, where he concludes that "outside intervention in several forms by neighboring nations has definitely internationalized the conflict": "Applicability of International Criminal Law to Events in the former Yugoslavia" (1994) 9 Am. U. J. of Int'l. L. and Pol'y 499 at 507. James C. O'Brien, supra note 44 at 639 argues that, despite the ostensible withdrawal of the JNA, it would be wrong to say the conflict was internal, given the extensive use of proxy groups. Theodor Meron, "War Crimes in Yugoslavia and the Development of International Law" (1994) 88 A.J.I.L. 78 at 81, warned that any attempt to apply the *Nicaragua* test to the conflict in Yugoslavia "would result in byzantine complexity, making prosecutions difficult and often impossible." He argued that the "unacknowledged, but clear, intervention in the

observers,[77] have concluded that the conflict remained an international armed conflict. The decision of the majority has been criticized as having "a flavour of Alice in Wonderland,"[78] and as "very disturbing" for international humanitarian law.[79]

If international law is to be respected, it must accord with common sense. It is of course proper to proceed cautiously in describing a

---

Bosnian conflict by Belgrade on behalf of the Serbs . . . could transform the conflict from internal to international even under classic principles of international law": Meron, *ibid.*, 81. See also George H. Aldrich, "Jurisdiction of the International Criminal Tribunal for the Former Yugoslavia" (1996) 90 A.J.I.L. 64.

75 In resolution 757 (1992), the Security Council condemned the failure of the FRY to comply with the requirements of resolution 752. Thus the Security Council did not believe that the restructuring of the forces amounted to a withdrawal.

76 Grave breaches of the Geneva Conventions are crimes of universal jurisdiction punishable by any state. (The Tribunal has concurrent jurisdiction over grave breaches committed in the territory of the former Yugoslavia since 1991, but states may prosecute in the absence of a request for deferral from the Tribunal: Art. 9 of the Statute). Some states, notably Germany and the Netherlands, have therefore prosecuted persons alleged to have committed grave breaches during the conflict in the former Yugoslavia. For example, Novislav Djajic, a Bosnian Serb, was sentenced to five years of imprisonment by a German court in May 1997 for the murder of 14 Muslims. Although the material events occurred in Bosnia in June 1992, after the purported withdrawal of the FRY forces, the German court reached the opposite conclusion from that of the Trial Chamber, holding that the armed conflict was international in character.

77 The Commission of Experts concluded that the entire conflict was an armed conflict of an international character: Interim Report of the Commission of Experts Established Pursuant to Security Council Resolution 780 (1992), UN Doc. S/25274. Roy Gutman, "Federal Army Tied to Bosnia Crimes," *Newsday* (Nov. 1, 1995), quotes a U.S. defence source as saying that "they just changed shoulder patches," and quotes Borisov Jovic, a top Milosevic aide, as admitting that the alleged "withdrawal" was a ruse to deflect western criticism.

78 Roy Gutman, "Confusion in War Crimes Case," *Newsday* (May 13, 1997).

79 Niccoló Figá-Talamanca, "A Blow to Human Rights," *The Tribunal*, Vol. 9, June/July 1997, criticizes the majority decision as "very disturbing" for international humanitarian law and inconsistent with customary law. The majority decision narrows the scope of the "grave breaches" regime and may therefore deter further prosecutions. The majority "set such a tough test for effective control that it would be almost impossible to hold States accountable for acts by their local agents," thus allowing states "to violate the Conventions with impunity if they act outside their own territory through local agents." "Many years of progress in human rights jurisprudence, establishing state accountability for torture or extra-judicial executions committed by para-military groups . . . would be reversed."

force as a *de facto* organ of a state, but given the unlikelihood of obtaining copies of actual orders, the position taken by the majority is an invitation to states to evade their obligations through even the most blatant use of proxy forces. If necessary, international law would benefit from a common sense presumption of control, even in the absence of proof of direct orders, where a proxy force is funded, equipped, supplied, and trained by an outside state, where there is constant communication and co-ordination of efforts, where the proxy force carries out operations planned by the state, and where the state continues to finance and supply the proxy force despite a clear pattern of violations of international humanitarian law.[80]

AFTERMATH OF THE *TADIC* JUDGMENT

The *Tadic* judgment was greeted by the press as an "historic verdict" that "marked a milestone" in the work of the Tribunal and the efforts to punish those responsible for war crimes and crimes against humanity during the conflict.[81] Despite the findings that the "grave breaches" provisions did not apply and that particular killings had not been proved beyond a reasonable doubt, the Office of the Prosecutor was pleased with the outcome, since the pivotal conviction was the persecution count.[82]

The defence filed notice of appeal of the *Tadic* judgment on June 3, 1997, on procedural grounds, alleging an unfair trial, insufficient cross-examination, insufficiently specific charges, and retroactivity.[83] The prosecutor also appealed against specific findings of the Trial Chamber, namely (1) the finding that the grave breaches provisions were inapplicable; (2) the finding that certain killings had not been proven beyond a reasonable doubt; (3) the finding as to the intent requirement for crimes against humanity; and (4) the

80 This would also be more consistent with the definition of aggression, *supra* note 73.

81 Tracy Wilkinson, "Bosnian Serb Found Guilty of Crimes against Humanity," *Toronto Star* (May 8, 1997) A2; See also Jocelyn Coulon, "Un jugement historique," *Le Devoir* (May 8, 1997) A1; Mirko Klarin, "The Tribunal Proves Itself," *The Tribunal*, Vol. 9, June/July 1997. Reactions in the territory of the former Yugoslavia differed: Dejan Anastasijevic, "Unimpressed in Belgrade," *The Tribunal*, Vol. 9, June/July 1997; Rasim Cerimagic, "Disappointment in Sarajevo, Paranoia in Pale," *The Tribunal*, Vol. 9, June/July 1997.

82 Wilkinson, *ibid.*

83 Tribunal, Press Release CC/PIO/208 (June 4, 1997).

finding that a discriminatory motive must be proven for crimes against humanity.[84]

Following a sentencing hearing, the Trial Chamber sentenced Dusko Tadic to twenty years in prison for his crimes. This included twenty years for acts of persecution (amounting to a crime against humanity) as well as concurrent sentences of six to ten years for other crimes against humanity and war crimes.[85] The sentence is also subject to appeal.[86] In sum, the *Tadic* judgment does indeed mark a milestone for the Tribunal, because it concludes the first criminal trial by an international tribunal in decades. The judgment sensibly develops the definition of crimes against humanity, although the additional requirement of discriminatory motive does not appear to have been required by the Statute or by previous instruments. The conclusion that the conflict was internal will continue to be the most controversial aspect of the judgment. Ultimately, perhaps the most important aspect of the judgment will be its contribution to the historic record in a credible and objective way.

Erdemovic Judgment

Procedural History and Facts

The *Erdemovic* judgment[87] arose from an appeal against a sentencing judgment rendered by Trial Chamber I in November 1996, in which Drazen Erdemovic was sentenced to ten years of imprisonment following a guilty plea to one count of a crime against humanity.[88]

The *Erdemovic* case is particularly challenging because of the tension between the extreme gravity of the crime and the compelling mitigating circumstances of the case. Drazen Erdemovic had been a member of a Bosnian Serb army detachment that was sent to

84 Tribunal, Press Release CC/P10/210 (June 9, 1997); See also Boris Heim, "Louise Arbour critique la règle de preuve du TPI," *Le Devoir* (June 10, 1997) A7.

85 Sentencing Judgment, *Prosecutor* v. *Dusko Tadic a/k/a "Dule,"* Trial Chamber, July 14, 1997, Case No. IT-94-1-T.

86 Tribunal, Press Release CC/PIO/235 (Aug. 13, 1997).

87 Judgment, *The Prosecutor* v. *Drazen Erdemovic*, Case No. IT-96-22-A, Appeals Chamber, Oct. 7, 1997 [hereinafter *Erdemovic* Appeal].

88 Sentencing Judgment, *The Prosecutor* v. *Drazen Erdemovic*, Case No. IT-96-22-T, Trial Chamber I, Nov. 29, 1996 [hereinafter *Erdemovic Sentencing* Judgment].

a collective farm and ordered to serve as an execution squad. Busloads of Bosnian Muslim men were brought to the farm and escorted in groups of ten to a nearby field, where they were shot and killed by the detachment. These summary executions resulted in the deaths of hundreds of Muslim civilians — clearly a crime of extreme gravity.

One mitigating factor was that Erdemovic pleaded guilty before the Tribunal, thereby demonstrating remorse and relieving the Tribunal of the burden of a full trial. In fact, the conviction was based entirely on Erdemovic's voluntary statements, since the Office of the Prosecutor did not have independent evidence of his involvement in the executions. For this reason, Erdemovic's defence counsel had advised him not to plead guilty, but Erdemovic nevertheless insisted on doing so, for reasons of conscience.[89] Furthermore, Erdemovic co-operated fully with the Office of the Prosecutor and testified in proceedings for the issuance of international arrest warrants against Karadzic and Mladic. In addition, his young age (he was twenty-three at the time of the crime), his low rank, and the evidence of his character were all substantial mitigating factors.

Of more importance during the appeal were the circumstances in which the crime was committed. Erdemovic stated that it was only when they arrived on-site that the members of the unit were informed that they were to massacre hundreds of Muslim men. Erdemovic promptly refused, but was threatened: "If you don't wish to do it, stand in the line with the rest of them and give the others your rifle so that they can shoot you." He then complied with the order to save his life.[90] Erdemovic reported that he later opposed a similar order from a lieutenant colonel to participate in the execution of 500 Muslim men, and in that case was able to avoid compliance because three of his comrades supported him when he refused to obey.

The Trial Chamber considered the severity of the crime as well as the compelling mitigating circumstances, and concluded that a

89 Separate and dissenting Opinion of Judge Stephen, *The Prosecutor* v. *Drazen Erdemovic*, Case No. IT-96-22-A, Appeals Chamber, Oct. 7,1997. at paras. 3-11 [hereinafter Stephen Opinion].

90 *Erdemovic* Appeal, *supra* note 87 at para. 7. As a further mitigating factor, it may be noted that he had a wife and a nine-month-old son.

ten-year sentence was appropriate.[91] On appeal, the Appeals Chamber was asked to reduce his sentence on the basis of duress or extreme necessity, and the Appeals Chamber raised of its own motion the question of the validity of his guilty plea. The Appeals Chamber decision is split into four separate opinions, with the majority concluding that the guilty plea was not informed and re-sending the matter to a Trial Chamber for a new pleading.

THE GUILTY PLEA

Reliance on a plea of guilty is contemplated in the Statute (Article 20, paragraph 3), and in the Rules of Procedure and Evidence (Rule 62).[92] The concept of a guilty plea proved to be a contentious issue in the development of Tribunal procedures, since the practice is unknown in civil law systems. It is therefore comforting that all five members of the Appeals Chamber, notwithstanding their diverse legal backgrounds, agreed that the concept of the guilty plea should find a ready place in an international criminal forum, such as the Tribunal. It was noted that enabling the accused and the prosecutor to avoid a lengthy trial is all the more indispensable in international proceedings, where trials are inevitably complex, evidence is difficult to collect, victim and witness protection is arduous, and where additional costs are incurred for translation and for transportation of witnesses from distant places.[93]

All of the judges agreed that the procedural "short-cut" of a guilty plea must not be allowed to curtail the rights of the accused.

91 Some commentators have questioned whether this sentence was too long, despite the severity of the crime, since this was a case with circumstances (age, duress, guilty plea, conviction based solely on voluntary statements) as favourable to the accused as possible. Thus a ten-year sentence under such circumstances could deter voluntary surrender by others.

92 Art. 20, para. 3, provides for the entry of a plea by the accused. Rule 62 contemplates a plea of guilty or not guilty, and in the case of a guilty plea, provides for the scheduling of a pre-sentencing hearing.

93 Separate and Dissenting Opinion of Judge Cassese, *The Prosecutor* v. *Drazen Erdemovic*, Case No. IT-96-22-A, Appeals Chamber, Oct. 7, 1997 at para. 8 [hereinafter Cassese Opinion]; Separate and Dissenting Opinion of Judges McDonald and Vohrah, *The Prosecutor* v. *Drazen Erdemovic*, Case No. IT-96-22-A, Appeals Chamber, Oct. 7, 1997 at para. 2 [hereinafter McDonald-Vohrah Opinion]. Judges McDonald and Vohrah also referred to the financial constraints of the United Nations, and Judge Cassese referred to the benefits to the accused of helping atone for his wrongdoing, avoiding the indignity and public exposure of a trial, and the expectation that the court will recognize his co-operative attitude.

They also agreed on the conditions applicable for acceptance of a guilty plea,[94] although they reached their conclusions by different routes:[95]

(1) The guilty plea must be *voluntary*: that is, it must not be the result of threats, inducements or promises and must be made by an accused who is mentally competent;

(2) The guilty plea must be *informed*: that is, the accused must understand the nature of the charges and the consequences of pleading guilty;

3) The guilty plea must be *unequivocal*: that is, it must not be accompanied by words contradicting an admission of criminal responsibility.

A majority of the Appeals Chamber found that Erdemovic's guilty plea was not an informed plea. Erdemovic and his lawyer were not advised of, and did not understand, the difference between a war crime and a crime against humanity, and, as a result, Erdemovic pleaded guilty to the more serious offence of a crime against humanity rather than the less serious charge of a war crime.[96] The case was therefore remitted to a Trial Chamber so that Erdemovic could be given the opportunity to re-plead. Judge Li in dissent questioned the majority's contention that crimes against humanity are intrinsically more serious than war crimes.[97]

94 McDonald-Vohrah Opinion, *ibid.*, para. 8; Cassese Opinion, *ibid.*, para. 10; Stephen Opinion, *supra* note 89 at para. 5; Separate and Dissenting Opinion of Judge Li, *The Prosecutor* v. *Drazen Erdemovic*, Case No. IT-96-22-A, Appeals Chamber, Oct. 7, 1997 at paras. 10-27. [hereinafter Li Opinion].

95 The different routes taken in the McDonald-Vohrah Opinion and the Cassese Opinion suggest a common law-civil law rivalry. The McDonald-Vohrah Opinion referred to the common law authorities as relevant material in the absence of other guidance on guilty pleas, and adopted a typical common law test. Judge Cassese strongly criticized the use of domestic law authorities, and, in particular, common law authorities, except as an extreme last resort. He then sought to derive an appropriate test from general principles and the spirit of the Statute, and, perhaps coincidentally, arrived at a test identical to that of Judges McDonald and Vohrah.

96 *Erdemovic* Appeal, supra notre 87 at para. 20; McDonald-Vohrah Opinion, *supra* note 93 at para. 15.

97 Li Opinion, *supra* note 94 at paras. 18-26. Judge Li persuasively argued that the gravity of a criminal act is determined by the intrinsic nature of the act itself and not by its classification under one category or another, since the harm done is exactly the same. Judges McDonald and Vohrah argued that crimes against

DURESS AS A DEFENCE TO MURDER

The issue of whether duress can amount to a defence to a crime against humanity divided the Appeals Chamber, just as the closely related issue of superior orders divided the Supreme Court of Canada in 1993.[98] Article 7, paragraph 4 of the Statute specifies that "superior orders" are not a defence but may be considered in mitigation of sentence. However, the Statute is silent with respect to duress.

While grappling with the issues, all five judges agreed that "superior orders" and "duress" are conceptually distinct (even though both may arise from the same fact situation) and the existence of "superior orders" is simply a factor to consider when examining a claim of duress.[99] All five judges agreed that duress may be available in some circumstances with respect to war crimes and crimes against humanity, but the contentious issue was whether duress could ever offer a complete defence to a crime involving the killing of innocent human beings. All five judges agreed that the existing international humanitarian law jurisprudence is inconclusive and that there is no established rule of customary international law settling this issue.

---

humanity are intrinsically more serious because "humanity comes under attack," that they make humanity a victim, and they consequently affect "each and every member of mankind." However, this basis seems all too metaphysical and places exceptional reliance on the *name* of the crime. A better argument is the fact that crimes against humanity involve the widespread or systematic perpetration of odious crimes, and are therefore generally more serious because of their heinousness and magnitude. However, Judge Li points out that war crimes can be equally severe, and that the gravity of the offence must be judged on a case-by-case basis. In any event, the idea that crimes against humanity are intrinsically more serious than war crimes is now an article of faith in the Tribunal jurisprudence, and it is noteworthy that, in the sentencing of Dusko Tadic, more severe sentences were imposed for acts characterized as crimes against humanity than for war crimes.

98 *R.* v. *Finta, supra* note 49.

99 This is a sensible distinction, because it is easy to envisage a superior order without duress (e.g., where there is no threat of immediate death for failure to obey the order), and it is also easy to envisage a situation of duress without superior orders (e.g., where the recipient of the threat is not in a subordinate-superior relationship with the issuer of the threat). *Finta* is inconsistent with this approach, because "superior orders" and "duress" considerations appear to be conflated in that decision.

Each of the opinions therefore turned to the domestic legal systems of the world for guidance, and found that domestic legal systems are divided on the issue. In the common law tradition, duress is available as a complete defence for many crimes but is excluded for murder, for which duress may only be considered as a mitigating factor.[100] In the civil law tradition, no specific exception is made for murder, and duress is a complete defence for all crimes, although in some systems it is necessary to show that the act was proportionate to the threat. The remaining legal systems of the world canvassed in the opinions were similar to the civil law tradition: duress is a complete defence if the criteria are met.

Judges McDonald, Vohrah, and Li concluded that duress cannot provide a complete defence for a soldier who committed crimes against humanity or war crimes involving the killing of innocent human beings. These judges regarded a "proportionality" assessment as completely inappropriate where the resulting acts involved the killing of innocent people. Where an accused sacrifices another to save his own life, a crime has been committed, although the duress may result in the mitigation of punishment. The judges considered this a clear, simple, and uniform approach designed to deter subordinates from killing innocent human beings.[101]

Judges Cassese and Stephen, dissenting, would have rejected a special distinction for crimes involving the killing of innocent human beings. They would have applied the general test developed by military tribunals following the Second World War, which required (1) an immediate threat of severe and irreparable harm to life or limb; (2) no adequate means of averting such evil; (3) the crime committed was not disproportionate to the evil threatened; and (4) the situation leading to duress must not have been voluntarily brought about by the person coerced. Both Cassese and Stephen argued that the proportionality requirement would be extremely difficult to satisfy where innocent human beings had

100 For example, the Canadian *Criminal Code*, R.S.C. 1985, c. C-46, as amended, excludes the defence of "compulsion by threats" for the crimes of high treason or treason, murder, piracy, attempted murder, sexual assault, sexual assault with a weapon, threats to a third party or causing bodily harm, aggravated sexual assault, forcible abduction, hostage taking, robbery, assault with a weapon or causing bodily harm, aggravated assault, unlawfully causing bodily harm, arson or an offence under ss. 280-330 (abduction and detention of young persons).

101 McDonald-Vohrah Opinion, *supra* note 93 at paras. 32-33; Li Opinion, *supra* note 94 at paras. 5-12.

been killed, and perhaps could never be satisfied where the accused had sacrificed another life to save his own. They emphasized, however, that not all situations involve a sacrifice of one life to save another. For example, in the instant case, the victims were certain to die regardless of what Erdemovic did. His choice was to die alongside them or to live. Had he refused, he would have forfeited his own life for no benefit to anyone and with no effect whatsoever. Both Cassese and Stephen believed that in such situations, where the accused's stark choice is between (1) many lives or (2) many lives *plus his own*, then the Trial Chamber should be allowed to assess whether the requirements for duress have been established.

Both viewpoints on the duress issue can marshall substantial arguments of policy and principle. The exclusion of the defence of duress for killing innocent civilians reinforces the prohibition against taking life, consistent with the dictum that one "ought rather to die himself, than to kill an innocent."[102] This approach recognizes the difficulty of the accused's situation by mitigating the punishment, but expresses society's disapprobation of the fact that the accused deliberately took the life of another. It also avoids the potential moral quagmire of "balancing" between various evils or choosing which life to preserve. Such an approach sends out a clear and unequivocal message to subordinates that they will be held responsible for their actions, and that they must resist manifestly unlawful orders or face legal repercussions. As noted by Judge Li, the primary purpose of international humanitarian law is to protect innocent lives, and to allow the defence of duress would encourage subordinates under duress to kill with impunity, rather than deter them.

On the other hand, the "proportionality" approach has the advantage of flexibility. Killing innocent human beings would almost never be justified under the "proportionality" test, but there might be extreme circumstances where we must recognize that the person truly had no moral alternative. The strict position of the majority is based on the repugnance of balancing lives, but Judges Cassese and Stephen question whether there is any balancing where the victims are certain to die, where no choice of the accused could alter their fate, and the accused's choice is merely whether to die with them or to live. Judges Cassese and Stephen ask whether criminal law requires a person forced into such a situation

102 McDonald-Vohrah Opinion, *ibid.*, para 71, Li Opinion, *ibid.* at para. 7, quoting the common law commentaries of Hale and Blackstone.

to forfeit his or her life for no benefit to anyone. Even if the *Erdemovic* situation does not meet the test, both Cassese and Stephen suggest other extreme situations where a person can hardly be expected to act differently. Is it the purpose of criminal law to punish individuals for conduct in situations where no one could be expected to act differently? Is it the purpose of criminal law to condemn individuals who, through no fault of their own, find themselves forced to choose the lesser of two evils? Finally, although sceptics argue that this approach to duress would permit law-breakers to confer immunity on their agents by threatening them, the stringent requirements of the test for duress[103] would prevent such obvious abuse of the defence.

Both approaches have significant advantages and disadvantages, and one's preference may ultimately depend on one's view of the fundamental purpose of criminal law. In the *Erdemovic* judgment, the majority of the Appeals Chamber has opted for the approach that killing of innocent human beings by soldiers cannot be justified by duress, and that exceptional circumstances are only a factor for mitigation of punishment.

Subpoena Orders: *Blaskic* Case

procedural history

On October 29, 1997 the Appeals Chamber handed down its decision on the power of the Tribunal to issue subpoenas to states and to individuals.[104] This issue arose in the context of the *Blaskic* proceedings, in the course of which *subpoenas duces tecum* (court orders for the production of documents) were issued on January 15, 1997, by the Tribunal. The orders were directed to the Republic of Croatia and the Croatian defence minister, as well as to the government of Bosnia and Herzegovina and the custodian of certain archives containing defence records.[105]

103 Notably the requirement of proportionality and the requirement that the person coerced does not knowingly enter into the situation of duress, e.g., by joining a unit known for violations of international humanitarian law.

104 Judgment on the Request of the Republic of Croatia for Review of the Decision of Trial Chamber II of July 18, 1997, *The Prosecutor* v. *Tihomir Blaskic*, Case No. IT-95-14-AR108*bis*, Oct. 29, 1997 [hereinafter Appeals Chamber Subpoena Judgment].

105 Specifically, the Custodian of the Records of the Central Archives of what was formerly the Ministry of Defence of the Croatian Community of Herceg Bosna.

Croatia promptly challenged the authority of the Tribunal to issue a subpoena to a sovereign state. Hearings on the issue were held in the spring of 1997, and in July 1997, the Trial Chamber issued a decision upholding the power of the Tribunal to issue subpoena orders to states or to individuals, including state officials.[106] The Trial Chamber held that a state may not avoid the production of evidence by categorically asserting that national security is at stake, and the Tribunal may hold *in camera* and *ex parte* hearings for the purpose of assessing the assertions of the state.

The Appeals Chamber granted Croatia's request for a review of the Trial Chamber's Decision in July, and following a motion by the prosecutor, confirmed its decision in August.[107] *Amicus curiae* briefs supporting the authority of the Tribunal were submitted by the governments of Canada and New Zealand (a joint brief), Norway, and the Netherlands.[108] An *amicus curiae* brief opposing the use of subpoenas was submitted by the government of China. Hearings were held in September, and the Appeals Chamber handed down its decision on October 29, 1997.

At stake was "one of the most crucial international legal issues since the Nuremberg Trials,"[109] since the power to compel states to turn over documents is essential if international criminal justice is to be effective. The unanimous decision by the Appeals Chamber was carefully balanced: although it rejected the use of the term "subpoena" with respect to states (and for this reason struck down

106 Decision on the Objection of the Republic of Croatia to the Issuance of Subpoenae *Duces Tecum, The Prosecutor* v. *Tihomir Blaskic,* Case No. IT-95-14-PT, Trial Chamber II, July 18, 1997 [hereinafter Trial Chamber Subpoena decision]. The alert reader may have noted at this point that there is no apparent consistency in the Tribunal's use of the terms "decision" and "judgment."

107 Decision on the Admissibility of the Request for Review by the Republic of Croatia of an Interlocutory Decision of a Trial Chamber (Issuance of *Subpoenae Duces Tecum*) and Scheduling Order, *The Prosecutor* v. *Tihomir Blaskic,* Case No. IT-95-14-AR108*bis,* July 29, 1997; and Decision on Prosecution Motion to Set Aside the Decision of the Appeals Chamber of 29 July 1997, *The Prosecutor* v. *Tihomir Blaskic, ibid,* Aug. 12, 1997.

108 In addition to the *amicus curiae* briefs submitted by governments, briefs were submitted by the Max Planck Institute for Foreign and International Criminal Law, Juristes sans frontières, and Alain Pellet, Ruth Wedgewood, Carol Elder Bruce, and Herwig Roggeman: Appeals Chamber Subpoena Judgment, *supra* note 104 at para. 17.

109 Juliet O'Neill, "In the Fight for International Justice," *Ottawa Citizen* (Sept. 14, 1997) A9.

the subpoenas at issue in the case), it upheld the essential power to issue orders for the production of evidence.

THE AUTHORITY TO ISSUE ORDERS FOR THE PRODUCTION OF EVIDENCE

The Appeals Chamber confirmed that the Tribunal can issue binding orders to states, including orders for the production of evidence. This conclusion is well-supported by the Statute and by general principles of international law. Article 29, paragraph 2(b), of the Statute provides that "[s]tates shall comply without undue delay with any request for assistance or an order issued by a Trial Chamber, including, but not limited to . . . the production of evidence." The Statute of the Tribunal was adopted by Security Council Resolution 827, which was an enforcement measure under Chapter 7 of the United Nations Charter, so United Nations Member States are therefore obliged to comply.[110] Resolution 827 requires all states "to co-operate fully with the International Tribunal and its organs" and specifically highlights the obligation to comply with requests or orders issued under Article 29 of the Statute. Accordingly, the Appeals Chamber easily concluded that "the obligation set out — in the clearest of terms — in Article 29 is an obligation which is incumbent on every Member State of the United Nations."[111]

The Appeals Chamber specified that orders for the production of evidence must (1) identify specific documents and not broad categories; (2) set out the reasons why such documents are considered relevant; (3) not be unduly onerous; and (4) give the state sufficient time for compliance.[112] Failure by a state to comply with an order may be noted by the Tribunal and reported to the Security Council.[113]

REJECTION OF THE TERM "SUBPOENA"

The Appeals Chamber held that the term "subpoena" cannot be applied or addressed to states and that the term should refer only to compulsory orders issued to individuals acting in their private

110 Arts. 2, 25, and 41 of the Charter of the United Nations.

111 Appeals Chamber Subpoena Judgment, supra note 104 at para. 26.

112 *Ibid.*, para. 32.

113 *Ibid.*, para. 33.

capacity.[114] This rejection of the term "subpoena" may surprise those familiar with the common law system, for whom the term may be synonymous with an order compelling the production of evidence or the testimony of a witness. However, the term generated tremendous controversy in the international setting. Since *subpoena* literally means "under penalty," the concern was raised that the term implied some power of the Tribunal to penalize states that failed to comply with subpoena orders — a power that is not contemplated in the Statute. Although both the prosecutor and the Trial Chamber emphasized that the term was not intended to imply any special powers,[115] the concern and controversy continued. Therefore, by rejecting the use of the term "subpoena" in the context of orders to states, the Appeals Chamber jettisoned this controversial term while affirming the authority of the Tribunal to issue "binding orders for the production of evidence." In this manner, the Appeals Chamber has cleverly rejected the controversial label but preserved the essential power.[116]

INDIVIDUALS AND STATE OFFICIALS

Another controversial issue was whether binding orders may be directed to specified state officials. The Appeals Chamber noted that customary international law permits each state to determine its internal structure and to designate the relevant officials to respond to a request.[117] More importantly, there was no provision in the Statute suggesting that the Tribunal can issue orders to specified state officials.[118] The Appeals Chamber therefore declined to expand the jurisdiction of the Tribunal.[119]

114 *Ibid.*, paras. 21 and 25.

115 Trial Chamber Subpoena decision, *supra* note 106 at paras. 58-64.

116 The words of Juliet Capulet (William Shakespeare, *Romeo and Juliet*, Act II, Scene II) are apposite:

> What's in a name? That which we call a rose
> By any other name would smell as sweet

117 Appeals Chamber Subpoena Judgment, *supra* note 104 at para 41.

118 *Ibid.*, para. 42.

119 The Appeals Chamber also described the practical difficulties that would otherwise arise. The Appeals Chamber noted that there are two hypothetical situations that could result in non-compliance: either (1) the state orders the official not to comply or (2) the state orders the official to comply but the official refuses. In the first situation, there would be little practical advantage

With respect to individuals acting in their private capacity, many provisions of the Statute and Rules imply an ancillary jurisdiction over individuals,[120] so the Appeals Chamber concluded that orders may be directed to individuals acting in their private capacity. The Appeals Chamber clarified that "individuals acting in their private capacity" could include state officials who, for instance, witnessed a crime before they took office, since the person's role in the Tribunal proceedings would be unrelated to their current functions as state officials.[121] Normally, the Tribunal will turn to the relevant national authorities to seek remedies or sanctions for non-compliance, but in cases where resort to national remedies would not prove workable, the Tribunal may invoke its own contempt power.[122]

NATIONAL SECURITY CONCERNS

The final issue that generated controversy was the difficult and sensitive issue of national security concerns. Croatia argued that the mere assertion by a state of national security as a privilege must be accepted by the Tribunal.[123] The prosecutor conceded that the Tribunal should give due regard to the legitimate security interests of a state, but argued that the assertion of privilege must be assessed by the Tribunal in order to determine its validity.[124]

Both the Trial Chamber and the Appeals Chamber rejected the suggestion that a mere assertion of privilege must be accepted by the Tribunal. To permit states to avoid disclosure by a unilateral

---

in directing an order to the official who would be bound by the instructions of his government (*ad impossibilia nemo tenetur*). In the second situation, the state would be obliged to compel the official, through national legal remedies, to comply with the order. The Appeals Chamber left open the possibility that, in the event of a persistent refusal by a state official to comply despite the orders of his or her government, the official might be regarded as no longer a part of the state apparatus and treated like a private individual, subject to all the available remedies and sanctions.

120 Such as the contempt power in Rule 77 of the Rules of Procedure and Evidence or the inherent contempt power of the Tribunal: Appeals Chamber Subpoena Judgment, *supra* note 104 at para. 48.

121 Ibid., paras. 46-51.

122 Ibid., paras. 57-60.

123 Brief on Appeal of the Republic of Croatia in Opposition to *Subpoenae Duces Tecum*, at 59-64; Trial Chamber Subpoena decision, supra note 106 at paras. 108-110.

124 Prosecutor's Brief in Response to the Brief of the Republic of Croatia; Trial Chamber Subpoena decision, ibid. at para. 110.

blanket assertion of confidentiality would invite abuse and would undermine the effectiveness of the Tribunal.[125] Thus, the Appeals Chamber confirmed that the Tribunal has the authority to scrutinize the validity of assertions of privilege, although the Tribunal "should not be unmindful of legitimate state concerns related to national security."[126]

The Appeals Chamber went on to suggest "possible modalities of making allowance for national security concerns."[127] The Tribunal may scrutinize the validity of assertions, taking into account "the degree of *bona fide* co-operation and assistance lent by the relevant State . . . as well as the general attitude of the State *vis-à-vis* the International Tribunal (whether it is opposed to the fulfilment of its functions or instead consistently supports and assists the International Tribunal)."[128] The state at issue may be invited to submit the relevant documents to the scrutiny of one judge designated by the Trial Chamber.[129]

Thus, the Appeals Chamber has suggested a procedure that avoids the potential for abuse inherent in unilateral blanket assertions of confidentiality, while striving to ensure due respect for the legitimate security concerns of states. Only time will tell if the procedure is indeed workable and effective.

CONCLUSION

Nineteen ninety-seven was a year of groundbreaking developments for the International Criminal Tribunal for the former

125 Appeals Chamber Subpoena Judgment, supra note 104 at paras. 64 and 65. The Appeals Chamber also observed that the crimes within the Tribunal's jurisdiction are generally related to armed conflict and military operation, so military documents will often be of crucial importance if international criminal proceedings are not to be stultified.

126 *Ibid.*, para. 67.

127 *Ibid.*, paras. 67-69.

128 *Ibid.*, para. 68.

129 Judge Karibi-White objected to this suggestion, since he believed the Statute did not permit the determination of such an issue by a single judge: Separate Opinion of Judge Adolphius G. Karibi-White, Case No. IT-95-14-AR 108*bis*. The Appeals Chamber also suggested an alternative streamlined procedure, where a state, acting *bona fide*, considers one or two documents to be of a sensitive nature and of scant relevance. In this limited circumstance, the responsible minister may simply submit a signed affidavit explaining the reasons for non-disclosure: Appeals Chamber Subpoena Judgment, *supra* note 104 at para. 68.

Yugoslavia. The arrest of four indictees and the voluntary surrender of another eleven indictees over the course of the year not only increases the number of indictees in custody but also heralds improved co-operation and support from the relevant states and entities as well as from the international community. The completion of the *Tadic* trial marks the first trial by an international tribunal in fifty years and the first judicial condemnation of ethnic cleansing. The Tribunal has refined its jurisprudence with respect to crimes against humanity, grave breaches of the Geneva Conventions, the conditions for a guilty plea, the defence of duress, and the power to issue orders for the production of evidence.

Following the dramatic increase in the number of indictees in custody and the corresponding increase in workload, the international community is intensifying its support for the Tribunal. This has taken the form of a substantial budget increase from the United Nations, and more direct forms of support such as financial contributions, seconded personnel, equipment, and programs of assistance such as enforcement of sentences and witness relocation.[130] For example, on December 17, 1997, the government of Canada announced a package of additional assistance including a financial contribution of $600,000, the secondment of personnel, and negotiation of a witness relocation agreement.[131] In 1998, the *Tadic* appeal will address many of the issues canvassed here. Several cases,

130 Italy and Finland have signed agreements providing for the enforcement of sentences in their territories: Tribunal, Press Releases CC/PIO/154 (Feb. 6, 1997) and CC/PIO/192 (May 8, 1997). The United Kingdom has offered to finance the construction of an interim courtroom and also became the first state to agree to provide witness relocation assistance to the Tribunal: Tribunal, Press Releases CC/PIO/228 (July 17, 1997) and CC/PIO/258 (Nov. 7, 1997). The United States and the Netherlands have also offered to build an additional courtroom in response to the surge in the demands upon the Tribunal: Tribunal, Press Release CC/PIO/282 (Jan. 8, 1998).

131 The package of additional assistance included: (1) a financial contribution of $600,000, the majority for the exhumation of mass graves (for collection of evidence) and the remainder to help finance the construction of a much-needed additional courtroom; (2) the secondment of five crime analysts to assist in investigations; (3) a list of Canadians available for recruitment and who possess the expertise and qualifications most urgently needed by the Tribunal; and (4) the negotiation of an agreement providing for the relocation of witnesses in danger: Aileen McCabe, "Canada Boosts Aid to War Crimes Probe," *Ottawa Citizen* (Dec. 18, 1997) A12; "Le Canada Aide le TPI" *Journal de Montréal* (Dec. 18, 1997); Tribunal, Press Release CC/PIO/280 (Dec. 22, 1997).

including *Blaskic*, *Celebici*, and *Aleksoviski* will address the issue of command responsibility. *Celebici* also represents the first international criminal trial on charges of rape and sexual assault since the Tokyo Tribunal. Thus, there is every reason to expect that the work of the Tribunal will be as interesting and productive in 1998 as it was in 1997.

Sommaire

Procès et progrès: développements majeurs en 1997 au Tribunal pénal international pour l'ex-Yougoslavie

L'année 1997 fut marquée par plusieurs développements importants au Tribunal pénal international pour l'ex-Yougoslavie. De nouvelles arrestations et des redditions volontâires ont augmenté la charge de travail du Tribunal et renforcé sa crédibilité. La décision Tadic *a clarifié le droit international humanitaire, en particulier en ce qui concerne les crimes contre l'humanité. La décision* Erdemovic *examine la défense de contraintes dans le cas de meutres de civils et le plaidoyer de culpabilité dans le droit international pénal et. La décision* Blaskic *se penche sur l'utilisation des subpoenas en droit international.*

Summary

Trials, Tribulations, and Triumphs: Major Developments in 1997 at the International Criminal Tribunal for the Former Yugoslavia

Nineteen ninety-seven was marked by several important developments at the International Criminal Tribunal for the former Yugoslavia. A series of arrests and voluntary surrenders have increased the Tribunal's workload and credibility. The landmark Tadic *judgment has clarified international humanitarian law, particularly with respect to crimes against humanity. The* Erdemovic *decision considered the defence of duress with respect to the murder of civilians and the use of guilty pleas in international criminal law. Finally, the* Blaskic *decision has considered the use of subpoenas in international law.*

Notes and Comments / Notes et commentaires

The Primacy of the Principle of Equitable Utilization in the 1997 Watercourses Convention

Background

As recently as the 1950s, there was no customary international law on the non-navigational uses of international water resources. This assertion is supported by the claims and counterclaims of the states then in serious conflict over three of the world's major international rivers — namely, the Indus, the Nile, and the Columbia. The upstream states argued that states had the right to deal with the waters in their territories as they pleased. In the case of the Indus, this argument was based on territorial sovereignty, thus echoing the Harmon doctrine.[1] In the case of the Columbia, the argument was based on the Boundary Waters Treaty of 1909.[2] The downstream states argued that they were entitled to receive the flow of the waters undiminished in quantity and quality, thus invoking a riparian rights view of the law that, in practice, would give them a right of veto over upstream water uses. In the end, the parties to these disputes settled the matters at issue by treaties that discounted the legal principles they had invoked.[3]

The great diversity of opinion expressed by those involved in these disputes about the relevant law made it impossible to assert

1 For this doctrine enunciated by Attorney-General Harmon of the United States, see *Treaty of Guadalupe-Hidalgo — International Law*, 21 Ops. Att'y Gen. 274 at 280-83 (1895).

2 Treaty relating to boundary waters and questions arising along the boundary between the United States and Canada, Jan. 11, 1909, 3 Stat. 2448; TS No. 548; III Redmond 2607.

3 The Indus Waters Treaty, Sept. 19, 1960, 419 UNTS 125; The Nile Waters Treaty, Nov. 8, 1959, 453 UNTS 51; The Columbia River Treaty, Jan. 17, 1961 and Jan. 23, 1964, 15 UST 1555; TIAS 5638; 542 UNTS 244.

with assurance that there was any customary international law governing international water resources at that time. This legal vacuum in an area of increasingly important human activity, however, could not continue for long. By the end of the 1960s, the principle of equitable utilization of transboundary waters had been generally accepted as a rule of customary international law, emerging mainly from the intensive studies of the Institute of International Law[4] and, in particular, of the International Law Association (ILA).[5] The principle had also been foreshadowed in the award in the *Lake Lanoux* case.[6]

The principle of equitable utilization emphasizes that a state cannot legally do as it pleases with the transboundary water resources in its territory. Its essence is that states must act reasonably in dealing with these waters. The principle is expressed best in Article 4 of the 1966 Helsinki Rules,[7] which states that "each basin state is entitled, within its territory, to a reasonable and equitable share in the beneficial uses of the waters of an international drainage basin." By Article 5 of the Rules, the share of a state is to be determined in the light of all relevant factors in each particular case.

An important event in the field of international water law occurred in 1970. Following the adoption of the Helsinki Rules in 1966, the Finnish delegation at the United Nations proposed that the General Assembly should adopt the Helsinki Rules as guidelines for states in using international water resources in their territories. Instead of doing so, however, the General Assembly in 1970 referred the law of the non-navigational uses of international watercourses to the International Law Commission (ILC) for study, with a view to its progressive development and codification.[8] Thus, the ILC began its work that culminated in 1994 in its adoption of a

4 Resolution on the Utilization of Non-Maritime International Waters (except for Navigation), adopted by the Institute of International Law at its Session at Salzburg (Sept. 4-13, 1961), 49 Annuaire de l'Institut de Droit International, Tome II, 381 (1961).

5 See Finnish Branch of the International Law Association, *The Work of the International Law Association on the Law of International Water Resources*, E. J. Manner and Veli-Martti Metsalampi, eds. (1988).

6 (1957), (France-Spain), 12 R.I.A.A. 281 (Award of Nov. 16, 1957), 24 I.L.R. 101.

7 Manner and Metsalampi, *supra* note 5 at 21.

8 General Assembly Resolution 2669 (XXV), Dec. 8, 1970; UN GOAR, 25th Sess., Supp. No. 28, at 127; UN Doc. A/8028 (1970).

set of draft articles on the topic. These articles were then submitted to the General Assembly with the recommendation that they be used as the basis for "the elaboration of a convention by the Assembly or by an international conference of plenipotentiaries."[9] The General Assembly referred the draft articles to a Working Group of the Whole of its Sixth Committee (Working Group). This body, having considered the articles in October 1996 and in March and April 1997, approved the Convention on the Law of the Non-Navigational Uses of International Watercourses (Watercourses Convention) and reported this to the General Assembly.[10] After detailed consideration of the Convention by a Working Group of the Sixth Committee, the General Assembly adopted it on May 21, 1997.[11] The Watercourses Convention will remain open for signature until May 20, 2000, and it will enter into force on the ninetieth day following the deposit of the thirty-fifth instrument of ratification, acceptance, approval, or accession with the UN secretary general.[12]

The Substantive Principles of the Watercourses Convention

The principles of law to be applied in the resolution of international water disputes are found chiefly in Articles 5, 7, 20, and 21 of the Watercourses Convention.[13] It is not easy, however, to discern from the text of these articles what the principles of law are. This is not surprising, for the articles are the product of committees composed of persons with very different views of the law.

From the reports of the ILC's five Special Rapporteurs on the topic of international watercourses and from the discussions in the ILC and later in the Working Group, those with different views can be divided into four categories. The first group supported the following propositions: no harm to ecosystems; no pollution harm to the environment or to other watercourse states; no harm to other

[9] Report of the International Law Commission on the work of its 46th session, May 2 - July 22, 1994, GAOR, 49th Sess., Supp. No. 10 (A/49/10), at 195-366. [hereinafter Report of the ILC.]

[10] UN Doc. A/51/869, Apr. 11, 1997, 36 I.L.M. 700 (1997) [hereinafter 1997 Convention].

[11] UN Resolution 51/229, May 21, 1997.

[12] 1997 Convention *supra* note 10 at Art. 36, para. 1.

[13] For the text of these articles, which will be referred to subsequently, see 1997 Convention, *supra* note 10.

watercourse states; and, if no harm, the benefits of utilizations to be shared in accordance with the principle of equitable utilization.

The second group supported the above four propositions but with the qualifying word "significant" added before "harm" in propositions two and three. The third group supported the first two propositions of the second group and the fourth proposition of the first two groups; that is to say, this group advocated applying the principle of equitable utilization unless there will be harm to ecosystems or significant pollution harm. The fourth group, on the other hand, advocated bringing all utilizations under the principle of equitable utilization, harm being an important factor to be taken into account in determining whether a utilization is reasonable and equitable.

The articles of the Watercourses Convention need to be examined closely to determine which of these competing views of the substantive law have prevailed.

ARTICLE 5

Article 5 of the Convention provides as follows:

1. Watercourse States shall in their respective territories utilize an international watercourse in an equitable and reasonable manner. In particular, an international watercourse shall be used and developed by watercourse States with a view to attaining optimal and sustainable utilization thereof and benefits therefrom, taking into account the interests of the watercourse states concerned, consistent with adequate protection of the watercourse.
2. Watercourse States shall participate in the use, development and protection of an international watercourse in an equitable and reasonable manner. Such participation includes both the right to utilize the watercourse and the duty to cooperate in the protection and development thereof, as provided in the present Convention.

The wording of Article 5 gives rise to two questions. The first is whether the concluding words of paragraph 1, namely "consistent with adequate protection of the watercourse," modify the scope of the principle of equitable utilization expressed in the article. All of the five Special Rapporteurs for the ILC's work on international watercourses took the view that the principle of equitable utilization was part of customary international law. Thus, one assumes that the article was intended to incorporate it. This assumption seems to be justified in the light of the ILC's commentary on Article 5, particularly the statement that "there is overwhelming support for the doctrine of equitable utilization as a general rule of law for the determination of the rights and obligations of States in this field."[14] Consequently, it seems reasonable to treat the second sentence of paragraph 1 as subservient to the first, its purpose being to emphasize that the protection of the watercourse is an important factor to be taken into account in applying the principle of equitable utilization.

This interpretation, however, may be questioned because of remarks made in the ILC's commentaries on Articles 20 and 21. Concerning Article 20, it is said:

> The obligation to "protect" the ecosystems of international watercourses is a specific application of the requirement contained in article 5 . . . to use and develop an international watercourse in a manner that is consistent with adequate protection thereof. In essence, it requires that watercourse states shield the ecosystems of international watercourses from harm or damage . . . [and] from a significant threat of harm . . . It requires that these ecosystems be protected in such a way as to maintain them as much as possible in their natural state.[15]

Concerning Article 21, paragraph 2, which deals with transboundary pollution that may cause significant harm to other watercourse states or their environment, it stated: "This paragraph is a specific application of the general principles contained in articles 5 and 7."[16]

If the provisions of Articles 20 and 21 impose a strict duty not to cause harm or significant harm, they can be reconciled with the provisions of Article 5 only in one of two ways: first, by holding that the clause "consistent with adequate protection of the watercourse" in Article 5 in effect incorporates by implicit reference the no harm rule in the subsequent articles and so overrides the principle of equitable utilization provided for in Article 5 to the extent that there is inconsistency between the articles; or, second, by presuming that any harm or significant harm, as the case may be, is unreasonable and inequitable, as Professor McCaffrey indicated in his Fourth Report to the ILC:

> [S]tating that . . . water uses that cause appreciable pollution harm to other watercourse States and the environment could well be regarded as being *per se* inequitable and unreasonable . . . [T]he Commission should likewise demonstrate its recognition of the importance of pollution prevention and environmental protection by adopting a rule of "no appreciable

14 Report of ILC, *supra* note 9 at 222.

15 *Ibid.*, 282.

16 *Ibid.*, 291.

pollution harm" that is not qualified by the principle of equitable and reasonable utilization.[17]

In this view, it is an irrebuttable presumption, in effect an absolute rule, that a use of the waters of an international watercourse that causes significant pollution harm or any harm to the ecosystem is *ipso facto* unlawful; it is unlawful not because it is in fact unreasonable and inequitable but because it is deemed to be so.

But facts do matter and, as Professor Lammers has written, "a strict application of the no substantial harm principle may in certain circumstances lead to results which are quite inequitable."[18] A law that sanctions unreasonable and inequitable results is, one would think, jurisprudentially and morally weak. Moreover, experience in other fields has shown that such laws are unlikely to be effective, even when there is well-established enforceable machinery. A more just and practical interpretation of Article 5, therefore, is that the second sentence of paragraph 1 only supplements the first sentence — that is to say, equitable utilization is the primary rule. This view, of course, leaves unanswered whether there is really any conflict between the provisions of Article 5 and Articles 20 and 21.

This interpretation of Article 5 finds support in the ILC's commentary on the article in its 1994 Report to the General Assembly, where it is stated:

> The second sentence of paragraph 1 elaborates upon the concept of equitable utilization . . . The expression "with a view to" indicates that the attainment of optimal utilization and benefits is the objective to be sought by watercourse States in utilizing an international watercourse . . . This goal must not be pursued blindly, however.[19]

As Special Rapporteur Schwebel wrote in his Third Report in commenting on the first version of the ILC's article on equitable utilization, this pursuit is qualified by the recognition that "the well-being of the peoples dependent upon the waters of the system, or the socio-economic development of the area, not to mention protection of the marine environment, may give certain measures of protection overriding priority."[20] Emphasis should be placed on the word "may" in Mr. Schwebel's statement; in a particular case,

17 UN Doc. A/CN.4/412/Add.2 (1988) at para. 13; II *Yearbook of the International Law Commision* 241 (1988) [hereinafter McCaffrey Report].

18 J. G. Lammers, *Pollution of International Watercourses: The Search for Substantive Rules and Principles of Law* 367 (The Hague: Martinus Nijhoff Publishers, 1984).

19 Report of the ILC, *supra* note 9 at 218-19.

20 UN Doc. A/CN.4/348, Dec. 11, 1981, at 58, para. 87.

certain measures of protection may, of course, be given priority because it would be unreasonable and inequitable not to do so in the light of all relevant factors.

The second question about Article 5 is the effect of the words "and sustainable," which were added to paragraph 1 by the Working Group of the Sixth Committee. These words are not seen as limiting the scope or priority of the principle of equitable utilization. Sustainable utilization is clearly an important factor among all of the other relevant factors to be taken into account in determining what is a reasonable and equitable utilization; like "optimal" utilization, it is an objective that must be kept in view by states in their reasonable pursuit of the benefits of an international watercourse. This interpretation is supported by the arguments made above about the force of the words "consistent with adequate protection of the watercourse."

ARTICLE 7

The relationship between the principle of equitable utilization on the one hand, and that of no harm or no significant harm on the other hand, has been, and continues to be, a subject of controversy. The first step in defining this relationship was taken by Mr. Schwebel in his Third Report to the ILC. After an exhaustive study, he proposed the adoption of the following article (Article 8 of his draft articles in his Third Report):

1. The right of a system State to use the water resources of an international watercourse system is limited by the duty not to cause appreciable harm to the interests of another system State, except as may be allowable under a determination for equitable participation. . . .
2. Each system State is under a duty to refrain from . . . any activity that may cause appreciable harm to the interests of another system State, except as may be allowable under paragraph 1 of this article.[21]

In this article, then, the priority of equitable utilization was explicitly established. This priority, however, was rejected almost immediately by the successor Special Rapporteur, Mr. Evensen, who proposed an article that retained the duty not to cause appreciable harm but omitted the exception clause in favour of equitable utilization.[22] Thus, he made the no appreciable harm rule dominant.

21 *Ibid.*, 104-105.

22 Art. 9 of his Draft Article: see II *Yearbook of the International Law Commision* 172 (1983).

Thereafter, the priority of the two principles was a controversial issue in the ILC. While the Special Rapporteurs who followed Mr. Evensen, namely Professor McCaffrey and Mr. Rosenstock, shared Mr. Schwebel's view, opinion among the membership of the ILC remained divided. In the ILC's Draft Articles of 1991, the Evensen view was adopted: Article 7 simply stated that "Watercourse States shall utilize an international watercourse in such a way as not to cause appreciable harm to other watercourse States."[23] This article, however, proved to be unacceptable and a new formula was sought. Under the guidance of Special Rapporteur Rosenstock, the ILC adopted the following version of Article 7 in its 1994 Draft Articles:

1. Watercourse States shall exercise due diligence to utilize an international watercourse in such a way as not to cause significant harm to other watercourse States.
2. Where, despite the exercise of due diligence, significant harm is caused to another watercourse State, the State whose use causes the harm shall, in the absence of agreement to such use, consult with the State suffering such harm over:
   (a) the extent to which such use is equitable and reasonable taking into account the factors listed in article 6;
   (b) the question of ad hoc adjustments to its utilization, designed to eliminate or mitigate any such harm caused and, where appropriate, the question of compensation.[24]

The interpretation of Article 7 is not free from doubt. At first glance, the commentary on the article seems to indicate that the ILC accepted the view that, in the last analysis, the dominant rule is equitable utilization. Consider, for example, these statements in the ILC's commentary on Article 7:

The fact that an activity involves significant harm, would not of itself necessarily constitute a basis for barring it. In certain circumstances "equitable and reasonable utilization" of an international watercourse may still involve significant harm to another watercourse State. Generally, in such instances, the principle of equitable and reasonable utilization remains the guiding criterion in balancing the interests at stake.[25]

23 Draft Articles on the Non-Navigational Uses of International Watercourses: Draft Report of the International Law Commission, UN GAOR, 43rd Sess. at 1, UN Doc. A/CN.4/L.463/Add.4 (1991).

24 Report of the ILC, *supra* note 9 at 236.

25 *Ibid.*

And again:

> The obligation of due diligence contained in Article 7 sets the threshold for lawful State activity. It is not intended to guarantee that . . . significant harm would not occur. It is an obligation of conduct, not an obligation of result.[26]

These statements seem to clearly assert the subordination of the no significant harm rule to the principle of equitable utilization. But do they do so? They were followed by this statement:

> What the obligation [to exercise due diligence] entails is that a watercourse State whose use causes significant harm can be deemed to have breached its obligation . . . only when it has intentionally or negligently caused the event which had to be prevented or has intentionally or negligently not prevented others in its territory from causing that event or has abstained from abating it.[27]

And again:

> A watercourse State can be deemed to have violated its due diligence obligation only if it knew or ought to have known that the particular use . . . would cause significant harm to other watercourse States.[28]

The obligation of a state to exercise due diligence to avoid causing harm to other watercourse states when it uses an international watercourse is not controversial. Suppose, however, that a use is within the right of a state under the principle of equitable utilization and is implemented with due diligence but with the knowledge that it will cause significant harm to another watercourse state. In that case, would that use be unlawful under Article 7, paragraph 1, since it would be a case of intentionally inflicted harm? On the basis of the statements just quoted, the utilization would seem to be unlawful.

Before giving a definitive answer to the question, however, Article 7, paragraph 2, must be considered. On its wording, this paragraph comes into play only after it has been determined by the application of paragraph 1 that, in spite of the exercise of due diligence, a utilization has caused significant harm. The paragraph has no bearing on the question of the lawfulness of the utilization, of whether it was done with or without due diligence, or whether it was done knowing that it would cause significant harm to other watercourse states. In other words, the paragraph is merely procedural, not

26 *Ibid.*, 237.

27 *Ibid.*

28 *Ibid*, 239.

substantive. Nevertheless, its opening words, "where, despite the exercise of due diligence," may assist in the interpretation of paragraph 1.

This interpretation that paragraph 2 is procedural is supported by the language of the paragraph that requires consultation with the state that suffers harm as a result of a use, over "the extent to which such use is equitable and reasonable." In reading paragraphs 1 and 2 of Article 7 together, therefore, one is justified in concluding that, notwithstanding the various statements made in the commentary, the article does not prohibit a use that is equitable and reasonable and done with due diligence, even though the use causes significant harm to other watercourse states. As far as Article 7 is concerned, then, the ILC in its 1994 Draft Articles ultimately sustained the priority of the principle of equitable utilization over the no significant harm rule.

The controversy over the relationship of equitable utilization and the no harm rule, however, did not end with the work of the ILC. Article 7 proved to be a most contentious issue as the Working Group sought to elaborate a convention based on the ILC's 1994 Articles. A perusal of the statements made about Article 7 during the discussions of the Working Group shows that some twenty-three states spoke in favour of the no harm or no significant harm rule while nineteen states spoke against that rule. In the end, the Working Group adopted an entirely new version of the article, but the division of opinion on the matter persisted, as evident from the voting on Articles 5, 6, and 7 as a package: 38 for, 4 against, 22 abstaining, and 129 not voting.[29]

The new Article 7 is as follows:

1. Watercourse States shall, in utilizing an international watercourse in their territories, take all appropriate measures to prevent the causing of significant harm to other watercourse States.
2. Where significant harm nevertheless is caused to another watercourse State, the State whose use causes such harm shall, in the absence of agreement to such use, take all appropriate measures, having due regard for the provisions of Articles 5 and 6, in consultation with the affected State, to eliminate or mitigate such harm and, where appropriate, to discuss the question of compensation.

The wording of this article is much improved over that of the ILC's version of it. By clearly stating that due regard must be had for the articles setting out the principle of equitable utilization, it

[29] UN Doc. A/C.6/51/NUW/CRP.94; A/C.6/51/SR.62, Apr. 4, 1997.

settles the issue of priority in favour of that principle. The essence of the article is this: if a state is acting within its rights as defined in Articles 5 and 6, it is under a duty to prevent, eliminate, or mitigate harm to other watercourse states by all appropriate, presumably reasonable, measures; in short, it must act without malice and with due diligence — a proposition that is not disputed.

The function of Article 7, as defined in the Watercourses Convention, therefore, is not to impose limits on the right of states to undertake equitable and reasonable utilizations under Articles 5 and 6, but on the implementation of these utilizations. Article 7 deals only with process.[30]

ARTICLES 20 AND 21

Although not placed among the general principles set out in Part II of the ILC's 1994 Draft Articles and in the Watercourses Convention, but instead in Part IV entitled Protection, Preservation and Management, Articles 20 and 21, at first glance, seem to contain important substantive legal principles that severely limit the rights of states under Article 5.

Article 20 of the Watercourses Convention provides that "Watercourse States shall, individually and where appropriate, jointly, protect and preserve the ecosystems of international watercourses." And Article 21 provides:

1. For the purpose of this article, "pollution of an international watercourse" means any detrimental alteration in the composition or quality of the waters of an international watercourse which results directly or indirectly from human conduct.
2. Watercourse States shall, individually and where appropriate, jointly, prevent, reduce and control the pollution of an international watercourse that may cause significant harm to other watercourse States or to their environment, including harm to human health or safety, to the use of the waters for any beneficial purpose or to the living resources of the watercourse. . . .

While the language of these articles is unambiguous, they leave open the question of the basis of the obligation of the states concerned. What constitutes a breach of the requirement in Article 20 to protect and preserve ecosystems, or of the requirement in

30 Professor McCaffrey takes this view of Art. 7 of the ILC's 1994 Draft Articles: see Stephen C. McCaffrey, "An Assessment of the Work of the International Law Commission" (1996) 36 Nat. Resources. J. 297, 309-10.

Article 21 to prevent, reduce, and control pollution that may cause the specified significant pollution harm? Is liability strict if harm is caused to the ecosystem of an international watercourse or if the pollution specified in Article 21, paragraph 2, is caused? Or does liability depend upon the failure to exercise due diligence? In other words, is the obligation one of result or one of conduct? These articles are silent on these questions.

The ILC, however, answered them in its commentary on Article 21 as follows:

> As with the obligation to "protect" ecosystems under article 20, the obligation to "prevent . . . pollution . . . that may cause significant harm" includes the duty to exercise due diligence to prevent the threat of such harm.[31]

This statement concerning Articles 20 and 21, equally applicable to Articles 22 and 23, was endorsed by the Working Group of the Sixth Committee and by the General Assembly in the following statement of understanding attached to the Watercourses Convention: "As reflected in the commentary of the International Law Commission, these articles impose a due diligence standard on watercourse states."[32] The obligation, then, is to act reasonably to achieve the objectives defined in these articles. To put the matter another way, the obligation is one of conduct, not of result.

This interpretation of Articles 20 and 21 raises again the relationship between them and Article 5, that is to say, whether equitable utilization is the first principle in the Watercourses Convention. Some of the language in the ILC's commentaries on Articles 20 and 21 lend support to the thesis that equitable utilization is the first principle. As mentioned in the discussion of Article 5 above, it is stated in these commentaries that Articles 20 and 21 are specific applications of Article 5. Particularly pertinent to the question is the following statement in the commentary on Article 21:

> The requirement that watercourse States "reduce and control" existing pollution reflects the practice of States, in particular those in whose territories polluted watercourses are situated. This practice indicates a general willingness to tolerate even significant pollution harm, provided that the watercourse State of origin is making its best efforts to reduce the pollution to a mutually acceptable level. A requirement that existing

[31] Report of the ILC, *supra* note 9 at 291-92.

[32] A/C.6/51/NUW/WG/L.4/Add.1, Apr. 3, 1997; and 1997 Convention, *supra* note 10 at 720.

pollution causing such harm be abated immediately could, in some cases, result in undue hardship, especially where the detriment to the watercourse State of origin was grossly disproportionate to the benefit that would accrue to the watercourse State experiencing the harm. On the other hand, failure of the watercourse State of origin to exercise due diligence in reducing the pollution to acceptable levels would entitle the affected State to claim that the State of origin had breached its obligation to do so.[33]

This statement recognizes that, in matters relating to the protection of ecosystems and of pollution of international watercourses, the interests of the states concerned must be balanced reasonably and equitably. This is, of course, the essence of the principle of equitable utilization.

THE NO HARM RULE BY ANOTHER ROUTE

The no significant harm rule, however, is resilient and does not yield first place readily. Even when it is accepted that the legitimacy of any use of an international watercourse depends upon its being equitable and reasonable, the rule may be given *de facto* dominance by accepting the argument that an act that causes significant harm is necessarily unreasonable and inequitable. This argument has in fact been made. As seen above, in his Fourth Report to the ILC, Professor McCaffrey wrote that "water uses that cause appreciable pollution harm to other watercourse States and the environment could well be regarded as being *per se* inequitable and unreasonable."[34] And in the commentary on Article 7, there is the statement that "A use which causes significant harm to human health and safety is understood to be inherently inequitable and unreasonable."[35]

These propositions may be acceptable as rebuttable presumptions, the burden of rebuttal being on the state causing the harm, but they are not acceptable as irrebuttable presumptions, for they would in effect confer on the no significant harm rule the status of an overriding principle of international water law. Equitable and reasonable utilization, implemented with due diligence, would cease to be the guiding principle of this branch of the law.

33 Report of the ILC, *supra* note 9 at 242.

34 McCaffrey Report, *supra* note 17 at para. 13.

35 Report of the ILC, *supra* note 9 at 242.

The Language of the Watercourses Convention

A regrettable feature of the ILC's 1994 Draft Articles and the Watercourses Convention is the looseness of their language. First, many of the crucial words in these documents lack precise meaning. Take, for example, the words ecosystems, environment, optimal, sustainable development, protection of the watercourse, preservation, appropriate measures, and so forth. Words like these can reasonably mean different things to different people. As Mr. Harris of the United States said in the discussion of the Convention in the Working Group: [T]here is no single definition of any of those principles that was acceptable to all States."[36] Second, apart from the difficulties caused by words with imprecise definitions, the syntax of many of the articles is awkward, leaving their meaning obscure; this is especially true in the case of Articles 5 and 7. And third, the intended meaning of some of the important articles can be gleaned only from the commentaries; for example, it is from the commentary on Article 21 that it is learned that the obligations under Articles 20 and 21 are ones of due diligence. Such an important qualification should have been made explicit in the body of the articles.

This failure to state clearly the principles of law set forth in the Watercourses Convention undoubtedly reflects the compromises that had to be made in order to reach an agreement. As a result of these compromises, however, the usefulness and influence of the Convention will likely be diminished.

The Gabčíkovo Case

The argument that the United Nations Watercourses Convention maintains the primacy of the principle of equitable utilization in international water law is supported by the judgment of the International Court of Justice (ICJ) in the *Case Concerning the Gabčíkovo-Nagymaros Project (Hungary/Slovakia)*.[37] This case involved the rights and obligations of the parties under the Treaty of September 16, 1977, and instruments related thereto between Hungary and Czechoslovakia concerning the construction and operation of the Gabčíkovo-Nagymaros System of Locks on the Danube River. Although the judgment is confined to the determination of those treaty rights and obligations, statements in it throw light on the

[36] UN Doc. A/C.6/51/SR.15 at 5.

[37] Judgment of Sept. 25, 1997, [1997] I.C.J. Rep. 3.

ICJ's perception of the customary law of international watercourses and of the provisions of the Watercourses Convention dealing with equitable utilization and the no significant harm rule.

The following statements from the judgment demonstrate the trend of the ICJ's thinking on the matter:

Paragraph 78: The suspension and withdrawal of that consent constituted a violation of Hungary's legal obligations . . . but that cannot mean that Hungary forfeited its basic right to an equitable and reasonable sharing of the resources of an international watercourse.

Paragraph 85: In 1929, the Permanent Court of International Justice, with regard to navigation on the River Oder, stated as follows: "[the] community of interest in a navigable river becomes the basis of a common legal right, the essential features of which are the perfect equality of all riparian States in the use of the whole course of the river" . . . Modern development of international law has strengthened this principle for non-navigational uses of international watercourses as well, as evidenced by the adoption of the Convention of 21 May 1997 . . . Czechoslovakia, by unilaterally assuming control of a shared resource, and thereby depriving Hungary of its right to an equitable and reasonable share of the natural resources of the Danube . . . failed to respect proportionality which is required by international law.

Paragraph 140: [The] Project's impact upon . . . the environment are of necessity a key issue . . . [N]ew norms and standards have been developed . . . Such new norms have to be taken into consideration, and such new standards given proper weight . . . This need to reconcile economic development with protection of the environment is aptly expressed in the concept of sustainable development.

Paragraph 141: It is for the Parties themselves to find an agreed solution that takes account of the objectives of the Treaty . . . as well as the norms of international environmental law and the principles of the law of international watercourses. The Court will recall in this context . . . [what] it said in the *North Sea Continental Shelf* cases.

Paragraph 142: The principle of good faith obliges the Parties to apply it in a reasonable way.

Paragraph 147: Re-establishment of the joint regime will also reflect in an optimal way the concept of common utilization of shared water resources for the achievement of the several objectives mentioned in the Treaty, in concordance with Article 5, paragraph 2, of the [Watercourses] Convention . . . according to which [quotation of Article 5 omitted].

Paragraph 150: In this case, the consequences of the wrongful acts of both Parties will be wiped out "as far as possible" if they resume their co-operation in the utilization of the shared water resources of the Danube, and if the multi-purpose programme . . . for the use, development and protection of the watercourse is implemented in an equitable and reasonable manner.

These statements lead to the conclusion that the ICJ took the view that the emerging norms for the protection of ecosystems and the protection of the environment from pollution and other hazards are not peremptory norms of international law, but nevertheless are to be taken seriously into account in the determination of international water resources issues. Equitable and reasonable sharing of these resources determines the lawfulness of their use; that this is so even under the terms of the Watercourses Convention can be deduced from the ICJ's language in its judgment in the *Gabčikovo-Nagymaros* case and the Court's invocation of Article 5 of that Convention.

Conclusion

Recognizing the difficulties in interpreting the Watercourses Convention, one nevertheless concludes that it adopts equitable utilization as the dominant principle governing the non-navigational uses of international watercourses, the principle that entitles watercourse states to a reasonable and equitable share of the benefits of the uses of the shared resource, and renders obligatory the exercise of due diligence by states in undertaking utilizations. At the same time, the Convention emphasizes that the sustainability of utilizations and the protection and preservation of these watercourses are important objectives that must be taken into account in determining the rights and duties of states under the principle of equitable utilization. This theme runs through the articles considered above.

The Convention, therefore, does not embody the notion that a project that is admittedly equitable and reasonable cannot be implemented if it will cause significant harm to other watercourse states; nor does it support the notion that a use that causes significant harm is *ipso facto* inequitable and unreasonable. Significant harm is subordinate to equitable utilization. This conclusion is supported by the recent decision of the International Court of Justice in the *Gabčikovo-Nagymaros* case.

Moreover, whatever the content and intent of the Watercourses Convention, its chequered history prevents it from being taken as credible evidence of customary international law. The record of the discussions in the ILC and in the Working Group of the Sixth Committee shows substantial disagreement over the substantive articles of the Convention. The extent of this disagreement among states is evident in the divided votes in the Working Group: on Articles 5, 6, and 7 as a package, it was 38 for, 4 against, 22 abstentions, and 129 states not voting;[38] on the Convention as a

[38] *Supra* note 29.

whole, it was 42 for, 3 against, 19 abstentions, and 130 states not voting.[39] Furthermore, the states that did not vote for the Convention in the Working Group are not all minor ones; China, France, and Turkey voted against it, and Argentina, Egypt, India, Israel, Pakistan, Russia, and Spain were among the abstainers. When the Convention came before the General Assembly for approval, the vote was 104 for, 3 against, and 27 abstaining.[40] In the face of this voting record, it would seem to be impossible to argue successfully that the provisions of the Convention are accepted as customary law by the international community. For states not party to the Convention, therefore, its provisions will at best serve only as guidelines, assisting in determining in a particular case whether a use of the waters of an international watercourse is reasonable and equitable under the customary international principle of equitable utilization.

In short, then, the attempt in the ILC and the United Nations General Assembly to advance international water law beyond the flexible principle of equitable utilization has failed. The interpretation of the Watercourses Convention advocated above leads to the conclusion that the general principles set forth therein are in harmony with the existing customary law on the subject, namely the principle of equitable utilization and that they have reaffirmed the soundness of this principle. Moreover, even if this interpretation is rejected, the general principles set forth in the Watercourses Convention are clearly the result of compromises and cannot be taken to be rules of customary international law universally binding on states.

CHARLES B. BOURNE
Founding Editor-in-Chief

Sommaire

La primauté du principe de l'utilisation équitable dans la Convention sur les cours d'eau de 1997

Durant une décennie, la Commission de droit international a débattu du lien entre le principe de l'utilisation équitable et le principe de la réduction des torts dans son travail sur les utilisations non-navigables des cours d'eau internationaux. La Convention, telle qu'adoptée par l'Assemblée générale le

39 UN Doc. A/C.6/51/SR.62/Add.1

40 UN Res. 51/229, *supra* note 11. Burundi, China, and Turkey voted against the Convention; notable among the abstainees were Argentina, Egypt, France, India, Israel, Pakistan, and Spain.

21 mai 1997, précise que le principe de l'utilisation équitable (qui prévoit le partage équitable et raisonnable de l'eau des cours d'eau internationaux) devient le principe fondamental substantif du droit international en matière des cours d'eaux. Un dommage suite à l'utilisation d'un cours d'eau international est un facteur indiquant si l'utilisation est, en effet, raisonnable, équitable et, donc, conforme à la Convention. Cette interprétation de la Convention correspond à l'évolution des principes de droit international coutumier en la matière. De plus, cette interprétation de la Convention est appuyée par l'arrêt récent de la Cour internationale de justice, Gabčíkovo.

Summary

The Primacy of the Principle of Equitable Utilization in the 1997 Watercourses Convention

The International Law Commission wrestled for over a decade with the relationship between the principle of equitable utilization and the no harm principle in its work on the law of the non-navigational uses of international watercourses. In its final Report to the UN General Assembly on this topic in 1994, the Commission presented a set of Draft Articles couched in obscure language that reflected the sharp differences of opinion on the matter and the compromises that had been made. This division of opinion about the relationship between these two principles persisted in the Working Group of the Sixth Committee of the General Assembly to which the Draft Articles were referred. Again, compromises were reached and the language of the substantive articles (in particular Articles 5, 7, 20, and 21) of the Watercourses Convention, adopted by the General Assembly on May 21, 1997, continues to be obscure and its meaning debatable.

It is argued here that in this Convention the principle of equitable utilization, which prescribes the reasonable and equitable sharing of the beneficial uses of the waters of an international watercourse, is made the primary substantive rule of international water law; harm caused by a utilization of these waters is, of course, an important factor to be taken into account in determining whether, in a particular case, the utilization is reasonable and equitable and, therefore, lawful. This interpretation of the Watercourses Convention brings it into harmony with customary international water law. It is an interpretation that finds support in the recent decision of the International Court of Justice in the Gabčíkovo *case.*

Les procédures d'accession à l'Organisation mondiale du commerce (OMC)

I Introduction

Le 1er janvier 1995, l'Accord de Marrakech instituant l'Organisation mondiale du commerce (l'Accord sur l'OMC) entrait en vigueur. L'intérêt marqué que portent les pays à ce nouvel accord est particulièrement frappant si l'on tient compte du nombre grandissant de pays Membre et de la longue liste de pays qui ont fait une demande d'accession à l'OMC. Le 30 janvier 1998, l'OMC comptait 132 Membres et trente pays avaient fait une demande d'accession à l'OMC.[1] Cet article examine les procédures d'accession à l'OMC et survole les droits et obligations des pays qui font une demande d'accession et des pays déjà Membres de l'OMC dans le cadre de ce processus d'accession.

L'Accord sur l'OMC comprend quelques vingt-cinq accords et protocoles sur des sujets divers qui élaborent les principes de base contenus dans l'accord du GATT. Le champ de compétence des accords de l'OMC dépasse de beaucoup celui du GATT. L'Accord de Marrakech instituant l'OMC constitue le point de départ des accords de l'OMC: il met en place une véritable organisation internationale, l'OMC. Ce premier accord est assez court et prévoit les

---

Les opinions exprimées dans cette note sont strictement personelles et ne lient aucunement le secrétariat de l'OMC. L'auteure tient à remercier Peter Milthorp, Geraldine Murphy, Moira Redecker et plus particulièrement Alain Richer pour leurs précieux commentaires. Toute erreur ne peut être imputée qu'à l'auteure.

1 Le 19 février 1998, le Conseil général a adopté la décision approuvant le Protocole d'accession et le rapport du Groupe de travail du Laos.

règles institutionnelles de base de l'OMC, soit les procédures d'accession, de retrait, de vote, d'amendement et d'autres dispositions d'application générale. Le résultat des autres négociations [a] été "annexé" à l'Accord instituant l'OMC. Cette formule juridique, l'utilisation d'"annexes," a permis de mettre en place un "Accord Unique" ("single undertaking").[2]

L'article II de l'Accord instituant l'OMC prévoit donc:

1. L'OMC servira de cadre institutionnel commun pour la conduite des relations commerciales entre ses Membres en ce qui concerne les questions liées aux accords et instruments juridiques connexes repris dans les Annexes du présent accord.
2. Les accords et instruments juridiques connexes repris dans les Annexes 1, 2 et 3 (ci-après dénommés les "Accords commerciaux multilatéraux") font partie intégrante du présent accord et sont contraignants pour tous les Membres.
3. Les accords et instruments juridiques connexes repris dans l'Annexe 4 (ci-après dénommés les "Accords commerciaux plurilatéraux") font également partie du présent accord pour les Membres qui les ont acceptés et sont contraignants pour ces Membres. Les Accords commerciaux plurilatéraux ne créent ni obligations ni droits pour les Membres qui ne les ont pas acceptés.

En adhérant à l'OMC, les pays doivent automatiquement et sans exception respecter tous les accords de l'OMC et ses annexes, et s'ils le désirent, les accords contenus à l'Annexe 4. À l'exception de l'Annexe 4, un pays qui adhère à l'OMC ne signe donc qu'un seul traité. Aucune réserve n'est autorisée:

5. Il ne pourra pas être formulé de réserves en ce qui concerne une disposition du présent accord. Il ne pourra être formulé de réserves en ce qui concerne des dispositions des Accords commerciaux multilatéraux que dans la mesure prévue dans lesdits accords. Les réserves

[2] Il existe une exception au concept d'"Accord Unique." Les parties contractantes au GATT étant incapables de former un consensus sur l'Accord sur les marchés publics et l'Accord sur les aéronefs civils, il a été décidé de mettre ces accords (de même que les accords sur la viande bovine et les produits laitiers qui depuis on été supprimés) dans une Annexe 4 distincte qui comprend les accords qui ne lient que les Membres qui y ont adhéré. Voir la décision du 10 décembre 1997, "Suppression de l'Accord international sur la viande bovine de l'annexe 4 de l'Accord sur l'OMC" et "Suppression de l'Accord international sur le secteur laitier de l'annexe 4 de l'Accord sur l'OMC" qui font suite aux décisions adoptées par le Conseil international des produits laitiers (IDA/8), et par le Conseil international de la viande bovine de mettre fin à leurs accords respectifs à compter du 1er janvier 1998 et invitant la Conférence ministérielle à supprimer ces accords de l'Annexe 4 de l'Accord sur l'OMC au moment où ils viendront à expiration.

> concernant une disposition d'un Accord commercial plurilatéral seront régies par les dispositions dudit accord.

De plus, un pays Membre doit être en mesure de respecter les normes contenues dans tous les accords de l'OMC dès le moment de son accession à l'OMC. Ceci n'exclut évidement pas l'application de périodes transitoires, si un accord en prévoit la possibilité.

> 4. Chaque Membre assurera la conformité de ses lois, réglementations et procédures administratives avec ses obligations telles qu'elles sont énoncées dans les Accords figurant en annexe.

Cette obligation est pertinente pour les pays qui accèdent à l'OMC puisque l'objet même du processus d'accession est de faire en sorte qu'ils modifient leur système juridique et leurs politiques commerciales pour les rendre conformes aux règles de l'OMC. Les résultats de ces négociations sont contenus dans le Protocole d'accession, le Rapport du groupe de travail et dans les Listes d'engagements qui y sont annexées. Tous les protocoles d'accession prévoient que les engagements pris dans le cadre du processus d'accession et consignés dans les documents d'accession font partie intégrante de l'Accord de l'OMC. Ceci signifie que la violation d'un engagement pris dans le cadre d'une accession constitue une violation de l'Accord de l'OMC qui peut donner lieu à une demande de règlement des différends. À titre d'exemple, le deuxième paragraphe du Protocole d'accession de la Mongolie prévoit ce qui suit: "Le présent protocole, qui comprendra les engagements mentionnés au paragraphe 61 du rapport du Groupe de travail, fera partie intégrante de l'Accord sur l'OMC."

L'objet du présent article est donc d'examiner le processus entourant la négociation de ces conditions spécifiques lors de l'accession d'un pays à l'OMC. Le cas de l'accession de la Mongolie sera par la suite étudié à titre d'exemple.

Il existe deux façons d'accéder à l'OMC. L'article XI prévoit la procédure d'accession pour les pays qui étaient déjà parties contractantes au GATT et l'article XII concerne les pays qui n'étaient pas déjà parties contractantes au GATT. L'article XI prévoit la procédure d'accession pour les Membres dits "originels."

II Accession à l'OMC pour les pays déjà parties contractantes au GATT: l'article XI de l'Accord de l'OMC

L'article XI de l'Accord de l'OMC prévoit ceci:

Article XI
Membres originels

1. Les parties contractantes au GATT de 1947 à la date d'entrée en vigueur du présent accord, et les Communautés européennes, qui acceptent le présent accord et les Accords commerciaux multilatéraux et pour lesquelles des Listes de concessions et d'engagements sont annexées au GATT de 1994 et pour lesquelles des Listes d'engagements spécifiques sont annexées à l'AGCS, deviendront Membres originels de l'OMC.
2. Les pays les moins avancés reconnus comme tels par les Nations Unies ne seront tenus de contracter des engagements et de faire des concessions que dans la mesure compatible avec les besoins du développement, des finances et du commerce de chacun d'entre eux ou avec leurs capacités administratives et institutionnelles.

Lors de l'entrée en vigueur de l'Accord sur l'OMC, le GATT comptait 126 parties contractantes.[3] En règle générale, il fallait donc que ces parties contractantes aient signé l'Acte final[4] et aient complété leurs négociations tarifaires et pris des engagements spécifiques au titre de l'Accord sur les Services avant le 1er janvier 1995. L'article XIV de l'Accord sur l'OMC prévoit qu'afin de bénéficier du statut de Membre originel, ces parties contractantes devaient avoir accepté l'Accord sur l'OMC dans les deux ans suivant son entrée en vigueur, soit avant le 31 décembre 1996.

1. Le présent accord sera ouvert à l'acceptation, par voie de signature ou autrement, des parties contractantes au GATT de 1947, et des Communautés européennes, qui sont admises à devenir Membres originels de l'OMC conformément à l'article XI du présent accord. Cette acceptation vaudra pour le présent accord et pour les Accords commerciaux multilatéraux qui y sont annexés. Le présent accord et les Accords commerciaux multilatéraux qui y sont annexés entreront en vigueur à la date fixée par les Ministres conformément au paragraphe 3 de l'Acte final reprenant les résultats des Négociations commerciales multilatérales du Cycle d'Uruguay et resteront ouverts à l'acceptation pendant une période de deux ans suivant cette date à moins

3 Voir l'appendice 1 au présent article qui contient la liste de tous les Membres actuels de l'OMC et la date effective de leur adhésion à l'OMC.

4 L'Accord instituant l'Organisation mondiale du commerce (dénommé dans le présent Acte final l'"Accord sur l'OMC"), les Déclarations et Décisions ministérielles, ainsi que le Mémorandum d'accord sur les engagements relatifs aux services financiers, joints en annexe, reprennent les résultats de leurs négociations et font partie intégrante de ce qui est l'Acte final. "En signant le présent acte final, les représentants *conviennent* (a) de soumettre pour examen, selon qu'il sera approprié, l'Accord sur l'OMC à leurs autorités compétentes respectives, en vue d'obtenir l'approbation de l'Accord conformément à leurs procédures; et (b) d'adopter les Déclarations et Décisions ministérielles."

que les Ministres n'en décident autrement. Une acceptation intervenant après l'entrée en vigueur du présent accord entrera en vigueur le 30e jour qui suivra la date de ladite acceptation.

Comme certains pays les moins avancés n'avaient pas complété les procédures de ratification de leur Listes de marchandises et de services, les parties contractantes adoptèrent la "Décision sur les mesures en faveur des pays les moins avancés" lors de la réunion ministérielle de Marrakech tenue en avril 1994. Cette décision octroyait aux pays suivants un délai supplémentaire de un an à compter du 15 avril 1994 pour compléter les procédures de ratification des listes d'engagements: Angola, Botswana, Burkina Faso, Burundi, République d'Afrique centrale, Tchad, Djibouti, Gabon, Guinée, Guinée-Bissau, Haïti, Lesotho, Malawi, Maldives, Mali, Mozambique, Rwanda, Sierra Leone, Îles Salomon, Togo et Zaïre.

Il a fallu prendre une décision particulière en ce qui concerne le Congo/Brazaville. Le Congo ne faisait pas partie des pays les moins avancés qui pouvaient bénéficier du délai supplémentaire qui leur était accordé. Toutefois, à cause de la situation de guerre civile qui y sévissait, le Congo a été la seule partie contractante du GATT qui n'a pas complété son processus de négociation des Listes. Le 24 avril 1997, le Conseil général a décidé d'adopter une décision qui permettait au Congo/Brazzaville de devenir Membre originel malgré le fait qu'il n'ait pas accepté l'Accord sur l'OMC avant le 31 décembre 1996. Cette décision est un exemple type du caractère pragmatique de l'OMC et, à ce titre, mérite d'être citée:

Considérant que le 25 février 1997 le gouvernement de la République du Congo a notifié à l'Organisation mondiale du commerce que le Parlement de la République du Congo a ratifié l'Accord de Marrakech instituant l'Organisation mondiale du commerce qu'il avait signé, sous réserve de ratification, le 15 avril 1994,

Considérant que le délai d'acceptation de l'Accord de Marrakech instituant l'Organisation mondiale du commerce est arrivé à expiration le 1er janvier 1997, deux ans après l'entrée en vigueur de l'Accord, ainsi qu'il est indiqué à l'article XIV:1 de l'Accord,

Considérant que la République du Congo est la seule partie contractante au GATT de 1947 restante qui était admise à devenir Membre originel de l'Organisation mondiale du commerce avant le 1er janvier 1997 et qui n'est pas encore Membre de l'Organisation,

Le Conseil général,

Décide de proroger avec effet rétroactif au 25 février 1997, date à laquelle le Directeur général a reçu notification de la ratification de l'Accord par la République du Congo, le délai prévu pour l'acceptation, par la République du Congo, de l'Accord de Marrakech instituant l'Organisation mondiale du commerce; la République du Congo serait ainsi réputée être Membre de l'Organisation à compter du 27 mars 1997, 30 jours après réception de la notification.[5]

C'est donc dire qu'outre la Communauté européenne, qui n'était pas une partie contractante en tant que telle, toutes les parties contractantes au GATT sont devenues Membres originels de l'OMC ayant complété le processus de ratification de leur listes et ayant accepté l'Accord sur l'OMC dans les délais impartis.[6] Ce statut de Membre originel n'offre, toutefois, aucun privilège. Les Membres originels sont soumis aux mêmes obligations que tous les autres Membres. Cette affirmation mérite toutefois deux qualifications. Comme nous le verrons dans la partie suivante de cet article, un pays qui n'était pas partie contractante au GATT peut se voir imposer, dans le cadre de son accession, des obligations additionnelles à celles prévues aux accords de l'OMC. De plus, un pays qui n'était pas partie contractante peut se voir refuser la possibilité de bénéficier de périodes transitoires, même si elles sont prévues aux termes de différents accords de l'OMC. Les Membres accédant à l'OMC aux termes de l'article XII (pays qui n'étaient pas parties contractantes) peuvent ne pas avoir exactement les mêmes droits et obligations que les Membres originels. Toutefois, cette affirmation nécessite une étude détaillée des dispositions spécifiques du Protocole d'accession de chaque pays accédant à l'OMC selon la procédure de l'article XII de l'Accord instituant l'OMC.

III Accession à l'OMC pour les pays qui n'étaient pas déjà parties contractantes au GATT: l'article XII de l'Accord instituant l'OMC

Aux termes de l'article XII de l'Accord instituant l'OMC, un État pourra accéder à l'OMC à des conditions à convenir entre lui et les Membres de l'OMC. C'est donc dire que l'accession de tout État est soumise à l'acceptation des Membres existants de l'OMC. L'article XII est formel:

1. Tout État ou territoire douanier distinct[7] jouissant d'une entière autonomie dans la conduite de ses relations commerciales extérieures et

5 Document WT/GC/W/54 contenant la décision adoptée par le Conseil général le 24 avril 1997 (WT/GC/M/19).

6 Voir la liste en appendice 1 qui mentionne les dates d'entrée en vigueur de l'Accord sur l'OMC pour tous les pays Membres originels.

7 Cette disposition vise notamment Hong Kong.

pour les autres questions traitées dans le présent accord et dans les Accords commerciaux multilatéraux pourra accéder au présent accord à des conditions à convenir entre lui et l'OMC. Cette accession vaudra pour le présent accord et pour les Accords commerciaux multilatéraux qui y sont annexés . . .

3. L'accession à un Accord commercial plurilatéral sera régie par les dispositions dudit accord.

Rien d'autre n'est prévu sur la procédure d'accession en tant que telle. Conformément à l'article XVI:1 de l'Accord instituant l'OMC,[8] la pratique du GATT a été maintenue et adaptée aux nouvelles exigences des accords de l'OMC. De façon générale, le processus d'accession prévoit l'examen du régime de commerce extérieur de l'État ou du territoire douanier distinct concerné. Cet examen débouche sur deux types de négociations. Des négociations multilatérales en vue de la conclusion d'un accord sur une décision et un protocole énonçant les modalités d'accession de l'État ou du territoire douanier distinct; et la négociation et l'établissement, pour cet État ou ce territoire douanier distinct, d'une liste de concessions et d'engagements à annexer au GATT de 1994 ainsi que d'une liste d'engagements spécifiques à annexer à l'Accord général sur le commerce des services (AGCS).

A LA DEMANDE D'ACCESSION[9] — ÉTABLISSEMENT D'UN GROUPE DE TRAVAIL

Lorsqu'un pays souhaite accéder à l'OMC, il doit présenter une requête en ce sens au Directeur général de l'OMC au titre de l'article XII. Cette communication est distribuée à tous les Membres. Le Conseil général examine alors la demande et détermine s'il convient d'établir un "groupe de travail." Le mandat des groupes de travail est en général le suivant: "Examiner la demande d'accession à l'OMC au titre de l'article XII; présenter au Conseil général/à la Conférence ministérielle des recommandations comportant éventuellement un projet de Protocole d'accession."

Tous les Membres intéressés peuvent être membres des groupes

8 "1. Sauf disposition contraire du présent accord ou des Accords commerciaux multilatéraux, l'OMC sera guidée par les décisions, les procédures et les pratiques habituelles des PARTIES CONTRACTANTES du GATT de 1947 et des organes établis dans le cadre du GATT de 1947."

9 Pour de plus amples détails sur la procédure d'accession voir le document WT/ACC/1 préparé par le Secrétariat de l'OMC.

de travail.[10] Le président du groupe de travail est désigné à l'issue de consultations menées par le président du Conseil général, auxquelles participent le requérant et les membres du groupe de travail. Une fois le groupe de travail établi, le Secrétariat informe le requérant des procédures suivies par les groupes de travail des accessions à l'OMC et de la prescription selon laquelle le requérant doit présenter un Mémorandum décrivant son régime de commerce extérieur en ce qui concerne plus spécifiquement des sujets figurant sur une liste standard,[11] sans nécessairement s'y limiter.

B PRÉSENTATION ET NÉGOCIATION DES COMPOSANTES DU RÉGIME DE COMMERCE EXTÉRIEUR DU PAYS REQUÉRANT

Le pays qui fait une demande d'accession doit d'abord présenter, pour distribution à tous les Membres, un Mémorandum décrivant en détail son régime de commerce extérieur et contenant des statistiques pertinentes. Parallèlement, des exemplaires du tarif douanier applicable, établi suivant la nomenclature du Système harmonisé (SH), et des autres lois et réglementations en rapport avec l'accession sont mis à la disposition des membres du groupe de travail. En règle générale, le requérant envoie un jeu complet des lois et réglementations pertinentes au Secrétariat. Si les textes sont courts, ils doivent être entièrement traduits par le requérant dans l'une des langues officielles de l'OMC (français, anglais et espagnol); s'ils sont longs, le requérant doit en fournir un résumé détaillé dans l'une des langues officielles. Le résumé ou les textes traduits sont distribués aux membres du groupe de travail et l'original est conservé au Secrétariat pour consultation.

Après la distribution du Mémorandum, les membres du groupe de travail sont invités à présenter par écrit des questions en vue de clarifier le fonctionnement du régime de commerce extérieur du requérant. Normalement, les réponses doivent également être communiquées par écrit et être regroupées et disposées par sujets conformément à la structure du Mémorandum. Suivant l'adéquation des renseignements fournis, plusieurs séries de questions-réponses peuvent être organisées avant la première réunion du groupe de travail. Les séries successives doivent être conçues pour choisir et clarifier les questions avant les réunions du groupe de travail, si nécessaire. À la demande de tout membre du groupe de

10 Ceci suit en fait la règle générale de l'OMC selon laquelle tous les Membres de l'OMC ont le droit d'être membres de tous les comités de l'OMC.

11 Voir l'Appendice 2 ci-après.

travail, le requérant fournit au groupe de travail des renseignements sur l'accession concernant toute matière jugée pertinente.

À la première réunion du groupe de travail, des représentants du requérant et des membres du groupe de travail examinent le Mémorandum et les questions et réponses communiquées en vue d'obtenir tout autre éclaircissement qui pourrait être nécessaire, compte tenu des diverses dispositions de l'Accord sur l'OMC et des Accords commerciaux multilatéraux. À la fin de chaque réunion du groupe de travail, le président fait généralement le point et indique les dispositions suivantes à prendre pour la préparation des réunions futures. Les Membres peuvent exiger que des changements législatifs ou autres soient effectués avant toute étape suivante du processus d'accession. C'est dans le cadre de ces négociations qu'un pays en développement doit négocier son droit à toute période transitoire. En effet, la pratique à ce jour veut que les pays en développement qui accèdent à l'OMC suivant la procédure de l'article XII, n'obtiennent pas automatiquement le droit aux périodes transitoires prévues aux différents accords multilatéraux. Le résultat de ces négociations multilatérales visant à consigner les engagements de l'État en processus d'accession constituera le Protocole d'accession.

Lorsque l'examen du régime de commerce extérieur est suffisamment avancé, les membres du groupe de travail peuvent engager des négociations bilatérales sur l'accès au marché concernant les marchandises et les services et sur les autres modalités à convenir. En pratique, les travaux d'investigation sur le régime de commerce extérieur et la phase de négociation peuvent se chevaucher et progresser en parallèle.

C NÉGOCIATION DES LISTES

Tout Membre de l'OMC doit prendre des engagements d'accès à son marché intérieur. Ces engagements couvrent trois champs: les mesures tarifaires, les engagements concernant l'accès au commerce des services et les engagements de réduction de subventions et autres formes de soutien dans le domaine agricole. Toutes ces négociations sont confidentielles et ont nécessairement des composantes bilatérales. Les négociations bilatérales peuvent être précédées d'un premier exercice de transmission d'information de la part du pays postulant, suivi de négociations bilatérales sur des aspects et secteurs précis, eu égard aux intérêts spécifiques de chacun des Membres. Les résultats de toutes ces négociations bilatérales sont par après "multilatéralisés."[12]

Aux termes du GATT de 1994, chaque pays Membre de l'OMC doit déposer des listes de concessions tarifaires qui sont négociées suivant les procédures et pratiques déterminées aux termes de l'article II et XXVIII(b) du GATT de 1994. De façon générale, ces négociations tarifaires visent la réduction et la consolidation des droits de douane qui sont perçues sur les marchandises par le pays faisant la demande d'accession. Il existe deux façon d'entamer le processus de négociation: les Membres intéressés présentent des demandes et le postulant fait ensuite des offres initiales ou, pour accélérer les choses, le postulant présente son projet de Liste de concessions et d'engagements qui servira de base pour les négociations.

L'État qui fait sa demande d'accession devra également prendre des engagements aux termes de l'Accord général sur le commerce des services (AGCS). Une description générale de la structure globale du marché et de la structure réglementaire des secteurs de services les plus importants dans le pays considéré doit donc être fournie dans le mémorandum sur le régime de commerce extérieur. Il est à noter que l'AGCS comprend deux sortes de dispositions. Les premières sont des obligations générales, dont certaines s'appliquent à tous les secteurs de services (nation la plus favorisée et transparence, notamment) et d'autres, uniquement à ceux qui sont inscrits dans les listes d'engagements. Les secondes sont des engagements spécifiques correspondant à des engagements négociés particuliers à chaque Membre. Tout comme les listes de marchandises, la négociation est enclenchée par les Membres intéressés qui présentent des demandes et l'État postulant présente ensuite un projet de Liste d'engagements spécifiques, ou alors ce dernier peut présenter un projet de Liste d'engagements et les Membres intéressés présentent ensuite des demandes.

Des négociations doivent également avoir lieu concernant les engagements aux termes de l'Accord sur l'agriculture. Généralement, le pays postulant doit compléter le formulaire standard permettant d'identifier les mesures de soutien interne, les subventions à l'exportation et autres composantes pertinentes aux termes de l'Accord sur l'agriculture. La description de toutes mesures maintenues par un gouvernement accédant à l'OMC devrait donc être

12 Sous réserve, à titre d'exemple, d'exemption du traitement de la nation la plus favorisée à l'endroit d'un Membre, comme cela est prévu à l'article II de l'AGS.

suffisamment détaillée pour que les Membres puissent se prononcer sur chacune des mesures en question eu égard aux critères pertinents énoncés dans l'Accord sur l'agriculture. Dans un deuxième temps les Membres intéressés entameront des négociations plus spécifiques, les résultats desquelles seront par la suite multilatéralisés.

Lorsque ces négociations bilatérales entre les Membres intéressés et le pays accédant sont terminées, les résultats sont examinés par tous les Membres qui bénéficieront de leur multilatéralisation en vertu du principe de base de la Nation la plus favorisée (sauf exemption négociée aux termes de l'article II de l'AGCS). Ces listes seront ensuite annexées au projet de Protocole d'accession, dont elles font partie intégrante.

D ADOPTION DU RAPPORT DU GROUPE DE TRAVAIL ET DU PROTOCOLE D'ACCESSION

Lorsque les négociations bilatérales et multilatérales sont terminées, le Secrétariat prépare un "rapport du groupe de travail" qui contient un résumé des discussions afférentes à cette accession. Le Protocole d'accession énonce les modalités d'accession convenues par le requérant et les membres du groupe de travail et ses dispositions sont donc fonction des circonstances propres au requérant. Ce rapport, de même que le Protocole d'accession, sont ensuite présentés au Conseil général pour approbation.

L'article XII prévoit que les instruments d'accession doivent être approuvés à la majorité des deux tiers des Membres de l'OMC:

> 2. Les décisions relatives à l'accession seront prises par la Conférence ministérielle. La Conférence ministérielle approuvera l'accord concernant les modalités d'accession à une majorité des deux tiers des Membres de l'OMC.

Toutefois, la pratique veut maintenant que les décisions d'accession soient prises par consensus ou, du moins, qu'un effort pour atteindre un consensus soit fait préalablement à tout vote. Cette nouvelle pratique a été adoptée à la suite de la première demande d'accession sous l'OMC, soit celle présentée par l'Équateur. L'Équateur a été le premier pays qui a fait une demande d'accession aux termes de l'article XII. Les négociations bilatérales et multilatérales ont été complétées en juin 1995. Le rapport du groupe de travail et le Protocole d'accession de ce pays ont été présentés au Conseil général en juillet de la même année. Conformément au texte de l'article XII et à la pratique du GATT, les Membres furent invités à voter au moyen de bulletins de vote dans les trente jours suivant l'envoi du bulletin de vote par la poste. L'accession ne pouvait donc être autorisée que si les deux tiers des Membres votaient en faveur de cette demande d'accession, ce qui impliquait qu'au moins quatre-vingt Membres devaient avoir retourné par la poste un vote favorable. Cette procédure, qui a eu lieu en août, aurait pu facilement occasionner des conséquences fâcheuses. Le nombre critique de quatre-vingt réponses favorables fut tout juste atteint à l'intérieur des délais impartis.

Riche de cette expérience, les Membres décidèrent que dorénavant les décisions en matière d'accession seraient prises par consensus. Le 15 novembre 1995, le Conseil général approuva la déclaration suivante du président du Conseil général:[13]

> Lorsque le Conseil général traitera de questions relatives à des demandes de dérogations ou à des accessions à l'OMC au titre des articles IX ou XII de l'Accord sur l'OMC, respectivement, il s'efforcera de prendre une décision conformément à l'article IX:1. Sauf disposition contraire, dans les cas où il ne sera pas possible d'arriver à une décision par consensus, la décision sur la question à l'examen sera prise aux voix conformément aux dispositions pertinentes des articles IX ou XII.
>
> La procédure ci-dessus n'empêche pas un Membre de demander un vote au moment où la décision est prise. En conséquence, si un Membre a un problème particulier concernant une décision qu'il est envisagé de prendre au sujet d'une demande de dérogation ou d'une accession à l'OMC, il devrait faire en sorte d'être présent à la réunion au cours de laquelle la question sera examinée. L'absence d'un Membre sera supposée impliquer qu'il n'a pas d'observations ou d'objections à formuler au sujet de la décision qu'il est envisagé de prendre sur la question.

Cette procédure d'approbation par consensus fut suivie pour les accessions de la Mongolie, de la Bulgarie et du Panama.

Une fois que la décision d'approuver le Protocole d'accession d'un pays est adoptée par le Conseil général, le pays requérant doit accepter ce Protocole et les engagements qui y sont contenus conformément à sa Constitution et sa procédure nationale. Le Protocole d'accession entre en vigueur trente jours après que le pays postulant l'ait accepté, soit par signature soit par dépôt de l'instrument de ratification si une approbation interne additionnelle est requise.

[13] Voir le Document WT/L/93.

IV L'ACCESSION DES PAYS QUI AVAIENT ENTAMÉ LE PROCESSUS D'ACCESSION DANS LE CADRE DU GATT DE 1947

A L'ACCESSION DES PARTIES CONTRACTANTES QUI N'AVAIENT PAS COMPLÉTÉ LA NÉGOCIATION DE LEUR LISTES

Certains pays qui sont devenus parties contractantes au GATT de 1947 dans le courant de 1994 n'ont pas été en mesure de mener à terme les négociations sur leurs projets de listes finales avant l'entrée en activité de l'OMC. Étant donné que ces parties contractantes avaient l'intention d'accepter l'Accord sur l'OMC conformément à l'article XIV de cet accord, et comme les Membres étaient désireux de faciliter l'accession de ces parties contractantes au titre de l'article XII selon des modalités identiques à celles qui auraient été d'application si elles avaient été en mesure d'achever les négociations sur leurs listes avant l'entrée en vigueur de l'Accord sur l'OMC, les Membres, le 31 janvier 1995, ont pris la décision suivante:

> Les parties contractantes au GATT de 1947 qui seront devenues parties contractantes dans le courant de 1994 et qui auront présenté leurs projets de listes à annexer au GATT de 1994 et à l'AGCS avant la date d'entrée en vigueur de l'Accord sur l'OMC mais qui n'auront pas été en mesure d'achever les négociations sur ces listes avant cette date, pourront soumettre au Conseil général, jusqu'au 31 mars 1995, les Listes négociées à annexer au GATT de 1994 et à l'AGCS. L'approbation de ces listes par le Conseil général sera considérée comme étant l'approbation des modalités d'accession par les Membres de l'OMC au titre de l'article XII, paragraphe 2, de l'Accord sur l'OMC.[14]

Les pays suivants ont à ce jour bénéficié de cette décision: Papouasie-Nouvelle-Guinée, Grenade, Qatar, Émirats Arabes Unis et Saint-Kitt-et-Nevis.

B L'ACCESSION DES PAYS POUR LESQUELS IL EXISTAIT DÉJÀ UN GROUPE DE TRAVAIL ÉTABLI DANS LE CADRE DU GATT DE 1947

À sa première réunion, le 31 janvier 1995,[15] le Conseil général décida que, lorsque des demandes d'accession à l'OMC au titre de l'article XII étaient présentées par des États et des territoires douaniers distincts pour lesquels il existait déjà un groupe de travail dans le cadre du GATT de 1947, les groupes de travail existants poursuivraient leurs travaux en tant que groupes de travail des accessions à l'OMC, avec un mandat type et leurs présidents actuels respectifs.

14 Voir la décision contenue dans le document WT/L/30.

15 WT/GC/M/1.

Ce fut notamment le cas des quatres premiers pays qui ont accédé depuis à l'OMC sous la procédure de l'article XII.

V La "non-application" des accords commerciaux multilatéraux entre certains membres[16]

Il est possible pour un Membre de l'OMC d'opposer la "Non-Application" à un pays accédant aux termes de l'article XII. Ceci signifie qu'un Membre peut demander de ne pas être tenu de respecter les dispositions de l'Accord sur l'OMC à l'égard d'un nouveau Membre. Cette demande peut tout aussi bien être présentée par le nouveau Membre. Cette possibilité existe même si des négociations bilatérales ont déjà eu lieu entre les deux pays.[17]

1. Le présent accord et les Accords commerciaux multilatéraux figurant aux Annexes 1 et 2 ne s'appliqueront pas entre un Membre et tout autre Membre si l'un des deux, au moment où il devient Membre, ne consent pas à cette application.

Ceci diffère du texte de l'article XXXV du GATT qui semblait prévoir qu'une partie contractante ne pourrait plus invoquer la non-application lorsqu'elle a entamé des négociations tarifaires avec le pays postulant:

Non-application de l'Accord entre des parties contractantes

1. Le présent Accord, ou l'article II du présent Accord, ne s'appliquera pas entre une partie contractante et une autre partie contractante
   a) si les deux parties contractantes n'ont pas engagé de négociations tarifaires entre elles,
   b) et si l'une des deux ne consent pas à cette application au moment où l'une d'elles devient partie contractante.
2. À la demande d'une partie contractante, les Parties Contractantes pourront examiner l'application du présent article dans des cas particuliers et faire des recommandations appropriées.

Toutefois, durant les négociations de l'Uruguay Round, le Conseil adopta une décision[18] qui a eu l'effet de modifier l'article XXXV en permettant à un pays qui avait entamé des négociations tarifaires de pouvoir continuer à soulever l'exception de la non-application:

16 Voir Wang Lei, "Non-Application Issues in the GATT and the WTO," J.W.T., vol.28, n° 2, avril 1994.

17 L'exception de non-application prend effet par simple notification au Conseil général avant l'adoption de la décision approuvant le rapport du Groupe spécial et le Protocole d'accession.

18 Voir le Document L/7435, décision adoptée le 23 mars 1994.

Interprétation de l'article XXXV

Les parties contractantes:

Eu égard aux dispositions liées du paragraphe 1 de l'article XXXV de l'Accord général sur les tarifs douaniers et le commerce;

Notant que, en invoquant l'article XXXV, une partie contractante d'une part, ou un gouvernement accédant à l'Accord général d'autre part, refuse d'appliquer l'Accord général, ou l'article II dudit Accord, à l'autre partie;

Désireuses de faire en sorte que les négociations tarifaires entre les parties contractantes et un gouvernement accédant à l'Accord général ne soient pas entravées par le refus d'accepter une obligation d'appliquer l'Accord général par suite de la participation à de telles négociations;

Décident ce qui suit:

Une partie contractante et un gouvernement accédant à l'Accord général sur les tarifs douaniers et le commerce pourront engager des négociations concernant l'établissement d'une liste de concessions dans le cadre du GATT par le gouvernement accédant sans préjudice du droit de chacun d'invoquer l'article XXXV à l'égard de l'autre.

Cette modification fut incorporée dans le nouvel article XIII de l'Accord de l'OMC.

L'entrée en vigueur de l'Accord sur l'OMC ne peut cependant être l'occasion d'invoquer cette clause de non-application entre pays qui étaient parties contractantes et qui deviennent Membres originels. Entre anciennes parties contractantes, l'exception de non-application n'est possible que si elle était déjà en vigueur dans le cadre du GATT 1947:

2. Le paragraphe 1 ne pourra être invoqué entre des Membres originels de l'OMC qui étaient parties contractantes au GATT de 1947 que dans les cas où l'article XXXV dudit accord avait été invoqué précédemment et était en vigueur entre ces parties contractantes au moment de l'entrée en vigueur pour elles du présent accord.

Le seul Membre de l'OMC qui maintien maintenant une exception de non-application, aux termes de l'article XIII de l'Accord sur l'OMC, est les États-Unis à l'égard de la Mongolie. Les pays suivants se prévalaient, le 8 décembre 1995, de l'article XXXV du GATT de 1947 (voir Tableau 1).

VI Le cas de la Mongolie

Quatres pays ont accédé à l'OMC[19] conformément à la procédure prévue à l'article XII, soit l'Équateur, la Mongolie, la Bulgarie, et le

[19] Pour une discussion critique du contenu des accords d'accession qui ont été conclus dans le cadre de l'OMC jusqu'à maintenant, voir Peter Milthorp, "Integration of FSU/economies in transition into the WTO," *Economics of Transition*, vol. 5(1), 1997 aux pp. 215-23.

TABLEAU 1

Pays se prévalant de l'article XXXV

A l'égard de	*Référence*	*Date*
Botswana	Japon (Succession)	août 1987
États-Unis	Hongrie (L3911)	septembre 1973
	Roumanie (L/3619)	novembre 1971
Guinée	Japon (Succession)	décembre 1994
Lesotho	Japon (Succession)	janvier 1988
Maroc	Israël (L/6192)	juin 1987
Tunisie	Israël (L/6713)	juillet 1990

Panama. Le 19 février 1998, le Conseil général devrait approuver le Protocole d'accession du Laos. À titre d'exemple, il peut être intéressant de se pencher un peu sur le processus d'accession de la Mongolie.

La Mongolie a fait sa demande d'accession le 17 juin 1991.[20] À sa réunion du 8 octobre 1991, le Conseil des Représentants du GATT a formé un groupe de travail chargé d'examiner la demande d'accession du gouvernement mongol au GATT au titre de l'article XXXIII et de présenter au Conseil des recommandations comportant éventuellement un projet de Protocole d'accession.[21] L'Ambassadeur d'Autriche, S.E. M. W. Lang, a été nommé président du Groupe de travail. En 1995, le gouvernement mongol a fait savoir qu'il avait décidé de négocier les modalités d'accession de la Mongolie à l'OMC au titre de l'article XII de l'Accord de l'OMC. Conformément à la décision adoptée par le Conseil général le 31 janvier 1995, le Groupe de travail de l'accession de la Mongolie au GATT de 1947 a été transformé en Groupe de travail de l'accession de la Mongolie à l'OMC.

Le Groupe de travail s'est réuni les 3 et 4 juin 1993, les 1er et 2 février, les 24 et 25 mai et les 3 et 4 novembre 1994 et le 26 juin 1996. Le Groupe de travail était saisi, comme base de discussion, d'un Mémorandum sur le régime de commerce extérieur de la Mongolie[22] ainsi que des questions posées par les Membres au sujet de ce régime et des réponses des autorités mongoles.[23]

20 Voir le document L/6886.

21 Voir les minutes de la réunion du Conseil du 8 octobre 1991, C/M/2152.

22 Voir les documents L/6943, L/6943/Add.1 et L/6943/Add.2.

23 Voir les documents L/7043/Rev.1 et Spec(93)28.

Après avoir examiné le régime de commerce extérieur mongol et compte tenu des explications données, des engagements pris et des concessions accordées par les représentants de la Mongolie, le Groupe de travail a conclu que la Mongolie devrait être invitée à accéder à l'Accord instituant l'OMC conformément aux dispositions de l'article XII. Il a établi à cette fin un projet de Protocole d'accession contenant notamment les Liste d'engagements spécifiques concernant les services[24] et des Listes de concessions et d'engagements concernant l'agriculture et les marchandises[25] annexées au Protocole d'accession. Les principaux engagements et points de discussion qui eurent lieu durant les négociations du groupe de travail de la Mongolie concernent:[26]

(1) Les réformes économiques, notamment la suppression des mesures de contrôle des prix et l'établissement d'un système de taux de change flottant ainsi que l'abolition et l'interdiction de monopoles.

(2) Une consolidation globale de son tarif à un taux général qui ne dépasse pas 30 %.

(3) Des engagements de rendre son régime fiscal en conformité avec les dispositions sur le traitement national prévues à l'article III.

(4) L'engagement qu'à compter de la date de l'accession, le pouvoir qu'avait le gouvernement de suspendre les importations et les exportations ou d'appliquer des prescriptions en matière de licences pouvant conduire à la suspension des échanges de produits soumis à licence soit utilisé en conformité avec les dispositions de l'Accord sur l'OMC, notamment les articles VI, XI, XVIII, XIX, XX et XXI du GATT de 1994 et les Accords multilatéraux sur l'agriculture, les mesures sanitaires et phytosanitaires, les procédures de licences d'importation et les obstacles techniques au commerce et que son gouvernement ne maintiendrait pas, après l'accession, de mesures non tarifaires à l'importation, notamment des interdictions, contingents, autorisations et licences, qui ne pourraient être justifiés au regard des dispositions de l'OMC. Il a été convenu que le Comité des licences d'importation examinerait la conformité

24 Voir WT/ACC/MNG/9/Add.2.

25 Voir le document WT/ACC/MNG/9/Add.1.

26 Voir le Rapport du Groupe de travail WT/ACC/MNG/9.

du régime de licences, au plus tard deux ans après l'accession de la Mongolie à l'OMC.

(5) L'engagement de supprimer au plus tard au 31 décembre 2002, de préférence de façon progressive, les mesures qui correspondaient à la définition d'une subvention prohibée donnée à l'article 3 de l'Accord sur les subventions et les mesures compensatoires, à savoir les subventions prévues par la nouvelle Loi sur l'investissement étranger, qui était entrée en vigueur le 1er juillet 1993.

(6) L'engagement de notifier l'existence de toutes les entreprises d'État et de mettre en oeuvre la Loi sur la privatisation qui prévoyait la privatisation progressive des avoirs de l'État et mettait en place un programme détaillé dans le secteur industriel, agricole et bancaire.

(7) L'engagement de n'appliquer aucune mesure incompatible avec l'Accord sur les Mesures d'investissement et de commerce dont les dispositions seraient respectées dès son accession, sans demander une période de transition.

(8) L'engagement que les lois mongoles en matière d'évaluation en douane soient maintenues totalement conformes à l'Accord de l'OMC sur la mise en oeuvre de l'article VII du GATT de 1994 sans aucune période de transition pour l'application de l'Accord. Si les services d'une entité d'inspection avant expédition étaient utilisés pour aider la Mongolie à mettre en oeuvre ses procédures douanières, le gouvernement mongol ferait en sorte que les activités de cette entité soient conformes aux Accords de l'OMC pertinents. Quant aux pratiques et aux formalités douanières, la Mongolie s'est engagée à se conformer, dès son accession, aux dispositions des articles VII, VIII et X du GATT de 1994 et à celles de l'Accord de l'OMC sur la mise en oeuvre de l'article VII du GATT.

(9) L'engagement d'appliquer à compter de la date de son accession à l'OMC, les dispositions des Accords commerciaux multilatéraux figurant à l'Annexe 1A de l'Accord sur l'OMC, notamment ceux sur les procédures de licences d'importation, les normes, les mesures antidumping et les subventions, et de recourir le moins possible aux dérogations à ces Accords prévues au bénéfice des pays en développement.

(10) L'engagement à compter de la date de son accession à l'OMC, si des zones franches étaient établies et si la production de ces zones était vendue dans le reste de la Mongolie, d'appliquer l'ensemble des taxes, droits de douane, redevances douanières et autres mesures normales de régulation des importations aux produits ou à leurs composants importés, et de respecter les dispositions de l'Accord de l'OMC sur les subventions et les mesures compensatoires lorsque la Mongolie accorderait des incitations pour l'établissement d'entreprises dans les zones franches.

(11) L'engagement que les lois mongoles dans le domaine des droits de propriété intellectuelle soient déjà conformes aux dispositions de l'Accord sur les aspects des droits de propriété intellectuelle qui touchent au commerce (ADPIC) et d'appliquer sans réserve les dispositions de l'Accord sur les ADPIC dès son accession à l'OMC, sans période transitoire.

(12) En matière de services, l'engagement de respecter l'AGS et plus particulièrement la Liste des engagements spécifiques annexée au Protocole d'accession.

(13) L'engagement de demander le statut d'observateur au Comité établi en vertu de l'Accord sur les marchés publics au moment de son accession en vue d'entamer les négociations pour en devenir membre.

(14) L'engagement d'effectuer toutes les notifications exigées par les dispositions pertinentes de l'Accord sur l'OMC.

Le rapport du groupe de travail de la Mongolie et son Protocole d'accession auquel furent annexées les listes d'engagements ont été présentés le 18 juillet 1996 au Conseil général de l'OMC qui adopta la décision suivante:

Le Conseil général,

Eu égard aux résultats des négociations menées en vue de l'accession de la Mongolie à l'Accord de Marrakech instituant l'Organisation mondiale du commerce, et ayant établi un Protocole d'accession de la Mongolie,[27]

Décide, conformément à l'article XII de l'Accord de Marrakech instituant l'Organisation mondiale du commerce, que la Mongolie pourra accéder à l'Accord instituant l'Organisation mondiale du commerce selon les modalités énoncées dans ledit Protocole.

27 Voir le texte du Protocole d'accession en appendice 3 (WT/ACC/MNG/11).

VII Conclusion

L'accession à l'OMC est un processus qui peut facilement durer trois à quatre ans et qui nécessite de la part des négociateurs du pays requérant une bonne compréhension des règles de l'OMC ainsi qu'une connaissance approfondie du système juridique et des politiques commerciales de leur pays. La longue liste des demandes d'accession est en soi la preuve qu'il est dans l'intérêt de tous les pays de se joindre à l'OMC. Que les raisons soient politiques ou économiques, l'accession au "Club de l'OMC" semble impérative.

Gabrielle Marceau
Division des affaires juridiques, Organisation Mondiale du Commerce

Summary

The Procedures for Accession to the World Trade Organization (WTO)

The great international interest for the WTO is evidenced by the importance of its membership and the long list of countries that have applied for accession. This note examines the new accession procedures under the WTO Agreement and discusses the rights and obligations of countries requesting such accession.

Sommaire

Les procédures d'acession à l'Organisation mondiale du commerce (OMC)

L'intérêt marqué que portent les états à l'Accord sur l'OMC est révélé par le nombre grandissant des pays qui en sont membres et par la longue liste des trente pays qui ont fait une demande d accession à l'OMC. Cet article examine les nouvelles procédures d'accession à l'OMC et survole les droits et obligations des pays qui font une telle demande d'accession.

Appendice 1

LISTE DES MEMBRES DE L'OMC ET LA DATE D'ENTRÉE EN VIGUEUR DE L'OMC

Gouvernement	*Entrée en vigueur/ Statut de Membre*
Afrique du Sud	1er janvier 1995
Allemagne	1er janvier 1995
Angola	1er décembre 1996
Antigua-et-Barbuda	1er janvier 1995
Argentine	1er janvier 1995
Australie	1er janvier 1995
Autriche	1er janvier 1995
Bahreïn	1er janvier 1995
Bangladesh	1er janvier 1995
Barbade	1er janvier 1995
Belgique	1er janvier 1995
Bélize	1er janvier 1995
Bénin	22 février 1996
Bolivie	14 septembre 1995
Botswana	31 mai 1995
Brésil	1er janvier 1995
Brunéi Darussalam	1er janvier 1995
Bulgarie	1er décembre 1996
Burkina Faso	3 juin 1995
Burundi	23 juillet 1995
Cameroun	13 décembre 1995
Canada	1er janvier 1995
Chili	1er janvier 1995
Chypre	30 juillet 1995
Colombie	30 avril 1995
Communauté européenne	1er janvier 1995
Congo	27 mars 1997
Corée	1er janvier 1995
Costa Rica	1er janvier 1995
Côte d'Ivoire	1er janvier 1995
Cuba	20 avril 1995
Danemark	1er janvier 1995
Djibouti	31 mai 1995
Dominique	1er janvier 1995

(Suite à la page suivante)

Liste des Membres de l'OMC et la date d'entrée en vigueur de l'OMC (*suite*)

Gouvernement	*Entrée en vigueur/ Statut de Membre*
Égypte	30 juin 1995
El Salvador	7 mai 1995
Émirats arabes unis	10 avril 1996
Équateur	21 janvier 1996
Espagne	1er janvier 1995
États-Unis	1er janvier 1995
Fidji	14 janvier 1996
Finlande	1er janvier 1995
France	1er janvier 1995
Gabon	1er janvier 1995
Gambie	23 octobre 1996
Ghana	1er janvier 1995
Grèce	1er janvier 1995
Grenade	22 février 1996
Guatemala	21 juillet 1995
Guinée	25 octobre 1995
Guinée-Bissau	31 mai 1995
Guyana	1er janvier 1995
Haïti	30 janvier 1996
Honduras	1er janvier 1995
Hong Kong	1er janvier 1995
Hongrie	1er janvier 1995
Îles Salomon	26 juillet 1996
Inde	1er janvier 1995
Indonésie	1er janvier 1995
Irlande	1er janvier 1995
Islande	1er janvier 1995
Israël	21 avril 1995
Italie	1er janvier 1995
Jamaïque	9 mars 1995
Japon	1er janvier 1995
Kenya	1er janvier 1995
Koweït	1er janvier 1995
Lesotho	31 mai 1995
Liechtenstein	1er septembre 1995
Luxembourg	1er janvier 1995
Macao	1er janvier 1995

(Suite à la page suivante)

LISTE DES MEMBRES DE L'OMC ET LA DATE D'ENTRÉE EN VIGUEUR DE L'OMC *(suite)*

Gouvernement	*Entrée en vigueur/ Statut de Membre*
Madagascar	17 novembre 1995
Malaisie	1er janvier 1995
Malawi	31 mai 1995
Maldives	31 mai 1995
Mali	31 mai 1995
Malte	1er janvier 1995
Maroc	1er janvier 1995
Maurice	1er janvier 1995
Mauritanie	31 mai 1995
Mexique	1er janvier 1995
Mongolie	29 janvier 1997
Mozambique	26 août 1995
Myanmar	1er janvier 1995
Namibie	1er janvier 1995
Nicaragua	3 septembre 1995
Niger	13 décembre 1996
Nigéria	1er janvier 1995
Norvège	1er janvier 1995
Nouvelle-Zélande	1er janvier 1995
Ouganda	1er janvier 1995
Pakistan	1er janvier 1995
Panama	6 septembre 1997
Papouasie-Nouvelle-Guinée	9 juin 1996
Paraguay	1er janvier 1995
Pays-Bas — Pour le Royaume en Europe et pour les Antilles néerlandaises	1er janvier 1995
Pérou	1er janvier 1995
Philippines	1er janvier 1995
Pologne	1er juillet 1995
Portugal	1er janvier 1995
Qatar	13 janvier 1996
République centrafricaine	31 mai 1995
République démocratique du Congo	1er janvier 1997
République dominicaine	9 mars 1995
République slovaque	1er janvier 1995
République tchèque	1er janvier 1995
Roumanie	1er janvier 1995

(Suite à la page suivante)

Liste des Membres de l'OMC et la date d'entrée en vigueur de l'OMC *(suite)*

Gouvernement	*Entrée en vigueur/ Statut de Membre*
Royaume-Uni	1er janvier 1995
Rwanda	22 mai 1996
Saint-Kitts-et-Nevis	21 février 1996
Sainte-Lucie	1er janvier 1995
Saint-Vincent-et-les-Grenadines	1er janvier 1995
Sénégal	1er janvier 1995
Sierra Leone	23 juillet 1995
Singapour	1er janvier 1995
Slovénie	30 juillet 1995
Sri Lanka	1er janvier 1995
Suède	1er janvier 1995
Suisse	1er juillet 1995
Suriname	1er janvier 1995
Swaziland	1er janvier 1995
Tanzanie	1er janvier 1995
Tchad	19 octobre 1996
Thaïlande	1er janvier 1995
Togo	31 mai 1995
Trinité-et-Tobago	1er mars 1995
Tunisie	29 mars 1995
Turquie	26 mars 1995
Uruguay	1er janvier 1995
Vénézuela	1er janvier 1995
Zambie	1er janvier 1995
Zimbabwe	3 mars 1995

Appendice 2

Modèle pour les aide-mémoire sur le régime de commerce extérieur

I. INTRODUCTION

Exposé des objectifs généraux du régime de politique commerciale du requérant et de leur relation avec les objectifs de l'OMC.

II. ÉCONOMIE, POLITIQUES ÉCONOMIQUES ET COMMERCE EXTERIEUR

(1) economie

(2) politiques économiques

(3) commerce extérieur des marchandises et des services: volume et valeur des échanges, exportations et importations, balance du commerce extérieur, structure des échanges, commerce par régions géographiques et dynamique du commerce, données statistiques en la matière et renseignements sur les publications (voir l'annexe 1)

(4) commerce intérieur des services, y compris valeur et composition des investissements directs étrangers

(5) renseignements sur les mouvements financiers en relation avec les nationaux travaillant à l'étranger, envois de fonds, etc.

(6) renseignements sur la croissance du commerce des marchandises et des services au cours des dernières années et prévisions pour les années à venir

III. CADRE POUR L'ÉLABORATION ET L'APPLICATION DES POLITIQUES AFFECTANT LE COMMERCE EXTERIEUR DES MARCHANDISES ET LE COMMERCE DES SERVICES

(1) attributions des pouvoirs exécutif, législatif et judiciaire

(2) entités gouvernementales responsables de l'élaboration et de la mise en oeuvre des politiques affectant le commerce extérieur

(3) partage des responsabilités entre le gouvernement central et les gouvernements sous-centraux

(4) eventuels programmes législatifs ou plans de modification du régime réglementaire

(5) lois et instruments juridiques (voir l'annexe 2)

(6) description des tribunaux ou procédures judiciaires, arbitraux ou administratifs, le cas échéant

IV. POLITIQUES AFFECTANT LE COMMERCE DES MARCHANDISES

(1) réglementation des importations

(2) réglementation des exportations

(3) politiques intérieures affectant le commerce extérieur des marchandises

(4) politiques affectant le commerce extérieur des produits agricoles

(5) politiques affectant le commerce extérieur dans d'autres secteurs

V. RÉGIME COMMERCIAL DE LA PROPRIÉTÉ INTELLECTUELLE

(1) généralités

(2) normes fondamentales de protection, y compris les procédures pour l'acquisition, le maintien et l'exercice des droits de propriété intellectuelle

(3) mesures visant à empêcher l'usage abusif de droits de propriété intellectuelle

(4) moyens de faire respecter les droits

(5) lois, décrets, réglementations et autres instruments juridiques concernant les points ci-dessus

(6) statistiques concernant les demandes de droits de propriété intellectuelle et l'octroi de ces droits, ainsi que toutes statistiques concernant les moyens de faire respecter ces droits

VI. RÉGIME COMMERCIAL DES SERVICES

(1) généralités
Description générale de la structure globale du marché et de la structure réglementaire pour les secteurs de services les plus importants (par exemple, services financiers, télécommunications, services professionnels, construction, tourisme, transports)

(2) politiques affectant le commerce des services
Indication générale des principales lois, réglementations, règles,

procédures, décisions et mesures administratives et des principaux autres instruments juridiques et description des mesures spécifiques affectant le commerce des services. On pourra faire, le cas échéant, des distinctions selon les modes de fourniture et/ou les secteurs:

Accès au marché et traitement national
Limitations ou conditions appliquées à l'accès au marché et au traitement national. Indiquer si elles sont appliquées sur une base horizontale (par exemple, mesures concernant le régime des investissements étrangers, le mouvement des personnes fournissant un service, la propriété immobilière et les conditions d'établissement) ou sur une base sectorielle
Traitement de la nation la plus favorisée
Indiquer toute mesure existante incompatible avec le traitement NPF

VII. BASE INSTITUTIONNELLE DES RELATIONS COMMERCIALES ET ÉCONOMIQUES AVEC LES PAYS TIERS

(1) accords bilatéraux ou plurilatéraux concernant le commerce extérieur des marchandises et le commerce des services
(2) accords d'intégration économique, d'union douanière et de libre-échange
(3) Accords d'intégration des marchés du travail
(4) Coopération économique multilatérale, participation aux organisations économiques multilatérales, programmes d'autres organisations multilatérales qui touchent au commerce

Doivent également être complétées deux formulaires concernant le régime agricole des pays requérants (WT/ACC/4) et les aspects relatifs à l'AGCS (WT/ACC/5).

Appendice 3

Protocole d'accession de la Mongolie à l'Accord de Marrakech instituant l'Organisation mondiale du commerce

L'Organisation mondiale du commerce (ci-après dénommée "l'OMC"), eu égard à l'approbation du Conseil général de l'OMC donnée en vertu de l'article XII de l'Accord de Marrakech instituant l'Organisation mondiale du commerce (ci-après dénommé "l'Accord sur l'OMC") et le gouvernement de la Mongolie (ci-après dénommé "la Mongolie"), *Prenant note* du rapport du Groupe de travail de l'accession de la Mongolie à l'OMC qui figure dans le document WT/ACC/MNG/9 et Add.1-2 (ci-après dénommé "le rapport du Groupe de travail"), *Eu égard* aux résultats des négociations sur l'accession de la Mongolie à l'OMC, *Conviennent* de ce qui suit:

Partie I: Dispositions générales

(1) À compter de la date à laquelle le présent protocole entrera en vigueur, la Mongolie accédera à l'Accord sur l'OMC conformément à l'article XII dudit accord et deviendra ainsi Membre de l'OMC.

(2) L'Accord sur l'OMC auquel la Mongolie accédera sera l'Accord sur l'OMC tel qu'il aura été rectifié, amendé ou autrement modifié par des instruments juridiques qui seront entrés en vigueur avant la date d'entrée en vigueur du présent protocole. Le présent protocole, qui comprendra les engagements mentionnés au paragraphe 61 du rapport du Groupe de travail, fera partie intégrante de l'Accord sur l'OMC.

(3) La Mongolie présentera chaque année au Secrétariat une notification sur la mise en oeuvre des engagements échelonnés assortis de dates définitives qui sont mentionnés aux paragraphes 10, 13, 20, 21, 23, 24, 29, 35, 42, 44, 45, 46, 48, 51, 54, 59 et 60 du rapport du Groupe de travail, en indiquant tout retard éventuel dans la mise en oeuvre et les raisons ayant motivé ce retard.

(4) Sauf dispositions contraires du paragraphe précédent ou des paragraphes mentionnés au paragraphe 61 du rapport du Groupe de travail:

(a) Les obligations découlant des Accords commerciaux multilatéraux annexés à l'Accord sur l'OMC qui doivent être mises en oeuvre au cours d'une période commençant au moment de l'entrée en vigueur dudit accord seront mises en oeuvre par la Mongolie comme si elle avait accepté cet accord à la date de son entrée en vigueur.

(b) Les notifications qui doivent être présentées au titre des Accords commerciaux multilatéraux annexés à l'Accord sur l'OMC dans un certain délai à compter de la date d'entrée en vigueur dudit accord seront présentées par la Mongolie dans le délai commençant à courir à compter de la date d'entrée en vigueur du présent protocole.

Partie II: Listes

(5) Les Listes annexées au présent protocole deviendront la Liste de concessions et d'engagements annexée à l'Accord général sur les tarifs douaniers et le commerce de 1994 (ci-après dénommé le "GATT de 1994") et la Liste d'engagements spécifiques annexée à l'Accord général sur le commerce des services (ci-après dénommé "l'AGCS") de la Mongolie. Les concessions et les engagements inscrits sur les Listes seront mis en oeuvre par étapes ainsi qu'il est spécifié dans les parties pertinentes des Listes.

(6) Dans le cas de la référence à la date du GATT de 1994 que contient le paragraphe 6a) de l'article II dudit accord, la date applicable en ce qui concerne les Listes de concessions et d'engagements annexées au présent protocole sera la date d'entrée en vigueur du présent protocole.

Partie III: Dispositions finales

(7) Le présent protocole sera ouvert à l'acceptation de la Mongolie, par voie de signature ou autrement, jusqu'au 31 décembre 1996.

(8) Le présent protocole entrera en vigueur le trentième jour qui suivra celui où il aura été accepté par la Mongolie.

(9) Le présent protocole sera déposé auprès du Directeur général de l'OMC. Le Directeur général de l'OMC remettra dans les moindres délais à chaque Membre de l'OMC et à la Mongolie une copie certifiée conforme du présent protocole et une notification d'acceptation dudit protocole par la Mongolie conformément au paragraphe 7.

(10) Le présent protocole sera enregistré conformément aux dispositions de l'article 102 de la Charte des Nations Unies.

Fait à Genève, le dix-huit juillet mil neuf cent quatre-vingt-seize, en un seul exemplaire, en langues française, anglaise et espagnole, les trois textes faisant foi.

Investor-State Dispute Settlement under NAFTA Chapter 11: The Shape of Things to Come?

INTRODUCTION

FOR MOST PURPOSES, individuals and private business organizations have no standing under international law. A complaint that a state has breached its international obligations can be made only by another state.[1] Historically, this was as true in the area of foreign investments as in any other. If a private investor experienced an injury as a result of an action by a state in breach of its international obligations, the investor's only means of redress was to seek to have its national government take action on its behalf.[2]

From the investor's point of view, this state of affairs has several drawbacks. It is often difficult to get one's national government to take action against another state. In addition to the limited resources that increasingly strained governments are working with, government policy regarding another state will be driven by a complex array of factors that may result in reluctance to take action

1 Bernd-Roland Killmann, "The Access of Individuals to International Trade Dispute Settlement" (1996) 13:3 J. Int'l Arbitration 143 at 144-7; Elihu Lauterpacht, "International Law and Private Foreign Investment" (1997) 4 Ind. J. Global Legal Studies 259.

2 Special tribunals have been established from time to time to adjudicate disputes between individuals or business enterprises and states arising out of particular situations. E.g., the Iran-United States Claims Tribunal was established by agreement between the United States and Iran to deal with complaints by American investors in connection with the revolution in Iran as a result of which the Shah's regime was overthrown. See C. N. Brower, "The Iran-United States Claims Tribunal" (1990) 224 Recueil des Cours 123. See generally, J. I. Charney, "Third Party Dispute Settlement and International Law" (1997) 36 Col. J. Transnational L. 65.

on a given complaint at any particular time. Even where a private party has sufficient influence and the requisite good timing to get his or her state to take action, there may be no forum competent to adjudicate the complaint. Resolution of the complaint will depend upon the uncertain and, typically, opaque process of diplomatic negotiation.[3]

The inadequacy of investor-state dispute settlement reflects the lack of an international consensus on the extent to which state sovereignty is, or should be, subject to substantive or procedural limitations when it comes to dealing with foreign investors. The divergence of view is most striking with respect to a state's power to expropriate the assets of foreign investors. In this regard, there is no international agreement on what procedures must be followed by a state before it can expropriate or on what compensation should be paid.[4]

Some countries have agreed to bilateral or multilateral commitments regarding substantive obligations protecting investors backed up by binding dispute settlement. Of greatest significance to Canada is Chapter 11 of the North American Free Trade Agreement (NAFTA),[5] which provides that, where one of the NAFTA states (Canada, the United States, or Mexico), acts contrary to its obligations under NAFTA in relation to a foreign investor, under the agreement, the investor may seek relief against the state in binding arbitration for any injury suffered. Since 1996 and 1997, four cases have been initiated under this process. The purpose of this comment is to describe the process under NAFTA Chapter 11 and to suggest some of the issues that may arise as it is increasingly resorted to by investors.

[3] Some states, including the United States and the European Union, have created procedures by which individuals and enterprises may make complaints about the behaviour of other states and under which states are obliged to consider bringing the complaints forward. Canada has no such procedure. See J. C. Thomas, "Advancement of Private Sector Commercial Interests through International Trade Dispute Settlement Procedures" (1996) 14th Int'l Trade Law Seminar (Department of Justice).

[4] The lack of international consensus was evidenced most recently by the suspension of negotiations on the Multilateral Agreement on Investment (MAI) sponsored by the Organization for Economic Co-operation and Development in April 1998. See *Multilateral Agreement on Investment, Consolidated Text and Commentary* (Paris: OECD, 1997): M. Drohan, "Nations Set to Bury MAI," *Globe and Mail* (Apr. 27, 1998) B-1.

[5] Done Dec. 17, 1992, reprinted in (1993) 32 I.L.M. 605 [hereinafter NAFTA].

Background: Overview of Multilateral and Bilateral Efforts to Improve Investor-State Dispute Settlement

In 1965, under the auspices of the World Bank, the International Center for the Settlement of Investment Disputes (ICSID) was established in Washington and the Convention on the Settlement of Investment Disputes between States and Nationals of Other States (ICSID Convention) was initiated in an attempt to provide a process for the resolution of investor-state disputes.[6] ICSID provides facilities and a set of arbitral rules for the resolution of disputes between investors from state parties to the ICSID Convention and other state parties to the Convention.[7] The center has jurisdiction, however, over a dispute only where both parties consent,[8] and relatively few disputes have been resolved using the ICSID process.[9]

In 1978, the Administrative Council of ICSID created an "Additional Facility," which permitted ICSID to provide facilities for disputes that were outside its jurisdiction because either the investor's state or the state complained against was not a party to the ICSID Convention.[10] Parties consenting to Additional Facility Arbitration participate in an arbitral process similar to the ICSID arbitration process. This process, too, has been little used.[11]

As foreign direct investment, especially in developing countries, increased, investors sought a more effective mechanism to resolve investor-state disputes as well as substantive standards to govern the

6 Convention on the Settlement of Investment Disputes between States and Nationals of Other States, done at Washington, Mar. 18, 1965, 575 UNTS 159, reprinted in 4 I.L.M. 532 (1965) [hereinafter ICSID Convention]. Canada is not a party to the ICSID Convention.

7 The mandate of ICSID is set out in Art. 1(2) of the ICSID Convention: "The purpose of the Centre shall be to provide facilities for conciliation and arbitration of investment disputes between Contracting States and nationals of other Contracting States in accordance with the provisions of this Convention."

8 ICSID Convention, *supra* note 6, Art. 25.

9 Since coming into force in 1966, ICSID has been used for only 42 arbitrations, and most of the completed cases were settled before an award was rendered. It must be acknowledged that disputes may have been resolved, in part, because of the possibility of resort to the ICSID process.

10 International Center for the Settlement of Investment Disputes, Additional Facility for the Administration of Conciliation, Arbitration and Fact-Finding Proceedings, created by the Administrative Council of ICSID, Sept. 27, 1978, reprinted in Document ICSID/11 (June 1979) [hereinafter Additional Facility Rules].

11 No final award has ever been made under the Additional Facility Rules, *ibid.*

investor-state disputes as well as substantive standards to govern the actions of states in relation to foreign investors. At the same time, many developing countries were turning away from reliance on the state as the sole engine of development, becoming more interested in attracting private foreign investment. As a consequence, these states became more willing to consider committing to a set of international rules safeguarding foreign investors, including investor-state dispute settlement. This community of interest has been the basis for the proliferation of bilateral investment protection treaties incorporating both standards of behaviour for host states and investor-state dispute settlement. Canada, for example, began negotiating bilateral investment protection agreements providing for investor-state dispute settlement in 1989 and has now signed such agreements with nineteen countries. The United States and other countries have been engaged in similar efforts. In total, there are now more than 1,300 bilateral investment agreements worldwide.[12]

The most significant development with respect to investor-state dispute settlement from a Canadian point of view, however, was the implementation of NAFTA in 1994.[13] NAFTA marked the first time that two developed countries had agreed to a comprehensive code governing state behaviour in relation to foreign investment, with detailed investor-state dispute resolution procedures. Furthermore, for the first time, Mexico agreed to be bound by these standards.

12 UN Centre for Transnational Corporations, *Bilateral Investment Treaties in the Mid 1990s* (forthcoming). This community of interest also made it easier for investors contracting with a state to include provisions requiring the state to submit to some form of arbitration should a dispute arise. It may yet facilitate the completion of the long-standing effort in the OECD to develop a MAI. As part of the Final Act embodying the Results of the Uruguay Round of Trade Negotiations in 1994 ((1994) 33 ILM 1), the contracting parties agreed to a very modest agreement dealing with some investment issues (the Agreement on Trade Related Investment Measures), and some parties made commitments regarding investment in the General Agreement on Trade in Services. At the Singapore Ministerial Meeting of the World Trade Organization in December 1996, a working group was set up to study trade and investment issues.

13 The U.S. is both the most significant destination for outward Canadian foreign investment and the origin of more foreign investment in Canada than any other source. An investor-state dispute settlement procedure on the NAFTA model was included in the recently concluded Canada-Chile Free Trade Agreement (Ch. G). See generally, J. Yrarrazavale C., "Foreign Investment under NAFTA: Implications for Chile" (1994) 25 Rev. Gen. du Droit 455 at 462.

Essentially, Chapter 11 gives investors a right to initiate binding dispute settlement proceedings against a NAFTA state that is alleged to be in breach of its obligations. Proceedings take place, at the investor's option, under one of the following sets of arbitral rules as modified by the provisions of Chapter 11:

(1) the United Nations Commission on International Trade Law Arbitration Rules (the UNCITRAL Rules);[14]

(2) the rules under the ICSID Convention (the ICSID Rules);[15] or

(3) the rules under the ICSID Additional Facility (the Additional Facility Rules).[16]

The investor-state provisions of Chapter 11 expand on the provisions of the standard United States bilateral investment treaty as well as the similar provisions in Canadian foreign investment protection agreements. They are also similar to the investor-state dispute settlement provisions proposed in the OECD's draft multilateral agreement on investment (MAI).[17]

Concurrent with this proliferation of international instruments providing a process for binding investor-state dispute settlement, the volume of foreign direct investment has continually increased, multiplying the circumstances in which investor state disputes may arise.[18] The inevitable consequence is that investor-state procedures are beginning to be used. As noted, the first four cases under NAFTA Chapter 11 have been commenced within the past two

14 Arbitration Rules of the UN Commission on International Trade Law, approved by the UN General Assembly, Dec. 15, 1976, UN GAOR, 31st Sess., Supp. No. 17 at 46, Ch. V, Sec. C, U. Doc. A/31/17, 1976, reprinted in *UNCITRAL Arbitration Rules* (New York: UN, 1977) [hereinafter UNCITRAL Rules].

15 The ICSID Rules are contained in the ICSID Convention, *supra* note 6, and the following rules created under the Convention and published by ICSID in *ICSID Basic Documents* (Washington: ICSID, 1985): Administrative and Financial Regulations; Rules of Procedure for the Institution of Conciliation and Arbitration Proceedings (Institution Rules); Rules of Procedure for Arbitration Proceedings (Arbitration Rules).

16 Additional Facility Rules, *supra* note 10.

17 *Supra* note 4. One important difference between NAFTA Chapter 11 and the draft MAI is that the latter also contemplates the option of arbitration under the rules of the International Chamber of Commerce (Draft MAI, *supra* note 4, Art. V.D.Z.C. iv.).

18 In OECD, "Financial Market Trends No. 67" (Paris: OECD, 1997), it is reported that foreign direct investment globally exceeded US $250 billion in 1996, following eight years of continuous growth.

years. Two are cases by American investors against Mexico and two are complaints by American investors against Canada.

Investor-State Dispute Settlement under NAFTA Chapter 11

SCOPE OF APPLICATION

Who Can Complain

NAFTA Investors

Investor-state dispute settlement is available to an investor (NAFTA Investor) of one of the state parties to NAFTA (NAFTA Party). A NAFTA Investor means:

(1) a NAFTA Party;

(2) a state enterprise of a NAFTA Party;

(3) a person who is a national of a NAFTA Party; or

(4) an enterprise constituted or organized under the laws of a NAFTA Party and a branch located in the territory of a NAFTA Party and carrying out business activities there.[19]

One of the most significant aspects of Chapter 11 is that each NAFTA Party has bound itself to participate in arbitration initiated by a private party in accordance with the procedures under Chapter 11 and to comply with any eventual arbitral award.[20] A NAFTA Party complained against may, nevertheless, refuse to participate in dispute settlement with a NAFTA Investor in limited circumstances. If the NAFTA Investor is an enterprise constituted or organized under the laws of a NAFTA Party but is owned or controlled by persons (referred to here as the ultimate investors), who are investors of a state or states not party to NAFTA, and the enterprise has no substantial business activities in the territory of the NAFTA Party under whose law it is constituted or organized, the NAFTA Party complained against may refuse to participate.[21]

[19] NAFTA, *supra* note 5, Art. 1139. "[E]nterprise" is defined in Article 201 as "any entity constituted or organized under applicable law, whether or not for profit, and whether privately owned or governmentally owned, including any corporation, trust, partnership, sole proprietorship, joint venture, or other association."

[20] NAFTA Art. 1122.

[21] NAFTA Art. 1113. In order to deny access on the second ground, notification to the NAFTA Party under whose laws the enterprise is constituted or organized

The overall effect of these provisions is to provide the benefits of Chapter 11 to a very wide range of participants in the economies of NAFTA Parties. For example, a subsidiary of an investor that is controlled by nationals of a state not party to NAFTA, but which is organized under the laws of, and has a substantial business presence in, a NAFTA Party is entitled to the full benefit of the investment chapter. Access to dispute settlement and the other benefits of Chapter 11 can be denied in these circumstances only where the NAFTA Party complained against does not maintain diplomatic relations with the state of the ultimate investor or is imposing some kind of international embargo in relation to the ultimate investor's state that would be violated if access to dispute settlement were given.[22] For example, the United States could refuse to participate in an arbitration initiated by a Mexican business if it were controlled by Cuban nationals.

Article 1101.1(c) provides that certain obligations in Chapter 11 apply to all investments within the territory of a NAFTA Party. All investors, not just NAFTA Investors, benefit from the provisions that prohibit NAFTA Parties from imposing certain performance requirements as a condition of permitting a foreign investment or from granting certain incentives to induce investment,[23] including relaxing environmental standards.[24] Nevertheless, only NAFTA Investors, subject to the limits set out above, have standing to initiate investor-state dispute settlement proceedings in relation to any alleged breach of these obligations.

The Requirement for an Investment

In order for a NAFTA Investor to initiate proceedings under Chapter 11, it must be seeking to make, be making, or have made

---

is required in accordance with Art. 1803. The NAFTA Party so notified may request consultations under Art. 2006. A NAFTA Party may deny all the benefits of Ch. 11 on the grounds described, not just access to dispute settlement.

22 Under NAFTA Art. 1113, a NAFTA Party may deny the benefits of Ch. 11 where (1) the NAFTA Party complained against does not maintain diplomatic relations with the ultimate investor's state; (2) the NAFTA Party complained against has put in place measures in relation to the ultimate investor's state that prohibit transactions with the ultimate investors or that would be violated or circumvented if access to dispute settlement were given.

23 NAFTA Art. 1106. See *infra* note 36 and accompanying text.

24 NAFTA Art. 1114.2.

an "investment."[25] Investment is very broadly defined to include ownership interests in enterprises, debt and equity securities issued by an enterprise, certain loans, all forms of real and personal property (including intellectual property), and interests that entitle the owner to share in income or profits or that arise out of commitments of capital or other resources. Claims to money arising solely from commercial contracts for the sale of goods and extensions of credit in connection with commercial transactions are excluded from the definition of investment.[26] Despite these exclusions, the definition clearly goes far beyond investments representing control of an enterprise to include much less significant interests such as portfolio investment and other sorts of relationships.

This comprehensive definition represents one of the significant differences between the Chapter 11 process and the ICSID Rules, the Additional Facility Rules, and the UNCITRAL Rules (these three sets of rules are sometimes referred to collectively as the Arbitral Rules in this article). Disputes subject to arbitration under the ICSID Rules must arise out of an investment, but "investment" is not defined. What constitutes an investment has arisen in several ICSID cases.[27] Christoph Schreuer has described "investments" for the purpose of the ICSID Rules as possessing, typically, the following features: (1) a long-term relationship; (2) expectation of return; (3) assumption of risk by both parties; (4) substantial value; and (5) significance to the state's economic development. He does not suggest, however, that these features must be present before an arbitration under the ICSID Rules can commence.[28]

Under the Additional Facility Rules, arbitrations need not arise only out of an investment, but the secretary-general of ICSID will approve a dispute for resolution under the Additional Facility Rules only if it relates to more than an ordinary commercial transaction.[29] The ICSID Administrative Council, in its commentary on the Additional Facility Rules, describes these transactions as those involving "long term relationships or the commitment of substantial resources on the part of either party, and . . . which are of special

25 NAFTA Art. 1139.

26 *Ibid.*

27 See C. Schreuer, "Commentary on the ICSID Convention: Art. 25" (1996) 11 ICSID Rev. Foreign Invt. L. J. 318 at 355-73.

28 *Ibid.*, 372-73.

29 Additional Facility Rules, *supra* note 10, Art. 4(3).

importance to the economy of the State party."[30] The UNCITRAL Rules were designed to be used for all types of commercial disputes and do not mention investment at all.

Because of the complete absence of case law so far, the breadth of the NAFTA investment definition cannot yet be stated with confidence. Nevertheless, it may be safely concluded that the NAFTA definition of investment is significantly broader than the existing definitions under the ICSID Rules and the Additional Facility Rules. Indeed, it brings under investor-state dispute settlement a range of business relationships, including, for example, licensing and franchising agreements and some services contracts that would not ordinarily be considered investments at all.

Claims on Behalf of Enterprises Controlled by a NAFTA Investor

A NAFTA Investor is not limited to seeking relief for injuries it has suffered directly. It may seek relief in relation to state actions affecting its investments in any form of corporation, trust, partnership, joint venture, or other association. A NAFTA Investor may make a claim as well, on behalf of an enterprise formed under the laws of another NAFTA Party that is a juridical person, such as a corporation, if the enterprise is owned or controlled by the NAFTA Investor, directly or indirectly.[31] Both being able to claim relief directly for an injury caused by an action in relation to an investment and being able to claim relief on behalf of an investment represent significant changes to the rules of international law that would otherwise apply. It had been held by the International Court of Justice that, as a matter of international law, a claim by an investor could not be made where the only injury was to a corporation in which an investor had an interest as a shareholder and the investor's losses were only incidental to the injury to the corporation.[32]

30 Comment (iii) to Art. 4 of the Additional Facility Rules, *ibid.* See also Schreuer, *supra* note 27 at 367-70.

31 NAFTA Art. 1117.

32 *Case Concerning Barcelona Traction, Light and Power Co.* (*Belgium* v. *Spain*), [1970] I.C.J. Rep. 3 (Preliminary Objections). In a subsequent case, the ICJ was more receptive to the protection of such interests, though the case was decided based on the interpretation of a provision of a Treaty of Friendship, Commerce and Navigation rather than on general principles of international law (*Case Concerning Elettronica Sicula Sp.A. (ELSI)* (*U.S.* v. *Italy*), [1989] I.C.J. Rep. 15 (Judgment)).

What Can Be Complained About

NAFTA Investors can initiate proceedings to pursue a claim that a NAFTA Party[33] has breached its obligations under Chapter 11 or that a state enterprise or state sanctioned monopoly has acted in a manner inconsistent with the NAFTA Party's obligations under certain provisions of Chapter 15[34] and the NAFTA Investor has incurred loss or damage arising out of the breach.[35] These obligations go far beyond traditional investor protection against expropriation and restrictions on the repatriation of funds.

The general categories of obligations imposed on NAFTA Parties by Chapter 11 are the following:

(1) NAFTA Investors must be accorded the better of national treatment and most favoured nation treatment by NAFTA Parties (Articles 1101, 1102, and 1103).

(2) Investments of NAFTA Investors must be given at least the minimum treatment required by international law, including "fair and equitable treatment and full protection and security" (Article 1105).

(3) NAFTA Parties may not impose specified performance requirements in connection with the establishment, acquisition, expansion, management, conduct, or operation of an investment of a NAFTA Investor or condition the receipt of an advantage on a subset of these requirements (Article 1106).

(4) NAFTA Parties may not require investments of NAFTA Investors to appoint to senior management positions individuals of any particular nationality (Article 1107).

33 Measures of state and provincial governments may be complained about as well, except to the extent that reservations have been taken under NAFTA Art. 1108(a)(ii). All provinces and states have taken very broad reservations: J. Johnson, *The North American Free Trade Agreement: A Comprehensive Guide* 297-323 (Toronto: Canada Law Book, 1994). Also, the national treatment obligation in relation to a state or province is only to provide treatment no less favourable than the most favourable treatment accorded by that state or province to investors and investments of investors of the NAFTA Party of which it forms a part (Art. 1102.3).

34 NAFTA Arts. 1502.3(a) and 1503.2.

35 NAFTA Arts. 1116 (claim by a NAFTA Investor on its own behalf) and 1117 (claim by a NAFTA Investor on behalf of an enterprise).

(5) NAFTA Parties must permit all financial transfers relating to an investment of a NAFTA Investor freely and without delay (Article 1109).

(6) NAFTA Parties must observe certain standards in connection with the expropriation of investments of NAFTA Investors relating to the purpose of the expropriation, the process to be followed, and the compensation to be paid (Article 1110).[36]

Certain exceptions to the application of these obligations are provided for, and reservations are permitted in some circumstances. No reservation may be taken, however, against the obligation to provide a minimum standard of treatment, the obligation to permit financial transfers, or the expropriation and compensation obligations. Each NAFTA Party has taken extensive reservations with respect to the other obligations.[37] Canada and Mexico retain their investment review regimes. In addition, as a result of the fact that the general exceptions in NAFTA Chapter 21, including the exemption for measures relating to national security, apply to Chapter 11, the power of the president of the United States to prohibit or reverse an acquisition of a United States business by a foreign investor if he believes it would harm national security is preserved.[38]

Where a claim relates to an investment in the financial services sector, it is governed by Chapter 14, the financial services chapter, not by Chapter 11. All of the dispute settlement provisions as well as the Chapter 11 obligations regarding transfers of funds, expropriation and compensation, and denial of benefits are incorporated by reference in Chapter 14.[39] As a result, NAFTA Investors in the financial services sector may resort to arbitration under the Chapter

36 The substantive standards of behaviour set for governments are discussed in more detail in D. M. Price, "An Overview of the NAFTA Investment Chapter: Substantive Rules and Investor-State Dispute Settlement" (1993) 27 Int'l Lawyer 727; and D. A. Gantz, "Resolution of Investment Disputes under the North American Free Trade Agreement" (1993) 10 Arizona J. of Int'l and Comp. L. 335.

37 See Johnson, *supra* note 33 at 297-323 and G. N. Horlick and A. L. Marti, "NAFTA Chapter 11B — A Private Right of Action to Enforce Market Access through Investment" (1997) 14:1 J. Int'l Arbitration 43 at 50-2.

38 This power is granted under the Exon-Florio amendment (s. 5021 of the Omnibus Trade and Competitiveness Act, 1988 (Pub. Law 100-418)). See Johnson, *supra* note 33 at 302-3.

39 NAFTA Art. 1401 does so by incorporating by reference Arts. 1109, 1110, 1111, and 1113-38 from Ch. 11.

11 rules in relation to actions of a NAFTA Party contrary to the Chapter 11 rules in these areas. Chapter 14 also includes certain specific exceptions to the obligations of the NAFTA Parties for measures relating to the safety, soundness, integrity, and financial responsibility of financial institutions, the protection of investors, and the stability of the financial system.

The potentially broad scope of what may be complained about under NAFTA Chapter 11 is demonstrated by the first case brought against Canada. The investor, Ethyl Corporation asserted, among other things, that its commercial interests had been expropriated by the federal government ban on the import and interprovincial transport of its gasoline additive, MMT. Ethyl's claim extended not just to the legislation itself. Ethyl has claimed that statements by the minister of the environment and the debate on the bill in the House of Commons represented an expropriation of its good will. Such a claim could not be made if Ethyl was a Canadian business for two reasons.

First, a Canadian business has no standing to make a claim against the Canadian government under Chapter 11. An investor of one NAFTA Party can only make a claim under NAFTA Chapter 11 in relation to a measure of *another* NAFTA Party.[40] This limitation excludes even a claim by a Canadian investor who has an investment in a United States business in which that business is affected by a Canadian government measure contrary to Chapter 11 that has injured the Canadian investor, perhaps by causing a decline in the value of the investor's investment. Not only could the Canadian investor not claim directly, but it would also be prevented from claiming on behalf of the investment — the United States business. There is nothing to prevent the United States business from complaining itself and seeking relief in the form of monetary damages that would have the effect of remedying the injury to the Canadian investor. In these circumstances, the Canadian investor could ensure that a Chapter 11 proceeding is initiated only if it controls the United States business.

Second, although Canada does have laws protecting all businesses against expropriation, the definition of expropriation for the purposes of these laws is much narrower than under Chapter 11. For there to be an expropriation requiring compensation, there must be more than a prohibition of an activity. There must be some

[40] NAFTA Arts. 1116.1 and 1117.1.

transfer of good will or other asset to the Crown.[41] No such transfer occurs in the MMT case. Under Chapter 11, acts "tantamount to expropriation" are included, creating a standard that is less certain and potentially much broader.

Several procedural issues arise in applying the substantive standards of behaviour in Chapter 11. Perhaps the most critical issue is when may an investor initiate the dispute settlement proceedings. Article 1101 provides that the scope of the investment chapter is limited to "measures adopted or maintained" by a NAFTA Party. Difficult questions arise with respect to what is a measure, and when is it adopted or maintained.

A measure is defined in Article 201(1) of the NAFTA as including "any law, regulation, procedure, requirement or practice." The definition, on its face, is not exhaustive. The claim in the MMT case vividly illustrates that arguments will be made that measures are not limited to rules and procedures with direct legal effect but extend to a wide range of other government actions. The issue of when a measure has been adopted is important for several reasons. In terms of the Chapter 11 process itself, the resolution of this issue will determine not only the circumstances in which a claim may be made by an investor but also the timing for doing so.[42] If "measure" is interpreted in this context as being adopted only on the date the legislation comes into force, the required six-month cooling off period, during which an investor may not initiate dispute settlement, would not start until that date. In circumstances like the MMT case, where the government ultimately did enact legislation, such an interpretation should only force a delay in the process.[43] Nevertheless, such a delay may be significant in cases where substantial, potentially irreversible, losses occur before the enactment of the legislation. Where, for example, a threatened law will eliminate a significant component of an investor's business, that business may be forced to close before the law is enacted. If government action

41 See R. Dearden, "Arbitration of Expropriation Disputes between an Investor and the State under the North American Free Trade Agreement" (1994) J. World Trade 113 at 117-20.

42 An investor must wait until at least six months have expired following "the events giving rise to a claim" before initiating Ch. 11 proceedings: see *infra* note 48 and accompanying text.

43 Where a claim is made that relies on pre-legislation government action followed by legislation, one question that arises is whether a failure to wait six months from the date of enactment is simply a procedural irregularity or a defect in the jurisdiction of the arbitral panel.

never proceeds to a legislative enactment or some other legally effective step, requiring such a step will bar the investor's claim entirely. On the other hand, allowing investors to seek relief on the basis of the minister's statements, as claimed in the MMT case, has very serious implications for the freedom of governments to initiate public debate on an issue.

Claims under Chapter 11 are also subject to a limitation period. They must be made within three years after the investor first acquired or should have first acquired knowledge of the breach and of the loss or damage.[44]

THE DISPUTE RESOLUTION PROCESS[45]

Initiation

The investor initiates a claim for arbitration under Chapter 11. In doing so, the investor must choose which set of Arbitral Rules apply. Until Canada and Mexico join the ICSID Convention, ICSID arbitration will not be available. Under the ICSID Rules, arbitrations must involve claims against state parties to the ICSID Convention by investors of convention states. Because the United States is a party to the ICSID Convention, claims against the United States by Canadian or Mexican investors and claims by American investors against Canada or Mexico can be dealt with under the Additional Facility Rules or UNCITRAL Rules. Disputes between Canadian investors and Mexico or between Mexican investors and Canada can only be arbitrated under the UNCITRAL Rules.[46]

44 NAFTA Art. 1116.2 (claim by a NAFTA Investor on its own behalf) and Art. 1117.2 (claim by a NAFTA Investor on behalf of an enterprise). None of the three sets of Arbitral Rules imposes a limitation period.

45 A substantial body of literature describes each of the three sets of Arbitral Rules referred to in Ch. 11: e.g., J. Paulsson "ICSID Arbitration: The Host State's Point of View" and W. Craig "ICSID Arbitration: The Foreign Investor's Point of View," chs. 14 and 15 in *Problems and Solutions in International Business* (Southwestern Legal Foundation, 1993); Thomas Brewer, "International Investment Dispute Settlement Procedures: The Evolving Regime for Foreign Direct Investment," (1995) 26 L. and Policy in Int'l Bus. 633. An excellent table comparing the three sets of rules and indicating the changes made by Ch. 11 is set out as an annex to Cheri Eklund, "A Primer on the Arbitration of NAFTA Chapter Eleven Investor-State Disputes" (1994) 11:4 J. Int'l Arbitration 135 at 159-71.

46 As noted earlier, the MMT case is proceeding under the UNCITRAL Rules while the two cases by American investors against Mexico are being dealt with

Before an investor initiates a claim for relief under Chapter 11, several conditions must be satisfied. First, the investor and the NAFTA Party complained against should have attempted to settle the claim through negotiation,[47] although such attempts are not mandatory. Second, at least six months must have passed since the events giving rise to the claim[48] and, at least ninety days before submitting the claim, the investor must have given the NAFTA Party a notice of the investor's intention to do so.[49]

In submitting a claim under Chapter 11, the investor must consent to arbitration in accordance with Chapter 11 and waive its right to initiate or continue any other dispute settlement procedure with respect to the injurious measure of the NAFTA Party.[50] If the claim is for loss or damage to an interest in an enterprise that is a juridical person owned or controlled by the investor, both the investor and the enterprise must consent and give such a waiver. Similarily, where an investor initiates proceedings on behalf of an enterprise, both must consent and give a waiver.[51] Under this scheme, it appears to be possible for an investor from one NAFTA Party to initiate a claim for an injury to it resulting from a measure of another NAFTA Party that affects a business in which the investor has an investment without the consent of the business, so long as the investor does not own or control the business. For example, a Canadian minority shareholder in a United States corporation could institute proceedings against the United States in connection with a United States government measure inconsistent with Chapter 11 that caused it an injury, such as a decline in share price, regardless of whether the United States corporation was interested in pursuing such a claim itself, and even in the face of the United States corporation's vigorous opposition.[52]

---

under the Additional Facility Rules. Who qualifies as an investor from one of the NAFTA Party states is discussed above, *supra* notes 19-32 and accompanying text.

47 NAFTA Art. 1118. There is no similar exhortation to negotiate in any of the Arbitral Rules.

48 NAFTA Art. 1120. None of the three sets of Arbitral Rules contains such a condition.

49 NAFTA Art. 1119. None of the three sets of Arbitral Rules contains such a condition.

50 NAFTA Art. 1121.1.

51 NAFTA Art. 1121.2.

52 This observation was made by G. N. Horlick and A. L. Marti, *supra* note 37 at 47.

The waiver does not extend to claims for injunctive, declaratory, or other extraordinary relief not involving the payment of damages under the law of the NAFTA Party complained against. The waiver is limited in this way because the final award that may be made under Chapter 11 is limited to monetary damages plus applicable interest or restitution of property in lieu thereof.[53] Claims for other types of relief may be pursued in other fora. The requirement for a consent and waiver from an enterprise cannot be raised where the NAFTA Party complained against has taken control of the enterprise.[54] Even though an investor is free to pursue relief in other fora, the scope for doing so will be limited because, outside the Chapter 11 process, an investor will not be able to claim relief based on a breach of the substantive standards set out in Chapter 11. Where there is no other basis for a claim, access to other remedies is effectively prevented. There is no bar, however, to an investor's home state initiating dispute settlement proceedings under NAFTA Chapter 20 in connection with a measure inconsistent with Chapter 11. Such state-to-state proceedings may result in the withdrawal of the measure.

As pointed out above, one of the distinctive features of Chapter 11 is that each of the NAFTA Parties has given its consent to arbitration in the NAFTA itself.[55] This consent is critical, since it gives the investor the ability to require a NAFTA Party to participate in the dispute settlement process and binds it to the result.

Appointment of Arbitrators

Under Chapter 11, arbitral tribunals consist of three arbitrators unless the parties otherwise agree. Each party appoints one arbitrator. The parties must agree on the appointment of the third member of the tribunal, who is the presiding arbitrator.[56] If a tribunal has not been constituted within ninety days of the date when a claim is

53 NAFTA Art. 1135.1. A tribunal may not award punitive damages (Art. 1135.3).

54 None of the Arbitral Rules contains restrictions on the remedies that may be granted: *infra* notes 72-77 and accompanying text.

55 Art. 1122 provides that the consent satisfies the jurisdictional requirements of the ICSID Convention and the Additional Facility Rules. It is also sufficient for the purposes of UNCITRAL arbitration.

56 NAFTA Art. 1123. In any event, this is essentially the same process as is contemplated in the Arbitral Rules: ICSID Rules, *supra* note 15, Art. 37(2); Additional Facility Rules, *supra* note 10, Art. 6; UNCITRAL Rules, *supra* note 14, Art. 5.

submitted to arbitration, the secretary-general of ICSID, on the request of either party, shall appoint any arbitrator not appointed. In appointing the presiding arbitrator, the secretary-general must choose from a roster of forty-five arbitrators, established by consensus of the NAFTA Parties, who are experienced in international law and investment matters and meet the requirements of each set of Arbitral Rules.[57] At the time of writing, the NAFTA parties had not struck a roster. If no member of the roster is available to serve, the secretary-general shall appoint an arbitrator from the panel of arbitrators maintained by ICSID. In either case, the secretary-general shall not appoint a presiding arbitrator who is a national of the NAFTA Party complained against or the NAFTA Party of the investor.[58] The appointment process can be a significant source of delay in investor-state proceedings.

All arbitrators must meet the standards set in the relevant set of Arbitral Rules. Although expressed in different language, in each set of Arbitral Rules it is provided that arbitrators must be independent and impartial. The ICSID Rules and the Additional Facility Rules also require competence.[59] Each of the three sets of Arbitral Rules sets out a procedure under which a party may challenge and seek the removal of an arbitrator on the basis of his or her failing to meet these requirements.[60]

57 These requirements are discussed below, *infra* notes 59-62 and accompanying text.

58 NAFTA Art. 1124. The provisions under the Arbitral Rules for appointment in default of an appointment by the parties that would apply in the absence of NAFTA, are similar. The ICSID Rules and the Additional Facility Rules allow 90 days, or such other period as the parties agree, before action by the appointing authority may be requested, and provide for appointments to be made by the Chairman of the Administrative Council of ICSID: ICSID Rules, *supra* note 15, Art. 38; Additional Facility Rules, *supra* note 10, Art. 6. In the case of ICSID arbitrations, all such appointments must be made from the ICSID Panel: ICSID Rules, *supra* note 15, Art. 40. Under the UNCITRAL Rules, only 30 days need to elapse before a party may request an appointing authority to appoint arbitrators: UNCITRAL Rules, *supra* note 14, Art. 7. If the parties have not agreed on an appointing authority, a party may request the secretary-general of the Permanent Court of Arbitration at The Hague to designate an appointing authority.

59 ICSID Rules, *supra* note 15, Art. 14; Additional Facility Rules, *supra* note 10, Art. 9; UNCITRAL Rules, *supra* note 14, Arts 9-10.

60 ICSID Rules, *ibid.*, Art. 57, Rule 9; Additional Facility Rules, *supra* note 10, Art. 16; UNCITRAL Rules, *supra* note 14, Arts 10-12.

None of the Arbitral Rules or Chapter 11 imposes requirements on arbitrators as detailed as those contained in the Code of Conduct governing panellists and others under NAFTA Chapters 19 and 20.[61] None provides the same level of disclosure of previous relationships with the parties nor imposes restrictions on the activities of members of tribunals after an award is issued, which are designed to ensure that nothing is done that might create the appearance that a member was not impartial. The application of the Code has been a significant issue in the context of disputes under Chapter 19 regarding domestic anti-dumping and countervailing duty decisions.[62] It remains to be seen whether there will be pressure from the NAFTA Parties to adopt a similar code of conduct for arbitrators in Chapter 11 cases.

Consolidation of Proceedings

Chapter 11 permits the consolidation of arbitral proceedings when claims have a question of law or fact in common and when it would be in the interests of the fair and efficient resolution of the claims that they be dealt with together. Any party seeking consolidation must make a request to the secretary-general of ICSID. The secretary-general must appoint a tribunal of three arbitrators to hear the consolidation request under the UNCITRAL Rules. If it determines that consolidation is appropriate, the tribunal assumes jurisdiction over the consolidated proceeding and any other tribunal ceases to have jurisdiction.[63]

61 Code of Conduct for the Dispute Settlement Procedures under Chapters 19 and 20 of NAFTA, Canada Gazette Part I, Jan. 22, 1994 (Code of Conduct). The Code of Conduct is established under NAFTA Art. 1909. I note that Ch. 11 proceedings are already referred to in the Code of Conduct, although the obligations in the Code do not apply to members of tribunals under Ch. 11. The ICSID Rules have been considered in several cases: See A. R. Parra, "The Rights and Duties of ICSID Arbitrators," (1995) ICC Int'l. Arbitration Bulletin (Spec. Supp.) 50.

62 In one of only three Ch. 19 cases to go to an Extraordinary Challenge Committee, a challenge to the independence of the two Canadian members of the panel was a significant issue (*Softwood Lumber*, ECC-94-1904-O1USA). The challenge was unsuccessful.

63 NAFTA Art. 1126. None of the Arbitral Rules contains a procedure for consolidation.

Place of Arbitration

Arbitrations may be held wherever the parties agree. In default of agreement, however, the only requirement in Chapter 11 is that tribunals must hold the arbitration in the territory of a NAFTA Party who is a party to the United Nations Convention on the Recognition and Enforcement of Foreign Arbitral Awards (New York Convention).[64] Canada, Mexico, and the United States are all parties to the New York Convention. A decision of a tribunal regarding the place of arbitration must be made in accordance with the Arbitral Rules under which the arbitration is proceeding.[65]

The decision of where to arbitrate will typically be driven by a host of considerations relating to the mutual convenience of the parties. It will also depend upon where appropriate facilities and support are available. The ICSID Secretariat provides support for disputes proceeding under the ICSID Rules and the Additional Facility Rules. While it only has its own facilities in Washington, ICSID has relationships with other arbitral organizations around the globe and so is capable of providing support in any major city in North America or beyond. For example, one of the proceedings against Mexico has held preliminary hearings in Vancouver, supported by the ICSID Secretariat under an agreement with the British Columbia International Commercial Arbitration Centre. The complaint against Canada under the UNCITRAL Rules is proceeding without any institutional support.

The NAFTA Secretariat, which provides support for other dispute resolution procedures under NAFTA, has facilities in Ottawa, Washington, and Mexico City and has substantial experience with the work of binational panels deciding dumping and countervailing duty cases under Chapter 19 as well as cases under Chapter 20 of NAFTA. The Secretariat could play a similarly effective role in connection with Chapter 11 proceedings governed by the UNCITRAL Rules or as a host for arbitrations under the ICSID

64 Done at New York, June 10, 1958, UN Doc. No. E/Conf. 26/9 Rev. 1; 330 U.N.T.S. 3 [hereinafter New York Convention].

65 NAFTA Art. 1130. Under the UNCITRAL Rules, the parties may agree on the place of arbitration and, if they do not, the tribunal decides (UNCITRAL Rules, *supra* note 14, Art. 16). The ICSID Rules require the parties to agree if the arbitration is to be anywhere other than the ICSID Centre in Washington (ICSID Rules, *supra* note 15, Art. 63). Under the Additional Facility Rules, the place of arbitrations is determined by the tribunal in consultation with the parties, but must be held in a state party to the New York Convention (Additional Facility Rules, *supra* note 10, Arts. 20-21).

Rules or the Additional Facility Rules. For it to do so, the Free Trade Commission established under NAFTA would have to direct the Secretariat to perform such a role and, in each case, the parties would have to agree to use the Secretariat.[66] No direction of the Free Trade Commission of this kind has been made to date.

Participation by Other NAFTA Parties

Once the NAFTA Party complained against has received a claim from an investor, it is obliged to deliver a notice to the other NAFTA Parties within thirty days of the date when the claim was submitted. It must also deliver copies of all pleadings to each other NAFTA Party.[67] Other NAFTA Parties are entitled to receive from the NAFTA Party complained against a copy of all evidence and written arguments submitted to a tribunal.[68]

A NAFTA Party is also entitled to participate in arbitral proceedings on written notice to the parties to the dispute in order to make submissions regarding questions about the interpretation of NAFTA.[69] Since the obligations that are the subject of dispute settlement under Chapter 11 are found in NAFTA, there will be a basis for such third party participation in most cases.

Not surprisingly, none of the three sets of Arbitral Rules creates a right for third parties to participate. This is an important distinction between the process under Chapter 11 and that under the Arbitral Rules governing disputes not subject to NAFTA. Each of the sets of Arbitral Rules is designed solely as a process to resolve disputes between parties. In contrast, the Chapter 11 dispute settlement involves the interpretation of a multilateral instrument — an issue in which all the NAFTA Parties have a stake. It is difficult to anticipate the effect of third party participation in the investor-state dispute settlement process. While one may imagine that, in some cases, the home state of an investor will become involved in support

66 The Free Trade Commission is established under Art. 2001 of NAFTA and consists of cabinet-level representatives of the three NAFTA Parties or their designates. Under NAFTA Art. 2002.3(c), the Free Trade Commission may direct the Secretariat to support the work of other committees and groups established under NAFTA and otherwise facilitate the operation of NAFTA.

67 NAFTA Art. 1127.

68 NAFTA Art. 1129. Where a NAFTA Party receives such material it must treat it as if it were the Party complained against. This means, in part, that the NAFTA Party must ensure that the material remains confidential.

69 NAFTA Art. 1128.

of the position of the investor, states may often seek to prevent rulings that will have the consequence of expanding the rights of investors within their own borders.

Applicable Law and Rulings by the Free Trade Commission

As noted, one significant difference between the process under Chapter 11 and the provisions of the Arbitral Rules is that, under Chapter 11, arbitral tribunals are to apply NAFTA, itself, and any applicable rule of international law. Where the Free Trade Commission, which was established under NAFTA, has interpreted a provision of NAFTA, the interpretation is binding on an arbitral tribunal.[70] Where a NAFTA Party asserts that a measure is within the scope of a reservation or exception set out in an Annex to NAFTA, the NAFTA Party may request the tribunal to refer the question to the Commission. The tribunal is obliged then to request an interpretation and the Commission is obliged to provide a written response within sixty days. If the Commission fails to respond within this time, however, the tribunal must decide the issue. If the Commission does respond, its interpretation is binding on the tribunal.[71] Since the Free Trade Commission is composed of cabinet level representatives of each NAFTA Party, it is possible that interpretations of the Commission may, in some cases, reflect political compromises that may not be in the interests of investors.

Interim Relief, Final Awards, and Costs

Before making a final award, a tribunal may take interim measures to preserve the rights of a party or to ensure that the tribunal's jurisdiction is made fully effective. These measures may include an order to preserve evidence in the possession of party. A tribunal's power in this regard is subject to a significant limitation: tribunals

70 NAFTA Art. 1131.

71 NAFTA Art. 1132. The basic rule under all three sets of Arbitral Rules for disputes not governed by NAFTA Ch. 11 is that the governing law is that agreed on by the parties. In default of agreement, the Additional Facility Rules and the UNCITRAL Rules provide that the tribunal shall determine the applicable law by using the conflict of laws rules that it considers appropriate: Additional Facility Rules, *supra* note 10, Art. 55; UNCITRAL Rules, *supra* note 14, Art. 33. Failing a designation by the parties, the Additional Facility Rules also provide for the application of international law rules that the tribunal decides are appropriate. Under the ICSID Rules, in default of agreement the law to be applied is the law of the state complained against and any applicable rules of international law: ICSID Rules, *supra* note 15, Art. 42(1).

may not order attachment or enjoin the measure alleged to constitute a breach of the obligations of the NAFTA Party complained against.[72] This limitation preserves the freedom of the NAFTA Parties to legislate as they choose, subject to an obligation to pay compensation to investors. As noted above, an investor is not barred from seeking attachment or an injunction in other fora. This right may be of limited value, however, since, in the absence of a specific consent from the state complained against, there is likely to be no other forum in which the investor can seek relief for a breach of the substantive standards of NAFTA Chapter 11, and no other standards may apply.[73]

Final awards against a NAFTA Party are limited to monetary damages plus applicable interest and restitution of property. Even if restitution is ordered, however, a NAFTA Party may opt to pay monetary damages and applicable interest instead. Punitive damages are expressly precluded.[74] Tribunals may award costs in accordance with the applicable Arbitral Rules.

None of the three sets of Arbitral Rules imposes limits on remedies available in final awards. Each, however, addresses the

72 NAFTA Art. 1134.

73 The Ch. 11 rules on interim relief vary the operation of the Arbitral Rules in several ways. Under the ICSID Rules and the Additional Facility Rules, interim relief may be limited or even excluded, if the parties agree. Such an agreement would now appear to be prevented by NAFTA. In the absence of an agreement under the ICSID Rules and the Additional Facilities Rules, the parties may request any type of interim relief from a tribunal. The same is true under the UNCITRAL Rules (*supra* note 14, Art. 26). Under NAFTA, however, relief cannot extend to suspending the measure complained about. Regarding interim relief from the courts, the ICSID Rules, the Additional Facility Rules, and the UNCITRAL Rules all expressly permit parties to seek interim relief from competent judicial authorities: (ICSID Rules, *supra* note 15, Art. 47, Rule 39(5); Additional Facility Rules, *supra* note 10, Art. 47; UNCITRAL Rules, *supra* note 14, Art. 26). In the case of the ICSID Rules, however, this is only permitted if the parties have provided for doing so in their consent to arbitration. Under NAFTA, the parties' ability to resort to judicial authorities is limited to proceedings for injunctive, declaratory, and other extraordinary relief. This conclusion is based on the NAFTA provision on interim measures, Art. 1134, which does not refer to resort to judicial authorities, and the investor and investment consent requirements in Arts. 1121 and 1122, which do not require a waiver of the right to initiate proceedings for these types of relief.

74 NAFTA Art. 1135.3. Where awards are made on the basis of claims on behalf of an investment, the award must go to the investment (Art. 1135.2).

issue of costs, leaving it to the discretion of the tribunal.[75] Since the procedures under Chapter 11 are self-financed, the costs may be substantial. This self-financing character distinguishes proceedings under Chapter 11 from those under Chapters 19 and 20.[76]

A NAFTA Party may not assert, as a defence or counterclaim, that the investor has received or will receive indemnification or other compensation for all or part of its alleged damages.[77] A NAFTA Party might otherwise have sought to raise such a claim, for example, where an investor was compensated for its loss by insurance, such as that available from the Export Development Corporation in Canada and similar agencies in the other NAFTA Parties. Similarly, NAFTA does not address subrogation of state agencies paying compensation to the investor. Apparently, an agency can initiate an action under Chapter 11 only where it can characterize the relationship under which compensation is to be paid as an investment.

REVIEW OF ARBITRAL AWARDS

No NAFTA provision deals with the review of arbitral awards.[78] Each of the three sets of Arbitral Rules provides for review, but in very different ways.

The ICSID Convention excludes the possibility of judicial review of an award.[79] Each state party to the ICSID Convention is obliged to give effect to this prohibition. As noted, currently only the United States is a party to the convention and, until another NAFTA Party joins, there can be no proceedings under the ICSID Rules. The ICSID Rules provide for an internal review on certain procedural grounds — for example: (1) where the tribunal is not properly constituted or manifestly exceeds its powers; (2) for corruption on the part of a tribunal member; (3) where the award fails to state the reasons upon which it is based; or (4) for a serious

75 ICSID Rules, *supra* note 15, Arts. 59-61, Rule 28; Additional Facility Rules, *supra* note 10, Art. 59; UNCITRAL Rules, *supra* note 14, Arts. 38-40.

76 This aspect of the Ch. 11 process was criticized in Gary N. Horlick and F. Amanda DeBusk, "Dispute Resolution under NAFTA: Building on the U.S.-Canada FTA, GATT and ICSID" (1993) 10:1 J. of Int'l Arbitration 51 at 55, citing the expense of the ICSID process.

77 NAFTA Art. 1137.3.

78 Art. 1136 conditions the enforceability of awards under Ch. 11 on the completion of proceedings to revise, set aside, or annul an award: see *infra* notes 88-94 and accompanying text.

79 ICSID Convention, *supra* note 6, Art. 53.

departure from a fundamental rule of procedure.[80] While these grounds may appear narrow, some commentators have noted that reviews of awards have become routine in ICSID cases and have sometimes resulted in delays extending to years.[81] Ultimately, review may lead to the annulment of an award.

By contrast, under the Additional Facility Rules and the UNCITRAL Rules,[82] awards may not be annulled, although tribunals may issue interpretations of awards and awards may be revised to correct clerical errors. Under the Additional Facility Rules, the ICSID Convention does not apply[83] and, as a result, arbitral decisions under the Additional Facility Rules, while final and binding,[84] may be subject to judicial review under national law. The same is true for UNCITRAL awards. Recourse against awards rendered pursuant to the Additional Facility Rules and the UNCITRAL Rules will be governed by the law of the forum and will be available in very limited circumstances. Under Canadian federal law and the laws of each province, the main grounds are as follows: (1) a party was not given proper notice of the appointment of an arbitrator; (2) the award deals with a dispute not contemplated by, nor falling within the terms of, the submission to arbitration; or (3) the award is contrary to the public policy of the state in which the award is sought to be enforced.[85] In Canada, the scope of these grounds has been interpreted narrowly.[86]

80 *Ibid.*, Art. 52.

81 E.g., Horlick and DeBusk, *supra* note 76 at 57, citing *Amoco* v. *Republic of Indonesia*, ARB/18/1 (Nov. 20, 1984) and *Klockner* v. *Republic of Cameroon* ARB/81/2 (May 17, 1990).

82 Additional Facility Rules, *supra* note 10, Schedule C, Arts. 56-58; UNCITRAL Rules, *supra* note 14, Arts. 35-7.

83 Additional Facility Rules, *ibid.*, Schedule A (Administrative and Financial), Art. 3.

84 Additional Facility Rules, *ibid.*, Art. 53; UNCITRAL Rules, *supra* note 14, Art. 53(4).

85 Commercial Arbitration Act, R.S.C. 1985, c. 17 (2nd Supp.), Art. 44. An example of provincial legislation is the International Commercial Arbitrations Act, R.S.O. 1990, c. I.9. These Acts implement the standards in the New York Convention.

86 E.g. *Quintette Coal Ltd.* v. *Nippon Steel Corp.*, (1991), 50 B.C.L.R. (2d) 207 (C.A.), leave to appeal to the Supreme Court of Canada refused (1990), 50 B.C.L.R. (2d) xxvii; *Schreter* v. *Gasmac Inc.* (1992), 7 O.R. (3d) 608 (Gen. Div.), additional reasons (1992), 89 D.L.R. (4th) 380. Both the Additional Facility Rules and the UNCITRAL Rules provide for proceedings to correct or seek an interpretation of an award (Additional Facility Rules, *supra* note 10, Arts. 56, 57; UNCITRAL Rules, *supra* note 14, Arts. 35, 36).

It will be interesting to see how the traditional reluctance of the courts to intervene on the basis of public policy will operate in Chapter 11 cases where the government measure complained about is designed to promote some important, generally recognized public policy. In the MMT case, for example, the measure complained about — a ban on the import and interprovincial transport of the gasoline additive MMT — has the ostensible purpose of protecting the Canadian environment. The investor, Ethyl Corporation, is asserting that its commercial interests have been expropriated by the federal government ban. If the environmental risk associated with the use of MMT was significant enough and the measure justifiable as a means of reducing the risk, would a court refuse to enforce an award on the basis of public policy? Each NAFTA Party's right to enact measures to protect the environment is expressly recognized in Chapter 11.[87] Nevertheless, a decision to refuse to enforce an award in these circumstances would severely undermine the Chapter 11 process. It would also be hard to justify because an award under Chapter 11 does not prevent the government from continuing the measure. It only requires the government to pay compensation to the injured investor. Nevertheless, the price associated with such a compensation award may be sufficiently high that the consequence of enforcing the award might be the repeal of the measure. In the MMT case, the compensation sought was US $251 million.[88]

ENFORCEMENT

NAFTA Chapter 11 contains a variety of provisions dealing with enforcement. The award has no binding force except between the disputing parties and in respect of the particular case.[89] Investors may not seek to enforce the award until the expiry of certain time periods ranging from three months after the award is rendered in the case of Additional Facility and UNCITRAL arbitrations to 120

87 NAFTA Art. 1114.1 provides as follows: "Nothing in the Chapter shall be construed to prevent a Party from adopting, maintaining or enforcing any measure otherwise consistent with this Chapter that it considers appropriate to ensure that investment activity in its territory is undertaken in a manner sensitive to environmental concerns."

88 In August 1998, it was disclosed that the Canadian government and the investor, Ethyl Corporation, had agreed to a settlement under which Canada would pay Ethyl US $13 million and would repeal the ban on MMT.

89 NAFTA Art. 1136.1.

days in the case of ICSID arbitrations.[90] Subject to this limitation, however, a NAFTA Party against which an award has been made is obliged under the terms of NAFTA to abide by the award without delay.[91] Each NAFTA Party must provide for the enforcement of the award in its territory.[92]

If an award is made under the ICSID Rules, the award is directly enforceable in all state parties to the ICSID Convention. There are no grounds upon which enforcement may be denied. In states not party to the ICSID Convention, an ICSID award may be enforced under the New York Convention and the Inter-American Convention on International Commercial Arbitration.[93] NAFTA Article 1122 provides that the consent of the NAFTA Parties in Chapter 11 satisfies the jurisdictional requirements of the New York Convention and the Inter-American Convention on International Commercial Arbitration. Awards under the Additional Facility Rules or the UNCITRAL Rules may also be enforced under these two conventions. Under each convention, a court in a state party to the convention must enforce the arbitral award as if it was an order of the court. The grounds upon which a court may refuse to enforce an award are essentially the same as those upon which a court may grant recourse against an award, as described in the previous section[94] and the same questions raised above regarding the scope of the public policy exception may arise.

If the NAFTA Party complained against fails to comply with a final award, another NAFTA Party whose investor was a party to the arbitration may request the Free Trade Commission to establish a state-to-state dispute settlement panel under Chapter 20 and seek a recommendation that the NAFTA party complained against abide by or comply with the final award. Upon the receipt of such a request, the Commission is bound to establish a panel.[95]

90 NAFTA Art. 1136.3.

91 NAFTA Art. 1136.2.

92 NAFTA Art. 1136.4.

93 Done at Panama, Jan. 30, 1975, O.A.S.T.S No. 42, reprinted 14 I.L.M. 336.

94 New York Convention, *supra* note 64, Art. V; Inter-American Convention on International Commercial Arbitration, *ibid.*, Art. 5.

95 NAFTA Art. 1136.5

PUBLICATION OF AWARDS

Under the three sets of Arbitral Rules, the publication of an award may take place only with the consent of both parties.[96] Under NAFTA, this rule is maintained for awards against Mexico, but Canada and the United States are permitted to disclose awards against them without the consent of the investor, and investors may similarly make an award public.[97]

CONCLUSION

Chapter 11 of NAFTA modifies the procedure to be followed under the Arbitral Rules in significant ways, such as by providing for consolidation, and for participation by NAFTA Parties in addition to the one complained against, as well as by providing recourse to the Free Trade Commission for binding interpretations of NAFTA. The most significant departures from the investor-state dispute settlement process under the ICSID Rules and the Additional Facility Rules are the extremely broad definition of investments subject to protection and the ability of an investor to force states to participate in binding arbitration.

A variety of issues regarding the Chapter 11 procedure will be worked out only as more cases are brought forward. These issues include the adequacy of the provisions of the Arbitral Rules dealing with the independence of tribunal members, the publication of awards, and the extent to which there will be pressure to put in place some form of institutional support for arbitrations under the UNCITRAL Rules. Perhaps the most interesting and significant issue is the extent to which the Chapter 11 process goes beyond levelling the playing field to put foreign investors in a better position than domestic firms. This will be determined by the interpretation placed by arbitral tribunals on the substantive standards of behaviour imposed by Chapter 11 as well as by the interpretation placed by courts asked to enforce awards made under Chapter 11 on the public policy ground for non-enforcement. The manner in which these issues and others are resolved will have significant implications, not just for the effectiveness of the Chapter 11

96 ICSID Rules, *supra* note 15, Rule 48(5); UNCITRAL Rules, *supra* note 14, Art. 32(5). The Additional Facility Rules do not address publication, but it has been suggested that agreement of the parties would be required: Eklund, *supra* note 45, at 157.

97 NAFTA Annex 1137.4. The secrecy of the Chapter 11 process has drawn significant public criticism in the wake of the settlement of the MMT case.

process, but also for the balance struck by Chapter 11 between the rights of investors and the freedom of states to make rules governing activities within their own borders. In turn, how the Chapter 11 process takes shape will have a significant impact on whether similar mechanisms will be put in place in a broader multilateral context.

J. ANTHONY VANDUZER
Faculty of Law, University of Ottawa

Sommaire

Le règlement des différends entre les États et les investisseurs en vertu du chapitre 11 de l'ALÉNA: un aperçu de l'avenir?

Il y a eu récemment une prolifération d'ententes internationales imposant des standards minimums à l'égard du traitement des investisseurs étrangers et, en plus, leur offrant des méthodes de règlement des différends lorsqu'un État fait outrage à ces standards. D'envergure pour le Canada est le chapitre 11 de l'ALÉNA qui indique, d'un part, les standards que doivent respecter les États et, d'autre part, le droit des investisseurs à l'arbritage obligatoire. En 1996 et 1997, les trois premiers arrêts ont été commencés en vertu de ce chapitre. Cet article examine la procédure décrite par le chapitre 11 et les inquiétudes que son utilisation par des investisseurs soulèvera.

Summary

Investor-State Dispute Settlement under NAFTA Chapter 11: The Shape of Things to Come?

Recently, there has been a proliferation of international agreements imposing minimum standards on states in respect of their treatment of foreign investors and allowing investors to initiate dispute settlement proceedings where a state violates these standards. Of greatest significance to Canada is Chapter 11 of the North American Free Trade Agreement, which provides both standards for state behaviour and the right to initiate binding arbitration. Since 1996, four cases have been brought under Chapter 11. This note describes the Chapter 11 process and suggests some of the issues that may arise as it is increasingly resorted to by investors.

Following Suit: A Comparison of Dispute Resolution Mechanisms under NAFTA Chapter 20 and the Canada-Israel Free Trade Agreement

Introduction

On November 24, 1994, following a meeting in Ottawa with the late Israeli prime minister, Yitzhak Rabin, Prime Minister Jean Chrétien announced the beginning of negotiations on a free trade deal between Canada and Israel. In 1996, the negotiators reached an agreement and the Canada-Israel Free Trade Agreement (CIFTA)[1] was born. The CIFTA was reviewed and signed by both governments on July 31, 1996, and took effect January 1, 1997. It is the first of its kind to be signed by Canada with a non-North American country; it is the second agreement Israel has signed with a North American country.

This comment compares the dispute settlement mechanisms in the North American Free Trade Agreement (NAFTA)[2] and the new CIFTA. An effective dispute resolution mechanism is essential in facilitating the proper operation and future success of international trade agreements. As Judge Lauterpacht of the International Court of Justice said, "most so-called conflicts of interests are due, not to economic necessities, but to the imperfections of international legal organization, in particular to the legal admissibility of force and the absence of judicial settlement."[3] The dispute resolution mechanisms under CIFTA and NAFTA are similar in many respects, but differences exist. The purpose of this comment is to mark the significance of these differences.

1 Not published. The text of the Agreement is available through the Information Centre at the Department of Foreign Affairs [hereinafter CIFTA].

2 Dec. 17, 1992, (1993) 32 I.L.M. 289 [hereinafter NAFTA].

3 H. Lauterpacht, *The Function of Law in the International Community* 250 (Connecticut: Archon Books, 1966).

CIFTA and NAFTA Mechanisms: General Overview

Chapter 8 of CIFTA and Chapter 20 of NAFTA set the dispute resolution procedures to be applied by the parties.[4] The two mechanisms cover disputes concerning the interpretation or application of the Agreements, alleged violations of the Agreements or impairments of benefits accorded by them. Both invoke a form of consultation to achieve resolution, the purpose of which is to resolve disputes by way of co-operation so that the end result is mutually acceptable to the parties.

When resolution cannot be achieved through consultation, the CIFTA Chapter 8 and the NAFTA Chapter 20 mechanisms provide for panel review of the issue. Both recognize that panel composition is important to the integrity of the settlement process and thus set out a selection process for choosing panellists. The review by an independent panel is aimed at guaranteeing impartiality, with the result that a resolution is more likely to be accepted by the disputing parties. Both mechanisms place time limits on each stage of the dispute settlement process to ensure an expedited process.

In the CIFTA and the NAFTA mechanisms, panel decisions are not binding under domestic law. In other words, the panels' findings under both mechanisms do not create new domestic law and are not enforceable through the courts of the losing party. In both Agreements, a complaining party can compel the other party to make its trade practices conform to a panel decision only by suspending the application of benefits of equivalent effect to the party complained against.

CIFTA and NAFTA Mechanisms: A Detailed Comparison

Jurisdiction

CIFTA Article 8.1 and NAFTA Article 2004 confer jurisdiction with respect to the resolution of disputes over the interpretation or application of the Agreements. This jurisdiction extends to actual or proposed measures of a party that are or would be inconsistent with the obligations of the Agreement in question. The dispute mechanisms are also designed for situations in which measures taken by one party are consistent with the obligations of the Agreements but the effects of such measures are unacceptable.

[4] NAFTA contains a number of mechanisms for resolving disputes between its parties. This comment concentrates on the general dispute mechanism in Chapter 20.

"Nullification or Impairment"

Under NAFTA Annex 2004 and CIFTA Annex 8.1, settlement may be sought where measures used by one party cause a "nullification or impairment"[5] of benefits that otherwise would reasonably have accrued to the other. This language, common to the two annexes, apparently dictates a low tolerance to measures taken by one party that are consistent with an Agreement but damaging to the other party.[6] Thus, in the two dispute mechanisms, although consistency between *measures* taken under an Agreement and the *provisions* of that Agreement is important, where the measures cause damage to benefits otherwise accruing to the other party, a remedy may be sought. Consequently, measures that are consistent with the Agreement under which they are invoked cannot detract from any benefit the Agreement was designed to grant.

A slight difference in the wording of the two provisions might affect the protection that each provides. Both mechanisms offer recourse to dispute settlement in which benefits reasonably expected to accrue to a party are impaired.[7] However, unlike the CIFTA provision, the NAFTA provision provides that what is reasonably expected to accrue is determined only by reference to the expectations of the complaining party and not by reference to those of the party complained against.[8] Consequently, the NAFTA provision seems to favour the complaining party more than does the CIFTA provision.[9]

5 This language is distinct from the language used in the Israel-United States Free Trade Area Agreement (1985) 24 I.L.M. 653 [hereinafter Israel-U.S. FTA]. In that agreement, Art. 19 provides that the dispute settlement mechanism applies in cases where measures taken by a party "severely distort the balance of trade benefits." CIFTA parties may have elected not to use this language because of fear that it would not provide clear guidelines as to the level of protection provided since measures can impair benefits while not changing their *balance*. This would occur, for example, when the party invoking the measure and the party against which the measure is taken are affected equally by the measure taken.

6 *Supra* note 2, Annex 2004(1) and *supra* note 1, Annex 8.1(1).

7 *Supra* note 2, Annex 2004(1) and *supra* note 1, Annex 8.1(1).

8 *Ibid.*

9 Here, CIFTA parties chose to follow the Israel-U.S. FTA which in Art. 19:1(a) provides that the benefits protected are those "accorded by [the] Agreement." Thus, like CIFTA, the Israel-U.S. FTA provides a more balanced approach to the benefits the Agreement protects.

Consultation and Co-operation

Both mechanisms require initial consultation. NAFTA Article 2003 requires parties to make every effort through co-operation and consultation to arrive at a mutually satisfactory resolution of any dispute.[10] CIFTA Article 8.6.(2) requires parties to make every attempt to arrive at a mutually agreeable resolution through consultation or other "consultative provisions of th[e] Agreement."[11] Though the language of the two articles is similar, a significant difference exists. NAFTA Article 2006(5)(a) states that consulting parties must provide sufficient information to enable full examination of how a measure might affect the operation of the Agreement. A similar provision under CIFTA requires disclosure of information "pertaining to any actual or proposed measure."[12] The CIFTA provision may prove too general in the future and its disclosure guidelines insufficient. However, this is unlikely, given that CIFTA Article 8.6(2) requires that any information relevant to a complete examination of the complaint must be disclosed. In summary, both mechanisms provide an effective consultation mechanism for resolving a "real" dispute — that is, a dispute in which parties evidence a sincere and substantial disagreement.[13]

THE NAFTA AND THE CIFTA COMMISSIONS

Both the CIFTA and the NAFTA Commissions are composed of senior representatives from the parties, and both are specifically charged with the responsibility of resolving disputes that arise over the interpretation and application of the Agreement in question.[14] Both mechanisms also provide that, should parties fail to resolve a matter within thirty days, a party may request in writing a meeting of the Commission.[15] Under both Agreements, the purpose of such a

[10] *Supra* note 2, Art. 2003. *See* also *supra* note 2, Art. 2006.

[11] *Supra* note 1, Art. 8.6(2).

[12] *Ibid.*, Art. 8.5(5).

[13] Contrasting these two mechanisms is the Israel-U.S. FTA, in which the consultation procedure is less specific. The lack of specificity, particularly regarding time tables, motivates trade officials to keep open channels of communication. However, it could be counterproductive if a party were tempted to stretch the process of consultations indefinitely under the belief that it would gain through delay.

[14] *Supra* note 2, Art. 2001 and *supra* note 1, Art. 8.2. The commissions also have responsibilities that are not related to their dispute resolution mechanisms.

[15] *Supra* note 2, Art. 2007(1) and *supra* note 1, Art. 8.7(1).

meeting is to resolve the dispute and avoid further action.[16] Both Agreements allow their commissions to call on technical advisers.[17] The NAFTA additionally allows its Commission recourse to conciliation, mediation, or any other dispute resolution procedure and to make recommendations necessary to assist parties to reach a mutually satisfactory resolution of the dispute.[18]

The CIFTA Commission's mandate is to resolve the dispute, but a provision allowing the CIFTA Commission to make recommendations does not exist. The CIFTA Commission can call only on technical advisers or on the assistance of a mediator.[19] While both Agreements provide for mediation, CIFTA requires that a mediator be acceptable to both parties.[20] This condition will likely create difficulties, since CIFTA does not prescribe a procedure for appointing a mediator where parties disagree over who will be appointed.

The NAFTA procedure is the more expeditious. The NAFTA Commission must convene within ten days of when a request for a meeting of the Commission is delivered; the CIFTA allows twenty days between delivery and first meeting.[21] Both commissions have thirty days after convening to resolve the dispute before it is referred to an arbitration panel.[22]

Panel Proceedings

If consultations fail and a commission is unable to resolve the dispute, then, upon request of a party, the dispute will be referred to an arbitral panel for resolution. Initiation of the arbitral process is similar under both Agreements. The party requesting arbitration must notify the other of its intention to initiate the panel procedure.[23] The CIFTA deems the delivery date of the notification to the other party to be the date the panel is established.[24] No similar provision exists in the NAFTA Chapter 20 mechanism, although the

16 B. Appleton, *Navigating NAFTA: A Concise User's Guide to the North American Free Trade Agreement* 147 (Scarborough: Carswell, 1994).

17 *Supra* note 2, Art. 2007(5)(a) and *supra* note 1, Art. 8.7(2).

18 *Supra* note 2, Art. 2007(5)(b, c).

19 *Supra* note 1, Art. 8.7(2).

20 *Ibid.*

21 *Supra* note 2, Art. 2008(4) and *supra* note 1, Art. 8.7(1).

22 *Supra* note 2, Art. 2008(1)(a) and *supra* note 1, Art. 8.9(2).

23 *Ibid.*

24 *Supra* note 1, Art. 8.9(2).

timetable for the panel proceedings refers to the delivery of the request as the starting point. The two mechanisms are therefore practically indistinguishable in this respect. This aspect of the procedure is important, since each party must comply with several obligations within a specified time. With a clear starting point, confusion and complaints over expiry of time requirements are minimized.[25]

Composition and Selection of the Panels

The time allowed for panel selection under the NAFTA Chapter 20 mechanism is thirty-five days from the time the panel is established,[26] and under CIFTA is forty-five days.[27] Both mechanisms require a roster of able and willing panellists to be maintained.[28] However, under the NAFTA Chapter 20 mechanism, this roster must be maintained by the parties; under CIFTA, this responsibility falls to the CIFTA Commission. Also, NAFTA Article 2009(1) requires that roster members be appointed by consensus, while the CIFTA Commission is free to appoint roster members by majority. These differences are likely sufficient to facilitate quicker roster formation under CIFTA.[29] Also, although the CIFTA Commission is composed of members of the parties, its mandate is primarily to resolve disputes. This circumstance is not duplicated by the NAFTA Chapter 20 mechanism. NAFTA parties must appoint a roster but are not otherwise compelled to agree on its composition. Furthermore, due to the political interests that inevitably intervene — especially since the parties are not charged to resolve disputes — roster selection runs a longer, more serpentine course. The Commission, being a body with a specific mandate to resolve disputes, is less susceptible to political interests, and the hurdle to the creation of a roster therefore does not require quite the leap that it does for those working under the NAFTA Chapter 20 provisions.

Under the NAFTA Chapter 20 provisions, the panel selection process involves a system by which one party selects two panellists

25 See Y. Baranes, "The Motivations and the Models: A Comparison of the Israel-U.S. Free Trade Agreement and the North American Free Trade Agreement" (1997) 17 New York Law School J. of Int'l and Comp. Law 145.

26 *Supra* note 2, Art. 2011.

27 *Supra* note 1, Annex 8.9(3).

28 *Supra* note 2, Art. 2009 and *supra* note 1, Annex 8.9.

29 Indeed, to this date NAFTA parties have been unable to agree on a roster for NAFTA Chapter 20 dispute settlement mechanisms.

from the nationals of the other's roster. The panel chair is mutually chosen by the parties within fifteen days of the request for a panel.[30] This selection process aims to guarantee high quality and unbiased panellists. Under CIFTA, each disputing party selects one member of the panel, and the selected panellist need not be a citizen of the other party. Although, theoretically, two panellists can be citizens of the same party, this is unlikely to occur because selection is performed through consultation with the other party.[31]

Selection of a chair is somewhat different under the two mechanisms. Under CIFTA, the chair is elected by the CIFTA Commission, while under the NAFTA Chapter 20 mechanism this responsibility falls to the parties.[32] Again, the CIFTA arrangement is the better. Since the CIFTA Commission must focus on candidate qualifications rather than on political interests, a chair will likely be elected more readily by the CIFTA Commission than by party deliberation.

Both Agreements specify a process for electing a chair in case of disagreement. Under the NAFTA Chapter 20 mechanism, if parties do not agree on a chair, "the disputing [p]arty chosen by lot shall select . . . as chair an individual who is not a citizen of that [p]arty."[33] Under CIFTA, if the commission is unable to agree on a chair, the chair is selected by lot from two nominees agreed upon by the parties.[34]

The CIFTA and the NAFTA Chapter 20 mechanism deal similarly with the qualifications and expertise of panellists.[35] Both provide that panellists are to be chosen strictly on grounds of objectivity, reliability, and sound judgment.[36] Both Agreements also require that panellists be independent and that they not be affiliated with,

30 *Supra* note 2, Art. 2011.

31 *Supra* note 1, Annex 8.9(3). This is not the case with the Israel-U.S. FTA, since the process neither prescribes limits to the nationality of the elected panel members nor requires that selection be performed through consultation between the parties. The likely reason for this is that, unlike the negotiators of the Israel-U.S. FTA, the negotiators of CIFTA and NAFTA did not suffer from the misleading belief that disagreements could always be resolved in a conciliatory atmosphere. A strong belief in consultation resulted from the particularly strong political relationship between the U.S. and Israel.

32 *Supra* note 2, Art. 2011 and *supra* note 1, Art. 8.9(3).

33 *Supra* note 2, Art. 2011(1)(b).

34 *Supra* note 1, Annex 8.9(3).

35 *Supra* note 1, Annex 8.9(1) and *supra* note 2, Art. 2009(2)(a).

36 *Ibid.*

or take instruction from, any party.[37] As one minor difference, the NAFTA Chapter 20 mechanism requires each panellist to be an expert or at least be experienced in law, international trade, or dispute resolution under international trade agreements.[38] CIFTA requires expertise of the panellist in the particular matter only where appropriate.[39] CIFTA's use of the words "where appropriate" will likely create impediments to selecting the panellists. The NAFTA provision avoids this risk by demanding expertise and experience from panellists in every dispute. Finally, under both mechanisms, panellists are subject to continuous examination and must comply with codes of conduct established under the respective Agreements.[40]

Rules of Procedure

Under both Agreements, model rules of procedure are established by the commission.[41] Both assure a right to at least one panel hearing and the opportunity to provide initial and rebuttal written submissions.[42] A NAFTA Chapter 20 panel may request information and technical advice from any person or body it deems appropriate, provided that the disputing parties agree to the request.[43] CIFTA provides that technical advisors may be called to assist the CIFTA Commission, but no specific provision allows the CIFTA panel to use such assistance.[44]

Both Agreements provide that any part of the panel's hearings, deliberations, and initial report, and all written submissions to, and communications with, the panel are confidential.[45] Confidentiality is essential to the hearing process. Sensitive information is submitted by the disputing parties to the panel for consideration and must be protected. Furthermore, an arbitration panel is likely to be more

37 *Supra* note 2, Art. 2009(2)(a), (b) and *supra* note 1, Annex 8.9(1).

38 Negotiators of both CIFTA and NAFTA Chapter 20 recognized the importance of the qualifications and expertise of panelists and, unlike the negotiators of the Israel-U.S. FTA, chose to include requirements for them.

39 *Supra* note 1, Annex 8.9(1) and *supra* note 2, Art. 2009 (2) (a).

40 *Supra* note 1, Annex 8.9(6) and *supra* note 2, Art. 2009(2)(c).

41 *Supra* note 2, Art. 2012(1) and *supra* note 1, Art. 8.9(5).

42 *Supra* note 2, Art. 2012(1)(a) and *supra* note 1, Art. 8.9(5)(a).

43 *Supra* note 2, Art. 2014.

44 *Supra* note 1, Art. 8.7(2).

45 *Supra* note 2, Art. 2012(1)(b) and *supra* note 1 Art. 8.9(5)(d).

independent if the personal opinions of the panel members are not subject to close public scrutiny. Confidentiality thus protects panellists in that they cannot be identified with a particular position taken during the deliberations. If the personal opinions of panellists were published, fear of public criticism addressed personally to the panellists might restrict their freedom in expressing thoughts that might not conform with public opinion.

Banning publication of the initial report allows the panel to consider properly the post-initial report comments submitted by the parties regarding the findings and recommendations in the initial report, and paves the way for the panel to make necessary changes in the final report without fear of criticism.

Reports and Decisions

General

Under both mechanisms, panel decisions are not binding under domestic law. That is to say, such decisions do not create new domestic law and are not enforceable through the courts of a losing party.[46] The NAFTA signatories and Israel have strong views on sovereignty and place a high priority on preserving it.[47] The non-binding system of dispute resolution therefore contrasts with the binding system applied in the European Union. Trade decisions can be more effectively enforced under the European system, but at a cost of partially surrendering members sovereignty. NAFTA, like CIFTA, was not designed to create a common market and thus opted for a looser and less intrusive arrangement.[48]

Time and Composition of the Reports

NAFTA Article 2016(2) and CIFTA Article 8.9(6) provide that an initial report must be presented within ninety days after a panel

46 Consequently, under CIFTA and NAFTA Chapter 20, a party can compel a losing party's trade practice to conform to an adverse panel decision only by suspending benefits accorded the losing party that are available as countermeasures by the agreements. Panel decisions requiring concessions from a losing party, therefore, have little prospect of being adhered to if these benefits are of less value than the concessions required.

47 J. R. Johnson, *The North American Free Trade Agreement: A Comprehensive Guide* 4 (Aurora: Canada Law Book, 1994).

48 *Ibid.*

is established.[49] While a NAFTA initial report must be based on submissions and arguments presented by parties and on any expert advice or scientific information placed before the panel,[50] CIFTA does not limit the bases of the initial report. This difference is likely of marginal significance, because a CIFTA panel will naturally limit its findings to any material presented to it during the dispute. Theoretically, however, the CIFTA initial report can be based on any other material available to the panel.

Both NAFTA Article 2016(2) (a, b, and c) and CIFTA Article 8.9(6) require an initial report to include findings of fact, determinations on the validity of the measure at issue, and recommendations for dispute resolution. Under Chapter 20 of NAFTA, a panel has thirty days to prepare and present a final report after presentation of the initial report.[51] Under CIFTA, this time period is sixty days.[52] The NAFTA parties may submit written comments on the initial report to the panel within fourteen days of presentation of the report.[53] CIFTA provides that, within thirty days of issuing the initial report, only a party disagreeing in whole or in part may submit written statements explaining its objections.[54] A party not objecting may do so only on request by the panel or by the CIFTA Commission. This discrepancy between the NAFTA and CIFTA provisions is insignificant because, in practice, only a disagreeing party or parties would submit comments requiring further examination of the issues.

Implementation of Panel Reports

NAFTA Article 2018(1) provides that disputing parties shall resolve the dispute on the basis of the report's findings and

49 The requirement that the panel provide an initial report does not exist in the Israel-U.S. FTA. This is a significant difference. In all three agreements, panel reports are final and not subject to appeal. However, while under both the CIFTA and the NAFTA Chapter 20 mechanism, parties may submit written comments to the panel on the conclusions of the initial report, and by doing so allow the panel to reconsider its initial report and make further examination when needed, under the Israel-U.S. FTA such a possibility does not exist. The one report released by a panel formed under the Israel-U.S. FTA is final and may not be re-examined even when re-examination is manifestly necessary.

50 *Supra* note 2, Art. 2016(1)(2).

51 *Ibid.*, Art. 2017.

52 *Supra* note 1, Art. 8.9(7).

53 *Supra* note 2, Art. 2016(4).

54 *Supra* note 1, Art. 8.9(7).

recommendations.[55] The respective CIFTA provision is slightly different. A report is submitted to the CIFTA Commission and, on receiving it, "the Commission shall agree on the resolution of the dispute which normally shall conform with the report of the panel."[56] Being a separate and independent body, the CIFTA Commission is in a better position than the NAFTA parties to agree on implementation measures. In practice, though, because the CIFTA Commission is composed of officials of the disputing parties, arriving at the required consensus might also prove difficult.[57] Both Agreements provide that disputes shall be resolved by removing a measure not conforming with the Agreement. If this is impossible, the losing party shall compensate the winning party;[58] the losing party decides whether a measure can be removed. Neither Agreement provides guidelines regarding the compensation that a party should pay if it decides to maintain a measure despite recommendations of the panel report. Consequently, the parties may face further difficulties in reaching agreement on this issue.

Publication

The publication of panel reports is important for two reasons. Publicizing a decision allows the winning party to foster sympathetic public opinion among other states as well as within the public of the opposing party.[59] Publication raises public awareness and any consequential public disapproval will pressure a party to conform. Publication also creates and permits the development of trade law. It becomes a factor in the creation of a responsible trade jurisprudence capable of providing guidance for future dispute settlements.[60]

NAFTA Article 2017(4) and CIFTA Article 8.9(8) provide that a panel report shall be published fifteen days after it is transmitted to

55 *Supra* note 2, Art. 2018(1).

56 *Supra* note 1, Art. 8.9(9).

57 *Ibid.*, Art. 8.2(5).

58 *Supra* note 2, Art. 2018(2) and *supra* note 1, Art. 8.9(9).

59 A. Azrieli, "Improving Arbitration under the U.S.-Israel Free Trade Agreement: A Framework for a Middle-East Free Trade Zone" 67 St. John's L. Rev. 187 at 232.

60 *Ibid.*, 233. In contrast to these two agreements, decisions under the Israel-U.S. FTA are not publicized and therefore cannot form part of such trade jurisprudence. It is unclear what the policy was which led the negotiators of the Israel-U.S. FTA to avoid publication of panel reports.

the Commission. CIFTA additionally provides that any separate opinions and any written party submissions shall also be published.[61] Since the initial report remains confidential after the conclusion of any CIFTA dispute, it remains to be seen how the above CIFTA provision will affect this confidentiality. Written views, which are to be published, usually refer to findings in the initial report.

Retaliation

Where a losing party refuses to implement panel recommendations, both Agreements allow the complaining party to suspend the application of benefits of equivalent effect until resolution of the dispute has been attained.[62] The CIFTA and the NAFTA Chapter 20 provisions are essentially identical. Both allow suspension of benefits by the winning party in the sector affected by a measure inconsistent with the obligations of the Agreements, or a measure that causes the nullification or impairment of any benefit that could reasonably be expected to accrue to the winning party.[63] Suspension of benefits in another sector is permitted by both Agreements if the complaining party considers it impractical or ineffective to suspend benefits in the same sector.[64]

Both Agreements provide that, on the written request of a disputing party, a panel may be established to determine whether the level of benefits suspended by the complaining party is manifestly excessive.[65] However, the two Agreements differ on panel composition. While the NAFTA Chapter 20 mechanism requires that a new panel be established, CIFTA specifically instructs the original panel to establish the benefit level.[66] The CIFTA provision seems more

61 *Supra* note 1, Art. 8.9(8).

62 *Supra* note 2, Art. 2019(1) and *supra* note 1, Art. 8.9(10).

63 *Supra* note 2, Art. 2019(2)(a) and *supra* note 1, Art. 8.11(a).

64 *Supra* note 2, Art. 2019(2)(b) and *supra* note 1, Art. 8.11(b).

65 *Supra* note 2, Art. 2019(3) and *supra* note 1, Art. 8.9(12). A system dealing with countermeasures does not exist in the Israel-U.S. FTA. That agreement refers to the issue of countermeasures only in general words by providing in Art. 19:2 that "the affected Party shall be entitled to take any appropriate measure." The Israel-U.S. FTA therefore is less instructive as to the level and kind of benefits that can be suspended. It is unclear who decides what constitutes an appropriate measure, and whether "appropriate" means compensatory in nature or any measure necessarily employed to enforce the other party to implement the panel decision.

66 *Supra* note 2, Art. 2019(3) and *supra* note 1, Art. 8.9(12).

effective for the simple reason that the original panel is familiar with the dispute. Recourse to a new panel under the NAFTA provision is also likely to result in additional costs and time. Finally, both provisions allow sixty days for the determination by the panel.[67] Since the CIFTA procedure involves panellists already familiar with the various aspects of the dispute, it is likely that the sixty-day period will be used more effectively under CIFTA than under NAFTA.

Conclusion

The new dispute resolution mechanism of CIFTA followed the NAFTA Chapter 20 model. Both mechanisms aim at achieving dispute resolution through consultations and arbitration. The resolution mechanisms in both Agreements are products of negotiations that did not suffer from having to account for political considerations. The goal of the negotiators was to achieve a result that ensures high-quality dispute resolution, and a means for re-examining decisions and procedures that guarantees impartiality.

The CIFTA negotiators relied heavily on the wording of the NAFTA Chapter 20 mechanism. In some areas, however, the CIFTA wording intentionally deviates from that of NAFTA Chapter 20. Those differences appear to be of minor significance and are not likely to impair significantly the efficiency of the CIFTA mechanism. In most of these areas, the differences will be reflected in both costs and time consumed in the decision process, but not in the quality of the decisions themselves. However, like NAFTA Chapter 20, CIFTA places time limits on each stage of the dispute settlement process to ensure speedy resolution.

Finally, Canada and Israel are truly committed to embarking on a new and enhanced trade relationship, and the CIFTA dispute resolution mechanism will advance this objective efficiently. NAFTA Chapter 20 provided a model for constructing a new dispute resolution mechanism that is likely to ensure the enforcement and ultimate success of the new trade agreement between Canada and Israel.

Yair Baranes
Faculty of Law, University of Saskatchewan

67 *Supra* note 2, Art. 2019(4) and *supra* note 1, Art. 8.9(13).

Sommaire

Une comparaison des régimes de règlement des différends du chapitre 20 de l'ALÉNA et de l'Accord de libre échange Canada-Israël

L'Accord de libre échange Canada-Israël suit le modèle de règlement des différends du chapitre 20 de l'ALÉNA: il existe donc plusieurs similarités entre les deux régimes. Touefois, dans certains domaines comme les consultations et la composition des Panels d'arbitrage, le régime de règlement des différends de l'Accord Canada-Israël diffère clairement de celui prévu à l'ALÉNA.

Summary

Following Suit: A Comparison of Dispute Resolution Mechanisms under NAFTA Chapter 20 and the Canada-Israel Free Trade Agreement

The Free Trade Agreement between Canada and Israel bases its dispute settlement mechanism on Chapter 20 of NAFTA. There are accordingly many similarities between the two regimes. In certain areas, however, such as consultations and Panel composition, the Canada-Israel dispute settlement regime was clearly intended to differ from the NAFTA regime.

Maxwell Cohen
(1910-1998)

IT IS WITH GREAT SADNESS that we record the passing of one of the founding editors of this *Yearbook* and one of the leaders in international law in Canada. Maxwell Cohen contributed the first article to the first volume of the *Canadian Yearbook of International Law*, entitled, "Some Main Directions of International Law: A Canadian Perspective." In it, he surveyed the state of international law practice and scholarship of the time, touching on such issues as boundary rivers, ocean resources, federalism, and the Arctic, and moving more broadly to the United Nations Charter and developments in international organization, to new states in international law, and to developments in economic regulation.

Twenty-five years later, Maxwell Cohen contributed the opening article to the *Yearbook*, returning to the theme of international law in Canada ("The Canadian Yearbook and International Law in Canada after Twenty-Five Years"). Both of these opening articles in the *Yearbook* are quintessentially Cohen — the breadth of interest, the felicitous phrase, the intertwining of the global and the local, and the ability to look ahead and see what existing trends mean for the future. Throughout his career, Maxwell Cohen as scholar and legal practitioner observed the events taking place in the international field and provided insights for us into what they might mean.

Maxwell Cohen was a man of ideas and imagination, a provocative writer, a stimulating colleague, and a humane and passionate believer in the importance of the discipline and practice of international law. His contributions were prodigious and his loss leaves a great gap in the field in Canada. He was a faithful member of the Editorial Board of the *Yearbook* and he will be missed by us all.

Maxwell Cohen's career in its many aspects has been chronicled by Professor R. St. J. Macdonald ("Maxwell Cohen at Eighty: International Lawyer, Educator, and Judge") in the *Canadian Yearbook of International Law*, vol. 27 at pages 3-56.

The Editors

Chronique de Droit international économique en 1996 / Digest of International Economic Law in 1996

I Commerce

préparé par
SOPHIE DUFOUR

LE PROCESSUS D'OUVERTURE DES frontières a franchi de nouveaux sommets au cours des années 1995 et 1996. Que ce soit au sein de l'Accord de libre-échange nord-américain (ci-après ALÉNA),[1] de l'Organisation mondiale du commerce (ci-après OMC)[2] ou de la zone de libre-échange des Amériques envisagée d'ici l'an 2005, le Canada a grandement contribué à ce processus, tel que nous le verrons dans les paragraphes qui suivent.

I L'ALÉNA DANS UNE PERSPECTIVE CANADIENNE: LES ÉVÉNEMENTS MARQUANTS SURVENUS EN 1995 et 1996

L'entrée en vigueur de l'ALÉNA, le 1er janvier 1994, s'est traduite par une augmentation significative des exportations canadiennes sur les sols américains et mexicains. Déjà, à la fin de 1994, celles-ci

Sophie Dufour est avocate, professeure à la Faculté de droit de l'Université de Sherbrooke (LL.B., Université Laval, Québec; LL.M., Osgoode Hall School of Law, York University, Ontario; LL.M., University of Cambridge, Angleterre; LL.D., Université Laval, Québec).

1 Accord de libre-échange nord-américain entre le gouvernement du Canada, le gouvernement des États-Unis d'Amérique et le gouvernement des États-Unis du Mexique, 17 décembre 1992, Ottawa, Approvisionnements et Services Canada, 1992 [ci-après *ALÉNA*].

2 Accord de Marrakech instituant l'Organisation mondiale du commerce, dans GATT, *Résultats des négociations commerciales multilatérales du cycle d'Uruguay — Textes juridiques*, Genève, GATT, 1994 aux pp. 6 et s. [ci-après *Accord sur l'OMC*].

affichaient une hausse respective de 22 et 31 pour cent.[3] Un an plus tard, elles croissaient à nouveau, de l'ordre de 13,9 pour cent vers les États-Unis et de l'ordre de 5,4 pour cent vers le Mexique et ce, malgré les rebondissements économiques subis par ce dernier en raison de la crise du peso, survenue au mois de décembre 1994.[4] Cette croissance s'est poursuivie en 1996: les exportations canadiennes destinées au marché américain augmentaient de 6 pour cent pour atteindre 223,5 milliards de dollars,[5] tandis que celles à destination des marchés mexicains connaissaient une hausse de 5,3 pour cent pour s'établir à 1,2 milliards de dollars.[6] Les importations canadiennes de marchandises en provenance des États-Unis et du Mexique ont, elles aussi, connu une augmentation importante. En effet, entre 1993 et 1996, les ventes américaines au Canada se sont accrues de 38 pour cent[7] tandis que celles originant du Mexique ont augmenté de 60 pour cent.[8] Tout en demeurant les principaux fournisseurs étrangers du Canada, les Américains ont dû laisser une place aux Mexicains qui occupent désormais le quatrième rang à cet égard.[9] Plus globalement, on peut noter qu'au cours des trois premières années de vie de l'ALÉNA, les échanges commerciaux entre les trois pays signataires ont connu une hausse significative de 13,8 pour cent.[10]

Il va sans dire que les règles adoptées dans le cadre de l'ALÉNA ont grandement contribué à clarifier les termes des échanges commerciaux intervenus entre les États-Unis, le Mexique et le Canada. L'existence de ces règles n'a toutefois pas réussi à empêcher la survenance de différends à l'intérieur de la zone nord-américaine de libre-échange au cours des trois premières années d'existence de l'accord. En pareilles situations, l'ALÉNA prévoit que les gouvernements concernés doivent s'efforcer de résoudre leur conflit à

3 Canada, Ministère des Affaires extérieures et du Commerce international, *L'ALÉNA et ce qu'il représente pour les investisseurs au Canada*, Ottawa, décembre 1996 à la p. 3.

4 *Ibid.*

5 Canada, Ministère des Affaires extérieures et du Commerce international, *ALÉNA: un partenariat au travail*, Ottawa, juin 1997 à la p. 5 [ci-après *ALÉNA: un partenariat au travail*].

6 *Ibid.* aux pp. 7-8.

7 *Ibid.* à la p. 5.

8 *Ibid.* aux pp. 6-7.

9 *Ibid.* à la p. 6.

10 *Ibid.* à la p. 4.

l'amiable. En cas d'échec des pourparlers, ces derniers doivent soumettre leur différend à un groupe spécial arbitral en vue d'en arriver plus rapidement et efficacement à un règlement.

Les dispositions du chapitre XIX de l'ALÉNA, applicables dans le cas où le différend porte sur la question de savoir si des droits antidumping ou compensateurs imposés par un partenaire de l'ALÉNA l'ont été en conformité avec ses lois nationales en la matière,[11] ont été invoquées à soixante-treize reprises[12] entre 1989 et 1996,[13] dans le cadre de la soumission de demandes d'examen par des groupes spéciaux arbitraux.

Prévue, pour sa part, au chapitre XX de l'ALÉNA, la procédure générale de règlement des différends liés à l'interprétation ou à l'application de l'accord avait fait l'objet de onze demandes de consultations à la fin de 1996.[14] Seule une d'entre elles a conduit à une décision du groupe spécial arbitral appelé à se prononcer sur la question soumise. Il s'agit de l'affaire concernant *Les tarifs appliqués par le Canada sur certains produits agricoles.*[15]

A LES TARIFS APPLIQUÉS PAR LE CANADA SUR CERTAINS PRODUITS AGRICOLES

Dans cette affaire, les États-Unis ont soutenu que les droits de douane désormais appliqués par le Canada sur certains produits agricoles originant de la zone de libre-échange nord américaine — produits laitiers, produits de la volaille, ovoproduits — excédaient les taux acceptés par ce dernier aux termes des dispositions de l'ALÉNA. Dès le 1er janvier 1995, le Canada a en effet commencé à transformer en équivalents tarifaires, à des taux variant entre 200 % et 300 %, les barrières non tarifaires appliquées aux produits du lait, de la volaille et des oeufs importés sur les marchés canadiens. Ce processus de transformation, plus couramment appelé tarification dans le jargon commercial international agricole, ne fait que

11 ALÉNA, *supra* note 1, art. 1904.2.

12 *ALÉNA: un partenariat au travail, supra* note 5 à la p. 3.

13 Il importe de se rappeler que les dispositions du c. XIX de l'ALÉNA s'inspirent en grande partie de celles prévues au même chapitre de l'Accord de libre-échange canado-américain (*Accord de libre-échange entre le Canada et les États-Unis d'Amérique,* 22 décembre 1987, R.T. Can. 1989 n° 3, c. 7 [ci-après ALÉ].

14 *ALÉNA: un partenariat au travail, supra* note 5 à la p. 3.

15 *Les tarifs appliqués par le Canada sur certains produits agricoles en provenance des États-Unis d'Amérique* (2 décembre 1996), CDA-95-2008-01 (c. 20 Groupe spécial) [ci-après *Les tarifs appliqués par le Canada sur certains produits agricoles*].

traduire l'engagement assumé par le Canada dans le cadre de l'Accord sur l'agriculture résultant des négociations commerciales multilatérales du cycle d'Uruguay (ci-après Accord sur l'agriculture).[16] En effet, aux termes des prescriptions de l'article 4.2 de cet accord,[17] les pays membres de l'OMC se sont engagés à ne plus imposer de restrictions à l'importation à l'encontre de produits agricoles étrangers afin de protéger la production agricole nationale. Seules les barrières tarifaires peuvent désormais être utilisées à cette fin. Or, en vertu de l'article 302 de l'ALÉNA, les parties se sont engagées à ne pas augmenter les droits de douane existants et imposés sur les produits originaires importés.[18]

Conformément à l'article 2006(4) de l'ALÉNA, les États-Unis entreprennent des discussions avec le Canada, dès le 2 février 1995, afin de résoudre ce conflit apparent entre l'article 302 de l'ALÉNA et l'article 4.2 de l'Accord sur l'agriculture.[19] Ces discussions se soldent cependant par un échec. Les États-Unis requièrent donc l'assistance de la Commission sur le libre-échange, suivant les termes de l'article 2007 de l'ALÉNA.[20] Aucun résultat positif ne résulte non plus de cette seconde démarche. En conséquence, au mois de juillet 1995, les États-Unis demandent la formation d'un comité d'arbitrage, conformément à l'article 2008 de l'ALÉNA. Constitué le 19 janvier 1996, le Comité s'efforce de résoudre la question à l'origine du conflit entre les États-Unis et le Canada. Celle-ci est formulée comme suit: "La question est de savoir si les droits de douanes imposés par le Canada sur certains produits agricoles en provenance des É.-U. pour raison de 'tarification,' conformément aux accords conclus lors des négociations d'Uruguay, enfreignent les clauses pertinentes de l'ALÉNA."[21]

16 Accord sur l'agriculture, dans GATT, *Résultats des négociations commerciales multilatérales du cycle d'Uruguay — Textes juridiques*, Genève, GATT, 1994 aux pp. 40 et s.

17 L'article 4.2 de l'*accord sure l'agriculture* est à l'effet suivant "[l]es Membres ne maintiendront pas de mesures du type de celles qui ont dû être converties en droits de douane proprement dits, ni ne recourront ni ne reviendront à de telles mesures, exception faite de ce qui est prévu à l'article 5 et à l'Annexe 5" [note de bas de page omise].

18 L'article 302(1) de l'ALÉNA se lit comme suit: "[s]auf disposition contraire du présent accord, aucune des Parties ne pourra augmenter un droit de douane existant, ni instituer un droit de douane à l'égard d'un produit originaire" (ALÉNA, *Supra* note 1).

19 *Les tarifs appliqués par le Canada sur certains produits agricoles*, *supra* note 15, par. 1.

20 *Ibid.*, par. 2.

21 *Ibid.*, par. 113.

Le Comité établit le point de départ de son analyse sur la base de l'article 710 de l'Accord de libre-échange canado-américain (ci-après ALÉ), lequel est incorporé à l'ALÉNA par le biais des paragraphes 1 et 4 de l'Annexe 702.1 de l'ALÉNA.[22] L'article 710 de l'ALÉ est à l'effet suivant:

> À moins de conventions contraires spécifiquement présentées dans ce Chapitre, les Parties conservent leurs droits et obligations concernant les produits agricoles, les aliments, les boissons et certains produits connexes en vertu de l'Accord général sur les tarifs douaniers et le commerce (GATT) et des accords négociés en vertu du GATT, y compris leurs droits et obligations en vertu de l'Article XI du GATT.[23]

Sur la base de l'article 102(2) de l'ALÉNA[24] et des articles 31 et 32 de la *Convention de Vienne sur le droit des traités de* 1969,[25] le Comité conclut que les termes de l'article 710 sont de nature prospective, c'est-à-dire qu'ils doivent être interprétés, non pas à la lumière des termes tels qu'ils existaient au moment de l'entrée en vigueur de l'ALÉ, mais tels qu'ils se sont développés à la suite des résultats des négociations commerciales multilatérales du cycle d'Uruguay.[26]

L'effet de l'article 710 de l'ALÉ est donc d'incorporer dans l'ALÉNA l'obligation qu'ont les parties, aux termes de l'article 4.2 de l'Accord sur l'agriculture, d'éliminer les barrières non tarifaires agricoles et de les remplacer par des équivalents tarifaires. Il en résulte une contradiction entre cette disposition et l'article 302(1) de l'ALÉNA, lequel, rappelons-le, interdit aux parties de relever

22 ALÉNA, *supra* note 1, par. 1 et 4 de l'Annexe 702.1: "1. Les articles 701, 702, 704, 705, 706, 707, 710 et 711 de l'*Accord de libre-échange entre le Canada et les États-Unis,* qui sont incorporés dans le présent accord et en font partie intégrante, s'appliquent entre le Canada et les États-Unis . . . 4. Les Parties reconnaissent que l'article 710 de l'*Accord de libre-échange entre le Canada et les États-Unis* incorpore les droits et obligations du Canada et des États-Unis au titre de l'Accord général en ce qui concerne les produits agricoles, les produits alimentaires, les boissons et certains produits connexes, y compris les exemptions prévues à l'alinéa (1)b) du Protocole portant application provisoire de l'Accord général et les dérogations accordées en vertu de l'article XXV de l'Accord général."

23 ALÉ, *supra* note 13.

24 ALÉNA, *supra* note 1, art. 102(2): "[l]es Parties interpréteront et appliqueront les clauses de cet accord à la lumière de ses objectifs établis au paragraphe 1 et conformément aux règlements applicables au droit international."

25 *Convention de Vienne sur le droit des traités,* 22 mai 1969, 1980 n° 37.

26 *Les tarifs appliqués par le Canada sur certains produits agricoles, supra* note 15, par. 118-24, 132-45.

leurs droits de douane existants.[27] L'article 710 de l'ALÉ doit, en pareil cas, avoir préséance sur l'article 302(1) de l'ALÉNA. Tel se dégage-t-il, en effet, de l'article 701(2) de l'ALÉNA, suivant lequel: "En cas d'incompatibilité entre la présente section et toute autre disposition du présent accord, la présente section l'emportera dans la mesure de l'incompatibilité."[28]

Par cette décision, rendue le 2 décembre 1996, le Comité d'arbitrage a ainsi donné raison au Canada en ces termes: "l'application de droits de douanes par le Gouvernement du Canada sur les produits agricoles en provenance des É.-U. est conforme aux dispositions de l'Accord de libre-échange nord-américain."[29] La réaction des États-Unis ne s'est pas fait attendre. La Représentante américaine du commerce, Charlene Barshefsky, et le Secrétaire américain à l'agriculture, Dan Glickman, ont, le jour même de la publication de la décision du Comité, émis une déclaration conjointe à l'effet suivant: "We are deeply disappointed that the panel supported Canada's view that it could apply extremely high tariff rates to imports of dairy, poultry, egg, barley and margarine products from the United States. The United States will do everything possible, consistent with our trade laws, to seek the ultimate elimination of these duties and to improve U.S. access to the Canadian market for dairy, poultry, egg, barley and margarine products."[30]

B LA SAGA DE L'ENTREPRISE AMÉRICAINE COUNTRY MUSIC TELEVISION

Depuis 1984,[31] Country Music Television (ci-après CMT), un service américain de télévision de musique *country* établi à Nashville (États-Unis), rejoint près de deux millions de foyers canadiens par l'entremise de 450 câblodistributeurs canadiens. CMT a ainsi assuré la promotion de nombreux artistes américains et canadiens,

27 Voir *supra* note 18 et texte correspondant.

28 ALÉNA, *supra* note 1.

29 *Les tarifs appliqués par le Canada sur certains produits agricoles*, *supra* note 15, par. 209.

30 United States, Office of the United States Representative, Executive Office of the President, *Joint Statement of the Acting U.S. Trade Representative and the Secretary of Agriculture Regarding Release of the NAFTA Panel Report on Canadian Agriculture Tariffs*, Washington, DC, 2 décembre 1996.

31 Canada, Conseil de la radiodiffusion et des télécommunications canadiennes, *Liste révisée de services spécialisés non-canadiens éligibles*, Ottawa, 11 juin 1984, Annexe.

non seulement sur le marché nord-américain mais, également, sur les marchés asiatiques, européens et latino-américains où il est également présent. Toutefois, depuis le 1er janvier 1995, les câblodistributeurs canadiens ne peuvent plus transmettre la programmation de CMT à leurs abonnés. Cette restriction imposée à l'endroit de CMT résulte d'une décision rendue le 6 juin 1994 par le Conseil de la radiotélévision et des télécommunications canadiennes (ci-après CRTC)[32] dans le cadre de laquelle ce dernier a octroyé une licence de radiodiffusion à New Country Network (ci-après NCN), un nouveau service canadien de télévision de musique *country* sur le marché canadien. Dans cette décision, le CRTC a, du même coup, retiré à CMT le droit qui lui avait été octroyé, dix ans auparavant, de diffuser ses programmes sur les marchés canadiens.[33] Ce retrait est demandé par NCN, qui n'est pas sans éprouver certaines inquiétudes à l'idée de devoir faire concurrence à CMT à compter du 1er janvier 1995, date de l'entrée en vigueur de sa licence d'exploitation.[34] Le CRTC, en faisant droit à la demande de NCN, agit en conformité avec sa politique applicable à l'endroit des services par satellite télédistribués par des entreprises étrangères admissibles, telles CMT: "[L]e Conseil a pour politique de se réserver le droit d'annuler l'autorisation de télédistribuer le service non-canadien dans les cas où il autorise un service canadien selon une formule qui entre en concurrence avec celle d'un service par satellite non-canadien autorisé."[35]

Le 6 février 1995, le Représentant du commerce des États-Unis, Mickey Kantor, décide d'entreprendre une enquête, aux termes de l'article 301 de la Loi sur le commerce de 1974,[36] à la demande de CMT, en vue de déterminer si la politique du CRTC consistant à refuser l'accès des marchés canadiens aux services de télévision non-canadiens concurrençant directement un service de télévision canadien est déraisonnable et constitue un fardeau et une restriction au

32 Canada, Conseil de la radiodiffusion et des télécommunications canadiennes, *Approbation du service de vidéoclips de musique country "The Country Network,"* Décision CRTC 94-284, Ottawa, 6 juin 1994 [ci-après *Décision CRTC 94-284*].

33 Canada, Conseil de la radiodiffusion et des télécommunications canadiennes, *Liste révisée des services par satellite admissibles,* Avis CRTC n° 1994-61, Ottawa, 6 juin 1994.

34 Décision CRTC 94-284, *supra* note 32 à la p. 5.

35 *Ibid.*

36 United States, *Trade Act of* 1974, Pub. L. n° 93-618, sanctionnée le 3 janvier 1975, cod. à 19 U.S.C. 2411 [ci-après *Trade Act of* 1974].

commerce américain.[37] En annonçant cette décision, Mickey Kantor a déclaré:

We consider the action taken against CMT to be a very serious matter. The CRTC's action amounted to the confiscation of CMT's business efforts over the past ten years to serve the Canadian market. We know of no other comparable action taken in other markets our industry serves and are especially concerned by such treatment in Canada . . . Canadian government support for the arts is a noble and worthwhile policy objective. However, it cannot be effectively achieved by discriminating against U.S. interests or by discouraging U.S. investment in Canada. CMT has given extraordinary exposure to Canadian artists in North America and Europe. While our principal concern is for U.S. interests, the CRTC action has also armed the interests of Canadian artists. The practice is as counterproductive as it is discriminatory.[38]

Le 22 juin 1995, les deux parties concernées, CMT et NCN, annoncent néanmoins avoir réussi à conclure un accord de principe en vue de mettre fin à leur différend et ce, par le biais de la formation d'un service canadien et unifié de télévision de music *country* portant le nom de *Country Music Television (Canada)*.[39] Aucune action en représailles n'est prise par le Bureau du représentant du commerce des États-Unis (ci-après USTR) bien que le 21 juin 1995 ait été fixé comme date ultime pour le déclenchement d'une telle action, dans le cas où aucun progrès n'aurait été réalisé pour mettre un terme à ce différend.[40] Les parties s'engagent à finaliser leur entente avant le 6 février 1996, date à partir de laquelle le USTR a le pouvoir de rendre une décision en vertu de l'article 301 à l'égard de la politique du CRTC relative aux services par satellite télédistribués par des entreprises non-canadiennes.

Le 6 février 1996, le USTR indique avoir déterminé, conformément à l'article 301, que ladite politique du CRTC est, à sa face

37 United States, Office of the United States Representative, Executive Office of the President, *USTR Kantor Announces* 301 Investigation of Certain Discriminatory Canadian Communications Practices, Washington, DC, 6 février 1995.

38 *Ibid.*

39 United States, Office of the United States Representative, Executive Office of the President, *Ambassador Kantor Announces Commercial Settlement in the U.S.-Canada Country Music Television Dispute*, Washington, DC, 22 juin 1995. En vertu de cet accord de principe, le nouveau service serait désormais accessible à près de six millions de foyers canadiens (*Ibid.*).

40 *Ibid.*

même, discriminatoire.[41] Cependant, étant donné l'avancement des pourparlers entre les parties concernées en vue de la création d'un service de télévision canadien et unifié de musique *country*, toute idée d'exercer une action en représailles contre le Canada est désormais écartée.[42] Une entente est effectivement signée entre CMT et NCN le 7 mars 1996, créant ainsi le service de télévision *Country Music Televison (Canada)*.[43] En annonçant la fin de ce différend, le Représentant du commerce américain, Mickey Kantor, s'est exprimé comme suit: "The only acceptable resolution of this issue was to restore Country Music Television's access to the Canadian market. This Administration will not tolerate discrimination against any U.S. industry. It is of special concern when it involves Canada, one of our largest export makets and our FTA partner."[44]

La résolution de ce conflit commercial ne suffit cependant pas à apaiser les craintes de l'administration Clinton, laquelle demeure préoccupée par la politique de radiodiffusion appliquée par le Canada. Cette politique est, en effet, clairement discriminatoire à l'égard des services non-canadiens. Pour cette raison, le USTR a décidé de continuer, conformément aux prescriptions de l'article 301, de surveiller non seulement la mise en oeuvre de l'entente relative à *Country Music Television (Canada)* par le gouvernement canadien mais, également, toute action susceptible d'être prise par ce dernier à l'endroit d'autres services américains de télévision visant à obtenir l'autorisation de distribuer leur programmation au Canada.[45]

C L'ENTENTE DE RECONNAISSANCE DES SERVICES DE GÉNIE ENTRE LES TROIS PARTENAIRES

Entre temps, le 5 juin 1995, les représentants des corporations américaines, canadiennes et mexicaines des ingénieurs signaient une entente historique sur les exigences requises en matière

41 United States, Office of the United States Representative, Executive Office of the President, *USTR Announces Determinations in Country Music Television Section* 301 Investigation of Canadian Broadcasting Policies, Washington, DC, 6 février 1996.

42 *Ibid.*

43 United States, Office of the United States Representative, Executive Office of the President, *USTR Announces Commercial Agreement in the U.S.-Canada Country Music Television Dispute*, Washington, DC, 6 février 1996.

44 *Ibid.*

45 *Ibid.*

d'octroi de permis de travail, temporaire ou permanent, dans les trois pays.[46] Il s'agit là du premier accord de reconnaissance mutuelle de services professionnels résultant des dispositions du chapitre 12 de L'ALÉNA.

Aux termes de la section A de l'Annexe 1210.5 du chapitre 12 de l'ALÉNA, les corporations professionnelles des trois pays sont encouragées à signer des ententes de reconnaissance mutuelle de leurs services.[47] Des dispositions spécifiques ont par ailleurs été prévues en vue de permettre aux ingénieurs d'exercer leur profession à titre temporaire sur le territoire des trois États.[48] La conjonction de ces dispositions conduit ainsi le United States Council for International Engineering Practice, le Conseil canadien des ingénieurs et le Comite Mexicano para la Practica Internacional de la Ingenierall à la conclusion de ladite entente.

Lors de la cérémonie de signature de l'entente, le Représentant du commerce américain, M. Kantor, a félicité les ingénieurs des trois pays d'avoir mené à terme cette négociation. Suivant ses termes: "Both the NAFTA and the GATS (the General Agreement on Trade in Services) seek to make it easier for professionals in one country to practice in another either temporarily or on a long-term basis. This is a success story and we all want to be . . . recognized as such."[49]

De fait, une telle entente devrait assurer une plus grande mobilité des ingénieurs sur le marché nord-américain. Cependant, son

[46] United States, Office of the United States Representative, Executive Office of the President, *USTR Announces Mutual Recognition Agreement Reached by Engineers under NAFTA*, Washington, DC, 5 juin 1995 [ci-après *Recognition Agreement Reached by Engineers under NAFTA*].

[47] ALÉNA, *supra* note 1, par. 2, section A de l'Annexe 1210.5: "[l]es Parties encourageront les organismes compétents sur leurs territoires respectifs à élaborer des normes et des critères mutuellement acceptables relativement à l'autorisation d'exercer et à la reconnaissance professionnelle des fournisseurs de services professionnels, et à présenter à la Commission [du libre-échange] des recommandations visant la reconnaissance mutuelle."

[48] *Ibid.*, par. 1, section C de l'Annexe 1210.5: "[l]es Parties se rencontreront dans un délai d'un an à compter de la date d'entrée en vigueur du présent accord en vue d'établir un programme de travail que chacune des Parties devra entreprendre, de concert avec ses organismes compétents, dans le but d'accorder l'autorisation d'exercer à titre temporaire sur son territoire aux ressortissants d'une autre Partie qui sont habilités à exercer comme ingénieurs sur le territoire de cette autre Partie."

[49] *Recognition Agreement Reached by Engineers under NAFTA*, *supra* note 46.

entrée en vigueur est conditionnelle à sa ratification par les gouvernements étatiques et provinciaux des États-Unis et du Canada, lesquels ont compétence sur la question des permis de travail de leurs ingénieurs.

D L'ENTENTE CANADO-AMÉRICAINE SUR LE BOIS D'OEUVRE DU 16 FÉVRIER 1996

Les relations canado-américaines ont enfin connu un dénouement majeur, le 16 février 1996, à la suite de la conclusion d'une entente de principe entre le gouvernement du Canada et le gouvernement des États-Unis visant à mettre un terme au différend concernant les exportations canadiennes de bois d'oeuvre sur le marché américain.[50] Fruit de négociations amorcées à partir du mois de décembre 1994, cette entente, entrée en vigueur le 1er avril 1996, comporte quatre objectifs principaux:

- Favoriser une croissance stable dans le marché nord-américain du bois d'oeuvre;
- Réduire les exportations canadiennes de bois d'oeuvre aux États-Unis de manière à maintenir les importations américaines de bois d'oeuvre canadien à des niveaux historiques;[51]
- Assurer un accès continu au marché américain aux producteurs canadiens de bois d'oeuvre; et
- Permettre aux Américains l'accès au bois d'oeuvre canadien dans les périodes de forte demande.[52]

Lors de l'annonce de la conclusion de cette entente, le Représentant du commerce des États-Unis a émis la déclaration suivante, qui

50 United States, Office of the United States Representative, Executive Office of the President, *U.S. and Canada Reach Agreement on Softwood Lumber*, Washington, DC, 16 février 1996 [ci-après *U.S. and Canada Reach Agreement on Softwood Lumber*].

51 *Ibid.* à la p. 2. Les importations canadiennes de bois d'oeuvre aux États-Unis occupaient, en 1995, 36 pour cent du marché américain, comparativement à 27 pour cent en 1991. Sur la période 1993-95, le volume des importations canadiennes a, quant à lui, augmenté de plus de 12 pour cent. Déjà grandement affectée par cette situation, l'industrie américaine de bois d'oeuvre a perdu encore quelques points sur le marché entre décembre 1994 et juin 1995. Pour les producteurs américains, cela correspond à plus de 400 millions de dollars de pertes de ventes. La croissance des importations américaines de bois d'oeuvre s'est par ailleurs traduite par une chute du prix du produit. Entre janvier 1994 et juin 1995, le prix est passé de 475 $ à 292 $ par 1000 pi² (mesure de planche).

52 *Ibid.* à la p. 1.

n'est pas sans révéler l'importance qu'a pris le dossier du bois d'oeuvre dans l'agenda des gouvernements canadien et américain au cours de la décennie 1986-1996: "The Agreement represents the culmination of a more than year-long effort by both countries to resolve our differences and avoid further acrimony over this long-standing bilateral dispute. There was no higher priority for our bilateral trade relationship with Canada than seeing these negotiations succeed. Our ability to do so is an historic accomplishment and clearly demonstrates the tremendous commitment we share to maintain our strong trading relationship."[53]

L'Administration Clinton s'est engagée à surveiller de très près la mise en oeuvre de cette entente. Toute faille dans son fonctionnement pourrait se traduire par les actions suivantes de la part du gouvernement américain:

- Institution d'une action commerciale en vertu de l'article 301 de la Loi sur le commerce de 1974[54] contre les importations canadiennes de bois d'oeuvre;

[53] *Ibid.* Déjà, en 1986, les États-Unis et le Canada avaient cherché à résoudre leur différend en concluant un Mémorandum d'entente en vertu duquel le Canada s'engageait à appliquer une taxe à l'exportation du bois d'oeuvre résineux vers les États-Unis de 15 pour cent jusqu'à ce que les provinces productrices visées aient ajusté certaines pratiques en matière de droits de coupe, assimilées par les Américains à des subventions. En 1991, le Canada met cependant fin, unilatéralement, au Mémorandum. Du même coup, le USTR initie une enquête visant à déterminer si les producteurs canadiens de bois d'oeuvre bénéficient de subventions. Deux décisions sont rendues par le USTR, l'une concluant à l'existence d'un préjudice, l'autre ordonnant l'imposition de droits compensateurs à l'encontre du bois d'oeuvre canadien exporté aux États-Unis. Le Canada interjette appel de ses deux décisions en vertu de la procédure de règlement des différends du c. 19 de l'ALÉ. Dans l'affaire *Certains produits de bois d'oeuvre du Canada,* USA-92-1904-02 (c. 19 Groupe spéc.), le groupe spécial, à l'unanimité, renvoie à trois reprises la décision du USTR sur le préjudice, confirmant ultimement une partie de la décision issue du renvoi. Le groupe spécial met fin à sa révision le 27 janvier 1995. Dans l'affaire *Certains produits de bois d'oeuvre du Canada,* USA-92-1904-01 (c. 19 Groupe spéc.), le groupe spécial renverse, par deux fois, avec deux dissidences chacune, la décision du USTR sur les droits compensateurs. Une demande est déposée par les États-Unis, aux termes de l'art. 1904.13 de l'ALÉ, afin d'instituer un comité pour contestation extraordinaire (*Certains produits de bois d'oeuvre du Canada,* CCE-1904-01USA (Comité con. extr.)). Le Comité, avec une dissidence, rejette la demande américaine et confirme les décisions du groupe spécial.

[54] *Trade Act of* 1974, supra note 36.

- Imposition immédiate de tarifs douaniers accrus sur les importations canadiennes de bois d'oeuvre;[55] et
- Imposition d'une caution en garantie sur toutes les importations canadiennes de bois d'oeuvre afin d'assurer la perception des tarifs douaniers.[56]

II L'implication du Canada sur la scène commerciale internationale au cours des années 1995 et 1996

A L'entrée en vigueur de l'OMC le 1er janvier 1995

La scène commerciale multilatérale a été marquée par un événement marquant en 1995, soit l'entrée en vigueur de l'OMC, le 1er janvier. Issue des négociations commerciales multilatérales du cycle d'Uruguay, l'OMC vient remplacer le Secrétariat de l'Accord général sur les tarifs douaniers et le commerce (ci-après GATT ou GATT de 1994)[57] et devient, pour ainsi dire, le socle sur lequel se fonde désormais le système commercial multilatéral.

Le Secrétariat de l'OMC, où travaillent environ 450 fonctionnaires, tous nationaux des pays membres, se trouve toujours à Genève, à l'instar de son prédécesseur. Élu pour une période de quatre ans, le Directeur général de l'OMC, Renato Ruggiero, est entré en fonction le 1er mai 1995. Le budget de l'OMC est évalué annuellement à environ 83 millions de dollars. Les contributions de chaque pays sont calculées sur la base de la part qu'il représente dans le volume total des échanges des membres.

L'OMC a essentiellement pour mission d'administrer et de mettre en oeuvre les accords commerciaux multilatéraux et plurilatéraux issus du cycle d'Uruguay; d'être une instance pour les négociations commerciales multilatérales; de régler les différends commerciaux; de surveiller les politiques commerciales des pays membres; et de coopérer avec les autres institutions internationales participant à l'élaboration des politiques économiques mondiales.

L'Accord de Marrakech instituant l'OMC (ci-après Accord sur l'OMC)[58] comporte tout juste seize dispositions. Il est composé de

55 Leur perception serait toutefois suspendue jusqu'à ce qu'une détermination de leur montant soit établie dans le cadre d'une enquête du USTR, instituée à la demande de l'industrie américaine de bois d'oeuvre.

56 *U.S. and Canada Reach Agreement on Softwood Lumber*, *supra* note 50 à la p. 3.

57 Accord général sur les tarifs douaniers et le commerce, 1er janvier 1948, R.T. Can. 1948 n° 31, dans GATT, *Résultats des négociations commerciales multilatérales du cycle d'Uruguay — Textes juridiques*, Genève, GATT, 1994 aux pp. 511et s. [ci-après *GATT de 1994*].

58 Accord sur l'OMC, *supra* note 2.

quatre annexes,[59] lesquelles contiennent les accords obtenus lors du cycle d'Uruguay en matière de marchandises[60] de services[61] et de droits de la propriété intellectuelle;[62] de règles et procédures régissant le règlement des différends;[63] de mécanisme d'examen des politiques commerciales;[64] d'autres accords commerciaux sur les aéronefs civils, sur les marchés publics, sur le secteur laitier et sur la viande bovine.[65]

Deux règles d'interprétation existent afin de déterminer le rang des sources juridiques contenues dans l'Accord sur l'OMC. D'abord, tout conflit entre l'Accord sur l'OMC et un accord multilatéral inséré en annexe doit être résolu en accordant la préséance à l'Accord sur l'OMC.[66] La priorité doit par contre être donnée à l'accord multilatéral dans le cas d'un conflit entre le GATT de 1994

59 Les accords contenus dans les trois premières annexes sont définis comme des accords multilatéraux engageant, par le fait même, tous les pays membres de l'OMC. Les accords contenus dans la quatrième annexe sont plutôt définis comme des accords plurilatéraux; cela signifie qu'ils ne lient que les pays membres qui les ont acceptés. L'Accord sur l'OMC doit être considéré comme un traité unique; à ce titre, il doit être accepté par chaque pays membre dans sa totalité, comme un seul engagement.

60 *Ibid.*, Annexe 1A. Le GATT continue d'exister sous la forme de GATT de 1994, lequel consiste en une version modifiée et mise à jour du GATT de 1947 et fait partie intégrante de l'Accord sur l'OMC. Le GATT, les instruments légaux et les décisions adoptées par les parties contractantes avant l'entrée en vigueur de l'OMC ont été incorporées par référence dans l'Annexe 1A de l'Accord sur l'OMC. Il s'ensuit que les quarante-sept années d'existence du GATT ont été reprises par l'OMC, y compris la jurisprudence et les nombreuses décisions des parties contractantes.

61 *Ibid.*, Annexe 1B.

62 *Ibid.*, Annexe 1C.

63 *Ibid.*, Annexe 2.

64 *Ibid.*, Annexe 3. À la suite de la Réunion ministérielle de mi-parcours tenue à Montréal en décembre 1988, le GATT a établi un mécanisme d'examen des politiques commerciales pour revoir périodiquement les politiques commerciales des États membres. L'expérience ayant été positive, l'Annexe 3 de l'Accord sur l'OMC a fait du mécanisme d'examen des politiques commerciales un élément permanent de la nouvelle Organisation. Sous l'égide du GATT, le mécanisme d'examen ne s'appliquait qu'aux seules politiques concernant le commerce des marchandises. Désormais, le mécanisme s'applique à tous les domaines couverts par les accords de l'OMC, y compris les services et les droits de propriété intellectuelle.

65 *Ibid.*, Annexe 4.

66 *Ibid.*, art. XVI.3.

et un accord multilatéral annexé.[67] En conséquence, le GATT de 1994 s'applique dans les seuls cas où il n'a pas été supplanté par les résultats du cycle d'Uruguay, tels qu'incorporés dans les autres accords multilatéraux.

L'organe suprême de l'OMC est la Conférence ministérielle.[68] Elle se réunit à tous les deux ans. La première conférence ministérielle a eu lieu à Singapour en décembre 1996.[69] Dans l'intervalle, ses fonctions sont exécutées par le Conseil général.[70] La Conférence ministérielle et le Conseil général ont le pouvoir de prendre une décision sur tous les sujets non spécifiquement assignés à d'autres organes. Par ailleurs, à la requête d'un pays membre, ils peuvent aussi prendre une décision sur une matière autrement assignée à un autre organe en vertu d'un accord multilatéral.[71]

Une plus grande cohésion est ainsi assurée à l'égard des décisions prises au sein de l'OMC. Les activités quotidiennes relèvent principalement du Conseil général, lequel est composé de représentants de tous les pays membres de l'OMC.[72] Outre les fonctions qui lui sont assignées par la Conférence ministérielle, le Conseil général se réunit sous deux autres formes possibles: d'une part, à titre d'Organe de règlement des différends afin d'assurer la supervision des procédures qui s'y rapportent;[73] d'autre part, à titre d'Organe d'examen des politiques commerciales, afin de procéder à des examens périodiques des politiques commerciales domestiques et extérieures des gouvernements des pays membres.[74]

B LA MISE EN OEUVRE DE L'ACCORD SUR L'OMC EN DROIT INTERNE CANADIEN

Le gouvernement canadien a promulgué, le 1er janvier 1995, le Projet de loi C-57, intitulé la *Loi portant mise en oeuvre de l'Accord*

67 *Ibid.*, Annexe 1A, note interprétative générale relative à l'Annexe 1A.

68 *Ibid.*, art. IV.1.

69 Voir *infra* notes 80-88 et texte correspondant.

70 *Ibid.*, art. IV.2.

71 *Ibid.*, art. IV.1.

72 *Ibid.*, art. IV.2. Le Niger est devenu le 128e membre de l'OMC lors de la clôture de la Conférence ministérielle de Singapour, le 13 décembre 1996. Voir à cet égard Anon., "Niger Becomes 128th Member of WTO" *Kyodo News International* (13 décembre 1996).

73 *Accord sur l'OMC, supra* note 2, art. IV.3.

74 *Ibid.*, art. IV.4.

instituant l'Organisation mondiale du commerce (ci-après Loi de mise en oeuvre).[75] Dans l'Énoncé canadien de mise en oeuvre de l'Accord sur l'OMC,[76] le gouvernement canadien expose les trois considérations l'ayant conduit à mettre en oeuvre l'Accord sur l'OMC:

- l'importance du commerce et de l'investissement à l'échelle mondiale pour le bien-être de tous les Canadiens;
- l'engagement de longue date du Canada envers un régime commercial et financier international à la fois équitable et ouvert; et
- le rôle crucial que jouent des règles et des procédures convenues afin d'assurer l'égalité des chances aux Canadiens dans un monde comportant des entités beaucoup plus importantes et plus puissantes.[77]

Conformément à l'article XVI de l'Accord sur l'OMC, le Canada a modifié certaines de ses lois afin de tenir compte des obligations énoncées dans les instruments constitutifs de l'Accord sur l'OMC. À titre d'exemples, les articles 74, 76, 77, 79, 80 et 92 de la Loi de mise en oeuvre ont modifié diverses dispositions du Tarif des douanes[78] de manière à y intégrer les réductions tarifaires consenties par le Canada, telles qu'elles figurent dans la Liste du Canada jointe au Protocole de Marrakech annexé au GATT de 1994.[79]

C LA CONFÉRENCE MINISTÉRIELLE DE SINGAPOUR

Tenue à Singapour du 9 au 13 décembre 1996, la première Conférence ministérielle de l'OMC a réuni les ministres du Commerce, des Affaires étrangères, des Finances et de l'Agriculture des gouvernements des pays membres. Cette Conférence visait à faire un bilan des travaux réalisés par l'OMC au cours de ses deux premières années d'existence et un examen de la mise en oeuvre des accords issus du cycle d'Uruguay.

Tous s'accordent pour dire qu'outre la question de l'investissement, celle de la dimension sociale de la libéralisation du commerce international (ci-après DSLCI) a figuré à la tête des discussions de la

75 L.C. 1994, c. 47 [ci-après *Loi de mise en oeuvre*].

76 Gaz. C. 1994.I.4847.

77 *Ibid.* à la p. 4848.

78 L.R.C. 1985, c. C-54.01.

79 Voir *Loi de mise en oeuvre, supra* note 75.

Conférence ministérielle de Singapour.[80] Quatre jours ont en effet été requis pour permettre aux 128 pays membres de l'OMC de parvenir à un consensus sur la question. En dépit des efforts déployés par les États-Unis,[81] la France[82] et d'autres pays développés[83] afin d'obtenir l'inclusion, dans la Déclaration ministérielle

80 Voir notamment J. Son et R. Etwareea, "OMC: le marchandage bat son plein à la Conférence de Singapour," *Journal de Genève et Gazette de Lausanne* (12 décembre 1996) 17; M. Battye, "WTO Row Places Labour Standards Firmly in Spotlight," *Reuter* (13 décembre 1996); Anon., "OMC: la Conférence de Singapour débouche sur une série de compromis," *Journal de Genève et Gazette de Lausanne* (13 décembre 1996) 11 [ci-après La Conférence de Singapour débouche sur une série de compromis]; P. Chaboudez, "OMC: la déclaration finale comprend un plan d'action en faveur des pays les moins développés. Sans mesure contraignante," *Tribune de Genève* (14-15 décembre 1996) 23 [ci-après La déclaration finale comprend un plan d'action en faveur des pays les moins développés]. Invité le 2 décembre 1996 par le Conseil général de l'OMC à s'adresser à la Conférence ministérielle de Singapour, le Directeur général du Bureau international du Travail, Michel Hansenne, s'est vu, dès le lendemain, retirer son invitation; l'Organisation a ainsi dû se contenter d'un statut d'observatrice, sans droit de parole. Cette décision a été prise par le Conseil général de l'OMC, à la suite des pressions exercées en ce sens par l'Inde, le Pakistan, l'Égypte et la Malaisie, soit quatre des nombreux pays en développement opposés à l'idée d'établir un lien entre le commerce et les normes du travail au sein de l'OMC. Voir à cet égard S. Nebehay, "ILO Chief Rebuffed by WTO on Trade-Labour Spat," *Reuter* (5 décembre 1996); M. Gultas, "Le Directeur général de l'OIT est indésirable à Singapour," *Journal de Genève et Gazette de Lausanne* (5 décembre 1996) 21; AFP, "À Singapour, la clause sociale bute sur un front d'opposition," *Journal de Genève et Gazette de Lausanne* (10 décembre 1996) 19; Bureau international du Travail, Conseil d'administration, Groupe de travail sur la dimension sociale de la libéralisation du commerce international, *Poursuite de la discussion sur le programme et le mandat du groupe de travail: (c) Conférence ministérielle de l'Organisation mondiale du commerce (Singapour, 9-13 décembre 1996)*, doc. GB.268/WP/SDL/1/3, 268e session, Genève, Bureau international du Travail, mars 1997, par. 2.

81 Voir OMC, *États-Unis — Déclaration de C. Barshefsky, Représentante des États-Unis pour les questions commerciales internationales par intérim*, Conférence ministérielle, Singapour, 9-13 décembre 1996, OMC doc. WT/MIN(96)/ST/5, 9 décembre 1996 à la p. 4.

82 Voir OMC, *France — Déclaration de Y. Galland, Ministre des Finances et du Commerce extérieur*, Conférence ministérielle, Singapour, 9-13 décembre 1996, OMC doc. WT/MIN(96)/ST/11, 9 décembre 1996 à la p. 3.

83 Au nombre des États membres ayant, à l'instar des États-Unis et de la France, choisi de se prononcer en faveur d'un rôle actif de l'OMC sur la question de la DSLCI, figurent le Canada, les Communautés européennes, la Norvège, la Belgique, la Suisse, l'Italie, les Pays-Bas, la Finlande, le Danemark et la Suède. Voir à cet égard OMC, *Canada — Déclaration de A. C. Eggleton, Ministre du*

de Singapour, du sujet dans le programme de travail de l'OMC, les pays récemment industrialisés et les pays en développement ont eu gain de cause. Fermement opposés à l'idée de la création d'un lien entre le commerce et les normes du travail ainsi que de la formation d'un groupe de travail à cet égard au sein de l'OMC, ces derniers[84]

Commerce international, Conférence ministérielle, Singapour, 9-13 décembre 1996, OMC doc. WT/MIN(96)/ST/1, 9 décembre 1996 à la p. 4; OMC, *Communautés européennes — Commission des Communautés européennes — Déclaration de Sir L. Brittan, Vice-Président de la Commission européenne,* Conférence ministérielle, Singapour, 9-13 décembre 1996, OMC doc. WT/MIN(96)/ST/2, 9 décembre 1996 à la p. 3; OMC, *Norvège — Déclaration de K. Nordheim-Larsen, Ministre de la Coopération pour le développement,* Conférence ministérielle, Singapour, 9-13 décembre 1996, OMC doc. WT/MIN(96)/ST/21, 9 décembre 1996 à la p. 2; OMC, *Belgique — Déclaration de S. E. P. Maystadt, Vice-Premier Ministre et Ministre des Finances et du Commerce extérieur,* Conférence ministérielle, Singapour, 9-13 décembre 1996, OMC doc. WT/MIN(96)/ST/61, 11 décembre 1996 aux pp. 2-3; OMC, *Suisse — Déclaration de S. E. J.-P. Delamuraz, Président de la Confédération,* Conférence ministérielle, Singapour, 9-13 décembre 1996, OMC doc. WT/MIN(96)/ST/109, 12 décembre 1996 à la p. 2; OMC, *Italie — Déclaration de A. Fantozzi, Ministre du Commerce extérieur,* Conférence ministérielle, Singapour, 9-13 décembre 1996, OMC doc. WT/MIN(96)/ST/10, 9 décembre 1996 aux pp. 2-3; OMC, *Pays-Bas, Déclaration de S. E. A. Van Dock-Van Weele, Ministre du Commerce extérieur,* Conférence ministérielle, Singapour, 9-13 décembre 1996, OMC doc. WT/MIN(96)/ST/48, 10 décembre 1996 à la p. 2; OMC, *Finlande — Déclaration de O. Norrback, Ministre des Affaires européennes et du Commerce extérieur,* Conférence ministérielle, Singapour, 9-13 décembre 1996, OMC doc. WT/MIN(96)/ST/20, 9 décembre 1996 à la p. 3; OMC, *Danemark — Déclaration de P. Nielson, Ministre de la Coopération pour le développement,* Conférence ministérielle, Singapour, 9-13 décembre 1996, OMC doc. WT/MIN(96)/ST/6, 9 décembre 1996 à la p. 2; OMC, *Suède — Déclaration de S. E. B. von Sydow, Ministre du Commerce,* Conférence ministérielle, Singapour, 9-13 décembre 1996, OMC doc. WT/MIN(96)/ST/35, 10 décembre 1996 à la p. 2.

84 La levée des boucliers des pays récemment industrialisés et des pays en développement sur la question de la DSLCI résulte principalement de pays comme le Brésil, la Thaïlande, l'Indonésie, l'Inde, le Pakistan, la Malaisie, l'Égypte, la Tanzanie, le Mexique, Hong Kong et les Philippines, lesquels ont clairement exprimé leur refus à l'idée d'introduire la question sous l'enceinte de l'OMC. Toutefois, certains pays développés, parmi lesquels l'Allemagne, le Royaume-Uni, l'Australie et l'Espagne ont choisi de se rallier à leur position. Voir à cet égard OMC, *Brésil — Déclaration de S. E. L. F. Lampreia, Ministre des Relations extérieures,* Conférence ministérielle, Singapour, 9-13 décembre 1996, OMC doc. WT/MIN(96)/ST/8, 9 décembre 1996 à la p. 3; OMC, *Thaïlande — Déclaration de S. E. A. Viravan, Vice-Premier Ministre et Ministre des Finances,* Conférence ministérielle, Singapour, 9-13 décembre 1996, OMC doc. WT/MIN(96)/ST/15, 9 décembre 1996 à la p. 3; OMC, *Indonésie — Déclaration de S. E. T. Ariwibowo, Ministre de l'Industrie et du Commerce,* Conférence minis-

ont réussi à réduire à sa plus simple expression le paragraphe de la Déclaration ministérielle portant sur les normes du travail. Celui-ci reconnaît expressément la juridiction de l'Organisation international du Travail (ci-après OIT) en la matière, rejette le recours aux normes du travail dans un dessein protectionniste, reconnaît comme légitime l'avantage comparatif des pays à bas salaires et souligne la volonté de l'OMC de continuer à collaborer avec l'OIT. Le quatrième paragraphe de la Déclaration ministérielle est ainsi formulé:

4. Nous renouvelons notre engagement d'observer les normes du travail fondamentales internationalement reconnues. L'Organisation internationale du Travail (OIT) est l'organe compétent pour établir ces

térielle, Singapour, 9-13 décembre 1996, OMC doc. WT/MIN(96)/ST/22, 9 décembre 1996 à la p. 3; OMC, *Inde — Déclaration de B. B. Ramaiah, Ministre du Commerce,* Conférence ministérielle, Singapour, 9-13 décembre 1996, OMC doc. WT/MIN(96)/ST/27, 9 décembre 1996 à la p. 4; OMC, *Pakistan — Déclaration de M. Z. Khan, Ministre du Commerce et Chef de la délégation pakistanaise,* Conférence ministérielle, Singapour, 9-13 décembre 1996, OMC doc. WT/MIN(96)/ST/29, 9 décembre 1996 aux pp. 4-5; OMC, *Malaisie — Déclaration de S. E. D.' S. R. Aziz, Ministre du Commerce international et de l'Industrie,* Conférence ministérielle, Singapour, 9-13 décembre 1996, OMC doc. WT/MIN(96)/ST/64, 11 décembre 1996 à la p. 2; OMC, *Égypte — Déclaration de S. E. A. Goueli, Ministre du Commerce et des Approvisionnements,* Conférence ministérielle, Singapour, 9-13 décembre 1996, OMC doc. WT/MIN(96)/ST/73, 11 décembre 1996 à la p. 2; OMC, *Tanzanie — Déclaration de A. O. Kigoda, Ministre de l'Industrie et du Commerce,* Conférence ministérielle, Singapour, 9-13 décembre 1996, OMC doc. WT/MIN(96)/ST/50, 10 décembre 1996 à la p. 3; OMC, *Mexique — Déclaration de H.B. Mendoza, Ministre du Commerce et du Développement industriel,* Conférence ministérielle, Singapour, 9-13 décembre 1996, OMC doc. WT/MIN(96)/ST/14, 9 décembre 1996 à la p. 2; OMC, *Hong Kong — Déclaration de D.Y. Chung-Yee, Ministre du Commerce et de l'Industrie,* Conférence ministérielle, Singapour, 9-13 décembre 1996, OMC doc. WT/MIN(96)/ST/19, 9 décembre 1996 à la p. 2; OMC, *Philippines — Déclaration de S. E. C. B. Bautista, Secrétaire au commerce et à l'industrie,* Conférence ministérielle, Singapour, 9-13 décembre 1996, OMC doc. WT/MIN(96)/ST/41, 10 décembre 1996 à la p. 3; OMC, *Allemagne — Déclaration de G. Rexrodt, Ministre de l'Économie,* Conférence ministérielle, Singapour, 9-13 décembre 1996, OMC doc. WT/MIN(96)/ST/13, 9 décembre 1996 à la p. 3; OMC, *Royaume-Uni, Déclaration de I. Lang, M. P., Président du Conseil du commerce, Chef du Département du commerce et de l'industrie,* Conférence ministérielle, Singapour, 9-13 décembre 1996, OMC doc. WT/MIN(96)/ST/9, 9 décembre 1996 à la p. 3; OMC, *Australie — Déclaration de S. E. T. Fisher, M. P., Vice-Premier Ministre et Ministre du Commerce,* Conférence ministérielle, Singapour, 9-13 décembre 1996, OMC doc. WT/MIN(96)/ST/26, 9 décembre 1996 à la p. 3; OMC, *Espagne — Declarationde S. E. R. de Rato y Figaredo, Deuxième Vice-Président, Ministre de l'Économie et des Finances,* Conférence ministérielle, Singapour, 9-13 décembre 1996, OMC doc. WT/MIN(96)/ST/66, 11 décembre 1996 à la p. 3.

> normes et s'en occuper, et nous affirmons soutenir les activités qu'elle mène pour les promouvoir. Nous estimons que la croissance économique et le développement favorisés par une augmentation des échanges commerciaux et une libéralisation plus poussée du commerce contribuent à la promotion de ces normes. Nous rejetons l'usage des normes du travail à des fins protectionnistes et convenons que l'avantage comparatif des pays, en particulier des pays en développement à bas salaires, ne doit en aucune façon être remis en question. A cet égard, nous notons que les Secrétariats de l'OMC et de l'OIT continueront de collaborer comme ils le font actuellement.[85]

Dans ses remarques finales à l'intention des ministres des États membres de l'OMC, le Président de la Conférence ministérielle, le Singapourien Yeo Cheow Tong, a apporté le commentaire suivant à l'endroit de ce paragraphe: "Des délégations ont dit qu'elles craignaient que ce texte ne donne à l'OMC compétence pour engager de nouveaux travaux sur le rapport entre le commerce et les normes du travail fondamentales. *Je veux assurer à ces délégations que cela ne se produira pas* [les italiques sont de nous]."[86]

Malgré les assurances de Yeo Cheow Tong à cet égard, nombreux sont ceux qui restent convaincus que les États-Unis et l'Union européenne — qui se sont d'ailleurs déclarés satisfaits de la

85 OMC, *Déclaration ministérielle de Singapour*, Conférence ministérielle, Singapour, 9-13 décembre 1996, OMC doc. WT/MIN(96)/DEC/W, 13 décembre 1996, para. 4. Sur la Déclaration ministérielle de Singapour, voir notamment S. Hishiyama, "WTO Makes Leap Toward Further Trade Liberalization" *Kyodo News International* (13 décembre 1996); F. Williams, "Singapore Deals Give a Boost to WTO" *Financial Times* (16 décembre 1996) 4; F. Williams, "WTO Refuses to Link Trade Measures to Labour Rights" *Financial Times* (13 décembre 1996) 8 [ci-après *WTO Refuses to Link Trade Measures to Labour Rights*]; *La Conférence de Singapour débouche sur une série de compromis, supra*, note 80; *La déclaration finale comprend un plan d'action en faveur des pays les moins développés, supra*, note 80; A. Friedman, "Trade Success in Singapore Helps WTO Come of Age" *International Herald Tribune* (14-15 décembre 1996) 1, 5; Anon., "The WTO's Successful Debut" *Wall Street Journal [Europe]* (16 décembre 1996) 6.

86 OMC, *Remarques finales de S. E. Y. C. Tong, Président de la Conférence ministérielle, Ministre du Commerce et de l'Industrie de Singapour*, Conférence ministérielle, Singapour, 9-13 décembre 1996, OMC doc. WT/MIN(96)/9, 13 décembre 1996, para. 8. L'opinion du Président de la Conférence ministérielle est d'ailleurs partagée par la plupart des pays en développement selon lesquels toute possibilité d'implication directe de l'OMC à l'endroit de la question de la DSLCI est écartée en raison des termes utilisés au quatrième paragraphe de la Déclaration de Singapour. Voir à cet égard M. Battye, "WTO Row Places Labour Standards Firmly in Spotlight" *Reuter* (13 décembre 1996); *WTO Refuses to Link Trade Measures to Labour Rights, ibid.*

substance du paragraphe concernant les normes du travail[87] — ne sont pas prêts de lâcher prise sur le sujet et continueront leur campagne afin d'introduire la question de la DSLCI au sein de l'OMC dans un avenir rapproché.[88]

D LES DIFFÉRENDS PORTÉS DEVANT L'OMC EN 1995 et 1996

Pour qu'un système commercial multilatéral fonctionne convenablement et sans frictions, il ne suffit pas d'y prévoir un ensemble convenu de règles. Les pays membres du système doivent, en plus, disposer de voies de recours en cas de violation des règles de base, et de moyens de régler leurs différends. L'élaboration d'un solide mécanisme multilatéral de règlement des différends, capable de combler certaines lacunes de l'ancien système du GATT, a donc été un des objectifs les plus importants des négociations du cycle d'Uruguay.

Le mécanisme de règlement des différends élaboré aux termes du *Mémorandum d'accord sur les règles et procédures régissant le règlement des différends* (ci-après MARPRRD)[89] est considéré comme l'une des grandes réussites de l'OMC. Érigé à partir des règles déjà existantes en cette matière dans le GATT,[90] il comporte des améliorations importantes faisant de lui un mécanisme d'une grande efficacité. Ainsi, la procédure de règlement des différends de l'OMC s'applique à tous les différends survenant entre deux ou plusieurs pays membres, quel que soit l'accord multilatéral à l'origine du conflit.[91] De plus, contrairement à l'usage développé dans le cadre du régime issu du cycle de Tokyo, les gouvernements ne peuvent plus exercer un droit de veto *de facto* et bloquer l'adoption des rapports émis par les groupes spéciaux.[92] Par contre, il leur est

87 Voir G. De Jonquières et F. Williams, "WTO's Tariff-Busting Deal Hailed as "Global Tax Cut" *Financial Times* (14-15 décembre 1996) 3. Le Vice-Président de la Commission européenne, Sir L. Brittan, a déclaré: "I think that the agreements [*sic*] on labour standards does mark a breakthrough . . . on this delicate but vital subject. We have put our foot in the door" (J. Macartney, "World Pact Signals Freer Trade in 21st Century" *Reuter* (13 décembre 1996)).

88 Voir à cet égard Anon., "Declaration Bars WTO Mandate on Trade-Labour Link" *Reuter* (13 décembre 1996).

89 Mémorandum d'accord sur les règles et procédures régissant le règlement des différends dans GATT, *Résultats des négociations commerciales multilatérales du cycle d'Uruguay — Textes juridiques*, Genève, GATT, 1994 aux pp. 427 et s.

90 *Ibid.*, art. 3.1.

91 *Ibid.*, Appendice 1.

92 *Ibid.*, notamment art. 23.

désormais possible d'interjeter appel des conclusions rendues par les groupes spéciaux devant le nouvel Organe d'appel créé à cette fin.[93]

Cette efficacité théorique est corroborée dans la pratique. En effet, entre le mois de janvier 1995 et le mois d'août 1996, cinquante-trois demandes de consultations ont été soumises concernant trente-sept questions[94] en vertu des dispositions du MARPRRD.[95] Sur ces trente-sept questions, onze ont été réglées à l'amiable.[96] Trois d'entre elles impliquaient le Canada à titre de partie plaignante.[97]

Ainsi, dans l'affaire *Communautés européennes — Droits sur les importations de céréales,*[98] le Canada a présenté une demande de consultations aux Communautés européennes, au mois de juillet 1995, au sujet de règlements adoptés par ces dernières afin de mettre en oeuvre certaines concessions accordées en matière agricole dans le cadre des négociations du cycle d'Uruguay.[99] Ces règlements avaient pour effet d'accroître de manière significative le prix à l'importation du blé canadien.[100] Un groupe spécial est établi le 11 octobre 1995. Bien qu'il n'y ait eu aucune notification officielle à cet effet, l'affaire semble avoir été réglée par voie bilatérale.

Par ailleurs, dans l'affaire *Corée — Mesures concernant l'eau en bouteille,*[101] le Canada a soutenu, dans sa demande de consultations du 8 novembre 1995, que les règlements coréens concernant la durée de conservation et la désinfection de l'eau embouteillée en Corée étaient incompatibles avec les articles III et XI du GATT de 1994,[102] les articles 2 et 5 de l'*Accord sur l'application des mesures*

93 *Ibid.*, art. 17.

94 Plus d'un pays membre peuvent en effet soumettre une demande de consultations à l'égard d'une même question.

95 Canada, Ministère des Affaires extérieures et du Commerce international, *L'Organisation mondiale du commerce: qu'est-ce qu'elle peut apporter au Canada?* Ottawa, décembre 1996 à la p. 4 [ci-après *L'Organisation mondiale du commerce: qu'est-ce qu'elle peut apporter au Canada?*].

96 *Ibid.*

97 *Ibid.*

98 OMC doc. WT/DS9, 10 juillet 1995.

99 *Ibid.*

100 *Ibid.*

101 OMC doc.WT/DS20, 8 nov. 1995 [ci-après WT/DS20].

102 GATT de 1994, *supra* note 57.

sanitaires et phytosanitaires[103] ainsi que l'article 2 de l'*Accord sur les obstacles techniques au commerce.*[104] Toutefois, le 24 avril 1996, les parties annonçaient être parvenues à régler leur différend.[105]

Enfin, dans le cadre de l'affaire *Communautés européennes — Désignation commerciale des pectinidés,*[106] le Canada, le Pérou et le Chili ont soumis une demande de consultations aux Communautés européennes au sujet d'un arrêté du gouvernement français édictant les noms officiels et la désignation commerciale des pectinidés.[107] Par cet arrêté, les pétoncles du Canada, du Pérou et du Chili ne pourraient plus être vendus sur le marché français sous la désignation de *coquilles Saint-Jacques.*[108] Or, de l'avis des plaignants, il n'existe aucune différence entre leurs produits et le produit français, que ce soit en termes de couleur, de taille, de texture, d'apparence et d'utilisation.[109] S'agissant donc, selon eux, de produits similaires, l'arrêté français contreviendrait aux articles I et III du GATT de 1994 ainsi qu'à l'article 2 de l'*Accord sur les obstacles techniques au commerce.*[110] Deux groupes spéciaux sont établis, l'un à la demande du Canada le 19 juillet 1995, l'autre à la demande du Pérou et du Chili le 11 octobre 1995.[111] Les groupes spéciaux n'ont cependant pas eu à émettre de conclusions sur les deux cas soumis puisque, le 5 juillet 1996, les parties notifiaient officiellement la résolution à l'amiable de leur différend.[112]

103 *Accord sur l'application des mesures sanitaires et phytosanitaires,* dans GATT, *Résultats des négociations commerciales multilatérales du cycle d'Uruguay — Textes juridiques,* Genève, GATT, 1994 aux pp. 72 et s.

104 *Accord sur les obstacles techniques au commerce,* dans GATT, *Résultats des négociations commerciales multilatérales du cycle d'Uruguay — Textes juridiques,* Genève, GATT, 1994 aux pp. 145 et s. [ci-après *Accord sur les obstacles techniques au commerce*].

105 WT/DS20, *supra* note 101.

106 OMC doc. WT/DS7 (plainte du Canada), WT/DS12 (plainte du Pérou), WT/DS14 (plainte du Chili) [ci-après *Affaire sur les coquilles Saint-Jacques*].

107 *Ibid.*

108 *Ibid.*

109 *Ibid.*

110 *Accord sur les obstacles techniques au commerce, supra* note 104.

111 *Affaire sur les coquilles Saint-Jacques, supra* note 106.

112 *Ibid.*

III La zone de libre-échange des Amériques: les efforts déployés par les États américains, en 1995 et 1996, en vue de sa création

Lors du Sommet des Amériques, tenu au mois de décembre 1994 à Miami (États-Unis), les chefs d'État des trente-quatre démocraties du continent américain[113] se sont engagés à créer une zone de libre-échange des Amériques (ci-après ZLÉA) au sein de laquelle les barrières au commerce et aux investissements seront progressivement éliminées ainsi qu'à finaliser les négociations s'y rattachant d'ici l'an 2005. Afin de donner suite au Sommet, deux réunions ont eu lieu en 1995 et en 1996, de manière à formuler et à mettre en oeuvre le plan de travail en vue de la création de la ZLÉA.

Tenue au mois de juin 1995 à Denver (États-Unis), la première réunion a d'abord été l'occasion, pour les ministres du Commerce des trente-quatre États participants, d'identifier les objectifs de la ZLÉA: "[La ZLÉA] respectera complètement les dispositions de l'Accord portant création de l'Organisation mondiale du commerce (Accord de l'OMC); elle sera équitable, aura une portée étendue et couvrira notamment tous les domaines mentionnés dans le Plan d'action du Sommet des Amériques; elle n'élèvera pas de barrières contre d'autres pays; enfin, elle représentera une entreprise unique comportant des droits et des obligations réciproques."[114]

Cette première réunion a également donné lieu à la mise sur pied de sept groupes de travail concernant les aspects économiques suivants: l'accès aux marchés; les procédures douanières et les règles d'origine; les investissements; les normes et barrières techniques au commerce; les mesures sanitaires et phytosanitaires; les subventions; l'antidumping et les droits compensateurs; et, enfin, les économies de petite taille.[115] Un Comité tripartite a par ailleurs été établi. Formé de l'Organisation des États américains, de la

[113] Antigua-et-Barbuda, Argentine, Bahamas, Barbade, Bélize, Bolivie, Brésil, Canada, Chili, Colombie, Costa Rica, Dominique, Équateur, El Salvador, États-Unis, Grenade, Guatemala, Guyane, Haïti, Honduras, Jamaïque, Mexique, Nicaragua, Panama, Paraguay, Pérou, République dominicaine, St-Vincent-et-Grenadines, Ste-Lucie, St-Kitts-et-Nevis, Suriname, Trinité-et-Tobago, Uruguay et Vénéezuela.

[114] Sommet des Amériques, Réunion ministérielle sur les échanges internationaux, *Déclaration ministérielle de Denver, Déclaration conjointe*, Denver, 30 juin 1995, par. 2.

[115] *Ibid.*, Annexe I.

Banque interaméricaine de développement et de la Commission économique pour l'Amérique latine et les Caraïbes, il vise à soutenir les efforts des États participants dans la mise en branle du processus.[116]

La seconde réunion a pour sa part eu lieu à Carthagène (Colombie), au mois de mars 1996.[117] Quatre nouveaux groupes de travail ont été créés en matière de passation des marchés publics, de droits de propriété intellectuelle, de services et de politique de concurrence.[118] En outre, cette réunion a conduit les trente-quatre ministres du Commerce du continent américain à s'interroger sur la possibilité de construire la ZLÉA à partir des bases économiques existantes. Cette interrogation s'est traduite par la déclaration suivante: "Nous avons examiné les méthodes qui permettent de construire la ZLÉA à partir des arrangements sous-régionaux et bilatéraux existants, afin d'élargir et de renforcer l'intégration économique de l'hémisphère et d'unifier les accords. Les méthodes sont diverses et complexes, et doivent être cohérentes avec l'Article XXIV du GATT 1994 . . . et l'Article V de l'[Accord général sur le commerce des services] . . ."[119]

Enfin, les ministres ont également convenu de l'importance de réaliser des progrès concrets, d'ici l'an 2000, afin de respecter l'objectif visant à compléter les négociations devant aboutir à la ZLÉA au plus tard en 2005.[120]

Ainsi qu'il nous a été permis de le constater à la lumière de ces événements, le Canada a, au cours des années 1995 et 1996, occupé une place de choix dans le processus de mondialisation des économies qui s'intensifie à une vitesse fulgurante. Le Canada ne peut, du reste, rester à l'écart de ce processus. Ainsi que l'a souligné l'ambassadeur John Weekes, représentant permanent du Canada auprès de l'Organisation mondiale du commerce et de l'Office des Nations Unies à Genève, dans le cadre d'une allocution présentée au mois d'octobre 1996:

> Il est devenu presque banal de parler de la mondialisation et du rythme rapide des progrès technologiques qui influent sur la vie courante de

116 *Ibid.*, par. 8.

117 Sommet des Amériques, Deuxième réunion ministérielle sur les échanges internationaux, *Déclaration conjointe*, Carthagène, 21 mars 1996.

118 *Ibid.*, par. 9.

119 *Ibid.*, par. 3.

120 *Ibid.*, par. 4.

tous les citoyens de la planète. Toutefois, il faut absolument reconnaître ces réalités pour être en mesure de gérer la politique étrangère du Canada à la veille du XXIe siècle. Le Canada exporte actuellement près de 40 p. 100 de son produit intérieur brut. De fait, le tiers des biens et services produits chaque année par les Canadiens sont exportés vers un pays seulement, les États-Unis. Il est évident que notre prospérité en tant que pays et notre puissance en tant que nation sont inextricablement liées à notre capacité de continuer à garder les marchés étrangers ouverts dans des conditions prévisibles.[121]

121 *Organisation mondiale du commerce: qu'est-ce qu'elle peut apporter au Canada?*, *supra* note 95 à la p. 1.

II Le Canada et le système monétaire international en 1996

préparé par

BERNARD COLAS

LA GLOBALISATION DES MARCHÉS financiers oblige des pays comme le Canada à repenser l'exercice de leur souveraineté. Elle met en évidence l'interdépendance entre pays industriels et économies émergentes ainsi que l'importance d'une action concertée au niveau international.

En 1996, le Canada a poursuivi, avec ses partenaires du Groupe des Sept, la mise en oeuvre des recommandations formulées au Sommet de Halifax l'année précédente.[1] Celles-ci visaient à favoriser la stabilité du système financier international. Pour ce faire, le Canada a encouragé le renforcement des institutions financières internationales (I) et l'action des organismes de surveillance des institutions financières (II).

I Institutions financières internationales

En 1996, le renforcement des institutions financières internationales s'est traduit par l'augmentation de leurs moyens financiers et de leur efficacité ainsi que par l'intensification de leur coopération.

A ACCROISSEMENT DE CAPITAL

En effet, le Canada a participé en 1996 à l'augmentation du capital de la Banque européenne pour la reconstruction et le

---

Bernard Colas est avocat de l'étude Byers Casgrain (Montréal), Docteur en droit, Président de la Société de droit international économique (SDIE).

1 B. Colas, "Le Canada et le système financier international en 1995" (1996) 34 A.C.D.I. 369.

développement (BERD) et de l'Association internationale de développement (IDA) ainsi qu'aux discussions relatives à l'augmentation du capital du Fonds monétaire international (FMI).

En avril 1996, la BERD a été autorisée à doubler ses dotations en capital pour les porter à 20 milliards d'ECU (34 milliards C).[2] Le Canada a déposé son instrument de souscription le 29 novembre 1996 et a souscrit 34 000 actions supplémentaires, soit 3,4 % du total, ce qui nécessitera un investissement de capital libéré total de 133 millions C entre 1998 et 2009.[3] Cette augmentation exprime la confiance des actionnaires quant à la pertinence de cette banque, vieille de cinq ans, et devrait lui permettre d'avoir assez de ressources pour répondre à la demande croissante des pays européens en transition.

La onzième reconstitution du capital de l'Association internationale de développement (IDA 11) s'est traduite par une injection de 22 milliards US.[4] L'engagement du Canada s'élève à 607 millions C.[5] Ces ressources supplémentaires doivent financer les crédits engagés du 1er juillet 1996 au 30 juillet 1999. Elles viennent en aide aux soixante-dix-neuf pays les plus pauvres de la planète qui représentent environ 57 % de la population mondiale.

Au sein du Fonds monétaire international (FMI), les pays membres n'ont pas encore réussi à s'entendre quant à l'ampleur de l'augmentation et de la répartition de la prochaine révision des quotes-parts, l'objectif étant de déterminer la quote-part des pays membres qui corresponde à leur position au sein de l'économie mondiale.[6] Ces États cherchent également à trouver une répartition équitable des droits de tirage spéciaux (DTS) afin de tenir compte des nouveaux membres, telle la Russie, qui n'ont pas participé aux allocations antérieures.[7]

2 *Rapport annuel de la Banque européenne pour la reconstruction et le développement* (1996) à la p. 5.

3 Ministère des Finances du Canada, *Rapport sur les opérations effectuées en vertu de la Loi sur l'Accord portant création de la Banque européenne pour la reconstruction et le développement* (1996) à la p. 9 [ci-après *BERD*].

4 Rapport annuel de la Banque mondiale (1997) à la p. 160.

5 Ministère des Finances du Canada, *Rapport sur les opérations effectuées en vertu de la Loi sur les accords de Bretton Woods et des accords connexes* (1996) à la p. 38 [ci-après *Bretton Woods*].

6 Rapport annuel du Fonds monétaire international (1997) à la p. 6 [ci-après *FMI*].

7 *Bretton Woods, supra* note 5 à la p. 10.

Toutefois, le groupe de travail du Groupe des Dix (G-10), présidé par le Canada et créé à la suite du Sommet de Halifax, est parvenu à obtenir l'appui de vingt-cinq pays pour doubler le montant de ressources accordées en vertu des accords généraux d'emprunts (entente de crédit qui appuie les ressources courantes du FMI). Cette entente a donné lieu à la création de nouveaux accords d'emprunt (NAE) qui s'élèvent à 34 milliards de DTS (environ 67 milliards C). Ces ressources seront fournies au FMI si ce dernier a besoin de ressources supplémentaires pour prévenir ou corriger les imperfections du système monétaire international ou pour traiter une situation exceptionnelle qui menace la stabilité du système. La part du Canada s'élève à 4,1 %, sous forme d'un engagement à consentir des prêts non budgétaires au FMI à partir de ses réserves internationales.[8]

Les NAE entreront en vigueur lorsqu'ils auront été entérinés par d'éventuels participants à des accords de crédit d'une valeur d'au moins 28,9 milliards de DTS, y compris les cinq membres adhérant aux accords de crédit les plus importants. Les NAE ne remplaceront pas les Accords généraux d'emprunt, qui demeureront en vigueur. Cependant, ils constitueront le premier et principal recours du FMI en cas de besoin de ressources supplémentaires.

Ces initiatives ont été complétées par des mesures destinées à renforcer leur efficacité.

B GESTION EFFICACE ET COORDONNÉE

Le Canada a pris position au sein des institutions financières pour qu'elles assainissent leur gestion financière et intensifient leur coopération. Il s'est opposé au relèvement des salaires du personnel de la BERD[9] et de la Banque mondiale.[10] Il est également intervenu au sein de la Banque mondiale pour favoriser une politique d'ouverture, de transparence et de réformes internes.[11]

Il a enjoint le FMI de trouver des façons plus rentables pour exécuter ses programmes[12] et a appuyé les mesures visant à renforcer la transparence de ses activités et la responsabilité qui en

8 *Bretton Woods, supra* note 5 à la p. 9.

9 *BERD, supra* note 3 à la p. 19.

10 *Bretton Woods, supra* note 5 à la p. 32.

11 *Rapport annuel de la Banque mondiale* (1997) à la p. 133.

12 *Bretton Woods, supra* note 5 à la p. 13.

découle. Le FMI a notamment amorcé, en octobre 1996, un processus d'évaluation indépendante. Cette évaluation a porté sur plusieurs éléments de programmes appuyés par la Facilité d'ajustement structurelle renforcée (FASR).[13] Rappelons que cette facilité offre une aide financière à des conditions de faveur à des pays à faible revenu aux prises depuis longtemps avec des problèmes de balance des paiements.

Enfin, le Canada a encouragé les efforts déployés par le FMI et la Banque mondiale pour mettre en oeuvre "l'Initiative d'allégement de la dette des pays pauvres très endettés" décidée en 1995.[14] Il a en outre salué les accords de coopération conclus entre ces institutions ainsi qu'avec l'Organisation mondiale du commerce (OMC), engagée en 1996 notamment dans d'intenses négociations pour la libéralisation des services financiers.[15]

L'intensification de la coopération entre institutions prend place également au niveau des organismes de réglementation des secteurs bancaires, des valeurs mobilières et des services d'assurance.

II Surveillance des institutions financières

Cette coopération souhaitée par les principaux pays industrialisés entre autorités réglementaires devient inévitable dans une économie mondialisée où les institutions financières ont de plus en plus facilement accès aux marchés étrangers.

A Ouverture aux banques étrangères

Le Canada n'y fait pas exception. Engagé dans des négociations pour la libéralisation des services financiers au sein de l'OMC, il ouvre progressivement son secteur financier aux banques étrangères.[16] En effet, le gouvernement canadien a fait circuler en 1996 un document de consultation qui propose de modifier la loi sur les banques et de permettre notamment aux banques étrangères d'ouvrir directement des succursales au Canada. Ces propositions ont été reprises dans la *Loi visant à modifier certaines lois relatives aux institutions financières*.[17]

13 *FMI, supra* note 6 à la p. 4.

14 *B. Colas, supra* note 1.

15 *Bretton Woods, supra* note 5 à la p. 11.

16 Ministère des Finances du Canada, *Documentation de consultation sur la politique d'accès des banques étrangères* (1996).

17 *Loi visant à modifier certaines lois relatives aux institutions financières*, L.C. 1997, c. 15, art. 76(ss) (sanctionnée le 25 avril 1997).

Le gouvernement a également créé en 1996 un Groupe de travail sur l'avenir du secteur des services financiers pour le conseiller sur l'orientation à donner à ses prochaines réformes réglementaires.[18] Il poursuit l'objectif d'intensifier la compétitivité du secteur financier canadien face à la concurrence internationale tout en maintenant la stabilité de son système par l'adoption de mesures prudentielles.

B MESURES PRUDENTIELLES

En 1996, le Canada a continué à participer aux travaux de comités réunis au sein de la Banque des règlements internationaux (BRI) à Bâle (Suisse). Ceux-ci ont donné lieu à l'adoption de nombreux textes dont certains ont déjà reçu application au Canada.

En effet, le Comité de Bâle sur le contrôle bancaire a élaboré, en étroite collaboration avec les autorités de pays hors G-10, un ensemble exhaustif de principes fondamentaux pour un contrôle bancaire efficace.[19] Ce document définit vingt-cinq principes de base indispensables à l'efficacité d'un système prudentiel et couvre les sept grands domaines suivants:

> Conditions préalables à un contrôle bancaire efficace, Agrément et structure de propriété des établissements, Réglementations et exigences prudentielles, Méthodes de contrôle bancaire permanent, Exigences en matière d'information, Pouvoirs institutionnels des autorités prudentielles, et Activité bancaire transfrontière.[20]

Ce dernier élément a fait l'objet d'un second document du Comité de Bâle. Adopté conjointement avec le Groupe *offshore* des autorités de contrôle bancaire, ce texte porte sur la surveillance des activités bancaires transfrontières et contient vingt-neuf recommandations destinées à renforcer l'efficacité de la surveillance, par les autorités prudentielles du pays d'origine et du pays d'accueil, des banques opérant hors des frontières nationales.[21] Le rapport réaffirme notamment le principe selon lequel les autorités du pays

18 Ministère des finances du Canada, *Le gouvernement communique des renseignements au sujet du Groupe de travail sur l'avenir du secteur des services financiers canadien*, 19 décembre 1996, Communiqué 96-101.

19 Comité de Bâle sur le contrôle bancaire, *Principes fondamentaux pour un contrôle bancaire efficace* (1996).

20 *Rapport annuel de la Banque des règlements internationaux* (1997) à la p. 188 [ci-après *BRI*].

21 Comité de Bâle sur le contrôle bancaire & Groupe offshore des autorités de contrôle bancaire, *Surveillance des activités bancaires transfrontières* (1996).

d'origine doivent avoir plein accès aux informations dont elles ont besoin et établit des procédures pour les inspections à l'étranger menées auprès des filiales des banques sous leur contrôle. Il traite aussi de la nécessité d'assurer que toutes les opérations bancaires transfrontières soient soumises à une surveillance efficace de la part des pays d'origine et d'accueil. Il formule, en outre, des recommandations pour le suivi des normes de contrôle des pays d'accueil et pour les pratiques relatives aux groupes dont la structure peut être à l'origine de lacunes prudentielles.

Ce même Comité de Bâle s'est également intéressé à la gestion du risque de taux d'intérêt.[22] Le document de consultation qu'il a préparé établit douze principes ayant valeur de normes que ses membres utilisent pour évaluer l'efficacité de la gestion de ce risque par les banques. Ces principes couvrent plusieurs domaines: suivi par le conseil d'administration et la direction générale; politiques et procédures adéquates de gestion; système de mesure et de surveillance; portée des contrôles; et méthodes à utiliser par les autorités prudentielles.[23]

Quant à l'Amendement à l'Accord sur les fonds propres adopté par le Comité de Bâle en janvier 1996,[24] il a été mis en oeuvre par le Canada. En effet, le Bureau du surintendant des institutions financières a émis une ligne directrice[25] sur les normes de fonds propres pour risques de marché qui reprend le texte de l'accord international commenté dans notre dernière chronique.[26]

Un second comité retient notre attention: le Comité sur les systèmes de paiement et de règlement. Il a adopté un rapport sur les risques de règlement dans les opérations de change.[27] Ce document fournit une définition claire du risque de règlement dans les opérations de change, une méthode pour le mesurer et une stratégie pour le réduire. Celle-ci encourage notamment les

22 Comité de Bâle sur le contrôle bancaire, *Principes pour la gestion du risque de taux d'intérêt* (1997).

23 *BRI, supra* note 20 aux pp. 189-90.

24 *Amendement à l'Accord sur les fonds propres pour son extension aux risques de marché*, 1996. Voir Banque des règlements internationaux, *66e rapport annuel*, 10 juin 1996, Bâle, Suisse, aux pp. 185-86.

25 *Ligne directrice sur les normes de fonds propres pour risque de marché; Rapport annuel du Bureau du surintendant des institutions financières*, (1996-97) à la p. 13.

26 *B. Colas, supra* note 1.

27 Comité sur les systèmes de paiement et de règlement, *Risques de règlement dans les opérations de change* (1996).

initiatives des établissements, groupements professionnels et banques centrales.

En 1996, les travaux de ce comité[28] ont incité le gouvernement canadien à moderniser son système de réglementation et de surveillance des institutions financières. En effet, l'entrée en vigueur en 1996 du projet de loi C-15[29] octroie notamment de nouveaux pouvoirs à la Banque du Canada afin qu'elle puisse contrôler la conception et le fonctionnement des principaux systèmes de compensation et de règlement au Canada.[30]

Dernier fait à souligner pour 1996. Ces différents comités de Bâle ont élargi leur coopération avec les pays hors Groupe des Dix (G-10) et ont poursuivi leurs travaux avec l'Organisation internationale des commissions de valeur (OICV) et l'Association internationale des contrôleurs d'assurance (AICA).[31]

Ainsi, le Canada en 1996 a poursuivi sa politique de coopération au niveau multilatéral afin de renforcer les institutions financières internationales et de compléter son arsenal de mesures prudentielles pour prévenir les risques systémiques.

28 Comité de Bâle sur le contrôle bancaire, *Multilateral Netting of Forward Value Foreign Exchange Transactions* (1996).

29 P.L. C-15, *Loi modifiant la législation sur les institutions financières et édictant une nouvelle loi*, 1e sess., 35e Parl., art. 162 qui édicte la *Loi sur la compensation et le règlement des paiements*, 1996.

30 *Rapport annuel de la Banque du Canada* (1996) à la p. 21.

31 *BRI, supra* note 20 à la p. 187.

III Investissement

préparé par
PIERRE RATELLE

I Actions multilatérales

A OMC

1 Examen des politiques du Canada en matière d'investissement étranger

Du 18 au 19 novembre 1996, l'Organe d'examen des politiques commerciales de l'Organisation mondiale du commerce (OMC) a examiné pour la quatrième fois, mais pour la première fois sous l'égide de l'OMC, la politique et les pratiques commerciales du Canada. Dans le cadre de cet examen, la discussion a porté notamment sur la politique du Canada en matière d'investissement.[1] Les participants ont en outre soumis un certain nombre de questions par écrit portant sur cette matière, et le représentant du Canada a communiqué, au cours de la réunion, des réponses complètes par écrit et s'est engagé à donner d'autres précisions le cas échéant.[2]

Pierre Ratelle est avocat spécialiste en droit des affaires internationales, Bourret Ratelle, s.e.p., Montréal; Docteur en droit international économique de l'Université de Paris 1 (Panthéon-Sorbonne); Chargé de cours en droit international public et en droit commercial international aux départements des sciences juridiques et des sciences politiques ainsi qu'à l'École des sciences de la gestion de l'Université du Québec à Montréal (UQAM); D.E.A. en droit international économique de l'Université de Paris 1 (Panthéon-Sorbonne); D.E.A. en droit international public et européen de l'Université de Paris 2 (Panthéon-Assas); LL.B. (Laval).

[1] Pour le contenu de la discussion, voir OMC, *Rapport annuel* 1997, vol. 1 aux pp. 183-85.

[2] *Ibid.* à la p. 181.

2 *Création d'un groupe de travail sur le commerce et l'investissement*

Du 9 au 13 décembre 1996 s'est tenue, à Singapour, la première conférence biennale ordinaire de l'Organisation mondiale du commerce à l'échelon ministériel.[3] Aux termes de cette conférence, les Ministres ont décidé de créer notamment un groupe de travail chargé d'examiner les liens entre le commerce et l'investissement.[4]

[3] Dans le cadre des préparatifs de cette conférence, le Secrétariat de l'OMC a rendu publique au mois d'octobre un rapport détaillé sur le commerce et l'investissement. On pouvait y lire notamment: "Vu la multiplication des liens réciproques d'ordre économique, institutionnel et juridique entre le commerce et l'investissement étranger direct (IED), les gouvernements Membres de l'OMC devraient-ils continuer à recourir aux accords bilatéraux IED ou devraient-ils créer un cadre multilatéral qui reconnaisse l'existence de ces liens et tienne compte des intérêts de tous les Membres de l'OMC — qu'il s'agisse des pays développés, des pays en développement ou des pays les moins avancés?" Voir OMC, "Commerce et investissement direct, Nouveau rapport du Secrétariat de l'OMC," 9 octobre 1996, Communiqué n° 57.

[4] "Compte tenu des dispositions existantes de l'OMC relatives aux questions se rapportant à la politique en matière d'investissement et de concurrence et du programme incorporé qui est prévu dans ces domaines, y compris aux termes de l'Accord sur les MIC, et étant entendu que les travaux entrepris ne préjugeront pas de l'opportunité d'engager des négociations à l'avenir, nous convenons aussi:

- d'établir un groupe de travail chargé d'examiner les liens entre commerce et investissement; et
- d'établir un groupe de travail chargé d'étudier les questions soulevées par les Membres au sujet de l'interaction du commerce et de la politique en matière de concurrence, y compris les pratiques anticoncurrentielles, afin de déterminer les domaines qui pourraient être examinés plus avant dans le cadre de l'OMC.

Chacun de ces groupes tirera parti des travaux de l'autre si nécessaire et s'inspirera aussi des travaux de la CNUCED et des autres enceintes intergouvernementales appropriées, sans préjudice de ceux-ci. En ce qui concerne la CNUCED, nous prenons note avec satisfaction des travaux entrepris conformément à la Déclaration de Midrand et de la contribution qu'ils peuvent apporter à la compréhension des questions. Dans la conduite des travaux de ces groupes, nous préconisons une coopération avec les organisations susmentionnées pour utiliser au mieux les ressources disponibles et pour s'assurer que la dimension développement est pleinement prise en considération. Le Conseil général suivra les travaux de chaque organe et déterminera après deux ans ce que chacun devrait faire par la suite. Il est clairement entendu que s'il y a des négociations futures sur des disciplines multilatérales dans ces domaines, elles n'auront lieu qu'après que les Membres de l'OMC auront pris par consensus une décision expresse à ce sujet." Voir *supra* note 1 à la p. 116, § 20.

Le ministre canadien du Commerce international a fait des déclarations sur cette problématique lors de la journée d'ouverture[5] et de clôture de cette conférence.[6]

B L'AMI DE L'OCDE

Dans le cadre de l'Organisation de Coopération et de Développement économiques (OCDE), les négociations concernant l'*Accord multilatéral sur l'investissement* (AMI) se sont poursuivies en 1996.[7] Le groupe de négociation sur l'AMI a d'ailleurs présenté un rapport détaillé sur l'état d'avancement des négociations à la réunion annuelle du Conseil de l'OCDE au niveau ministériel qui s'est tenue les 21 et 22 mai.[8] Aux termes de cette réunion, le Conseil a réaffirmé sa volonté de parvenir à la conclusion de l'AMI lors de sa prochaine réunion en 1997.[9]

C ALÉNA

Les membres du Groupe de travail sur l'investissement et les services (GTIS)[10] ont fait de nombreuses consultations pendant

5 Voir Ministère des Affaires extérieures et du Commerce international, "Discours d'ouverture de l'honorable Art Eggleton, ministre du Commerce international, à la conférence ministérielle de l'Organisation mondiale du commerce à Singapour," 9 décembre 1996, Déclaration nº 96/55.

6 Voir Ministère des Affaires extérieures et du Commerce international, "La Conférence pose les jalons d'un système multilatéral consolidé," 13 décembre 1996, Communiqué nº 247.

7 Au sujet du contenu de l'AMI, voir P. Ratelle, "Investissement" (1996) 34 A.C.D.I. aux pp. 384-86.

8 Pour le contenu du rapport, voir (http://www.oecd.org/daf/cmis/mai/mairap96.htm).

9 "9. Ministers stress that strengthening the open and rules-based multilateral system will give renewed impetus to ongoing multilateral trade liberalisation efforts, and will map future directions for the multilateral trading system in support of sustainable real growth, employment and development. To that end they commit to: . . . (vi) further the progress made so far in the negotiation of a Multilateral Agreement on Investment (MAI): reach an agreement by the Ministerial meeting in 1997, with high standards of investment liberalisation and protection and effective dispute settlement procedures and aim at achieving a higher level of liberalisation; engage in an intensified dialogue with non-member countries, in particular those interested in acceding to the MAI." Voir (http://www.oecd.org/news_and_events/reference/nw96-53a.htm).

10 Environ 30 comités et groupes de travail ont été mis sur pied pour la mise en

1996 afin d'achever la notification des réserves de l'Annexe I concernant les mesures non conformes existantes de leurs entités infranationales, conformément aux articles 1108(2) et 1206(2) de l'ALÉNA.[11]

II Actions bilatérales

A ACCORD DE LIBRE-ÉCHANGE AVEC LE CHILI

Le 5 décembre 1996, le Canada a signé un accord de libre-échange avec le Chili.[12] Les chapitres G et H de la partie III de cet

oeuvre de l'*Accord de libre-échange nord-américain* (ALÉNA). Ces comités et groupes de travail sont composés de représentants des trois États contractants. Le GTIS a été établi par les ministres du Commerce de l'ALÉNA lors de leur réunion du 14 janvier 1994 à Mexico. Le GTIS concentre ses activités sur la mise en oeuvre notamment du c. 11 (Investissement). Il se penche sur des questions telles que: (1) le développement des services professionnels en ce qui concerne les ARM pour les conseillers juridiques, ingénieurs, architectes et autres professionnels étrangers; (2) les procédures de l'Annexe I pour les réserves des États ou des provinces d'ici à janvier 1997; (3) les questions techniques se rapportant au chevauchement des Annexes I et II.

11 Ce travail a entraîné au niveau ministériel un échange de lettres et de pièces qui a formé un accord de la Commission du libre-échange le 31 mars 1996. Cet accord avait pour effet de prolonger indéfiniment la réserve concernant toutes les mesures non conformes existantes des États et provinces sur l'investissement et les services non financiers qui contreviennent à l'ALÉNA. Les "mesures existantes" sont définies comme étant celles qui étaient en vigueur le 1er janvier 1994. À l'origine, l'ALÉNA contenait une clause d'antériorité s'appliquant à toutes les mesures non conformes existantes pour une période de deux ans prenant fin le 1er janvier 1996. Cette échéance a été repoussée au 31 mars 1996 par un échange de lettres entre les ministres du Commerce. En outre, pour des raisons de transparence, les parties à l'ALÉNA ont soumis des listes des mesures non conformes existantes en vigueur au niveau infranational. La Commission du libre-échange a également convenu de l'interprétation suivante: "L'inscription d'une mesure à l'annexe I est sans préjudice de tout recours ultérieur à l'effet que l'annexe II puisse s'appliquer à ladite mesure ou à une de ses applications." Voir Ministère des Affaires extérieures et du Commerce international, "Rapport du Groupe de travail de l'ALÉNA sur l'investissement et les services," dans (http://www.infoexport.gc.ca/nafta/11-f.asp).

12 Voir Ministère des Affaires extérieures et du Commerce international, "Des sociétés canadiennes annoncent des investissements importants alors que le Canada et le Chili signent un Accord de libre-échange," 17 décembre 1996, Communiqué no 251. Le Canada a signé un tel accord avec le Chili principalement parce que l'administration américaine n'était pas en mesure d'obtenir l'aval du Congrès américain concernant l'adhésion sans restriction du Chili à l'ALÉNA. Un des buts visés par le Canada consiste en fait à conclure un accord intérimaire afin de faciliter l'adhésion éventuelle du Chili à l'ALÉNA. Voir

accord contiennent des dispositions exhaustives en matière d'investissement qui s'inspirent de celles prévues dans l'ALÉNA.[13] Parallèlement à cet accord, et à l'instar de l'ALÉNA, les deux pays ont signé des accords de coopération dans les domaines de l'environnement et du travail.[14]

B CONVENTIONS D'INVESTISSEMENT

Pendant l'année en cours, le réseau canadien de conventions bilatérales sur la promotion et la protection des investissements (CPPI)[15] a pris de l'expansion par rapport à l'année précédente. D'abord, le Canada a conclu sans les ratifier des CCPI avec la Roumanie,[16] l'Équateur,[17] la Barbade,[18] le Venezuela,[19] le Panama[20]

Ministère des Affaires extérieures et du Commerce international, "Le Canada et le Chili négocieront des accords de coopération dans les domaines de l'environnement et du travail dans le cadre de l'accord commercial bilatéral provisoire," 29 février 1996, Communiqué n° 26.

13 Nous traiterons en détail du contenu de ces dispositions dès que cet accord entrera en vigueur au Canada.

14 Voir Ministère des Affaires extérieures et du Commerce international, "Déclaration conjointe du président du Chili, M. Eduardo Frei, et du premier ministre du Canada, M. Jean Chrétien, à l'occasion de la signature de l'Accord de libre-échange entre le Canada et le Chili," 18 novembre 1996, Déclaration n° 96/49.

15 Les CCPI sont des accords bilatéraux réciproques visant à promouvoir et à protéger les investissements étrangers par des droits et des obligations exécutoires concernant le traitement national, le traitement selon le principe de la nation la plus favorisée, l'expropriation, le transfert de fonds, les mesures relatives aux investissements liés au commerce, la transparence et le règlement des différends entre investisseurs et États et entre États.

16 Voir *Accord entre le gouvernement du Canada et le gouvernement de la Roumanie pour l'encouragement et la protection des investissements,* signé à Bucarest, le 17 avril 1996.

17 Voir *Accord entre le gouvernement du Canada et le gouvernement de la République de l'Équateur pour la promotion et la protection réciproques des investissements,* 29 avril 1996, R.T. Can. 1997 n° 25 (signé à Quito).

18 Voir *Accord entre le gouvernement du Canada et le gouvernement de la Barbade pour la promotion et la protection réciproques des investissements,* 29 mai 1996, R.T. Can. 1997 n°4 (signé à Bridgetown).

19 Voir *Accord entre le gouvernement du Canada et le gouvernement de la République du Vénézuela concernant la promotion et la protection des investissements,* signé à Caracas, le 1er juillet 1996.

20 Voir *Traité entre le gouvernement du Canada et le gouvernement de la République de Panama pour l'encouragement et la protection des investissements,* signé à Guatemala, le 12 septembre 1996.

et l'Égypte.[21] Ensuite, les CCPI conclues l'année précédente avec les Philippines et la Trinité-et-Tobago sont entrées en vigueur.[22] Ces CCPI se fondent sur le nouveau modèle canadien, lequel incorpore des dispositions clés du chapitre de l'ALÉNA sur les investissements.[23]

III Actions unilatérales

A NOUVEAUX SEUILS DE LIC

Au titre de l'article 14(2) de la *Loi sur Investissement Canada* (LIC),[24] de nouveaux seuils d'examen doivent être calculés à chaque année pour les investisseurs membres de l'OMC, ou, le cas échéant, pour tout investisseur ultimement contrôlé par un pays membre de l'OMC (autre que le Canada), et entrent en vigueur le 1er janvier de chaque année. Le montant représente le calcul de la moyenne du produit intérieur brut nominal (PIB) aux prix du marché pour des périodes spécifiques, tel que publié par Statistiques Canada, multiplié par le montant déterminé pour l'année précédente. Pour 1996, le montant était de 168 millions de dollars.[25]

B RIPOSTE À LA LOI HELMS-BURTON

Suite à l'entrée en vigueur de la loi américaine Helms-Burton (LHB),[26] le Canada y a réagi en modifiant sa *Loi sur les mesures*

21 Voir *Accord entre le gouvernement du Canada et le gouvernement de la République arabe d'Égypte pour l'encouragement et la protection des investissements,* 13 novembre 1996, R.T. Can. 1997 n°31 (signé au Caire).

22 Voir *Accord entre le gouvernement du Canada et le gouvernement des Philippines sur la promotion et la protection des investissements,* 9 novembre 1995, R.T. Can. 1996 n° 46; *Accord entre le gouvernement du Canada et le gouvernement de la Trinité-et-Tobago pour l'encouragement et la protection des investissements (avec Annexe),* 11 septembre 1995, R.T. Can. 1996 n° 22.

23 Des CCPI suivant le nouveau modèle ont également été conclues avec l'Ukraine, la Lettonie et l'Afrique du Sud. Au sujet des CPPI antérieures à 1996, voir P. Ratelle, "Investissement" (1996) 34 A.C.D.I. 381-82; (1995) 33 A.C.D.I. 361; (1994) 32 A.C.D.I. 298-99; (1993) 31 A.C.D.I. 337-38; (1992) 30 A.C.D.I. 337; (1991) 29 A.C.D.I. 446-47; (1990) 28 A.C.D.I. 453-54.

24 L.R.C. 1985, c. 28 (1er suppl).

25 Voir Gaz. C. 1996.I.1048.

26 Le projet de LHB (ou *Cuban Liberty and Democratic Solidarity (Libertad) Act* de 1996) a été adopté par le Sénat américain le 5 mars et par la Chambre des

extraterritoriales étrangères (LMEÉ).[27] Les modifications à la LMEÉ entreront en vigueur le 1er janvier 1997.[28] Le Canada a également eu des consultations avec les États-Unis à ce sujet dans le cadre de l'ALÉNA, et a abordé la question dans le cadre d'organisations internationales comme l'ONU, l'OEA et l'OCDE.[29] Enfin, le Canada a annoncé qu'il participerait, en tant que tierce partie, à la contestation de la LHB par l'Union européenne devant un groupe spécial de l'OMC.[30]

---

représentants le 6 mars. Le président Bill Clinton lui a donné force de loi le 12 mars. Le Titre III de la LHB permet aux nationaux des États-Unis qui revendiquent la propriété de biens expropriés par Cuba de poursuivre des nationaux étrangers, y compris canadiens, devant les tribunaux américains. Si la société poursuivie n'a pas d'actif aux États-Unis, le plaignant américain pourrait tenter de faire appliquer le jugement par les tribunaux canadiens. Le Titre IV de la LHB permet au gouvernement américain de refuser l'admission aux dirigeants d'entreprises canadiennes, ainsi qu'à leurs conjoints et à leurs enfants, qui, selon le département d'État, sont réputées avoir fait le "trafic" de biens visés par une réclamation américaine. Le 15 juillet 1996, le président américain a annoncé la suspension pour six mois du droit de poursuite en vertu du Titre III, et décidera de proroger ou non cette suspension le 16 janvier 1997. Voir Ministère des Affaires extérieures et du Commerce international, "Le Canada encouragé par la décision du président américain sur la Loi Helms-Burton," 16 juillet 1996, Communiqué n° 127.

27 Voir *Loi modifiant la Loi sur les mesures extraterritoriales étrangères*, S.C. 1996, c. 28, laquelle a reçu la sanction royale le 28 novembre 1996 et doit entrée en vigueur le 1er janvier 1997. La LMEÉ modifiée: (1) garantira que les jugements rendus en vertu de la LHB ne seront ni respectés ni reconnus au Canada; (2) permettra aux Canadiens de recouvrer devant les tribunaux canadiens toute somme payée en vertu de la LHB ainsi que leurs frais judiciaires et les dommages subséquents — prescription appelée "clause de récupération"; (3) donnera au procureur général du Canada l'autorité de modifier une annexe énumérant les lois étrangères inadmissibles contraires au droit international. Voir Ministère des Affaires extérieures et du Commerce international, "La loi visant à contrer la loi Helms-Burton entre en vigueur le 1er janvier 1997," 30 décembre 1996, Communiqué n° 261.

28 *Ibid.*

29 *Ibid.*

30 Voir Ministère des Affaires extérieures et du Commerce international, "Le Canada appuie la requête de l'Union européenne visant la constitution d'un groupe spécial sur la loi Helms-Burton dans le cadre de l'OMC," 21 novembre 1996, Communiqué n° 214.

Canadian Practice in International Law / La pratique canadienne en matière de droit international public

At the Department of Foreign Affairs in 1996-97 / Au ministère des Affaires étrangères en 1996-97

compiled by / préparé par
PHILIPPE KIRSCH

HUMAN RIGHTS

Child Labour: International Legal Framework

On January 23, 1996, the Legal Bureau wrote:

The following is a brief review of the principal international instruments relevant to the issue of child labour. Also discussed are the instruments applicable to forced or compulsory labour that might be relevant when dealing with certain situations including child labour. If necessary, a more complete analysis of these instruments could be provided at a later date. This memo will deal firstly with legal instruments relevant to child labour,

---

Philippe Kirsch, Q.C., is a legal advisor in the Department of Foreign Affairs and International Trade. The extracts from official correspondence contained in this survey have been made available by courtesy of the Department of Foreign Affairs and International Trade. Material appearing in the House of Commons Debates is not included. Some of the correspondence from which extracts are given was provided for the general guidance of the inquirer in relation to specific facts that are not often described in full in the extracts contained in this compilation. The statements of law and practice should not necessarily be regarded as a definitive statement by the Department of Foreign Affairs and International Trade of that law or practice.

both binding and not binding on Canada. Secondly, it will address more general instruments that could have application to the situation of child labour.

(1) Child Labour

(a) International legal instruments to which Canada is a party

The International Covenant on Economic, Social and Cultural Rights (ICESCR) (Article 10(3)) provides that "children and young persons should be protected from economic and social exploitation" and that "their employment in work harmful to their morals or health or dangerous to life or likely to hamper their normal development should be punishable by law." It also mentions that States should set age limits below which the paid employment of child labour should be prohibited. In addition, the right of everyone to the enjoyment of just and favourable conditions of work is detailed in Article 7.

The Convention on the Rights of the Child (CRC), adhered to by over 180 states, recognizes (in Article 32(1)) the "right of the child to be protected from economic exploitation and from performing any work that is likely to be hazardous or to interfere with the child's education, or to be harmful to the child's health or physical, mental, spiritual, moral or social development." Article 32(2) obliges State Parties to "take legislative, administrative, social and educational measures to ensure the implementation of the present article" and specifically calls on State Parties to:

(a) provide for a minimum age or minimum ages for admission to employment,
(b) provide for appropriate regulation of the hours and conditions of employment,
(c) provide for appropriate penalties or sanctions to ensure the effective enforcement of the present article.

With regard to Article 32(2)(a), the question arises as to whether State Parties are required to set a general minimum age of employment, or whether it is sufficient if they prohibit children from working during school hours, or in particular forms of employment that might be harmful to them. Canada adopted the second interpretation in its defence of its first report under the CRC in May 1995 before the Committee on the Rights of the Child. Canada's position was not commented upon by the Committee.

Canada's obligations with regard to these international instruments is to ensure the implementation of the provisions in domestic law. Other State Parties have the same obligations, subject to whatever reservations they might have made. It is important to note that the above-mentioned provisions do not have as their objective the prohibition or elimination of child labour. Rather, they aim at regulating child labour, and at prohibiting the exploitation of children and certain types of child labour detrimental to the child's development.

(b) Other international instruments non-legally binding on Canada

The provisions of the Convention on the Rights of the Child mentioned above are drawn from standards set by the Minimum Age Convention

(ILO 138), which Canada has not ratified. Article 2 provides that States shall specify "a minimum age for employment or work." The ILO Committee of Experts has confirmed that the Convention requires setting a minimum age for all employment or work subject to specified exceptions and that it is insufficient to prohibit employment of children during school hours or to limit minimum age provisions to selected sectors of the economy and occupations.

When Canada presented its report to the Committee on the Rights of the Child, Canada explained that it had not ratified the Minimum Age Convention because Canadian laws and practice do not meet the Convention's requirements and will not in the foreseeable future. For example, no jurisdiction in Canada prohibits work for young persons under the school leaving age to the full extent required by the Convention, and no jurisdiction in Canada prohibits all work, including light work, for children under 13 years of age.

There is however considerable compliance in Canada with the underlying principles of the ILO Convention No. 138. Canadian jurisdictions generally:

- have protective legislation specifying conditions under which children under the school leaving age can be employed;
- prohibit the employment of children under the school leaving age during school hours; and
- prohibit work outside school hours for young people under specified ages, in specific occupations and situations which are likely to be injurious to their health, education or welfare.

(2) Forced or Compulsory Labour

(a) International instruments binding on Canada

Although the following instruments do not apply to child labour specifically, they would be relevant to the worst cases of child exploitation. As discussed above there is a distinction to be made between child labour and the exploitation of children.

The Universal Declaration of Human Rights (Article 4) states that "no one shall be held in slavery or servitude: slavery and the slave trade shall be prohibited in all their forms." Similarly, the International Covenant on Civil and Political Rights (Article 8) provides that no one shall be held in slavery, servitude or required to perform forced or compulsory labour.

Canada is a party to both the Slavery Convention (signed at Geneva on September 25, 1926 and amended by the Protocol of December 7, 1953) which defines slavery as "the status or condition of a person over whom any or all of the powers attaching to the right of ownership are exercised," and the Supplementary Convention on the Abolition of Slavery, Slave Trade, and Institutions and Practices Similar to Slavery, which refers to the Slavery Convention and complements it.

Article 1 of the Supplementary Convention calls on State Parties to take measures towards the abolition of a number of institutions and practices such as debt bondage, which it defines as the "status or condition arising by a pledge by a debtor of his personal services or of those of a person under his control as security for a debt, if the value of those services as reasonably assessed is not applied towards the liquidation of the debt or the length and nature of those services are not respectively limited and defined" (Article 1 (a)). Another practice falling in the same section is "any institution or practice whereby a child or young person under the age of 18 is delivered by either or both of his natural parents or by his guardian to another person, whether for reward or not, with a view to the exploitation of the child or young person or of his labour" (Article 1 (d)). A United Nations publication (Fact Sheet No. 14 on Contemporary Forms of Slavery), makes the following comments on debt bondage:

> Debt bondage can hardly be distinguished from traditional slavery because it prevents the victim from leaving its job or the land he tills until the money is repaid. Although in theory a debt is repayable over a period of time, a situation of bondage arises when in spite of all his efforts, the borrower cannot wipe it out. Normally, the debt is inherited by the bonded labourer's children. Sharecropping is a familiar way of leading debt borrowers into debt bondage.

The obligation to take measures towards the abolition of debt bondage and other practices should be understood not only in terms of adopting domestic measures but also in terms of making efforts in the international arena. In fact, one of the preambular paragraphs of the Supplementary Convention mentions the need for the intensification of "national as well as international efforts towards the abolition of slavery, the slave trade and institutions and practices similar to slavery."

(b) Instruments non-legally binding on Canada

ILO Convention (No. 29) Concerning Forced Labour also addresses the issue of compulsory labour; however Canada is not a party. Article 2 defines forced or compulsory labour as "all work or service which is exacted from any person under the menace of any penalty and for which the said person has not offered himself voluntarily."

There also exist a number of General Assembly and Commission of Human Rights resolutions on the rights of the child, conclusions and recommendations issued by the Committee on the Rights of the Child, Special Rapporteurs reports and recommendations, and reports by the Working Group on Contemporary Forms of Slavery that could be looked at in a more exhaustive study of the subject. This body of work, while not legally binding, provides a solid basis for reenforcement of the existing international legal obligations. It is often used to strengthen human rights standards incrementally and therefore is an important tool.

In conclusion, the majority of relevant existing legal instruments aim at the regulation of child labour and at prohibiting the exploitation of child labour, and not at the complete abolition of child labour unless it is tantamount to slavery. The obligations undertaken by State Parties relate to the domestic implementation of the norms provided in these instruments. As is the case with most human rights instruments, the obligations are undertaken by State Parties towards their own populations. This is not to say, however, that taking measures towards increasing international respect for and implementation of these norms should not be an objective of State Parties to the conventions.

INTERNATIONAL ECONOMIC LAW

Settlement of Disputes

In his comments on the Appellate Body Report in Canada — Certain Measures Concerning Periodicals, on July 30, 1997, the Ambassador of Canada to the World Trade Organization in Geneva wrote:

Opening Remarks

Canada acknowledges, in accordance with Articles 16.4 and 17.14 of the Understanding on Rules and Procedures Governing the Settlement of Disputes (DSU), that the Panel and Appellate Body reports are adopted and unconditionally accepted by the parties to the dispute, unless the Dispute Settlement Body (DSB) decides by consensus not to adopt the reports. Nonetheless, Canada notes that the adoption procedure is without prejudice to the right of Members to express their views. Consequently, Canada wishes to express its views on the reports of the Panel and the Appellate Body, and to underline the importance to Canada of a number of issues raised in this case.

It is with respect for the fundamental importance of the dispute settlement system that Canada expresses its great disappointment with the report of the Appellate Body, and with certain aspects of the Appellate Body's deliberations. Canada's observations may be reflected in the future discussions that Members may have in the context of the review of the DSU.

Canada has a vested interest in an open, respected and stable system for international trade. However, as international trade leads to an increasingly globalized and homogeneous world, it will be culture that will preserve the distinctiveness of WTO Members and ensure their ongoing sovereignty. The Government of Canada is therefore committed to maintaining effective policies and policy instruments in support of cultural development.

Print-based media are still a primary means of communication in Canada and around the world. Of all the different types of print-based media, periodicals in particular are timely and topical publications. Periodicals that are created for and in response to the needs of the Canadian market are not like periodicals that are created for and reflect the needs, interests and perceptions of the markets of other countries. It is not realistic for Canada, or for any Member of the WTO for that matter, to rely upon, nor even expect, media products from other countries to attempt to reflect its own reality. For it is in this reality that our sovereign distinctiveness as a country is determined. It is therefore critically important that a way be found, within the rules-based trading system, for WTO Members to be able to develop and maintain policies that promote their own unique culture and identity.

Expeditiousness and Fairness

The dispute settlement provisions in the WTO Agreement ensure greater expeditiousness and fairness in the application of trade rules.

Canada was at the forefront of the reform of the dispute settlement process during the Uruguay Round negotiations and continues to support these goals.

Expeditiousness is a constant preoccupation of the DSU working procedures that provide strict time-frames for DSB decisions. Ensuring an expeditious dispute settlement system must not result, however, in neglect of the fundamental principles of fairness.

Canada expresses disappointment with the handling of basic fairness requirements by the Appellate Body. Basic fairness requires an opportunity to argue and be heard. The determination of substitutability, competitiveness and protectionism under Article 3:2, second sentence, of the GATT 1994 is a point of critical importance to the interpretation of the GATT 1994 and to the outcome of this case. Argument was neither submitted to nor solicited by the Appellate Body on these points. Had an opportunity been provided to submit a full written and oral argument, there would be no basis for a claim of lack of procedural fairness.

The Appellate Body found that it could complete the analysis of Article 3:2 of the GATT 1994 in this case, provided that there was sufficient basis in the "Main Arguments" part of the Panel Report to allow the Appellate Body to do so. The Appellate Body, therefore, relied on the summary of arguments from the Panel report with respect to Article 3:2, second sentence of the GATT 1994. This is no substitute for a full written and oral argument on appeal.

The Appellate Body based its decision on a test that was not dealt with in the Panel report, that was not raised on appeal, and that was accordingly not addressed in the written or oral arguments of the parties. No notice was given to the parties of the intention of the Appellate Body to base its decision on a test that did not form the basis of the appeal under Article 17, paragraph 6 of the DSU. The Appellate Body, therefore, rendered its decision without the benefit of written or oral argument by the parties, and without providing a proper opportunity to the parties to submit such argument. The procedure adopted by the Appellate Body amounts to a denial of the right to be given notice and to be heard on all relevant issues.

The Appellate Body relied on the *United States-Gasoline* case, where it considered the chapeau to Article 20 after deciding that one of the subparagraphs of Article 20 was applicable. This was simply a two-step analysis of a single legal provision. Any ruling on whether an exception in Article 20 applies automatically involves a consideration of the chapeau. The two sentences of Article 3:2 of the GATT 1994, in contrast, are distinct obligations with different coverage and rules, and have been clearly treated as such in prior decisions, including the *Japan-Alcoholic Beverages* case.

In reviewing Canada's appeal of the Panel's decision on the excise tax as a services measure, the Appellate Body inferred that because Canada did not appeal the ruling on Tariff Code 9958, the excise tax should be considered a tax on a good. It is inappropriate, as a matter of fairness, to draw prejudicial inferences from decisions not to appeal distinct issues.

GATT / GATS

With respect to Canada's arguments on the application of GATT disciplines to services measures, Canada is most disappointed in the

Appellate Body's ruling. A coherent interpretation of the GATT 1994 and the GATS together, giving meaning to all the treaties' provisions, is essential for future compliance by Members with all their obligations and commitments in respect of trade in goods and services.

When the Appellate Body is asked to rule on the relative scope of the two agreements, it is important to apply careful and deliberate reasoning for Members to understand how it arrived at its decision. In this case, the Appellate Body was asked to rule on the applicability of the GATT and GATS provisions to the excise tax. We are disappointed that the Appellate Body did not provide considered reasoning on the question of the excise tax as a measure affecting advertising services. Instead, the decision on this critical point appears to rest largely on the Appellate Body's interpretation of policy linkages between the tax on advertising and the border measure targeting magazines *per se.*

It is clear from the report of the Appellate Body that WTO Members have to reflect upon the issue of the relationship between obligations under the GATT 1994 and commitments under the GATS. In the absence of agreement among Members on the respective scope of the two Agreements, we will face an increasing number of disputes that leave the Appellate Body to make this determination. Canada points to the recent *EC-Bananas* decision, and underscores the need for further attention to this issue, if our work in the services area is to make meaningful progress.

GATT Article 3

The Appellate Body considered that no decision on the "like products" issue could properly be made because of the absence of any adequate analysis in the Panel report. If it was impossible to make a determination of "likeness" for the purpose of Article 3:2, first sentence, in view of the absence of an adequate analysis in the Panel report, then *a fortiori* it was also impossible to determine whether the products were "directly competitive or substitutable" for the purpose of the second sentence. The Panel report contained no analysis of the second sentence at all, which is also to be addressed on a case-by-case basis, according to the *Japan-Alcoholic Beverages* case. Canada questions the Appellate Body's decision to refuse to rule on an issue because the Panel analysis is inadequate, but then to rule on a separate issue that the Panel failed to analyze at all.

The Appellate Body's finding on the "like products" issue was, in part, based on its analysis of the *Sports Illustrated* and *Harrowsmith* examples, neither of which was relevant to the case. This indicates a fundamental misunderstanding of the facts. The *Sports Illustrated* split-run was a *domestic* and not an imported product. This was common ground between the parties. The Appellate Body also based its conclusion on the fact that the U.S. edition of *Harrowsmith Country Life,* a Canadian-owned periodical formerly published in the United States, had ceased production. Since this product was never exported to Canada, and was not destined for a Canadian readership, it cannot be sustained that the closure of the U.S. edition amounts to a protective application of the tax. Thus the measure was to have an effect only on a domestic operation.

The Appellate Body assumed at page 19 of their Report that the words "directly or indirectly" in Article 3:2, first sentence, must also apply to Article 3:2, second sentence "given the broader application of the latter." While the second sentence is broader in its product coverage, it clearly is not broader in respect of the taxation measures to which it applies.

The statement quoted from the Panel report at pages 26-27 of the Appellate Body report shows that magazines need both circulation and advertising revenue, and that a shortfall of advertising will affect editorial quality. It does *not* show that magazines are directly competitive or substitutable as consumer products. We contend that the quotation at page 27 of the Appellate Body report from the Report of the Task Force on the Canadian Magazine Industry does not provide sufficient evidence on which to base such a conclusion when weighed against the countervailing evidence that the relevant magazines were very "poor substitutes" as consumer products. It is our view that all that is left of the analysis on this issue is a political statement whose probative value, either as a matter of economics or of law, is minimal.

"Funded" Postal Rates

The Appellate Body said that their textual interpretation was supported by the context of Article 3:8(b) examined in relation to Articles 3:2 and 3:4 of the GATT 1994. But the Appellate Body did not make any examination of the context of the producers' subsidy exemption in relation to national treatment disciplines. Further, the Appellate Body relied on the object and purpose of Article 3:8(b) to draw their conclusions in respect of "funded" rates. Unfortunately, the Appellate Body did not then explain what the object and purpose were nor did it conduct any analysis of them. As a result, this decision fails to provide sufficient reasoning to enable us to understand why the "funded" postal rates could not benefit from the exemption allowed in Article 3:8(b).

Conclusion

Canada's commitment to the dispute settlement system remains firm. It is Canada's intention to continue to abide by the rules and procedures governing the settlement of disputes. Canada will inform the DSB of our intentions in respect of implementation of the recommendations and rulings of the DSB by August 29, 1997. However, in lieu of making its statement at the meeting required by Article 21(3) of the DSU, Canada will inform the DSB by letter transmitted to the Chairman for circulation to the Members of the DSB. We have spoken with the United States, the other party in this case, and we both agree that our respective rights and obligations will be preserved through this approach, as if the meeting under Article 21(3) had been held.

In their concluding remarks, the panellists stressed "that the ability of any Member to take measures to protect its cultural identity was not at issue in the present case." This ability is not to be taken for granted. In the Canadian context, where we share a common language and the world's longest undefended border with a neighbour ten times our size, it is our unique challenge to "protect our cultural identity" with no possibility of achieving the economies of scale available to producers of cultural products and services that reinforce the American identity. While many aspects of the Canadian problem are unique, we believe all Members have an interest in addressing the issue squarely. For its part, Canada is committed to policies and measures to strengthen the viability of Canadian cultural industries, bearing in mind the need to ensure that Canada's rights and obligations as a WTO Member are respected.

INTERNATIONAL ENVIRONMENTAL LAW

Precautionary Principle

In its submissions to the World Trade Organization in the *Beef Hormones* case, Canada wrote:

The EC has cited the "precautionary principle" as a "general principle of international law." Canada notes that this "principle" was not presented as part of the "Legal Discussion" in either of the EC submissions. Apart from a cursory reference to the "precautionary approach" in the EC's first oral submission, the EC did not attempt to demonstrate how the "precautionary principle" affects, in its view, the interpretation of the treaty rules contained in the SPS Agreement and the GATT 1994.

Canada submits that the precautionary approach or concept is an *emerging* principle of international law, which may in the future crystallize into one of the "general principles of law recognized by civilized nations" within the meaning of Article 38(1)(c) of the Statute of the International Court of Justice. However, in Canada's view it has not yet attained the status of a general principle of international law, nor that of a rule of customary international law. The reason for characterizing the precautionary approach as "an emerging principle of international law" is that it is not clear whether one deals with a policy approach or a legal principle.

The precautionary approach is of relatively recent origin. There is not one agreed definition of the precautionary approach. It has found its expression in different provisions in treaties and other international instruments that vary considerably in content. In the US-EC Panel, the United States defined the precautionary approach as "call[ing] for taking action based on preliminary or inconclusive scientific information where it may be imperative to act in the absence of conclusive scientific information." It gave the example of global climate change and how, in that instance, preliminary scientific information indicated the need to act as a precaution even though a full scientific understanding had not yet been achieved. The United States also stated that "to invoke the precautionary principle, there still must be some scientific information indicating a risk, not . . . mere speculation." Canada agrees with these observations.

The precautionary approach has not crystallized into a rule that dictates a certain course of action in specific instances. Rather, it has found concrete expression in various treaties and other instruments related to the protection of the environment cited in chapter 3 of Freestone and Hey, *The Precautionary Principle and International Law* (1996).

The non-absolute nature of the precautionary approach is exemplified by principle 15 of the Rio Declaration on Environment and Development, which provides:

> In order to protect the environment, the precautionary approach shall be widely applied by States according to their capabilities. Where there are threats of serious or irreversible damage, lack of full scientific certainty shall not be used as a reason for postponing cost-effective measures to prevent environmental degradation.

Thus even in the non-legally binding Rio Declaration, the precautionary approach was qualified in several respects. Furthermore, the Rio Declaration did not reject a scientific approach to the assessment of environmental risks. Principle 17 of the same Declaration provides:

> Environmental impact assessment, as a national policy instrument, shall be undertaken for proposed activities that are likely to have a significant adverse impact on the environment and are subject to a decision of a competent national authority.

The EC has cited the language of Article 130r(2) of the Treaty Establishing the European Community as evidence of its adherence to the precautionary approach. Article 130r(3) makes it clear, however, that the precautionary approach is not an absolute guide in the formulation of EC environmental policy. The text provides as follows:

> In preparing its policy on the environment, the Community shall take account of:
>
> · available scientific and technical data;
> · environmental conditions in the various regions of the Community;
> · the potential benefits and costs of action or lack of action;
> · the economic and social development of the Community as a whole and the balanced development of its regions.

Thus the precautionary approach is not absolute and any guidance it provides must be balanced against other policy objectives in the drafting of specific measures.

Birnie and Boyle, in *International Law and the Environment*, arrived at the following conclusion regarding the "precautionary principle":

> Despite its attractions, the great variety of interpretations given to the precautionary principle and the novel and the far-reaching effects of some applications suggest that it is not yet a principle of international law. Difficult questions concerning the point at which it becomes applicable to any given activity remain unanswered and seriously undermine its normative character and practical utility, although support for it does indicate a policy of greater prudence on the part of those states willing to accept it.

Although this was written in 1992, Canada submits that this conclusion is still valid.

When the SPS Agreement was being negotiated, governments were aware of the precautionary approach as it was being developed in the field of international environmental law. The inclusion of Article 5(7) in the SPS Agreement, which permits WTO Members to proceed with the adoption of provisional measures on the basis of available pertinent information, is an expression of the precautionary approach in the SPS Agreement. Thus the precautionary approach was taken into account when the internal balance of rights and obligations within the SPS Agreement was struck.

The EC has conceded that its import ban is *not* based on Article 5(7) of the SPS Agreement. The EC appears to suggest, however, that the precautionary concept could somehow override certain provisions in the text of the SPS Agreement. Canada rejects any such suggestion. Any intimation by the EC that the precautionary concept would somehow justify the adoption of measures under the SPS Agreement that are not based on scientific evidence runs counter to fundamental canons of treaty interpretation laid down in Articles 31 and 32 of the Vienna Convention on the Law of Treaties and would amount to a revision of the SPS Agreement. This is so even if the precautionary approach could be said to have attained the status of a general principle of international law. Thus, the precautionary approach or principle cannot be invoked by the EC to override the obligations of the SPS Agreement.

Dispute Settlement

In a memorandum on dispute resolution under the North American Agreement on Environmental Co-operation, dated June 12, 1997, the Legal Bureau wrote:

The North American Agreement on Environmental Co-operation (NAAEC), the so-called "environmental side accord" to the North American Free Trade Agreement, entered into force on January 1, 1994. Its Parties are Canada, the United States, and Mexico. The NAAEC seeks to protect the North American environment by ensuring that each Party effectively enforces its environmental laws.

Part 5 of the NAAEC provides for binding dispute settlement by establishing a multi-stage process to address situations where one Party alleges that another Party has displayed a "persistent pattern of failure" to "effectively enforce its environmental law."

The first stage is consultation pursuant to Article 22. The consulting Parties are required to "make every attempt to arrive at a mutually satisfactory resolution of the matter through consultations."

If the consulting Parties fail to resolve the matter within 60 days of delivery of a request for consultations, either Party may request a special session of the Council of the Commission for Environmental Co-operation (CEC) to examine the dispute. The Council comprises the NAAEC Environment Ministers or their designees. The Council must convene within 20 days of the request to "endeavour to resolve the dispute promptly." In doing so, the Council may call on technical advisors, create working groups or expert groups, or have recourse to good offices, conciliation, mediation, or other dispute resolution procedures.

If the matter is unresolved within 60 days after the Council has convened, the Council, at the request of any consulting Party and by a two-thirds vote, convenes an arbitral panel under Article 24.

The arbitral panel, if established, would comprise five members. The disputing Parties are to "endeavour to agree on the chair of the panel within 15 days after the Council votes to convene the panel." If they cannot agree on the chair within this period, then "the disputing Party chosen by lot shall select within five days a chair who is not a citizen of that Party." Within 15 days of the selection of the chair, the remaining panellists are chosen through the process of "reverse selection." Each disputing Party selects "two panellists who are citizens of the other disputing Party." Panellists are "normally" to be selected from a tri-laterally-agreed roster of expert panellists. This roster has yet to be established. The panel's procedures would likely include written and oral argument, although the Rules of Procedure required by the NAAEC have yet to be established. Within 180 days of the selection of the last panellist, the panel presents to the disputing Parties an initial report containing:

(a) findings of fact;
(b) its determination as to "whether there has been a persistent pattern of failure by the Party complained against to effectively enforce its environmental law," or any other determination requested in the terms of reference; and
(c) if the panel concludes that there has been a persistent failure to enforce environmental law, its recommendations for the resolution of the dispute, "which normally shall be that the Party complained against adopt and implement an action plan sufficient to remedy the pattern of non-enforcement."

The panel would consider any comments the disputing Parties may wish to make, and then present the final report within 60 days of the initial report. The final report is published five days after it is transmitted to the Council.

After receiving the report, the disputing Parties may agree on a mutually satisfactory plan to remedy the problem. If the Parties are unable to agree, or if one Party believes that the other is not implementing an action plan, the panel may impose an action plan and/or fines on the offending Party. The monetary enforcement assessment can, depending on the circumstances, be substantial. Annex 34 of the NAAEC provides that, for the first year after the entry into force of the NAAEC, the monetary enforcement assessment could have gone as high as US $20 million. Thereafter, any monetary assessment shall be no greater than .007 per cent of the total trade in goods between the Parties during the most recent year for which data are available. If the Party does not pay the fine, the other Party may suspend NAFTA benefits. However, the suspension of trade benefits provisions are not applicable to Canada since Annex 36A of the NAAEC provides that decisions of arbitral panels may be enforced directly in a Canadian court.

INTERNATIONAL HUMANITARIAN LAW

Deportations and Forcible Transfers from Occupied Territories

In a memorandum dated July 31, 1997, the Legal Bureau wrote:

Article 49 of the Fourth Geneva Convention contains a general prohibition on the forcible transfers or deportations of protected persons:

> Individual or mass forcible transfers, as well as deportations of protected persons from occupied territory to the territory of the Occupying Power or to that of any other country, occupied or not, are prohibited, regardless of their motive.

The Article does provide an exception for the evacuation of a population for security or military reasons:

> Nevertheless, the Occupying Power may undertake total or partial evacuation of a given area if the security of the population or imperative military reasons so demand. Such evacuations may not involve the displacement of protected persons outside the bounds of the occupied territory except when for material reasons it is impossible to avoid such displacement. Persons thus evacuated shall be transferred back to their homes as soon as the hostilities in the area in question have ceased.

It is our view that this exception should be read narrowly and would not necessarily apply to the deportation or forcible transfers of individuals, referred to in the first paragraph. This interpretation is supported by the Commentary on the Geneva Conventions:

> Unlike deportation and forcible transfers, evacuation is a provisional measure entirely negative in character and is, moreover, often taken in the interests of the protected persons.

As the prohibition on the deportation of protected persons from occupied territories is unqualified, the next question is which persons would be considered as "protected persons." Article 4 of the Fourth Geneva Convention states:

> Persons protected by the Convention are those who, at a given moment and in any manner whatsoever, find themselves, in the case of a conflict or occupation, in the hands of a Party to the conflict or Occupying Power of which they are not nationals.

Persons who are covered by the other three Geneva Conventions, in particular those who would fall within the category of prisoner of war (POW), i.e. members of the armed forces, militia, and organized resistance movements, are not considered "protected persons."

In summary, the Fourth Geneva Convention contains an absolute prohibition on deportation of "protected persons," i.e. civilians, whether they are considered to be security risks or not, from occupied territories.

Humanitarian Intervention

In a memorandum dated November 13, 1996, the Legal Bureau wrote:

Humanitarian intervention is a concept which developed in the 19th century to provide legal justification for interference by one or more States in the internal affairs of another State. The basis for humanitarian intervention was given as the fundamental shared concern for the minimum conditions of survival for all humanity. In fact, in all cases that this was used as the justification for unilateral action by a State, it was not accepted by the international community as the true motivation. In this manner, the concept of humanitarian intervention was discredited.

The legality of humanitarian intervention has always been controversial. Since the advent of the UN Charter, the principle has enjoyed little support among States. Indeed, both paragraphs 4 and 7 of Article 2 of the Charter along with subsequent legal instruments suggest that humanitarian intervention is not incorporated into modern international law. It is also difficult to find support for the doctrine in the post-Charter behaviour of States. For its part, Canada has never endorsed humanitarian intervention as an exception to the principle of non-intervention in the domestic affairs of States unless carried out collectively under the auspices of the UN Security Council's Chapter 7 powers.

INTERNATIONAL LEGAL CO-OPERATION

Mutual Assistance in Tax Matters

On February 9, 1996, the Legal Bureau wrote:

As a general proposition, States may agree by treaty to provisions for recovery of tax claims. This was done by Canada and the United States in the March 17, 1995, Protocol to the 1980 Double Taxation Agreement, by provision of the new Article 26A (Assistance in Collection). In this 1995 Protocol, the Parties agreed to assist each other in the collection of revenue claims in the territory of the other Party. There is a restriction — a requesting state can only ask for assistance if the taxpayer is a citizen of the requesting State or a corporation organized under the laws of the requesting State. Thus, for example, Canada could ask the United States for assistance in collecting taxes from Canadian citizens or corporations in the United States, but not from U.S. citizens or corporations.

At international law, a State cannot use the courts of another State to recover penalties or taxes without the permission of the latter State. This is particularly true for revenue claims. For example, this doctrine was accepted by the Supreme Court of Canada in denying enforcement of a U.S. judgment for taxes (*United States* v. *Harden*, [1963] S.C.R. 366).

The rationale for the rule seems based on a concept of sovereignty: "[it is] the assertion of the right to have its sovereign powers in regard to penalties and taxes respected and enforced that constitutes the infringement of the sovereignty of the State of the forum and therefore is contrary to international law" (F. A. Mann, "Conflict of Laws and Public Law," Recueil des Cours 132 (1971) at 166).

A Canadian commentator on the *Harden* decision thought that the there was another reason for the public policy of not enforcing foreign tax claims. He believed that there was a desire to avoid the political and diplomatic embarrassment of declining to enforce a particular foreign tax claim on the grounds that it was oppressive or otherwise objectionable. The safer course was to avoid this situation by declining to enforce any foreign tax claim. As this position would lead to tax evasion, he proposed that there be reciprocal enforcement of judgment statutes (K. Lysek, "Foreign Revenue Laws: United States v. Harden," (1964) *Canadian Yearbook of International Law,* 245.)

Whatever the merit in this analysis of the underlying rationale for the public policy, the conclusion that the executive, and not the courts, should take action to avoid tax evasion is sound. While not a reciprocal enforcement of judgments statute, the treaty arrangements providing for mutual administrative assistance have a similar result.

INTERNATIONAL ORGANIZATIONS

Co-operation between the Council of the NAAEC and the NAFTA Free Trade Commission

On June 4, 1997, the Legal Bureau issued a legal opinion on Article 10(6) of the North American Agreement on Environmental Co-operation (Agreement) as follows:

Article 10(6) provides for co-operation between the Council, the governing body for the Agreement, and its equivalent for the North American Free Trade Agreement (NAFTA), the NAFTA Commission. The aim of the Article is to help the NAFTA Commission achieve the environmental goals and objectives of the NAFTA. This Article reads as follows:

> The Council shall co-operate with the NAFTA Free Trade Commission to achieve the environmental goals and objectives of the NAFTA by:
>
> (a) acting as a point of inquiry and receipt for comments from non-governmental organizations and persons concerning those goals and objectives;
>
> (b) providing assistance in consultations under Article 1114 of the NAFTA where a Party considers that another Party is waiving or derogating from, or offering to waive or otherwise derogate from, an environmental measure as an encouragement to establish, acquire, expand, or retain an investment of an investor, with a view to avoiding any such encouragement;
>
> (c) contributing to the prevention or resolution of environment-related trade disputes by:
>
> (i) seeking to avoid disputes between the Parties,
>
> (ii) making recommendations to the Free Trade Commission with respect to the avoidance of such disputes, and

(iii) identifying experts able to provide information or technical advice to NAFTA committees, working groups and other NAFTA bodies;

(d) considering on an ongoing basis the environmental effects of the NAFTA; and

(e) otherwise assisting the Free Trade Commission in environment-related matters.

We are of the opinion that the implementation of Article 10(6) is under the authority of the Council. The Council is required to achieve the goals and objectives of this Article in co-operation with the NAFTA Commission. As such co-operation has to be seen in the broader context of the NAFTA Commission's obligation to implement NAFTA, including its environmental goals and objectives, it is within the authority of the NAFTA Commission to decide what to do with this co-operation. However, the Council is not subject to the authority of the NAFTA Commission in its activities under Article 10(6).

Paragraph 10(6)(a) provides that the Council will act as a point of inquiry and receipt for public comments on the environmental goals and objectives of the NAFTA. It is clearly a Council action that is triggered by a third-party and not by the NAFTA Commission.

By virtue of paragraph 10(6)(b), the Council shall co-operate with the NAFTA Commission "by providing co-operation in consultations under Article 1114 of the NAFTA." Based on the fact that it is "inappropriate to encourage investment by relaxing domestic health, safety or environmental measures," Article 1114(2) of the NAFTA provides for consultations between a Party alleged to have offered such encouragement and the Party making the allegation. As the two Parties are engaged in consultations without having to rely directly on the NAFTA Commission, it would seem logical that these two Parties are able to call upon the Council's co-operation without having to rely on a decision by the NAFTA Commission. Furthermore, paragraph 10(6)(b) fits perfectly under the Council's function to "promote and facilitate co-operation between the Parties with respect to environmental matters" (see paragraph 10(1)(f)). In conclusion, we are of the opinion that this paragraph is triggered by each consultation initiated pursuant to Article 1114 of the NAFTA. Of course, the Parties involved in the consultations are free to decide on the extent to which the Council's co-operation will be considered.

Paragraph (c) calls for the Council's contribution in "the prevention or resolution of environment-related trade disputes." Although it is clear to us that this paragraph is not solely triggered by public comments made pursuant to paragraph (a), the wording of the text does not provide guidance as to when paragraph (c) will be triggered. In other words, paragraph (c) is unclear on the circumstances and procedures relating to involvement of the Council in the avoidance or the settlement of an environment-related trade disputes. We also note that the NAFTA Commission is mandated by Article 2001 of the NAFTA to "resolve disputes that may arise" and to supervise their implementation. This Article and paragraph (c) appear to constitute an overlap between the mandate of the NAFTA Commission and the Council. However, these two provisions could be interpreted in a consistent manner as the Council's mandate is to co-operate and not to resolve disputes. It would be appropriate to establish mechanisms and guidelines for the relation between the Council by the NAFTA Commission for "the prevention or resolution of environmental-related trade disputes."

Paragraph 10(6)(d) provides for an ongoing consideration of "the environmental effects of the NAFTA." The use of the term "ongoing" indicates that this paragraph is a continuous obligation. Such an obligation started upon the entry into force of the Agreement and will be completed only at its expiration. Therefore, we are of the opinion that this paragraph is already triggered.

Headquarters for the World Customs Organization

On December 2, 1996, the Legal Bureau wrote:

The headquarters for the World Customs Organization (WCO) is in Brussels. The WCO was founded in 1952 as the Customs Co-operation Council (CCC, which remains the official name). From the founding of the WCO in Brussels, the Government of Belgium has paid one-half of the headquarters rent. In 1995, Belgium decided that it would no longer do so. Accordingly, proposals have been made to move the headquarters to a new location, as financially advantageous offers have been received from Germany and the Netherlands. A number of issues arise in respect of any proposed move. In particular, there are legal issues relating to application of the provisions of the Convention Establishing the Customs Co-operation Council (CTS 1971/38) . . .

Article 7(a) of the CCC Convention provides that: "The headquarters of the Council shall be in Brussels." [W]e . . . conclude that this provision could be amended by application of Article 20 of the Convention. Article 20 provides for amendments to the Convention. However, all Contracting Parties to the Convention (i.e. the WCO members) must agree. In the circumstances, no timely unanimous agreement to such a change to the Convention seems possible.

Apart from the process provided for the amendments to the CCC Convention . . .[there is a question] of possible application of provisions of the Vienna Convention on the Law of Treaties (CTS 1980/37). We [are of the] opinion that the relevant articles of the Vienna Convention do not apply.

Briefly, the relevant provisions are in Articles 61 and 62. Article 61 provides that provisions of a treaty may cease to apply in the event of supervening impossibility of performance. That is not the case here.

Article 62 provides that a fundamental change in circumstances may be grounds for terminating a treaty, but only if those circumstances were essential to a Party consenting to be bound by the treaty and if the effect of the change is to radically transform the obligations under the treaty. An argument has been made that Belgium's 1995 decision to refuse to bear half the rent constitutes such a fundamental change in circumstance. As noted, we agree . . . that, given the circumstances of the negotiation of the CCC Convention, this is not the case.

Given that the WCO headquarters shall remain in Brussels until such time as the CCC Convention is amended, the question has arisen as to what functions of the WCO can be carried on elsewhere. Article 7(b) of the CCC Convention provides: "The Council, the Permanent Technical Committee and any committees established by the Council may meet elsewhere than at the headquarters of the Council, if the Council so decides." We agree with the conclusion of the Danish opinion that this provision authorizes the movement out of Brussels of some of the activities of Council. A decision by Council to do so would only require a vote of two-thirds of the Members present at the meeting.

Differences arise in just what amount of Council activity could be moved out of Brussels before that city was no longer WCO headquarters. [One] view is that the Council should keep "some activity" there, in order to demonstrate that the headquarters of the Council is still in Brussels. Then there are more extreme views. [Another] opinion is that Article 7(b) of the CCC Convention is intended only to cover occasional meetings and not the relocation of a main activity. In [this] view, such main activity of the WCO includes the Secretariat and the majority of meetings. [Yet another] view, however, is that the Secretariat could be moved leaving only "extremely limited (mailbox)" activity in Brussels.

The question becomes one of assessing how much activity could be moved out of Brussels before, in fact, the headquarters has moved. The general rule of interpretation of treaties (Vienna Convention, Article 31(1)) is that "a treaty shall be interpreted in good faith in accordance with the ordinary meaning to be given to the terms of the treaty in their context and in light of the object and purpose." There is no agreed definition of "headquarters" in international law as a guide to the ordinary interpretation of the term. Professor Pellet proposed a definition of "siège" (which is the translation of headquarters in the CCC Convention): "Terme désignant le lieu (ville ou pays) où sont établis et fonctionnent un organe international, une institution internationale ou certains organes de celle-ci." Using the Vienna Convention rule of interpretation, [a consulted scholar] considered that the reference to "sont établis et fonctionnent" meant that the headquarters has to be in the place where the significant activity of the WCO is conducted. He concluded that Brussels would no longer be the headquarters if all the Secretariat's management bodies had been transferred (i.e. the . . . "mailbox" proposal). However, [the scholar] saw nothing to prevent most Secretariat members moving from Brussels.

An analogy might be made to domestic law considerations of the "domicile" of a company. For certain purposes, notably taxation, courts determine corporate domicile. This is done by reference to the place where effective control of the corporation is exercised, not the place of the registered office. Domicile is a question of fact, decided by consideration of the course of business of the company, including the residence of management. A similar analysis of the proposal to move all but the "mailbox" out of Brussels would lead to a conclusion that the "domicile" of the WCO had moved. Such a *de facto* change of headquarters would be contrary to the provisions of the CCC Convention.

While the "mailbox" proposal is not acceptable, there is no definitive legal answer on what functions of the Secretariat and Council could be moved from Brussels without constituting a change in headquarters.

INTERNATIONAL RIVERS

Navigation Rights in the St. Lawrence Seaway

On March 11, 1996, the Legal Bureau wrote:

Navigation rights in the St. Lawrence River and the Great Lakes have, historically, been an important aspect of the bilateral relationship, evidenced by the many bilateral agreements between the United States and the United Kingdom throughout the 19th and early 20th centuries. Although these rights were not specifically mentioned in the 1783 United States-United Kingdom Treaty of Peace [unless otherwise indicated, all of the subsequent referenced agreements are bilateral agreements between the United States and the United Kingdom], establishing the international boundary in the Great Lakes and St. Lawrence River, the Jay Treaty of 1794 provided for rights to navigate the contiguous boundary waters for the purposes of trade and commerce. As well, the British provided limited rights to small American vessels to navigate the St. Lawrence, confining the privilege to "small vessels trading *bona fide* between Montreal and Quebec."

Pursuant to the Treaty of Ghent of 1814, two Commissioners were appointed to settle the remaining boundary disputes. The result of that effort was codified in a treaty settlement of 1842. This agreement provided for wide rights of free navigation in various places along the boundary waters for vessels of both Parties. As well, the Treaty of Washington of 1871 provided unequivocal rights of navigation for American citizens "from, to, and into the sea" along the St. Lawrence "subject to any laws and regulations . . . of Canada, not inconsistent with such privileges of navigation." British subjects were granted similar rights on the Stikine, Yukon and Porcupine Rivers as well as full navigational rights on Lake Michigan.

The current boundary waters regime was established by the Boundary Waters Treaty of 1909 between the United States and the United Kingdom (on behalf of Canada). This agreement provides the legal framework for both navigational and non-navigational boundary issues arising between the neighbouring countries. Of particular relevance is Article 1:

> The High Contracting Parties agree that the navigation of all navigable waters shall forever continue free and open for the purposes of commerce to the inhabitants and to the ships, vessels, and boats of both countries equally, subject, however, to any laws and regulations of either country, within its own territory, not inconsistent with such privilege of free navigation and applying equally and without discrimination to the inhabitants, ships, vessels, and boats of both countries.

It is further agreed that so long as this treaty shall remain in force, this same right of navigation shall extend to the waters of Lake Michigan and to all the canals connecting boundary waters, and now existing or which may hereafter be constructed on either side of the line . . .

While this Article asserts the rights of free navigation for vessels of either country, it is silent on the issue of the navigational rights for third-party vessels. The agreement does not assure navigational rights other than for those of the vessels of the Contracting Parties.

Not until 1954 were the navigational rights of third-Party vessels considered, in an Exchange of Notes between Canada and the United States concerning the construction of the St. Lawrence Seaway. Paragraph 6(a) of this agreement provides that "both Governments will use their best endeavours to avoid placing unreasonable restrictions on the transit of passengers, shipping and trade in the international section of the St. Lawrence Seaway." While the language used in this provision is hortatory ("use . . . best endeavours") rather than binding, sub-paragraph (b) provides a more explicit reference to third-party vessels:

> It is further agreed that each Government will consult the other before it enacts any new law or promulgates any new regulation, applicable in the respective national parts of the international section of the St. Lawrence River, which might affect Canadian or United States shipping, or shipping of third-country registry proceeding to or from Canada or the United States respectively.

The obligation of consultation, while not inhibiting the enactment of legislation restricting the navigational rights of third-party vessels, suggests that the other Party should be granted an opportunity to respond to proposed restrictions prior to their enactment.

Despite the condition of consultation in the case of proposed legislation, nothing in the bilateral treaty regime prevents either State, at its discretion, from prohibiting a third-party vessel from entering its internal waters.

The absence of any explicit third-party navigational rights on the St. Lawrence and Great Lakes underlines the position of Canada and the United States that the waters of these bodies are national and do not have an international character. This approach is reflected not only in the various bilateral treaties but also in the operational regulations of the Seaway. The Joint Regulations of the St. Lawrence Seaway of 1960 specify that the use of the Seaway is a privilege granted by the governments through the regulatory agencies. As Article 3 provides, "except as provided in these Regulations, no vessel shall transit the Seaway." Article 7 of the Regulations provides that every vessel wishing to enter the Seaway must report to the Seaway Authority. Moreover, the Authority has the right to deny access to the Seaway for reasons ranging from vessel condition to perceived crew incompetence (Article 5).

Clearly, the bilateral boundary water regime between Canada and the United States has not affected the rights of either country to exercise its rights of territorial sovereignty to refuse the entry of third-party vessels in its internal waters. As a matter of practice, both States act co-operatively to permit the usage of the Seaway by other States and to consult each other when restrictions on transit are proposed. Nonetheless, none of the bilateral agreements dealing with navigation and boundary waters issues prevents either Party from refusing navigational rights to third-Party vessels wishing to transit through the St. Lawrence Seaway.

TREATIES

Denunciation of Treaties

In a memorandum of September 4, 1997, on the legal validity of North Korea's withdrawal from the International Covenant on Civil and Political Rights [ICCPR], the Legal Bureau wrote:

In summary, a good case can be made that the "denunciation" of the Covenant by the [Democratic People's Republic of Korea] (DPRK) is of no legal effect and that it remains bound by its provisions. We note, however, that the issue of whether or not the ICCPR is subject to denunciation has not been subject to a clear pronouncement in international law or jurisprudence. Furthermore, in the absence of a precedent — and other states' reactions to it — there is no extant state practice on this point.

The Process of "Denunciation" at International Law

Neither of the Covenants (ICCPR or ICESCR) contains an express provision for denunciation by a State Party. Accordingly, denunciation would have to proceed in accordance with the international law of treaties. The Vienna Convention on the Law of Treaties [VCLT] contains the following provision:

Article 56: *Denunciation of or withdrawal from a treaty containing no provision regarding termination, denunciation or withdrawal*

1. A treaty which contains no provision regarding its termination and which does not provide for denunciation or withdrawal is not subject to denunciation or withdrawal unless:
   (a) it is established that the parties intended to admit the possibility of denunciation or withdrawal; or
   (b) a right of denunciation or withdrawal may be implied by the nature of the treaty.
2. A party shall give not less than twelve months notice of its intention to denounce or withdraw from a treaty under paragraph 1.

Canada and South Korea are parties to the VCLT, while the DPRK is not. Its provisions are, however, widely regarded as reflecting the customary international law of treaties. Two questions therefore arise from the absence of a denunciation clause in the ICCPR.

Did the Parties intend to admit the possibility of denunciation or withdrawal?

The intent of states parties, where not expressly stated, may be deduced from a number of circumstances. The VCLT enumerates these:

Article 31: *General Rule of Interpretation*

1. A treaty shall be interpreted in good faith in accordance with the ordinary meaning to be given to the terms of the treaty in their context and in the light of its object and purpose.
2. The context for the purpose of the interpretation of a treaty shall comprise, in addition to the text, including its preamble and annexes:
   (a) any agreement relating to the treaty which was made between all the parties in connection with the conclusion of the treaty;
   (b) any instrument which was made by one or more parties in connection with the conclusion of the treaty and accepted by the other parties as an instrument related to the treaty.
3. There shall be taken into account together with the context:
   (a) any subsequent agreement between the parties regarding the interpretation of the treaty or the application of its provisions;
   (b) any subsequent practice in the application of the treaty which establishes the agreement of the parties regarding its interpretation;
   (c) any relevant rules of international law applicable in the relations between the parties.

Thus, the UN Charter, which — unlike the Covenant of the League of Nations — does not provide for the unilateral withdrawal by State Parties, was the subject of an Interpretative Declaration that was approved by the Plenary of the founding conference and which confirmed a right of withdrawal in a number of circumstances. There is no similar instrument in existence in respect of the ICCPR.

In the *Certain Expenses* case (which addressed the question whether expenses for peacekeeping operations, which were not provided for by the Charter, were appropriately paid out of the general assessment) the International Court of Justice took recourse to a review of the "purposes and principles" of the UN Charter in order to read into the Charter a not otherwise expressed "intent" of the drafters to provide for initiatives such as peacekeeping. Accordingly, a review of the purposes of the ICCPR — as expressed in the preamble — can provide a useful insight into the intention of the State Parties concerning their own ability to revoke the ICCPR's provisions. In our view, the references in the preamble to "the obligation of States under the Charter of the United Nations to promote universal respect for, and observance of, human rights and fundamental freedoms" as well as the references to "inherent dignity" and "equal and inalienable rights" and to the goals of the Universal Declaration are evidence of the Parties' acknowledgement of the fundamental and irrevocable nature of these rights.

The First Optional Protocol to the ICCPR, which expressly and with procedural detail provides for denunciation, usefully illustrates the point that, where the Parties do intend to allow for denunciation, they will do so expressly.

Finally, the absence of a precedent for the denunciation of the ICCPR or ICESCR by a State Party suggests that state practice (Article 31(3)(b)) argues against the availability of denunciation.

Is a right of denunciation "implied by the nature of the treaty"?

In our view, the nature of the ICCPR seems to preclude such an implication, which is more readily made in the context of instruments that regulate the conduct of State Parties as between themselves, usually based on mutual concessions, such as a mutual legal assistance treaty, the GATT, or an oil exploration agreement. The Covenants, on the other hand, oblige State Parties unilaterally to protect and implement the fundamental rights of persons, the existence of which is already recognized as customary international law and cannot thus be denied. Finally, academic views on the denunciability of the Covenants confirm that their "nature" would appear to preclude the implication that these treaties are denounceable (see, e.g., Paul Sieghart, *The International Law of Human Rights,* at §12).

A further analogy concerning the "nature" of the ICCPR can be drawn in respect of its own derogation provisions. The Covenant provides for derogability only of certain of its provisions, and then only in "times of emergency which threatens the life of the nation." As a result, even armed conflict, or the exercise of a State's right at international law to the use of force in self-defence, cannot operate to vitiate certain central provisions of the ICCPR (Articles 6, 7, 8(1) and (2), 11, 15, 16, and 18). It would therefore be difficult to argue that unilateral denunciation by a State Party — in a fit of political pique at that — could achieve the same end.

It should be noted in this context that both the European and Inter-American Conventions on Human Rights contain denunciation clauses. In our view, however, this does not suggest that their *nature* makes them denounceable. Their status as regional instruments gives them a more specialized character; we understand that all of the parties to both conventions are also parties to the ICCPR, which would still operate if they denounced the regional instrument. Moreover, we would argue that the very presence of denunciation clauses in these instruments suggests that such explicit provision are necessary in human rights instruments, precisely because of their special nature.

Conclusion

In conclusion, there are strong arguments in favour of the view that the ICCPR is not an instrument that can be denounced unilaterally by a State Party. Moreover, it should be noted that the substantive provisions of the ICCPR — in particular those tracking the Universal Declaration and/or the expressly non-derogable rights, but not the reporting obligations — have entered into customary international law. Accordingly, even if the denunciation of the ICCPR by the DPRK were to be of legal effect, the DPRK would remain under an obligation at international law not to contravene its provisions.

Treaties and Estoppel

In a memorandum dated October 28, 1996, the Legal Bureau wrote:

At the heart of the matter is whether Canadian acquiesence will constitute an estoppel that will, to one extent or another, prevent Canada from objecting in the future. The doctrine of estoppel, which arises from private law, is essentially as follows: (1) a statement of fact which is clear and unambiguous; (2) this statement must be voluntary, unconditional, and authorized; and (3) there must be reliance in good faith upon the statement either to the detriment of the party so relying on the statement or to the advantage of the party making the statement (Professor Bowett, (1957), BY 176 at 202, cited in Ian Brownlie, *Principles of Public International Law*, 4th edition, (1990) at 641). Put in the context of international relations, M. N. Shaw, in *International Law*, 3rd ed. (1991) at 299 states "Estoppel is a legal technique whereby states deemed to have consented to a state of affairs cannot afterwards alter their position." There is ample precedent for the doctrine of estoppel having been adopted in international law, and I. C. MacGibbon, in "Estoppel and International Law," *International Law Quarterly*, 468-513 at 501, has asserted that an estoppel can be based as much [on] an acquiesence of one party to another's statement or conduct as [on] a positive statement from the party itself.

The doctrine is substantially incorporated into international law through the 1969 Vienna Convention on the Law of Treaties (CTS 1980 No. 37, the Vienna Convention) to which Canada is a Party but the United States is not, but which, in our view, correctly states general principles of customary international law in a way binding to both states. In particular, Article 26 provides that "Every treaty in force is binding upon the parties to it and must be performed by them in good faith." Accordingly, Canada, as any state, must be consistent and, cannot, as Lord McNair commented "blow hot and cold" (5 *British Yearbook of International Law* 496-97 (1924)). Secondly, it is possible that an estoppel can be created through a course of conduct by treaty parties that constitute either a subsequent *agreement* regarding the interpretation of the treaty or the application of its provisions {Article 31(3)(a)} or any subsequent *practice* in the application of the treaty which establishes the agreement of the parties regarding its interpretation 31(3)(b)}.

Federal State Clause (Provincial Implementation)

In a memorandum regarding the proposed Draft Convention on the Recognition of Qualifications Concerning Higher Education in the European Region, being then prepared by the Council of Europe and UNESCO, dated November 5, 1996, the Legal Bureau wrote:

Since Canada is a state where primary, if not exclusive, jurisdiction for education rests with the provinces, our approach to the drafting of the Convention should ensure that this jurisdictional fact is fully accommodated in the Convention. The current draft largely succeeds in this regard. Under Article 2.2, a state such as Canada will be required to deposit a declaration setting out our constitutional position vis-à-vis education (see our Declaration made pursuant to the [UNESCO Convention for the Recognition of Studies, Diplomas and Degrees concerning Higher Education in the States belonging to the Europe Region (CTS 1990 No. 20)] for a precedent). More importantly, Article 11.5 provides that Canada may specify the territories and provinces to which the Convention may be applied. Thus, if any province does not wish to implement the provisions of the Convention, our accession can effectively exclude its application to that province.

Implementation of Treaties in Domestic Law

In a memorandum regarding proposed amendments to domestic legislation intended to implement international obligations, dated August 13, 1996, the Legal Bureau wrote:

The current draft legislation takes the approach of incorporating by reference the provisions of both the Convention and Protocol and has a substantive provision . . . that gives these annexed provisions "the force of law." This approach raises the issue of whether it accomplishes the desired goal of implementing Canada's obligations only and represents good legislative drafting practice.

For those provisions of the Convention and Protocol that touch directly on the obligations of State Parties, we expect that the simple process of giving the force of law to the Articles in question, as set out in the Annex, should be sufficient. That being said, it is true that the Convention and Protocol were not drafted or intended to be taken as domestic legislation . . . [W]e would suggest that consideration be given to drafting Canadian obligations arising from the Convention and Protocol in a legislative form, and attaching the provisions of the Convention and Annex for purposes of interpretation. Our problem with the current approach is two-fold. First, as a general matter, we are reluctant to adopt directly into Canadian law the texts of international conventions which are the result of many compromises and often are not drafted with the precision required in domestic legislation. We would prefer to ensure that our understanding of the substance of the provision is accurately reflected in language consistent with the main body of Canadian legislation. Secondly, we are concerned that the draft bill goes beyond and seeks to give the force of Canadian law to matters outside of Canadian domestic law, and does not resolve issues raised but not definitively dealt with in the Convention and Protocol.

Retroactivity of Treaties

In a memorandum dated August 27, 1996, the Legal Bureau wrote:

[Y]ou requested our views on appropriate drafting to ensure that the new HQ agreement with [an International Organization] could be applied from a particular date prior to the probable date of actual signing and entry into force.

In particular, you indicated that negotiations were proceeding on a new headquarters agreement with [the Organization] which you expect to sign and bring into force later in the Fall. However, it is both the Canadian government's and [the Organization's] desire to make enforceable the provisions of the Agreement from October 15, when [the Organization] actually enters the new premises and rental provisions of the Agreement under negotiation need to be applied.

In our view, this can be accomplished by two mechanisms that should provide sufficient protection for the Canadian government. The Agreement should provide in its "entry into force" provisions that it comes into force on signature, *but with effect* from October 15, 1996 (assuming that the signature takes place later than that date). That will provide for authoritative and binding obligations from October 15, once the agreement is actually signed. For this period, i.e., between October 15 and the actual date of signature, you should also consider concluding an Exchange of Notes after the agreement text is finalized and initialled that refers to the initialled agreement and indicates the intention of both the Government of Canada and [the Organization] to provisionally apply all or some of its provisions until the actual date of signature and entry into force.

USE OF FORCE

International Legal Obligations and Nuclear Co-operation

In August 1997, the Legal Bureau wrote:

Article 3 of the Treaty on the Non-Proliferation of Nuclear Weapons (NPT) provides that each non-nuclear-weapon State party to the NPT undertakes to accept safeguards for the exclusive purpose of verification of the fulfilment of its obligations assumed under the NPT with a view to preventing diversion of nuclear energy from peaceful purposes to nuclear weapons or other nuclear explosive devices. State parties are not to undertake to provide certain material and equipment to any non-nuclear-weapon State unless the source or special fissionable material is subject to the safeguards required by Article 3.

Article 3 therefore requires safeguards for transfers . . . The requirement for Article 3 safeguards is on transfers to any non-nuclear-weapon State. It is not only to . . . States that are party to the NPT. The wording of Article 3 differs in this regard to other obligations contained in the NPT. As a result of Canada's adherence to the NPT and as part of its obligations under the NPT, safeguards would be required on any transfer to [another State].

In the 1970s, two non-treaty initiatives were undertaken by a number of States to support the non-proliferation regime.

The first one, known as the Zangger Committee, is comprised of States which are all parties to the NPT. The Zangger Committee's aim was to establish a uniform approach to the implementation of the obligations contained in Article 3.2 of the NPT by defining the items which require the application of IAEA safeguards (i.e., the Zangger List). This list was formally accepted by individual Zangger member States, and was given effect through respective domestic export control legislation. Zangger member States informed the Director General of the IAEA of their decisions to act in conformity with the list. All member States of the IAEA were also informed. Although the Zangger list has no status at international law, individual member States have adopted national arrangements unilaterally.

Canada has implemented its Zangger commitments in the Export Control List of the Export and Import Permits Act and in the Atomic Energy Control Act. The export of any Zangger item requires a permit and a licence. Certain conditions must be met before these are issued . . . The Zangger List does not create a new obligation, it provides guidance as to the interpretation of the NPT's requirement for safeguards on transfers.

The second initiative, often referred to as the Nuclear Suppliers' Group (NSG), includes States that are parties to the NPT and others that are not. The NSG has produced a set of guidelines for the export of nuclear material, equipment or technology and a set of guidelines for the transfer of nuclear-related dual-use equipment, material and related technology.

The NSG Guidelines on Nuclear Transfers set forth additional conditions applicable to the export of nuclear material, equipment and technology to any non-nuclear-weapon country. There is a requirement of formal government assurances explicitly excluding uses that would result in any nuclear explosive device. Article 4 of the NSG Guidelines for Nuclear Transfers requires that:

(a) Suppliers should transfer trigger list items or related technology to a non-nuclear-weapon State only when the receiving State has brought into force an agreement with the IAEA requiring the application of safeguards on all source and special fissionable material in its current and future peaceful activities.

(b) Transfers covered by paragraph (a) to a non-nuclear-weapon State without such a safeguards agreement should be authorized only in exceptional cases when they are deemed essential for the safe operation of existing facilities and if safeguards are applied to those facilities. Suppliers should inform and, if appropriate, consult in the event that they intend to authorize or deny such transfers.

(c) (exception for agreements drawn up before April 3, 1992).

(d) Under agreements to which the policy referred to in paragraph 4(a) does not apply (see paragraph 4(b) and (c)), suppliers should transfer trigger list items or related technology only when covered by IAEA safeguards with duration and coverage provisions in conformity with IAEA doc. GOV/1621. However, suppliers undertake to strive for the earliest possible implementation of the policy referred to in paragraph 4(a) under such agreements.

(e) Suppliers reserve the right to apply additional conditions of supply as a matter of national policy.

Article 4(a) requires full-scope safeguards on all transfers of items identified by the NSG trigger list. The only exception permitted from full-scope safeguards is in the event of exceptional circumstances where the transfers are deemed essential for the safe operation of an existing facility. To date this exception has only been used once, by Belgium, for the export of a trigger list item to KANUPP, the CANDU reactor in Pakistan. Notwithstanding the exception for facility-specific safeguards in specific circumstances in Article 4(b), there is nonetheless a commitment to work toward the implementation of full-scope safeguards.

. . . NSG commitments would not permit the transfer of any trigger list item to [another State] unless full-scope safeguards were implemented. The only possibility for such a transfer would be if the requirements of the exception set out in paragraph 4(b)are met.

The NSG Guidelines also make provision for consultations to ensure that any transfer does not contribute to risks of conflict or instability. There is a mechanism to deal with the situation where an NSG supplier believes that there has been a violation of the understandings resulting from the Guidelines. The Guidelines reiterate the need for prudence in considering transfers, having regard to all the circumstances of each case, including any risk that technology transfers might result in unsafeguarded nuclear materials.

The NSG has also established guidelines for the transfer of nuclear-related dual-use equipment, material and related technology. Member States undertake to establish an export licensing arrangement for the transfer of specified equipment, material and related technology.

The NSG trigger list, as the Zangger List, has no status at international law. Individual NSG member States have made a political commitment to abide by the NSG Guidelines and trigger list. Canada has implemented its NSG commitments through the Export Control List of the Export and Import Permits Act and the Atomic Energy Control Act. The export of any NSG item requires a permit and a licence. Certain conditions must be met before these are issued. In addition to specifying which items should be controlled, the NSG guidelines set out factors which should be taken into account in determining whether the required export documentation (i.e., permit and licence) should be issued.

Parliamentary Declarations in 1996-97 / Déclarations parlementaires en 1996-97

compiled by / préparé par
DAVID AUBRY

1 *Le Commerce / Trade*

(a) Helms-Burton

Hon. Lloyd Axworthy (Minister of Foreign Affairs): . . . the legislation being presented to the House today at second reading is basically a defensive measure to allow Canadians to protect themselves against parts of that act and to demonstrate that we will provide a basic tool kit for Canadians and to ensure that their interests are protected . . . The Helms-Burton bill is an attempt by the United States to unilaterally decide the rules of the game for other countries. That runs counter to the basic principles on which an international economy or an international society can work. We have debated in the House in the past weeks the importance of a fundamental rule of law to govern the action between individuals. The rule of law is also important in governing the relationships between nations if we want to develop an open international economy for trade, investment, telecommunications, commerce and culture. We have learned our lessons over the past 40 or 50 years that the best way to do that is to come to an agreement on basic laws that we agree to, basic principles that we adhere to. If there are to be changes to those, nations come together to negotiate and discuss them and arrive at some consensus.

The Minister of Trade has been actively involved in the development of a World Trade Organization. It is an enormously important development for the world. The whole premise is that there have to be rules by which countries abide. If one country, especially an extremely powerful country, perhaps the most powerful country in the world, begins to adopt a unilateral approach that it can declare on its own, without any consideration for the rights of other individuals or states, then it begins to break down the international system that we have laboured so diligently in the last half century to build. It is ironic that the United States has, over that 50 years, been a leader in developing those rules. Not only has it been a leader, but it has been a beneficiary. Perhaps no country in the world has

David Aubry est à le Faculté de droit à l'Université d'Ottawa / Faculty of Law, University of Ottawa.

gained more of its economic strength by helping to open up the international system. Yet at the very time of the rhetoric and the pronouncements in various fora around the world by United States representatives of a need to put rules into globalization and ensure that we expand and augment our openness, its Congress passed a law which basically tells Canadians: "We will decide for you what your policy will be in relation to a third party. And if you do not adhere to what we decide is right, then we will penalize your companies and your individuals." It makes absolutely no sense. It is totally contrary to the interest of the international community and is certainly contrary to the interests of Canada. I would dare say, it is contrary to the interests of the United States.

. . . We have not argued the question of whether the United States policy toward Cuba is right or wrong. We do not agree with it. We have a different approach. But it is certainly their right how they want to deal with another country. We will use all avenues and venues to talk with the United States and other countries about how we can work together to improve and make the system in Cuba more open. For the United States to tell us how to carry out our policies and, if we do not agree with them, to impose a penalty, is an enormous step backward both in our relationships and also in terms of the wider international community . . .

One of the things we can take some satisfaction from is that in Title III, which is the part of the Helms-Burton bill which gives the right to U.S. companies to sue foreign companies that they believe may have been involved in confiscated property in Cuba, the United States President has deferred the implementation of that part of the act as he has a right to do under the legislation. He has not totally deferred it. Canadian companies are still accruing liability under that portion but a deferment on a six month by six month basis is not good enough . . .

The direction to become unilateral arbiters of what is right and wrong is not given by divine right to one state alone. We must begin to work in the area of co-operation, consensus building and rule making in the international community. That is how countries like us survive and that is how the international community will survive.

We do not simply by our opposition to the Helms-Burton bill in any way ignore the responsibilities of Canadians to begin to conduct our relationships with Cuba in a way that will promote and encourage a more open system. I can say to the House we are actively engaged in developing discussions, dialogues and initiatives that down the road we believe will help to work in that country, to have a more open market system economically and a system of government that will provide more transparency and accountability.

We in no way withdraw from our responsibilities as a member of the international community to help promote human rights, democratic development and more accountability particularly in our own hemisphere. We happen to believe that our approach of engaging in that kind of active involvement with the Cuban people and the Cuban government is a much more effective and useful way to proceed.

It is not simply a matter of Helms-Burton by itself. It is also the right to maintain, develop and promote a more active engagement, to build bridges with the Cuban government and the Cuban people. In that way we can help make transitions in our own hemisphere and promote the fact that we are able and willing to work with our fellow countries in this hemisphere in the promotion of a better system of government, better economic development and a system in the hemisphere that will recognize the rule of law . . .

(House of Commons Debates, September 20, 1996, pp. 4485-94)
(Débats de la Chambre des Communes, le 20 septembre 1996, pp. 4485-94)

Hon. Arthur C. Eggleton (Minister for International Trade): . . . certain fundamental principles must be respected. The freedom to maintain our own foreign policy and trading relationships is one of them, as my colleague the Minister of Foreign Affairs has so correctly pointed out. Canadians have the right to expect that their government will act to respond to threats to our sovereignty and this government is fully prepared to accept that responsibility.

. . . [T]wo sections of the act are particularly offensive. Title III allows U.S. citizens with claims on expropriated property in Cuba to sue foreign nationals, such as Canadians, in the United States courts. If the company has no assets in the United States that it can seize upon, an American could try to come to the Canadian judicial system and ask the courts to enforce the ruling and seize assets here. Title IV of the act allow the U.S. government to deny entry to executives of companies which the U.S. state department deems to be trafficking in property subject to a U.S. claim. This ban extends also to the families, the children of these executives. The amendments that we are proposing will strengthen FEMA in two ways. It will permit the attorney general to block any attempt by a foreign claimant to enforce a judgment under a law such as Helms-Burton, and it will give Canadians recourse to Canadian courts if awards are made against them in American courts. It is our hope that they will never need to be employed . . .

Americans know that trade is bringing the world together as never before. With the free exchange of goods and investment comes a greater openness to new ideas and new approaches. Again and again history has shown us that closer trade links lead to closer relations between nations. So freer trade and a clear system of rules to enforce it are important objectives and ones that this government is fully in support of.

. . . Helms-Burton is unacceptable because it flouts long established international legal practices for settling disputes between nations regarding claims by foreign investors who have had their property expropriated. These established practices have served the world well in the past. By choosing to ignore them now, Helms-Burton sets a dangerous precedent.

If the U.S. behaves in this way today, what is to stop other countries from adopting similar measures tomorrow? If such an international free-for-all ensues, we will undo much of what has already been achieved in bringing trade under international rules.

(House of Commons Debates, September 20, 1996, pp. 4485-94)
(Débats de la Chambre des Communes, le 20 septembre 1996, pp. 4485-94)

M. Stéphane Bergeron (Verchères): . . . ma question s'adresse au ministre du Commerce international. Au début du mois, l'Union européenne annonçait son intention de déposer une plainte officielle devant l'Organisation mondiale du commerce concernant la Loi américaine Helms-Burton à portée extraterritoriale. Le lendemain, le Canada déclarait qu'il allait participer à ce processus initié par les Européens. Compte tenu que le Canada a justifié sa participation à la plainte européenne par le fait qu'il devait protester contre la loi américaine, comment le ministre explique-t-il que le Canada n'ait pas encore demandé la formation d'un groupe spécial en vertu de l'ALÉNA pour régler définitivement ce différend?

Hon. Arthur C. Eggleton (Minister for International Trade): . . . as I indicated previously, we continue with the protest under NAFTA, but we are also in a position to join many other countries in having this matter adjudicated before the WTO. We are readying to prepare a case in support of the European Union. One of the strengths of the position Canada has put forward is that we have been able to get the support of countries right around the world that know the action by the United States is wrong. We will continue to work with those countries in a unified way to continue in our action, and the WTO is a good forum for the next step.

M. Stéphane Bergeron (Verchères): . . . l'article 4 de la Loi américaine Helms-Burton, que ce gouvernement n'a toujours pas tenté de contrer, par ailleurs, interdit l'entrée aux États-Unis de gens d'affaires canadiens et de leurs familles, sous prétexte que leurs compagnies feraient le trafic des propriétés américaines à Cuba. Le ministre ne convient-il pas que la meilleure façon de contrer cet article de manière définitive est de demander la formation d'un groupe de travail spécial en vertu de l'ALÉNA?

Hon. Arthur C. Eggleton (Minister for International Trade): . . . the two issues, both title III and title IV, are intertwined and will be dealt with together, in terms of the WTO and the NAFTA. We will also be continuing at the OECD where there is a multilateral agreement on investment. This is . . . key to the investment rules, the protection of Canadian company assets in other countries. We will continue to work with other countries. We will continue to use a number of forums to protest Helms-Burton and to get the message across clearly to the United States and other countries that unilateral extraterritorial action attempting to impose their will, their foreign trade policy on Canada or any other country is totally unacceptable.

(Débats de la Chambre des Communes, le 29 Octobre 1996, p. 5807)
(House of Commons Debates, October 29, 1996, p. 5807)

M. Benoît Sauvageau (Terrebonne): La semaine dernière, les États-Unis et l'Union européenne concluaient une entente au sujet du différend qui les oppose relativement à la loi Helms-Burton. Cette entente prévoit un éventuel assouplissement de l'application de cette loi en échange de la suspension de la poursuite européenne devant l'Organisation mondiale du commerce et de la mise en place de règles globales prévenant l'investissement de compagnies dans des propriétés expropriées par d'autres gouvernements. Compte tenu que le *Bilan des réalisations des libéraux* stipule que le Canada a été l'animateur de l'opposition internationale face à la Loi Helms-Burton, le ministre peut-il nous expliquer comment il se fait que le Canada ne soit pas partie prenante de l'entente intervenue la semaine dernière entre l'Union européenne et les États-Unis?

Hon. Arthur C. Eggleton (Minister of International Trade): We are pursuing our consultations about this subject with the United States. The Americans are conscious of our strong opposition to this legislative measure and we are pursuing our consultations. In the context of the negotiations with the European Union, the objective consisted of creating a new forum which has no ties with the World Trade Organization, with which the United States refuse to collaborate, but is related to the OECD with which the United States [agreed] to discuss. It is a useful decision because Canada introduced the question of a multilateral agreement on the investments during those discussions. In fact, Canada was the first to mention the question of extraterritoriality and the Helms-Burton Act, and we shall continue to talk in more details about this subject.

M. Benoît Sauvageau (Terrebonne): Étant donné que le ministre refuse toujours de contester la Loi Helms-Burton devant l'ALÉNA et considérant qu'il n'est nullement garanti que les négociations à l'OCDE iront à un accord, le ministre peut-il nous dire ce qui l'empêche de loger une plainte devant l'ALÉNA?

Hon. Arthur C. Eggleton (Minister of International Trade): As for NAFTA, yes it is still possible for us to use it. If the negotiations get bogged down, if the United States refuse to discuss . . . the Helms-Burton Act and this type of unilateral measure, we shall use it.

(Débats de la Chambre des Communes, le 15 avril 1997, p. 9603)
(House of Commons Debates, April 15, 1997, pp. 9745-46)

(b) Marketing Boards / Les offices de commercialisation

M. Michel Gauthier (chef de l'opposition): . . . À la suite de la décision préliminaire qui est rendue dans le dossier controversé des oeufs, du lait et de la volaille, une décision qui doit être confirmée bientôt, le premier ministre entend-il faire des représentations auprès du président américain, avant qu'il ne soit trop tard, pour ne pas que le Canada se retrouve dans la situation dans laquelle il s'est retrouvé dans le dossier du bois d'oeuvre, c'est-à-dire obligé de négocier à rabais une entente qui finit par faire mal? Dans le domaine du bois, l'entente, si imparfaite soit-elle, nuit aux producteurs de bois et les fait souffrir durement. L'entente du lait, des oeufs et de la volaille pourrait être de cet ordre, si le premier ministre n'intervient pas rapidement, de façon proactive auprès du président.

Le très hon. Jean Chrétien (premier ministre, Lib.): . . . dans le dossier des oeufs et de la volaille, nous avons discuté de ce problème à plusieurs reprises avec les Américains. Notre position est claire, nous avons déterminé que les offices de commercialisation qui existent au Canada ont le droit d'exister en vertu des accords que nous avons signés avec eux et aussi en vertu des accords du GATT qui ont été renégociés il y a un an. Alors, nous croyons que notre position est tout à fait conforme aux accords conclus avec les Américains. S'ils veulent défier ces accords, des recours sont prévus dans l'ALÉNA et aussi dans les règles du GATT pour défendre nos droits. Nos positions sont claires et, en ce moment, les accords existent entre les deux pays; ils ont été signés en bonne et due forme.

(House of Commons Debates, November 6, 1996, pp. 6183-84)
(Débats de la Chambre des Communes, le 6 novembre 1996, pp. 6183-84)

(c) Canada-Israel Free Trade Agreement

Hon. Arthur C. Eggleton (Minister for International Trade): . . . I am pleased to commence the debate on second reading for the bill with respect to Canada-Israel free trade.

Cet accord historique est à la fois important et symbolique. Important parce qu'il constitue le premier accord de libre-échange signé par le Canada avec un pays n'appartenant pas au continent américain, et symbolique parce qu'il apporte un nouveau témoignage de notre attachement à [la] libéralisation du commerce à l'échelle du globe.

It sends a very clear message. Canada is ready, willing and able to trade with the world. With this agreement we will stand on the same footing as the European Union and the United States, both of which have already signed free trade agreements with Israel. For the first time we will have direct access to the Israeli market without having to funnel our trade through the United States or any other country. The globalization of markets is one of the great waves of history and it is one Canada cannot afford to and does not intend to watch from the shores. In today's ever changing world no nation, however rich or powerful, can long remain isolated from the great economic currents of this day. Markets are opening up, barriers are falling down and free movement of goods, services and ideas is becoming simply unstoppable . . .

The free trade agreement with Israel represents another step toward our goal of freer trade worldwide. It is clear proof that Canada is prepared to match our rhetoric on free trade with concrete actions . . .

Before turning to some of the main features of the agreement, let me state clearly something important. While the agreement is between Canada and the Government of Israel, we intend to extend the same benefits to the Palestinians. We will be meeting with Palestinian officials to examine the best ways to go about this . . .

First, under this agreement all tariffs will be removed from industrial products beginning on January 1, 1997, all industrial product tariffs. At Canada's request, the only exception is that women's swimwear and, at Israel's request, certain cotton fabric will continue to be subject to tariffs. Even here however the tariffs are scheduled to be phased out over two and one-half years. Second, duty free access or low duties will be applied to a variety of agricultural and fisheries products exported by either country. For Canada such exports include grains, grain products, beef, salmon, maple syrup, alcoholic beverages and various processed foods. Third, the agreement also provides clear and straightforward rules of origin, a key component of any successful trading relationship. I would point out that these rules of origin are generally less restrictive than those under the NAFTA, reflecting the structure and openness of our respective economies. Fourth, to resolve any disputes that might arise under the agreement, both sides have agreed to be governed by a binding dispute settlement mechanism. It is worth emphasizing the areas that are not covered by the agreement. As we would expect, supply managed dairy, poultry and egg producers are excluded. Cultural industries are also exempt. So too is the auto pact. Other areas of trade such as trade in services and government procurement continue to be governed by the multilateral rules being established through the World Trade Organization.

(House of Commons Debates, October 9, 1996, pp. 5311-18)
(Débats de la Chambre des Communes, le 9 octobre 1996, pp. 5311-18)

(d) Canada-Chile Free Trade Implementation Act

Mr. Ron MacDonald (Parliamentary Secretary to Minister for International Trade): . . . Bill C-81 is enabling legislation for the Canada-Chile Free Trade Agreement. It is an important milestone for us because it broadens the access to Canadian products and services under a free trade regime into Latin American and South American countries . . . In the last decade there has been an explosion in trade deregulation. If we look around the globe we see the emergence of different trade groups like the European Union and the Mercosur block in South America. In North America we initially had the free trade deal with the United States which was then extended to Mexico and was known as the NAFTA.

This is a good deal for Canada. It is a deal that has good support around the House of Commons. It immediately reduces the import duty for about 75 per cent of the goods that Canada exports to Chile. For the rest of the goods, by and large with one or two exceptions, over the next five years a zero tariff will be applied. The deal also allows us to do a couple of other things which I will cover quickly. It gives us a very good dispute settlement mechanism which is similar to the deal we have with the United States. On trade remedies, where I will draw the line, we have agreed in this deal that there is no room in a free trade association for anti-dumping laws to be applied. This is a great victory for Canada. This deal is a great victory for the people of Chile. I look forward to support from all members of the House to have this speedily passed at second reading and referred to a committee so that on June 2 this free trade deal will come in force for the benefit of all people of Canada and Chile.

Mr. Jim Silye (Calgary Centre): . . . when the Liberals ran in the last election their three big issues were jobs, jobs, jobs; get rid of the GST and renegotiating NAFTA. We all know that they did not renegotiate NAFTA. They signed it the way it was presented. They made the mistake of not sticking to their original principles and by not adhering to their commitment to hold the agreement up until there was a satisfactory dispute settlement mechanism. That has really cost this country severely. It has caused a severe problem in international trade and trade with our partners because the Americans are taking advantage of us every chance they get. We would not have the dispute over softwood lumber. It would have been settled. Settlements would be a lot faster if there was a proper dispute settlement mechanism in place in the NAFTA. Based on the comments in his speech that he feels this is a good deal with Chile because it is the same as the one Canada has with the States, I submit we are not happy with the one with the United States . . .

Mr. Ron MacDonald (Parliamentary Secretary to Minister for International Trade): . . . the hon. member has asked a very important question. He alluded to the fact that the dispute settlement mechanism under NAFTA simply does not work. I would like to sit down and show my hon. colleague that the dispute settlement mechanism has worked very well. Of the disputes that have gone full term, Canada has won over 90 per cent of them. I believe the deal we have negotiated has protected Canadian industries.

(House of Commons Debates, February 4, 1997, pp. 8153-55)
(Débats de la Chambre des Communes, le 4 fevrier 1997, pp. 8153-55)

(e) Multilateral Agreement on Investment

Mr. Chris Axworthy (Saskatoon-Clark's Crossing): As everyone knows, the Liberals promised not to sign the NAFTA without the conclusion of parallel agreements on labour and the environment. The government did not respect this promise like many others and nevertheless signed the NAFTA. Canada is actually playing an important role in the negotiation of the multilateral agreement of the OECD on investment, an agreement which will stop Canada from fixing job objectives for the new foreign investments in Canada. Yesterday, the Minister of International Trade said that the Liberals will not sign the agreement unless the disposition to that effect is eliminated.

Hon. John Manley (Minister of Industry, Minister of the Agency of Economic Promotion of Atlantic Canada, Minister of the Economic Diversification of Western Canada and Minister of the Federal Bureau of Regional Development (Quebec)): The government will lead in a very prudent way the negotiations concerning the multilateral agreement on investment. We have established a certain number of criteria which we have very efficiently applied these last few years in the study of investments made by Investment Canada or in regard of our cultural policies. We are searching for ways to open the investments in Canada but also those of Canadians elsewhere, and we know that this will allow our companies to enjoy a better access in markets and an increase in exports.

(House of Commons Debates, April 8, 1997, pp. 9452-53)
(Débats de la Chambre des Communes, le 8 avril 1997, pp. 9452-53)

2 *Les différends internationaux et le maintien de la paix / International Disputes and Peacekeeping*

(a) Middle East / Le Moyen-Orient

M. Pierre de Savoye (Portneuf): . . . ma question s'adresse au ministre des Affaires étrangères. La position du gouvernement canadien sur la crise au Proche-Orient est apparue pour le moins confuse, vendredi dernier, alors que le ministre de la Coopération internationale a refusé d'engager le gouvernement quant à la fermeture du tunnel de Jérusalem. Dans le contexte où le Conseil de sécurité a adopté une résolution demandant la fermeture du tunnel, le ministre peut-il clairement indiquer à cette Chambre quelle position défend son gouvernement dans la crise actuelle?

L'hon. Lloyd Axworthy (ministre des Affaires étrangères): . . . dans le discours que j'ai prononcé pendant la réunion du Conseil de sécurité, j'ai mentionné l'importance qu'il y ait une période d'accalmie au Moyen-Orient, particulièrement pour s'assurer de réduire les incidents qui pourraient dégénérer en grands conflits, et aussi de maintenir la fermeture du tunnel pendant la période de discussions et de négociations entre les deux parties.

M. Pierre de Savoye (Portneuf): . . . pendant que le président palestinien conditionne sa participation au Sommet à des engagements fermes de la part d'Israël, l'État hébreu refuse, quant à lui, de fermer le tunnel, déploie des chars de combat en Cisjordanie, et menace de désarmer les policiers palestiniens. Devant cette impasse, je demande au ministre s'il peut indiquer à cette Chambre quelle attitude précisément entend prendre le gouvernement canadien?

Hon. Lloyd Axworthy (Minister of Foreign Affairs): . . . I have already explained that we have made our views known very clearly to the Security Council on Friday night. I had direct discussions with the acting Israeli ambassador at the UN on Friday. We expressed our very strong concern that the two parties come back to the negotiating table. The president of the United States has now invited the head of the Palestine authority and the new prime minister of Israel to do that. Negotiations are underway now to determine the meeting.

I think it is really in the interests of all Canadians, not just the Government of Canada, to express strongly their great hope and earnest feelings about the importance of the two parties coming back to the table and continuing to follow the Oslo accords so there can continue to be negotiations toward peace in that area.

(House of Commons Debates, September 30, 1996, p. 4862)
(Débats de la Chambre des Communes, le 30 septembre 1996, p. 4862)

Mme Suzanne Tremblay (Rimouski-Témiscouata): . . . dans le domaine des affaires étrangères, il y a un autre problème d'importance. Dans le contexte où les tensions s'aggravent au Moyen-Orient, le premier ministre du Canada a-t-il l'intention de soulever, auprès du président américain, l'urgence de relancer le processus de paix en Israël et l'autorité palestinienne avant que la crise politique actuelle ne dégénère encore davantage?

Hon. Lloyd Axworthy (Minister of Foreign Affairs): . . . beginning on Tuesday next week I will be in Cairo at the middle eastern major summit meeting. I hope to have direct discussions with the foreign minister of Israel and the representative of the Palestinian authority as well as other leaders from the Middle East. We will certainly make very clear our strong support for continuation of the peace process, our commitment to help them develop economically and to provide the kind of support we need internationally on a multilateral basis to search for the right solutions for peace in that area.

(House of Commons Debates, November 6, 1996, p. 6184)
(Débats de la Chambre des Communes, le 6 novembre 1996, p. 6184)

Mme Monique Guay (Laurentides): La tension continue de monter au Proche-Orient, où hier, le ministre israélien de la Défense a prévenu que si les frictions entre les Palestiniens et l'armée israélienne se poursuivaient, Israel n'aurait, et je cite, "aucun problème pour reconquérir Hébron ou une autre ville palestinienne." Compte tenu que cette déclaration risque de mettre le feu aux poudres et de faire basculer de manière irréversible le processus de paix issu des Accords d'Oslo, le ministre peut-il nous dire quelles actions le Canada entent prendre pour sauvegarder la paix au Proche-Orient?

Hon. Lloyd Axworthy (Minister of Foreign Affairs): The tensions which are increasing in the Middle East preoccupy us a lot. We continue to incite all the parties to find ways to apply the peace process established in Oslo in order to solve their differences and to respect their commitment.

Mme Monique Guay (Laurentides): Le ministre entend-il renouveler, à la lumière du nouveau contexte, l'opposition canadienne au sujet israélien de construire de nouvelles colonies juives à Jérusalem-Est?

Hon. Lloyd Axworthy (Minister of Foreign Affairs): We have always maintained that the attempts aimed at creating new colonies are contrary to resolutions adopted by the United Nations. It is what we have always declared and our position has not changed.

(House of Commons Debates, April 11, 1997, p. 9603)
(Débats de la Chambre des Communes, le 11 avril 1997, p. 9603)

(b) L'Afghanistan / Afghanistan

Mme Madeleine Dalphond-Guiral (Laval-Centre): . . . ma question s'adresse au ministre des Affaires étrangères. Il y a quelques jours, les intégristes islamiques ont pris le pouvoir à Kaboul, et la situation est devenue intolérable pour les femmes là-bas. Des femmes sont battues, tuées et traitées en esclave par ceux qui ont maintenant le contrôle du pays. Comment le gouvernement canadien compte-t-il réagir face à cette situation tragique en Afghanistan?

Hon. Lloyd Axworthy (Minister of Foreign Affairs): There is very little we can do other than to join the international community in expressing our great outrage at the travesties of justice that are taking place. The matter was discussed at the Security Council this weekend. Expressions of concern have been raised and we join in those very strongly. We will do anything we can do to assist the United Nations and other bodies to try to bring about some form of calm and an end to the violence in that area.

Mme Madeleine Dalphond-Guiral (Laval-Centre): . . . est-ce que le gouvernement canadien peut prendre, devant cette Chambre, un engagement ferme, comme il l'a déjà fait en Afrique du Sud, de ne pas reconnaître le régime des Talibans, compte tenu du fait qu'il contrevient à des valeurs fondamentales et chères au peuple québécois et canadien?

Hon. Lloyd Axworthy (Minister of Foreign Affairs): Mr. Speaker, certainly in any recognition we would take into account the values, the stands and the behaviour of the recipient state. I will certainly take the hon. member's point of view as a strong representation.

(House of Commons Debates, September 30, 1996, p. 4863)
(Débats de la Chambre des Communes, le 30 septembre 1996, p. 4863)

(c) La Région des Grands Lacs africains / Great Lakes Region of Africa

Mme Madeleine Dalphond-Guiral (Laval-Centre): . . . ma question s'adresse au ministre des Affaires étrangères. Alors qu'une catastrophe humanitaire sans précédent se prépare dans l'est du Zaïre, des rebelles tutsis auraient annoncé aujourd'hui un cessez-le-feu unilatéral de trois semaines afin de permettre aux réfugiés qui le désirent de regagner le Rwanda. Pour le moment, l'aide humanitaire d'urgence demeure toutefois bloquée. Un appel dramatique est donc lancé pour la création de couloirs humanitaires afin de sauver de la mort des milliers, peut-être des centaines de milliers de personnes. Le ministre peut-il faire le point sur la situation qui prévaut actuellement dans l'est du Zaïre, où plus d'un million de civils sont victimes des combats et sur les démarches visant à créer des corridors pour permettre aux organismes humanitaires de venir en aide aux réfugiés?

L'hon. Lloyd Axworthy (ministre des Affaires étrangères):. . . tout d'abord, je voudrais dire que le gouvernement du Canada a appuyé fortement les efforts de l'ambassadeur Chrétien pour trouver une solution et faire des recommandations qui visent une conciliation dans la région des grands lacs africains. Deuxièmement, nous avons indiqué que grâce aux efforts de ma collègue, la secrétaire d'État responsable de l'Afrique, nous sommes en train de considérer des modalités afin d'aider les groupes africains qui proposent un corridor, un refuge, un sanctuaire en Afrique. Et aussi, mon collègue, le ministre de la Coopération internationale, considère également l'aide humanitaire, selon les demandes des groupes et autres organisations. Généralement, nous avons répondu par un effort actif de la part des Canadiens, et j'espère que le cessez-le-feu réussira, grâce aux efforts diplomatiques.

Mme Madeleine Dalphond-Guiral (Laval-Centre): . . . dans le contexte du sommet régional prévu demain à Nairobi, d'importantes pressions sont exercées sur l'Afrique du Sud pour qu'elle suspende ses ventes d'armes au Rwanda. Compte tenu des liens privilégiés entre le Canada et l'Afrique du Sud, le ministre s'engage-t-il à demander lui aussi à l'Afrique du Sud de geler toute livraison d'armes au Rwanda?

Hon. Lloyd Axworthy (Minister of Foreign Affairs): . . . we have expressed our deep concern about the sale of arms, not just by South Africa but by many western countries that are also engaged in the sale of arms in that region. It is something that I think has contributed substantially to the problem and we will follow through with our efforts. We are also undertaking very strong efforts with the government of Rwanda to begin to more actively prosecute the war criminal trials. Until that particular problem is met, the return of the refugees from Zaire becomes increasingly difficult. A number of efforts have to take place. I give the House full assurance that we are fully engaged in this file. The secretary of state has just returned from Africa. We will continue to use all our efforts to try to find some solution and particularly to help the approximately one million people who are now being faced with this enormous disruption to their lives. As Canadians we want to do the best we possibly can for that region.

Mr. John English (Kitchener): . . . my question is for the Minister of Foreign Affairs. Canadians are deeply concerned about the tragedy that is unfolding in the areas of Rwanda, Burundi and Zaire. Can the Minister of Foreign Affairs further explain what activities the international community and Canada can undertake at this point to improve the terrible situation there?

Hon. Lloyd Axworthy (Minister of Foreign Affairs): . . . first to provide further explanation, the mission of Ambassador Chrétien is being fully supported by a number of Canadian diplomats in our missions in the African area. As well, we are providing a support service here and logistical support. In addition, as I mentioned, our secretary of state has just returned from Africa where she met with a number of African states, and we intend to follow through with any form of available assistance we might provide if there is to be some form of decision to allow for safe corridors.

Last week the Minister for International Co-operation and I announced a new strategy for the Government of Canada and the Canadian people, what we call peacebuilding. It will allow us to mobilize Canadian resources of a variety of kinds, to fit themselves into areas of post-conflict where there is turmoil and disruption taking place. It is a kind of civilian peacekeeping operation which will allow us to have a rapid response so that we do not continue to suffer the kinds of tragedies that we have seen in Rwanda, Burundi or Zaire. We have to be able to develop new mechanisms to respond to these new realities and we are taking the lead in our own country and promoting the idea of peacebuilding in international organizations.

(House of Commons Debates, November 4, 1996, pp. 6060-61)
(Débats de la Chambre des Communes, le 4 novembre 1996, pp. 6060-61)

Mme Suzanne Tremblay (Rimouski-Témiscouata): Au lendemain de la réélection du président Clinton et du Sommet de Nairobi, le premier ministre va-t-il proposer au président américain une demande conjointe du Canada, des États-Unis et de la France, auprès du Conseil de sécurité, afin de mettre rapidement en place une force humanitaire multinationale chargée de mettre fin au drame atroce que vivent actuellement les réfugiés du Zaïre? Nous n'avons rien contre la diplomatie, mais, comme le rappelle encore ce matin Bernard Kouchner, le temps presse et des gens sont en train de mourir.

L'hon. Lloyd Axworthy (ministre des Affaires étrangères): . . . le Canada a fait preuve de leadership et d'initiative en ce qui concerne les chefs régionaux africains. En effet, nous sommes prêts à étudier soigneusement les propositions des chefs africains pour un sanctuaire, pour le corridor et pour les forces neutres. Avec la mission spéciale de l'ambassadeur Chrétien, nous aurons l'occasion d'examiner les propositions immédiatement afin de déterminer les types de ressources et d'engagements de toute la communauté internationale.

M. Michel Gauthier (chef de l'opposition): . . . Lorsque le premier ministre nous dit que pour les réfugiés qui sont retournés au Rwanda, il n'y a pas nécessité d'intervention militaire d'aucune façon, je voudrais lui demander si le gouvernement canadien a obtenu du gouvernement rwandais des assurances à l'effet que la sécurité de ces personnes serait véritablement assurée. À notre avis, ce n'est pas évident que le retour de ces gens au Rwanda signifie nécessairement la pleine et entière sécurité.

Le très hon. Jean Chrétien (premier ministre): . . . lorsque des citoyens reviennent dans leur pays, ce sont des citoyens rwandais qui rentrent chez eux. Les autorités locales nous assurent que les dispositions sont prises pour les aider à réintégrer la vie normale dans leur pays. C'est à l'intérieur de leur propre pays.

Miss Deborah Grey (Beaver River): . . . Will the Prime Minister explain to the House just what our mission to Central Africa is and what efforts he is making to ensure the safety of our Canadian troops?

Right Hon. Jean Chrétien (Prime Minister): . . . the mandate is very clear. The mandate has been given to an international force to go into Central Africa to help provide food, medication, shelter and other needs to the refugees. At this time we are all on the side of Zaire. I am happy to see that the representative of the third party realizes that probably half of the refugees are back in their country of Rwanda and others are moving. At this moment a survey is being made by a team in eastern Zaire to evaluate the situation to find out what is happening to the refugees who are still there. We are told by the Government of Rwanda that it will open the southern part to let the refugees into Rwanda in the days to come. By the end of the operation we will know if there are still some Rwandan refugees in Zaire. If there are none, the problem will become strictly humanitarian. As I said earlier, the Government of Rwanda is willing and eager to receive help from all the countries that want to contribute to this settlement of the people coming back home after two or three years. It may be that in the next three or four days we will be in a position where the armed forces will not be required any more. At this moment the Canadian soldiers who are in Kigali are completely safe and in no danger.

They are awaiting the evaluation that will be made by General Baril and the other military officials involved. They will be meeting in Stuttgart, Germany on Thursday or Friday and the decision will be made at that time about what kind of forces and who outside Canada will be contributing[.]

(House of Commons Debates, November 19, 1996, pp. 6444-45)
(Débats de la Chambre des Communes, le 19 novembre 1996, pp. 6444-45)

3 Les relations diplomatiques / Diplomatic Relations

(a) China

Mr. Jim Hart (Okanagan-Similkameen-Merritt): . . . Last week the defence minister gave Chinese generals special tours of our military bases and today Canadians were shocked to learn that the government is ignoring its own environmental laws and providing interest free loans to sell CANDU reactors. Behind closed doors cabinet has jigged the Canadian Environmental Assessment Act to allow this sale. Instead of scrapping Canada's environmental laws to benefit China, should Canada not urge China to change its law?

Hon. Arthur C. Eggleton (Minister for International Trade): . . . first of all, we are not providing any interest free loans. This is a regular commercial operation. In fact, AECL is expected to make money on it. One hundred Canadian companies will profit from this. It will mean some 27,000 person years in employment. With respect to the environment there is absolutely no diminishing of the Canadian Environmental Assessment Act. That act was never intended to apply to the Export Development Corporation's commercial financing operations in foreign countries, and so it does not apply. Over the years that AECL has produced the CANDU-6 reactor, it has done a great deal of environmental work on it and in fact it is the safest, most reliable, most environmentally efficient nuclear reactor in the world.

(House of Commons Debates, November 8, 1996, p. 314)
(Débats de la Chambre des Communes, le 8 novembre 1996, p. 314)

(b) Hong Kong

M. René Laurin (Joliette): À quelques mois de la rétrocession de Hong Kong à la Chine, celle-ci vient d'annoncer qu'elle prévoyait reserrer les règles de démonstrations populaires, en plus d'interdire, pour les partis politiques, tout contact avec l'étranger. Cette situation est pour le moins inquiétante en regard des libertés dont jouiront les Chinois de Hong Kong après la rétrocession. Le ministre peut-il nous dire si le Canada prévoit prendre des mesures contre la Chine pour éviter, après la rétrocession, une érosion des droits de la personne et des libertés fondamentales des Chinois vivant actuellement à Hong Kong?

Hon. Lloyd Axworthy (Minister of Foreign Affairs): Not later than today, during breakfast, the Secretary of State to Asia and myself have met Mr. Lu Ping, the Chinese minister in charge of the transition in Hong Kong. We have attracted his attention on our preoccupations about the proposed changes. Those changes have still not been brought and are still being examined in the Parliament of Hong Kong. We have certainly expressed our point of view. We think that a maximum of uniformity must be maintained concerning the freedom of the press, the right to protest and the right of political parties to maintain their autonomy.

(House of Commons Debates, April 21, 1997, pp. 9995-9996)
(Débats de la Chambre des Communes, le 21 avril 1997, pp. 9995-9996)

4 *War Crimes / Crimes de guerre*

(a) Deportation of war criminals

Mr. Ian McClelland (Edmonton Southwest): Like millions of Canadians, I was both appalled and embarrassed when Irving Abella of the Canadian Jewish Congress told the television program "60 minutes" that former Liberal Prime Minister Pierre Trudeau would not prosecute war criminals living in Canada. My question is for the Prime Minister. Does this reprehensible abdication of responsibility continue to be the Liberal government policy as evidenced by recent botched deportation proceedings and foot dragging?

Hon. Allan Rock (Minister of Justice and Attorney General of Canada): In January 1995, a few months after the Supreme Court of Canada had decided the *Finta* case, that is very difficult to proceed through the criminal law, this government committed itself to start, by April 1997, twelve deportation and denaturalization cases where there was evidence of complicity in war crimes. We have now started ten of those cases. The other two will be started by our target date of April of this year. That is evidence of this government's commitment.

(House of Commons Debates, February 3, 1997, p. 7579)
(Débats de la Chambre des Communes, le 3 février 1997, p. 7579)

(b) Former Yugoslavia / l'ex-Yougoslavie

Mrs. Val Meredith (Surrey-White Rock-South Langley): Two months ago, in a response to a question I asked on actual war criminals in Canada, the Parliamentary secretary of the Minister of Citizenship and Immigration said that measures were taken about this subject, that the concerned persons would be expelled and that they would not stay in our country. We learn now that, when Canada generously greeted authentic refugees from the Bosnian war, he accepted at the same time a certain number of persons suspected of being war criminals. Can the Minister explain to the House the measures which have been taken in regards to those persons suspected of being war criminals and state the date of their expulsion from Canada?

L'hon. Lucienne Robillard (ministre de la Citoyenneté et de l'Immigration): Oui, le Canada a joué un rôle dans réinstallation des réfugiés de l'ex-Yougoslavie et, oui, nous avons été fidèles à notre tradition généreuse au Canada d'accepter des réfugiés qui étaient persécutés ou qui vivaient des conditions difficiles dues à des conflits dans leur pays d'origine. Chaque fois que nous avons accueilli des réfugiés, nous l'avons fait avec notre esprit d'ouverture. Selon les informations que nous avons à ce jour, parmi ces personnes que nous avons accueillies depuis 1993 dans notre pays, au-delà de 19 000 personnes, nous n'avons pas d'information confirmant ce que la député du Parti réformiste vient d'avancer aujourd'hui même.

Mrs. Val Meredith (Surrey-White Rock-South Langley): It is very interesting; the collaborators of the minister made a list of 250 persons suspected of being actual war criminals when the representatives of the Bosnian government say that the representatives of Canada never consulted their list of persons suspected of being war criminals before accepting the applicants of refugee status from Bosnia. Now we know that some of these individuals are in Canada, it is not likely that they will face justice in the near future because of the absence of a treaty of extradition with Bosnia.

L'hon. Lucienne Robillard (ministre de la Citoyenneté et de l'Immigration): Ce gouvernement est au premier rang des pays qui ont mené la guerre aux criminels de guerre contemporains. À plusieurs égards, même les décisions qui ont été rendues par nos tribunaux jouent un rôle de jurisprudence au plan mondial. Concernant l'ex-Yougoslavie, le Canada aide même les tribunaux internationaux pour poursuivre les gens qui ont pu commettre des crimes contre l'humanité.

(House of Commons Debates, April 15, 1997, pp. 9746-47)
(Débats de la Chambre des Communes, le 15 avril 1997, pp. 9746-47)

(c) International Court of Justice / Cour internationale de Justice

Hon. Warren Allmand (Notre-Dame-de-Grâce): Within a few weeks the United Nations will vote to establish a permanent international criminal court to try individuals who commit serious violations of human rights and crimes against humanity, including genocide and ethnic cleansing. I know the government supports this measure but it requires an amendment to our domestic legislation to permit the referral of accused Canadians to the new international court. In order to give impetus to a positive vote at the UN, when will Canada amend its domestic legislation to facilitate this matter?

Hon. Lloyd Axworthy (Minister of Foreign Affairs): . . . if I might be allowed to provide an answer for the hon. member, at the United Nations general assembly this fall in the statement we totally endorsed the idea of an international court and indicated that we would do everything possible to facilitate its development.

(House of Commons Debates, November 8, 1996, p. 6314)
(Débats de la Chambre des Communes, le 8 novembre 1996, p. 6314)

Mme Maud Debien (Laval-Est): Les crimes de génocide qui ont été commis, entre autres, en ex-Yougoslavie et au Rwanda, ont conduit à la création de tribunaux internationaux provisoires. Or, on sait très bien que d'autres crimes de même nature se perpétuent ailleurs dans le monde. Puisque, comme le disait si bien Amnistie Internationale, "on ne crée pas des tribunaux temporaires pour régler des problèmes permanents," le ministre entend-il prendre le leadership auprès de la communauté internationale quant à la création d'une cour criminelle internationale permanente?

L'hon. Lloyd Axworthy (ministre des Affaires étrangères): Pendant le discours que j'ai prononcé à l'Assemblée générale des Nations Unies en septembre dernier, j'ai expliqué directement et clairement que le Canada appuie l'établissement d'une cour criminelle internationale permanente.

Mme Maud Debien (Laval-Est): On sait que le Canada a déclaré qu'il allait faire de l'arrestation des criminels de guerre en Bosnie une priorité. Or, il ne faudrait pas oublier que près de 100 000 personnes croupissent dans les prisons rwandaises sans être jugées. En attendant que la communauté internationale mette sur pied une cour permanente avec l'appui du Canada bien sûr, comme vient de le dire le ministre, celui-ci ne croit-il pas qu'une priorité devrait être accordée également à la bonne marche du Tribunal international au Rwanda, et surtout à son fonctionnement, selons les règles les plus strictes du droit?

Hon. Lloyd Axworthy (Minister of Foreign Affairs): I certainly agree with the sentiments expressed by the hon. member about the real imperative and necessity of prosecuting war criminals. As you know, Mr. Speaker, Canada has been given the honour of having Judge Louise Arbour as the chief prosecutor for the international war crimes tribunal. In a meeting with Judge Arbour about a month ago, she expressed the same concern as the hon. member does about the need to prosecute more actively in Rwanda for war crimes issues.

(House of Commons Debates, November 22, 1996, pp. 6612-13)
(Débats de la Chambre des Communes, le 22 novembre 1996, pp. 6612-13)

5 *Land Mines*

Ms. Marlene Caterall (West Ottawa): Canada plays a very important role in the banning of land mines. Did the conference held in Ottawa this week allow us to realize true progress in that regard? Is there a reason to hope that we can stop this plague which land mines represent?

Mr. Francis Leblanc (Parliamentary Secretary of the Minister of Foreign Affairs.): The conference had the objective of reuniting countries from every region of the world sharing the same ideas to aim at the global ban of heinous weapons which are anti-personnel mines. The conference already had a proven effect. The number of countries which committed themselves to favour this ban went from about 14 a year ago, to 47 today in time to participate at this conference. We hope that a bigger number of countries will quickly follow this movement to allow the United Nations to pass a very energetic resolution on these weapons this fall.

(House of Commons Debates, October 4, 1996, p. 5115)
(Débats de la Chambre des Communes, le 4 octobre 1996, p. 5115)

Treaty Action Taken by Canada in 1996 / Mesures prises par le Canada en matière de traités en 1996

compiled by / préparé par
ANDRÉ BERGERON

I BILATERAL

Argentina
Agreement between the Government of Canada and the Government of the Argentine Republic for Co-operation in the Peaceful Uses of Nuclear Energy. Ottawa, June 21, 1994. *Entered into force* July 24, 1996. CTS 1996/19.

Australia
Agreement between the Government of Canada and the Government of Australia Concerning the Protection of Defence Related Information Exchanged between them. Canberra, October 31, 1996. *Entered into force* October 31, 1996. CTS 1996/31.

Austria
Supplementary Agreement to the Agreement on Social Security between Canada and the Republic of Austria. Vienna, September 12, 1995. *Entered into force* December 1, 1996. CTS 1996/25.

Barbados
Agreement between the Government of Canada and the Government of Barbados for the Promotion and Protection of Investments (with Annex). Bridgetown, May 29, 1996.

Belgium
Treaty between the Government of Canada and the Government of the Kingdom of Belgium on Mutual Legal Assistance in Criminal Matters.Brussels, January 11, 1996.

Protocol amending the Agreement on Social Security between Canada and Belgium, signed at Brussels on May 10, 1984. Brussels, March 11, 1996.

Brazil
Agreement between the Government of Canada and the Government of the Federative Republic of Brazil for Co-operation in the Peaceful Uses of Nuclear Energy (with Annexes). Brasilia, May 22, 1996.

Chile
Free Trade Agreement between the Government of Canada and the Government of the Republic of Chile. Santiago, December 4, 1996.

Agreement on Social Security between the Government of Canada and the Government of the Republic of Chile. Ottawa, November 18, 1996.

Agreement between the Government of Canada and the Government of the

---

André Bergeron is treaty registrar in the Legal Advisory Division at the Department of Foreign Affairs / Greffier des Traités, Direction des consultations juridiques, Ministère des Affaires étrangères.

Republic of Chile for the Avoidance of Double Taxation of Income from the Operation of Ships and Aircraft. Santiago, July 30, 1992. *Entered into force* January 1, 1996. CTS 1996/5.

Czech Republic
Agreement between the Government of Canada and the Government of the Czech Republic on Air Transport (with Annex). Prague, March 13, 1996. *Entered into force* March 13, 1996. CTS 1996/12.

Ecuador
Agreement between the Government of Canada and the Government of the Republic of Ecuador for the Promotion and Protection of Investments (with Annex). Quito, April 29, 1996.

Egypt
Agreement between the Government of Canada and the Government of the Arab Republic of Egypt for the Promotion and Protection of Investments (with Annex). Cairo, November 13, 1996.

European Community
Agreement between the Government of Canada and the Government of the European Community constituting an Agreement on the Terms of Settlement of the World Trade Organization Dispute "EC — Trade Description of Scallops (WT/DS7)." Geneva, June 25, 1996. *Entered into force* June 25, 1996. CTS 1996/37.

Exchange of Letters between the Government of Canada and the European Community on the Conclusion of Negotiations under Article XXIV:6. Brussels, December 30, 1995 and July 25, 1996. *Entered into force* July 25, 1996. CTS 1996/34.

Agreement for the Conclusion of Negotiations between the Government of Canada and the European Community under Article XXIV:6. Brussels, July 25, 1996. *Entered into force* July 25, 1996. CTS 1996/43.

Agreement between Canada and the European Community Establishing a Co-operation Programme in Higher Education and Training (with Annex). Brussels, December 19, 1995. *Entered into force* January 1, 1996. CTS 1996/4.

Agreement for Scientific and Technological Co-operation between Canada and the European Community (with Annex and Appendix). Halifax, June 17, 1995. *Entered into force* February 27, 1996. CTS 1996/24.

France
Agreement between the Government of Canada and the Government of the French Republic on the Recognition and Enforcement of Judgments in Civil and Commercial Matters and on Mutual Legal Assistance in Maintenance. Ottawa, June 10, 1996.

Hong Kong
Exchange of Notes between the Government of Canada and the Government of Hong Kong constituting an Agreement to Amend the Air Services Agreement signed at Hong Kong, June 24, 1988. Hong Kong, May 23 and December 19, 1996. *Entered into force* December 20, 1996. CTS 1996/38.

Exchange of Notes between the Government of Canada and the Government of Hong Kong constituting an Agreement to Extend the Canada/Hong Kong Agreement Concerning the Investigation of Drug Trafficking and Confiscation of the Proceeds of Drug Trafficking, done in Hong Kong November 14, 1990. Hong Kong, January 9 and January 11, 1996. *Entered into force* January 11, 1996.

Hungary
Treaty between Canada and the Republic of Hungary on Mutual Assistance in Criminal Matters. Budapest, December 7, 1995. *Entered into force* September 1, 1996. CTS 1996/18.

Protocol to the Tax Convention between the Government of Canada and the Government of the Republic of Hungary, signed on April 15, 1992. Budapest, May 3, 1994. *Entered into force* April 26, 1996. CTS 1996/10.

India

Agreement between the Government of Canada and the Government of the Republic of India for the Avoidance of Double Taxation and the Prevention of Fiscal Evasion with Respect to Taxes on Income and on Capital (with Protocol). Delhi, January 11, 1996.

Indonesia

Air Transport Agreement between the Government of Canada and the Government of the Republic of Indonesia (with Annex and Protocol). Jakarta, January 17, 1996.

International Fund For Ireland

Protocol to the Agreement between the Government of Canada and the International Fund for Ireland. Ottawa and Belfast, March 27, 1996. *Entered into force* March 27, 1996. CTS 1996/11.

Israel

Free Trade Agreement between the Government of Canada and the Government of the State of Israel (with Annexes). Toronto, July 31, 1996.

Kazakhstan

Agreement between the Government of Canada and the Government of the Republic of Kazakhstan for the Avoidance of Double Taxation and the Prevention of Fiscal Evasion with Respect to Taxes on Income and on Capital (with Protocol). Almaty, September 25, 1996.

Lithuania

Convention between the Government of Canada and the Government of the Republic of Lithuania for the Avoidance of Double Taxation and the Prevention of Fiscal Evasion with Respect to Taxes on Income and on Capital. Vilnius, August 29, 1996.

Luxembourg

Agreement between the Government of Canada and the Government of the Grand-Duchy of Luxembourg Regarding Audio-Visual Co-Production (with Annex). Luxembourg, March 4, 1996. *Entered into force* March 4, 1996. CTS 1996/13.

Malaysia

Agreement between the Government of Canada and the Government of Malaysia on Air Transport (with Annex). Kuala Lumpur, January 18, 1996. *Entered into force* January 18, 1996. CTS 1996/6.

Mexico

Agreement on Social Security between Canada and the United Mexican States. Ottawa, April 27, 1995. *Entered into force* May 1, 1996. CTS 1996/17.

Morocco

Amendment to the General Agreement between the Government of Canada and the Government of the Kingdom of Morocco Concerning Economic and Technical Cooperation. Rabat, December 16, 1996. *Entered into force* December 16, 1996. CTS 1996/39.

Agreement of Co-operation regarding the Transfer of Persons Incarcerated under Sentence between the Government of Canada and the Government of the Kingdom of Morocco. Rabat, May 4, 1987. *Entered into force* December 1, 1996. CTS 1996/32.

Netherlands

Exchange of Notes constituting an Agreement between the Government of Canada and the Government of the Kingdom of the Netherlands Concerning Canadian Use of the Netherlands' Facilities as a Staging Base. Ottawa, January 17 and 20, 1995. *Entered into force* September 3, 1996. CTS 1996/21.

Exchange of Notes Constituting an Agreement Replacing the Agreement between the Government of Canada and the Government of the Kingdom of the Netherlands for the Training of Netherlands Armed Forces in Canada, done in The Hague on December 4 and 5, 1986. Ottawa, December 24, 1996.

New Zealand

Agreement on Social Security between the Government of Canada and the Government of New Zealand. Ottawa, April 9, 1996.

Pakistan
Agreement between the Government of Canada and the Government of the Islamic Republic of Pakistan on Air Transport (with Annex). Islamabad, January 15, 1996. *Entered into force* January 15, 1996. CTS 1996/3.

Panama
Agreement between the Government of Canada and the Government of the Republic of Panama for the Promotion and Protection of Investments. Guatemala City, September 12, 1996.

Philippines
Agreement between the Government of Canada and the Government of the Republic of the Philippines for the Promotion and Reciprocal Protection of Investments (with Annex). Manila, November 9, 1995. *Entered into force* November 13, 1996. CTS 1996/46.

Poland
Agreement between the Government of Canada and the Government of the Republic of Poland on Film and Television Co-Production (with Annex). Ottawa, May 27, 1996.

Romania
Agreement between the Government of Canada and the Government of Romania for the Promotion and Reciprocal Protection of Investments (with Annex). Bucharest, April 17, 1996.

Slovakia
Agreement between the Government of Canada and the Government of the Slovak Republic for Co-operation in the Peaceful Uses of Nuclear Energy (with Annexes). Bratislava, October 22, 1996. *Entered into force* October 22, 1996. CTS 1996/30.

Slovenia
Agreement between the Government of Canada and the Government of the Republic of Slovenia for Co-operation in the Peaceful Uses of Nuclear Energy (with Annexes). Ljubljana, May 31, 1995. *Entered into force* April 17, 1996.

Saint Lucia
General Agreement between the Government of Canada and the Government of Saint Lucia on Development Co-operation (with Annexes). Saint Lucia, March 4, 1987. *Entered into force* July 19, 1996.

St. Vincent and the Grenadines
General Agreement between the Government of Canada and the Government of St. Vincent and the Grenadines on Development Co-operation (with Annexes). St. Vincent, February 26, 1987. *Entered into force* April 17, 1996.

Sweden
Convention between Canada and Sweden for the Avoidance of Double Taxation and the Prevention of Fiscal Evasion with Respect to Taxes on Income. Stockholm, August 27, 1996.

Switzerland
Treaty between Canada and the Swiss Confederation on Extradition. Berne, October 7, 1993. *Entered into force* March 19, 1996. CTS 1996/15.

Agreement between the Government of Canada and the Government of the Swiss Confederation Regarding the Transfer of Forfeited Assets. Ottawa, December 17, 1996. *Entered into force* December 17, 1996.

Trinidad and Tobago
Agreement between the Government of Canada and the Government of the Republic of Trinidad and Tobago for the Reciprocal Promotion and Protection of Investments (with Annex). Toronto, September 11, 1995. *Entered into force* July 8, 1996. CTS 1996/22.

Convention between the Government of Canada and the Government of the Republic of Trinidad and Tobago for the Avoidance of Double Taxation, the Prevention of Fiscal Evasion with Respect to Taxes on Income and the Encouragement of International Trade and Investment. Washington, September 28, 1966. *Entered into force* March 1, 1967. CTS 1967/5. *Terminated* February 8, 1996.

Convention between the Government of Canada and the Government of the

Republic of Trinidad and Tobago for the Avoidance of Double Taxation, the Prevention of Fiscal Evasion with Respect to Taxes on Income and the Encouragement of International Trade and Investment. Toronto, September 11, 1995. *Entered into force* February 8, 1996. CTS 1996/7.

Ukraine

Agreement between Canada and Ukraine on Mutual Assistance in Criminal Matters. Ottawa, September 23, 1996.

Convention between the Government of Canada and the Government of Ukraine for the Avoidance of Double Taxation, and the Prevention of Fiscal Evasion with Respect to Taxes on Income and on Capital. Kiev, March 4, 1996.

United Nations

Agreement between the Government of Canada and the United Nations University concerning the United Nations University International Network on Water Environment and Health. Hamilton, September 20, 1996. *Entered into force* September 20, 1996. CTS 1996/27.

Agreement between the Government of Canada and the Secretariat of the Convention on Biological Diversity concerning the Headquarters of the Convention Secretariat. New York, October 25, 1996. *Entered into force* October 25, 1996. CTS 1996/28.

United States of America

Agreement between the Government of Canada and the Government of the United States of America on Co-operation in Comprehensive Civil Emergency Planning and Management, signed in Ottawa on April 28, 1986 (with annex). Ottawa and Washington, August 12, 1996.

Softwood Lumber Agreement between the Government of Canada and the Government of the United States of America. Washington, May 29, 1996. *Entered into force* May 29, 1996. CTS 1996/16.

Exchange of Notes between the Government of Canada and the Government of the United States of America constituting an Agreement concerning the North American Aerospace Defence Command (NORAD). Washington, March 11, 1981. CTS 1981/31. *Terminated* March 28, 1996.

Exchange of Notes between the Government of Canada and the Government of the United States of America constituting an Agreement to Extend the North American Aerospace Defence Command (NORAD) Agreement for a five-year period. Washington, March 19, 1986. CTS 1986/34. *Terminated* March 28, 1996.

Exchange of Notes between the Government of Canada and the Government of the United States of America constituting an Agreement to Extend the North American Aerospace Defence Command (NORAD) Agreement for a five-year period. Washington, April 30, 1991. CTS 1991/19. *Terminated* March 28, 1996.

Exchange of Notes between the Government of Canada and the Government of the United States of America constituting an Agreement to Extend the North American Aerospace Defence Command (NORAD) Agreement for a further five-year period. Washington, March 28, 1996. *Entered into force* March 28, 1996 with effect from May 12, 1996. CTS 1996/36.

Exchange of Notes between the Government of Canada and the Government of the United States of America constituting an Agreement with respect to Environmental Issues. Washington, October 7 and 9, 1996. *Entered into force* October 9, 1996. CTS 1996/35.

Exchange of Notes between the Government of Canada and the Government of the United States of America constituting an Agreement on the Training of Mission Specialists. Ottawa, August 31, 1995 and May 17, 1996. *Entered into force* May 17, 1996. CTS 1996/26.

Exchange of Notes between the Government of Canada and the Government of the United States of America constituting an Agreement Concerning the Torso Rotation Experiment (with Memorandum of Understanding). Ottawa, June 19, 1996. *Entered into force* June 19, 1996. CTS 1996/41.

Second Supplementary Agreement amending the Agreement between the Government of Canada and the Government of the United States of America with respect to Social Security. Ottawa, May 28, 1996.

Uruguay

Agreement between Canada and the Oriental Republic of Uruguay on Mutual Assistance in Criminal Matters. Ottawa, July 10, 1996.

Venezuela

Agreement between the Government of Canada and the Government of the Republic of Venezuela on Audio-Visual Co-Production. Caracas, February 15, 1996. *Entered into force* October 21, 1996. CTS 1996/33.

Agreement between the Government of Canada and the Government of the Republic of Venezuela for the Promotion and Protection of Investments (with Annex). Caracas, July 1, 1996.

Treaty between the Government of Canada and the Government of the Republic of Venezuela for the Serving of Penal Sentences. Caracas, January 24, 1994. *Entered into force* January 1, 1996. CTS 1996/2.

Vietnam

Agreement between the Government of Canada and the Government of the Socialist Republic of Vietnam on Trade and Commerce. Hanoi, November 13, 1995. *Entered into force* January 25, 1996. CTS 1996/9.

Agreement on Economic Co-operation between the Government of Canada and the Government of the Socialist Republic of Vietnam. Ottawa, June 21, 1994. *Entered into force* March 20, 1996. CTS 1996/45.

II MULTILATERAL

Adoption

Convention on Protection of Children and Co-operation in Respect of Inter-Country Adoption. The Hague, May 29, 1993. *Signed* by Canada April 12, 1994. *Ratified* by Canada December 19, 1996.

Aviation

Convention on the Marking of Plastic Explosives for the Purpose of Detection. Montreal, March 1, 1991. *Signed* by Canada March 1, 1991. *Ratified* by Canada November 29, 1996.

Copyright, Industrial Property

Accession by Canada to Articles 1 to 12 (the "substantive" provisions) of the Stockholm Act (1967) of the Paris Convention for the Protection of Industrial Property, done at Paris March 20, 1883, revised at Stockholm July 14, 1967. *Acceded to* by Canada February 23, 1996. *Entered into force* for Canada May 26, 1996.

Defence

Exchange of Notes constituting an Agreement concerning the Agreement of June 19, 1951 between the parties to the North Atlantic Treaty (NATO) regarding the Status of Their Forces, the Supplementary Agreement of August 3, 1959 and the Agreements related thereto. Bonn, September 12, 1994. *Signed* by Canada September 12, 1994. *Ratified* by Canada March 7, 1995. *Entered into force* for Canada September 18, 1996. CTS 1996/47.

Agreement on the Status of Missions and Representatives of the Third States to the North Atlantic Treaty Organization. Brussels, September 14, 1994. *Ratified* by Canada May 28, 1996.

Agreement among the States Parties to the North Atlantic Treaty and other States Participating in the Partnership for Peace Regarding the Status of Their Forces. Brussels, June 19, 1995. *Signed* by Canada October 13, 1995. *Entered into force* for Canada June 1, 1996. CTS 1996/29.

Environment

United Nations Convention to Combat Desertification in Those Countries Experiencing Serious Drought and/or Desertification, particularly in Africa. Paris, June 17, 1994. *Signed* by Canada October 14, 1994. *Ratified* by Canada December 1, 1995. *Entered into force* for Canada December 27, 1996.

Labour

Convention Concerning Labour Statistics (ILO No. 160). Geneva, June 25, 1985. *Ratified* by Canada November 22, 1995. *Entered into force* for Canada November 22, 1996. CTS 1996/8.

Mutual Legal Assistance

Inter-American Convention on Mutual Assistance in Criminal Matters. Nassau, May 23, 1992. *Signed* by Canada June 3, 1996. *Ratified* by Canada June 3, 1996. *Entered into force* for Canada July 3, 1996.

Narcotics

Anti-Doping Convention (with Appendix). Strasbourg, November 18, 1989. *Signed* by Canada March 6, 1996. *Entered into force* for Canada May 1, 1996. CTS 1996/14.

Navigation — Safety

International Convention on Salvage. London, April 28, 1989. *Ratified* by Canada November 14, 1994. *Entered into force* for Canada July 14, 1996.

Nuclear (IAEA)

Convention on Nuclear Safety. Vienna, September 20, 1994. *Signed* by Canada September 20, 1994. *Ratified* by Canada December 12, 1995. *Entered into force* for Canada October 24, 1996. CTS 1996/44.

Nuclear

Comprehensive Nuclear Test-Ban Treaty. New York, September 10, 1996. *Signed* by Canada September 24, 1996.

Postal Matters

Acts of the 16th Congress of the Postal Union of the Americas, Spain and Portugal. Mexico City, September 15, 1995. *Signed* by Canada September 15, 1995. *Entered into force* for Canada January 1, 1996.

Patents

Strasbourg Agreement Concerning the International Patent Classification. Strasbourg, March 24, 1971. *Acceded to* by Canada January 11, 1995. *Entered into force* for Canada January 11, 1996.

Budapest Treaty on the International Recognition of the Deposit of Microorganisms for the Purpose of Patent Procedure, done on April 28, 1977, as amended Budapest, April 28, 1977. *Acceded to* by Canada June 21, 1996. *Entered into force* for Canada September 21, 1996. CTS 1996/29.

Telecommunications

Final Acts of the Plenipotentiary Conference of the International Telecommunication Union. Kyoto, October 14, 1994. *Acceptance* by Canada October 9, 1996. *Entered into force* for Canada October 9, 1996.

Final Acts of the Conference of the International Telecommunication Union. Geneva, November 17, 1995. *Acceptance* by Canada October 9, 1996. *Entered into force* for Canada October 9, 1996.

Amendment to the Agreement Relating to the International Telecommunications Satellite Organization "INTELSAT" (Art. 22-d). Singapore, April 4, 1995. *Acceptance* by Canada January 24, 1996. *Entered into force* for Canada September 11, 1996. CTS 1996/49.

Amendment to the Agreement Relating to the International Telecommunications Satellite Organization "INTELSAT" (Art. 17-f). Copenhagen, August 31, 1995. *Entered into force* for Canada October 16, 1996. CTS 1996/48.

Telecommunications — Radio

Inter-American Convention on an International Amateur Radio Permit (with Annex). Montrouis, June 6, 1995. *Entered into force* for Canada February 23, 1996. CTS 1996/40.

Timber

International Tropical Timber Agreement, 1994 (with Annexes). Geneva,

January 26, 1994. *Signed* by Canada May 3, 1995. *Ratified* by Canada May 23, 1996.

Trade

Exchange of Notes between Canada, the United States of America, and Mexico amending Annex 401, Annex 403.1, and Table 308.1.1 of Annex 308.1 of the North America Free Trade Agreement. Ottawa, Washington, and Mexico City, November 6, 1995. *Entered into force* for Canada January 1, 1996. CTS 1996/42.

Trade — GATT

Agreement on Government Procurement. Marrakesh, April 15, 1994. *Signed* by Canada April 15, 1994. *Ratified* by Canada December 22, 1995. *Entered into force* for Canada January 1, 1996.

Transfer of Offenders

Inter-American Convention on Serving Criminal Sentences Abroad. Managua, June 9, 1993. *Signed* by Canada July 8, 1993. *Ratified* by Canada on June 4, 1995. *Entered into force* for Canada April 13, 1996. CTS 1996/23.

I BILATÉRAUX

Argentine

Accord de Coopération entre le gouvernement du Canada et le gouvernement de la République d'Argentine concernant les utilisations pacifiques de l'énergie. Ottawa, le 21 juin, 1994. *En vigueur* le 24 juillet, 1996. RTC 1996/19.

Australie

Entente entre le gouvernement du Canada et le gouvernement de l'Australie relative à l'échange et à la protection de l'information en matière de défense. Canberra, le 31 octobre 1996. *En vigueur* le 31 octobre 1996. RTC 1996/31.

Autriche

Accord supplémentaire à l'Accord sur la sécurité sociale entre le Canada et la République d'Autriche. Vienne, le 12 septembre 1995. *En vigueur* le 1er décembre 1996. RTC 1996/25.

Barbade

Accord entre le gouvernement du Canada et le gouvernement de la Barbade pour la promotion et la protection réciproque des investissements (avec Annexe). Bridgetown, le 29 mai, 1996.

Belgique

Traité d'entraide judiciaire en matière pénale entre le gouvernement du Canada et le gouvernement du royaume de Belgique. Bruxelles, le 11 janvier 1996.

Protocole portant amendement à l'Accord de sécurité sociale entre le Canada et la Belgique. Bruxelles, le 11 mars 1996.

Brésil

Accord de coopération entre le gouvernement du Canada et le gouvernement de la République fédérative du Brésil concernant les utilisations pacifiques de l'énergie nucléaire (avec Annexes). Brasilia, le 22 mai 1996.

Chili

Accord de libre-échange entre le gouvernement du Canada et le gouvernement de la République du Chili. Santiago, le 4 décembre 1996.

Accord sur la sécurité sociale entre le gouvernement du Canada et le gouvernement de la Rpublique du Chili. Ottawa, le 18 novembre 1996.

Accord entre le gouvernement du Canada et le gouvernement de la République du Chili tendant à éviter la double imposition sur les revenus provenant de l'exploitation des transports maritime et aérien. Santiago, le 30 juillet 1992. *En vigueur* le 1er janvier 1996. RTC 1996/5.

Communautés Européennes

Échange de Lettres entre le gouvernement du Canada et les Communautés européennes constituant un Accord comportant les termes du règlement du différend en instance devant l'Organisation mondiale du commerce "CE-Dénomination de vente des Pectinidés (WT/DS7)." Genève, le 25 juin

1996. *En vigueur* le 25 juin 1996. RTC 1996/37.

Échange de Lettres entre le Canada et la Communauté Européenne constituant un Accord concernant la conclusion des négociations dans le cadre de l'article 24:6. Bruxelles, le 30 décembre 1995 et le 25 juillet 1996. *En vigueur* le 25 juillet 1996. RTC 1996/34.

Accord concernant la conclusion des négociations entre le Canada et la Communauté Européenne dans le cadre de l'article 26:6. Bruxelles, le 25 juillet 1996. *En vigueur* le 25 juillet 1996. RTC 1996/43.

Accord entre le Canada et la Communauté Européenne établissant un programme de coopération dans le domaine de l'enseignement supérieur et de la formation (avec Annexe). Bruxelles, le 19 décembre 1995. *En vigueur* le 1er janvier 1996. RTC 1996/4.

Accord de coopération scientifique et technologique entre le Canada et la Communauté Européenne (avec Annexe et Appendice). Halifax, le 17 juin 1995. *En vigueur* le 27 février 1996. RTC 1996/24.

Équateur

Accord entre le gouvernement du Canada et le gouvernement de la République de l'Équateur pour la promotion et la protection réciproques des investissements (avec Annexes). Quito, le 29 avril 1996.

Égypte

Accord entre le gouvernement du Canada et le gouvernement de la République arabe d'Égypte pour l'encouragement et la protection des investissements (avec Annexe). Le Caire, le 13 novembre 1996.

États-Unis d'Amérique

Échange de Notes entre le gouvernement du Canada et le gouvernement des États-Unis d'Amérique constituant un Accord modifiant l'Accord de coopération concernant la planification et la gestion civile d'urgence sur une base globale, signé à Ottawa le 28 avril 1986 (avec Annexe). Ottawa et Washington, le 12 août 1996.

Accord sur le bois d'oeuvre résineux entre le gouvernement du Canada et le gouvernement des États-Unis d'Amérique. Washington, le 29 mai 1996. *En vigueur* le 29 mai 1996. RTC 1996/16.

Échange de Notes entre le gouvernement du Canada et le gouvernement des États-Unis d'Amérique constituant un Accord concernant l'organisation et le Commandement de la Défense aérospatiale de l'Amérique du Nord (NORAD). Washington, le 11 mars 1981. *Terminé* le 28 mars 1996. RTC 1981/31.

Échange de Notes entre le gouvernement du Canada et le gouvernement des États-Unis d'Amérique constituant un Accord prolongeant l'Accord du Commandement de la Défense aérospatiale de l'Amérique du Nord (NORAD) pour une période de cinq ans. Washington, le 19 mars 1986. *Terminé* le 28 mars 1996. RTC 1986/34.

Échange de Notes entre le gouvernement du Canada et le gouvernement des États-Unis d'Amérique constituant un Accord prolongeant l'Accord du Commandement de la Défense aérospatiale de l'Amérique du Nord (NORAD) pour une période de cinq ans. Washington, le 30 avril 1991. *Terminé* le 28 mars 1996. RTC 1991/19.

Échange de Notes entre le gouvernement du Canada et le gouvernement des États-Unis d'Amérique constituant un Accord prolongeant l'Accord du Commandement de la Défense aérospatiale de l'Amérique du Nord (NORAD) pour une autre période de cinq ans. Washington, le 28 mars 1996. *En vigueur* le 28 mars 1996 avec effet du 12 mai 1996. RTC 1996/36.

Échange de Notes entre le gouvernement du Canada et le gouvernement des États-Unis d'Amérique constituant un Accord concernant les questions environnementales (avec Appendice). Washington, les 7 et 9 octobre 1996. *En vigueur* le 9 octobre 1996. RTC 1996/35.

Échange de Notes constituant un Accord entre le gouvernement du Canada et le gouvernement des États-Unis d'Amérique sur l'entraînement des spécialistes de mission du Canada. Ottawa, le 31 août 1995 et le 17 mai 1996. *En vigueur* le 17 mai 1996. RTC 1996/26.

Échange de Notes constituant un Accord entre le gouvernement du Canada et le gouvernement des États-Unis d'Amérique sur l'expérience de rotation du torse (avec Mémoire d'entente). Ottawa, le 19 juin 1996. *En vigueur* le 19 juin 1996. RTC 1996/41.

Deuxième Accord supplémentaire modifiant l'Accord entre le gouvernement du Canada et le gouvernement des États-Unis d'Amérique en matière de sécurité sociale. Ottawa, le 28 mai 1996.

France

Convention entre le gouvernement du Canada et le gouvernement de la République française relative à la reconnaissance et à l'exécution des décisions judiciaires en matière civile ou commerciale ainsi qu'à l'entraide judiciaire en matière de pensions alimentaires. Ottawa, le 10 juin 1996.

Hong Kong

Échange de Notes entre le gouvernement du Canada et le gouvernement de Hong Kong constituant un Accord modifiant leur Accord sur les services aériens, signé à Hong Kong le 24 juin 1999. Hong Kong, les 23 mai et 19 décembre 1996. *En vigueur* le 20 décembre 1996. RTC 1996/38.

Échange de Notes constituant un Accord prorogeant l'Accord Canada-Hong Kong concernant les enquêtes sur le trafic des drogues et la confiscation du produit du trafic des drogues, fait à Hong Kong le 14 novembre 1990. Hong Kong, les 9 et 11 janvier 1996. *En vigueur* le 11 janvier 1996.

Hongrie

Traité d'entraide judiciaire en matière pénale entre le Canada et la République de Hongrie. Budapest, le 7 décembre 1995. *En vigueur* le 1er septembre 1996. RTC 1996/18.

Protocole à la convention fiscale entre le gouvernement du Canada et le gouvernement de la Republique de la Hongrie, signée le 15 avril 1992. Budapest, le 3 mai 1994. *En vigueur* le 26 avril 1996. RTC 1996/10.

Inde

Accord entre le gouvernement du Canada et le gouvernement de la République de l'Inde en vue d'éviter les doubles impositions et de prévenir l'évasion fiscale en matière d'impôts sur le revenu et sur la fortune (avec Protocole). Delhi, le 11 janvier 1996.

Indonésie

Accord entre le gouvernement du Canada et le gouvernement de la République d'Indonésie sur le transport aérien (avec Annexe et Protocole). Jakarta, le 17 janvier 1996.

Israël

Accord de libre-échange entre le gouvernement du Canada et le gouvernement de l'État d'Israël (avec Annexes). Toronto, le 31 juillet 1996.

Kazakstan

Convention entre le gouvernement du Canada et le gouvernement de la République du Kazakstan en vue d'éviter les doubles impositions et de prévenir l'évasion fiscale en matière d'impôts sur le revenu et sur la fortune (avec Protocole). Altamy, le 25 septembre 1996.

Le Fond International Pour l'Irlande

Protocole à l'Accord intervenu entre le gouvernement du Canada et le Fonds international pour l'Irlande. Ottawa et Belfast, le 27 mars 1996. *En vigueur* le 27 mars 1996. RTC 1996/11.

Lituanie

Convention entre le gouvernement du Canada et le gouvernement de la République de la Lituanie en vue d'éviter les doubles impositions et de prévenir l'évasion fiscale en matière d'impôts sur le revenu et sur la fortune. Vilnius, le 29 août 1996.

Luxembourg
Convention entre le gouvernement du Canada et le gouvernement de la République du Grand-Duché de Luxembourg concernant la coproduction audiovisuelle (avec Annexe). Luxembourg, le 4 mars 1996. *En vigueur* le 4 mars 1996. RTC 1996/13.

Malaisie
Accord entre le gouvernement du Canada et le gouvernement de la Malaisie sur le transport aérien. Kuala Lumpur, le 18 janvier 1996. *En vigueur* le 18 janvier 1996. CTS 1996/6.

Mexique
Accord sur la Sécurité sociale entre le Canada et les États-Unies du Mexique. Ottawa, le 27 avril 1995. *En vigueur* le 1er mai 1996. RTC 1996/17.

Maroc
Accord entre le gouvernement du Canada et le gouvernement du Royaume du Maroc constituant un Accord modifiant leur Accord concernant la coopération économique et technique (avec Annexe). Rabat, le 16 décembre 1996. *En vigueur* le 16 décembre 1996. RTC 1996/39.

Accord de coopération relatif au transfèrement des condamnés détenus entre le gouvernement du Canada et le gouvernement du Royaume du Maroc. Rabat, le 4 mai 1987. *En vigueur* le 1er décembre 1996. RTC 1996/32.

Nations Unies
Accord entre le gouvernement du Canada et l'Université des Nations Unies concernant le réseau international pour l'eau, l'environnement et la santé de l'Université des Nations Unies. Hamilton, le 20 septembre 1996. *En vigueur* le 20 septembre 1996. CTS 1996/27.

Accord entre le gouvernement du Canada et le Secrétariat de la Convention sur la diversité biologique concernant le siège du Secrétariat. New York, le 25 octobre 1996. *En vigueur* le 26 octobre 1996. RTC 1996/28.

Nouvelle-Zélande
Accord sur la sécurité sociale entre le gouvernement du Canada et le gouvernement de la Nouvelle-Zélande. Ottawa, le 9 avril 1996.

Pakistan
Accord sur le transport aérien entre le gouvernement du Canada et le gouvernement de la République islamique du Pakistan (avec Annexe). Ismalabad, le 15 janvier 1996. En vigueur le 15 janvier 1996. RTC 1996/3.

Panama
Traité entre le gouvernement du Canada et le gouvernement de la République du Panama pour l'encouragement et la protection des investissements (avec Annexe). Guatemala City, le 12 septembre 1996.

Pays-bas
Échange de Notes constituant un Accord remplaçant l'Accord entre le gouvernement du Canada et le gouvernement du Royaume des Pays-Bas concernant l'utilisation par le Canada d'installations néerlandaises comme base d'étape. Ottawa, les 17 et 20 janvier 1995. *En vigueur* le 3 septembre 1996. CTS 1996/21.

Échange de Notes constituant un Accord remplaçant l'Accord entre le gouvernement du Canada et le gouvernement du Royaume des Pays-Bas pour l'entraînement au Canada d'unités des Forces Armées des Pays-Bas, fait à La Haie les 4 et 5 décembre 1986. Ottawa, le 24 décembre 1996.

Philippines
Accord entre le gouvernement du Canada et le gouvernement de la République des Philippines pour l'encouragement et la protection réciproque des investissements (avec Annexe). Manille, le 9 novembre 1995. *En vigueur* le 13 novembre 1996. RTC 1996/46.

Pologne
Accord entre le gouvernement du Canada et le gouvernement de la République de Pologne sur la coproduction cinématographique et

télévisuelle (avec Annexe). Ottawa, le 27 mai 1996.

Roumanie

Accord entre le gouvernement du Canada et le gouvernement de la Roumanie pour l'encouragement et la protection des investissements (avec Annexe). Bucharest, le 17 avril 1996.

République Slovaque

Accord de coopération entre le gouvernement du Canada et le gouvernement de la République Slovaque (avec Annexe). Bratislava, le 22 octobre 1996. *En vigueur* le 22 octobre 1996. RTC 1996/30.

République Tchèque

Accord entre le gouvernement du Canada et le gouvernement de la République Tchèque sur le transport aérien (avec Annexe). Prague, le 13 mars 1996. *En vigueur* le 13 mars 1996. RTC 1996/12.

Saint-Vincent-et-Grenadines

Accord général entre le gouvernement du Canada et le gouvernement de Saint-Vincent-et-Grenadines sur la coopération au développement (avec Annexes). Saint-Vincent, le 26 février 1987. *En vigueur* le 17 juillet 1993.

Sainte-Lucie

Accord général entre le gouvernement du Canada et le gouvernement de Sainte-Lucie sur la coopération au développement (avec Annexes). Sainte-Lucie, 4 mars 1987. *En vigueur* le 19 juillet 1993.

Slovénie

Accord de coopération entre le gouvernement du Canada et le gouvernement de la République de Slovénie concernant les utilisations pacifiques de l'énergie nucléaire (avec Annexes). Ljubljana, le 31 mai 1995. *En vigueur* le 17 avril 1996.

Suède

Convention entre le Canada et la Suède en vue d'éviter les doubles impositions et de prévenir l'évasion fiscale en matière d'impôts sur le revenu. Stockholm, le 27 août 1996.

Suisse

Traité d'extradition entre le Canada et la Confédération Suisse. Berne, le 7 octobre 1993. *En vigueur* le 19 mars, 1996. RTC 1996/15.

Accord entre le gouvernement du Canada et le gouvernement de la Confédération Suisse au sujet du transfert de fonds confisqués. Ottawa, le 17 décembre 1996. *En vigueur* le 17 décembre 1996.

Trinité-et-Tobago

Accord entre le gouvernement du Canada et le gouvernement de la République de Trinité et Tobago pour la promotion et la protection réciproque des investissements (avec Annexe). Toronto, le 11 septembre 1996. *En vigueur* le 8 juillet 1996. RTC 1996/22.

Convention entre le gouvernement du Canada et le gouvernement de la Trinité et Tobago en vue d'éviter les doubles impositions et de prévenir l'évasion fiscale en matière d'impôts sur le revenu et d'encourager le commerce et les investissements internationaux. Washington, le 28 septembre 1966. En vigueur le 1er mars 1967. RTC 1967/5. *Terminé* le 8 février 1996.

Convention entre le gouvernement du Canada et le gouvernement de la Trinité et Tobago en vue d'éviter les doubles impositions et de prévenir l'évasion fiscale en matière d'impôts sur le revenu et d'encourager le commerce et les investissements internationaux. Toronto, le 11 septembre 1995. *En vigueur* le 8 février 1996. RTC 1996/7.

Ukraine

Traité d'entraide judiciaire en matière pénale entre le Canada et l'Ukraine. Ottawa, le 23 septembre 1996.

Convention entre le gouvernement du Canada et le gouvernement de l'Ukraine en vue d'éviter les doubles impositions et de prévenir l'évasion fiscale en matière d'impôts sur le revenu et sur la fortune. Kiev, le 4 mars 1996.

Uruguay
Traité d'entraide judiciaire en matière pénale entre le Canada et la République orientale de l'Uruguay. Ottawa, le 10 juillet 1996.

Vénézuela
Accord entre le gouvernement du Canada et le gouvernement de la République du Vénézuela sur la coproduction audiovisuelle. Caracas, le 15 février 1996. *En vigueur* le 21 octobre 1996. RTC 1996/33.

Accord entre le gouvernement du Canada et le gouvernement de la République du Vénézuela pour la promotion et la protection des investissements (avec Annexe). Caracas, le 1er juillet 1996. En vigueur le 20 janvier 1998.

Accord entre le gouvernement du Canada et le gouvernement de la République du Vénézuela sur l'exécution des sentences pénales. Caracas, le 24 janvier 1994. *En vigueur* le 1er janvier 1996. RTC 1996/2.

Vietnam
Accord de commerce entre le gouvernement du Canada et le gouvernement de la République socialiste du Vietnam. Hanoï, le 13 novembre 1995. *En vigueur* le 25 janvier 1996. RTC 1996/9.

Accord de coopération économique entre le gouvernement du Canada et le gouvernement de la République socialiste du Vietnam. Ottawa, le 21 juin 1994. *En vigueur* le 20 mars 1996. RTC 1996/45.

II MULTILATÉRAUX

Adoption
Convention sur la protection des enfants et la coopération en matière d'adoption internationale. La Haye, le 29 mai 1993. *Signée* par le Canada le 12 avril 1994. *Ratifiée* par le Canada le 19 décembre 1996.

Aviation
Convention sur le marquage des explosifs plastiques et en feuilles aux fins de détection. Montréal, le 1er mars 1991. *Signée* par le Canada le 1er mars 1991. *Ratifiée* par le Canada le 29 novembre 1996.

Bois
Accord international de 1994 sur les bois tropicaux (avec Annexes). Genève, le 26 janvier 1994. *Signé* par le Canada le 3 mai 1995. *Ratifié* par le Canada le 23 mai 1996.

Brevets
Arrangements de Strasbourg concernant la classification internationale des brevets, modifié le 28 septembre 1979. Strasbourg, le 24 mars 1971. *Adhésion* du canada le 11 janvier 1995. *En vigueur* pour le Canada le 11 janvier 1996.

Traité de Budapest sur la reconnaissance internationale du dépôt des micro-organismes aux fins de la procédure en matière de brevets, fait le 28 avril 1977, tel que modifié. Budapest, le 28 avril 1977. *Adhésion* du Canada le 21 juin 1996. *En vigueur* pour le Canada le 21 septembre 1996. RTC 1996/29.

Commerce
Échange de Lettres entre le Canada, les États-Unis d'Amérique et les États-Unis mexicains modifiant l'annexe 401.1, l'annexe 403.1 et le tableau 308.1.1 de l'annexe 308.1 de l'Accord de libre-échange de l'Amérique du Nord. Ottawa, Washington, Mexico, le 6 novembre 1995. *En vigueur* pour le Canada le 1er janvier 1996. RTC 1996/42.

Commerce — GATT
Accord sur les marchés publics. Marrakesh, le 15 avril 1994. *Signé* par le Canada le 15 avril 1994. *Ratifié* par le Canada le 22 décembre 1995. *En vigueur* pour le Canada le 1er janvier 1996.

Défense
Échange de Notes constituant un Accord modifiant l'Accord constitué par l'Échange de Notes du 25 septembre 1990 relatif à la Convention du 19 juin 1951 entre les États parties au

Traité de l'Atlantique Nord (OTAN) sur le statut de leurs forces et à l'Accord supplémentaire du 3 août 1959 complétant ladite Convention, y compris les Accords qui s'y rapportent. Bonn, le 12 septembre 1994. *Signé* par le Canada le 12 septembre 1994. *Ratifié* par le Canada le 7 mars 1995. *En vigueur* pour le Canada le 18 septembre 1996. RTC 1996/47.

Accord sur le statut des missions et des représentants d'États tiers auprès de l'Organisation du Traité de l'Atlantique Nord. Bruxelles, le 14 septembre 1994. *Ratifié* par le Canada le 28 mai 1996.

Convention entre les États parties au Traité de l'Atlantique Nord et les autres États participant au partenariat pour la paix sur le statut de leurs forces. Bruxelles, le 19 juin 1995. *Signée* par le Canada le 13 octobre 1995. *Ratifiée* par le Canada le 1 juin 1996. RTC 1996/29.

Droit d'auteur (Propriété industrielle)
Adhésion par le Canada aux articles 1 à 12 (les dispositions de fond) de l'Acte de Stockholm (1967) de la Convention de Paris pour la protection de la propriété industrielle, faite à Paris le 20 mars 1883 et révisée à Stockholm le 14 juillet 1967. *Adhésion* du Canada le 23 février 1996. *En vigueur* pour le Canada le 26 mai 1996.

Entraide en matière pénale
Convention interaméricaine sur l'entraide en matière pénale. Nassau, le 23 mai 1992. *Signée* par le Canada le 3 juin 1996. *Ratifiée* par le Canada le 3 juin 1996. *En vigueur* pour le Canada le 3 juillet 1996.

Environnement
Convention des Nations Unies sur la lutte contre la désertification dans les pays gravement touchés par la sécheresse et/ou la désertification, en particulier en Afrique. Paris, le 17 juin 1994. *Signée* par le Canada le 14 octobre 1994. *Ratifiée* par le Canada le 1er décembre 1995. *En vigueur* pour le Canada le 27 décembre 1996.

Navigation — Sauvetage
Convention sur le sauvetage. Londres, le 28 avril 1989. *Ratifiée* par le Canada le 14 novembre 1994. *En vigueur* pour le Canada le 14 juillet 1996.

Nucléaire (AIÉA)
Convention sur la sûreté nucléaire. Vienne, le 20 septembre 1994. *Signée* par le Canada le 20 septembre 1994. *Ratifiée* par le Canada le 12 décembre 1995. *En vigueur* pour le Canada le 24 octobre 1996.

Nucléaire
Traité d'interdiction complète des essais nucléaires. New York, le 10 septembre 1996. *Signé* par le Canada le 24 septembre 1996.

Questions Postales
Actes du XVIe congrès de l'Union postale des Amériques, de l'Espagne et du Portugal. Mexico, le 15 septembre 1995. *Signés* par le Canada le 15 septembre 1995. *En vigueur* pour le Canada le 1er janvier 1996.

Stupéfiants
Convention sur le dopage (avec Annexe). Strasbourg, le 18 novembre 1989. *Signée* par le Canada le 6 mars 1996. *En vigueur* pour le Canada le 1er mai 1996. RTC 1996/14.

Télécommunications
Actes finals de la Conférence de plénipotentiaires de l'Union internationale des télécommunications. Kyoto, le 14 octobre 1994. *Acceptation* par le Canada le 9 octobre 1996. *En vigueur* pour le Canada le 9 octobre 1996.

Actes finals de la Conférence de l'Union internationale des télécommunications. Genève, le 17 novembre 1995. *Acceptation* par le Canada le 9 octobre 1996. *En vigueur* pour le Canada le 9 octobre 1996.

Amendement à l'Accord relatif à l'Organisation internationale de télécommunications par satellites "INTELSAT" (art. 22-d). Singapour, le 4 avril 1995. *Acceptation* par le Canada le 24 janvier 1996. *En vigueur* pour le Canada le 11 septembre 1996. CTS 1996/49.

Amendement à l'Accord relatif à l'Organisation internationale de télécommunications par satellites "INTELSAT" (art. 17-f). Copenhagen, le 31 août 1995. *En vigueur* pour le Canada le 16 octobre 1996. CTS 1996/48.

Télécommunications — Radio
Convention interaméricaine relative à un permis international de radioamateur (avec Annexe). Montrouis, le 6 juin 1995. *En vigueur* pour le Canada le 23 février 1996. RTC 1996/40.

Transfèrement des délinquants
Convention interaméricaine sur l'exécution des décisions pénales à l'étranger. Managua, le 9 juin 1993. *Signée* par le Canada le 8 juillet 1994. *Ratifiée* par le Canada le 4 juin 1995. *En vigueur* pour le Canada le 13 avril 1996. RTC 1996/23.

Travail
Convention concernant les statistiques du Travail (OIT No 160). Genève, le 25 juin 1985. *Ratifiée* par le Canada le 22 novembre 1995. *En vigueur* pour le Canada le 22 novembre 1996. RTC 1996/8.

Cases / La jurisprudence

Canadian Cases in Public International Law in 1996-97 / La jurisprudence canadienne en matière de droit international public en 1996-97

compiled by / préparé par
KARIN MICKELSON

Extradition — Interpretation of Term "Jurisdiction"

State of Romania. v. *Cheng* (1997), 114 C.C.C. (3d) 289. Nova Scotia Supreme Court.

The seven detainees, Taiwanese nationals who were officers of the Taiwanese-registered container vessel *Maersk Dubai,* were accused of throwing three Romanian stowaways overboard while the vessel was on the high seas, in two separate incidents during two separate voyages from Spain to Canada. After the vessel's arrival at the Port of Halifax, a number of its Filipino crew members reported the incidents to Canadian authorities, who proceeded to arrest the seven officers. The State of Romania requested their extradition on charges of murder.

The focus of MacDonald J.'s analysis is on the role of the extradition judge being limited to the committal of a "fugitive" as defined in Section 2 of the *Extradition Act,* R.S.C. 1985, c. E-23. He notes that while the obligation to extradite is derived from international treaties, the authority to extradite comes from statute, and that the authority of the extradition judge is limited to the parameters of that statute. Section 2 defines "fugitive" as including "a person

Karin Mickelson is at the Faculty of Law at the University of British Columbia.

being . . . in Canada . . . who is accused . . . of an extradition crime committed within the jurisdiction of a foreign state." The question that arises, according to MacDonald J., is the following: "Does this mean a crime committed within the territorial boundaries of the Requesting State as the Detainees assert; or does it mean a crime which the Requesting State has jurisdiction to prosecute as Romania asserts?" (at 315). If the latter interpretation is chosen, the decision of the Supreme Court of Canada in *R.* v. *Lépine*, [1994] 1 S.C.R. 286 [noted in (1994) 32 Canadian Yearbook of International Law 357] would prevent the extradition judge from considering the validity of Romania's jurisdictional claim. If the former interpretation is preferred, then the judge must consider whether the crimes are alleged to have occurred within the territory of Romania.

Given the numerous meanings associated with the term "jurisdiction" in Canadian jurisprudence, a resort to interpretive aids is warranted. MacDonald J. considers the original meaning rule, the general principle that statutes should be interpreted so as to conform with Canada's international treaty obligations deference to treaty obligations, the specific impact of the Extradition Treaty between Canada and Romania, and the definition of "foreign state" contained in the Extradition Act. MacDonald J. interprets the first two as requiring that the Extradition Act be interpreted so as to reflect Canada's extradition treaty obligations at the time when the legislation was first enacted. An examination of the extradition treaties in existence at that time reveals that in eleven out of thirteen treaties, "fugitive" was defined as someone who had committed or was accused of committing a crime within the "territory," as opposed to the "jurisdiction" of the requesting State. While the treaty with the United States at that time referred to "jurisdiction," it was interpreted to mean "territorial jurisdiction." The Canada-Romania treaty, concluded in 1893, also provides for the extradition of persons alleged to have committed offences within the "territory" of the requesting state. Finally, "foreign state" in the Extradition Act is defined in geographical (i.e., territorial) terms.

Thus, the term "jurisdiction" as contained in the definition of "fugitive" must be read as meaning "territorial" jurisdiction, which, MacDonald J. goes on to state, must be read in light of the late nineteenth-century understanding of territory as limited to the geographical boundaries of the State. In order for the detainees to be "fugitives" under the Extradition Act, then, it must be alleged that they committed crimes within the geographical boundaries of the State of Romania. Since no such allegations had been made, they could not be considered "fugitives," and thus, MacDonald J. holds that he lacks jurisdiction to commit them for extradition.

N.B.: Despite the conclusion reached, MacDonald J. goes through an exhaustive review of the evidence, reaching the conclusion that had a different interpretation of jurisdiction been arrived at, there was ample evidence to justify extradition.

Treaties — Domestic Application

Baker v. *Canada (Minister of Citizenship and Immigration)*, [1997] 2 F.C. 127, (1996), 142 D.L.R. (4th) 554. Federal Court of Appeal.

This was an appeal from the decision by Simpson J., noted in (1996) 34 Canadian Yearbook of International Law 455. The applicant, a Jamaican citizen, had entered Canada in 1981 as a visitor and had thereafter worked illegally for eleven years. During that time she had four children, all of whom are Canadian citizens. In September 1993, she applied for landing on humanitarian and compassionate grounds, pursuant to s. 114(2) of the Immigration Act, R.S.C. 1985, c. I-2. That request was denied, and Simpson J. dismissed the application for judicial review of that decision. Simpson J. also certified a question as to whether given that the Immigration Act does not expressly incorporate the language of Canada's international obligations with respect to the Convention on the Rights of the Child, federal immigration authorities must treat the best interests of the Canadian child as a primary consideration in assessing an application under s. 114(2).

Writing for the Court of Appeal, Strayer J.A. notes that there are two aspects to this issue, namely whether the Convention imposes this obligation on officials directly or whether it does so indirectly by having created a legitimate expectation that such priority will be given. In considering these questions, basic constitutional and administrative law principles must be kept in mind. Prominent among these is the notion that a treaty made by the executive branch does not have legal effect over rights and obligations within Canada unless implemented by statute. The Convention on the Rights of the Child has not been adopted by either federal or provincial legislation. Legislation implementing a treaty should be interpreted by reference to the treaty, but the Immigration Act is not legislation implementing the Convention. The general principle that courts should interpret all legislation so as to avoid, if possible, interpretations that would put Canada in breach of its international obligations cannot be applied to bring about unconstitutional results.

A consideration of subsection 114(2) makes it clear that Parliament has granted discretion to the Minister in determining whether there are "humanitarian" or "compassionate" grounds upon which to waive a deportation order. There is no legislative attempt to define these terms or to give an ordering of their priority. On the basis of the separation of powers, the executive cannot by the indirect means of undertaking an international obligation alter a law of Parliament that confers virtually unfettered discretion. Nor could the executive by such international arrangements alter rights and obligations within the jurisdiction of the provincial legislatures — a result that would logically follow from the appellant's argument that the norms of the Convention must be applied even in the absence of legislation.

Strayer J.A. goes on to note that the Convention norms invoked by the appellant do not apply to her situation. For example, Article 3 of the Convention provides that "in all actions concerning children . . . the best interests of the child shall be a primary consideration." The immigration proceedings in question could at best be seen as "affecting" the appellant's children rather than "concerning" them.

The appellant also made an argument based on legitimate expectations, arising out of the commitment made by the federal executive, through ratification of the Convention, to conduct all public administration consistently with the requirements of the Convention. Quite apart from the conclusion that the Convention does not on its face apply to the situation of the appellant, Strayer J.A. notes that the use of the doctrine of legitimate expectations put forward by the appellant is not permissible. The appellant was arguing not only for the procedural right to have the best interests of the children taken into account (which Simpson J. had found to have happened), but for a substantive right to have the best interests of the children given priority over other considerations. However, the doctrine of legitimate expectations creates no substantive rights. Strayer J.A. notes that this conclusion obviates the need to consider "the interesting question of whether the ratification of multilateral conventions can in any realistic sense be regarded as a meaningful representation to all Canadians that public affairs will thereafter be conducted in accordance with those conventions."

Treaties — Domestic Application

Jose Pereira E Hijos, S.A. v. *Canada (Attorney General),* [1997] 2 F.C. 84. Federal Court Trial Division.

The plaintiffs were the owner and captain of the Spanish fishing vessel *Estai,* which was seized on the high seas by Canadian authorities in March 1995 pursuant to the Coastal Fisheries Protection Regulations, [C.R.C., c. 413] as amended by P.C. 1995-372, dated March 3, 1995, SOR/95-135, made under the Coastal Fisheries Protection Act, R.S.C. 1985, c. C-33 as amended. The plaintiffs claimed damages for trespass, assault, malicious prosecution, and negligent navigation. The defendants objected, *inter alia,* to allegations relating to international law found in the statement of claim and the reply to the defendant's demand for particulars, asserting that the plaintiffs sought to establish that international law principles should have priority over the domestic law of Canada, in particular the Coastal Fisheries Protection Regulations.

MacKay J. notes that the principles concerning the application of international law in Canadian courts are well settled. Accepted norms of customary law are applied as part of domestic law unless they are in conflict with domestic law and, in construing domestic law, courts will seek to avoid conflict with those norms. Norms arising from international conventions become part of the law of Canada only by legislative enactment. The plaintiffs accept these principles, but seek the opportunity to establish at trial that the amended Regulations are unlawful for a number of reasons, including that they are beyond the authority granted to the Governor in Council under the Coastal Fisheries Protection Act. MacKay J. considers this claim to be arguable and states that the Court will not bar the plaintiffs' opportunity to raise it for determination at trial. Nonetheless, that issue may be raised without reference in the pleadings or particulars to specific international treaties or conventions, which, in so far as they are considered a source of law, will be applied only if they are specifically incorporated in Canadian domestic law. To the extent that international treaties are considered authority for international law principles, it is unnecessary to plead them specifically, in the same way that it is unnecessary to plead other authority. MacKay J. directs that references to particular conventions be struck from the statement of claim and the reply to demand for particulars. MacKay J. does not direct striking out reference to "established principles of international law" in the statement of claim, characterizing this as part of the factual description of the applicable legal regime.

Treaties — Interpretation of Statutes Incorporating International Obligations

Sinnapu v. *Canada (Minister of Citizenship and Immigration)*, [1997] 2 F.C. 791. Federal Court Trial Division.

In 1993, the Immigration and Refugee Board determined that the applicants, a Tamil couple from Sri Lanka, were not Convention refugees because of the existence of an internal flight alternative. In their application for judicial review of the decision to remove them to Sri Lanka, the applicants argued, *inter alia*, that because of the situation of internal conflict existing in that country, their return would violate Canada's statutory obligations under the Geneva Conventions Act, R.S.C., 1985, c. G-3.

According to McGillis J., Sri Lanka is engaged in an internal conflict to which common Article 3 of the 1949 Geneva Conventions and the customary law of armed conflicts apply. However, since Canada has no involvement whatsoever in that dispute, common Article 1 of the Conventions does not impose upon Canada an obligation to ensure that the parties to that conflict respect common Article 3. Even if Canada does have such an obligation under common Article 1, it would not affect the application of laws pertaining to immigration. This interpretation of Canada's obligations would not change if it were determined that the conflict in Sri Lanka is of an international character.

Canadian Cases in Private International Law in 1996-97 / La jurisprudence canadienne en matière de droit international privé en 1996-97

compiled by / préparé par
JOOST BLOM

A Jurisdiction / Compétence des tribunaux

1 Common Law and Federal

(a) Jurisdiction *in personam*

Constitutional limits on taking jurisdiction

Cook v. *Parcel, Mauro, Hultin & Spaanstra, P.C.* (1997), 143 D.L.R. (4th) 213, leave to appeal refused July 1997, 147 D.L.R. (4th) vii (S.C.C.). British Columbia Court of Appeal.

The British Columbia-resident former directors and officers of a British Columbia company sought a declaration from the British Columbia Supreme Court that certain documents in possession of a Colorado law firm, which United States regulatory agencies were trying to obtain, were protected by solicitor-client privilege. The law firm had acted for the British Columbia company and certain of its subsidiaries, including one that had operated a gold mine in Colorado from 1982 to 1993. The agencies were seeking evidence in relation to alleged criminal and civil environmental wrongs committed in the mining company's operations. The law firm was taking the position that it was not in a solicitor-client relationship with the applicants as distinct from their company. The applicants obtained an *ex parte* order for service of process *ex juris* on the law firm under British Columbia Rule 13(3), which permits an order to be made in any case in which the Rules of Court do not allow service *ex juris*

Joost Blom is at the Faculty of Law at the University of British Columbia.

without leave. The firm applied to have the service set aside, and for a declaration that the British Columbia court lacked jurisdiction.

The Court of Appeal, affirming the chambers judge, held that the court had no jurisdiction because there was no real and substantial connection between the province and the facts giving rise to the litigation. There was only a tenuous connection between British Columbia and the Colorado law firm or the subject matter of the litigation. The closest and most real connection was with Colorado, and its law ought to govern the issues. The directors and officers were seeking not only declaratory but also injunctive relief and were thereby seeking to bind the Colorado courts and to challenge the territoriality principle of that state. It was hardly conceivable that a Colorado court would enforce any order made in British Columbia that supported the conclusion that jurisdiction did not exist. Moreover, the proper law to be applied to the nature and extent of the privilege claimed was the law of Colorado.

The chambers judge had held that British Columbia was also *forum non conveniens*, but the Court of Appeal did not find it necessary to discuss that point.

Note. The "real and substantial connection" criterion for jurisdiction is a constitutionally based inherent limitation on the powers of the courts of the provinces. It derives in part from the limitation of provincial legislative authority to the administration of justice "in the province" (s. 92(14) of the Constitution Act, 1867), and in part from the comity owed by each province's legal system to those of the others, an obligation that the Supreme Court has found to be implicit in the constitutional structure of Canada: see *Morguard Investments Ltd.* v. *De Savoye*, [1990] 3 S.C.R. 1077 (noted in 29 Canadian Yearbook of International Law 536 (1991)) and *Hunt* v. *T & N Plc.*, [1993] 4 S.C.R. 289 (discussed in 32 Canadian Yearbook of International Law 385 (1994). In a given case, the real and substantial connection requirement may impliedly restrict the very broad powers of service that most provinces' rules of court provide. Even apart from the constitutional element, it is extremely doubtful that a British Columbia court has jurisdiction to issue an injunction restraining conduct outside the province by a non-resident person who has not submitted to the court's jurisdiction.

Defendant's presence or residence in the jurisdiction

Note. A non-resident defendant who was compelled to come to Alberta to defend a lawsuit was granted an order of immunity from service in another lawsuit, on the basis that the grant of immunity would expedite the administration of justice: *G.(C.)* v. *L.(C.)* (1996), 39 Alta. L.R. (3d) 23, 1 C.P.C. (4th) 33 (Q.B. (Master)).

Service ex juris — *grounds*

National Bank of Canada v. *Clifford Chance* (1996), 4 C.P.C. (4th) 276. Ontario Court, General Division.

The plaintiff lenders had provided financing for a construction project in England. The defendant, a firm of London solicitors, had provided the plaintiffs with an opinion concerning the security that the borrowers had given in the form of a pledge of shares. The plaintiffs brought an action against the defendants in Ontario, alleging breach of contract, professional negligence, negligent misrepresentation, and breach of fiduciary duty because the opinion had proved incorrect. The defendants argued that service *ex juris* was not authorized by the Ontario Rules of Civil Procedure or, alternatively, that the Ontario Court should decline jurisdiction on the ground of *forum non conveniens.*

The court held that service *ex juris* was proper for certain of the claims. The claim in negligent misrepresentation fell within Rule 17.02(g) ("tort committed in Ontario") because the alleged tort had occurred in Toronto, where the plaintiffs had received the opinion at the closing of the deal and had authorized the advance of the funds. The claim in professional negligence for the drafting of the opinion could not be brought under Rule 17.02(h) ("damages sustained in Ontario arising from a tort or breach of contract, wherever committed") because the financial harm caused to the plaintiffs by the opinion was suffered in England. The mere recording of the loss in Ontario did not alter the location of the damage. The conractual claims fell under Rule 17.02(f)(i) ("contract made in Ontario") because the defendants' acceptance of the plaintiffs' offer of a retainer was received in Ontario. They also fell under Rule 17.02(f)(iv) ("breach of the contract has been committed in Ontario") because the allegedly faulty opinion was delivered to the plaintiffs in Ontario. Since the damage from the breach of contract was suffered in England, the contractual claims, like the professional negligence claim, could not be made to fit under Rule 17.02(h).

Although it therefore had jurisdiction over certain of the claims, the court held that it was *forum non conveniens.* This was a classic international transaction with numerous connecting factors to

Ontario and England; both countries had a real and substantial connection to the litigation. The location of witnesses and evidence was fairly evenly divided between Ontario and England. However, the dispute was about the performance by English solicitors of obligations relating to an opinion they gave on English law. The opinion was delivered in connection with a construction project entirely located in England and was concerned with the validity of expected security, all of which was also located in England. England was clearly the more appropriate forum.

Note. See also *McFaul* v. *Richler* (1996), 30 B.L.R. (2d) 226 (B.C.S.C.) (service *ex juris* in wrongful dismissal claim upheld because the alleged dismissal took place in the province); *Gray* v. *Dow Corning Canada Inc.*, [1996] 6 W.W.R. 185, 143 Sask. R. 55 (Q.B.), aff'd, [1996] 8 W.W.R. lxii, 148 Sask. R. 78 (C.A.) (service *ex juris* in tort and contract claims against a manufacturer of breast implants upheld because the alleged tort, negligent failure to warn, was committed in the province and either the breaches of contract or the damage suffered from them was located in the province). In *Jackson* v. *Flett*, [1997] 6 W.W.R. 179, 154 Sask. R. 223 (Q.B.), service *ex juris* on an alleged sexual harasser, most of whose alleged acts took place in Manitoba, was held available because Saskatchewan was *forum conveniens* for the claim, which ought to be joined to an action already begun against the harasser's employer — a corporation that did business in Saskatchewan and over which the court had jurisdiction as of right.

Attornment to the jurisdiction

Note. See *Trans-Continental Textile Recycling Ltd.* v. *Flairius Enterprises S.A.* (1995), 106 F.T.R. 278 (Prothonotary); *Georgetown Wire Co.* v. *Gemini Structural Systems Inc.* (1997), 200 A.R. 285 (C.A.).

Declining jurisdiction — exclusive choice of forum clause

Sarabia v. *The "Oceanic Mindoro,"* [1997] 2 W.W.R. 116, 26 B.C.L.R. (3d) 143, leave to appeal refused (May 22, 1997) (S.C.C.). British Columbia Court of Appeal.

The plaintiff seaman brought an action in British Columbia for injuries that he had suffered in an accident on board his ship while it was in Vancouver harbour. The defendants, Philippine shipowners, relied on a term of the plaintiff's employment contract that incorporated certain standard terms, which included, as Philippine law required, an exclusive choice of forum clause in favour of an employment compensation tribunal in the Philippines. The clause covered all disputes "arising out of" the employment agreement. The defendants conceded that, if the clause applied to the plaintiff's claim, the action should be stayed. The British Columbia Court of Appeal held that the clause applied. The language clearly included tort claims arising outside the Philippines that arose out of the employment relationship. Other choice of forum cases had construed "arising out of" as including contract-related tort claims. Forum selection clauses, the court thought, should be given much the same deference as arbitration clauses. The plaintiff had the burden of showing that there was strong cause to override the choice of forum. The plaintiff, in other words, had to overcome the principle of respecting private agreements between the parties, as well as the comity of nations. The plaintiff in this case had not met this onus.

ABN Amro Bank Canada v. *Krupp Mak Maschinenbau GmbH* (1996), 135 D.L.R. (4th) 130. Ontario Divisional Court.

The plaintiff bank had supplied financing to a failed commercial venture, as part of which a German firm, the defendant, was to supply technology for a propulsion system to be installed in a Canadian Coast Guard ship. As security the plaintiff had taken an assignment of assets from the Canadian company set up for this venture. The assets included a technology licensing agreement with the defendant. This agreement contained an arbitration clause. The plaintiff sued the defendant for having conspired, with the Canadian businessman who owed the Canadian company, to trick the plaintiff. The alleged deception related to the defendant's supposedly having contributed equity capital to the project, as the conditions of the plaintiff's loan required, without the contribution actually taking place. The defendant sought a stay of the court proceedings on the ground of the arbitration clause. The plaintiff argued that the alleged fraud rendered the arbitration agreement null and void or inoperative, within the meaning of Article 8 of the UNCITRAL Model Law on International Commercial Arbitration (implemented in Ontario by the International Commercial Arbitration Act, R.S.O. 1990, c. I.9), with the result that the court was not obliged to stay the judicial proceeding.

The majority of the Ontario Divisional Court, reversing the motions judge, ordered the proceeding stayed. The bank as assignee of the licensing agreement was bound by the arbitration clause. Article 8 did not oblige a court to deal with a claim that the arbitration agreement was inoperative or null and void. This was because the issues might be integrally related to the merits of a dispute that would otherwise have to be arbitrated and Article 16 provided an arbitrator with jurisdiction, concurrent with the courts', in respect of the validity of the arbitration agreement in order that, where appropriate, one forum might be available to resolve the entire dispute between the parties: *Gulf Canada Resources Ltd.* v. *Arochem Int'l Ltd.* (1992), 66 B.C.L.R. (2d) 113 (C.A.). A motions court was *prima facie* not a particularly appropriate forum to decide the issue whether the plaintiff's claim of fraud was made out, and it was appropriate for the jurisdiction to do so under Article 8 to be declined. The dissenting judge thought that the issue of fraud ought to have been dealt with by the motions judge, given that the affidavit evidence of fraud was uncontradicted by the plaintiff. The majority thought the pleadings did not allege fraud clearly enough to put the plaintiff on notice that the validity of the arbitration agreement would be the focus of the hearing on the motion requesting arbitration.

Note. Exclusive choice of forum clauses were also enforced in *Can-Am Produce & Trading Ltd.* v. *The "Senator"* (1996), 112 F.T.R. 255 (Prothonotary); *National Bank of Canada* v. *Halifax Ins. Co.* (1996), 173 N.B.R. (2d) 145 (Q.B.); *Holo-Deck Adventures Ltd.* v. *Orbotron Inc.* (1996), 8 C.P.C. (4th) 376 (Ont. Gen. Div.); and *DiPaolo Machine Works Ltd.* v. *Prestige Equipment Corp.* (1996), 5 C.P.C. (4th) 175 (Ont. Gen. Div.). In two cases, the clause was denied effect on the ground that it did not unambiguously apply to the dispute: *Jian Sheng Co.* v. *Great Tempo S.A.* (1997), 129 F.T.R. 55 (Prothonotary); *Schleith* v. *Holoday* (1997), 31 B.C.L.R. (3d) 81 (C.A.). In the latter case, the clause stipulated that all disputes arising out of the contract should be "litigated at the discretion and election of First Marathon only in a court in Toronto, Ontario." The action was brought against First Marathon. The court said the clause was open to the construction that it only applied to claims by First Marathon, not claims against it. In any event, First Marathon had not made any election when the plaintiff commenced the action. The case points up the pitfalls of trying to give one party the right to elect the forum, without careful drafting of the clause.

Declining jurisdiction — defendant served within the jurisdiction

Sarafi v. *The "Iran Afzal,"* [1996] 2 F.C. 954, 111 F.T.R. 256. Federal Court, Trial Division.

The plaintiff, an Iranian citizen, served the defendant ship in Canada in an action claiming unpaid wages he had earned while working for the owning shipping line before it had been nationalized by the Iranian state, as well as for damages for the loss through the nationalization of the shares he had owned in the line. The shipowners relied on sovereign immunity and, alternatively, on the Canadian court being *forum non conveniens.*

The defence of sovereign immunity failed, because the ship being sued was used by the state shipping line in a commercial activity. Section 7 of the State Immunity Act, R.S.C. 1985, c. S-18, which denies immunity in proceeedings relating to ships so used, applied regardless of whether the claim actually related to the activities of that ship (which it did not, as the plaintiff had not served on the ship). The action was, however, stayed on the ground of *forum non conveniens.* Iran was the jurisdiction with the closest connection to the action and it was the natural forum for the disposition of the claims. The employment contract was governed by Iranian law and the nationalization program that had cost the plaintiff his shares was carried out under Iranian law. The fact that the plaintiff had obtained security for the enforcement of a Canadian judgment was not an essential consideration where there was no question as to the defendant's capacity to pay if the plaintiff succeeded in the alternative forum.

Note. The argument of *forum non conveniens* failed in *Mundaca Investment Corp.* v. *Keats* (1996), 144 Nfld. & P.E.I. R. 77 (Nfld. S.C.) because it was found that the defendant did not genuinely desire a trial in the other forum, Florida. It also failed in *Garrett* v. *Cameco Corp.*, [1997] 10 W.W.R. 393, 151 Sask. R. 86 (Q.B.), because the alternative forum, Kyrgyzstan, was not clearly more appropriate for a personal injury action arising out of the accidental death of Saskatchewan residents while in that country. The principal defendant was a Saskatchewan corporation that owned the Kyrgyzstan businesses for whom the deceased had been working. Actions were stayed in *Royal Ins. Co. of Canada* v. *Detroit Diesel-Allison British Columbia Ltd.* (1997), 43 C.C.L.I. (2d) 11 (B.C.S.C.) (a *lis alibi pendens* situation — issues in the action were also the subject of proceedings in California, which involved the same parties as well as others); and

ABB Power General Inc. v. *CSX Transportation* (1996), 47 C.P.C. (3d) 381 (Ont. Gen. Div.).

Declining jurisdiction — defendant served ex juris

Dennis v. *Salvation Army Grace General Hospital Board* (1997), 156 N.S.R. (2d) 372. Nova Scotia Court of Appeal.

The plaintiff mother, who lived at the time in Newfoundland, had given birth in the defendant hospital in St. John's, Newfoundland, to a daughter who was born with brain damage and damage to her central nervous system. The mother and the infant daughter brought an action in Nova Scotia, where they now resided, against the hospital and the attending physicians, claiming their negligence had resulted in the injuries to the daughter. The defendants argued that Nova Scotia was *forum non conveniens*. The Nova Scotia Court of Appeal, reversing the chambers judge, held that the action should not be stayed. Newfoundland had not been shown to be clearly the more appropriate forum. The evidence as to the damage to the infant plaintiff was in Nova Scotia. The plaintiffs would be subjected to an undue burden if they had to travel to Newfoundland, expecially since the infant plaintiff was severely handicapped. The factors that favoured trial in Newfoundland were that it was the place of the tort and that it would be more convenient for the attendance of witnesses from the hospital and for the production of the hospital's documents. These were, however, insufficient to make Newfoundland a clearly more appropriate forum.

Note. A similar result was reached in an Ontario resident's lawsuit in Ontario against a college in the United States for injuries suffered in a fall there (*Dunlop* v. *Connecticut College* (1996), 50 C.P.C. (3d) 109 (Ont. Gen. Div.)). An additional factor in that case was that a stay would have put the plaintiff at a disadvantage because the limitation period in Connecticut had already run. In *Santo Domingo Estate* v. *Kenora (Town)* (1996), 111 Man. R. (2d) 124 (Q.B.), the continuing loss to the the plaintiff widow in Manitoba was sufficient to justify continuing an action there for the accidental death of her husband in, and allegedly through the negligence of, the defendant Ontario town. In *Hunt* v. *Durdle* (1996), 153 N.S.R. (2d) 223 (N.S.T.D.), by contrast, the court stayed an action by a woman who sued a Newfoundland apartment landlord for injuries she had received in a fall on the stairs while visiting her son. The alleged tort had occurred in Newfoundland and virtually all the evidence and witnesses were located there.

Contract actions in which *forum non conveniens* was argued were the following. In *Entertainment & Sports Corp.* v. *Ice Hockey Federation of Russia* (1996), 201 A.R. 305 (Q.B.), the contract was made in Alberta, in English, on the plaintiff Alberta corporation's letterhead. The court held that Alberta was the appropriate forum for an action against the Russian party for breach of the contract. In *McFaul* v. *Richler* (1996), 30 B.L.R. (2d) 226 (B.C.S.C.) the action was not stayed because it was connected to another claim that could probably not be heard in the alternative forum. In *Craig Broadcast Systems Inc.* v. *Frank N. Magid Associates Inc.*, [1997] 3 W.W.R. 509, 116 Man. R. (2d) 312 (Q.B.), an action against Iowa-based consultants was not stayed, because they had assiduously sought the plaintiff's business in Manitoba and because their advice had related to a Canadian broadcasting licence application. No stay was granted in *Gilmour* v. *Barry-Wehmiller Co.* (1996), 34 O.R. (3d) 305 (Gen. Div.), although the action was on a contract expressly governed by Missouri law, because the defendant was an Ontario company and other claims on alleged oral contracts and on torts might well be governed by Ontario law. Third party claims were not stayed in *Occidental Chemical Corp.* v. *Sovereign Gen. Ins. Corp.* (1997), 32 O.R. (3d) 277 (Gen. Div.), although the claims were against Alberta solicitors for advice given there. The third party proceeding was allowed to continue because of its relationship to the principal action that the claimant against the solicitors had to defend in Ontario. An unusual additional factor, to which the court gave some weight, was that one of the defendant solicitors was now an Alberta Queen's Bench judge, which raised some concern about possible bias if the action was heard in Alberta.

A claim against two California corporations, arising out of their sale to the Ontario plaintiff of a virtual reality amusement ride, was stayed in *Holo-Deck Adventures Ltd.* v. *Orbotron Inc.* (1996), 8 C.P.C. (4th) 376 (Ont. Gen. Div.). There was a choice of forum agreement and, even if there had not been, the plaintiff had not shown that Ontario was a more appropriate forum than California. The court put the onus on the plaintiff because the defendant was a non-resident. The question of onus is a confused one. In many other cases, courts assume that as long as service *ex juris* is authorized without leave, even a non-resident defendant has the onus of showing that the alternative forum is clearly more appropriate. See, for instance, the *Dennis* case, noted immediately above, and *Wall* v. *679927 Ontario Ltd.* (1997), 156 N.S.R. (2d) 360 (C.A.), decided by the same court on the same day.

In *Geac Computer Corp.* v. *Park* (1996), 45 C.P.C. (3d) 99 (Ont. Gen. Div.), an action against the United States-resident vendors of a business was not stayed because the suggested alternative forum, Texas, had not been shown to be clearly more appropriate for the trial. It was relevant that the contract for the sale of the business was governed by Ontario law. The court refused to give decisive weight to the fact that some of the defendants in the Ontario action had previously begun their own proceedings in Texas against the Ontario plaintiffs, who had raised in their Texas counterclaims exactly the same claims they were now making in Ontario. *Canadian Life & Health Ins. Compensation Corp.* v. *Blue Cross of Atlantic Canada* (1997), 156 N.S.R. (2d) 384 (C.A.), was a case in which the *lis alibi pendens* argument was successful and a stay was granted; parallel proceedings in New Brunswick were between the same parties and concerned exactly the same issues.

A tort claim arising out of commercial dealings was not stayed in *Krupp Mak Maschinenbau GmbH* v. *Black* (1996), 149 N.S.R. (2d) 297 (T.D.), mainly because the claims related to funds allegedly taken from a Nova Scotia company now in bankruptcy, and the bankruptcy was being administered by the Nova Scotia court. See also *Aquino* v. *Machula* (1996), 149 Sask. R. 37 (Q.B.), where the alleged economic torts, arising from immigration-related investment schemes, were committed outside the province but most of the defendants were resident in the province.

See also *Cook* v. *Parcel, Mauro, Hultin & Spaanstra, P.C.*, noted above under the heading, "constitutional limits on jurisdiction," *National Bank of Canada* v. *Clifford Chance*, noted above under the heading, "service *ex juris*-grounds," and *Nicholas* v. *Nicholas*, noted below under (c) Matrimonial Proceedings: Divorce and corollary relief.

(b) Actions relating to property

Movables — intangible — debt — jurisdiction to garnish — situs

Delaire v. *Delaire*, [1996] 9 W.W.R. 469, 147 Sask. R. 161. Saskatchewan Queen's Bench.

A wife had obtained a court order in British Columbia for maintenance against the husband. Both parties were now living in British Columbia but had formerly resided in Saskatchewan. The husband had a registered retirement savings plan (RRSP) with a brokerage firm that had an office in Saskatchewan, but the RRSP was not kept at a Saskatchewan branch. The wife brought an action in Saskatchewan on the British Columbia order, under the Enforcement of Maintenance Orders Act, S.S. 1984-85-86, c. E-9.2, claiming a garnishing order against the brokerage firm in respect of the RRSP.

The court held that a beneficial interest in a trust was not garnishable and, alternatively, that if the RRSP was considered a debt the court had no jurisdiction to garnish it. Two theories could be found in the cases as to the jurisdiction to garnish. One was that jurisdiction depended upon personal jurisdiction over the debtor. The other was that jurisdiction existed if the situs of the debt was in the province. Here the locus of the debt should be the test for ability to garnish the debt. This was supported by four reasons. First, if personal jurisdiction was used as the test, the debtor might be subject to garnishing proceedings in other provinces in respect of the same debt. Second, the court's power to discharge the garnishee from liability to the judgment debtor would be limited. Third, the court might not be able to determine questions like set-off as between the garnishee and the judgment debtor, because the relevant items would be extraprovincial. And, fourth, the personal jurisdiction theory, based simply on an ability to serve the defendant within the province, was falling out of favour. An RRSP was located, by analogy with the location of an ordinary debt, in the province of the branch where the account was kept, which was outside Saskatchewan.

Matrimonial property

Simard v. *Simard* (1997), 29 B.C.L.R. (3d) 270. British Columbia Supreme Court.

In an application by a wife for a division of family assets under the Family Relations Act, R.S.B.C. 1996, c. 128, one of the issues was whether the British Columbia court had jurisdiction to order a division of the husband's Canadian Armed Forces pension. The husband lived in Ontario and had not attorned to the court's jurisdiction. Some earlier cases suggested that in such circumstances the court could not order the division of a pension outside the province: *Key* v. *Key* (1985), 1 R.F.L. (3d) 150 (B.C.S.C.); *Britten* v. *Britten* (1983), 50 B.C.L.R. 131, 37 R.F.L. (2d) 329 (S.C.).

Murphy J. noted that the judges in these cases may have been concerned about how, as a practical matter, to bind the pension administrators to accept the claimant spouse as a beneficiary. Since those cases had been decided, however, federal public service pensions, at least, were subject to legislation that removed this difficulty (Pension Benefits Division Act, S.C. 1992, c. 46). The judge also referred to the Supreme Court of Canada's view that the necessary basis for a court's jurisdiction was a real and substantial connection to the forum that warrants the exercise of jurisdiction. He decided that the claimant wife's long residence in British Columbia supplied a real and substantial connection that justified the taking of jurisdiction to divide the defendant husband's Armed Forces pension, notwithstanding that the husband lived in Ontario and was disputing the court's jurisdiction.

Note. Another issue in matrimonial property division cases is how a court can deal with immovables outside the province. Traditionally, it is beyond a court's power to adjudicate respecting title to a movable outside the jurisdiction: *British South Africa Co.* v. *Companhia de Moçambique*, [1893] A.C. 602 (H.L.). In *Macedo* v. *Macedo* (1996), 19 R.F.L. (4th) 65 (Ont. Gen. Div.), the court, as part of a division of property under the Family Law Act, R.S.O. 1990, c. F-3, ordered the husband to sell certain property in Portugal and share the proceeds equally with the wife, or purchase her interest in the property for $57,000. The court held that, although it could not deal directly with the title to a foreign immovable, it had jurisdiction to make a personal order against the owner requiring the property to be transferred.

In another matrimonial property action, *Ravida* v. *Ravida Estate* (1996), 22 R.F.L. (4th) 217, 13 E.T.R. (2d) 112 (Ont. C.A.), an equalization payment was ordered to be made by the executor of the deceased spouse's estate. The order required the executor to secure the payment against the assets of certain corporations incorporated in Florida. The executor contended that to liquidate the assets of those corporations would expose her to liability under the law of Florida to the creditors of the corporations or of the estate. The court held that the executor had provided insufficient evidence that this was really so, and upheld the order.

Bankruptcy and insolvency

Note. In *Microbiz Corp.* v. *Classic Software Systems Inc.* (1996), 45 C.B.R. (3d) 40 (Ont. Gen. Div.), a Canadian distributor of a United States company's products sought to sue the American company in Ontario for amounts owing to it. The defendant relied on the fact that the claim was contrary to a plan of reorganization approved by a United States court in bankruptcy. The American judgment approving the reorganization was recognized by the Ontario court, on the ground that there was a real and substantial connection between the United States court and the subject matter of the proceedings, and that the defendant had attorned to the United States court's jurisdiction by filing proofs of claim in the proceedings.

(c) Matrimonial proceedings

Divorce and corollary relief

Nicholas v. *Nicholas* (1996), 139 D.L.R. (4th) 652, 24 R.F.L. (4th) 358. Ontario Court of Appeal.

The parties were born in Trinidad and their four children were born there, but in the late 1970s the family moved to Ontario. The husband continued to do business in Trinidad. The parents planned to return to Trinidad permanently once the children were through their education. The parents separated in 1993. The husband filed a petition for divorce in Trinidad. Shortly afterwards the wife filed a divorce petition in Ontario, claiming custody of the children, child and spousal support, and a division of property. The court gave an order for the husband to be served *ex juris*. The Trinidad court granted a decree *nisi* of divorce. At about the same time, the husband sought a stay of the Canadian proceedings under Rule 17.06 of the Ontario Civil Procedure Rules, on the ground of *forum non conveniens*. The Ontario Court of Appeal, affirming the decision of the motions judge, granted the stay. Trinidad was the appropriate forum for the proceedings, which, since custody was no longer in issue, was solely about money and property issues. These would be more conveniently dealt with in Trinidad, where there were numerous assets including two homes and the husband's substantial business assets. The expert opinion evidence was to the effect that the wife would not be at a juridical disadvantage there. Although the wife had regarded Ontario as her home for the past sixteen years, the parties still looked on Trinidad as their permanent home. It was not necessary to determine which party had the onus of proof on the question of *forum non conveniens*, because it was clear that Trinidad had the closest connection to the dispute.

Note. See also *Alexiou* v. *Alexiou* (1996), 41 Alta. L.R. (3d) 90, 188 A.R. 149 (Q.B.). In that case the requirement under the Divorce Act, R.S.C. 1985, c. 3 (2nd Supp.), s. 3, that either spouse have been ordinarily resident in the province for one year immediately preceding the petition, was met although the relevant party, the husband, had been living in Canada on a visitor's visa for most of that year. Although the court therefore had jurisdiction in divorce, it chose to decline it. Greece was a more appropriate forum. The parties had lived most of their life in Greece, the matrimonial assets were located there, friends and relatives lived there, the wife had her job there and lived there with the children, and the husband, an Orthodox priest who had been suspended from his position at a Canadian church, had better prospects of employment there than in Canada. Moreover, the wife had already applied to the Greek court for custody and support, and the husband had accepted the court's jurisdiction. Neither party would suffer a disadvantage if the divorce proceedings took place in Greece.

(d) Infants and children

Custody — existence of jurisdiction

Note. Jurisdiction in custody is defined by statute in some provinces and left to the common law in others. Ontario and Saskatchewan are two of the provinces with a statutory definition. In *F.(P.)* v. *F.(S.)* (1997), 29 R.F.L. (4th) 59 (Ont. Gen. Div.), the court held that it had jurisdiction because the children were habitually resident in Ontario. They had come to Ontario with their mother from California, with the father's consent, and stayed there, again with the father's consent, when the marriage broke up. In *L.(G.)* and *L.(L.)* (1996), 149 Sask. R. 32 (Q.B.), and *McGeoch* v. *Lasiuk* (1996), 146 Sask. R. 246 (Q.B.), the jurisdictional criteria in s. 15(1)(b) of the Children's Law Act, S.S. 1991, c. C-8.1, were not met because the children were not habitually resident in Saskatchewan and the exceptional circumstances that were necessary to justify taking jurisdiction over a non-habitually resident child were not present.

If custody is sought as corollary relief under the Divorce Act, R.S.C. 1985, c. 3 (2nd Supp.), the jurisdictional tests in s. 3 for divorce proceedings must be met. Under s. 3, either party must have been ordinarily (the French version says habituellement) resident in the province for one year immediately preceding the petition. See *Antonini* v. *Antonini* (1996), [1997] 1 W.W.R. 168, 149 Sask. R. 279 (Q.B.), where this requirement was not met. The alternative of taking jurisdiction in custody under the Children's Law Act, S.S. 1991, c. C-8.1, was not available either, because the children were not habitually resident in Saskatchewan. Section 5 of the Divorce Act defines jurisdiction in proceedings to vary a corollary order. See *Warr* v. *Warr* (1996), 146 Sask. R. 60 (Q.B.), in which the applicant wife's ordinary residence in the province at the commencement of the variation proceedings was the ground for jurisdiction. If the other parent opposes jurisdiction and the child has a more real and substantial connection with another province, the court can transfer the proceeding to that province. In *Warr* v. *Warr* the closest connection was with Saskatchewan, especially since the connections with Nova Scotia were due to the father's having wrongfully removed the children there.

Custody — declining jurisdiction

Note. In many cases, the issue of jurisdiction in custody is decided on grounds of *forum non conveniens.* The court may decline jurisdiction on condition, for example, that interim custody is to be exercised by the spouse that sought to invoke the local court's jurisdiction, pending a resolution of the custody issue by the foreign court. See *Anderson* v. *Sullivan* (1996), 22 B.C.L.R. (3d) 319 (C.A.) (jurisdiction not declined, notwithstanding that proceedings were already under way in Ontario; the children had all their connections with British Columbia); *Simmons* v. *Jamieson* (1997), 159 N.S.R. (2d) 113 (jurisdiction declined in favour of court in Ohio, unless that court itself declined jurisdiction); *F.(C.L.)* v. *N.(M.)* (1997), 155 Sask. R. 59 (Q.B.) (jurisdiction declined in favour of court in Texas, to which mother and child had recently moved); and *P.(G.)* v. *P.(L.)* (1996), 142 Sask. R. 161 (Q.B.) (jurisdiction declined in favour of court in Manitoba, to which mother and child had moved despite a previous order issued in Saskatchewan restraining the mother from taking the child from the province).

Access rights — control by court — movement of child out of jurisdiction

Gordon v. *Goertz,* [1996] 2 S.C.R. 27, 134 D.L.R. (4th) 321. Supreme Court of Canada.

As part of a divorce in 1993, the mother was awarded custody of the parties' young daughter, with generous rights of access being granted to the father. In 1995, the mother, a dentist, wished to move to Australia to study orthodontics. The father applied to the Saskatchewan court for variation of the custody order to give him custody of the child or else to restrain the mother from removing the child from Saskatoon, Saskatchewan. The Supreme Court of Canada, affirming with a variation the decisions below, held that the access rights should be varied to permit the mother to move to Australia, with a right to the father to have access in Australia and also to exercise access rights in Canada. According to s. 17(5) of the Divorce Act, R.S.C. 1985, c. 3 (2nd Supp.), the judge must base a variation decision on the best interests of the child. Variation was possible whenever there was a material change in circumstances affecting the child. Such a material change was present here, both in the fact that the father had had even more extensive contact with his child than the original order contemplated, and in the mother's desire to move to advance her career. If the threshold of material change in circumstances is met, the child's best interests must be determined afresh on all the evidence. In this case, that involved balancing the reasons for keeping her in her mother's custody against the desirability of preserving her contact with her father.

Two of the nine judges concurred in the result but disagreed with the majority's view that on a variation application, once the material change was established, the best interests of the child should be approached *de novo*. Rather, they would have applied a presumption that the custodial parent's wish to move should be given effect unless the access parent shows that the change in residence would be detrimental to the child's interests to an extent that justifies a variation of access or, if the child's interests could not be accommodated in any other way, an order that the child remain in the jurisdiction.

Note. This case was applied in *Woodhouse* v. *Woodhouse* (1996), 29 O.R. (3d) 417, 20 R.F.L. (4th) 337 (C.A.). The mother was enjoined from moving to Scotland with the children because of the prejudice to the father's rights of access. The trial judge had concluded that the children's best interests would not be adversely affected by the mother's economic circumstances in Canada compared with Scotland. The judge also had doubts, from the mother's past actions, as to whether she would comply with any Ontario access order once she was in Scotland. The mother's wishes were entitled to great weight, but there was no presumption that they should be given effect.

Child abduction — Hague Convention

Note. See *Thorne* v. *Dryden-Hall* (1997), 148 D.L.R. (4th) 508, 35 B.C.L.R. (3d) 121 (C.A.) (child held to have been wrongfully removed by the mother from United Kingdom because the mother was subject to a court order not to remove the child without the father or the court's permission, these powers to determine residence being "rights of custody" under the Convention); *Hoskins* v. *Boyd*, [1997] 6 W.W.R. 526, 34 B.C.L.R. (3d) 121 (C.A.) (return of half-aboriginal child to a non-aboriginal environment in Oregon, where the father lived and from which the child had been wrongfully removed, held not to pose a "grave risk of physical or psychological harm," which must be an intolerable situation going beyond the normal disruption to be expected from the removal of a small child; court not concerned with determining the best interests of the child as under a custody application; child ordered returned); *Kinnersley-Turner* v. *Kinnersley-Turner* (1996), 24 R.F.L. (4th) 252, 94 O.A.C. 376 (C.A.) (child held to have been wrongfully removed from England to Ontario because the English court had jurisdiction to award custody; child ordered returned); *Morris* v. *Nevins* (1996), 92 O.A.C. 232 (Div. Ct.) (children's removal from Ontario to England held wrongful because the Ontario court had jurisdiction to award custody in pending proceedings); *Antonini* v. *Antonini* (1996), [1997] 1 W.W.R. 168, 149 Sask. R 279 (Q.B.) (child held wrongfully removed from California because under California law the parents had joint custody; child ordered returned, subject to conditions).

(e) Antisuit injunctions

Hudon v. *Geos Language Corp.* (1997), 100 O.A.C. 336, 10 C.P.C. (4th) 92. Ontario Divisional Court.

The plaintiff was employed by the defendant Japanese corporation to teach English in Japan. She took a short holiday to China and was injured in an accident there, with the result that she was rendered disabled. She returned to Ontario. She brought an action in Ontario against the Japanese corporation and its British Columbia corporate affiliate, claiming that the defendants had promised or represented that the Japanese corporation would provide medical insurance coverage, which it had not done. The defendants applied for a stay on the ground of *forum non conveniens*. The application was dismissed. The defendants did not appeal from the dismissal but did commence proceedings in Japan for a declaration that under Japanese law, which expressly governed the plaintiff's contract, they were not liable for failing to provide holiday medical insurance. The plaintiff applied to the Ontario Court for an antisuit injunction against the Japanese corporation continuing the proceedings in Japan.

The Divisional Court held that the injunction should be granted, applying the principles in *Amchem Products Inc.* v. *British Columbia (Workers Compensation Board)*, [1993] 1 S.C.R. 897 (noted in 31 Canadian Yearbook of International Law 405 (1993)). An antisuit injunction could be sought notwithstanding that no permanent injunction was claimed in the action, and notwithstanding that the foreign proceedings did not constitute an actionable wrong. The fact that the plaintiff did not first take proceedings in Japan to stay the Japanese action was not in itself a sufficient ground for denying the injunction. The fact that an Ontario court had already decided that Ontario was an appropriate forum was an important, though not conclusive, factor in deciding whether an injunction should be issued. The reasons for the conclusion that Ontario was an appropriate forum included the facts that many of the witnesses with respect to the alleged misrepresentations were resident in Ontario; that evidence of Japanese law could be given by experts; and that the defendant had failed to show that preventing it from proceeding in Japan would deprive it unjustly of any legitimate juridical advantage. On the other hand, the plaintiff had a strong personal advantage from being able to proceed in Ontario because she was a permanently disabled person for whom travel to Japan would be difficult. Therefore, the two conditions in *Amchem* were met. Japan was *forum non conveniens* by Canadian standards, and an injustice would result if the continuation of the proceedings there was not enjoined.

Note. See also *Droit de la famille-*2398, noted below under 2 Québec, (b) Injonctions contre les poursuites-*forum non conveniens.*

2 Québec

(a) Entrée en vigueur des nouvelles règles relatives à la compétence des tribunaux québécois

Note. Veuillez voir *Mayor* c. *Dionne* (1994), [1996] R.L. 79 (C.S.).

(b) Règles de compétence du tribunal québécois

Actions personnelles — article 3148 C.C.Q.

Note. Veuillez voir *Melrose Int'l Trading Ltd.* c. *IBP Inc.*, [1996] R.J.Q. 1407 (C.Q.) (aucun des cas prévus à l'Article 3148 était applicable; le tribunal québécois n'avait pas compétence); *Morales*

Moving & Storage Co. Inc. c. *Chatigny Bitton,* [1996] R.D.J. 14 (Que. C.A.) (contrat de transport de certains biens meubles de Miami à Montréal; dommages causés aux biens; action contre les transporteurs, qui n'avaient aucune place d'affaires au Québec; préjudice survenu lors de la remise des meubles à la propriétaire au Québec; tribunal avait compétence).

(c) Compétence exceptionnelle

Action à l'étranger impossible-mesures provisoires ou conservatoires-protection d'une personne en cas d'urgence-Articles 3136, 3138 et 3149 C.C.Q.

Thériault c. *Gauvreau,* [1996] R.J.Q. 2328. Cour supérieure du Québec.

Les parties faisaient vie commune et étaient domiciliées au Nouveau-Brunswick. L'intimée, alors qu'elle était en vacances au Québec, a pris les dispositions nécessaires pour s'y faire avorter. Le requérant a déposé au Québec une demande d'injonction interlocutoire enjoignant à son conjointe de ne pas se soumettre à un avortement. Celle-ci s'opposait à la recevabilité de cette demande, invoquant l'absence de compétence des tribunaux québécois, la non-existence du droit à l'injonction pour les motifs mis de l'avant par la Cour suprême dans l'arrêt *Tremblay* c. *Daigle,* [1989] 2 R.C.S. 530, le fait que l'injonction aurait comme effet d'empêcher d'accomplir un geste permis légalement et la non-applicabilité de la Charte des droits et libertés de la personne, L.R.Q., c. C-12, aux personnes non domiciliées au Québec.

La Cour a décidé qu'elle était compétent mais a accueilli la requête en irrecevabilité. Quant à la question de compétence, le juge a précisé qu'en matière de recours personnels, les articles 3134 *et seq.* C.C.Q. posent comment principe que la compétence des tribunaux du Québec se limite aux cas où l'une des parties en cause y a son domicile. Le principe souffre toutefois un certain nombre d'exceptions, notamment celles prévues aux articles 3136 ("[l']action à l'étranger se révèle impossible ou [qu'on] ne peut exiger qu'elle y soit introduite"), 3138 ("l'autorité québécoise peut ordonner des mesures provisoires ou conservatoires, même si elle n'est pas compétente pour connaître du fond du litige"), et 3140 ("En cas d'urgence ou d'inconvénients sérieux, les autorités québécoises sont compétentes pour prendre les mesures qu'elles estiment nécessaires à la protection d'une personne qui se trouve au Québec ou à la protection de ses biens s'ils y sont situés"). En raison de la nature du présent débat, de l'urgence qui le caracterisait et des divers inconvénients susceptibles de résulter d'une décision à effet dilatoire, les tribunaux québécois avaient compétence.

(d) Élection de for

Compétence du tribunal québécois en présence d'une clause d'élection de for

Lamborghini (Canada) Inc. c. *Automobili Lamborghini S.P.A.* (1996), [1997] R.J.Q. 58. Cour d'appel du Québec.

En 1994, Lamborghini Canada a intenté contre Lamborghini Italia une action en injonction et en dommages-intérêts à la suite de rupture pare cette dernière d'un contrat d'agence générale conclu en 1986 pour la commercialisation et la vente d'automobiles au Canada. Lamborghini Italia répliqua par un moyen déclinatoire basé sur une clause d'election de for, conférant compétence exclusive au tribunal civil de Bologne, en Italie. La Cour supérieure a accueilli la requête pour exception déclinatoire.

La Cour d'appel a rejeté l'appel de Lamborghini Canada. Lorsque Lamborghini Canada a entamé ses procédures, le Code Civil du Québec était déjà en vigueur et ses règles visant la détermination de la compétence des tribunaux québécois en droit international privé s'appliquaient. Le dernier alinéa de l'article 3148 C.C.Q. permet, à première vue, de reconnaître la validité et l'effet de la clause d'élection de for en litige. Le fait que Lamborghini Canada se soit estimée protégée contre les effets de la clause d'élection de for par l'état du droit lorsqu'elle a signé cette clause ne devait pas empêcher que l'article 3148 C.C.Q. prenne effet en vertu de l'article 7 de la loi transitoire (Loi sur l'application de la réforme du Code civil, L.Q. 1992, c. 57).

Lamborghini Canada proposait, comme en première instance, une interprétation large de l'article 3136 C.C.Q. qui ferait correspondre celui-ci non pas au concept de forum de nécessité, mais à celui de forum de convenance (art. 3135 C.C.Q.) et permettrait ainsi à un tribunal québécois de demeurer compétent quant à un litige si certains facteurs tels que les inconvénients pour les parties, le coût du litige et les difficultés de la conduite d'une procès à l'étranger justifiaient une telle conclusion. La Cour d'appel a expliqué que l'article 3136 C.C.Q. exprime une règle d'exception basée sur l'impossibilité démontrée d'avoir accès au tribunal étranger et correspondant précisément au concept de forum de nécessité. En l'espèce, ni les coûts et les inconvénients reliés à un procès en Italie ni l'inquiétude de Lamborghini Canada, estimant que sa position tactique sera affaiblie si elle doit plaider devant le tribunal italien, n'en justifiaient l'application.

Clause compromissoire — contrat de travail

Note. Veuillez voir *Dominion Bridge Corp.* c. *Knai,* [1997] R.J.Q. 1637 (C.S.). Une demanderesse qui avait opté pour la soumission de son droit d'action à une autorité québécoise plutôt d'aller en arbitrage ne pouvait pas retirer cette option, étant donné que le défendeur l'avait suivi sur ce terrain. En outre, la demanderesse ne pouvait se prévaloir de la clause d'arbitrage prévue au contrat. Selon l'article 3149 C.C.Q., cette stipulation qui s'inscrivait dans le contrat d'emploi du défendeur lui était inopposable, car le for qui y était désigné était situé hors du Québec à moins qu'il ne s'y soumette volontairement, ce qui n'était pas le cas en l'instance (article 3148 C.C.Q.).

(e) *Forum non conveniens*

Moyen déclinatoire — article 3135 C.C.Q.

Note. Veuillez voir *Droit de la famille* — 2378, [1996] R.J.Q. 2993 (C.S.) (requête en annulation de pension alimentaire et d'arrérages; les tribunaux québecois étaient compétents, parce que les deux parties résidaient au Québec, mais les tribunaux ontariens étaient mieux à même de trancher le litige dans le contexte tout à fait exceptionnel des circonstances spécifiques au dossier et, en particulier, plusieurs ordonnances et jugements provisoires de la Division générale de la Cour d'Ontario et l'intervention à plusieurs reprises de la Cour d'appel de l'Ontario). Veuillez voir aussi *Lorenzetti* c. *McLachlan,* [1996] R.J.Q. 1311 (C.S.) (une demande de précisions ne constitue pas un empêchement à invoquer ensuite l'article 3135 C.C.Q., mais en l'espèce, rien n'indiquait que l'intérêt de la justice commandait que le tribunal québécois décline sa compétence).

Moyen déclinatoire — article 3135 C.C.Q. — faillite

Note. Veuillez voir *Reklitis (Syndic de),* [1996] R.J.Q. 3035 (C.S.). La Cour a décidé que l'article 3135 C.C.Q. ne s'applique pas dans le cadre d'une procédure intentée sous l'empire de la Loi sur la faillite et l'insolvabilité (Can.). De toute façon, en l'espèce, la Cour supérieure était mieux placée que l'autorité judiciaire étranger (grecque) pour trancher le litige, qui incluait une requête en révision d'un contrat de vente d'immeubles situés en Grèce. Le recours intenté par le syndic ne visait pas la nullité du contrat mais une condamnation pécuniaire à l'encontre de la soeur du débiteur personnellement. Le débiteur, sa soeur, le syndic, la masse des créanciers et toutes les parties en cause résidaient au Québec.

Injonction contre les poursuites

Droit de la famille-2398, [1996] R.J.Q. 1010. Cour supérieure du Québec.

Les parties ont été conjoint de fait et, pendant des huit dernières années de leur union, elles ont résidé en Ontario. En 1991, la défenderesse a réclamé devant les tribunaux ontariens un soutien alimentaire aux termes de la Loi sur le droit de la famille (Ontario), ainsi que la moitié de tous les éléments d'actif du requérant (essentiellement situés au Québec), en vertu de la doctrine du "constructive trust." Le demandeur a demandé au tribunal ontarien de décliner compétence au motif que le "constructive trust" et l'enrichissement sans cause sont des doctrines comparables, ce que le tribunal a refusé de faire. Plusieurs décisions interlocutoires ont été rendues, des interrogatoires hors cour ont été effectués et la défense a été produite, mais la cause n'est pas inscrite. En février 1994, l'épouse légitime du demandeur a intenté une action en séparation de corps à Laval. Ce dernier a alors demandé la mise en cause de la défenderesse dans cette instance, et ses conclusions à cet égard visaient à faire constater que le tribunal québécois était compétent et que la défenderesse ne l'avait nullement enrichi. Dans cette optique, les parties étant maintenant domiciliées au Québec, le demandeur réclamait une injonction permanente afin de faire suspendre ou de faire cesser les procédures judiciaires commencées en Ontario par la défenderesse. Celle-ci invoquait l'irrecevabilité de la requête au motif que l'on ne peut pas empêcher des procédures judiciaires par voie d'injonction.

La Cour a décidé que l'action en injonction était recevable en vertu de la doctrine du *forum non conveniens*, codifiée à l'article 3135 C.C.Q. Si cet article permet expressément la suspension d'instance, par laquelle un tribunal québécois décline sa compétence en faveur d'un tribunal étranger, il n'écarte pas l'injonction contre les poursuites, qui est la seconde modalité d'exercice du *forum non conveniens* en common law. Cette modalité provient du pouvoir inhérent de la Cour supérieure de prononcer ces injonctions dans des circonstances exceptionnelles malgré le libellé de l'article 758 du Code de procédure civile. En effet, en matière de droit international privé, l'injonction ne vise pas le tribunal étranger mais uniquement le ressortissant devant le tribunal. En introduisant le *forum non conveniens* dans le code civil, le législateur ne pouvait qu'avoir voulu permettre l'injonction dans le cadre du droit international privé, car conclure autrement reviendrait à priver le justiciable québécois de l'une des deux voies de droit ouvertes pour l'application de cette doctrine. Ce serait là l'acceptation dans le droit québécois d'une doctrine principale tout en y refusant une modalité d'exercice.

L'injonction elle-même ne pouvait toutefois être accordée. Il s'agissait d'un recours qui, en vertu de la règle de la courtoisie, ne doit être accordé qu'en des circonstances exceptionnelles, qui n'étaient pas ici réunies. Entre autres choses, il faillait mettre en balance la perte d'avantages subie par le demandeur à l'étranger et les inconvénients et les avantages que subirait le défendeur devant le tribunal étranger au cas où l'action serait jugée devant ce tribunal. Or, l'examen de la décision ontarienne refusant de décliner compétence, selon les règles comparables aux ceux du Québec, permettait de conclure que cette décision avait été raisonnable. Que le tribunal soit situé en Ontario n'était pas un inconvénient majeur puisqu'il siègeait non loin de la frontière du Québec. Aux termes de la Loi sur le droit de la famille, les conjoints de fait se doivent des aliments, ce qui n'est pas le cas au Québec, et, d'autre part, le "constructive trust" semblait d'application plus large que l'enrichissement sans cause québécois. Si le litige devait être entendu au Québec et si ses tribunaux déterminaient que le droit ontarien n'est pas applicable, il en résulterait donc la perte d'un avantage juridique légitime pour la défenderesse. Ceci permettrait au tribunal de refuser l'injonction, même si le juge conclue que la décision du tribunal ontarien était déraisonnable. De plus, selon l'article 3094 C.C.Q., la défenderesse ne pourrait, sur la base de sa cohabitation avec le demandeur pendant huit ans en Ontario, invoquer devant un tribunal québécois le droit ontarien puisque les deux parties étaient maintenant domiciliées au Québec. En outre, on ne pouvait pas conclure qu'une injustice grave résulterait de l'omission par le tribunal ontarien de se récuser. Finalement, la demande du demandeur était tardive étant donné que, pendant un an et demi depuis que ce recours existe, les procédures ont continué de progresser normalement en Ontario.

(f) Enfants et mineurs

Garde d'enfant — violation du droit de garde — loi sur les aspects civils de l'enlèvement international et interprovincial d'enfants

Droit de la famille — 2545, [1996] R.J.Q. 2509. Cour d'appel du Québec.

Les parties se sont mariées au Québec en 1989 et avaient deux enfants, âgés respectivement de six ans et de quatre ans. Elles avaient toutes deux la citoyenneté canadienne quoique l'intimé soit égyptien de naissance. En 1992, elles ont quitté le Québec pour la Californie en raison de'importantes difficultés financières. Par la suite, les relations entre les parties se sont détériorées et, le 18 janvier 1996, l'appelante est revenue au Québec avec les enfants, à l'insu de son mari. Celui-ci a alors intenté une action en divorce en Californie et a obtenu une ordonnance interdisant le déplacement des enfants hors des États-Unis. Le juge a alors précisé que la garde des enfants serait confiée au père, si la mère et les enfants étaient absents à la date fixée pour une audience d'urgence. Lors de celle-ci, l'intimé a reçu signification des procédures en séparation de corps intentées par l'appelante au Québec. Le juge californien a noté l'absence de l'appelante et la présence d'un avocat californien la représentant aux seules fins de contester la compétence du tribunal. Le juge a décidé que les tribunaux californiens étaient compétents pour entendre l'affaire et a fixé la date de l'audience. Entre-temps, la Cour supérieure du Québec a confié la garde provisoire des enfants à l'appelante jusqu'à une certaine date. Au jour fixé, l'intimé a présenté une requête en exception déclinatoire, qui a été rejetée au motif que les parties n'avaient pas établi leur domicile en Californie. La garde des enfants a alors été confiée à l'appelante. Quelques jours plus tard, un tribunal californien a attribué la garde des enfants à l'intimé. Par la suite, le premier juge a fait droit à la requête présentée par ce dernier en vertu de l'article 18 de la Loi sur les aspects civils de l'enlèvement international et interprovincial d'enfants, L.R.Q., c. A-23.01, après avoir conclu qu'il y avait eu déplacement illicite des enfants au sens de cette loi puisque ceux-ci avaient leur résidence habituelle en Californie. Le juge a ordonné le retour des enfants à Californie.

L'appel est accueilli, avec dissidence, par la Cour d'appel. La Loi sur les aspects civils de l'enlèvement international et interprovincial d'enfants a pour objet l'application au Québec de la Convention de La Haye sur les aspects civils de l'enlèvement international d'enfants (1980). Or, c'est à la lumière des objectifs et de la philosophie de cette convention qu'il faut analyser les dispositions pertinentes de la loi et les appliquer. La solidarité internationale en matière de protection des enfants commande une interprétation relativement uniforme de la convention partout dans le monde. Ni la loi ni la convention définissent le concept de "résidence habituelle". Aux yeux de la communauté internationale, la "résidence habituelle" doit être comprise comme une notion de pur fait. La réalité des enfants doit seule être prise en considération et les souhaits ou intentions de leur parents ne doivent pas peser dans la balance. Le premier juge avait donc raison de conclure que la "résidence habituelle" des enfants, le 18 janvier 1996, était la Californie et que leur déplacement au Canada, en violation du droit de garde attribué au père-et conjointement à leur mère-par le droit de la Californie, était illicite au sens de la loi et de la convention.

Les exceptions à l'obligation d'assurer le retour des enfants au lieu de leur "résidence habituelle" prévues dans la convention doivent être interprétées restrictivement. L'intérêt de l'enfant déplacé, au sens qu'on donne à cette notion en matière de garde d'enfant au Québec, n'est pas mentionné explicitement dans la convention ni dans la loi comme critère de l'objectif qui vise à assurer le retour de l'enfant. Au sens de la convention et de la loi, l'intérêt de l'enfant déplacé s'étudie sous l'angle plus étroit des exceptions. Il n'y avait pas lieu d'intervenir pour modifier la décision du premier juge, selon qui un risque grave de danger physique ou psychologique (article 21(2) de la Loi), si les enfants seront retournés à la Californie, n'existait pas. De plus, le premier juge avait assorti son ordonnance de retour de diverses conditions pour assurer que ce retour se fasse le mieux possible. Le juge dissident croyait que l'article 21(2) de la Loi paraît plus large et susceptible de viser les situations où le retour placerait l'enfant dans une situation grave, susceptible de porter préjudice à son développement, en créant une situation que la loi qualifie d'intolérable. Selon ce juge, l'ordre de renvoi devait être refusé au motif qu'il y avait un risque grave que les enfants seraient privés de contacts durables et continus avec leur mère.

B Procedure / Procédure

1 Common Law and Federal Law

(a) Interlocutory orders in interjurisdictional cases

Order to disclose evidence

Note. See *Brar* v. *Sidhu* (1997), 33 B.C.L.R. (3d) 59 (S.C. (Master)), in which the court held it had no jurisdiction to order a husband, resident in Alberta, to disclose information and documents that related to the British Columbia-resident wife's application in British Columbia to vary a child maintenance order. Under the circumstances of the case there was no way to compel obedience to any such order.

Mareva injunction

Note. In *Leaton Leather & Trading Co.* v. *Ngai* (1997), 32 B.C.L.R. (3d) 14 (S.C.), an action on a Hong Kong judgment against a debtor now resident in British Columbia, the judgment creditor obtained a Mareva injunction against the debtor's disposing of his sole substantial asset — namely his home — which he had put up for sale. The court rejected the argument, supported by statements in some cases, that there should be no injunction to restrain a disposal that was motivated by considerations other than a desire to avoid payment of the judgment. The relevant factor was whether there was a real risk that the disposal would render a judgment nugatory. For the sequel, see *Leaton Leather & Trading Co.* v. *Kong*, noted below under C. Foreign Judgments, 1. Common Law and Federal, (d) Defences applicable to enforcement by action or registration: violation of natural justice.

(b) Evidence obtained abroad for local proceeding

Manner of obtaining evidence — fundamental rights

R. v. *Terry*, [1996] 2 S.C.R. 207, 135 D.L.R. (4th) 214. Supreme Court of Canada.

The accused was arrested by police in California under a warrant issued in extradition proceedings to have the accused returned to Canada to stand trial for murder. He made a statement to police in California. The contents of this statement, and a knife that California police had found in his girfriend's apartment as a consequence of the statement, were tendered in evidence at his trial in Canada.

The accused argued that the evidence was inadmissible because the police in the United States, while complying with United States law in giving him the "Miranda warning," had failed to warn him immediately upon his detention that he had the right to counsel, thus contravening a fundamental right granted by s. 10(b) of the Canadian Charter of Rights and Freedoms. He contended that this violation rendered the evidence inadmissible according to s. 24(2) of the Charter.

The Supreme Court of Canada, affirming the courts below, held the evidence was admissible because there had been no breach of the Charter. The requirements of the Charter did not apply to United States police when detaining the accused under a United States arrest warrant. A state is only competent to enforce its laws within its own boundaries. The principle that criminal law applies only within the country's territory is particularly true of the process enacted to enforce it. The gathering of evidence is governed by the law of the country under whose law the investigation is carried out, and no other. It was not unfair to treat evidence gathered abroad differently from that gathered in Canada. People expect to be governed by the law of the state where they currently reside. Nor did policy considerations require that foreign police comply with the Charter requirements. It was the accused, not Canadian police, who decided that he should go abroad. Canadian police had an incentive to insist on high standards from the foreign police because of the risk that, otherwise, evidence could be excluded on the ground that its use would violate the principles of fundamental justice or render the trial unfair. Any attempt to bind foreign police by Canadian law would be impossible to regulate. Even if the American police could be considered in some sense as "agents" of the Canadian police, they would be governed by California law so long as they operated in California.

(c) Proof of foreign law

Statutory law from another province

Note. See *Berthelot* v. *Rioux* (1996), 177 N.B.R. (2d) 144 (Q.B.), in which the legislative requirement, that the court accept an official printed version of another province's statute as proof of the contents of the statute, was held not to require the court to give effect to a rule in a Québec statute unassisted by further evidence. The court required the party relying on the statute to provide evidence on the interpretation of the legislation.

(d) Evidence obtained locally for foreign proceeding

Letters rogatory

Note. In *Fecht* v. *Deloitte & Touche* (1996), 28 O.R. (3d) 188 (Gen. Div.), a United States court had issued letters rogatory to the Ontario Court, for the production of documentary evidence by the auditors of a Canadian firm that was the defendant in a class action suit in the United States court for violation of United States securities laws. The court refused the request because it was far too broad and would clearly include irrelevant material. The court had no power to narrow the terms of the request. The court also thought that enforcement would be prejudicial to a business citizen of Canada and an infringement upon Canadian sovereignty. However, the court stated that the power to enforce letters rogatory did extend to the pre-trial discovery of non-parties to the foreign litigation. Moreover, the right to examine non-parties would not necessarily be limited to the same extent as under Ontario law, although the Ontario rule should not be disregarded entirely.

2 Québec

Administration de la preuve — Application du droit étranger — obligation au secret

Arab Banking Corp. c. *Wightman*, [1996] R.J.Q. 1715. Cour supérieure du Québec.

Certain representatives, who were being examined on discovery before plea, took a series of objections to questions put to them. They relied upon obligations of secrecy imposed by the laws of Germany and Switzerland upon banks in each of those jurisdictions. They argued that these rules ought to be applied, notwithstanding that Québec law governed issues of evidence according to s. 3130 C.C.Q.: "Evidence is governed by the law applicable to the merits of the dispute, subject to any rules of the court seised of the matter which are more favourable to the establishment of evidence."

The bank representatives invoked, in particular, s. 3079 C.C.Q., which says: "Where legitimate and manifestly preponderant interests so require, effect may be given to a mandatory provision of the law of another country with which the situation is closely connected. In deciding whether to do so, consideration is given to the purpose of the provision and the consequences of its application."

The court was prepared to assume that the provisions in question were mandatory as regards each of Germany and Switzerland, although the evidence as to the consequences of breach of the provisions was less than conclusive. There was a close connection with Germany and Switzerland because each of the banks had its principal place of operation in the country in question. The purpose of the provisions, to ensure bank secrecy, carried a different and much diminished weight in Canada than in some other countries. The consequences of applying the secrecy rules would be contrary to the interests of justice. The bank in each instance had selected the Québec court as the forum. It chose to litigate in a jurisdiction where bank secrecy had a very limited application. If the individuals' testimony were subject to the rules of secrecy as they maintained, the banks would be justified in withholding information that might otherwise be material and admissible, thus conferring upon them a potential advantage or upon the defendants a disadvantage, or both. The "legitimate and manifestly preponderant interests" that might require application of the secrecy laws were not made out. On the contrary, the public interest required that all relevant evidence be available to the court. The argument that comity required respect for the bank secrecy laws of other countries was rejected on the ground that comity was not a matter of absolute obligation and, in this case, had to give way to the greater public interest of requiring the unrestricted testimony of the witnesses in question.

C *Foreign Judgments / Jugements étrangers*

1 Common Law and Federal Law

(a) Conditions applicable to enforcement by action or registration

Jurisdiction of original court — attornment to the jurisdiction

Note. In *Fulford* v. *Reid*, [1997] 1 W.W.R. 118, 6 C.P.C. (4th) 224 (Man. Q.B.), the Manitoba-resident defendant in an Ontario defamation action had taken no step in the proceeding except to send a letter to the plaintiff's lawyer. The letter disputed the Ontario court's jurisdiction but also stated defences. The plaintiff's lawyer filed the letter with the Ontario court as a defence and then had the defence struck. Registration of the judgment in Manitoba was set aside on the ground that sending the letter of defence to the lawyer did not constitute a submission to the Ontario court's jurisdiction.

Jurisdiction of original court — real and substantial connection between the forum and the facts giving rise to the litigation

Note. According to *Morguard Investments Ltd.* v. *De Savoye*, [1990] 3 S.C.R. 1077 (noted in 29 Canadian Yearbook of International Law 536 (1991)), a default judgment given against a non-resident of the originating jurisdiction must be recognized if there is a sufficient connection between the originating jurisdiction and the parties or the subject matter of the litigation. This principle has been applied in a number of cases in which foreign sellers of goods brought an action in the foreign country against Canadian buyers who had not paid for the goods. The buyers did not defend. The default judgments were held enforceable against the buyers in Canada: *Gorman-Rupp of Canada Ltd.* v. *Electrical Industries Western Ltd.* (1996), [1997] 1 W.W.R. 118, 44 Alta. L.R. (3d) 146 (Q.B.); *J.B.S. Tooling Co.* v. *Upward Tool Group Inc.* (1996), 6 C.P.C. (4th) 191 (Ont. Gen. Div.) (judgment registered under Canada-U.K. Convention); *Confection C.M.P. Inc.* v. *Gravel* (1995), 44 C.P.C. (3d) 301 (Ont. Gen. Div.). The same conclusion was reached in cases where foreign lenders sued Canadian borrowers in the country where the borrowers had borrowed the money: *Commercial Agency* v. *Jarvis* (1996), 46 C.P.C. 223 (Alta. Q.B. (Master)); *First American Bank & Trust (Receiver of)* v. *Garay* (1996), 49 C.P.C. (3d) 326 (Ont. C.A.) (action on guarantee).

In *Morrissette* v. *Performax Systems Ltd.* (1997), 115 Man. R. (2d) 55 (C.A.), a Québec court gave default judgment against a Manitoba corporation and three individuals, resident in Manitoba, who allegedly owned and ran the corporation. The Manitoba court held that the judgment was enforceable against the corporation but not against the individuals, because there was no evidence to show facts amounting to a real and substantial connection between themselves, as distinct from their company, and Québec. For this purpose it was assumed that the law of Québec, with respect to what facts will implicate a shareholder in personal liability, was the same as that of Manitoba.

Note also that in *United States of America* v. *Ivey* (1996), 139 D.L.R. (4th) 570 (Ont. C.A.), aff'g (1995), 130 D.L.R. (4th) 674 (Ont. Gen. Div.) (noted in 34 Canadian Yearbook of International Law 492 (1996)), leave to appeal was refused by the Supreme Court of Canada (1997), 145 D.L.R. (4th) vii.

Finality of the judgment

Note. Under the Court Order Enforcement Act, now R.S.B.C. 1996, c. 78, s. 29(6)(e), a judgment from a reciprocating state is not registrable if an "appeal is pending" before the foreign court. (The pendency of an appeal does not preclude an action at common law, although it is usually grounds for staying enforcement of a resulting judgment.) In *Dunton* v. *Whitewater West Recreations Ltd.* (1996), 136 D.L.R. (4th) 56, [1997] 4 W.W.R. 98 (B.C.S.C.), the judgment debtor under a default judgment from Colorado had unsuccessfully applied to have the Colorado court set the judgment aside. It had filed a notice of intent to appeal from the court's dismissal of that application. The court held that this was a pending appeal from the judgment within the meaning of the statute.

(b) Defences applicable to enforcement by action or registration

Violation of natural justice

Leaton Leather & Trading Co. v. *Kong* (1997), 147 D.L.R. (4th) 377. British Columbia Supreme Court.

The defendant and others were sued in Hong Kong on guarantees they had given of a Hong Kong corporation's debts. The proceedings were conducted in English. The plaintiff applied for summary judgment. The defendant, Ngai, received notice of the application but his English was limited. He appeared in court without a lawyer to present evidence on behalf of all the defendants. The plaintiff's lawyer applied for judgment on the basis that Ngai had not provided affidavits three days before the hearing. Ngai, through a translator, explained that he had no money for a lawyer but he had evidence to present that would refute the plaintiff's affidavit evidence. The court said that Ngai could not pretend to know nothing about procedure because he had filed a statement of defence. Judgment was granted in favour of the plaintiff without Ngai being allowed to present his evidence. Ngai was unaware of the possibility of an appeal and did not appeal. He subsequently became resident in British Columbia. The plaintiff brought an action in British Columbia on the Hong Kong judgment.

Saunders J. held that the judgment was unenforceable because it was obtained contrary to the principles of natural justice. If the judgment debtor was unrepresented, a recognizing court might be compelled to act with greater attention to the fullness of the hearing than in the case of a judgment debtor who had had counsel. In this case, granting judgment against an unrepresented litigant who has attended with documents, without either considering the documents or hearing the litigant or adjourning to permit the litigant to put the material in proper form, was effectively to deny the party the opportunity of substantially presenting his case before the court. The disadvantage of the defendants as unrepresented parties was deepened by the need to translate the Hong Kong court's comments because English was not their first language. Judgment was granted without consideration of any of the merits of the defence. The judgment fell within the limited class of cases that offend the rules of natural justice. The failure to take an appeal stemmed from the same ignorance of legal procedure that led to the judgment against the defendants without consideration of the merits of their case. There was no reason in principle why a failure to appeal would make enforceable in a foreign jurisdiction a judgment gained by denying a litigant the right to be heard.

Note. Successful defences on the ground of natural justice are extremely rare in the reported cases. This is the first Canadian example known to the writer. A more typical case is *National American Ins. Co.* v. *Leong* (1996), 49 C.P.C. (3d) 246 (B.C.S.C.). In that case, the defendants had lost their right to appeal a judgment against them in defended proceedings in Washington State because they had filed a notice of appeal that was not signed by any of the defendants, and by the time they attempted to correct this omission the time for filing the notice had expired. The British Columbia court held that the original judgment was properly registered under the Court Order Enforcement Act, R.S.B.C. 1996, c. 78. There was no fundamental flaw in the proceedings or irregularity of a serious nature. The defendants had been given fourteen days' notice to show cause why their appeal should not be dismissed because of the procedural fault, and they had failed to respond. Moreover, the American court, with all the relevant facts before it, had exercised its discretion in refusing to allow extension of the time to appeal.

(c) Registration under uniform reciprocal enforcement of judgments legislation or an international convention

Defences — judgment debtor not ordinarily resident or carrying on business in original jurisdiction

Note. See *Ellerbrok* v. *Hortico Inc.* (1996), 44 C.P.C. (3d) 1

(N.S.C.A.), and *Davis & Co.* v. *Dunn* (1996), 2 C.P.C. (4th) 347 (N.W.T. S.C.), in both of which the defence succeeded.

Defences — appeal pending

Note. See *Dunton* v. *Whitewater West Recreations Ltd.* (1996), [1997] 1 W.W.R. 112, 6 C.P.C. (4th) 224 (see above, under (a) Conditions applicable to enforcement by action or registration: finality of the judgment).

(d) Registration under uniform reciprocal enforcement of maintenance orders legislation

Note. In *Smibert* v. *Smibert*, [1996] 10 W.W.R. 326 (Sask. Q.B.), a Saskatchewan-resident wife sought to register, under the Reciprocal Enforcement of Maintenance Orders Act, S.S. 1983, c. R-4.1, a maintenance order given as part of a divorce judgment in Alabama. This was held impossible, since final orders could only be registered against a debtor who was resident in Saskatchewan at the time of registration; the husband had not been in Saskatchewan for many years. See also *Grim* v. *Dubé* (1997), 28 R.F.L. (4th) 332 (N.B.Q.B.), on the meaning of "final order" under the uniform legislation.

2 Québec

Note. Veuillez voir *Mutual Trust Co.* c. *Ubani*, [1996] R.L. 173 (C.S.).

D Choice of Law (including Status of Persons) / Conflits de lois (y compris statut personnel)

1 Common Law and Federal

(a) Characterization

Substance and procedure

Note. In *Tolofson* v. *Jensen*, [1994] 3 S.C.R. 1022 (noted in 33 Canadian Yearbook of International Law 458 (1995)), the Supreme Court of Canada, reversing a long-standing but illogical common law rule, held that limitations statutes should be characterized as substantive, irrespective of whether their wording was in terms of barring the remedy ("no action shall be brought" or the like) or extinguishing the right. This change in the law has led to a rash of cases in which victims of motor vehicle accidents that took place in provinces with short limitation periods have retroactively lost their right to sue, despite the fact that, until December 1994 (the date of the *Tolofson* decision), they might reasonably have expected that the longer limitation statute of their home province would apply because it was procedural. Courts have expressed their sympathy for the victim, but have felt bound to uphold the common law fiction that the common law is never changed, it is merely revealed to have been different at all times from what everybody thought. Therefore, the change from the application of the *lex fori* (for procedural limitation rules) to the *lex loci delicti* (which governs substantive issues in tort actions) has been held to have effect even in actions that were commenced — as then permitted by the *lex fori*'s limitation rule — before December 1994. See *Brill* v. *Korpaach Estate* (1997), 148 D.L.R. (4th) 467, [1997] 8 W.W.R. 511 (Alta. C.A.), leave to appeal refused 152 D.L.R. (4th) vi (S.C.C.); *Stewart* v. *Stewart* (1997), 145 D.L.R. (4th) 228, [1997] 5 W.W.R. 353 (B.C.C.A.); *Hendsbee* v. *Khuber* (1995), 148 N.S.R. (2d) 270, 47 C.P.C. (3d) 258 (T.D.).

See also *Holt Cargo Systems Inc.* v. *ABC Containerline N.V. (Bankrupt)* (1997), 127 F.T.R. 244, 46 C.B.R. (3d) 169 (F.C.T.D.) (validity of maritime lien held a substantive issue that depended on the proper law of the agreement under which the lien was said to have arisen, in this case the law of the United States); *Bakker* v. *Van Adrichem*, [1997] 5 W.W.R. 151, 30 B.C.L.R. (3d) 199 (C.A.) (a rule about the defendant's confirmation of the cause of action restarting the limitation period, held substantive); *Horseshoe Club Operating Co.* v. *Bath* (1997), 35 B.C.L.R. (3d) 110 (S.C.) (gaming legislation of *lex fori* providing that all contracts by way of gaming or wagering were void, held substantive and inapplicable to gambling debt incurred in Nevada); *Bachand* v. *Roberts* (1996), 38 C.C.L.I. (2d) 151 (Ont. Gen. Div.) (provision in insurance policy referring to "all costs taxed against the insured" held to mean costs according to the law of the place where action was brought (Ontario), not costs according to the law of the place where the accident occurred (Virginia); the question was one of procedure).

Succession and construction of a will

Note. See *Re Fulford Estate* (1996), 146 Nfld. & P.E.I.R. 348 (P.E.I. T.D.), in which the construction of a will was held governed by the law of Prince Edward Island but the rules of succession were determined by the law of Ontario as the deceased's last domicile. The particular issue could be characterized as either construction or succession. However, the result was the same irrespective of which law was applied.

(b) Torts

Place of the tort

Stewart v. *Stewart Estate*, [1996] 8 W.W.R. 624, 24 B.C.L.R. (3d) 141. Northwest Territories Supreme Court.

The plaintiff, a resident of the Northwest Territories, brought an action there against the defendant, also resident there, for damages arising out of the death of the plaintiff's daughter in a motor vehicle accident in the Yukon. The defendant relied on a one-year limitation period for claims under the Yukon's Fatal Accidents Act, R.S.Y. 1986, c. 64. The plaintiff argued for the application of the two-year limitation period in the corresponding legislation in the Northwest Territories (Fatal Accidents Act, R.S.N.W.T. 1988, c. F-4). Schuler J., applying *Tolofson* v. *Jensen*, [1994] 3 S.C.R. 1022 (noted in 33 Canadian Yearbook of International Law 458 (1995)) held that Yukon law applied as the *lex loci delicti*. The plaintiff was wronged when his daughter was killed. The defining activity that constituted the wrong was the defendant's negligence, which resulted in the death, not the harm to the plaintiff's interests in the Northwest Territories. In the circumstances, the application of the *lex loci delicti* rule did not result in an injustice that would justify making an exception to the rule.

Note. The *lex loci delicti* rule was also applied in *Leonard* v. *Houle* (1996), 3 C.P.C. (4th) 222, 21 M.V.R. 212 (Ont. Gen. Div.), in which the plaintiff was injured in a car crash that resulted from a police chase of a stolen car that began in Ottawa, Ontario, and ended in the collision with the plaintiff's car across the river in Hull, Québec. Alleged negligent acts by the Ottawa police and the Hull police that took place in Québec were not actionable because of the bar under Québec law to civil suits arising out of automobile accidents. Alleged negligent acts of the Ottawa police that took place in Ontario would be governed by Ontario law, and the action was allowed to proceed with respect to those acts only.

Right of subrogation

Note. In *Cowley* v. *Brown Estate* (1997), 147 D.L.R. (4th) 282 (*sub nom. Cowley* v. *Brown*), [1997] 7 W.W.R. 380 (Alta. C.A.), the question was whether, in an Alberta action for damages arising out of a motor vehicle accident in Alberta, the court should apply a Saskatchewan law that gave the victim a right to sue for medical expenses that had been paid by the Saskatchewan government and gave the province a right of subrogation in respect of such expenses. The court decided the answer was yes. The victim's right to treatment and who was obliged to pay for it were issues governed by the law of Saskatchewan as the province in which the expenses were incurred. The province's right of subrogation was a private matter between the victim and the source of collateral benefits, which again was a relationship governed by Saskatchewan law.

(c) Property

Movables — tangible — transfer inter vivos

Note. In *Canadian Imperial Bank of Commerce* v. *A. K. Construction (1988) Ltd.* (1996), 11 P.P.S.A.C. (2d) 280 (Alta. Q.B. (Master)), a security interest that was perfected in Alberta was held to have continued perfected, notwithstanding that the collateral had been put in the hands of a Minnesota firm to be sold and the creditor had failed to register a financing statement in Minnesota within 15 days of learning that this had happened. The 15-day rule, in s. 7(3) of the Personal Property Security Act, S.A. 1988, c. P-4.05, applies only to a creditor's learning that the debtor has "transferred an interest in the collateral" to a person in another jurisdiction. The transfer to the Minnesota company was for the purposes of sale by them as agents or bailees, not a transfer of an interest in the collateral to them. The creditor's security position in Alberta, when the goods returned there, was therefore unimpaired.

Matrimonial property

Note. See *Adam* v. *Adam* (1996), 25 R.F.L. (4th) 50 (Ont. C.A.), applying Zimbabwe law, as the law of the spouses' last common habitual residence, to determine the division of property. The choice of law rule is contained in s. 15 of the Family Law Act, R.S.O. 1990, c. F-3.

2 Québec

Statut personnel

Divorce en étranger — reconnaissance

Note. Veuillez voir *Droit de la famille*-2054, [1997] R.J.Q. 1124 (C.S.), dans lequel la Cour a décidé qu'un jugement de divorce prononcé en Algérie ne pouvait pas être reconnu. L'article 3167 C.C.Q., qui obligerait à reconnaître le jugement vu que les époux avaient la nationalité algérienne, devait être déclaré inapplicable en matière de divorce, car il contrevient à l'article 22 de la Loi sur la divorce, S.R.C. 1985, c. 3 (2e suppl.), selon lequel un jugement étranger de divorce est reconnu à la condition que l'un des ex-époux ait résidé habituellement dans le pays étranger pendant au moins l'année précédant l'introduction de l'instance. Le jugement est porté en appel.

Book Reviews / Recensions de livres

Ethics and Authority in International Law. By Alfred P. Rubin. Cambridge: Cambridge University Press, 1997. Pp. 228.

This is a complex and important work. Professor Rubin identifies two "inspirations" for the book. The first was a panel at the 1973 American Society of International Law Annual Meeting at which he was asked why the United States did not arrest and try "before its own courts various officials of the Government of South Viet Nam who had been photographed committing what seemed obvious violations of the 'positive' laws of war" (at xi). The second was in 1981-82 when Rubin, while examining the concept of piracy, found (at xii) that concepts of "universal crime" and "universal jurisdiction" were seriously wanting.

I think it is easier to appreciate Professor Rubin's complex arguments if I first state his overall conclusions and prescriptions and then outline some of the steps that led him to these conclusions. Rubin himself believes that baroque music provides the best analogy for understanding the operation of the international legal order:

> Baroque music features independent instruments playing independent melodies in counterpoint, coming together at key places, each fitting the coming-together into its own melody. In a baroque fugue, a single simple melody is repeated in different keys, at different tempi and with different melodic embellishment. The analogy to a state asserting a rule of law and hearing its own assertion played to it in unforeseen circumstances and with unforeseen variations seems compelling (at 204).

Rubin (at 204) sees states playing counterpoint and fugue and "coming together at key points . . . even if at times the disharmonies of some melodic lines are disturbing to all." He calls this situation the "baroque dualist-positivist model" (at 205), and offers four ways to move towards a functioning international legal order within the constraints of this model (at 205-6):

(1) continued institution-building through treaty by which each member of the community yields a degree of its discretion . . . in return for the benefits of community decision-making
(2) of particular use in the human rights area, disaggregating the notion of a "legal" order to make "non-legal" remedies more obviously a useful reaction to tensions in the system with which no positivist system can cope without paying a price probably too high for realistic discussion
(3) accepting that "international law" is a "foreign" legal order to any municipal system, applying choice-of-law techniques within the existing positivist legal order
(4) accepting as inevitable in a positivist legal order that there are some problems that cannot be solved by the application of "law," and that some "reprogramming" and education divorced from "rule-making" and "enforcement" in their usual senses might be the only effective responses.

Professor Rubin begins (at 6) with a thorough discussion of naturalism and positivism, which "have dominated juristic thinking from earliest days." He provides lucid definitions along with cogent analyses of the origins of these concepts. Naturalism "assumes that rules of human behavior derive ultimately from outside the will of mankind" (at 6). In contrast (at 15), positivism "emphasizes human discretion as the source of law." Rubin finds both approaches inadequate and (at 20) recommends "toning down the traditional rhetoric and differentiating moral indignation from legal argumentation."

Chapter 2 undertakes the modest task of describing the international legal order! Rubin begins with the natural law model, examining the contributions of Samuel von Pufendorf, Christian Wolff, Emerich de Vattel, Jean Jacques Burlamaqui, Francisco Suarez, Alberico Gentili, and Richard Zouche. He is satisfied with neither the naturalist nor the positivist approach (at 54):

> In sum, what passes for scholarship in jurisprudential writings is usually either naturalist elaboration of principles that are asserted as if self-evident but with no necessary connection to wisdom or truth, or positivist works merely descriptive or empirical.

Rubin discusses the work of some of the early positivists — for example, Cornelisz Bynkershoek — and addresses the issues related to dualism, especially in the period that led up to the American Revolution.

Chapter 3, entitled "Theory and Practice Come Together," concentrates on the United States experiences, especially from the Articles of Confederation through the middle of the nineteenth century. The language adopted in the Constitution empowered Congress "[t]o define and punish Piracies and Felonies committed on the High Seas, and Offenses against the Law of Nations" (at 74). Rubin (*ibid.*) finds this a natural law approach that does not "conform to the practical experiences of statesmen." The expression "law of nations" was acceptable to both the natural and the positive law camps, although (at 83), they held different understandings, "many of them incompatible with the others."

Professor Rubin deals extensively with piracy, which he sees as a issue in which international law's reach exceeded its grasp. The first American federal statute dealing with piracy, passed on April 30, 1790, granted sweeping powers that Rubin decries (at 86):

> There is no indication how far the jurisdiction of the American tribunals is supposed to reach; if to apply to foreigners in foreign vessels, then there is an assumption of jurisdiction that surely the new country would not have been willing to concede to French or British officials stopping American ships on the high seas when no national interest of France or Great Britain had been affected.

Next, Rubin analyzes the slave trade. He agrees with Chief Justice John Marshall in the *Antelope* case (1825), calling Marshall's opinion "a triumph of 'dualism' and 'positivism.'" Although Marshall found the slave trade morally reprehensible, he nonetheless wrote in *Antelope* (at 105, quoting 23 US {10 Wheaton} 64, 113 at 126-7 (1825)):

> The principle common to (the British) cases is that the legality of the capture of a vessel engaged in the slave trade depends on the law of the country to which the vessel belongs. If that law gives its sanction to the trade, restitution will be decreed; if that law prohibits it, the vessel and cargo will be condemned as good prize.

Rubin has no patience for British hypocrisy, citing (at 129) their "refusal to concede reciprocal authority to those foreign countries acting under identical moral imperatives to those activating British rhetoric."

Chapter 4, entitled "Putting It Together," deals with positivism in modern times. Rubin points to the PCIJ Statute's *ex aequo et bono* provision as evidence of the ascendancy of positivism. His interpretation of *ex aequo et bono* (at 140) is "if the parties did not agree that the court should apply the rules of morality . . . the court lacked the authority to intermix those considerations with its analysis of the positive law." That Rubin's hero is Sir Hersch Lauterpacht is exemplified in his description of the way Sir Hersch "ingeniously (also ingenuously) suggested that the basis for a rule nullifying coerced treaties lay already (in 1927) in Article 10 of the Covenant of the League of Nations, playing treaty-based, positivist, procedural obstacles in the way of legal recourse to force by member states of the League" (at 142). Rubin is not as taken with Professor (later ICJ Judge) Philip Jessup, whose ideas "were not, or could not be, made the basis for a living international legal order" (at 144).

Professor Rubin does not believe that the interdependent, international economic world of the late twentieth century will ameliorate the problems that inspired this book. In fact, he suspects that it may strain the existing system further. Neither does he place much stock in the trend that many see "towards a more benign, co-operative, international institution-centered model" (at 154). He believes this is wishful thinking that has existed in much the same form for hundreds of years.

I find Rubin's discussion of reprogramming — which he offers as a solution — to be the most problematic element of the book. He defines reprogramming in this way (at 149):

> Reprogramming means offering alternatives that make it in our interest to act more benignly when threatened. Dispute-resolution mechanisms must be put in place and made attractive to statesmen; solutions that do not transform a losing case into a total disaster, as the "legal" order frequently transforms a close case into an absolute "victory."

His advice here is interesting, even profound, but — to paraphrase Rubin himself — if reprogramming were this easy it would have been accomplished hundreds of years ago (see the reference to Plato and Aristotle at 185). Furthermore, the co-operative model advocates, whom Rubin criticizes as ivory tower idealists, believe they are proposing precisely what he defines as reprogramming.

These few criticisms do not detract from a very significant work by a meticulous scholar — a scholar who uses at least three distinct levels of "sic." International law academics need books of this type that force us to introspection and towards a more rigorous reconciliation of "desirable" with "feasible." Every international scholar should read *Ethics and Authority in International Law.* It is valuable on many levels — for one example, as a review of some of the classics of international law that are often forgotten as we undertake increasingly narrow research on topics of current interest. The subject of the book is important and timeless. It also is timely, but I wish its timeliness had been established earlier so that more readers would make the effort to appreciate this major contribution, for which we owe Professor Rubin a debt of gratitude. Sir Hersch would approve.

John King Gamble
Pennsylvania State University

The Handbook of Humanitarian Law in Armed Conflicts. Sous la direction de Dieter Fleck. Oxford: Oxford University Press, 1995. Pp. xvi, 589. ISBN 0-19-825835-6, 202.50 $ CAN.

Comme le soulignait la Chambre d'appel du Tribunal pénal international pour l'ex-Yougoslavie dans la décision interlocutoire dans l'affaire *Tadic*, la démonstration de l'existence d'une règle coutumière de droit international humanitaire soulève une difficulté fondamentale, à savoir la quasi-impossibilité d'établir un dossier de la pratique des troupes sur le champ de bataille, faute de témoins. La manière de résoudre ce dilemme, selon le Tribunal, consiste à "s'appuyer essentiellement sur des éléments comme les déclarations officielles des États, les manuels militaires et les décisions judiciaires."[1] Fort de cette conclusion, le Tribunal invoque dans le cadre de sa discussion du droit coutumier applicable aux conflits armés internes divers manuels militaires, et au premier lieu le nouveau manuel allemand adopté en 1992.[2] Il s'inscrit ainsi dans une pratique bien établie par les tribunaux alliés au lendemain de la seconde guerre mondiale, qui avaient fait un large usage des manuels militaires américain et britannique pour prouver l'existence de normes coutumières telle l'impossibilité d'invoquer la défense d'ordre supérieur.

Avec ce *Handbook of Humanitarian Law in Armed Conflicts*, Dieter Fleck met enfin à la disposition du grand public le texte du nouveau manuel allemand. Il s'agit, bien sûr, non seulement de la simple publication du manuel lui-même, mais aussi de la traduction du commentaire de ce manuel préparé par un groupe d'experts universitaires et publié en langue allemande en 1994. L'un et l'autre — le manuel et le commentaire — constituent des contributions importantes au développement du droit international humanitaire.

1 Décision relative à l'appel de la défense concernant l'exception préjudicielle d'incompétence, *Le Procureur* c. *Dusko Tadic*, Affaire n° IT-94-1-AR72, Chambre d'appel, 2 octobre 1995, par. 99.

2 *Ibid.*, par. 118, 131; *Humanitäres Völkerrecht in bewaffneten Konflikten — Handbuch* (Federal Ministry of Defense, August 1992).

D'abord le manuel militaire, en soi, représente un énoncé à jour de la position d'une puissance militaire importante sur le droit humanitaire en vigueur. L'événement est remarquable surtout parce que ce genre d'exercice reste extrêmement rare malgré une évolution significative du droit international dans ce domaine au cours des dernières décennies. L'adoption du manuel allemand résulte d'un processus long et complexe ayant impliqué des consultations nombreuses avec des universitaires, des praticiens et des membres des forces armées de divers pays.[3] Le manuel décrit, en dix chapitres couvrant environ 150 pages dans sa version originale, les principales règles du droit humanitaire. On passe ainsi en revue le développement historique et les bases juridiques du droit humanitaire (chapitre 1), les règles régissant la conduite des hostilités, y compris la distinction combattant/non-combattant, les méthodes de combats, la protection de la population civile, des prisonniers de guerre, des blessés, malades et naufragés, du personnel religieux, et des biens culturels, ainsi que le droit de la guerre sur mer (chapitres 2-10), le droit de la neutralité (chapitre 10), et finalement les principes de mise en oeuvre du droit humanitaire (chapitre 12).

Le texte du manuel colle généralement d'assez près aux dispositions des principales conventions en la matière, y inclus les deux protocoles de 1977 et la Convention de 1980 sur les armes conventionnelles. Le manuel constitue ainsi une interprétation intéressante de ces instruments internationaux dont le contenu reste très souvent vague. Parfois, par contre, il s'écarte des textes pour adopter des positions difficiles à concilier avec les conventions. Ainsi, par exemple, la notion de combattant telle qu'on la retrouve à l'article 43(2) du Protocole 1 de 1977 recouvre les "membres des forces armées d'une Partie à un conflit (autre que le personnel sanitaire et religieux . . .)." Cela signifie donc que tous les membres des forces armées sont des combattants, sauf l'exception mentionnée entre parenthèses.[4] Le manuel allemand édicte plutôt, au paragraphe 301, que les forces armées d'une partie à un conflit regroupe à la fois des combattants et des non-combattants, ces derniers comprenant par exemple les juges, les fonctionnaires, et le personnel

[3] Voir D. Fleck, "Military Manual on International Humanitarian Law Applicable in Armed Conflict. Consultations of Government Experts in Koblenz (Germany), 7-11 October 1991," (1991) 4 Humanitäres Völkerrecht — Informationsschriften 213-15.

[4] Voir *Commentaire des Protocoles additionnels du* 8 juin 1977 aux Conventions de Genève du 12 août 1949, Yves Sandoz et al., éd. (Genève: CICR, 1986), para. 1677.

de soutien (par. 313). Il s'agit du maintien d'une distinction que l'on retrouvait à l'article 3 du Règlement concernant les lois et coutumes de la guerre sur terre annexé à la quatrième convention de La Haye de 1907, mais que l'on avait voulu éliminer avec l'adoption de l'article 43 du Protocole 1. On indique par cette prise de position que, pour l'État allemand, il reste légitime de différencier diverses catégories de membres des forces armées, et que les "militaires non-combattants," donc non habilités à se battre, peuvent être considérés comme combattants illégitimes s'ils participent activement aux hostilités. Comme ces non-combattants ne jouissent d'aucune protection particulière et peuvent être l'objet d'attaques directes, l'utilité d'une telle distinction n'apparaît pas très claire.

On pourra regretter que les auteurs du manuel allemand n'aient pas jugé utile d'incorporer au texte les éléments de la pratique militaire et judiciaire, desquels ils se sont inspirés pour rédiger les règles. Le manuel militaire britannique de 1958, rédigé de main de maître par le duo (successif) Oppenheim-Lauterpacht, reste donc sans équivalent de par son riche répertoire de la pratique des États dans le domaine des lois et coutumes de la guerre. Il faut dire que le manuel original est accompagné de deux autres volumes, l'un regroupant les textes des conventions pertinentes et l'autre une collection de cas pratiques avec solutions devant servir à illustrer les règles adoptées dans le manuel.[5] Malheureusement, ce dernier volume ne paraît pas avoir été publié commercialement, et donc il est difficile de savoir si les cas sont tirés de la pratique des États.

Pour compenser un peu l'absence de références à la pratique des États, les rédacteurs du manuel allemand ont eu l'heureuse idée de demander à un groupe d'universitaires de préparer un commentaire paragraphe par paragraphe du manuel. Dans cette version augmentée de presque six cents pages, onze auteurs (D. Fleck, M. Bothe, H. Fischer, H-P Gasser, C. Greenwood, W. Heintschel von Heinegg, K. Ipsen, S. Oeter, K.J. Partsch, W. Rabus et R. Wolfrum) nous offrent leurs réflexions sur le contenu du manuel. Les auteurs se sont sentis à des degrés divers liés par le texte du manuel: certains s'en écartent assez considérablement pour offrir une analyse plus générale de la matière, comme par exemple Christopher Greenwood qui s'excuse de la mention de la prohibition de l'emploi de la force (article 2(4) de la Charte des Nations unies) au paragraphe 101 pour aborder en détail les liens entre cette disposition et le droit humanitaire, dans le cadre d'une discussion très

[5] Zdv 15/3 *Textsammlung*; Zdv 15/4 *Sammlung von Fällen mit Lösungen.*

intéressante. D'autres commentent encore la position spécifique de l'Allemagne, par exemple les obligations conventionnelles de ce pays de s'abstenir de recevoir, manufacturer ou transférer des armes nucléaires discutées par Stefan Oeter. Le tout offre un tour d'horizon impressionnant de l'état du droit international humanitaire, bien que l'exercice reste essentiellement académique plutôt qu'un compendium de la pratique.

Il faut donc saluer la publication de ce *Handbook of Humanitarian Law in Armed Conflicts* comme un événement heureux, qui contribuera, on l'espère, au développement cohérent de ce domaine du droit international. Ce serait peut-être verser dans un optimisme injustifié que de souhaiter que cette prise de position par l'Allemagne entraîne dans sa foulée la réanimation des efforts du Canada pour rédiger son propre manuel du droit des conflits armés, restés moribonds depuis le dernier avant-projet datant de 1984.

RÉNÉ PROVOST
Faculté de droit et Institut de droit comparé, Université McGill

Droit des conflits armés: Recueil des conventions, résolutions et autres documents. Par Dietrich Schindler et Jiri Toman. Genève: Comité international de la Croix-Rouge et Institut Henry-Dunant, 1996. Pp. xliii, 1470. ISBN 2-88044-033-5, 83 $ CAN.

Enfin! C'est sûrement ce que se sont exclamés les internationalistes oeuvrant dans le domaine du droit international humanitaire lors de la publication de cette magnifique collection de documents divers sur le sujet. Jusqu'ici, en effet, l'on devait se contenter des publications de la Croix-Rouge qui, si elles couvrent les instruments essentiels, ne mettaient pas à la disposition des chercheurs francophones un éventail de documents comparable à ce que leurs collègues anglophones avaient à portée de la main grâce aux éditions en anglais du même volume ou encore de la collection éditée par Adam Roberts et Richard Guelff.[1] Le nouveau volume propose une collection de documents en français qui devrait satisfaire aux

[1] D. Schindler et J. Toman, éd., *The Law of Armed Conflicts: A Collection of Conventions, Resolutions and Other Documents*, 3e éd. (Genève: Nijhoff & Henry-Dunant Institute, 1988); A. Roberts et R. Guelff, éd., *Documents on the Laws of War*, 2e éd. (Oxford: Oxford University Press, 1989).

besoins courants et moins courants de ses usagers. On y retrouve bien sûr les textes des grandes conventions, avec toutes les réserves, déclarations et communications faites par les États lors de la signature ou la ratification, mais aussi des documents quasi introuvables ailleurs, par exemple l'arrangement de Nyon de 1937 portant sur la guerre sous-marine lors de la guerre civile en Espagne, ou encore le projet de convention sur la protection des populations civiles préparé par le CICR en 1956 mais auquel il ne fut jamais donné suite. Le volume est aussi notable en ce qu'il contient des versions françaises de documents habituellement disponibles uniquement en anglais, tel le Manuel Lieber préparé pour l'armée américaine en 1863 mais qui a exercé une influence bien au-delà des frontières de ce pays, ou encore le Manuel de San Remo sur le droit international applicable aux conflits armés sur mer élaboré par un groupe d'experts en 1994. Avec pas moins de cent sept documents couvrant presque 1500 pages en caractères petits mais très lisibles, on est à peu près sûr d'y trouver tout ce qui est d'intérêt. Offert à un prix tout-à-fait raisonnable, ce volume devrait constituer un achat indispensable pour tout chercheur sérieux dans le domaine du droit humanitaire.

RÉNÉ PROVOST
Faculté de droit et Institut de droit comparé, Université McGill

Obligations Erga Omnes and International Crimes: A Theoretical Enquiry into the Implementation and Enforcement of the International Responsibility of States. Par André de Hoogh. La Haye/Londres/Boston: Kluwer Law International, 1996. Pp. xxiii, 465. ISBN 90-411-0232-9, CAN $251.44.

Depuis le dictum de la Cour internationale de Justice dans l'affaire de la *Barcelona Traction* à propos des obligations *erga omnes*, les internationalistes se sont longuement interrogés sur la portée à accorder à ce concept.[1] En effet, il n'était pas clair quelles conséquences devaient découler de la qualification d'obligations souscrites "envers la communauté internationale dans son ensemble" par rapport à des droits dont, vu leur importance, "tous les États peuvent être considérés comme ayant un intérêt juridique à ce

1 *Barcelona Traction, Light and Power Company, Limited (Belgique* c. *Espagne), deuxième phase,* [1970] C.I.J. Rec. 3.

[qu'ils] soient protégés."[2] À ces complications intrinsèques au concept même d'obligation *erga omnes* est venu s'ajouter la difficulté de situer ce dernier par rapport à d'autres institutions nouvelles du droit international comme les normes *jus cogens* et les crimes internationaux définis dans l'article 19 du projet de la Commission de droit international sur la responsabilité des États.

La curiosité des internationalistes a été immédiatement piquée par le prononcé de la Cour internationale, suscitant de très nombreux articles, mais pendant longtemps aucun ne s'est hasardé à rédiger une monographie entièrement consacrée à ce sujet par trop mystifiant. André de Hoogh vient pallier à cette lacune doctrinale avec la publication de sa thèse de doctorat, en compagnie d'ailleurs d'au moins deux autres thèses récentes sur le même sujet.[3]

Ce long ouvrage se divise en six chapitres qui présentent de manière systématique le concept d'obligations *erga omnes* et ses liens avec la notion de crime international de l'État. Le premier chapitre colle d'assez près au passage de l'affaire *Barcelona Traction*, et constitue une analyse minutieuse de ce que la Cour international a voulu dire en mentionnant que les États avaient un "intérêt juridique" à la protection des droits correspondants aux obligations *erga omnes.* On différencie ainsi les simples intérêts des intérêts juridiques, puis les intérêts juridiques des droits des États. L'auteur fait ensuite le lien entre le concept d'obligation *erga omnes* et ceux de normes *jus cogens* et crimes internationaux de l'État.

La Cour, dans le fameux passage cité ci-dessus, réfère à l'intérêt *des États*, alors que l'idée d'obligations "souscrites envers la communauté internationale dans son ensemble" soulève immédiatement la question du rôle possible des Nations Unies, personnification de cette communauté. Le second chapitre examine ce problème sous l'angle de la personnalité internationale de l'ONU et de la portée légitime de ses intérêts juridiques. On y fait le lien entre les pouvoirs conférés au Conseil de sécurité en vertu de l'article 39 de la Charte des Nations Unies et la protection de la paix et la sécurité internationale, le droit des peuples à disposer d'eux-même, et les droits fondamentaux de la personne humaine, c'est-à-dire les trois exemples d'obligations *erga omnes* mentionnés par la Cour dans

2 *Ibid.*, par. 33.

3 Voir C. Annacker, *Die Durchsetzung von erga omnes Verpflichtungen vor dem Internationalen Gerichtshof* (Hamburg: Kovac, 1994); M. Ragazzi, *The Concept of International Obligations Erga Omnes* (Oxford: Clarendon, 1997).

Barcelona Traction. La conclusion à laquelle en arrive M. de Hoogh est à l'effet que le Conseil de sécurité peut considérer dans chacun de ces cas qu'il y a menace ou rupture de la paix internationale, mais que la pratique du Conseil révèle qu'il ne le fera pas de manière systématique.

De ces éléments préliminaires, l'analyse passe ensuite au chapitre trois à l'examen de l'obligation de réparation de l'État auteur d'un crime international. On y fait un tour d'horizon des règles classiques de l'obligation de réparation et de leur application aux suites de la violation d'obligations *erga omnes.* L'auteur en conclut que tout État lié par la norme violée peut légitimement intercéder auprès de l'État auteur de la violation, et que cette intercession ne peut être considérée comme une intervention dans les affaires internes de ce dernier. Par contre, le droit à la restitution et à la compensation est réservé à l'État directement affecté par la violation, bien que, comme on le constate par la création de la Commission de compensation des Nations Unies suite à l'invasion du Koweit par l'Iraq, il est possible de donner une portée assez large au concept d'"État affecté" par la violation d'une obligation *erga omnes.*

Les conditions du recours par les États à des contre-mesures suite à la violation d'obligations *erga omnes,* sujet du chapitre quatre, constitue peut-être le terrain le plus fertile de toute la thèse de M. de Hoogh tant il est sujet à controverse. Il débute par un exposé de la fonction des contre-mesures, dans lequel il souligne que celles-ci doivent être envisagées d'abord comme un moyen d'obtenir réparation pour le ou les États affectés par la violation d'une norme *erga omnes,* rejetant toute suggestion que ces réactions à l'illicite puissent jouer un quelconque rôle punitif. Se tournant ensuite vers la nature cette fois des contre-mesures, de Hoogh adopte l'analyse de Kelsen pour les qualifier de mécanisme de responsabilité collective, mais critique la position de la Commission du droit international selon laquelle la contre-mesure exclurait l'illicéité même de la mesure. Pour lui, on ne peut nier l'illégalité de la contre-mesure; on doit plutôt considérer que le fait internationalement illicite confère à l'État-victime un droit secondaire de non-respect d'une obligation due à l'État-auteur de la violation initiale (mais non aux États tiers). Inversement, il y a perte du droit de ce dernier État d'invoquer la responsabilité de l'État-victime pour non-respect de la norme violée à titre de contre-mesure. L'auteur se penche au passage sur le dilemme de l'auto-qualification des faits, centrale au droit des contre-mesures en raison du nécessaire constat préalable de la commission d'un fait internationalement illicite. Il rejette la proposition d'Arangio-Ruiz de conditionner la prise de contre-mesures à la constatation judiciaire de l'existence d'un fait illicite car, selon lui, la nature des crimes internationaux de l'État amoindrit la difficulté de qualification. Pour lui, par exemple, il est facile d'identifier l'auteur d'un acte d'agression ou de génocide. La pratique, pourtant, ne manque pas de fournir des exemples de profonds désaccords à ce sujet, par exemple les interventions soviétique en Afghanistan et américaine en Grenade ont fait l'objet de qualifications factuelles nettement divergentes.[4] Ici comme ailleurs, cependant, M. de Hoogh reste fidèle au sous-titre de son livre et s'en tient à une analyse purement théorique qui réfère peu à la pratique étatique.

Les deux derniers chapitres du livre recoupent des thèmes qui ont fait l'objet de débats importants dans des contextes autres que celui des crimes internationaux, soient le droit de recourir à des contre-mesures impliquant l'emploi de la force et la possibilité de porter un différend à la Cour internationale de Justice. Se référant aux arguments souvent soulevés pour soutenir la légalité de l'intervention d'humanité, l'auteur plaide pour une interprétation téléologique de l'article 2(4) de la Charte des Nations Unies qui autoriserait une réaction armée à la commission d'un crime international. Cette réaction peut être individuelle en cas d'agression armée, de par le droit de légitime défense collective, mais doit être autorisée par le Conseil de sécurité dans le cas d'autres crimes internationaux. La discussion du recours possible à la Cour internationale de Justice, quant à elle, ne soulève que peu de questions spécifiques aux obligations *erga omnes* et crimes internationaux. L'analyse survole ainsi des difficultés "classiques" reliées au caractère optionnel de la juridiction de la Cour, à l'existence d'un différend, aux liens entre la Cour et le Conseil de sécurité, et au pouvoir de la Cour d'ordonner des mesures conservatoires.

Monsieur de Hoogh nous livre ici une thèse touffue, résultat d'un labeur manifestement intense de recherche et une large utilisation des sources doctrinales. Le coeur de l'analyse constitue une dissection méthodique des travaux de la Commission du droit

[4] Voir, par exemple, M. Reisman et J. Silk, "Which Law Applies to the Afghan Conflict?" (1988) 82 Am. J. Int'l L. 459 à la p. 496. Pour une réflexion plus poussée sur le sujet, voir D. Alland, *Justice privée et ordre public international* (Paris: Pedone, 1994) aux pp. 84-125.

international, dont on ne s'écarte que peu dans la discussion, jusqu'au point de parfois se perdre dans un méandre de détails qui diluent la force de l'argumentation principale. La densité de l'oeuvre se double d'une manipulation incertaine de la syntaxe anglaise, qui obscurcit sans doute la pensée de l'auteur et rend souvent ardue la compréhension du texte. Dans ses commentaires des travaux de la CDI et des décisions de la Cour internationale, l'auteur fait feu de tout bois et critique d'une manière quelquefois paternaliste les Ago et Arangio-Ruiz, sans toujours se justifier pleinement. Il n'en reste pas moins que le livre de M. de Hoogh constitue une contribution utile au développement et à une plus grande compréhension des concepts encore mal cernés d'obligations *erga omnes* et de crimes internationaux.

RÉNÉ PROVOST
Faculté de droit et Institut de droit comparé, Université McGill

Introduction to International Organizations. Edited by L. Louis-Jacques and J. S. Korman, for the American Association of Law Libraries. 1996. Dobbs Ferry: Oceana. Pp. xxiii and 574. ISBN 0-379-21351-6.

Much is heard nowadays, both on the national and international level, of the importance of freedom of information. Somewhat less is heard of the extent to which over-publication may result in a secrecy more intense than any flowing from the days of secret diplomacy. Even before the proliferation of international organizations that now exists, the United Nations had issued so much paper that it was well-nigh impossible for scholars to find their way around if they wished to do any serious research regarding the activities of international organizations. As the years have passed, the situation has hardly improved. Each new organization that was added to the body of international control contributed its own mass of material to the paper mountain.

Any effort, therefore, that facilitates access to, and proper use of, this material is to be welcomed. *Introduction to International Organizations* published by Oceana on behalf of the American Association of Law Libraries makes a significant contribution in this respect.

While the volume is primarily intended for law librarians, it will prove of assistance to other researchers seeking literature concerning international organizations, their structure, operation, publications, and documentation. The first six papers, described under the general rubric "A Primer," provide general information, including a lengthy section on "Tapping (US) Federal Government Sources for Information by and about International Government Organizations," to which are attached forty-five "Exhibits" covering such matters as Fact Sheets on the Council of Europe, "Who Belongs to What," American Foreign Policy — Current Documents, Foreign Relations of the United States, and the like. What is becoming of major significance today is the extent to which the activities of international organizations impinge upon, or require the enactment of, national legislation. This is covered in a specific essay indicating the types of documents that the various organizations put forth, and which are relevant from this point of view.

Some 190 pages are concerned with searching for and using United Nations documents, with particular reference to "UN Bibliographical and Background Tools in Hardcopy and Online" as well as "Electronic Sources of UN Information." Information of this kind will probably prove of the greatest assistance to ordinary researchers, including those doing graduate work.

As to the specific organizations, three papers deal with the European Community — one on the legislative process and its documents and publications; another on material online for legal researchers; and, most useful, a selected bibliography of secondary resources. A similar bibliography is provided for the Council of Europe, together with a piece devoted to the Council's publications.

In the final group of papers, one deals with the OAS and its documentation, and a second with research issues and the legal literature relating to NAFTA, including Canadian implementation (at 529). (But what is meant by the statement at 526 that "NAFTA is not a treaty. It is a trade agreement"? Perhaps the writer should read the Vienna Convention on the Law of Treaties!). Third, there is a short selective guide to sources relevant to human rights NGOs, including information on bibliographies and encyclopedias, as well as the names and addresses of some of the leading NGOs in the field. It is perhaps unfortunate that organizations such as Médecins sans Frontières and the International Committee of the Red Cross are omitted from the list and, with the exception of the International Commission of Jurists, no non-American address is given.

For those concerned with the literature of and by international organizations, the volume provides at least a partial introductory resource.

L. C. Green
US Naval War College

Dictionnaire de Droit international pénal: Termes choisis. Par Anne-Marie La Rosa. Publications de l'Institut Universitaire de Hautes Études Internationales. Genève: Presses Universitaires de France, 1998. Pp. xii, 118, F.Fr. 180.

Comme son titre l'indique, cet ouvrage s'attache à clarifier les concepts essentiels d'une discipline juridique en plein développement et vraisemblablement appelée à en connaître d'autres encore à mesure que des juridictions — internationales ou nationales, d'ailleurs — seront saisies de poursuites incriminant des personnes présumées coupables d'infractions de nature criminelle au regard du droit international, en particulier de la branche régissant la conduite des hostilités dans les conflits armés.

Dans le vocabulaire juridique courant, en effet, la criminalité internationale recouvre des réalités bien diverses faisant de plus en plus l'objet de conventions et accords transnationaux. Pour sa part, l'auteur — une jeune juriste québécoise, actuellement en poste au BIT (Bureau International du Travail), et ayant auparavant oeuvré auprès du TPIY (Tribunal Pénal International pour l'Ex-Yougoslavie) — a préféré concentrer sa démarche sur la terminologie relative aux actes illégaux commis lors de violences conflictuelles et à leur répression dans le cadre du droit international.

Même si, pour obéir aux règles de l'art dans le domaine lexicographique, les termes sont naturellement présentés dans leur ordre alphabétique, Mme La Rosa offre également au lecteur un ordonnancement thématique dans une courte table des matières permettant fort utilement d'embrasser d'un coup d'oeil l'ensemble des trente-trois entrées selon une classification conceptuelle les répartissant respectivement sous l'une ou l'autre des trois rubriques: général; incriminations et notions afférentes; règles et principes inhérents à la répression pénale internationale.

Force est de constater que l'auteur ne se contente pas de donner de simples définitions: chacune des expressions traitées fait l'objet d'un petit article explicatif, comportant les références pertinentes à la jurisprudence, aux textes conventionnels ou résolutoires, aux documents de conférences, ouvrages de doctrine; autrement dit, à toutes les sources susceptibles de guider les chercheurs consultant l'ouvrage vers la documentation appropriée. Il y a là pour eux, sans conteste, une économie de temps fort appréciable car la densité du travail accompli à cet égard est d'une minutie exemplaire.

En outre, l'intérêt de l'ouvrage réside aussi dans la contextualisation historique des vocables juridiques répertoriés ainsi que les rapprochements établis avec des locutions connexes. À titre d'exemple, l'émergence de l'infraction de crime contre l'humanité est, bien sûr, située dans le cadre du Statut du Tribunal militaire international de Nuremberg, mais elle est également reliée (pp. 17-18) à la clause de Martens insérée dans les préambules des Conventions de la Haye de 1899 et de 1907 qui place en tout temps les belligérants et les populations sous l'empire, notamment, des lois de l'humanité. De même, apprend-on (p. 18) qu'en 1915 les gouvernements français, britannique et russe avaient qualifié de "crime contre l'humanité" les massacres à grande échelle frappant les Arméniens de Turquie et avaient initialement projeté d'en tenir responsables tous les membres du gouvernement turc et leurs agents impliqués dans la commission de ces actes.

Par ailleurs, l'objectivité des données — inhérente à un dictionnaire — n'empêche pas l'auteur, à l'occasion, de faire état de situations susceptibles de soulever des interrogations quant à la volonté des États d'assurer une mise en oeuvre effective du droit international par des sanctions appropriées de ses violations. À cet égard, l'évocation (p. 58) du renoncement des Alliés, au lendemain de la Première guerre mondiale, à juger, en vertu des articles 228 et 229 du Traité de Versailles, les 890 criminels par eux réclamés, est significative de la versatilité et de l'inconstance des gouvernements en la matière. Lorsque des procédures sont engagées dans un cadre national, comme ce fut le cas dans l'affaire Llandovery Castle, les peines prononcées peuvent paraître en-deçà de la gravité de l'infraction: telle nous semble la condamnation à quatre ans de réclusion de deux lieutenants dont la culpabilité fut établie dans l'exécution d'un ordre manifestement illégal, à savoir le torpillage d'un navire-hôpital britannique et le coulage des canots de sauvetage pour faire disparaître les témoins du crime.

Cet épisode illustre bien la difficulté de juger et sanctionner de manière appropriée des militaires ayant contrevenu aux règles du Droit international humanitaire (DIH), comme si l'état de guerre pouvait constituer une circonstance atténuante pour les délinquants alors même que ce corpus juridique vise précisément à atténuer les effets des conflits pour les victimes, voire en éliminer les excès inutiles. Or, dans le cas du Llandovery Castle, c'est le principe de distinction — pierre angulaire du DIH — qui a été enfreint et, par rapport à une telle règle cardinale, l'on s'attendrait à une peine ayant valeur dissuasive pour l'avenir. Ce n'est malheureusement point l'état des choses et, une cinquantaine d'années plus tard, les responsables du massacre de My Lai commis par une compagnie de militaires américains contre la population civile désarmée d'un village vietnamien ne recevront pas davantage une sanction à la hauteur des violences et violations commises.

On le voit, la lecture du dictionnaire ouvre la voie à la réflexion sur l'observation de la mise en oeuvre encore aléatoire du droit pénal international. Certes, l'instauration de juridictions pénales internationales pour juger des crimes commis dans les conflits de l'ex-Yougoslavie et du Rwanda constitue un progrès notable; toutefois les tergiversations marquant le processus de création d'une Cour criminelle internationale permanente ne manquent pas de faire craindre la perpétuation d'une justice *ad hoc* destinée aux seules catégories de combattants et responsables politiquement ciblés par les puissances du Conseil de Sécurité et plus singulièrement par ses membres permanents. Voilà qui constituerait un grave préjudice à l'établissement d'un état de droit dans le cadre de la société internationale.

Or, la précision du travail entrepris par Anne-Marie La Rosa révèle tout le potentiel régulateur des comportements d'un droit pénal international qui s'avère manifestement être le corollaire indispensable de l'ensemble des instruments conventionnels relatifs aux conflits armés et à la conduite des hostilités. Voire, par delà même les situations conflictuelles, le crime de génocide et le crime contre l'humanité reçoivent désormais une acception sans lien avec l'existence d'une guerre (respectivement pp. 47 et 21), ce qui signifie que les responsables d'actes relevant de ces catégories d'infractions au droit international devraient pouvoir être jugés en dehors de toute menace à la paix et la sécurité internationales qui a fondé, en vertu du Chapitre VII de la Charte, la création par voie résolutoire des TPI de La Haye et d'Arusha. Faut-il rappeler, d'ailleurs, que la Convention pour la prévention et la répression du crime de génocide, dont c'est bientôt le cinquantième anniversaire, avait prévu (article VI) la possibilité de traduire les personnes accusées de génocide devant la cour criminelle internationale dont l'établissement n'était pas supposé être renvoyé aux calendes grecques.

Il faut donc savoir gré à l'auteur de ce dictionnaire d'avoir réussi à faire une oeuvre de clarification et de compilation tout en préservant à une matière aussi importante son caractère dynamique et vivant. Aussi, la consultation de l'ouvrage est-elle rendue d'autant plus utile que les différentes entrées comportent des renvois aux termes synonymes, le cas échéant, ainsi qu'aux articles complémentaires. Et, pour en faciliter le maniement, un index des termes choisis en dresse le portrait d'ensemble avec tous les renvois et synonymes.

Publié à point nommé, nul doute que le dictionnaire de droit international pénal soit appelé à connaître le succès qu'il mérite tant auprès des étudiants et chercheurs que dans les sphères gouvernementales et des praticiens appelés à se pencher sur cette branche du droit.

KATIA BOUSTANY
Département des Sciences Juridiques, UQAM

Combattants et prisonniers de guerre en droit islamique et en droit international humanitaire. Par Ameur Zemmali. Paris: Éditions A. Pedone, 1997, 1998. Pp. 519, F.Fr. 260.

À l'heure où des violences extrêmes — si tant est qu'il y ait vraiment des degrés dans la violence — sont commises contre des populations civiles, en particulier en Algérie, par des groupes armés se revendiquant de l'Islam, l'ouvrage de Monsieur Ameur Zemmali vient fort heureusement apporter une contribution sereine et réfléchie à la connaissance d'un système juridique encore bien mal appréhendé par les internationalistes occidentaux.

La barbarie, faut-il le rappeler, n'est pas l'apanage des religions; en revanche, l'ordre religieux a presque toujours créé et souvent informé un ordre juridique (voir Santi Romano) destiné à régir les comportements et rapports humains. Aussi est-ce dans le substrat axiologique que monsieur Zemmali va rechercher à travers le corpus juridique islamique les règles qui ont constitué avant la lettre un droit humanitaire spécifique, pour ensuite aborder une démarche comparative avec le droit international humanitaire contemporain.

Mais, alors que ce dernier résulte d'outils conventionnels explicitement élaborés aux fins de réglementer la conduite des hostilités dans les situations conflictuelles, les normes islamiques dans ce domaine doivent être dégagées d'un ensemble de sources propres au droit musulman. C'est le grand mérite d'Ameur Zemmali d'avoir relevé un tel défi.

Juriste d'origine tunisienne, formé au droit international humanitaire (DIH) lors de ses études supérieures à Genève, puis devenu conseiller juridique et délégué du CICR, monsieur Zemmali va allier sa connaissance approfondie du droit musulman à celle, théorique autant que pratique, du DIH.

Pour la clarté de l'exposé et sa bonne compréhension, l'auteur commence par familiariser ses lecteurs avec les vocables, concepts, sources et écoles du droit islamique. Ainsi, dans un chapitre introductif d'une soixantaine de pages, sont expliqués, en une première section, l'ensemble des termes (*Chari'a, Fiqh, Qanun, Sunna,* etc.) qui participèrent à l'élaboration du droit islamique dès les origines de la prédication coranique; la deuxième section est consacrée à ce qui est identifié, à juste titre, comme "le droit international islamique" et où sont notamment abordées deux institutions majeures des rapports internationaux dans la perspective de l'Islam: d'une part, la distinction entre le *Dar al-Islam* et le *Dar al-Harb,* et, d'autre part, le *jihad* dont il évoque la fonction actuelle dans le contexte de situations conflictuelles contemporaines.

Ce travail de déblaiement terminologique est fort important pour l'appréhension du reste de l'ouvrage car la référence à ces concepts et sources du droit islamique y est inévitablement fréquente.

Par la suite, dans sa démarche comparative entre le DIH, entendu au sens strict du droit international moderne, et les règles applicables aux conflits armés en vertu du droit musulman, monsieur Zemmali traitera donc en deux parties successives du statut de deux catégories de personnes: le combattant et les prisonniers de guerre.

En ce qui concerne la notion de combattant, il est notable que le principe de distinction entre combattants et non-combattants avait très tôt fait l'objet dans la doctrine islamique d'un grand débat quant à sa portée (pp. 63 et s.) sans que son applicabilité comme telle fût en cause. En droit international il faudra attendre l'oeuvre codificatrice de la deuxième moitié du XIXe siècle, puis celle du présent siècle pour voir ce principe fondamental être définitivement consacré et développé dans différents textes du droit des conflits armés et du DIH (pp. 76-95).

L'auteur souligne bien, dans une section particulière, que la fonction du principe de distinction est la protection des personnes ne prenant pas part aux combats, laquelle résulte en droit islamique à la fois du Coran comme tel que de la tradition établie par le Prophète lui-même envers ses Compagnons (pp. 97-98). Le principe de distinction vise également la protection des biens et, à cet égard, les développements de l'ouvrage tendent à montrer que, dès le départ, le droit musulman énonce, à l'instar du droit des conflits armés actuel, l'inviolabilité de certains biens parallèlement à la préoccupation qu'il a eue de réglementer la prise de butin de guerre et sa répartition (pp. 104-11).

Mais une chose est l'affirmation du principe, une autre est sa mise en oeuvre. Et sur ce plan, monsieur Zemmali est amené à analyser les diverses causes d'atténuation de la distinction entre combattants et non-combattants — la nécessité militaire, la guerre totale — ainsi que les manifestations de cette atténuation, notamment celles qui constituent des violations du principe de distinction soit dans le cadre de guerres de libération nationale et de guerres civiles (Afghanistan, Libéria, Somalie, Angola, Rwanda), soit dans celui d'autres conflits récents ou actuels (Moyen-Orient, les deux guerres du Golfe, les situations conflictuelles de l'ex-Yougoslavie).

Quant à la notion de combattant, en tant que telle, l'auteur la traite à travers la particularité sémantique du terme arabe de "*mujahid*" dont il maintient l'emploi "pour montrer la spécificité du combattant musulman" (pp. 195 et s.), lequel n'est admis à faire partie des forces combattantes de l'Islam que s'il jouit de certaines qualités éthiques et a la capacité de remplir les devoirs d'une telle charge fondée sur une morale explicitée par le Prophète dans le Coran (pp. 204-14). L'on est quelque peu à distance, ici, des attributs techniques sous-tendant la qualité de combattant selon le droit de la Haye et le droit de Genève.

Par ailleurs, Ameur Zemmali s'interroge sur le statut de combattant dans les conflits armés non internationaux et, pour cela, dresse une typologie des conflits internes en Islam parmi lesquels se range l'apostasie impliquant un reniement de l'Islam et se distinguant sous cet angle du brigandage de grand chemin classé lui aussi dans cette même catégorie de conflits. Là encore, les règles applicables concernent un ordre de préoccupation fort différencié par rapport à celui qui a informé l'élaboration du corpus juridique relatif aux combattants des conflits armés non internationaux en DIH et qui demeure bien succinct du fait de la réticence persistante des États à admettre l'extension de protections spécifiques à des personnes perçues par eux uniquement sous l'angle de la menace à l'ordre établi. Aussi, monsieur Zemmali est-il amené à analyser l'absence de définition du combattant des conflits internes dans le Droit international humanitaire et le sens de l'obligation de traitement humain minimal (pp.262-81).

Comme les situations de combat sont susceptibles d'entraîner la captivité de certains, la deuxième partie de l'ouvrage est consacrée aux prisonniers de guerre dont le statut est, rappelle l'auteur, la conséquence de celui de combattant.

Dans un premier chapitre mettant en évidence le caractère protecteur du statut de prisonnier, l'auteur s'attache à montrer qu'il existe deux approches de la notion de prisonnier de guerre: celle du droit islamique, qui apparaît comme globale et s'entendant de tous les membres des forces ennemies capturés par la partie adverse (pp. 288-94) et celle du DIH qui identifie six catégories déterminées de personnes mais laisse subsister, par ailleurs des "cas douteux"; ce qui porte l'auteur à évoquer la pratique contemporaine et les exemples particuliers du cas Noriega et de l'affaire des Irakiens internés au Royaume-Uni lors de la deuxième guerre du Golfe. C'est également à partir de différentes situations qu'il examine l'application des règles et procédures mettant fin à la condition de prisonnier de guerre.

En outre, monsieur Zemmali s'attarde sur le problème du statut de l'espion et du mercenaire capturés pour constater que le droit islamique leur octroie, dans certaines circonstances, la qualité de prisonnier de guerre, alors que le DIH la leur dénie de manière générale. Il convient de noter, toutefois, que le bénéfice du traitement de prisonnier de guerre à l'égard du mercenaire demeure plus ambigu car si, dans la pratique des premières batailles livrées par eux, les Musulmans ne faisaient pas de distinction entre "mercenaires" et "autres combattants", les États musulmans contemporains qui, à l'instar des autres États, réprouvent le mercenariat, traduisent une telle condamnation, en droit, "par le refus de reconnaître au mercenaire le statut de combattant ou de prisonnier de guerre" (p. 389).

L'ouvrage s'achève sur la revue des garanties s'attachant au statut de prisonnier de guerre et soulève donc, notamment, les questions liées à l'exécution des captifs et à l'esclavage des prisonniers de guerre.

Par la clarté de l'exposé et le caractère méthodique de la démarche comparative, le travail de monsieur Zemmali élargit incontestablement la réflexion sur les problèmes de mise en oeuvre des règles du droit des conflits armés car les exemples puisés à travers l'Histoire révèlent tour à tour combien la conquête de notre humanité demeure laborieuse et n'est jamais définitivement acquise.

Il ne suffit pas, en effet, que les sociétés et les autorités souscrivent à des règles de droit destinées à introduire le respect de la dignité humaine là où la violence des armes déchaîne, de diverses manières, la part féroce et toujours barbare sommeillant en chacun; encore faut-il que ces règles soient connues de tous, ou du plus grand nombre à tout le moins, afin d'imprégner durablement les esprits et — tel est bien l'effet escompté — les comportements des individus placés aux différents échelons des situations conflictuelles et des confrontations armées. D'où l'importance de la diffusion du droit humanitaire, fût-il islamique ou international.

En véritable délégué du CICR, Ameur Zemmali le sait fort bien. Aussi, par son ouvrage, a-t-il du même coup amorcé un excellent travail de diffusion dont il faut espérer que sauront en tirer bénéfice tant les universitaires s'intéressant au DIH que, surtout, les autorités et militaires de quelque nature ou qualité, comme également les praticiens sur ce qu'il est convenu d'appeler le terrain humanitaire.

Katia Boustany
Département des Sciences Juridiques, UQAM

Les frontières maritimes internationales: Essai de classification pour un tour du monde géopolitique. Par G. Labreque. Collection Raoul Dandurand. Montréal: Harmattan, 1998. Pp. 444. ISBN 2-89489-039-7, 56,50 $ CAN.

Georges Labreque est avocat et professeur de droit international et de géographie politique au Collège royal militaire du Canada. Il a obtenu sa licence en droit à l'Université Laval et est titulaire d'une licence, d'une maîtrise et d'un doctorat en géographie délivrés par la même université. À cette riche carrière académique s'ajoute une expérience professionnelle tout aussi remarquable puisqu'il a exercé la profession d'avocat pendant une dizaine d'années et a été régisseur du logement du gouvernement du Québec. Il est actuellement sur une autre piste ambitieuse de recherche portant sur les concepts d'intégrité territoriale et de reconnaissance internationale.

Juriste doublé du géographe, Labreque aborde dans son ouvrage un sujet d'actualité brûlante du droit international public, les espaces maritimes et leurs délimitations subséquentes entre États limitrophes. Sa méthodologie a consisté à dresser une typologie des frontières maritimes internationales. Ayant fait le constat des lacunes de la cartographie, il plaide pour une nouvelle carte du monde géopolitique basée sur un ordre fonctionnel où toutes les frontières maritimes sont analysées dans leurs cadres régionaux et suivant plusieurs typologies.

Le cadre conceptuel de cette étude permet au lecteur de saisir, à prime abord, les complexités géographiques et juridiques des frontières maritimes du monde entier. Sont ici définis les éléments distinctifs entre frontières maritimes et frontières terrestres, entre frontières et territoires, entre frontières et limites. Après avoir défini une frontière maritime internationale, l'auteur s'interroge sur une classification des frontières maritimes internationales. Pour y parvenir, il répertorie toutes les frontières maritimes du monde, les décrit dans leurs cadres régionaux et les compare selon plusieurs typologies, par exemple, génétiques, fonctionnelles, morphologiques, relationnelles ou instrumentales. Chaque frontière est analysée suivant plusieurs considérations d'ordre politiques, stratégiques, historiques, juridiques, économiques, environnementales, géographiques, insulaires, géologiques, géomorphologiques et suivant les méthodes et les techniques de délimitation employées dans chaque cas.

Dans le premier chapitre, Labrecque aborde les problèmes relatifs à la territorialisation des espaces maritimes en décrivant, dans leurs aspects juridiques et géographiques, les différentes zones maritimes sous juridiction nationale (eaux intérieures, eaux archipélagiques, mer territoriale, zone contiguë, zone économique exclusive, plateau continental). En ce qui a trait aux limites extérieures des différentes zones maritimes, on relève que les législations nationales en la matière restent, dans une grande proportion, conformes aux règles du droit international, à quelques exceptions près où ces limites s'écartent des dispositions de la Convention de 1982 sur le droit de la mer.

Le chapitre II de l'ouvrage traite du second aspect de la territorialisation, à savoir l'opération proprement dite de la délimitation des espaces maritimes entre États côtiers adjacents ou opposés. La délimitation se distingue de la limitation maritime, ce dernier étant l'opération qui conduit au partage des espaces maritimes selon des facteurs juridiques et géographiques et des considérations géomorphologiques, géologiques, biogéographiques, environnementaux, historiques, économiques, culturels, géopolitiques et la considération tenant à la conduite des parties. On peut dire que la jurisprudence à l'égard de tous ces facteurs reste discriminatoire dans la mesure où elle établit une hiérarchie entre ceux-ci. En effet, si la géographie reste le principal facteur à considérer dans tout processus de délimitation maritime, tous les autres facteurs ci-haut mentionnés ne sont qu'accessoires, passagers et subjectifs. Dans la jurisprudence, de tels facteurs n'entrent pas directement en ligne de compte pour les États impliqués dans un différend sur une frontière maritime objective et permanente.

Le chapitre III est consacré à l'étude des diverses typologies des frontières maritimes qui, quoique définies de façon claire et simple, seront, pour nombre d'entre elles, mises au rancart, jugées sans pertinence scientifique. Les chapitres IV, V, VI, VII et VIII abordent l'analyse des frontières maritimes dans leurs cadres régionaux. C'est en Amérique que les premières frontières maritimes au-delà de la mer territoriale ont été tracées; cependant, celles-ci n'ont pas les mêmes caractéristiques ou en présentent très peu. Quant aux points de similitude, il a fallu les rechercher dans les trois sous-ensembles américains, à savoir les frontières maritimes en Amérique du Sud, en Amérique Centrale et en Amérique du Nord. Le constat est qu'en Amérique, toutes les frontières maritimes sont multifonctionnelles, presque toutes agréées, achevées et uniséquentielles. Les seules exceptions concernent les frontières maritimes du Canada qui sont pour les unes décidées (Affaires du *Golfe du Maine et Saint Pierre et Miquelon*) et pour les autres inachevées.

En Europe, le processus de délimitation s'avère plus complexe eu égard aux caractéristiques géographiques particulières de cette région. Il existe cependant un point commun aux frontières européennes: elles sont presque toutes unifonctionnelles du fait de la renonciation par les États concernés à leur juridiction exclusive en matière de pêche. On observe toutefois que les limites extérieures des différentes zones maritimes ne sont pas toutes uniformes et que le processus de délimitation ne connaît pas le même état d'avancement dans les cinq sous-ensembles européens, à savoir dans la Mer Baltique, dans la Mer du Nord, dans l'Atlantique, dans la Méditerranée, et dans la Mer Noire. Dans cette dernière sous-région, les frontières sont en général soit décidées, soit agréées et elles sont de surcroît de nature multifonctionnelle et unifonctionnelle.

En Afrique, la géographie des côtes est d'une simplicité telle qu'elle devait faciliter le processus de délimitation des espaces maritimes entre États africains. Les limites extérieures des mers territoriales sont très hétérogènes, oscillant entre les limites de 12 milles et 200 milles marins. Quant à la délimitation proprement dite, elle constitue un processus qui ne fait que commencer. À l'instar des autres régions maritimes, l'auteur divise le continent africain en quatre régions ou quatre sous-ensembles: sont décrites les frontières maritimes en Méditerranée, de l'océan Atlantique, de l'Océan Indien et enfin de la Mer Rouge. La simplicité physique de la géographie et l'exploitation sans retard des ressources de la mer au large des côtes africaines constituent deux facteurs qui donneront l'*impetus* au processus de délimitation des espaces maritimes africains.

En Asie, l'auteur relève d'une part qu'il existe des difficultés à établir des caractéristiques communes aux frontières maritimes de cette région, et d'autre part, qu'il s'agit d'un processus de délimitation dont l'avancement est à la traîne. Il a donc fallu rechercher les éléments explicatifs de ce lent processus de délimitation maritime dans les sous-ensembles régionaux de l'Asie. On peut mentionner cependant une caractéristique commune aux accords asiatiques de délimitation maritime: il s'agit de l'uniformité des limites extérieures des mers territoriales revendiquées par les États.

L'Océanie, quant à elle, avec ses considérables étendues maritimes, se caractérise par ses nombreuses zones de chevauchement. En général, la limite extérieure de la mer territoriale est fixée à douze milles marins. Le processus de délimitation n'est pas si avancé dans la mesure où, sur cinquante frontières potentielles, seulement quatorze ont été délimitées. La plupart des frontières maritimes océaniennes mettent aux prises des États en situation d'opposition. De sorte que, sur les quatorze frontières maritimes actuellement délimitées, douze l'ont été suivant la méthode de l'équidistance.

À tout considérer, on peut relever que cet ouvrage a le mérite de traiter à la fois du droit de la délimitation maritime (droit international) et de la géographie des océans. En cela, cette étude se veut, à notre avis, un appel à l'interdisciplinarité pour ce qui est de la compréhension du milieu marin. Cet ouvrage tend à concilier les sciences géographiques et les sciences juridiques où toutes deux se penchent sur un même objet de connaissance: la Mer. Celle-ci s'accommode difficilement des études parcellaires et sectorielles. La mer est en soi indivisible. Dans ses objets, elle est multiforme. Pour sa connaissance ou sa compréhension, elle fait appel à la multidisciplinarité. Le droit qui encadre son processus de délimitation dominé par les révélations cartographiques ou géographiques, tend de plus en plus et de mieux en mieux vers un meilleur raffinement, sinon vers une plus grande certitude ou davantage de prévisibilité. Ce droit est appelé à se développer et se préciser au fur et à mesure des différends qui seront soumis à la CIJ, au Tribunal d'arbitrage, et au Tribunal du droit international de la mer. Sans conteste, le juge international aura matière à jugement d'autant que sur 450 zones de chevauchement, seulement 150 sont actuellement délimitées.

Quand on achève la lecture de cet ouvrage qui, sans aucun doute, apportera beaucoup à la théorie générale des frontières maritimes internationales, on a le sentiment d'être doublement instruit de sciences juridiques et géographiques. Le plus grand mérite de cet ouvrage, hormis la profondeur des analyses, les belles illustrations cartographiques et une référence bibliographique bien ciblée, est d'avoir fait du régionalisme maritime, sinon de la région maritime, le support principal de son étude et à partir duquel il a élaboré son essai classificatoire des frontières maritimes internationales. Il aurait toutefois fallu, le croyons-nous, mettre ce régionalisme en perspective en insistant davantage sur l'approche de l'exploitation commune ou conjointe des ressources de la mer, approche qui passe pour être non seulement une pratique émergente des États, mais qui est perçue comme un moyen pragmatique de résolution des différends frontaliers sur mer. Certes, tel n'est pas le premier propos de cette étude, mais un regard plus insistant, même dans la conclusion de cette analyse, sur l'approche dite de la "zone de développement conjoint" des ressources que nous qualifions de partageables (unité de gisement, stock conjoint ou chevauchant) aurait certainement pu conforter une doctrine qui milite en faveur de cette tendance. Au total, on peut se rendre compte que cet ouvrage est le fruit d'un travail fouillé, méthodique et agréable à lire. Le style est simple et structuré, ce qui facilite la compréhension d'une matière aussi complexe que celle de la délimitation des espaces maritimes. Après l'ouvrage de Prosper Weil *Perspectives du droit de la délimitation maritime*, qui fait office d'oeuvre pionnière dans la littérature sur le droit de la délimitation maritime, il faudra compter désormais avec celui de Labrecque.

CISSÉ YACOUBA
Faculté de droit, Université d'Ottawa

Analytical Index / Index Analytique

THE CANADIAN YEARBOOK OF INTERNATIONAL LAW

1997

ANNUAIRE CANADIEN DE DROIT INTERNATIONAL

(A) Article; (NC) Notes and Comments; (Ch) Chronique; (P) Practice; (BR) Book Review

(A) Article; (NC) Notes et commentaires; (Ch) Chronique; (P) Pratique; (BR) Recension de livre

Index of Cases / Index de la jurisprudence